UNITED STATES ARMY IN WORLD WAR II

The War Department

WASHINGTON COMMAND POST: THE OPERATIONS DIVISION

by

Ray S. Cline

MILITARY INSTRUCTION

119001

OFFICE OF THE CHIEF OF MILITARY HISTORY

UNITED STATES ARMY

WASHINGTON, D.C., 1951

This volume, one in the series UNITED STATES ARMY IN WORLD WAR II, is the second to be published in the subseries THE WAR DEPARTMENT. The volumes in the over-all series are closely related and present a comprehensive account of the activities of the Military Establishment during World War II. A list of the subseries is appended at the end of this volume.

Library of Congress Catalog Card Number: 51–61201

Reprinted 1970

For sale by the Superintendent of Documents, U.S. Government Printing Office
Washington, D.C. 20402 - Price $5.75

UNITED STATES ARMY IN WORLD WAR II

Kent Roberts Greenfield, General Editor

Advisory Committee

James P. Baxter	William T. Hutchinson
President, Williams College	University of Chicago
Henry S. Commager	S. L. A. Marshall
Columbia University	Detroit News
Douglas S. Freeman	E. Dwight Salmon
Richmond News Leader	Amherst College
Pendleton Herring	Col. Thomas D. Stamps
Social Science Research Council	United States Military Academy
John D. Hicks	Charles H. Taylor
University of California	Harvard University

*Historical Division, SSUSA**

Maj. Gen. Orlando Ward, Chief

Acting Chief Historian	Stetson Conn
Chief, World War II Group	Col. Allison R. Hartman**
Editor-in-Chief	Hugh Corbett
Chief Cartographer	Wsevolod Aglaimoff

*Redesignated Office of the Chief of Military History, 28 March 1950.
**Succeeded by Col. Thomas J. Sands, 3 March 1950.

iii

The History of
THE WAR DEPARTMENT

. . . to Those Who Served

Foreword

This is the eighth of some hundred contemplated volumes covering the Army's part in World War II. This particular volume is written from the viewpoint of the Staff of the Army's high command. The Operations Division of the General Staff was the general headquarters within the General Staff with which General Marshall exercised his over-all Army command. Its history presents problems which are likely to arise in future wars. These problems may not all be solved by an Army staff in the future in view of current unification, but what they were and how they were solved is of interest not only to the soldier, but to the diplomat and statesman as well as others.

Dr. Ray S. Cline was a Junior Fellow at Harvard and served in the Office of Strategic Services. In 1946 he was assigned to the Operations Division of the War Department General Staff to write its history. The result shows a great amount of effective research and understanding from within that Division. Its viewpoint is from within and emphasizes the action taken by the Division in carrying out the policies of the high command.

In reading this book, its point of view must be kept in mind and at the same time the fact that General Marshall's character and military knowledge dictated the decisions must not be lost sight of. It must be further remembered that he was in touch with commanders in the field in making these decisions and had great respect for their views. General Marshall's views will be presented more fully in other volumes on the Army high command.

Washington, D. C.
15 January 1951.

ORLANDO WARD
Maj. Gen., U. S. A.
Chief of Military History

Preface

This volume is the history of a military staff. It describes the way a number of men worked together, defined their common responsibilities, and carried out their common aims. It also explains the ways in which the group as a whole changed and the ways in which it remained unchanged during the course of years as its individual members came and departed. In short, it is an institutional biography. It traces the origins, development, and mature characteristics of the Operations Division of the War Department General Staff. This Division was the principal staff agency of the high command in the U. S. Army during World War II.

Since the Operations Division, on its establishment in March 1942, inherited the staff and responsibilities of a predecessor agency, the War Plans Division, this history treats both staffs, but describes the wartime institution more fully and systematically. The attention paid the War Plans Division and other parts of the Army contemporaneous with it is intended only to provide the information necessary to an understanding of developments in the World War II period. Similarly, the information about the many agencies and staffs that came in contact with the Operations Division (or OPD, as it was usually called) is presented merely to illuminate the work the OPD did.

The Operations Division was charged with the responsibility under the Chief of Staff for the Army's part in the strategic planning and direction of operations in World War II. The Department of the Army plans to deal with the strategy story in other volumes of the series. The groundwork for these prospective volumes has already been laid down in a series of monographs written by the author and his associates, and this material has been freely used where needed for the present volume. Some examples of the things OPD did have been chosen to illustrate the kind of staff OPD was.

Army officers will argue for years whether OPD was a "good thing." The narrative here presented cannot settle any such argument, but it is designed to show that a serious military problem existed and that the creation of OPD provided a solution to it—not the only possible solution and not necessarily the best solution, but a solution. It is my hope to provide officers of the armed forces and other interested readers with information in which they may find precedents and analogies bearing on various possible solutions of their own problems in the future. The volume in its present form is based on a longer and more fully annotated version that may be consulted in the Office of the Chief of Military History, U. S. Army.

For the preparation of this work my associates and I have had complete freedom of access to the files in the Department of the Army. Documentary research has been supplemented by ample opportunity to interview a great many of the men whose work is here recorded. A common problem for all historians of World War II is the sheer mass of the records. Those of OPD alone filled several vault rooms. Even with a good deal of research assistance, it is impossible for a single historian within a span of three years to canvass and assess all of the available documentary material on a given subject. This work records the first round of the battle with the documents and provides through its footnotes a guide for future scholars. A combined bibliographical note and guide to footnotes will be found at the end of the volume.

I have tried in general to follow the common usage of the English language. After three years of reading in Army files, I am not altogether sure how well I have succeeded. Like other large government institutions in the United States, the Army normally conducts its business in a vocabulary of administrative or official prose. This technical language has its uses, and some of the terms that Army officers habitually employ cannot be translated unambiguously. For this reason I have chosen in many cases to follow the usage of the men whose work is described.

Credit for initiating work on this volume belongs to Maj. Harvey A. DeWeerd, Associate Editor of the *Infantry Journal* in 1945 and now Professor of History in the University of Missouri. On 8 October 1945 Major DeWeerd was authorized by Lt. Gen. John E. Hull, then Chief of OPD, to prepare a history of the Division. Two OPD officers were assigned to aid Major DeWeerd. Lt. Col. John B. Morgan, assistant executive of OPD during the latter part of the war, served for about six months as research associate and special adviser on the complex administrative ways of the War Department. Maj. Darrie H. Richards worked on this project as an associate historian for more than two years, contributing not only scholarship but also reliable guidance to information about Army doctrine and custom.

After a few weeks of exploratory research, Major DeWeerd invited me to join him as an associate historian. Before the project was well under way, the condition of Major DeWeerd's health required him to leave Washington. In January 1946 I took over professional direction of the OPD historical project, and on 29 March 1946 was formally authorized to continue the preparation of a history of OPD. This project remained in the Operations Division (Plans and Operations Division after June 1946) until July 1947, when it was transferred to the Historical Division (redesignated Office of the Chief of Military History in March 1950) and integrated with the Army history in which this volume now appears.

The author owes a debt of gratitude, notable both in its magnitude and in the sense that it cannot be repaid, to two civilian associate historians, Maurice Matloff and Edwin M. Snell. As Mr. Snell, Mr. Matloff, and Major Richards progressed with research on Army strategic planning, their findings became more and more useful in developing a working hypothesis about wartime military staff work in

Washington. Both in the formulation of ideas and the discovery of facts this aid has been invaluable. Furthermore, Mr. Matloff and Mr. Snell collaborated in the research and writing for Chapter XII, "The Midwar International Military Conferences," and Chapter XV, "Links with the Overseas Theaters." Final responsibility for these chapters, as for others, rests with the author, but credit for most of the work on Chapter XII is due to Mr. Matloff and on Chapter XV to Mr. Snell. Mr. Matloff also carried out original research on countless topics essential to the completion of the volume, and Mr. Snell rendered invaluable aid as an uncompromising critic and craftsman with regard to both matter and form of the entire text.

The acknowledgment given above indicates that research and writing for this history was planned as a true team enterprise. In the author's opinion only a co-operative effort can achieve scholarly results in a reasonable length of time from research on any broad topic in the fertile but nearly unbroken fields of contemporary government documents. This volume is much more substantial than it would have been had the facts and judgments in it been discovered by only one historian and sifted through only one mind. The author's task of research and writing has been greatly lightened by the co-operation of his entire staff. In addition to those already mentioned the staff included, during the main period of work on this volume, Mrs. Helen McShane Bailey, whose research on Army personnel and administrative policies was invaluable, and Mrs. Evelyn Cooper, Miss Grace Waibel, Miss Martha Kull, Mr. Martin Chudy, Mrs. Virginia Bosse, Miss Variana Albright, Miss Marcelle Raczkowski, Mr. William Oswald, and Mrs. Edna Jernigan.

To the many officers of the Operations Division who gave every support and encouragement to this work as well as invaluable historical information, I express grateful acknowledgment. Among them are several whose assistance has been especially notable: Brig. Gen. Thomas North and Col. William A. Walker, under whose administrative direction the history was launched; the wartime War Plans Division and OPD chiefs, Lt. Gen. Leonard T. Gerow, General of the Army Dwight D. Eisenhower, Gen. Thomas T. Handy, and Lt. Gen. John E. Hull; and Col. George A. Lincoln, Col. William W. Bessell, Jr., and Col. Vincent J. Esposito, who made detailed and illuminating comments on the complex work of OPD in the later war years.

Credit is also due to those records experts who were familiar with the wartime document files and who gave unstinted assistance to the author and his associates. Miss Alice M. Miller and Mr. Joseph Russell, custodians of the OPD files, and Mrs. Clyde Hillyer Christian and Mr. Robert Greathouse of the Historical Records Section, Adjutant General's Office, where most OPD records were placed while this volume was in progress, were particularly helpful.

Within the Historical Division the Chief Historian, Dr. Kent Roberts Greenfield, has been unsparing of his time and special knowledge. The chiefs of the Division, Maj. Gen. Harry J. Malony and Maj. Gen. Orlando Ward, have made valuable comments out of their personal experience, especially on the pre-Pearl Harbor period. Dr. Stetson Conn, acting Chief Historian during the absence of Dr. Greenfield, provided most helpful suggestions and guided the manuscript through the review process with skill and understanding. Col. Allison R. Hartman, Chief of the World War II Branch, has advised and assisted in the work at every stage. The volume was shepherded through the technical and production maze by Lt. Col. Harrison M. Markley, Chief of the Production Control Section, World War II Branch. Final editing has been done by Mr. W. Brooks Phillips, Associate Editor; copy editing by Miss Mary Ann Bacon; and indexing by Miss Martha Kull. To all of these, and to other members of the Historical Division who have assisted in this work as a part of their common enterprise, I wish to express my sincere appreciation.

I am indebted in a very special way to those former members of the Historical Division who encouraged me by their example and advice to enter the special field of military history, in particular to Professor Charles H. Taylor, Professor Walter L. Wright, Professor Roy Lamson, Col. John M. Kemper, and Col. Allen F. Clark, Jr. Most of all, in this respect as in every other, my special thanks are due to my wife, Marjorie Wilson Cline, whose editorial writing on the Historical Division's early AMERICAN FORCES IN ACTION series first aroused my interest in the Army historical program. Finally, the author is deeply indebted to the Society of Fellows, Harvard University, and especially to its Chairman, Professor C. Crane Brinton, for extending an already long leave of absence to include the period of research on this volume.

Washington, D. C.   RAY S. CLINE
13 October 1950.

Contents

Charts

Illustrations

All pictures in this volume are from U. S. Army photographs.

WASHINGTON COMMAND POST:
THE OPERATIONS DIVISION

589727 O–61—2

CHAPTER I

The Army High Command Before Pearl Harbor

Some of the greatest generals in World War II, far from striking the classic posture of the man on horseback, issued their military orders from the quiet of their desks and fought their decisive battles at conference tables. Strategic plans and policies fixing the essential character of the conflict were worked out in the capital cities of the warring nations. In Washington, as in London, Moscow, Berlin, and Tokyo, military leaders had to deal with urgent world-wide problems that transcended the problems of the individual battlefronts. Using new systems of rapid communication, they kept in touch with the movements of armies and set the patterns of grand strategy as effectively as the Caesars and Napoleons of the past. In so doing they had to reconcile divergent views about the employment of ground, sea, and air forces in the common effort. They had to assist in the delicate process of balancing military requirements of all kinds with the political, social, and economic programs of their national governments. Finally, they had to help adjust differences of military policy among the Great Powers in the coalition. The "fog of war," which traditionally has obscured and confused the scene of maneuver, quickly settled over this military work at the capital of the United States.

President Franklin D. Roosevelt and, in the last months of the war, President Harry S. Truman necessarily acquitted much of the tremendous responsibility of wartime Commander in Chief through the highest-ranking professional officers in the three fighting services. The highest position in the Navy was held initially by Admiral Harold R. Stark, Chief of Naval Operations, and after March 1942 by Admiral Ernest J. King, Chief of Naval Operations and Commander in Chief, United States Fleet. Throughout the entire war the military leaders of the Army were Gen. George C. Marshall, Chief of Staff, United States Army, and Gen. Henry H. Arnold, Commanding General, Army Air Forces. The latter organization was administratively a subordinate part of the Army but enjoyed almost complete independence in developing resources and techniques in the special field of air combat and air bombardment. Admiral King, General Marshall, General Arnold, and a personal representative (sometimes called chief of staff) of the President, Admiral William D. Leahy, constituted the U. S. Joint Chiefs of Staff committee during most of World War II. This committee not only guided the efforts of all three services in support of the common objective but also represented the United

States in continuous military staff work with Great Britain and, much more intermittently, in negotiations with the military leaders of the Soviet Union. The prestige that it enjoyed came in considerable part from the fact that the committee effectively represented the armed services whose chiefs constituted its membership. Its decisions were binding because they were carried out under the authority of each service chief in his own department and because in many cases they were given formal approval by the President.

The Chief of Staff of the U. S. Army, on the basis of the deliberations and decisions of the military high command of the United States, gave strategic direction to the efforts of the huge American ground and (Army) air forces that helped to fight and win World War II. Although strategy came to be determined almost entirely in interservice and coalition councils, the Chief of Staff was responsible for the Army's actions, first in helping to work out common strategic plans and then in carrying them out as agreed. He was the principal Presidential executive agent of the Army's "strategy, tactics, and operations," as well as immediate adviser of the Secretary of War in developing and supervising the entire Military Establishment.[1] The full weight of this office fell on one man, General Marshall.

In the task of planning for and employing an army of eight million men engaged in military operations all over the globe, General Marshall leaned most heavily on one division of the General Staff. It was first called the War Plans Division (WPD) because it was primarily concerned with strategic planning, but in March 1942 it

was given new powers in directing military operations and was renamed the Operations Division. Usually called "OPD," it was "charged with the preparation of strategic plans and coordination of operations throughout the world."[2] The second function was unprecedented in General Staff assignments of responsibility. In fact, OPD was unique in the history of American military institutions. It served as General Marshall's Washington command post from which he issued orders establishing U. S. Army commands all over the world, deploying millions of American troops to the theaters of war and setting the general strategic pattern of their military efforts. Its officers participated in the national and international staff work that lay behind the strategic decisions of the American and Allied high command. It was the staff that first clearly formulated and most strongly advocated some of the essential elements of the grand strategy actually followed in World War II, most notably the central military project of massing American and British forces for the invasion of Europe across the English Channel. In all of these roles OPD acted only as a single and, indeed, very small part of a military organization whose success depended on the efficiency of its leader, the Chief of Staff, and the competence of every staff and unit in the Army.

The Chief of Staff in World War II, for the first time in the history of the U. S. Army, exercised control over all the Army's wartime activities. The strategic instructions he issued not only governed the conduct of military operations in the theaters of war but also co-ordinated them with mobilization, training, equipment, supply, and replacement capacities in the United

---

[1] AR 10–15, par. 11, 13 Jul 42, sub: GS Orgn and Gen Dvs.

[2] *Biennial Report of the Chief of Staff of the United States Army, July 1, 1941 to June 30, 1943 to the Secretary of War,* p. 35.

States. He had both responsibility and authority to co-ordinate all Army activities and direct them toward the primary aim of winning the war. For this purpose he needed a staff capable of studying carefully the operations of the Army in combat and of issuing instructions to all Army agencies as deemed necessary to insure that strategic plans could and would be carried out. OPD's work under General Marshall, which aimed at "getting things done" as well as helping to devise plans and policies, indicated that it was feasible, through efficient, aggressive staff action, to centralize supervision of the vast and complex business of modern warfare.[3]

For some years before World War II, the U. S. Army had been teaching its officers a consistent doctrine concerning command and staff work. This doctrine was designed for tactical units of all sizes engaged in combat and in supporting activities in the field. The headquarters where the Chief of Staff was doing his work, the War Department, for a variety of reasons did not conform to these principles laid down for field commands.[4] During 1940 and 1941 General Marshall turned for help to the staffs and agencies already existing in the War Department or already provided for in legislation and regulations governing the Army. These staffs and agencies were not equipped to meet the critical situation as it actually developed in the hectic years of mobilization, rearmament, and training. Perhaps in time they might have met it and in some fashion have coped with the graver tests of war. Instead, however, from the effort, confusion, accomplishment, and error of 1941 the outlines of a plan for a new Army command post in Washington began to emerge, with a staff modeled more closely than any previous War Department agency on the lines of a general staff in the field. General Marshall finally established such a strategic and operations command post, which served him throughout World War II.[5] The Operations Division came into being and developed as the concrete embodiment of this idea in staff work for the support of the high command of the U. S. Army.

General Marshall's six-year tour of duty as Chief of Staff and ranking officer in the U. S. Army had begun in 1939. A graduate of the Virginia Military Institute in 1901, General Marshall entered the Army at the age of twenty-one as an infantry second lieutenant in February 1902. During World War I he spent two years in France as a high staff officer, reaching the temporary rank of colonel, principally with the First Army and at the general headquarters of the American Expeditionary Force. He returned to the United States in 1919 and served as aide-de-camp to General Pershing during that officer's tenure as

---

[3] Simpson Board Report, 28 Dec 45, title: Rpt of Bd of Offs on Orgn of WD, P&O 020, WD, 2.

[4] See pp. 6–8 below.

[5] The present volume, under the subseries title The War Department, presents the life history of a staff, the story of the development of WPD into OPD, and a description of the mature characteristics of OPD. A few extended case histories illustrate in detail at critical stages in its development the process of planning and making military decisions. For the most part, concrete examples of what is summary and abstract in this volume will be presented in subsequent volumes of the series containing a narrative of the Army's strategic planning and direction of military operations during World War II. Specific references to them are not included in this volume, but many of the generalizations about strategic planning herein are based on the voluminous research already undertaken in the presentation of the strategy volumes.

For the history of the Office of the Chief of Staff during the prewar period, see the volume in this series, Mark S. Watson, *Chief of Staff: Prewar Plans and Preparations* (Washington, D. C., 1950).

Chief of Staff, 1921–24. He attained the permanent rank of brigadier general in the peacetime Army in 1936, and in July 1938 he was ordered to Washington as chief of the War Plans Division. He became Deputy Chief of Staff on 16 October 1938, and less than a year later succeeded General Craig as Chief of Staff. He first received the title of Acting Chief of Staff on 1 July 1939, and then, upon the effective date of his predecessor's formal retirement, 1 September 1939, he acquired the full authority and rank (four-star general) of the Chief of Staff. He held that post until 20 November 1945, receiving in the meantime one of the four special Army appointments to five-star rank, with the title of General of the Army, conferred by Congress in December 1944.

During the first thirty months of his duty as Chief of Staff, German and Italian aggression in Europe and Japanese aggression in the Far East were bringing the threat of war closer and closer to the United States. General Marshall devoted himself to the urgent task of expanding the Army and training its ground and air forces to meet the grave challenge of the times. In preparing for the eventuality of war and making strategic plans, as in mapping out the course of military operations after war came, General Marshall enjoyed the confidence and support of his civilian superiors, Secretary of War Henry L. Stimson, President Roosevelt, and President Truman. The Secretary worked closely and harmoniously with the Chief of Staff, exercising essential civilian control over the Military Establishment. The President, as Chief Executive, shaped national policy in the light of the advice on military affairs that Secretary Stimson and General Marshall gave him. As Commander in Chief, determining strategic policy, he relied very heavily on General Marshall's views, whether expressed in his capacity as military head of the Army or as member of the interservice high command.

The advice the Chief of Staff gave on matters within his sphere of professional competence was valuable precisely insofar as it reflected his understanding of the capabilities of the Army and to the extent that he could bring about military performances commensurate with national needs. As the Army grew in size eightfold within two years, reaching a total strength of 1,500,000 in 1941, and as the outbreak of hostilities seemed nearer and nearer, General Marshall had to deal with military problems of unprecedented scope and complexity. He plainly needed staff assistance of the finest kind for the task at hand and the trials ahead.

Principles of Command

The idea of the new command post, nourished at its roots by orthodox General Staff doctrine, grew out of the unorthodox character of the Army's high command in Washington in 1939, 1940, and 1941. An understanding of this doctrine and of the structure of the high command is essential to the story of the development of OPD. The U. S. Army, particularly through the system of service schools that flourished between World War I and World War II, had tried to formulate and codify principles that would aid its officers to carry out their military duties efficiently and systematically despite the complexities and difficulties which they recognized to be inherent in the "human nature" of the "war-making machine" of which they were a part.[6]

---

[6] WD Manual for Comdrs of Large Units (Prov): Opns, 10 Apr 30, p. 1.

According to the Army's formulation of principle, the idea of command is central in all military organizations and effort. By the exercise of command the officer in charge of any unit controls its military action. A chain of command links the commanders of small military units through the commanders of successively larger organizations to the highest level of authority. The high command, the top level of military authority, tries to provide adequate material resources, or to distribute them wisely when they are inadequate, and to insure the proficiency of individual officers and men throughout the hierarchy. Its primary function is to make plans and then issue orders that insofar as possible gear the actions of every element of the organization into a unified military effort. The exercise of command, to be effective, requires the formulation of clear-cut decisions governing the conduct of all of the Army's ramified activities. The decisions must reflect an intelligent appraisal of the specific situations which they are intended to meet. Finally, instructions embodying these decisions must be conveyed speedily and clearly to the men who are required to carry them out.[7]

In this context the chain of command is a chain of military ideas expressed in the form of orders. Primarily the ideas are either strategic, prescribing military mis-

sions or objectives, or tactical, prescribing military maneuvers aimed at accomplishing some mission. At the highest level of command, ideas are mainly strategic. They are cast in very broad terms chosen to provide a common frame of reference for many military enterprises. Though comparatively simple in form, they are also most complex to arrive at and most intertwined with other, nonmilitary affairs. They are difficult to formulate precisely and to convey clearly to subordinate elements.

The U. S. Army, like other armies, recognizes that every officer who commands the common effort of more than a few men needs some kind of staff to assist him.[8] In small units it may be merely an informal, part-time group of immediate military subordinates acting in a secondary, advisory capacity. In large military organizations, especially in combat units in the field, it ordinarily has to be an agency formally constituted for the sole purpose of assisting in the exercise of command.

In a field command, some staff officers customarily relieve their commander of administrative or technical duties, in particular making plans according to his desires and establishing programs for providing the combat troops with all types of military supplies and for rendering other special services such as transport, ordnance, and medical aid. Other officers in the field, called general staff officers, devote themselves mainly to supplying the commander with information, helping him to reach strategic and tactical decisions, and conveying these decisions to subordinates. They may suggest feasible solutions to him, usually recommending a concrete line of action. When specifically instructed to do

---

[7] The principal sources of the ideas presented in this section, in addition to the 1930 Manual for Comdrs of Large Units (n. 6), were: (1) WD Fld Serv Regulations: Larger Units (FM 100–5), 22 May 41; (2) WD Stf Offs Fld Manual (FM 101–5), 19 Aug 40; (3) WD Fld Serv Regulations: Larger Units (FM 100–15), 29 Jun 42.
A convenient summary of doctrine contained in these publications, with some historical background and analysis, was prepared in 1937 for use in the Command and General Staff School, Fort Leavenworth, Kansas, and entitled Command and Staff Principles (Tentative) (hereafter cited as Command and Staff Principles).

[8] Command and Staff Principles, pp. 10, 15.

so, when previously established policy dictates the solution, or in emergencies, they make decisions in the name and with the authority of the commander. In every circumstance they provide instructions in detail for the guidance of subordinates in the chain of command. Finally, they supervise the execution of orders, that is, by direct inspection or observation they ascertain that military action conforms to the commander's intent and does actually meet the situations which originally required a command decision.[9]

A commander and his entire staff, in conventional U. S. Army usage, constitute a headquarters, the physical place and administrative entity where orders are received from higher authority and issued in appropriate form to the entire command. In the field, for the convenience of the commander who has to concentrate on the military operations of a campaign, the headquarters of a large command is often split into two parts, the forward echelon, usually referred to as the command post, and the rear echelon. The staff agencies immediately required by the commander to assist him in conducting tactical operations work with him in the command post, while the staffs with primarily administrative or technical duties usually remain in the rear echelon.[10] Ordinarily the general staff or a portion of it stays with the commander. Decisions reached at the command post of course govern administrative, technical, and supply policies.

In comparatively small commands the relationship of commander, staff, and subordinate levels of authority is usually personal and direct. The commander of a large military organization cannot be ac-

quainted with all the activities of the many units for whose efficient performance he is responsible. Orders are given in the form of written correspondence, often dispatched over great distances between officers who seldom, if ever, see one another. Consequently, efficient work by the general staff, with its comprehensive duties, requires a clear definition of responsibilities, sound organization of individual officers' efforts, and careful elaboration of procedures for both formulating and disseminating the military ideas essential to command. In large commands, therefore, an officer is appointed chief of the staff and co-ordinates its work. The chief of staff is the principal adviser and executive agent for the commander.[11]

The application of these principles of command and staff work in the U. S. Army was quite uniform by the beginning of World War II except in its highest command and its highest staff. There a unique situation existed, partly because of the great difficulty of co-ordinating the work of the military organization with other institutions of the nation, partly because of historical accident in the development of laws and traditions governing the Army, and partly because of loose thinking and looser terminology applied to the complex problems of higher staff work. Legally only the President exercised command of the entire Army and, with the help of the Secretary of War, established policies controlling its activities. The Chief of Staff was merely the adviser and executive agent of the President and Secretary of War, and literally the chief of the War Department General Staff. Nevertheless, as the ranking professional soldier of the U. S. Army, he possessed a kind of military authority that no civilian

---

[9] *Ibid.*, p. 18.
[10] WD Fld Serv Regulations: Opns (FM 100–5), 22 May 41, p. 33.

[11] Command and Staff Principles, pp. 27–28.

could have, and a trend of many years' duration had resulted by the beginning of World War II in the effective centralization of responsibility for the Army as a whole in the hands of the Chief of Staff.

This responsibility comprehended two separate though closely related spheres of Army activities. The first of these spheres included all military operations, that is, the tactical movements of units in combat and the performance of services, such as transport and supply, directly supporting the fighting forces in the theaters of war. A second sphere of military activity in modern times has loomed large in the background of every field of combat. The conduct of sustained military operations on a large scale in an industrial age requires the establishment of a vast, semimilitary organization well behind the battle lines. In wartime its function is to mobilize men and materials, train and equip units, transport forces to combat theaters and supply them there, evacuate, hospitalize, and replace casualties, and finally to maintain administrative controls over the workings of the whole Army, including the combatant forces. In peacetime this kind of organization has to keep its skeleton framework intact and draft plans for the emergency expansion of the whole Army. Since most of these nonoperational tasks have to be performed in or directed from the homeland, the source of men and materials, the Army calls the area in which they take place the zone of interior. Before World War II the War Department, the U. S. Army's permanent headquarters organization in the zone of interior, primarily concerned itself with this job of mobilizing military resources of all kinds and furnishing them in an orderly fashion to the theaters of operations for commitment to battle. Be-

cause of the complexity of these functions and the fact that they are only semimilitary in character, it has always been very hard to define and assign the command and staff responsibilities in the War Department.

As warfare increased in scale, the need grew to bring military operations in the combat theaters and activities in the zone of interior under the control of a single military authority. In the U. S. Army the creation of the General Staff in 1903 began a trend toward placing the burden of satisfying this need squarely on the shoulders of the Chief of Staff. In the following years, particularly after the end of World War I, the Chief of Staff came to occupy a position of vast responsibility. Acting under the authority of the President and Secretary of War, he was charged with planning, developing, and supervising the entire Army, which included all zone of interior agencies, the defensive garrisons of outlying bases of the United States—principally in the Panama Canal area, Hawaii, and the Philippines—and the tactical units, which in time of war were to be expanded to provide the combatant element of expeditionary forces.

In the years before the entry of the United States into World War II, the Chief of Staff exercised this Army-wide authority with the assistance of a number of military agencies, each answerable directly to him. No parallel development had taken place to provide for him a single staff appropriately empowered and organized to keep all these commands and agencies working along the same line. Many Army agencies rendered various kinds of staff assistance. The General Staff aided the Chief of Staff in co-ordinating activities of the Army, but even members of the War Department General Staff did not regard its responsibilities as entirely coextensive with those of the Chief of Staff.

In time of peace, in the 1920's and early 1930's, the only prospective overseas theaters of military operations were the outlying territorial possessions of the United States. The defensive garrisons in some of these bases had a strength of only a few hundred each, and as late as mid-1939 they had a total strength of less than 50,000 officers and men.[12] A single officer could and did command the entire Army without the support of the kind of well co-ordinated staff work considered essential in the commands of most of his subordinates. As German and Japanese military moves threatened to plunge the U. S. Army into combat in many scattered theaters of war, the attention of the Chief of Staff was stretched dangerously thin over his rapidly increasing forces.

Territorial and Tactical Elements of the Army in 1941

Until the Pearl Harbor attack of 7 December 1941 put the Army unequivocally on a war footing, General Marshall, like his predecessors, controlled most routine Army activities through territorial commands directly responsible to the Chief of Staff. These commands were of two main types: first, the corps area into which the continental United States (including Alaska) was divided for purposes of military administration and, second, the overseas departments.

There were nine corps area commands. They had been established by provision of

the National Defense Act as amended in 1920, and originally provided the only administrative machinery for local mobilization of forces in emergency and for routine control of other activities, including training of Regular Army units in the continental United States. The formal activation of field armies (tactical units) in 1932 removed from the corps areas as such the responsibility for administrative control and field maneuvering of tactical elements of the Army. These armies, to which the bulk of the tactical units of the ground army were assigned, operated directly under the command of the Chief of Staff, acting in the special capacity of Commanding General, Field Forces, formally granted him in 1936 Army Regulations.[13] Until 1940 four of the nine corps area commanders acted in a dual capacity as army commanders, and their staffs served them in both capacities. At that time the Second Corps Area (New York) was headquarters for the First Army, the Sixth Corps Area (Chicago) for the Second Army, the Eighth Corps Area (San Antonio) for the Third Army, and the Ninth Corps Area (San Francisco) for the Fourth Army. In 1940, the four armies received commanders and staffs separate from those of the corps areas.[14] Thereafter the corps area commanders, although they retained responsibility for administrative control and training of nontactical units, had as their primary job the provision of administrative and supply services for Army

---

[12] *Annual Report of the Secretary of War, 1939,* App. B, p. 53. Strength as of 1 July 1939 in the Hawaiian Department, the Panama Canal Department, the Philippine Department, Alaska, and Puerto Rico totaled 47,189 officers and men. Cf. *Annual Report of the Secretary of War, 1941,* App. B, p. 96. By 1 July 1941 there were 128,988 officers and men in the overseas bases and Alaska.

[13] Ltr, CofS to CGs Corps Areas and Depts, 9 Aug 32, sub: Establishment of Fld Armies, AG 320.2 (8–6–32), 1–a.

[14] (1) AG ltr, 3 Oct 40, sub: Orgn, Tng, and Administration of Army, AG 320.2 (9–27–40) M–C. (2) Army Directory, 20 Oct 40. (3) Army Directory, 20 Oct 41.

installations and tactical units in the United States.[15]

The overseas departments, unlike the corps areas, continued to have both administrative and operational (tactical) responsibilities throughout the period between the wars and during World War II. The departments, four in number in the pre-Pearl Harbor years, controlled all Army activities in Hawaii, the Philippines, the Panama Canal area, and the Puerto Rican area. In addition, the department commanders were immediately responsible for directing military operations by tactical units assigned to defend these four vital outlying base areas of the United States.

The tactical chain of command was distinct, if not always separate, from the chain leading from the War Department down to the territorial agencies. General Marshall exercised command of the Army as a fighting force through tactical headquarters responsible for training units and eventually for employing them in combat or in support of combat. The commanders of overseas departments and their staffs acted in both administrative and tactical capacities. Combat units were assigned directly to the departments for defensive deployment and, in event of war, for military operations.

The actual field forces in July 1939 constituted the mere skeleton of a combat force. There were theoretically nine infantry divisions in the Regular Army in the continental United States, but their personnel, scattered about in small units among various Army posts, provided the equivalent of only three and one-half divisions operating at half strength.[16] There were two divisions in Hawaii and the Philippines among the overseas department garrisons. It was impossible to organize tactical units larger than division size.

Expansion from this low point was rapid. Successive increments were added to the Regular Army in rhythm with the recurring crises abroad. The entire National Guard was mobilized and called into the active service of the United States. The induction of citizen soldiers began soon after the passage of the Selective Service Act of August 1940. By mid-1941 the four field armies contained twenty-nine infantry and cavalry divisions at nearly full strength, totaling over 450,000 officers and men. An armored force, established on 10 July 1940, had grown to comprise four divisions with a total strength of over 40,000 officers and men.[17] With combatant air units, the four armies and the armored force constituted the field forces of the U. S. Army.

In 1935 a military organization called the General Headquarters Air Force had been established to organize and command in combat the comparatively small number of tactical air units being trained, equipped, and supplied by the Air Corps, a so-called bureau in the War Department. Total Air Corps strength in July 1939 amounted to 22,000 officers and men. It had on hand about 2,400 aircraft of all types, including sixteen heavy bombers, and reckoned its combat units by squadrons, which numbered about eighty. By July 1941 the Air Corps had increased in size almost eightfold to 152,000 officers and men and had established four defensive air forces in the continental United States and two addi-

---

[15] The corps area continued to do similar work during World War II under the more appropriate name of service commands and under the jurisdiction of the then recently established Services of Supply rather than directly under the Chief of Staff. See WD GO 35, 22 Jul 42.

[16] *Biennial Report of the Chief of Staff of the United States Army, July 1, 1939, to June 30, 1941 . . .*, p. 2.

[17] *Ibid.*, p. 9.

tional air forces in overseas bases, Hawaii and Panama. The latter were an advance guard of the dozen combat air forces which eventually carried the air war to the enemy. By this time the Army had on hand about 7,000 aircraft of all types, including 120 heavy bombers, and was planning in terms of 55 to 70 combat groups of 3 or 4 squadrons each. These Army air units, organized as a virtually autonomous striking arm under the superior direction of the Chief of Staff, together with the four field armies, provided the nucleus of the combat units that protected the bases of the United States and moved across the Atlantic and Pacific to help win World War II.[18]

The Army could hardly absorb the thousands of untrained recruits it received in 1940 and 1941 and at the same time maintain or raise its combat efficiency, as it badly needed to do. In the continental United States the basic training of individuals and small units, together with the necessary construction, procurement, and administrative expansion, demanded the attention of Regular Army officers and men, in addition to that of their auxiliaries from the organized Reserve and National Guard. In overseas outposts there was less dilution of trained units by recruits. The garrisons in the overseas departments, the units most exposed to attack, expanded only about threefold during this two-year period, while the forces in the continental United States increased nearly tenfold.

The imminence of war brought about several changes in the structure of the Army.

For years war planning had been built around "M Day," when general mobilization of forces should begin. In the uneasy atmosphere of world affairs in 1939 and 1940, mobilization was a political matter of both domestic and diplomatic importance. Technically the United States never had an M Day for World War II. Nevertheless, the German triumphs in western Europe in mid-1940 brought about a vast though slow mobilization of American armed forces. These forces had to be trained before they could be employed. The Chief of Staff was responsible for the task of training the new Army, as he was for every other Army activity.

Consequently General Marshall faced the prospect of a multitude of decisions concerning the mobilization of men and materiel, strategic development of troops, and continuous strategic planning. The menacing international situation was steadily increasing the work of the entire War Department. Some of the requisite decisions concerning troop training were of the kind that called for speed and vigor of execution rather than for careful and deliberate planning. What was needed, particularly for the job of building a powerful tactical force out of the peacetime army, was an operating service of the kind for which the General Staff was wholly unadapted.[19] There was widespread dissatisfaction on the one hand with the amount of "operating and administrative duties" in which the War Department was involved and on the other with the "time killing system of concurrences" which tended to slow down War Department action.[20]

[18] For number of aircraft on hand, see *Army Air Forces Statistical Digest, World War II,* 1945, p. 135. For 1941 plans on combat groups, see W. F. Craven and J. L. Cate, *Plans and Early Operations,* Vol. I, THE ARMY AIR FORCES IN WORLD WAR II (Chicago, 1948), pp. 104–05 (hereafter cited as Craven and Cate, AAF I).

[19] *Handbook for the War Department General Staff,* 1923, p. 6.

[20] Memo, WPD for TIG, 10 Jul 40, sub: **WD Orgn as Affecting WPD,** WPD 2160–4. This expression of criticism almost coincided with the activation of GHQ.

Under these circumstances General Marshall decided to exercise his command of ground units in tactical training through a new agency, which he designated General Headquarters, U. S. Army (GHQ). Activated on 26 July 1940, GHQ was assigned the specific function of decentralizing activities under the Chief of Staff and assisting him in his capacity as Commanding General, Field Forces.[21] Brig. Gen. Lesley J. McNair became Chief of Staff, GHQ, and set up offices for the new staff at the Army War College building in Washington. The physical separation of General McNair's staff from the Munitions Building, where General Marshall and most of the staffs worked, was itself both a practical and psychological barrier to smooth integration with War Department activities.

The name GHQ, a time-honored Army designation for a headquarters controlling operations in the field, particularly the highest headquarters in an area or command, was misleading. General McNair's mission covered only the training of the combat forces, that is, the four field armies, the GHQ Air Force (until the creation of the Army Air Forces on 20 June 1941), the Armored Force, and miscellaneous GHQ reserves. In practice this assignment made GHQ a kind of operating agency for the G–3 Division of the General Staff, the part of the War Department responsible for making plans and issuing General Marshall's instructions governing troop organization, training, and routine movements.

For the time being General Marshall continued to exercise tactical command of the ground combat forces, other than those in training, through the War Department, under his authority as Chief of Staff and as advised by the General Staff.[22] Nevertheless, he made clear his intention of expanding GHQ functions progressively in conformity with the basic idea of a powerful GHQ and with formal Army plans for establishing such a command in the event of mobilization for war. As thus conceived the designation of GHQ was not a misnomer. Few Army officers saw any reason to doubt that the staff which handled the countless details connected with training troop units for tactical operations would in time direct those troops in combat. Determination of the status of GHQ in controlling Army operations, particularly in relation to the War Department, was one of the most pressing questions General Marshall had to try to solve when war came to the United States late in 1941.[23]

Another change in Army organization reflecting the international situation was the establishment of base commands as semiterritorial, semitactical organizations. For the most part these bases were on islands along the North Atlantic coastline and in the Caribbean area. Several were British territory leased to the United States in the destroyer-base transaction concluded by the President in 1940. By mid-1941 a number of areas containing vital U. S. Army bases had been set up as independent commands, each responsible for the administration and defense of the bases in it. The largest base

---

[21] AG ltr, 26 Jul 40, sub: General Headquarters, AG 320.2 (7–25–40) M (Ret) M–OCS.

[22] This fact was emphasized in the clearest possible terms in the War Department letter a few months later, AG ltr, 13 Dec 40, sub: GHQ Trs and Armies, AG 320.2 (12–5–40) M–P–M.

[23] The GHQ concept and the World War II institution established in conformity with it are discussed in Chapters II and IV. For General Marshall's plans to expand GHQ functions, see memo, Actg ACofS WPD for CofS, 12 Aug 40, sub: Allocation of Responsibilities Between WPD and GHQ, WPD 3209–5.

commands were in Newfoundland, Greenland, and Bermuda.

Originally all of the base commands reported to the Chief of Staff. Early in 1941, however, pursuant to a General Staff study, the Puerto Rican Department, the Panama Canal Department, and the several base commands that had been established in British Caribbean territory were integrated for purposes of general defensive planning under the newly constituted Caribbean Defense Command.[24] This consolidation introduced a new type of command in the Army. Only a few weeks later the local headquarters of Army troops stationed in Alaska was redesignated the Alaska Defense Command. The Army organization in Alaska, while not exactly analogous to the overseas departments or to the consolidated department and base command structure in the Caribbean, had a more active and comprehensive mission than a local base command.[25] In March the War Department put the new designation to further use when it set up within the continental United States four defense commands to "coordinate or to prepare and to initiate the execution of all plans for the employment of Army Forces and installations in defense against enemy actions." [26]

These new agencies—the Caribbean, Alaska, Northeast (later Eastern), Central, Southern, and Western Defense Commands—varied in practical military importance approximately as Army activities in each area centered in a defensive mission. The Caribbean Defense Command operated in a region where defense of the Panama Canal was the paramount task and where sustained hostile action was always possible. It was an active command with combatant ground and air forces assigned to it.[27] The Alaska Defense Command was also an active defense outpost but was under the control of the Commanding General, Fourth Army, and conducted its defensive planning under the supervision of the same officer as Commanding General, Western Defense Command.

The operational functions of the continental defense commands were potential rather than actual until such a time as hostilities opened. In constituting them, the War Department designated each of the commanders of the four field armies as commanding general of one of the continental defense commands and, in effect, charged them with organizing separate staffs to plan defense measures for the areas in which the armies were training. The objective was to "integrate the army command" with "what might later be a theater command."

The defense commands thus were created to fix responsibility for peacetime planning of regional defense and, in case of hostilities, to assure continuity between planning and the direction of defensive operations. The corps area headquarters already were fully occupied with their primary functions of supply and administration and did not con-

---

[24] (1) Memo, WPD for CofS, 19 Dec 40, sub: Caribbean Def Cmd, WPD 4440–1. The Chief of Staff approved this study 4 January 1941. (2) AG ltr, 9 Jan 41, sub: Caribbean Def Cmd, AG 320.2 (1–8–42) M–C.

[25] AG ltr, 4 Feb 41, sub: Designation of Alaska Def Cmd, AG 320.2 (12–20–42) M (Ret) M–C. Alaska was in the Ninth Corps Area and under the Western Defense Command when that agency was constituted on 17 March 1941.

[26] (1) Memo, WPD for CofS, 13 Mar 41, sub: Def Plans—Continental U. S., WPD 4247–9. (2) AG ltr, 17 Mar 41, same sub, AG 320.2 (2–28–41) M–WPD–M. Initially the commanding generals of the four continental defense commands were concurrently the commanding generals of the four field armies.

[27] For the unique status of the Caribbean Defense Command, see Revised Jt Army and Navy Bsc War Plan—Rainbow 5, Annex I, par. 2.

trol tactical troops, while the field armies were supposed to be able to move out of their training areas at any time to engage in offensive military operations. The responsibility of the defense commands for regional defense measures could not be made to include operational control over troops or installations without seriously interfering with the normal handling of supplies and training. The extent to which it might become necessary to give operational control to the defense commands therefore was left to be determined by specific circumstances in case of actual hostilities. In the meantime the commanding general of a defense command, being also in command of the field army in the area, was in a position to correlate planning for defense with activities already going on in the area, and to act promptly in case of hostilities.[28]

Provision for air defenses of the continental United States was made on a separate basis. The Chief of Staff decided in February 1941 that the "Air defense set-up should be in time of peace under the direction and control of the Commanding General of the GHQ Air Force."[29] Accordingly the directive that created the defense commands also established the four continental air forces, centralizing control of air defense measures conducted by them under the GHQ Air Force. After the creation of the Army Air Forces in June 1941, its chief became responsible for the "organization, planning, training and execution of active air defense measures, for continental United States."[30]

Later in 1941 Army organizations responsible for defending the United States were further supplemented by new commands in the two outlying areas, Iceland and the Philippines, where American troops were stationed farthest from the continental United States and closest to the zones of combat or potential combat. Although their missions were defensive, their proximity to actual or threatened enemy action gave a special military status to the forces in Iceland and the Philippines beyond that of a base command or even a department. Had hostilities involving the United States already begun, the two new commands probably would have been designated theaters of operations. As it was, they were constituted more nearly like task forces, temporary commands established for specific missions, despite the fact that the missions were not exclusively or at the time even primarily tactical. Their official designations were U. S. Forces in Iceland, commanded by Maj. Gen. Charles H. Bonesteel, and U. S. Army Forces in the Far East, commanded by Lt. Gen. Douglas MacArthur. The former was responsible for assisting in the defense of Iceland, a vital base on the North Atlantic convoy route and outpost of the Western Hemisphere. The latter, which included the troops formerly assigned to the Philippine Department and the forces of the Philippine Army, was given the task of organizing the defense of the Philippines and preparing ground and air forces to oppose with as much strength as

[28] Notes on Conferences in OCS, I, 207–08, 227–28, 239–40, WDCSA Rcds. These entries contain lengthy explicit statements by the Chief of Staff at conferences of 14 and 19 February 1941 on the nature of the defense commands.

[29] Memo, DCofS for WPD, 28 Feb 41, sub: Def Cmds and Air Def Set-up, WPD 4247–9.

[30] Memo for file, 30 Jun 41, WPD 4247–18. The memorandum contained an agreed statement by General Arnold, Brig. Gen. Carl Spaatz, and Brig. Gen. Leonard T. Gerow, as follows: "Active operations will be controlled by G. H. Q. These operations will be directed by appropriate commanders, either ground or air, as may be dictated by the situation."

possible any Japanese attack on American forces in the Far East.

With the organization of these theater-type commands, the U. S. Army was moving far toward the kind of organization it was to establish in the event of war. Yet the formal maintenance of peaceful relations with other powers and the defensive orientation of national policy inhibited any sharp break with the institutions and procedures of the peacetime Army. As a result, the rapid growth of the Army and the establishment of new military agencies to meet new military situations had created an extraordinarily complex structure under the Chief of Staff.

Origins and Development of the General Staff

The central headquarters of the Army at the beginning of World War II was the War Department. Through it the Chief of Staff supervised the mobilization and administration of the growing Army. Its components in 1940 and 1941 were the offices of the chiefs of the arms and services—successors of the old War Department bureaus—and the War Department General Staff. In a certain sense the arms and services constituted the administrative and technical staff of General Marshall's headquarters, and the General Staff assisted him in formulating plans and issuing orders to all organizations under his control. The structure of high command and the patterns of higher staff work in the U. S. Army at the beginning of World War II had been set by the developments of the past four decades. Legislation, regulations, and tradition alike placed the military chief of the Army and the Army's highest staffs apart from other military organizations. General Marshall necessarily worked within that structure as

best he could, for the most part using officers and staffs as he found them to meet situations as they arose. Only within this general framework of law and custom could he gradually make judicious rearrangements in organization and functions and trace new procedural patterns to replace the old ones that were inadequate.

Before the creation of the General Staff, the President of the United States, Commander in Chief of all the armed forces by provision of the Constitution, entrusted command of the combatant army, the "troops of the line," to a professional soldier called Commanding General of the Army. The Secretary of War was the special adviser to the President on all Army matters, but his primary responsibility extended only to the "fiscal affairs of the Army" as distinct from "its discipline and military control." [31] The commanding general had no effective authority over the semimilitary services upon which the success of military operations by the line soldiers so greatly depended. [32] Special bureaus, as they were traditionally called, performed such services for the Army, which primarily consisted of engineering, ordnance, signal, medical, transportation, supply, and general administrative work.

Each of these War Department bureaus

---

[31] Regulations for the Army of the United States 1901, Art. XXVII.

[32] (1) *Annual Report of the Secretary of War, 1903*, p. 5. The Secretary (Elihu Root) declared that the old system caused "almost constant discord and a consequent reduction of efficiency." (2) H Com on Mil Affairs, 69th Cong, 2d sess, hearings, *The National Defense: Historical Documents relating to the Reorganization Plans of the War Department and to the Present National Defense Act*, Part I, pp. 77–103. Pages cited contain statements by Lt. Gen. J. M. Schofield, Commanding General, 1889–95. This document, a convenient collection of testimony on Army affairs during the first two decades of the twentieth century, is cited hereafter as *Historical Documents*.

commissioned specialist officers in its own branch of the Army and controlled their subsequent careers. The bureaus supervised the noncombatant tasks performed by their officers and men in all Army organizations, including tactical units, above the brigade level. They developed, procured, and distributed the military equipment and supplies which the Army used and on which it subsisted. The Adjutant General's Department, one of the most powerful of the bureaus, kept all official records and issued all the formal orders emanating from the War Department under the authority of the President or the Secretary of War. Thus the bureaus controlled much of the manpower, all of the matériel, and most of the administration of the Army. They composed the administrative and technical staff advising the Secretary of War on policies in their special fields, and in addition were the operating agencies that actually performed the duties required under the policies they helped devise. The bureau chiefs reported directly to the Secretary of War and, especially because they had permanent tenure, enjoyed an almost independent status in the Army. Thus co-ordination of military and semimilitary aspects of War Department work could take place nowhere except in the Office of the Secretary of War. There was no professional soldier with authority broad enough to help accomplish such co-ordination. There was no staff concerned with military affairs and military operations as distinct from specialized combat, technical, administrative, or supply tasks.[33]

Experience in time of war had never highly recommended this system of Army control. It became less and less satisfactory as success more and more came to depend on the efficient mobilization and movement of vast quantities of increasingly specialized equipment and supplies for the support of the combatant troops. At the end of the nineteenth century the Spanish-American War showed that existing machinery for planning and managing the military effort was inadequate for the complexities of modern war.[34]

Elihu Root, Secretary of War 1899–1904, undertook to recommend a remedy for the deficiencies of Army organization. He worked for many months to convince the Congressional military affairs committees that the War Department as then constituted could not provide the information required or effect the co-ordination necessary for efficient prosecution of war. In 1902 Secretary Root reported to the President:

The most important thing to be done now for the Regular Army is the creation of a general staff. . . . Our military system is . . . exceedingly defective at the top. . . . We have the different branches of the military service well organized, each within itself, for the performance of its duties.

But when we come to the coordination and direction of all these means and agencies of warfare, so that all parts of the machine shall work true together, we are weak. Our system makes no adequate provision for the directing brain which every army must have to work successfully. Common experience has shown that this can not be furnished by any single man without assistants, and that it requires a body of officers working together under the direction of a chief and entirely separate from and independent of the administrative staff of an army (such as the adjutants, quartermasters, commissaries, etc., each of whom is engrossed in the duties of his own special de-

---

[33] For Army organization before the creation of the General Staff, see Regulations for the Army of the United States, 1901. Cf. *Annual Report of the Secretary of War, 1919*, p. 61.

[34] S Doc 221, 56th Cong, 1st sess, *Report of the Commission Appointed by the President to Investigate the Conduct of the War With Spain.*

partment). This body of officers, in distinction from the administrative staff, has come to be called a general staff.[35]

In accordance with this analysis and recommendation, the Secretary of War urged the passage of legislation creating a general staff to advise and assist the Secretary of War in integrating the work of the bureaus with combat needs and to develop sound military programs and plans.

The general staff idea finally overcame Congressional reluctance, which may have been based partly on public fear of a central staff system commonly identified with Prussian militarism and certainly was based partly on the determined opposition from bureau chiefs whose eminence it threatends.[36] An Army general staff corps came into being on 15 August 1903.[37] Its

strength, including the Chief of Staff, amounted to forty-five officers, who were to be detailed for approximately four-year tours of duty from other branches of Army service. The old title of Commanding General of the Army ceased to exist. The Chief of Staff took over his responsibility for the troops of the line and in addition assumed the crucial extra prerogative of supervising and co-ordinating the technical, administrative, and supply bureaus of the War Department.

The law authorizing the reorganization of the Army embodied Secretary Root's idea of a planning and co-ordinating staff, one which, he said, "makes intelligent command possible by procuring and arranging information and working out plans in detail, and . . . makes intelligent and effective execution of commands possible by keeping all the separate agents advised of the parts they are to play in the general scheme." [38] Spelled out in detail, the duties of the new staff were as follows:

. . . to prepare plans for the national defense and for the mobilization of the military forces in time of war; to investigate and report upon all questions affecting the efficiency of the Army and its state of preparation for military operations; to render professional aid and assistance to the Secretary of War and to general officers and other superior commanders, and to act as their agents in informing and coordinating the action of all the different officers who are subject under the terms of this act to the supervision of the Chiefs of Staff.[39]

The significance of this assignment of tasks to the General Staff depended upon the

[35] Annual Report of the Secretary of War, 1902, pp. 42–43.

[36] The General Staff concept was far from new. The German General Staff had been in operation for almost a century. In Secretary of War Newton D. Baker's opinion, expressed at the end of World War I, American delay in adopting the idea derived to a great extent from the traditional fear that it represented a kind of militarism which might involve the United States unnecessarily in war. See his analysis in Annual Report of the Secretary of War, 1919, pp. 61–62. Secretary Baker also pointed out that, besides the inevitable opposition from the bureau chiefs, the General Staff concept suffered because the "high degree of centralization which an effective General Staff employs inspired many Members of Congress with the fear that it would grow to be a tyrannical and arbitrary power."

[37] Secretary Root's account of the creation of the General Staff, Annual Report of the Secretary of War, 1903, pp. 3–8, and Apps. A, B, C, D, and E. Maj. Gen. W. H. Carter, Assistant Adjutant General in 1902, was the Army officer most prominent in work on General Staff legislation. Secretary Root paid special tribute to his services. General Carter declared that he originally convinced Secretary Root of the need for a "board of directors to plan and coordinate" for the Army. See S Doc 119, 68th Cong, 1st sess, Creation of the American General Staff: Personal Narrative of the General Staff System of the American Army, pp. 2–14.

The contemporary writing of a British student of

military organization may have helped spur the General Staff movement in the United States, as it did in Great Britain. See Spenser Wilkinson, Brain of an Army (London, 1895).

[38] Annual Report of the Secretary of War, 1902, p. 46.

[39] PL 88, 58th Cong, An Act to Increase the Efficiency of the Army.

vesting of broad powers in its chief. The law was fairly specific:

> The Chief of Staff, under the direction of the President or of the Secretary of War, under the direction of the President, shall have supervision of all troops of the line and of The Adjutant General's, Inspector General's, Judge Advocate's, Quartermaster's, Subsistence, Medical, Pay, and Ordnance Departments, the Corps of Engineers, and the Signal Corps. . . . Duties now prescribed by statute for the Commanding General of the Army . . . shall be performed by the Chief of Staff or other officer designated by the President.[40]

Only the ambiguity of the word "supervision," selected to describe the kind of control he exercised over all Army forces, beclouded the statement of the superior position of the Chief of Staff. In any case, regardless of arguments that later were to arise over the precise meaning of "supervision," the terms of the new legislation permitted the relationship between the Chief of Staff and Secretary of War to be redefined in a way that made for harmony rather than discord. The new Army Regulations drafted to carry out the provisions of the reorganization act read:

> The President's command is exercised through the Secretary of War and the Chief of Staff. The Secretary of War is charged with carrying out the policies of the President in military affairs. He directly represents the President and is bound always to act in conformity to the President's instructions.
> The Chief of Staff reports to the Secretary of War, acts as his military adviser, receives from him the directions and orders given in behalf of the President, and gives effect thereto.[41]

Secretary Root dwelt on the fact that the new law did not impair civilian control of the Army. In the words of his report for 1903:

> We are here providing for civilian control over the military arm, but for civilian control to be exercised through a single military expert of high rank, who is provided with an adequate corps of professional assistants to aid him in the performance of his duties, and who is bound to use all his professional skill and knowledge in giving effect to the purposes and general directions of his civilian superior, or make way for another expert who will do so.[42]

The creation of the General Staff Corps was a great advance toward centralization and professionalism in the administration of military affairs, but the General Staff encountered many difficulties in its early years. For instance, Secretary Root had silenced some of his initial critics by emphasizing its lack of either executive or administrative authority.[43] This very emphasis contributed to the tradition, wholeheartedly supported by the older administrative and technical bureaus, that "supervision" of the execution of War Department instructions or policies by the Chief of Staff or by the General Staff in his behalf did not entail any kind of intervention in or even detailed observation of the actual workings of subordinate agencies. Until World War I the General Staff confined itself almost exclusively to formulating general policies and plans and left their execution to the troop units and to the bureaus, the operating or performing elements of the Army.[44]

---

[40] Ibid.

[41] Regulations for the Army of the United States, 1904, Art. LIX.

[42] Annual Report of the Secretary of War, 1903, p. 6.

[43] Annual Report of the Secretary of War, 1902, p. 46.

[44] A full account of the early and middle period of General Staff history, 1904–19, is given in Maj. Gen. Otto L. Nelson, Jr., National Security and The General Staff (Washington, D. C., 1946), pp. 73–273. For an example of General Staff difficulty with one of the older bureaus, see the account of the 1911 controversy between Maj. Gen. Leonard Wood, Chief of Staff, and Maj. Gen. F. C. Ainsworth, The Adjutant General, in Nelson, pp. 138–66.

During World War I the General Staff, particularly after its reorganization in 1918, showed a great deal of vigor, exerting increasingly detailed supervision and control over the technical and administrative services. The Chief of Staff at the time, Gen. Peyton C. March, was willing to admit the inadvisability of having the General Staff do the work of the bureaus. He defended his staff's inclination to do so because of an urgent need to solve practical supply and transportation difficulties that no amount of policy planning would remedy.[45] Nevertheless, the General Staff was vulnerable to criticism within the terms of its own philosophy.

Early in World War I the General Staff was handicapped in developing an effective program of any kind because of the rapid rotation of officers in the position of Chief of Staff.[46] General March, however, who took over the duties of Chief of Staff on 4 March 1918, remained on duty until 30 June 1921. At the beginning of his tenure he promptly approved a previously expressed opinion that the "organization of the War Department as it existed at the be-

ginning of the war was in many respects entirely inadequate to meet the requirements of the situation." [47] Accordingly he undertook a thorough reorganization along the general lines already marked out a few weeks before he took office.[48]

This 1918 reorganization as finally carried out revamped the General Staff and affirmed the powers of the Chief of Staff in relation to other officers and to the bureaus. It gave the General Staff something comparable to its post-World War I structure. Staff functions were divided among four divisions: (1) Military Intelligence, (2) War Plans, (3) Operations, and (4) Purchase, Storage, and Traffic. Each division was headed by an officer called a director.[49] In addition, the 1918 reorganization strengthened the staff by clarifying the authority of its chief. War Department General Order 80, 26 August 1918, provided:

The Chief of the General Staff is the immediate adviser to the Secretary of War on all matters relating to the Military Establishment, and is charged by the Secretary of War with the planning, development and execu-

---

[45] *Report of the Chief of Staff, U. S. Army, 1919,* p. 23. Even General Pershing admitted that the weakness of the bureaus was the principal cause of the trouble but also blamed overzealous, poorly trained General Staff officers. See statement by General Pershing in *Historical Documents,* p. 367.

[46] *Report of the Chief of Staff, U. S. Army, 1918,* p. 6. Maj. Gen. H. L. Scott became Chief of Staff on 16 November 1914 and retired 21 September 1917. Gen. T. H. Bliss was Chief of Staff from 22 September 1917 until General March was assigned, but he was absent from Washington a great deal of the time. Thus, Maj. Gen. John Biddle was Acting Chief of Staff from 29 October 1917 until 16 December 1917. General Bliss returned and served from 16 December until 9 January 1918, when he left for France. General Biddle again served in acting capacity from 9 January until 3 March 1918. On 4 March, General March became Acting Chief and on 20 May was confirmed as Chief of Staff, which post he retained until after the end of the war.

[47] *Report of the Chief of Staff, U. S. Army, 1919,* p. 15. General March was particularly concerned about the lack of consolidation and co-ordination. There were nine different systems of estimating requirements, five sources of supplies for organizations to be equipped, five different systems of property accountability, and ten different agencies for handling money accounts with five different systems of fiscal accounting. See *Report of the Chief of Staff, U. S. Army, 1919,* pp. 15–17.

[48] WD GO 80, 26 Aug 18. This reorganization followed the line of development initiated by WD GO 14, 9 Feb 18 and WD GO 36, 16 Apr 18. For a brief summary of General Staff organization, see OPD Hist Unit Study A.

[49] War Department reorganization in 1946 reverted to the 1918 title of "director" for heads of General Staff Divisions. The term was chosen in 1946 to indicate that a certain amount of supervisory "operating activity" was proper for the General Staff so long as administrative detail had been delegated.

tion of the Army Program. The Chief of Staff by law (act of May 12, 1917) takes rank and precedence over all the officers of the Army, and by virtue of that position and by the authority of and in the name of the Secretary of War, he issues such orders as will insure that the policies of the War Department are harmoniously executed by the several Corps, Bureaus, and other agencies of the Military Establishment and that the Army Program is carried out speedily and efficiently.

This language, at least according to General March's interpretation, made the Chief of Staff the superior of the commander of the American Expeditionary Forces.[50]

Nevertheless, throughout World War I the authority of the Chief of Staff was confused by the fact that General John J. Pershing exercised virtually independent command over Army forces in France, the single important theater of operations. Army Regulations drafted in accordance with the 1903 legislation creating the position of the Chief of Staff explicitly stated that the President had authority to delegate command of all or part of the Army to an officer other than the Chief of Staff, and President Woodrow Wilson had exercised this prerogative.[51] General Pershing considered that he "commanded the American Expeditionary Forces directly under the President" and that "no military person or power was interposed between them."[52] In view of this attitude, of the magnitude of the job to be done in France, and of the indisputable paucity of qualified staff officers, General Pershing built up an independent staff in the theater to help him

direct military operations.[53] For most purposes the War Department was simply a mobilization and supply agency in the zone of interior, in a position of authority parallel perhaps with the American Expeditionary Forces (AEF) but clearly not superior. Since the effort of the United States was primarily made in one theater, in which liaison with Allied forces was maintained on the spot, military operations were conducted successfully without any very close co-ordination between the theater of operations and the General Staff. As a result of these circumstances, the end of World War I found the command situation considerably confused despite the special eminence given the Chief of Staff in General Order 80 of 1918. The General Staff was handicapped by this fact as well as by its other limitations.

The War Department After World War I

The Army underwent a thorough reorganization after the end of World War I. The National Defense Act, as revised on 4 June 1920, laid down the principal elements of the system which was to last almost unchanged for twenty years. It established the framework for wartime mobilization of a citizen "Army of the United States," including, besides men who might be drafted, Regular Army, National Guard,

---

[50] Gen. Peyton C. March, *The Nation at War* (New York, 1932), p. 266.

[51] Regulations for the Army of the United States, 1904, Art. LIX.

[52] James G. Harbord, *The American Army in France* (Boston, 1936), p. 111.

[53] (1) Statement by General Pershing in *Historical Documents,* p. 367. (2) John J. Pershing, *My Experiences in the World War* (New York, 1931), I, 16.
There were particularly stormy disagreements in regard to the supply program and the number of troops to be sent to France, subjects with which both the Chief of Staff and the commanding general of AEF were intimately concerned. See: (1) March, *The Nation at War,* p. 253; (2) Pershing, *My Experiences in the World War,* II, 186–87, 190–92, 223.

and Reserve components.[54] General Pershing became Chief of Staff on 1 July 1921 and helped rebuild the Regular Army in accordance with its central place in the new pattern. Several additional branches of the service, including the four combat components of the line, the Infantry, the Cavalry, the Coast Artillery, and the Field Artillery, were established by law on an administrative level with the service bureaus. The independent power of all the bureaus was permanently reduced in one important respect by the inauguration of a single promotion list for most officers instead of the former system of separate lists in each branch.[55]

Within this Army framework, the General Staff assumed something very close to its World War II form in accord with the recommendations of a board convened to study this problem. General Pershing enthusiastically approved the findings of the board, which was headed by Maj. Gen. James G. Harbord, his deputy. The new staff organization went into effect on 1 September 1921 and became part of basic Army Regulations in November of the same

year.[56] The General Staff was given as its primary responsibility the preparation of plans for "recruiting, mobilizing, supplying, equipping, and training the Army for use in the national defense." It was also required to "render professional aid and assistance to the Secretary of War and the Chief of Staff." Functional assignment of responsibilities represented the results of World War I experience both in the zone of interior and in France. Four "G" divisions, called G-1, G-2, G-3, and G-4, dealt respectively with the personnel, intelligence, mobilization and training, and supply aspects of General Staff work.[57] A fifth staff unit, called the War Plans Division, was assigned broad responsibilities for strategic planning. It was instructed also to be ready to "provide a nucleus for the general headquarters in the field in the event of mobilization," provision of such a nucleus having been called for in the Harbord Board report.[58] The division heads each received the title of Assistant Chief of Staff.

General Pershing's replacement of General March as Chief of Staff in 1921 brought an end for the time being to the practical situation that had obscured the import of Army orders defining the authority of the Chief of Staff. General Pershing himself held the rank of "General of the Armies," and would unquestionably command the

---

[54] The effect of the new act was described for the benefit of the Army in WD GO 31, 18 Jul 21. For an explanation of the tremendous improvement this system effected over traditional American military policy with respect to manpower and the use of militia, see John McAuley Palmer, *America in Arms* (New Haven, 1941). Compare this volume with Maj. Gen. Emory Upton's *Military Policy of the United States* (Washington, D. C., 1907), an older classic text recommending a different mobilization system.

[55] The completely new branches were Air Service, Chemical Warfare Service, and Finance Department. Infantry, Cavalry, and Field Artillery (components of the "troops of the line") were simply given the status of branches with bureau chiefs. Coast Artillery had been a bureau since 1908. For official designation of branches in 1921, see **WD GO 24, 17 Jun 21.**

[56] General Pershing appointed the Harbord Board immediately after he became Chief of Staff (see WD SO 155-0, 7 Jul 21). Extracts from the minutes and memoranda of the Harbord Board and committees are in *Historical Documents*, pp. 568-648. The recommendations of the board were put into effect by WD GO 41, 16 Aug 21, embodied without significant change in AR 10-15, 25 Nov 21. For Pershing's approval, see his memo for TAG, 16 Aug 21, no sub, AG 020 (7-6-21).

[57] The "G" terminology was derived from usage of AEF general staff divisions, which had adopted it from the French Army.

[58] WD SO 155-0, 7 Jul 21.

field forces in the event of a mobilization during his tenure. The Harbord Board wished also to avert any possibility in the future of two great, nearly independent commands such as those exercised by the Chief of Staff and the commanding general of the AEF in 1917 and 1918. Its subcommittee assigned to draft recommendations on the GHQ problem came to the conclusion that it was highly desirable for the Chief of Staff to be designated to command in the field in the event of mobilization.[59] This committee stated that all its recommendations rested on the "working basis" that "it must be possible to assign the Chief of Staff to command in the field." [60]

Despite the apparent desires of the members of the Harbord Board, the positive designation of the Chief of Staff as commanding general of the combatant army in the field did not go into either the General Orders or the Army Regulations implementing the Harbord recommendations. In subsequent peacetime years the U. S. Army was small and its largest tactical unit was the division. According to military usage the "field forces" did not actually exist until a number of divisions had been organized for tactical purposes into one or more field armies.[61] General Pershing and his two successors, Maj. Gen. John L. Hines and Gen. Charles P. Summerall, did not press the issue of formal title. About ten years later, when field armies were activated as skeleton tactical organizations contain-

ing the combatant troops, the term Commanding General, Field Forces, came into official use as a second title for General MacArthur, who was Chief of Staff from November 1930 until October 1935. Finally in 1936, during the tenure of Gen. Malin Craig, the dual designation of the Chief of Staff appeared in print in formal Army Regulations. They then included the stipulation that the "Chief of Staff in addition to his duties as such, is in peace the Commanding General of the Field Forces and in that capacity directs the field operations and the general training of the several armies, of the overseas forces, and of G. H. Q. units." [62]

Although these Army Regulations, still in effect at the beginning of World War II, specifically reserved for the President the power to select an Army officer other than the Chief of Staff to assume high command in the field, President Roosevelt from the beginning made it clear in his handling of Army affairs that General Marshall was the superior officer to whom he would turn for advice and who would be held responsible for the Army's conduct in the war.[63] This fact, plus the intimate understanding with which General Marshall and Secretary of War Stimson worked together throughout the period of hostilities, made the Chief of Staff's position unassailable. General Marshall delegated tremendous responsibilities and powers to his field generals and relied greatly on their individual initiative and capacities for success. Nevertheless, he retained in his own hands, insofar as it could remain with one man in a coalition war,

[59] Memo, Brig Gen Fox Connor, etc. for Maj Gen Harbord, 13 Jul 21, sub: Reasons for Establishing Nucleus of GHQ Within WDGS, *Historical Documents*, p. 576.

[60] Preliminary Rpt of Com, 11 Jul 21, title: Nucleus for GHQ in Fld in Event of Mobilization, *Historical Documents*, p. 572.

[61] WD Fld Serv Regulations: Opns (FM 100–5), 22 May 41, p. 2.

[62] AR 10–15, par. 1, 18 Aug 36, sub: GS Orgn and Gen Dys. See note on Designation of Commanding General, Field Forces, OPD Hist Unit Study B.

[63] For 1942 definition of superior position of the Chief of Staff, see Ch. VI.

control of the Army's conduct of military operations. It was significant that he exercised his command from Washington, where he also had effective authority over the Army's zone of interior programs. Thus General Marshall had a far broader responsibility than his predecessors in World War I. Moreover, he faced the new and intricate problems of a struggle involving many great industrial nations and joint operations by ground, sea, and air forces employing modern weapons. Yet at the outset he had to discharge that responsibility with the assistance of the same organization and under the same procedural traditions as had been established soon after the end of World War I.

In 1940 and 1941 the chiefs of the arms and services, who performed dual functions as heads of operating agencies and as administrative or technical staff advisers, still reported directly to the Chief of Staff. All officers continued to be commissioned in one of these arms or services—that is, the Infantry, Field Artillery, etc.—and enlisted men "belonged" to the branch to which they were currently assigned. Procurement and distribution of equipment and other supplies, training of officers and some specialized units, and administrative management of the bulk of Army affairs, were still the functions of the successors to the bureaus.

The offices of the chiefs of the services paid, fed, equipped, rendered legal and medical service to, and did the administrative work for the Army as a whole. The principal branches in the service category (excluding the service arms) at the beginning of World War II were Adjutant General's Department, Inspector General's Department, Judge Advocate General's Department, Quartermaster Corps, Finance Department, Medical Department, Ordnance Department, and Chemical Warfare Service. Two of these branches, Ordnance and Chemical Warfare, developed actual weapons of war. Four, including Ordnance, Chemical Warfare, the Medical Department, and the Quartermaster Corps, organized special units for assignment to the larger Army units or headquarters requiring their particular services.

In these latter respects the services resembled the combatant branches, the five arms and, more especially, the two service arms. The combat army was built around the Air Corps and the team of ground force combat arms, the Infantry, Cavalry, Field Artillery, and Coast Artillery. These branches were responsible for developing equipment, training personnel, and organizing units for the specialized job that each branch performed in actual combat. They produced the troops of the line of the old Army. The service arms—the Corps of Engineers and the Signal Corps—similarly developed equipment, trained technicians, and formed considerable numbers of units for combat service, but their primary mission was to develop efficiency in the performance of their particular specialized functions in support of the "line" Army.

The growth of a comparatively independent military organization, the Army Air Forces, out of one of the branches constituted the most radical change in War Department organization before World War II. The Air Service, which became a branch of the Army in 1918, received the name "Air Corps" in 1926. Like the ground combat branches, the Air Corps was responsible for developing its own kind of equipment and for training personnel to use it. In 1935 it developed the GHQ Air Force, the combatant air establishment, which represented the end product of Air Corps supply and training work in the same way that the field armies were the end product of the work of the other arms and service arms. The creation of an integrated combatant air force marked an important stage in the growth of the Army's air force toward acquiring a strategic mission of its own, air operations to destroy the enemy's will and capacity to fight by air bombardment, in addition to its conventional tactical mission of supporting operations by ground armies. The designation in October 1940 of the chief of the Air Corps, General Arnold, to act concurrently as Deputy Chief of Staff for Air gave the air arm a voice on the high command level as well as the "bureau" level and the combatant level of the War Department. The mutual understanding of General Marshall and General Arnold made an operational success of an administrative arrangement that was at best complex and awkward.

In June 1941 the combatant air organization, renamed the Air Force Combat Command, and the Air Corps were grouped together to form the Army Air Forces under General Arnold as chief.[64] The new organization was intended to have, "so far as possible within the War Department, a complete autonomy similar in character to that exercised by the Marine Corps of the Navy." [65] Thenceforth throughout World War II the air force of the United States constituted a special and largely autonomous entity within the Army.

The special needs of the air arm and the policy of employing its special power, particularly as a long-range striking force, had to be correlated with the needs, particularly for support aircraft, and the strategic objectives of the ground elements of the Army. The Chief of Staff, assisted by the General Staff, continued to exercise broad supervisory control over the air forces in an effort to develop for the Army as a whole a balanced program of production, training, and military operations. Consequently, the General Staff, with Air officers serving on it, was in effect a joint or interservice staff responsible under the Chief of Staff for the employment of two complementary military weapons, the ground and the air arms.[66]

During 1940 and 1941 the War Department General Staff assisted the Chief of Staff in co-ordinating the whole of the military machine under his control, the territorial and tactical organization and the arms and services insofar as they were operating agencies. In all, about one hundred officers were serving on the General Staff in mid-1939 and more than twice that many by mid-1941.[67]

In supervising their work in particular and Army activities as a whole, the Chief of Staff in 1939 had the assistance of the Deputy Chief of Staff, who regularly handled budgetary, legislative, and administrative matters, and had authority to act

---

[64] AR 95–5, 20 Jun 41. See also Craven and Cate, AAF I, Ch. IV.

[65] For the expression quoted, see diary, Brig Gen Leonard T. Gerow, entry for 13 Jun 41, noting a conference with representatives of other General Staff Divisions, the "Air Service," and GHQ, Item 1, Exec 10.

For a contemporary statement of the degree and kind of autonomy which the Army Air Forces enjoyed, see memo, OCS for WPD, etc., 24 Jun 41, no sub, WPD 888–116.

[66] For a presentation of the Army Air Forces point of view on its drive toward autonomy, see Craven and Cate, AAF I. See also Watson, *Chief of Staff: Prewar Plans and Preparations,* Ch. IX.

[67] (1) Statistical Summary, WDGS Asgmts (1903–46), Papers 1 and 3, Item 10, OPD Hist Unit file. (2) Memo, G–1 for CofS, 4 May 39, sub: Increase, WDGS, AG 320.2 (4–17–39). (3) Cf. *Annual Report of the Secretary of War,* 1939, App. B. In this statistical summary, 232 General Staff Corps officers are listed, but about half were in the field with troops.

for the Chief of Staff in his absence.[68] In 1940 two new deputies, one for air matters and one for equipment, supply, and other G–4 activities, were appointed to help get command decisions on a great many questions which were clogging the General Staff machinery and which had to be disposed of in order to get ahead with the rapid expansion of the Army.[69] The Chief of Staff was further aided by the Secretary of the General Staff, who kept records for the immediate Office of the Chief of Staff and his deputies, initiated staff action as required by them, and supervised the routing of papers and studies to and from the appropriate staff divisions.[70] Co-ordination of General Staff work for the most part had to be done by the Chief of Staff himself, although he was assisted in the process by his principal deputy. This latter officer periodically met with the War Department General Council, which consisted of the Assistant Chiefs of Staff, G–1, G–2, G–3,

G–4, and WPD, as well as the chiefs of arms and services. Increasingly in the 1939, 1940, and 1941 emergency, the Chief of Staff settled problems simply by calling staff officers concerned into informal conference and reaching a decision therein.[71]

General Staff Doctrine and Procedure

The United States, in setting up its General Staff Corps in 1903, had created a unique institution with its own characteristic procedures.[72] Like most higher military staffs of the nineteenth and twentieth centuries, the new General Staff derived a great deal of its functional theory and terminology from the Prussian system. In German usage the *Generalstab* had been understood to be almost literally the "General's Staff," that is, a staff versed in

---

[68] (1) AR 10–15, par. 2, 25 Nov 21, sub: GS Orgn and Gen Dys. (2) AR 10–15, par. 2, 18 Aug 36, same sub.

[69] (1) Notes on Conferences in OCS, I, 92, WDSCA rcds. At this conference, 1 October 1940, the Chief of Staff observed in connection with the appointment of additional Deputy Chiefs of Staff, that "things are getting very complicated here because of the lack of understanding on the part of some people as to how things work in the War Department." (2) Memo, SGS for All GS Divs, TAG, and Chiefs of Arms and Servs, 30 Oct 40, sub: Apmt of Add DCofS, WPD 4382. Maj. Gen. William Bryden was the principal Deputy Chief of Staff. General Arnold handled Air matters. Maj. Gen. R. C. Moore handled armored force problems and questions connected with housing, equipping, and transporting the expanding Army.

[70] AR 10–15, par. 3, 18 Aug 36, sub: GS Orgn and Gen Dys. From 3 July 1939 to 30 August 1941 the secretary was Brig. Gen. Orlando Ward. For the extent of the secretary's activities during the mobilization period, see the extensive file of informal memos between the Secretary and the Chief of Staff, 1930–42, in WDCSA Notes on Conferences, WDCSA Binders 1–37.

[71] For quite informal records of General Council and other conferences held by the Deputy Chief or the Chief of Staff, see Notes on Conferences in OCS, Vols. I and II, WDCSA rcds. These notes kept by the Secretary of the General Staff were the early counterpart of the formal minutes of the General Council kept after the March 1942 reorganization.

[72] Scholarly analysis of General Staff doctrine has often been concerned with theoretical distinctions rather than concrete problems of military administration. An evaluation of the modern General Staff and a guide to some of the writing in this field is provided in an article by Dallas D. Irvine, "The Origin of Capital Staffs," *Journal of Modern History*, X, No. 2 (June 1938), pp. 161–79. A recent brief survey of the development of military staffs from a practical, descriptive point of view is presented in a book by Lt. Col. J. D. Hittle, *The Military Staff: Its History and Development* (Harrisburg, 1944).

There is one very useful modern history of the General Staff in the U. S. Army: Major General Otto L. Nelson, Jr., *National Security and The General Staff* (Washington, D. C., 1946). It covers the General Staff from its origin in 1903 through World War II. It deals of course only in small part with WPD and OPD. Readers may profitably consult the work, however, for the background against which WPD worked and OPD developed.

generalship, or a staff concerned with military operations. In contrast, the phrase as usually interpreted in the U. S. Army conveyed the correct but rather vague idea of a staff with "general" rather than specific responsibilities.[73] Army Regulations and Army practice emphasized that the highest general staff, the War Department General Staff, had as its primary concern general planning and policy making.

Until 1903 the Army's technical, administrative, and supply agencies collectively had been termed the "General Staff." [74] After 1903 and through 1941 they still constituted both in numbers and in established prestige a major part of the War Department. The early activities of the General Staff, particularly during World War I, fastened its attention on the zone of interior, where mobilization and supply were the major tasks. The bureaus were handling these tasks, as they always had, and the main contribution of the General Staff was the preparation of basic studies on organization, training, production, transportation, and supply.[75] The many high-ranking officers who returned from France after World War I to take important positions in the War Department under General Pershing naturally tended to assume automatically that the General Staff served best when it devoted itself primarily to the zone of interior and did not interfere much with the conduct

of military operations in the field. The unwritten, unquestioned law preserving broad discretionary powers for the commander of an overseas theater became and remained one of the basic traditions of the Army. Between the operating agencies in the zone of interior and the overseas commands, the General Staff was squeezed into a narrow compass. Its avenue of escape was to rise above operating at home and operations abroad. Thus Army Regulations from 1921 through 1941 defined the basic duty of the General Staff as the preparation of "necessary plans for recruiting, mobilizing, organizing, supplying, equipping, and training the Army." [76] Once its area of responsibility had been marked out as coincident with these military programs and once its role there was confined to a very general planning, the General Staff developed appropriate procedural traditions.

The War Department manual for staff officers current at the beginning of World War II stated categorically: "A staff officer as such has no authority to command." [77] This statement did not alter the fact that the general staff of any commander could act with his authority, insofar as he approved, not only in devising plans and issuing orders, but also in observing the "execution of orders to insure understanding and execution in conformity with the commander's will." [78] In a field command, the general staff officers with combat troops had a strong incentive and ample opportunity to perform this final function of command. In the General Staff there was much less emphasis on seeing that things were done than on

---

[73] Palmer, *America in Arms*, p. 125. General Palmer succinctly stated the implications of what in effect was an adaptation of German usage to patterns of American culture and military tradition. A realization of this divergence from German concepts was only beginning to spread among higher ranking Army officers in the years before World War II.

[74] E.g., *Legislative History of the General Staff of the Army of the United States . . . from 1775 to 1901* (Washington, D. C., 1901).

[75] (1) *Report of the Chief of Staff, U. S. Army, 1916*, pp. 5, 83. (2) *Report of the Chief of Staff, U. S. Army, 1917*, pp. 4–5, 10.

[76] (1) AR 10–15, par. 1, 25 Nov 21, sub: GS Orgn and Gen Dys. (2) AR 10–15, par. 4a, 18 Aug 36, same sub.

[77] WD Stf Offs Fld Manual (FM 101–5), 19 Aug 40, p. 5.

[78] *Ibid.*, p. 6. See elaboration of this idea in Command and Staff Principles, pp. 28–29.

helping determine how they should be done. Army Regulations emphasized the point that the General Staff was not supposed to do the actual work called for in the plans it was making. They specifically stated: "The divisions and subdivisions of the War Department General Staff shall not engage in administrative duties for the performance of which an agency exists, but shall confine themselves to the preparation of plans and policies (particularly those concerning mobilization) and to the supervision of the execution of such plans and policies as may be approved by the Secretary of War." [79]

In other words the General Staff was designed first and foremost to think about military activities and, to a smaller extent, to see that they were conducted in conformity with approved thinking; but it was not at all to participate in them. Normally it merely furnished memoranda approved by the Chief of Staff or the Secretary of War to The Adjutant General, who issued official instructions on behalf of the War Department to the Army agencies concerned, principally the arms and services and the tactical headquarters such as the field armies and the overseas departments. These organizations were responsible for performing the military duties necessary to carry out plans and policies. Such executive or administrative tasks, including training and mounting garrison defenses (the peacetime equivalent of military operations), were not staff duties, and the General Staff tried not to take part in them. Often the problems it spent months in studying concerned picayune matters, but this fact was a reflection of the smallness of the Army and the severe fiscal limitations put upon it in peacetime. They were viewed as problems of

general significance according to the perspective of the time.

True, the General Staff was supposed to supervise the execution of plans and policies it had helped formulate in order to observe the results. This supervision provided the basis for future staff recommendations and, if faulty execution of orders was discovered, made it possible to correct the deficiency through appropriate command channels. But the kind of direct inspection or observation that enabled a general staff in the field to check on compliance with orders was not always feasible for the War Department. In technical and administrative work, about the only way to be certain that War Department policy was carried out in practice was to become intimately acquainted with the performance of the work in detail. The General Staff could not consistently take such action, not only because the subordinate agencies would object but also because it was too small to assume such a burden.

Comparing data on troop dispositions, unit strength, training problems, and levels of supply in the overseas commands against current plans and policies was easier, but securing up-to-date information of the kind required was still a difficult task. Correspondence with the troop commanders, especially with the overseas departments, was slow. It was also voluminous. Misunderstandings of intent and fact in written instructions and reports were hard to avoid, to detect, and to remedy. Travel to and from outlying bases on temporary duty was restricted by the necessity for economy. Under these circumstances the War Department could not effectively control tactical movements designed to carry out strategic plans or specific strategic instructions emanating from Washington.

---

[79] AR 10–15, par. 4b, 18 Aug 36.

For all these reasons, as well as for more adventitious or personal ones that may have existed, officers on duty in the General Staff as a rule did not intervene in the conduct of Army affairs by subordinate agencies, whether operating staffs in the zone of interior or tactical commands in the field. A clear-cut case of disregard of approved policy anywhere in the Army plainly warranted intervention in order to make the Chief of Staff's orders effective. It was a common presumption, however, that senior commanders in the field knew their responsibilities and how to discharge them, as did the chiefs of the arms and services, and that they did not require constant surveillance by a staff officer in Washington.

Continuous and systematic checking of all Army activities to ascertain compliance in detail with War Department instructions— "following-up," as Army officers called it— was left largely to the exertions and judgment of individual officers. This responsibility was neither reflected in the internal organization of the General Staff nor emphasized in its traditions. To a great extent the General Staff in the early years of General Marshall's leadership was still working on the assumption that had been noted by General Pershing in 1923 as basic to its work:

It is evident that proper General Staff procedure must be slow, even when there is substantial agreement as to what action is desirable. When there are conflicting ideas and interests, as there usually are when dealing with important questions, the different ideas must be investigated and threshed out with the greatest care, with the result that the time required to obtain a decision is multiplied many times. This necessary slowness of procedure in General Staff work makes it essential and proper that the General Staff should confine itself entirely to matters of the broadest policy. Its procedure is wholly unadapted to an operating service.[80]

The procedure to which these official remarks referred was mainly concerned with the formal memorandum, usually called more descriptively the staff study. Concurrence by any of the five staff divisions and by any of the chiefs of the arms and services, depending on whether the matter was of primary concern to them, might be, and very often was, required before a particular General Staff study could be approved. Specific approval by the Chief of Staff or the Secretary of War was secured in every important case and in many comparatively trivial ones before any of the Assistant Chiefs of Staff issued instructions for carrying out the plan or policy recommended in any staff study.[81] There was nothing wrong with this procedure in principle, or with the tradition it reflected. As long as the Army was small and there was no immediate emergency, these procedures did not handicap the Army in carrying on its routine activities. The War Department worked slowly but satisfactorily.

By the time the emergency of World War II came, habits of War Department General Staff officers had tended to solidify in the forms established during the 1920's and early 1930's. After 1939 the Army was no longer able to enjoy the luxury of thinking about military operations in the distant future. Ready or not, it might have to carry them out on a moment's notice. More and more often the staff divisions violated

---

[80] Handbook for the War Department General Staff, 1923, p. 6.

[81] For administrative instructions concerning staff studies, see the "Green Book," a General Staff manual, 1941, title: Instructions for Preparation of Papers, Item 4, OPD Hist Unit file.

For concurrences, see WPD adm memo, 23 May 32, sub: Concurrences, Paper 139, Item 2A, OPD Hist Unit file.

their own traditions and descended from their theoretically ideal plane of high abstraction to see that certain urgent steps were taken in building the new Army. It was characteristic that when the threat of war thus spurred the General Staff to new vigor, the most frequent criticisms were offered, even by staff officers, on the grounds that it was operating too much, concerning itself with the details of Army administration.[82] Yet the overwhelming danger, dimly seen or felt as the crisis developed, was that the Chief of Staff might, as a result of enemy action, find himself suddenly in command of one or more active theaters of operations. Each of the overseas bases was a potential combat zone. The General Staff, whether planning as it was supposed to do or operating as it often did, was unsuited to act as a field-type general staff in helping direct military operations. So long as the General Headquarters envisioned in 1921 was only a theory, as it had remained for nearly twenty years, the Chief of Staff would have no staff specifically instructed and carefully organized to help him control military activities in these areas of danger and in all the theaters of operations that would develop in case of war.

The United States Government was pledged to a policy of seeking peace at nearly any cost after war broke out in Europe in 1939. The Army was in no condition to conduct major military operations. These circumstances gravely complicated the task of building and managing a first-class fighting force. But a weakness potentially more crippling was inherent in the structure of the high command. In 1932 when he was Chief of Staff, General MacArthur pointed it out: "The War Department has never been linked to fighting elements by that network of command and staff necessary to permit the unified tactical functioning of the American Army." [83] The situation had not changed materially in the next eight years. Moreover, General MacArthur had promptly diagnosed the ultimate Army need that led to the creation of a new central staff to support the high command in World War II. He urged adoption of a system through which the "Chief of Staff, in war, will be enabled to center his attention upon the vital functions of operating and commanding field forces" and which would serve to "link in the most effective manner military activities in the Zone of the Interior to those in the Theater of Operations." [84] Achievement of this goal still lay ahead in **mid-1941.**

---

[82] E.g., memo, WPD for TIG, 10 Jul 40, sub: WD Orgn as Affecting WPD. WPD 2160–4.

[83] Ltr, CofS to CGs of the Four Armies, 22 Oct 32, sub: Development of Four Fld Armies, AG 320.2 (8–6–32), 1–a.

[84] *Ibid.*

CHAPTER II

The War Plans Division

Between the two world wars the chief activating agent in the system of Army high command was the War Plans Division of the General Staff. General Pershing and his principal advisers, notably General Harbord, had recommended integrating the staff function of strategic planning with that of assisting in the command of military operations. They proposed to accomplish this result by establishing a special group of staff officers who had the twofold duty of drawing up strategic plans in time of peace and of going into the field to help carry them out in time of war.[1] In accord with this plan WPD was constituted as the fifth division of the General Staff in 1921.

Strategic Planning Agency for the Army

As established, WPD was "charged, in general with those duties of the War Department General Staff which relate to the formulation of plans for the use in the theater of war of the military forces, separately or in conjunction with the naval forces, in the national defense."[2] This definition of responsibility, which survived in Army Regulations until after the entry of the United States into World War II, brought out the three main features of WPD's work. First, it had no duties beyond the normal General Staff type of duties, a limitation which had special meaning in view of the plans and policies tradition of the General Staff. Second, it nevertheless had a sphere of responsibility quite different from the rest of the General Staff, namely the formulation of strategic plans for military operations. Finally, it was the sole staff agency which represented the Army in interservice strategic planning.

In elaborating this general assignment of duties, the 1921 Army Regulations also specifically charged WPD with the "preparation of plans and policies and the supervision of activities concerning" three major Army problems which continued to be part of WPD's staff responsibility until after Pearl Harbor. These duties were as follows: "[1] Estimate of forces required and times at which they may be needed under the various possible conditions necessitating the use of troops in the national defense. [2] The initial strategical deployment (plans and orders for the movement of troops to execute the initial deployment to be the duty of G–3). [3] Actual operations in the theater of war."[3] The first two in-

---

[1] These two functions of WPD, as determined in the 1921 reorganization of the War Department, are described in the two sections that immediately follow.

[2] AR 10–15, par. 12, 25 Nov 21, sub: GS Orgn and Gen Dys.

[3] (1) *Ibid.* (2) AR 10–15, 18 Aug 36. In addition to assigning to WPD these three broad duties, the 1921 regulations specifically charged the Division with five duties of lesser strategic importance. Three of these were rather tenuously related to strategic planning and were transferred to other staff divisions between 1921 and 1941. The other two duties still assigned to WPD in 1941 were: "Location and armament of coast and land fortifications" and "Consultation with the Operations and Training Division (G–3) and the Supply Division (G–4) on major items of equipment."

volved the broadest kind of military planning that the Army did in peacetime. The third duty, though virtually dormant during the peacetime years of the 1920's and 1930's, indicated the main direction of WPD's interest. While the term theater of war included areas potentially as well as actually involved in warfare, theoretically actual operations would not begin until theaters of operations had been designated.[4] None was so designated until Pearl Harbor brought a conclusive end to the uneasy 1940–41 period of transition from peace to war. In the years between the wars, Army officers assumed that a staff for controlling combat operations in the field would be set up outside the General Staff by the time hostilities should begin. Nevertheless, in the interim WPD had a general responsibility for such staff control of operations on behalf of the high command.

From the beginning WPD's broad responsibilities made its position exceptional. The G–1, G–3, and G–4 Divisions of the General Staff were each concerned with devising general plans for some specific aspect of mobilizing men and material resources in the zone of interior. WPD's activities centered on planning in general outline the actual operations which the Army would have to conduct in the field and support from the zone of interior. The G–2 Division, with its clearly delineated task of collecting and disseminating information about potential enemies or potential areas of operations, was like WPD in taking a broad view of warfare. The primary responsibility, however, for translating this military intelligence into terms of strategic plans for Army operations did not belong to G–2 but to WPD.

Moreover, WPD was widely recognized as having primary staff interest in problems related to the defense of overseas bases, which at the outbreak of war were most likely to become zones of combat. A lecture prepared by WPD officers in 1925 stated:

It is the accepted theory that the War Plans Division naturally is concerned mainly with affairs in the Theater of Operations and that the other Divisions of the War Department General Staff are concerned mainly with affairs in the Zone of Interior. It is this responsibility for planning for the Theater of Operations which makes the foreign garrisons of special interest to WPD. At present all matters of policy concerning our foreign garrisons are referred to WPD.[5]

To fulfill responsibilities so closely related to the basic Army objective—military operations—WPD needed to take account in general of the war-waging capacity of the Army, which in turn reflected the political and economic resources and policies of the United States.

WPD devoted itself, when necessary, to studying staff problems that did not fall into any one of the functional spheres of responsibility of the other divisions. The successive Chiefs of Staff, beginning in 1921 with General Pershing, referred many of the most general and most complex studies to it for final recommendation.[6] While the Secretary of War and the Chief of Staff, under the President, had the final responsibility for representing the Army in the spheres of national policy and international relations, WPD drew up plans, made rec-

---

[4] For definition of terms, see WD Fld Serv Regulations: Opns (FM 100–5), 22 May 41, p. 1.

[5] Lecture, title: WPD—Its Gen Functions and Opns, WPD 2389. This lecture was prepared by WPD officers for delivery at the Army War College by Brig. Gen. H. A. Smith but was not delivered. It is a good summary of early WPD opinion about its duties.

[6] Lecture, Maj George V. Strong, 8 Oct 27, Army Industrial College, title: Orgn and Functions of WPD, GS, and Jt Army and Navy Bd, WPD 2722–1.

ommendations, and on occasion participated in deliberations in those spheres. Its officers were staff agents for the Army, particularly for the Chief of Staff, in joint Army-Navy planning, and they studied closely the military phases of international negotiations engaged in by the United States between the wars.[7] As a result of all these factors, WPD took its place during the period between the wars as the part of the Army that looked at Army problems with a perspective comparable to that of the Chief of Staff himself.[8] As World War II approached, General Marshall placed increasing reliance on this particular staff division, as chief of which he himself had briefly served in 1938.[9]

WPD and the GHQ Concept

In addition to its strategic planning activities, WPD as originally conceived had to be ready to meet its responsibility for providing a nucleus of personnel for a GHQ in the field should mobilization for war occur.[10] The GHQ system was planned by the Harbord Board in accord with the Army's experience in World War I, it was recommended by General MacArthur in the 1930's, and it was the Army's approved solution for meeting the extraordinary demands that would be made on the high command in wartime. It would serve as a

---

[7] For American interservice planning, see Ch. III. For accomplishments and activities in the interservice and international field in the immediate pre-Pearl Harbor period, see Ch. IV.

[8] In describing liaison maintained by WPD with other governmental departments, WPD's executive officer in 1939 mentioned State, Treasury, Interior, Agriculture, Commerce, and Justice. This officer declared: "The work of the Division is generally speaking on a far broader basis than is found in any other agency of the War Department." Lecture, Lt Col W. H. Walker, 13 Dec 39, Army Industrial College, title: WPD, WDGS, WPD 2722-5.

589727 O-61—4

field-type staff agency separate from the General Staff and the technical and administrative agencies of the War Department. Through it the commanding general of the field forces would be able to exercise command of Army forces engaged in military

---

[9] Between 1921 and the end of 1940 eleven officers served as chiefs of the Army's strategic planning agency, as follows:

Briant H. Wells (O–463) b. 1871	
Sep 1921–Oct 1923	
Stuart Heintzelman (O–774) 1876	
Dec 1923–Jul 1924	
Leroy Eltinge (O–502) 1872	
Jul 1924–Apr 1925	
Harry A. Smith (O–335) 1866	
Jul 1925–May 1927	
George S. Simonds (O–764) 1874	
Sep 1927–Sep 1931	
Joseph P. Tracy (O–390) 1874	
Sep 1931–Aug 1932	
Charles E. Kilbourne (O–858) 1872	
Sep 1932–Feb 1935	
Stanley D. Embick (O–766) 1877	
Mar 1935–May 1936	
Walter Krueger (O–1531) 1881	
May 1936–Jun 1938	
George C. Marshall (O–1616) 1880	
Jul 1938–Oct 1938	
George V. Strong (O–1908) 1880	
Oct 1938–Dec 1940	

WPD's first Assistant Chief of Staff held the rank of colonel for one year, but subsequently he was made a brigadier general. His successors either were brigadier generals or were promptly promoted to that rank after their appointments as Assistant Chief of Staff. For organization and personnel in WPD as a whole, see OPD Hist Unit Study C.

[10] AR 10–15, par. 7d(2), 25 Nov 21. For the careful reflections of Army officers on the proposed GHQ system as of 1939, see Army War College rpt, 14 Oct 39, sub: Orgn for High Comd, Rpt of Com 9, G–3 Course at Army War College, National War College Library. See particularly pp. 88–90. The report stated, p. 89: "All officers of the War Department who were interviewed by members of the Committee in regard to this regulation (i.e., AR 10–15, covering Commanding General, Field Forces, GHQ, and the General Staff) professed themselves as satisfied with the present version and considered its provisions desirable." Also: "It appears that the present text of Army Regulations (10–15) conforms to the principles of the Harbord Board."

operations. According to Army doctrine as of 1921, the Chief of Staff probably would himself serve as commanding general of the field forces and move into the field in a major theater of operations, presumably overseas or at least outside the boundaries of the continental United States. The assumption in the 1920's was that, once there, he would follow General Pershing's precedent of directing operations in virtual independence of the War Department, which in turn would devote all energies to the zone of interior functions of mobilizing men and material resources. Since it was to be hoped that he would either retain his position as Chief of Staff or be succeeded in that position by the incumbent Deputy Chief of Staff, friction between the Army in Washington and a general headquarters overseas could be controlled and minimized.

The Harbord Board particularly desired to integrate responsibility for high-level planning in peacetime with the direction of operations in time of war. The subcommittee of the Harbord Board appointed to study the question agreed: "The War Department is, and of course must remain the President's agency in deciding the political-strategical aspects of any particular war. But once these have been decided, the same officers who in peace have prepared the plans as to the strategical distribution of troops should be the principal staff officers charged with execution of further operations." [11] Therefore the Harbord Board provided that the "War Plans Division shall be so organized as to enable it, in the event of mobilization, to furnish the nucleus of the general staff personnel for each of the General Staff Divisions required at the Gen-

eral Headquarters in the Field." [12] The intent of the Harbord Board plan was that, in the event of a general mobilization, the War Plans Division "as a whole would sever its connections with the War Department and go into the field as the nucleus of G. H. Q." [13]

Working on a static conception of politicical-strategical planning of a kind that could be settled once and for all at the beginning of a war, the Harbord Board made no provision for continuous interaction between strategic plans and military operations. Consequently it left unclear how a close relationship could be maintained between operations in the field on the one hand and new developments in War Department and national planning on the other, although new ideas and policies affecting the course of the fighting were bound to develop from time to time in the event of a long war. No specific administrative techniques were devised and set down in writing whereby the commanding general of the field forces, however unlimited his authority, could in fact keep strategic plans and military operations in harmony with zone of interior programs. Relations between GHQ and the General Staff, both of which might be serving the same man in different but closely interrelated capacities, were left undefined.

The considerable prestige which WPD soon came to enjoy cast some doubt on the wisdom and feasibility of the 1921 provisions in respect to WPD and the nucleus of GHQ. The first specific suggestion that WPD would have a continuing usefulness in time of war, as a General Staff agency to assist the Chief of Staff in giving strategic direction to Army activities, appeared somewhat incidentally in a memorandum on per-

---

[11] Memo, Brig Gen Fox Conner, etc. for Maj Gen Harbord, 13 Jul 21, sub: Reasons for Establishing Nucleus of GHQ within WDGS, *Historical Documents*, p. 575.

[12] WD GO 41, 16 Aug 21.
[13] Memo, WPD for CofS, 30 Jun 24, sub: Annual Rpt of ACofS WPD for FY Ending June 30, 1924, WPD 1347-2.

sonnel prepared by the first WPD chief, Col. Briant H. Wells (brigadier general 4 December 1922), in December 1921. In justifying the retention of twelve officers on duty in WPD, he expressed the opinion that should hostilities occur, the functions of his Division would increase rapidly rather than diminish. He foresaw that in such a situation it would "become, under the Chief of Staff, the strategical directing body of the War Department General Staff." [14]

Whatever their individual theories about establishing a GHQ, Army leaders after 1921 generally agreed that it would be inadvisable to disrupt the work of WPD in time of national emergency. Both General Wells and Brig. Gen. Stuart Heintzelman, who in 1923 became the second WPD chief, pointed out to the Chief of Staff that WPD would have to continue to function in time of war with at least a part of its trained personnel in order to avoid putting the burden of a great deal of unfinished business on the other General Staff Divisions at a particularly critical time. Especially important would be WPD's work in interservice planning with the Navy. "Furthermore," General Heintzelman observed, "at the initiation of operations it will be important that someone thoroughly familiar with plans should be with the War Department as well as with G. H. Q." [15]

Efforts to define the functions to be performed by WPD after the establishment of GHQ also clearly indicated that the Division would continue to be vitally needed in time of war. A WPD officer, speaking at the Army War College as early as 1924, indicated almost precisely the operational responsibility that OPD was to be given in World War II. He said that in time of war "there should be some agency in the War Department to see to it that the point of view of the Theater of Operations is not lost sight of . . . [War Plans Division] should guard the interests of the Theater of Operations, anticipate its needs, and make every effort to see that its demands are met." [16]

In 1933 WPD officers prepared a study of the Division's postmobilization functions. In their opinion war would bring heavy responsibilities to WPD. It would be a "primary liaison agency of the War Department" and would provide membership for the joint Army-Navy boards and committees as well as for any other "governmental super-agencies, inter-departmental committees, or special War Department committees which have responsibilities affecting the military strategy of the war." WPD would "carry through to conclusion any modification of the pertinent strategic plan," would "keep informed of the progress of the initial strategical deployment," and would conduct a "survey of possible developments of the international political and military situations." Upon the basis of the knowledge gained in all these activities, it would complete "such strategical plans as the situation required," and revise them or develop new plans "as a continuing function." The War Department Mobilization Plan, 1933, specifically provided for the continuance of WPD after mobilization. Furthermore, a revision of Army Regulations 10–15 was then under consideration in order to make them "conform to the War De-

---

[14] Memo, WPD for G–1, 16 Dec 21, sub: Minimum No of RA Offs Required for WPD, WPD 392.

[15] (1) Memo, WPD for CofS, 30 Jun 24, sub: Annual Rpt of ACofS WPD for FY Ending June 30, 1924, WPD 1347–2. (2) Cf. memo, n. 12.

[16] Lecture, Lt Col E. M. Offley, 15 Dec 24, Army War College, title: G–1 Activities, WPD GS, WPD 2160–2.

partment Mobilization Plan, 1933, whereby the duties of the Commanding General of the Field Forces and of the Chief of Staff in the War Department are to be centered in one head." [17]   The revision of Army Regulations 10–15 that appeared in 1936 formally embodied this latter provision.[18]

In 1936 Brig. Gen. Walter Krueger, who preceded General Marshall as WPD chief, summed up the case for WPD as a permanent, that is peacetime and wartime, General Staff agency with extensive responsibilities.   While paying tribute to the tradition that WPD should not indulge in "interference in the proper functions of some high command or of some other agency of the War Department," General Krueger stressed the conviction that, in event of a major conflict, the Army would need "a group in the General Staff of the War Department capable of advising the Chief of Staff on the broad strategical aspects of the war."   If WPD were not used as the agency for this job, he predicted, it should "be one formed by the Chief of Staff and used by him directly." [19]   By 1938, although the GHQ concept remained a basic element in Army planning for war, the indispensability of some kind of War Plans Division in Washington had become so evident that the commitment to furnish the nucleus of GHQ meant merely that WPD would supply three or four officers for the G–3 Division of GHQ.[20]

War Planning: 1921–40

During the first two years of its existence, WPD established a pattern of work which persisted for the next twenty years.   The officers on the staff prepared voluminous studies for use at the international conferences on limitation of armaments, drafted and distributed to other Army agencies several strategic plans for the employment of military forces in the case of certain hypothetical war situations, and represented the Army in joint Army-Navy planning.[21] WPD also worked on the basic War Department mobilization plans, but after 1923 primary responsibility for this kind of planning was transferred to G–3.   This transfer resulted in a clarification of WPD's responsibility in line with a practical distinction which emerged from preliminary discussion of the issue.   Brig. Gen. Hugh A. Drum, then Assistant Chief of Staff, G–3, stated:

The War Department Mobilization Plan, the Corps Area Department and Unit plans all pertain to activities of the Zone of Interior, the mission of these plans being the mobilization of troops and their prompt preparation for entering the theater of operations.   While the War Plans Division is very much concerned in the development of these plans, its primary function is that of establishing the basis for the mobilization, that is to say, the estimate of the troops required for theaters of operations

---

[17] WPD draft memo, WPD for CofS, — Nov 33, sub: Dys of WPD WDGS After M–Day, and draft appendices, WPD 2160–3.   This memorandum, prepared by Maj. P. J. Mueller, was not dispatched.
[18] See Ch. I.
[19] WPD adm memo, 24 Oct 36, sub: Dys of WPD of WDGS in War, WPD 1199–211.
[20] See AG ltr, 8 Apr 38, sub: Annual Mobilization Asgmts of RA Offs, AG 320.2 (3–26–38) (Exec) W.P.

[21] Memo, WPD for CofS, 9 Aug 22, sub: Annual Rpt of ACofS WPD for Period 1 Sep 21–30 Jun 22, WPD 821–1.   Originally 14 officers were assigned for duty with WPD as constituted in 1921.   The number was cut to 12 in 1922, and strength remained at 11 or 12 officers, 1922–39.   By the end of 1940 it reached 22.   See OPD Hist Unit Study C.   All information presented in this history concerning officer personnel and personnel assignments in WPD and OPD is taken from the several officer personnel lists compiled by the author.   This information is not footnoted in the text.   For detailed personnel studies and a note on sources, see App. A and OPD Hist Unit Studies D, F, and K.

and the times and places for their concentration.[22]

In this sense war planning as distinct from mobilization planning was the functional core of all WPD's work throughout the existence of the Division under that name. Originally this function involved literally the writing of formal plans describing in considerable detail the missions to be accomplished and the forces to be employed under some particular military situation. Once approved by the Chief of Staff, they provided a strategic outline of military operations to be undertaken by Army commanders whenever the President or the Chief of Staff should order a particular plan into effect. Later, planning came to mean, in addition, staff participation in strategic deliberations, particularly in the interservice and international sphere, which led to formal command decisions binding on the Army.[23]

In every kind of planning the objective was to reach an agreement on specific military operations which would achieve the strategic objective sought and which would also reflect an intimate appreciation of the Army's mobilization, organization, equipment, training, supply, and replacement capacities. The other General Staff Divisions were almost completely occupied with these matters, and close collaboration with them was essential. In the peacetime years Army strategy had to be tailored to available resources more often than the reverse. In many cases, particularly as World War II came closer, G–4, G–3, or G–1 took

the lead, in accordance with their assigned staff functions, in radically altering the Army's strategic capabilities by recommending and securing, through the efforts of the Chief of Staff and his civilian superiors, new munitions procurement policies, new troop organization schedules, or new manpower programs for the Army. But WPD always performed the staff function of defining and developing the strategic factors in these as in all other kinds of Army planning.

Theoretically, and to a great extent in fact, the main enterprise of WPD during the 1920's and 1930's was the preparation of the "color" plans. The philosophy of these early war plans derived from the classic General Staff ideal of being prepared with detailed military plans for action in any conceivable emergency. Each emergency situation was given a particular color as a code name, which usually also applied to the principal nation visualized as an enemy in that particular situation. The existence of a plan in no way reflected any real anticipation of hostilities involving the nation or nations for which the plan was named. In fact, in the peacetime atmosphere of the years when most of the color plans were drawn up, there was no immediate menace to the United States. The emergency situations visualized were either highly improbable or of comparatively minor importance. It is true, of course, that such situations were the only ones then foreseen as possible causes for a declaration of war by the Congress or support of a war by the people of the United States. Even the minor operations contemplated probably would have strained the resources of the skeleton Army of the years 1921–40.

The keynote of all war planning before 1939 was the strategic concept, required

---

[22] Memo, G–3 for CofS, 20 Dec 23, sub: Change in Sec. XIV, Bsc Plan, WD Mobilization Plan, 1923, copy in WPD 1199–8.

[23] For a detailed description of the formal procedures of Army war planning, see lecture, Brig Gen Krueger, 3 Jan 38, Army Industrial College, title: War Plans and War Planning, WPD 2722–3.

by national policy, of defense of the United States by the United States alone against any and all combinations of foreign powers. Thus of the ten or twelve color plans current and approved in the years between the wars, the one which occasioned the most staff work was not, properly speaking, a war plan at all but instead a "National Position in Readiness" plan called BLUE (United States).[24] Of the others only two called for general mobilization of the armed forces, and these two represented highly improbable developments in international affairs, namely a war against RED (British Empire) or against a coalition of RED and ORANGE (Japan). The most significant plan from a strategic point of view was the ORANGE plan proper, which visualized a major conflict that, although primarily naval, would require the mobilization of more than a million men in the Army. The other war plans provided for actions in comparatively minor emergencies.[25]

In all cases the color plans were simple outlines of missions to be accomplished and Army forces to be mobilized, concentrated, and used in combat in the event that military operations became necessary under the circumstances presupposed in any one of the plans. As strategic planning in a broad sense, the early war plans, with the exception of ORANGE, were virtually meaningless because they bore so little relation to contemporary international political and military alignments. They were valuable, however, as abstract exercises in the technical process of detailed military planning, pro-

viding useful training for the officers who drew them up. By 1940 the color plans had been largely superseded by the more comprehensive RAINBOW plans, which provided a variety of military courses of action to meet the real strategic situation imposed by Axis aggression.[26]

Making the detailed military calculations needed to draft formal war plans, regardless of how limited their usefulness as current strategic policy might be, required painstaking work on the part of the whole General Staff. A statement on the complex process of war planning was formulated by WPD early in 1940 for use in a course of instruction in war planning given at the Army War College. It read as follows:

The War Plans Division is not the only war planning agency of our General Staff. Our entire General Staff is a war planning agency organized on functional lines: namely Personnel, Military Intelligence, Operations and Training, Supply, and War Plans. The War Plans Division is in a sense the keystone division of the General Staff, in so far as war plans are concerned, since it provides contact with the Navy in formulating Joint Basic war plans, and is charged with preparing the basic part of the Army Strategic Plans.[27]

Four representative staff actions of the 1930's that involved WPD were summarized for the Deputy Chief of Staff's information in September 1936 by Colonel Krueger (brigadier general 1 October 1936) who had just become division chief. To illustrate WPD's activities, Colonel Krueger selected two cases involving the study and resolution of issues that had arisen concerning the distribution of equipment among several interested Army agencies, a

---

[24] WPD 870. The entire file is correspondence on BLUE plan.

[25] For an outline of eleven early "color" plans approved by the Secretary of War, see WPD Book, 9 Jan 31, title: Strategical Plans Outline, Item 1, Exec 4. The color plans are filed as obsolete registered documents of Plans & Operations Division, GSUSA, in Classified Files, AGO.

[26] For RAINBOW plans, see Ch. IV.

[27] Army War College study, 1939–40, title: Notes on War Planning, App. 4, Item 2A, Exec 4. A detailed chart in this study gives a clear idea of how intricate and long-drawn-out were the steps in completing a joint war plan.

third case involving extra-War Department negotiations, for which WPD was responsible, and a final case of pure war planning. The actions were described as: (1) replacement of airplanes for overseas departments; (2) pack artillery in the Hawaiian Department; (3) War Department participation in the development of civil airways and landing fields in Alaska; and (4) procedure for co-ordinated action within the General Staff for the development of an Army strategical plan.

These four cases indicated in what sense WPD was the "keystone division of the General Staff." In solving the airplane problem, WPD consulted G–3, G–4, and the Air Corps to reach a compromise that would satisfy the commanding generals of the Panama Canal, Hawaiian, and Philippine Departments as well as the GHQ (combatant) Air Force in the United States. In disposing of two batteries of 75-mm. howitzer pack artillery, WPD had to reconcile the views of the same three department commanders, the Commanding General, Fourth Army, the Chief of Field Artillery, the Chief of Ordnance, The Quartermaster General, G–3, and G–4. The third case was comparatively simple since WPD not only had general authority to deal with extra-War Department problems, but also in this instance was explicitly directed by the Secretary of War and the Chief of Staff to "formulate the basis for action" upon a request from the Secretary of Interior for Army Signal Corps assistance in the Alaska airways program. Nevertheless, WPD consulted the Chief Signal Officer and the Chief of the Air Corps for technical information, G–1 and G–3 concerning personnel, G–4 concerning funds and equipment, and the Budget Advisory Committee concerning legislation. Finally, even in drafting a war plan, WPD worked closely with G–1, G–2, G–3, and G–4, these divisions drafting sections in accordance with their functional duties.[28]

As these four cases indicated, WPD was the "keystone" of the General Staff only in the sense that it had an interest in almost all kinds of Army affairs in which the Chief of Staff's authority had to be exercised, and had primary interest in those issues that most directly affected the Army's ultimate purpose, military operation. But however active or influential it might be as a result, the Division worked in accordance with prescribed General Staff procedures, conferring with all interested agencies, securing their concurrences to proposed solutions, and centering all activities around the final memorandum for the Chief of Staff's approval. Nor was the Division unique in playing such a role of co-ordinator. In staff actions that could be defined as problems primarily concerning personnel, organization and training, or procurement and supply, G–1, G–3, and G–4 respectively played similar roles.

Staff Authority

Whatever difference there was between WPD and the other divisions of the General Staff when it came to exercising delegated authority on behalf of the Chief of Staff, it enjoyed by virtue of its exceptional knowledge of his ultimate objectives in the broad sphere of military operations. The heads of all the divisions had the same discretionary authority. General Staff regulation provided: "The Assistant Chiefs of Staff, in charge of the divisions of the General Staff . . . are authorized on matters

[28] For all the foregoing, see memo, WPD for DCofS, 23 Sep 36, sub: Request of DCofS for Synopsis of Four Problems Handled by WPD, WDGS, WPD 3956.

under their supervision to issue instructions in the name of the Secretary of War and the Chief of Staff." [29]   Under this authority, WPD might issue instructions that had the force of authority in matters bordering between policy and execution of policy. The Division would first have to be confident that the case in question should be treated as requiring a secondary action necessary to carry out approved War Department policy rather than as raising a new issue for decision by the Chief of Staff. The fact that the Division had reached this conclusion was bound to influence the other divisions of the General Staff, who were apt to let the ruling stand.

Nevertheless, WPD's authority to make such decisions was obscure. If any Army agency, particularly one of the other staff divisions, took exception to the actions in question, the whole policy had to remain in abeyance until submitted to the Chief of Staff. The WPD chief thus had no grant of power to co-ordinate the work of the entire General Staff in the interests of supporting the strategic plans of the Army. A thorough canvassing of this question took place in 1925, when the Division chief's authority was subjected to particularly searching inquiry. The result of the whole study, in which WPD officers took a leading part, was to confirm the idea that WPD was on a level with, not superior to the other General Staff Divisions, and that it had to refer all basic policy decisions to the Chief of Staff rather than to try to co-ordinate the work of the rest of the General Staff. The consensus of the General Staff reflected very closely the line taken by WPD:

No additional authority and responsibility should be given to the Assistant Chief of Staff, WPD, with a view to more expeditious and

economical General Staff action. The authority granted by Par. 6, AR 10–15, is ample. In fact, as indicated below, the full authority granted by this paragraph has never been exercised by any Chief of the War Plans Division.

In my opinion, the Assistant Chief of Staff, WPD cannot properly and advantageously take final action concerning any type of cases now referred to the Chief of Staff and Deputy Chief of Staff for action. . . .

The following wording of Par. 6, AR 10–15, is suggested as more clearly expressing what is believed to be real intent of the paragraph, and as in accordance with the actual practice of the War Plans Division, which is thought to be correct:

The Deputy Chief of Staff and the Assistant Chiefs of Staff in charge of the divisions of the General Staff hereinafter provided for, are authorized on matters under their supervision to issue instructions in the name of the Secretary of War and the Chief of Staff, *except that basic policies, plans and projects,* and such other matters as may be required by supplementary instructions issued by the Chief of Staff, shall be submitted for approval by higher authority.[30]

This doctrine was invoked in a concrete case at about the same time. The issue was whether or not WPD had to get the Chief of Staff's approval to annexes and appendices of formal war plans which had already been approved by the Chief of Staff or whether these supplementary documents could be prepared by the various staff divisions "under the direction and coordination of the War Plans Division." [31]   The orthodox War Department opinion was set forth by a distinguished senior officer, Maj. Gen. Fox Conner, then Assistant Chief of Staff, G–4. He categorically asserted:

While it is believed that great differences between the several Divisions of the General

---

[29] AR 10–15, par. 6, 25 Nov 21.

[30] Memo, WPD for DCofS, 3 Aug 25, sub: Responsibilities of ACSofS, atchd as incl L of memo, Maj A. W. Lane for DCofS, 2 Sep 25, sub: Economy in Administration of GS, WPD 2220–2.

[31] Memo, WPD for CofS, 6 Nov 25, sub: Preparation of War Plans, WPD 2390.

Staff will be infrequent these differences will arise from time to time. When they do arise direction and co-ordination should not be left to the War Plans Division nor to any other Division of the General Staff. Direction and coordination as between General Staff Divisions is strictly a function of the Chief of Staff and any departure from this principle is regrettable from every point of view.[32]

By the end of 1939 the Chief of Staff and some of the officers in WPD were beginning to be disturbed over the limitations of staff procedure at a time of world crisis. General Marshall observed in a memorandum written shortly after he had assumed the duties of Chief of Staff: "It occurs to me that the current routine procedure of the War Department General Staff might have to be materially altered in the event of a war emergency."[33] Lt. Col. Thomas T. Handy and Lt. Col. Walton H. Walker of WPD, who drafted replies to this memorandum, stated: "Many questions now presented to

the Chief of Staff do not require a decision by him. They could and should be acted upon by a division of the General Staff after being properly coordinated with other divisions."[34] Nevertheless, throughout the period between the wars WPD did not exceed the limits of authority placed on the General Staff by traditional doctrine. It was not a central staff in co-ordinating Army-wide activities. It had neither authority nor incentive to act for the Chief of Staff in the day-to-day process of trying to link staff planning with military execution or operation of plans by subordinate agencies or commands. In peacetime such a staff was little needed, or at least the lack of it caused no disasters. In time of growing emergency the peacetime system put an enormous burden on the Chief of Staff, his deputies, and the Secretary of the General Staff, the officers who in their own persons were responsible for achieving co-ordination among Army plans and policies.

---

[32] Memo, G–4 for CofS, 16 Nov 25, sub: Preparation of War Plans, WPD 2390.

[33] Memo, CofS for WPD, 17 Aug 39, no sub, WPD 3963–1.

[34] Memo, WPD for CofS, 30 Sep 39, sub: Modification of GS Procedure, WPD 3963–1.

CHAPTER III

Early Interservice and International Staff Planning

The hurried mobilization of a big Army in 1940 and 1941 in some ways was a simple task in comparison with planning to use it in a big war, that is, a coalition war fought by large forces using all kinds of modern weapons and modern systems of communications. It was clear by the time of the fall of France in mid-1940 that, should the United States be drawn into war, American armed forces would have to engage in large-scale operations involving the close collaboration of air, sea, and ground forces with one another and with the armed forces of other nations. As soon as the United States reached a stage of military preparedness demanded by the approach of war, General Marshall found that many of his decisions on Army problems could not be made without reference to similar problems and decisions in the Navy. In the same way, both Army and Navy planning for the future came to hinge more and more on the military situation and the actual strategic plans of potential allies. In other words, nearly all of the most important decisions that had to be made in anticipating as well as in conducting such military operations could not be reached by the Army alone but had to be settled on a national or international plane of authority.

Making and carrying out the many decisions of this kind that materially affected the U. S. Army entailed a great deal of work by civilian and military staffs in Washington. Of these, WPD was only one and in fact one of the smallest. Yet in the Army the immediate influence of WPD grew steadily during the pre-Pearl Harbor period, if for no other reason, because its officers had become the principal support of the Chief of Staff in his strategic planning efforts outside the Army. The character of the impending conflict increased the importance of this part of WPD's staff work far beyond anything visualized in the 1920's.

In the process of military planning as of 1941, WPD might on its own initiative make a study and prepare recommendations bearing on the strategy that the Army ought to follow in the event of war. It was necessary to secure concurrences from the four other divisions of the General Staff insofar as their responsibilities were involved, and obtain the approval of the Chief of Staff and the Secretary of War. Other agencies inside and outside the War Department, especially the agencies of the Navy Department, were at the same time making their own plans and recommendations. Many of these recommendations required early decision, especially those dealing with the training of troops and the procurement and distribution of munitions. All of them somehow had to be adjusted and readjusted to one another in order to formulate a national strategic policy and program, which at the same time had to be co-ordinated with the plans of politically associated foreign powers, especially those of Great Britain. The Secretary of War and the Chief of Staff were the primary agents for the Army in the planning of national military policy. Of the War Department staffs which served them in one way or another and represented them in dealing with other agencies and with representatives of foreign powers, WPD shared most fully in their knowledge of strategic probabilities and best reflected their growing preoccupation with the development of Army units to meet the threat of war.

WPD officers had long maintained a liaison with most of the executive agencies, particularly with the State and Navy Departments. They sat on several interdepartmental committees, prepared reports and briefs for the use of the Chief of Staff in discussions outside the War Department, and when not sitting on these committees studied the deliberations of those who were working on such matters. The liaison was most imperfect, viewed in relation to the needs of World War II as they actually developed, but the principle of liaison existed. Moreover, the Army planners were able to carry on their work, not in isolation from conflicting or diverging ideas, but in an intellectual environment shared with planners in the State and Navy Departments. This association sometimes simplified, frequently complicated, and always was a conditioning factor in the Army's strategic planning.

Politico-Military Co-ordination

President Roosevelt, in order to determine national policy with respect to World War II, co-ordinated the ideas and work of the three agencies principally concerned—the State, War, and Navy Departments. He conferred with the three Secretaries of these departments in Cabinet meetings and at special "War Council" meetings at the White House attended by the Secretaries and the senior military advisers.[1] The President kept the main strands of national policy in his own hands, and his Cabinet assistants advised him as individuals rather than as a body. In addition to attending meetings at the White House, Secretary of War Henry L. Stimson, Secretary of the Navy Frank Knox, and Secretary of State Cordell Hull began holding informal weekly conferences in 1940, but this "Committee of Three" was designed primarily to keep the civilian heads of the three agencies abreast of one another's and the President's problems rather than to help solve them.[2]

In April 1938 a Standing Liaison Committee was formed by the State, War, and Navy Departments. This committee was suggested by Secretary Hull, and President Roosevelt heartily approved the idea. In accordance with the President's wishes, the committee consisted of the Chief of Staff, the Chief of Naval Operations, and the Under Secretary of State.[3] In view of the Chief of Staff's role, WPD had to work on some of the problems before they reached

---

[1] S Doc 244, 79th Cong, 2d sess, *Investigation of the Pearl Harbor Attack: Report of the Joint Committee on the Investigation of the Pearl Harbor Attack,* pp. 43–44.

[2] (1) *Ibid.,* p. 44. (2) Henry L. Stimson, *On Active Service in Peace and War* (New York, 1947), p. 563. The "Committee of Three" reorganized its conferences and put them on a slightly more formal basis late in the war. Minutes were kept throughout 1945 and were frequently distributed to the OPD chief. See copies of some of these minutes in ABC 334.8 Far East (9 Nov 44), 4.

[3] (1) Memo, FDR for Secy State, 4 Apr 38. (2) Ltr, Secy State to SW, 8 Apr 38. (3) Memo, ASGS for TAG, copies of (1), (2), and (3) filed with minutes of meetings of Standing Liaison Committee, Vol. I, WDCSA rcds.

the Standing Liaison Committee, and by 1941 the Division was preparing briefs on issues about which it was "necessary to refresh the mind of the Chief of Staff" before liaison meetings.[4] General Marshall very strongly supported the aim, not always but frequently achieved, of "having the State Department in joint plans so that our foreign policy and military plans would be in step."[5] National policies and interests involving the State Department as well as the armed services were usually described as politico-military affairs, and the committee's jurisdiction could not be defined more specifically. The Standing Liaison Committee dealt primarily with political and military relationships in the Western Hemisphere. It continued to meet until mid-1943, but its influence in general policy planning declined rapidly after the outbreak of hostilities.[6]

The President's dominant role in politico-military matters was absolutely clear. His public speeches, particularly during the early days when anti-Axis policy was being crystallized, nearly always marked the beginning of new phases in American diplomacy and military preparedness. The ideas in them often may have been advanced by almost anyone in his circle of official advisers, but the decision as to timing and phrasing was the President's own or at least was influenced only by some one of his personal, more or less anonymous White House assistants, among whom Harry L. Hopkins was prominent in quasi-military matters.[7] Above all it was the President who had to calculate the political risks to which he felt he could afford to commit himself and the U. S. Government by any military action. These risks lay both in the field of foreign relations and in that of domestic public opinion. Ultimately the success of any strategic policy depended upon the confidence which the governments of friendly nations and the people of the United States placed in the Roosevelt administration.

Although General Marshall and WPD were continually studying military plans in the strict sense, the Army's besetting problems in the two and one-half years just before the United States entered the war centered rather in the mobilization of manpower and the expansion of industrial production. Neither of these subjects was of primary staff concern to WPD or of sole concern in the Army. They were political and economic problems of the first magnitude. The Congress had to solve the first one, as it did by the passage of the Selective Service Act in 1940 and by its subsequent extension. The President solved or tried to solve the second by the establishment of a series of executive agencies concerned with munitions production and economic stabilization. The National Defense Advisory Commission of 1940; the Office of Production Management created in January 1941, under William S. Knudsen and Sidney Hillman; and the Supply, Priorities, and Allocations Board set up in August 1941 under Donald Nelson, were the forerunners of the powerful War Production Board

---

[4] WPD adm memo, 18 Apr 41, sub: Meeting—Standing Liaison Com, Paper 110, Item 2A, OPD Hist Unit file.

[5] Notes on Conferences in OCS, I, 70, WDCSA rcds.

[6] Min of meetings Standing Liaison Committee, four volumes (15 Feb 38–14 Jun 43), WDCSA rcds.

[7] See Secretary Stimson's tribute to Mr. Hopkins in his diary, 5 March 1941: "The more I think of it, the more I think it a godsend that he should be at the White House." Stimson, *On Active Service in Peace and War*, p. 334. On Hopkins' role, see also Robert E. Sherwood, *Roosevelt and Hopkins: An Intimate History* (New York, 1948).

finally established 16 January 1942 with Mr. Nelson as chairman.[8]

WPD had little to do directly with any of these agencies. Procurement was handled by the Army technical services, particularly the Ordnance Department, under the guidance of War Department G–4, and the Under (initially called Assistant) Secretary of War. This civilian official, Robert P. Patterson throughout Secretary Stimson's tenure, was responsible for "supervision of the procurement of all military supplies and other business of the War Department pertaining thereto and the assurance of adequate provisions for the mobilization of matériel and industrial organizations essential to wartime needs." [9] Nevertheless, military requirements recommended by the General Staff and especially the requirements contemplated in WPD's strategic planning were basic to industrial mobilization scheduling. Conversely, WPD's specific military proposals were always limited by the actual level of munitions production expected.

In like manner, military programs for equipping and training troops depended on the final distribution of munitions once they were manufactured. Here, too, the President controlled policy as to the sale of armaments to Great Britain and other anti-Axis Powers in 1940 and later the distribution of munitions and other supplies under the Lend-Lease Act of March 1941. At first he worked through the administrative machinery of the Treasury Department under Secretary Henry L. Morgenthau and later through the lend-lease administrative agencies successively headed by Mr. Hopkins, Maj. Gen. James H. Burns, and Edward R. Stettinius, Jr. The Secretary and Under Secretary of War, as well as the technical services and the G–4 Division of the General Staff, were deeply concerned with the foreign sales and lend-lease program.[10] WPD officers occasionally became involved in planning the actual release of specific articles of military equipment, trying to assess the strategic importance of weapons and their use by foreign powers. Most of the proceedings in this matter, as in administration of national economic policy, were carried on outside the War Department.

In advising on military strategy, Army leaders stayed well within the limits set by the national policy, as announced by the President, of extending aid "short of war" to countries resisting aggression. Military preparedness, insofar as it fell within the jurisdiction of the War Department, was correspondingly restricted. Military leaders could not act on the assumption, which would have resolved many of their difficulties, that the national policy of the United States would eventually have to encompass war. With each new development they could only revise their calculations of the likelihood that the United States would be drawn into open hostilities in the immediate future and correspondingly revise their plans for disposing such forces as would have become available for strengthening the defenses of the Western Hemisphere and outlying bases of the United States. The basic premise on which WPD, during 1939,

---

[8] (1) *Industrial Mobilization for War: History of the War Production Board and Predecessor Agencies: 1940–1945* (Washington, D. C., 1947), Vol. I. (2) Donald M. Nelson, *Arsenal of Democracy* (New York, 1946).

[9] Natl Def Act, 4 Jun 20, as quoted in AR 5–5, 15 Aug 28. For Assistant Secretary's and Under Secretary's work, especially in the critical period 1939–41, see: (1) *Annual Report of the Secretary of War, 1940,* pp. 1–10; (2) *Annual Report of the Secretary of War, 1941,* pp. 21–46.

[10] (1) Edward R. Stettinius, Jr., *Report to Congress on Lend-Lease Operations: Mar. 11, 1941–Dec. 31, 1942.* (2) Stettinius, *Lend-Lease: Weapon for Victory* (New York, 1944).

1940, and 1941, studied the risks of hostile action which the United States obviously was running, was set down in July 1940: civilian authorities should determine the "what" of national policy, and professional soldiers should control the "how," the planning and conduct of military operations.[11]

As the President put the country more and more on a war footing, the views of the Army more and more corresponded with, and in turn influenced, national policy. Increasing popular awareness of the gravity of the crisis caused a steady trend in the direction of military preparedness. The appointment to office in mid-1940 of Secretary of War Stimson, well known to be a staunch proponent of American preparedness and resistance to aggression, marked the seriousness of the situation and helped subsequently to insure a strong cabinet presentation of the Army's views. At the suggestion of Mr. Hopkins in April 1941, Maj. Gen. Stanley D. Embick, Army elder statesman, and General Marshall entered into a series of discussions at the White House designed to "begin the education of the President as to the true strategic situation—this coming after a period of [the President's] being influenced by the State Department." Even then, General Marshall noted, Army planners had to recognize and adjust their thinking to the fact that the President was governed by public opinion as well as by professional military opinion.[12] Whether or not the State Department approved of the Army's "education" of the President in early 1941, by the end of November Secretary of State Hull informed the President, Secretary Stimson, and Secretary Knox that, as a result of Japanese intransigence, the "safe-

guarding of our national security" was "in the hands of the Army and Navy." [13]

Joint Board Machinery

The importance of the more strictly military problems of co-operation between the War and Navy Departments had been recognized long before the advent of World War II. In July 1903 the two secretaries established a joint board for "conferring upon, discussing, and reaching common conclusions regarding all matters calling for the co-operation of the two services." The initial membership comprised four Army and four Navy officers designated by name rather than office. The board took on considerable importance in Army-Navy affairs for a time, particularly under the sponsorship of President Theodore Roosevelt, but gradually declined in prominence until in 1914 President Wilson issued oral orders for suspension of its meetings.[14]

After World War I the Secretaries of War and Navy reorganized the institution, formally named the Joint Army-Navy Board but still usually called simply "The Joint Board," and ordered it to hold meetings to "secure complete co-operation and co-ordination in all matters and policies involving joint action of the Army and Navy relative to the national defense." The membership of the Joint Board was reduced to six in number, designated by office rather than name: the Chief of Staff, the director of the

---

[11] Memo, WPD for CofS, 23 Jul 40, no sub, WPD 635–50.

[12] Notes on Conferences in OCS, II, 310, WDCSA rcds.

[13] S Doc 244, 79th Cong, 2d sess, *Investigation of the Pearl Harbor Attack: Report of the Joint Committee on the Investigation of the Pearl Harbor Attack,* p. 45.

[14] (1) Hq of Army GO 107, 20 Jul 03. (2) Memo, WPD for ASW, 27 Aug 37, sub: Relations Between Army and Navy, WPD 3740–1. This paper, prepared by General Krueger and Colonel Gerow, said the board functioned in the years before 1914 with indifferent success.

Operations Division (G–3), the director of the War Plans Division, the Chief of Naval Operations, the Assistant Chief of Naval Operations, and the director of the War Plans Division of the Office of Naval Operations.[15] After its reinstitution the Joint Board remained in operation continuously with mission unchanged. The composition of the board, however, changed twice. In 1923 the Deputy Chief of Staff, whose position had been set up by the Harbord reorganization in 1921, replaced the G–3 representative for the Army. In July 1941, in view of the increasing importance being attached to the air forces of both services, the Deputy Chief of Staff for Air (General Arnold) and the chief of the Bureau of Aeronautics of the Navy were added.[16] A co-ordinating secretary for the board was supplied alternately by the two services, the Army furnishing a WPD plans officer for this position in the immediate pre-Pearl Harbor period.[17]

In July 1939 the President put the Joint Board on a new administrative footing by directing it to exercise its functions under the "direction and supervision" of the President as Commander in Chief as well as under that of the two secretaries. The same order transferred to Presidential supervision the Joint Economy Board, which was concerned with administrative organization; the Joint Munitions Board, which co-ordinated the procurement of Army and Navy munitions and supplies; and the Aeronautical Board, which attempted to adjust policies on the development of aviation by the two services.[18]

The Joint Board became increasingly active in 1940 and 1941, making exploratory studies of almost every aspect of common Army and Navy interest and arriving at some far-reaching policy decisions in this field. It completed a number of joint strategic plans which brought together and defined general and specifically interservice elements in Army and Navy plans for identical operational situations. With the establishment of the Joint Intelligence Committee on the eve of Pearl Harbor, the Joint Board system was developing some of the character of a rudimentary interservice high command.[19] For a few weeks thereafter it attempted to function as such, making operational recommendations to the President concerning immediate military actions necessary as a result of the Pearl Harbor attack.

Throughout its existence the Joint Board was not a staff agency but simply a committee to make recommendations in the interests of interservice co-operation. It

---

[15] WD GO 94, 25 Jul 19.

[16] (1) WD GO 29, 2 Aug 23. (2) JB 301, ser 702, 2 Jul 41, sub: Change in Membership of JB.

[17] Memo for rcd, 19 Dec 41, sub: WPD Membership on Departmental and Interdepartmental Bds, Coms, and Commissions, WPD 3797–8.

[18] EO, 5 Jul 39, *Federal Register*, Doc 39–2343. See also: (1) Jt Planning Com Rpt, 17 Jul 39, sub: Mil Order of 5 Jul 39, JB 346, ser 646; (2) memo for rcd, Secy JB, 20 Jul 39, with JB 346, ser 646; (3) ltr, G. C. Marshall, Actg SW and Charles Edison, Actg SN to President, 14 Aug 39, filed with JB 346, ser 646. For the Jt Army-Navy Munitions Bd, see WD GO 51, 29 Nov 22.
WPD supplied a member for the Aeronautical Board as well as for the JB. See: (1) WD GO 20, 30 Jun 24; (2) WD GO 17, 2 Apr 42.

[19] For establishment of Joint Intelligence Committee, which was approved by the Joint Board in September 1941, ordered by the Chief of Staff in October, and finally accomplished by G–2 and the Navy's intelligence unit 3 December 1941, see: (1) JB 329, ser 710, 10 Sep 41, sub: Coordination of Int and Establishment of Central Info Gp as Agency of JB; (2) min of JB Meetings, 19 Sep 41; (3) memo, CofS for AAF and G–2, 20 Oct 41, sub: Jt Int Com, WPD, 4584–3 (the action on this memorandum was taken by General Gerow); (4) min of meetings 1st Jt Int Com, 3 Dec 41, copy filed WPD 4584–6.

was unlikely to reach conclusions on matters on which the Army and Navy were diametrically opposed. Its rulings had only the force of the authority which its members and their civilian department heads chose to exercise independently in their respective agencies except in the most important or urgent cases, upon which it was possible to get formal approval by the President. The Joint Board continued to exist on paper throughout the war, and on occasion it met to deal with issues that were considered unfinished business left over from prewar Army-Navy deliberations.[20] In theory it merely made a temporary transfer of its responsibilities when the members of the Joint Board and its subordinate committees began conducting their business in the parallel system set up under the Joint Chiefs of Staff early in 1942.[21] As long as the board remained operative, WPD (or OPD) was represented on it by its chief, and acted as the War Department agency for carrying out Joint Board decisions.[22] The existence of the Joint Board and WPD's connection with its work provided the essential precedents in Army experience for interservice planning organization and technique in World War II.

An integral part of the Joint Board organization after 1919 was a Joint Planning Committee, organized to "investigate, study, and report" on matters before the board. Originally the committee was intended to consist of three or more members from WPD and three or more members from the War Plans Division of the Office of the Chief of Naval Operations.[23] After the Joint Planning Committee had dropped far behind in its work because of the steadily increasing volume of national defense plans that had to be drawn up in 1939 and 1940, it underwent a reorganization in personnel and in operating method. In May 1941 the Joint Planning Committee was reduced to two permanent members, the Assistant Chief of Staff, WPD, and the director of the Navy War Plans Division, both of whom also sat as members of the Joint Board. Thus reduced in size, the committee was authorized to assign work to a new, permanent Joint Strategic Committee, "composed of at least three members of the Army War Plans Division and the Navy War Plans Division, whose primary duties would be the study and preparation of joint basic war and joint operations plans." In addition, whenever it saw fit, the committee could appoint working committees from the two divisions. Actually, the reorganization amounted to recognition that the Joint Planning Committee would be a device whereby the work of the Army and Navy planning staffs could be utilized and to some extent directed by the Joint Board for interservice co-ordination.[24] This approach

---

[20] An example was the attempt to revise the Joint Board publication of 1935, *Joint Action*. See n. 23.

[21] For official description of the Joint Board system at the beginning of U. S. participation in the war, see WD GO 6, 23 Jan 42. For Joint Chiefs of Staff, see Ch. VI.

[22] Guides for WPD Officers to Supplement the Green Book, 1941, a semiofficial handbook of administrative methods, Item 4, OPD Hist Unit file.

[23] (1) WD GO 94, 25 Jul 19. (2) Cf. lecture, Maj G. V. Strong, Army Industrial College, 8 Oct 29, title: Orgn and Functions of WPD, GS, and Jt Army-Navy Bd, WPD 2722-1. See also *Joint Action of the Army and Navy* (Washington, 1935), par. 128. This publication, prepared by the Joint Board in 1927 and revised in 1935, was issued by the Government Printing Office. It recorded the principal agreements about interservice collaboration until the approach of World War II spurred Army-Navy planning.

[24] (1) JB 301, ser 689, 5 May 41, sub: Reorgn of Jt Planning Com. (2) WPD adm memo [May 41], sub: Orgn and Functions of WPD, Paper 103, Item 2A, OPD Hist Unit file. WPD considered that by virtue of the May reorganization, the "entire per-

proved sufficiently adaptable to provide the pattern for the planning committees set up under the Joint Chiefs of Staff early in 1942.

International Military Collaboration

If interservice staff co-operation had its weaknesses in the pre-Pearl Harbor period, systematic military collaboration on the international plane was even less in evidence. Coalition warfare has usually been marked by a considerable reserve between the military staffs of nations perhaps only temporarily allied, and the United States was not even at war until the end of 1941. Under this circumstance the degree of liaison established with one power, Great Britain, was a remarkable achievement. It paved the way for the British-American combined staff system of World War II, a unique accomplishment in co-operative effort by the military staffs of two great sovereign powers.

Initially American relations with Great Britain, as with other nations, were maintained exclusively through diplomatic representatives, with military attachés functioning primarily as foreign intelligence reporters for the Army. Special military missions were sent to some of the Latin American countries but for the most part these dealt with either training technique or intelligence. In 1941, when lend-lease became a major political and military factor in the relations of the United States with friendly nations, several missions with Army members in control were sent to various

countries at war with Germany and Japan. But the President handled lend-lease under his own authority, and he dispatched civilian personal representatives, such as Mr. Hopkins, Averell H. Harriman, and Lauchlin Currie, as well as military missions, to supervise initial, basic negotiations with Great Britain, the Soviet Union, and China, the principal recipients of American assistance. Until Pearl Harbor, therefore, the Army had very little to do with international negotiations even when they affected American military plans and capabilities. Although this circumstance did not necessarily result in the adoption of policies unwise from a military point of view, it greatly limited the field in which Army planners were free to recommend strategic policy, especially Army policy which was interrelated with the distribution of American munitions.

A special situation existed with regard to British-American military relations, particularly important because many of the strategic objectives of the two nations were identical or could be reconciled. The President's sympathetic semipersonal correspondence with Prime Minister Winston S. Churchill in the United Kingdom's darkest days, the post-Dunkerque transfer of obsolete American arms to Great Britain, and the 1940 exchange of American destroyers for bases leased in British territory in the Western Atlantic, all served to establish an extraordinarily cordial association between the heads of the two governments in 1940 and 1941.[25]

In more narrowly military matters, the Army and the Navy began early in 1941 to take the lead in staff liaison with the British.

---

sonnel of the War Plans Division become temporary working members of the Joint Planning Committee."

The paper reorganizing the planning committee was approved by the Joint Board 8 May 1941. See memo, Lt Col W. P. Scobey, Secy JB for ACofS WPD, 9 May 41, sub: Reorgn of Jt Planning Com, filed with JB 301, ser 689.

[25] For initiation of correspondence, see Winston S. Churchill, *The Gathering Storm* (Boston, 1948), pp. 440–41.

The services were permitted to do so partly as a result of the mutual British-American political confidence which had been established, and partly because the President himself wished to avoid any appearance of committing the United States to a military course of action before Congress had declared war. Conferences in January, February, and March, generally known as the ABC–1 conversations, were the first of the formal British-American strategic discussions, and they were conducted under the auspices of the armed services rather than those of the State Department. American interests were represented by a committee of U. S. Army and Navy officers, two of whom were WPD planners.[26] Related conversations, specifically concerning the Pacific and the Far East and including Netherlands as well as British representatives, were conducted in Singapore on a similar plane, though with less success, by Army and Navy officers on duty in the Pacific. These international staff conversations did much to give shape to American strategic thinking in 1941. They were briefed and analyzed for General Marshall by WPD, which attempted to bring its planning into line with the military thinking of potential allies either by promoting the U. S. Army point of view or modifying it in the interests of acceptable compromise.

As a result of the successful conference between the British and U. S. representatives early in 1941, a method for continuous exchange of staff ideas came into existence. The United States dispatched observer groups of Army and Navy officers to Great Britain to provide systematic liaison with the British military leaders in London. On their part, the British established a staff group in Washington, the British Joint Staff

Mission, to represent the three armed services of Great Britain. Originally termed simply a military mission but later for purposes of secrecy publicly called the "Advisors to the British Supply Council in North America," it was set up in June 1941 under the leadership of Admiral Sir Charles J. C. Little, Lt. Gen. H. C. B. Wemyss, and Air Chief Marshal Sir Arthur T. Harris.[27] WPD acted as the War Department liaison agency with the British mission in all matters concerning Army ground or air plans, operations, organization, and supply.[28] It coordinated all Army work relevant to British-American discussions and advised the Chief of Staff and the Secretary of War on British studies and recommendations.[29] This arrangement for dealing with British-American military affairs in Washington established the ground work for a system of international staff and command co-ordination. The extent of co-operation achieved between the two countries under this arrangement was demonstrated by the August 1941

---

[26] See Ch. IV.

[27] (1) Note, Secy British Mil Mission in Washington, 18 May 41, sub: Apmts to British Mil Mission in Washington, incl with memo, WPD for CofS, 20 May 41, same sub, WPD 4402–10. (2) Memo, WPD for G–4, 8 Jul 41, sub: Methods of Collaboration Between U. S. Army and Navy and British Mil Mission in Washington, WPD 4402–29.

[28] For designation of WPD as Army liaison, see: (1) memo, WPD for CofS, 13 May 41, sub: Liaison with British, WPD 4402–10; (2) AG ltr, 26 Jul 41, sub: Liaison with British Jt Stf Mission in Washington, AG 334.8 British Supply Council in North America (7–9–41) MC–E–M.

[29] (1) Draft Joint Board paper, 16 May 41, title: Collaboration Between U. S. Mil Servs and British Mil Mission in Washington, WPD 4402–29. (2) For approval by the Chief of Staff and Chief of Naval Operations, see ltr, Secy for Collaboration to Secy British Mil Mission, 3 Jun 41, sub: Methods of Collaboration . . ., WPD 4402–29. (3) For British approval, see ltr, Jt Secys British Mil Mission in Washington to Secy for Collaboration, 10 Jun 41, no sub, WPD 4402–29.

conference between the President and the Prime Minister. American officers, including a WPD planner, and the chiefs of the British armed services discussed common strategy while the civilian representatives of the two great anti-Axis Powers were agreeing on the political and social principles, set forth in the "Atlantic Charter." It was from this working liaison between American and British military staffs that the Combined Chiefs of Staff structure developed after Pearl Harbor. The close identification of WPD with the British Joint Staff Mission foreshadowed the prominent role its successor agency would play in later British-American planning deliberations.

CHAPTER IV

Developments in 1941

By 1941 WPD had come to occupy a somewhat anomalous position in the War Department. Army Regulations and traditional Army doctrine gave to the Division no authority superior to that of the four other General Staff Divisions, likewise responsible for recommending plans and policies to the Chief of Staff.[1] On the other hand the preparation of war plans in conformity with interservice and international deliberations was becoming the most comprehensive and crucial kind of Army staff work. As the world situation became more unstable and the foreign relations of the United States more uncertain, the Chief of Staff depended increasingly upon advice and assistance from WPD, whose responsibilities were most nearly coextensive with his own multiple responsibilities as military head of the War Department, commander of all Army forces, and senior military representative of the Army in the national high command.

WPD started out in the year 1941 with a new chief, Brig. Gen. Leonard T. Gerow, who entered on duty 16 December 1940.[2]

General Gerow led WPD through a critical phase in which it more than doubled in size and carried a constantly mounting load of staff work. After the Pearl Harbor disaster, he devoted himself to trying to meet General Marshall's urgent needs for help in directing the Army's first moves in World War II. When he turned over his desk to Brig. Gen. Dwight D. Eisenhower on 15 February 1942, WPD had gained valuable experience and improved its organization in readiness for the new responsibilities it was shortly to assume as OPD.

General Gerow plunged into the voluminous staff work incident to solving the many problems confronting the Army in the pre-Pearl Harbor period. His necessarily close working relationship with General Marshall

---

[1] See Ch. II.

[2] General Gerow was fifty-two years old when assigned as WPD chief in 1940. He graduated from the Virginia Military Institute and accepted a commission in the Infantry in 1911, ten years after General Marshall's graduation from the same school. Until April 1935 he had served in the Infantry continuously except for about three years (1918–21) when he was on duty with the Signal Corps, mostly in France during and shortly after World War I. He reported to WPD as a major, was shortly pro- moted to the rank of lieutenant colonel, became Division executive under General Krueger in May 1936, and worked in that capacity until his tour ended in March 1939. In less than two years he was recalled to Washington to take over WPD. For approximately a year he served with the title of Acting Assistant Chief of Staff. The modifying term "Acting" was necessary because, having left the Division only twenty months before, he could not meet the peacetime requirement for two years of service with troops just previous to formal administrative action reassigning an officer to a regular detail in the General Staff Corps. On 24 December 1941 he finally received the formal designation of Assistant Chief of Staff. He became a permanent colonel 1 September 1940 and a temporary brigadier general 1 October 1940. From WPD General Gerow moved on to a career in the field with combat forces. He successively commanded the 29th Infantry Division, the V Corps (which he led ashore in Normandy in June 1944), and the Fifteenth Army in Europe. He held the rank of lieutenant general at the end of hostilities.

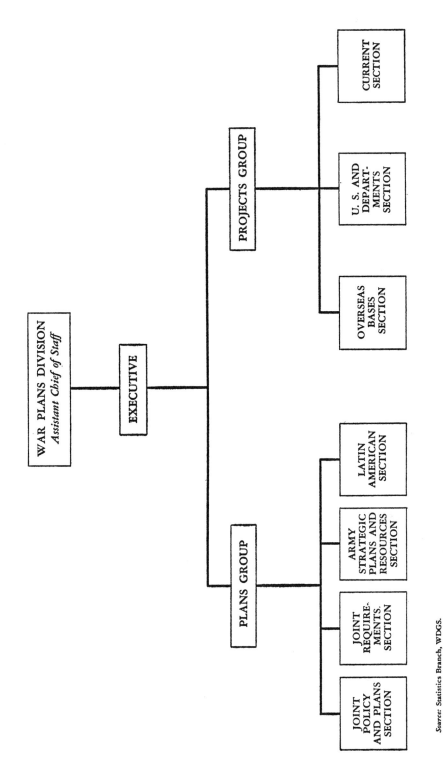

WAR PLANS DIVISION
Assistant Chief of Staff

EXECUTIVE

PLANS GROUP

PROJECTS GROUP

JOINT POLICY AND PLANS SECTION

JOINT REQUIRE-MENTS. SECTION

ARMY STRATEGIC PLANS AND RESOURCES SECTION

LATIN AMERICAN SECTION

OVERSEAS BASES SECTION

U. S. AND DEPART-MENTS SECTION

CURRENT SECTION

Source: Statistics Branch, WDGS.

Chart 1. War Plans Division, War Department General Staff: 15 September 1941

in national and international strategic planning tended to bring on him and on WPD more and more duties, especially those which had to be attended to at once and did not clearly fall within the sphere of responsibility of any particular Army staff or agency as defined by Army Regulations.

Organization, Duties, and Strength of WPD

Functional assignments within WPD in 1941 were set forth in a long administrative memorandum formulated in May of that year. It stated: "The general duties of this Division relate to the formulation of plans and general policies affecting the employment of our military forces in war, separately, or in conjunction with Naval forces." [3]

To perform these duties, the Division was divided into two groups, the Plans Group and the Projects Group.[4] An important share of WPD's duties was performed by the Joint Policy & Plans Section of the Plans Group. It provided Army representatives as needed for the Joint Strategic Committee, the Army-Navy planning group responsible to the reorganized Joint Planning Committee. In joint planning, as in Army planning, these officers were in effect reporting to the Assistant Chief of Staff, WPD, who was one of the two members of the new Joint Planning Committee as well as a member of the Joint Army-Navy Board. Within or through the Joint Board system, the Joint Policy & Plans officers dealt with all "matters of strategic policy and plans that involve the Navy or the Navy and associated powers." For many years WPD had assumed

the responsibility of following up Army action to see that joint Army-Navy Board decisions had been put into effect.[5] In mid-1941 the WPD chief in addition received specific authority to "take final War Department action on joint matters" that did not affect basic policy and on which there was no disagreement with the Navy Department.[6] This interservice work, plus the extensive strategic planning incident to exploratory British-American staff conferences and other military liaison established with Great Britain and the Soviet Union in 1941, placed a heavy burden on the handful of WPD planners assigned to these duties. In addition the Joint Policy & Plans Section supplied most of the officers who sat on the many boards and committees on which WPD was represented.[7] Finally, this section had the assignment of following national and international developments in order to "anticipate important strategic problems . . . and to prepare in advance appropriate studies." This work "set up

---

[3] WPD adm memo, May 41, sub: Orgn and Functions of WPD, WPD 3354–55. Several quotations from this memo are contained in succeeding paragraphs without separate citations.

[4] See the accompanying chart.

[5] There is no record of an official grant of authority to WPD to perform this function. However, no other agency could possibly have done it because WPD maintained the only Army file of Joint Board papers. For dependence on members of the Army Joint Planning Committee for supervision of "follow-up action by the Army on Joint Board decisions," see informal memo, Lt Comdr S. F. Bryant, USN, no addressee, 6 May 24, sub: Jt Planning Com and JB Procedure, copy filed Misc Folder 19, JB files, P&O.

By 1941 procedural custom had solidified sufficiently for WPD to state, without citation of authority: "WPD is the War Department agency designated to implement The Joint Board decisions." See Guides for WPD Officers to Supplement the Green Book, Item 4, OPD Hist Unit file.

[6] For WPD authorization to take action on certain Joint Board cases, see memo, WPD for CofS, 22 May 41, sub: Jt Army and Navy Procedure, WPD 3963–3.

[7] Memo for rcd, 19 Dec 41, sub: WPD Membership on Departmental and Interdepartmental Bds, etc., WPD 3797–8. WPD was represented on thirteen boards and committees at the end of 1941.

the basic requirements" for the planning undertaken by the whole Plans Group.

The Army Strategic Plans & Resources Section of the Plans Group was responsible for translating these general ideas on national and international strategy into specific Army terms in the light of current combat resources. The aspect of its work that pertained to resources was steadily becoming more important as the U. S. Army lost its peacetime character and grew rapidly in size. The Chief of Staff had to be kept informed as to where all the troop units were, how they could be employed, and at what time. The informal "bookkeeping" system on Army resources developed by this section shortly before Pearl Harbor met a very real need.[8]

The Joint Requirements & Technical Liaison Section of the Plans Group worked on the interservice and international level somewhat as the resources unit did on the Army level. It translated approved strategy into policies governing the distribution of munitions among friendly powers in accordance with lend-lease principles and the "best national interests of the United States." Finally, the Latin American Section of the Plans Group dealt with all problems of "military collaboration with Latin American Republics" except the allocation of arms and equipment, which was handled by the Joint Requirements & Technical Liaison Section.

The Projects Group, the second main element in the organization of WPD as of mid-1941, was an anomaly. It had a general responsibility for studying local Army problems in the light of Army plans whenever they were referred to the General Staff. It recommended War Department actions to improve the defensive capacity of overseas

possessions, particularly with respect to personnel allocations, armament, and fixed installations, but it had no clear authority and did not presume to interpose on its own initiative in order to direct the undertaking of specific measures for the current defense of any of the local commands, which were entrusted to senior officers directly responsible to General Marshall.[9] It assisted the Chief of Staff in exercising his operational command of the field forces only upon explicit instructions, not as a matter of routine, continuous responsibility.

Two of the Projects Group's three sections were named for areas. Initially they were called the Overseas Bases Section and the Continental U. S. and Departments Section but later in the year were redesignated the Atlantic Section and the Pacific Section. They handled all matters concerning projects within their respective areas, but the only specific action open to officers in these sections was "coordination where necessary" with other agencies.[10] In fact, when in special circumstances General Marshall or the Secretary of War specifically ordered General Gerow to issue instructions to the field concerning military operations, the WPD chief usually turned to the Plans Group for assistance. What the two area-oriented sections of the Projects Group actually did was simply to advise the Division on policies concerning allocation of defensive installations and

---

[8] E.g., see WPD charts, Tab C, Item 7, Exec 4.

[9] (1) For an explanation of the "Overseas Defense Projects" drafted by General Gerow in an earlier period, see memo, WPD for G–1, 24 Feb 39, sub: Increase in Almt of Commissioned Pers for WPD, WPD 3354–25. (2) Cf. memo, WPD for TAG, 26 May 37, sub: Jt Plan for Def of Panama Canal, WPD 1621–10.

[10] WPD adm memo, May 41, sub: Orgn and Functions of WPD, WPD 3354–55. Cf. orgn chart, 30 Jun 41, in Orgn Survey of WPD, WDGS, 26 Jul 41, atchd to ltr, A. H. Onthank to CofS, envelope with OPD 321.19 OPD.

combat resources to the overseas bases, especially in the Panama Canal, Puerto Rican, Hawaiian, and Philippine Departments. Finally, the Current Section of the group performed much the same function in studying general War Department policy on such matters as Army organization, equipment scheduling, and aviation development.[11] It was referred to as a miscellaneous unit, a term which in many ways applied to the entire Projects Group.

Throughout 1941, in keeping with its steadily expanding duties, WPD continued to grow in size as well as to readjust its organization to accommodate the variety of tasks the Division was performing for the Chief of Staff. General Gerow began requesting officer reinforcements early in the year. They arrived from time to time but never in numbers sufficient to catch up with the Division's work. In June the Division requested authorization for a ceiling strength of 54 of which 43 would be Regular Army and 11 Reserve officers.[12] Six months later, on the eve of the Pearl Harbor attack, WPD was approaching this ceiling, having reached a strength of 48 officers, including General Gerow.[13] This total represented slightly more than a 100-percent increase from the strength on 31 December 1940.

The selection of the officers needed to fill the Division's roster was a constant problem for the Division chief and his executive officer. The competition for the best Regular officers was keen in 1941, a period of rapid growth throughout the Army. Many officers requested never were made available to WPD. Some were requested on two or more separate occasions before they were finally assigned. General Gerow tried persistently to get officers who needed little training and testing. The basis of selection was personal acquaintance on the part of officers already in the Division, service record, and military education, probably in most cases in that order of importance. In 1941 the methodical canvassing of available candidates, with special emphasis on their efficiency ratings, was less in evidence than selection of a promising officer recommended to General Gerow or his executive.[14]

By 1941 WPD and the rest of the War Department had grown so much that the paper work involved in dispatching Division business had become voluminous and complex. This fact placed a heavy load on the civilian staff, especially on a few members whose knowledge of records and procedures helped the many new officers to make themselves quickly at home in their jobs. The entire civilian complement, which totalled only eight in 1939, had reached a total of about sixty by 7 December 1941.[15]

---

[11] For detailed study of WPD's organization and personnel, January–December 1941, see OPD Hist Unit Study E.

[12] (1) Memo, WPD for CofS, 7 Feb 41, sub: Pers Reqmts for WPD, WPD 3354–47. (2) Memo, WPD for CofS, 24 Jun 41, sub: Dtl of Add Offs for Dy in WPD, WPD 3354–55.

[13] WPD adm memo, 5 Dec 41, sub: Orgn, WPD, Paper 20, Item 2A, OPD Hist Unit file. This list properly does not include General McNarney, still in England though nominally assigned to WPD.

[14] For personnel procurement in general in this period, see WPD 3354 (Pers Asgmt) as a whole. For a good example, see: (1) note, Brig Gen Gerow for Lt Col W. P. Scobey, Sep 41, WPD 3354–2; (2) list, Sep 41, sub: Dtl of Offs to WPD, WPD 3354–2; (3) memo, WPD for G–1, 9 Sep 41, sub: Request for Dtl of Offs, WPD 3354–2.

[15] (1) List, 24 Mar 39, title: Employees by Name, Gr, Rate of Pay, and Divs, OCS, G–1 file 15466–12A, filed with G–1/16054–5, G–1 file, Army Dept Rcds Br. The other staff divisions had considerably larger civilian staffs. (2) WPD Civ Pers roster, 24 Nov 41, Paper 79, Item 2A, OPD Hist Unit file. (3) WPD Civ Pers roster, 18 Dec 41, Paper 78, Item 2A, OPD Hist Unit file.

War Planning: 1941

The early defensive deployment of the Army, which began well before Pearl Harbor, required WPD to act for the Chief of Staff in a variety of cases too critical to be left un-co-ordinated among the many War Department agencies and too detailed for General Marshall to supervise personally. Much of this staff work went on within the framework of interservice and international planning. Above all, WPD aided and advised the Chief of Staff by drafting detailed Army plans for putting into effect military preparations and movements on which agreement had been reached in interservice and international conferences.

It undertook to advise the Chief of Staff and, through him, the Secretary of War and the President on the military resources that the United States ultimately would have to mobilize to insure the defeat of the Axis Powers. In all these tasks the Division was exercising its traditional planning function, though it was less concerned with the formal war plans designed to meet hypothetical contingencies and moved toward continuous participation in Army-Navy and British-American deliberations on current strategic issues.

The character of war planning done by WPD in the immediate pre-Pearl Harbor period had changed considerably from that of the color plan years. By 1941 American national policy and Army planning entered a new, more realistic phase. The color plans, though some were still in effect, were rapidly becoming obsolete.[16] Their place

was taken by the RAINBOW plans, especially by RAINBOW 5, a comprehensive war plan dealing with the specific menace to the security of the United States which German, Italian, and Japanese aggression constituted. Like all top-level Army war plans, RAINBOW 5 was an approved staff study.[17] It made certain assumptions about the position of the United States with relation to other countries and laid down the course of action to be followed as well as ways and means to carry it out. It provided the general framework of War Department policy and strategy. It was distributed to a limited number of subordinate War Department agencies as a basis for the development of detailed supplementary plans. Unlike the older color plans, RAINBOW 5 rested upon assumptions which were significant in the light of international conditions at the time of its approval. In many ways it reflected the WPD thinking that had helped in the formulation of national military policy by the Joint Board.

War Department RAINBOW 5 was the most important end product of the strategic thinking that started in the fall of 1938 when military and governmental leaders of the United States first began to act and plan on the assumption that Axis aggression might threaten American security. In May and June 1939, a two-month-long exchange of memoranda, letters, and directives among

---

[16] As late as December 1941, WPD officers were assigned custody of Registered War Plans (color plans) of the static type developed in the 1920's, prepared, that is, without reference to the current international situation. Seven color plans were current at the time. See list, 1 Dec 41, title: WPD Custodians of Registered Documents, Tab B, Item 7, Exec 4.

[17] War Department RAINBOW 5 consisted of two registered plans: War Department Operations Plan RAINBOW 5 (WPD WDOP–R5) and War Department Concentration Plan RAINBOW 5 (WPD WDCP–R5–41). The War Department plans are closely connected with and based upon the same premises as Joint Army and Navy Basic War Plan RAINBOW 5 (JBWP–R5). Copies of the various RAINBOW plans and drafts are among the obsolete registered documents of Plans and Operations, GSUSA, in classified files, AGO.

WPD planners, Navy planners, the Chief of Staff, and the Chief of Naval Operations took place. Some were written by these individuals in their service capacities and some in their capacities as members of the Joint Board and Joint Planning Committee. This exchange resulted in Joint Board authorization for the preparation of five new basic war plans, to be called RAINBOW plans. The composite recommendations in all these papers provided that the five plans would outline the appropriate military action to perform the following missions, respectively:

RAINBOW 1: Prevent the violation of the letter or spirit of the Monroe Doctrine by protecting that part of the territory of the Western Hemisphere from which the vital interests of the United States can be threatened, while protecting the United States, its possessions, and its seaborne trade.

RAINBOW 2: Provide for the hemispheric defense mission described in RAINBOW 1 and "sustain the interests of Democratic Powers in the Pacific, . . . provide for the tasks essential to sustain these interests, and . . . defeat enemy forces in the Pacific."

RAINBOW 3: Provide for the hemispheric defense mission described in RAINBOW 1 and protect the "United States' vital interests in the Western Pacific by securing control in the Western Pacific, as rapidly as possible consistent with carrying out the missions" in RAINBOW 1.

RAINBOW 4: Provide for the hemispheric defense mission described in RAINBOW 1 and, unlike RAINBOW 1, carry out this mission by planning for projecting such U. S. Army forces as necessary to the southern part of the South American continent or to the eastern Atlantic.

RAINBOW 5: Provide for the hemispheric defense mission described in RAINBOW 1 and also send the "armed forces of the United States to the Eastern Atlantic and to either or both of the African or European Continents, as rapidly as possible consistent with carrying out the missions" in RAINBOW 1, "in order to effect the decisive defeat of Germany, or Italy, or both." This plan originally assumed "concerted action between the United States, Great Britain, and France." [18]

As a result of these joint Army-Navy actions, WPD drew up many studies and specific plans. It participated in preparing the first prerequisite to hemisphere defense planning, Joint Basic War Plan—RAINBOW 1, submitted to the Joint Board on 27 July 1939 and orally approved by the President on 14 October 1939. Detailed Army Operations and Concentration Plans, RAINBOW 1, were completed by WPD and approved by the Chief of Staff in July 1940.[19]

On 7 June 1940 the Joint Board approved the Joint Basic War Plan—RAINBOW 4, and WPD was faced with a large task in the preparation of subsidiary plans. The problem was solved by attaching a group of nine officers, made available by the closing of the Army War College, to WPD for temporary duty to work on the detailed

---

[18] The situations postulated in RAINBOWS 1, 3, 4, and 5 are set forth in the Draft of Joint Board Directives submitted in JB 325, ser 642, 11 May 39, sub: Jt Army and Navy Bsc War Plans. The situation postulated in RAINBOW 2, added to this list as a result of a recommendation by the Joint Planning Committee, was set forth in JB 325, ser 642, 23 Jun 39, sub: Alternative Situations Set Up in Directive for Jt RAINBOW Plans. The original directives issued by the Joint Board were drafted by the chief of WPD and his Navy counterpart. This procedure was suggested in memo, WPD for CofS, 2 May 39, sub: JB 325, ser 634, WPD 4175–1.

[19] (1) JB 325, ser 642/JB 325, ser 642–1, 9 Apr 40, sub: Jt Army and Navy Bsc War Plans—RAINBOW. (2) Memo, WPD for CofS, 10 Jul 41, sub: WD Oper Plan RAINBOW 1, 1940, and WD Concentration Plan, 1940, WPD 4175–11.

Army plans for RAINBOW 4. This group, known as the War Planning Committee, was stationed at the War College. It continued to work on RAINBOW 4 plans during the fall and winter of 1940–41, while the regular staff of WPD concentrated its attention to the development of RAINBOW 5.[20]

The overwhelming importance of RAINBOW 5 plans at every level soon became clear. In April 1940 revisions suggested by the Joint Planning Committee and approved by the Joint Board raised the priority for developing RAINBOW 5 since it was the most comprehensive plan still applicable after the outbreak of war in Europe.[21] As changes in the international situation and the elaboration of American strategy in British-American staff talks made the provisions of the first four RAINBOWS obsolete, they were dropped. RAINBOWS 2 and 3 were canceled at the Joint Board meeting on 6 August 1941. Full indorsement of the principle that the military menace of Germany was paramount had destroyed the value of those two plans. Not until 4 May 1942 did the Joint Board officially recognize the effect of Pearl Harbor by canceling RAINBOWS 1 and 4, which provided simply for hemisphere defense. But at the outbreak of war, 7 December 1941, RAINBOW 5 was the formal plan that went into effect. Though even RAINBOW 5 in many ways was inadequate for the crisis then at hand, it provided a substratum of strategic agreement on which the subsequent development of British-American plans was based.

All this preliminary study and work on national strategy had served to solidify military opinion in general and WPD thinking in particular. While its chief officers were working on the joint planning level, WPD co-ordinated all War Department ideas on the problems at hand.[22] Officers of the Division were busy on various aspects of RAINBOW 5 during most of 1940.[23]

Early in 1941 RAINBOW 5 became entwined with strategic deliberations aimed at integrating American plans for the eventuality of open war against the Axis with the current strategy of Great Britain, the principal power with which the United States probably would be associated in such a war. On 14 December 1940 the Joint Planning Committee, of which Col. Joseph T. McNarney was the Army member, received instructions from the Joint Board to draw up a paper for the guidance of American representatives at a conference with British military leaders. The paper was to include a general statement of the "probable nature and extent of naval and military operations . . . in case the United States should undertake a major offensive in the Atlantic, and a defensive in the Pacific, in support of Great Britain against the Axis." [24] This supposition of the nature of possible hostilities coincided with the assumptions of RAINBOW 5, then in the

---

[20] See correspondence in WPD 4175, especially memo, WPD for G–1, G–2, G–3, and G–4, sub: Color Plans, RAINBOW, WPD 4175–13.
[21] JB 325, ser 642/JB 325, ser 642–1, 9 Apr 40, sub: Jt Army and Navy Bsc War Plans—RAINBOW.

[22] Memo, WPD for G–1, G–2, G–3, and G–4, 17 Jun 40, sub: Color Plans, RAINBOW, WPD 4175–13.
[23] WPD files contain studies on "Main Courses of Action to Meet a RAINBOW No. 5 Situation" prepared as early as May 1940. See RAINBOW 5 Development File in OPD Registered Documents. The fall of France virtually nullified this work. For later WPD activities, see: (1) memo, WPD for G–2, 14 Dec 40, sub: RAINBOW 5, WPD 4175–18; (2) memo, WPD for CofAC, 18 Dec 40, sub: Data for RAINBOW 5, WPD 4175–18; (3) memo, Gen Marshall for Rear Admiral H. R. Stark, 29 Nov 40, sub: Tentative Draft, Navy Bsc War Plan—RAINBOW 3, WPD 4175–15.
[24] JB 325, ser 674, 14 Dec 40, sub: Jt Instrs for Army and Navy Representatives for Holding Stf Convs with British, Including Agenda for Convs.

WPD planning mill. In the first half of 1941 the basic War Department plan was integrated with the interservice RAINBOW plan and with the British-American staff planning initiated with ABC–1 concerning co-operation in the event of American entry into the war.

WPD researches and studies made themselves felt at both the interservice and British-American levels through General Gerow and Colonel McNarney. On 26 December General Gerow suggested to General Marshall that the Army representatives at the conferences be led by former WPD chief General Embick, and include the Assistant Chief of Staff, G–2, Brig. Gen. Sherman Miles. Also, General Gerow said the "potential importance of these Staff Conferences to future war planning makes it desirable to include in the representation two members of the War Plans Division." He recommended himself, as head of the Division, and Colonel McNarney, whom he described as "thoroughly familiar with present and prospective war plans and . . . particularly well qualified to discuss air operations." The Chief of Staff approved these suggestions.[25]

During January 1941 WPD worked on preparations for the meeting. The Joint Planning Committee prepared carefully phrased instructions for the American conferees. General Gerow submitted these papers in draft form to General Marshall on 14 January, recommending approval. They were ready for consideration by the Joint Board on 21 January and were approved with minor changes by the President on 26 January. These instructions, given to the British delegates at the first

meeting, 29 January 1941, contained a statement in the name of the Chief of Staff and the Chief of Naval Operations concerning the purpose of the conversations and the basic military position of the United States.[26]

All the resources of Army planning were brought to bear on making the staff conversations a success. The initial meeting took place on 29 January 1941. Fourteen plenary meetings were held between that date and 27 March 1941, the last day of the conference. General Gerow kept the Chief of Staff informed about tentative understandings which he and Colonel McNarney were helping to work out.[27] The conferees made steady progress and on the last day of the talks "formally adopted by unanimous agreement" a document containing: (1) a basic British-American war plan to be followed if the United States entered the war and (2) a summary of the fundamental strategic policies agreed upon by the military representatives. Usually referred to by its short title, ABC–1, this document and a supplementary section on air collaboration, called ABC–2, formed a testament of American strategic preparedness on the international level.[28]

---

[25] (1) Memo, WPD for CofS, 26 Dec 40, sub: Army Representatives for Stf Convs with Great Britain, WPD 4402. (2) Ltr, TAG to Maj Gen Embick, 30 Dec 40, AG 334.8 (12–26–40).

[26] (1) JB 325, ser 674, 21 Jan 41, sub: Jt Instrs . . . (2) Memo, FDR, 26 Jan 41, copy filed JB 325, ser 674, P&O rcds. (3) For WPD action, see memo, WPD for CofS, 14 Jan 41, sub: Stf Convs with British, WPD 4402–1. (4) Brig Gen Gerow's personal ABC–1 papers, Item 11, Exec 4.

[27] For a note on the use of U. S. Army forces, e.g., see memo, WPD for CofS, 5 Mar 41, sub: US-British Stf Convs, WPD 4402–3.

[28] (1) US-British Stf Convs: Rpt and Annexes, 27 Mar 41, Short Title ABC–1. (2) US-British Stf Convs: Air Collaboration, 29 Mar 41, Short Title ABC–2. For minutes of ABC–1 meetings and an extensive collection of papers considered at the conference, see five folders filed WPD 4402–89. According to War Department oral tradition, "ABC" as a designation for British-American staff agreements was a derivation from the phrase "American-British Conversations."

Although ABC–1 specifically stated that it constituted no political commitment of the United States to either a belligerent or nonbelligerent policy, it laid down the first principles of British-American co-operation "should the United States be compelled to resort to war." In the first place, the high commands of both countries would "collaborate continuously in the formulation and execution of strategical policies and plans which shall govern the conduct of the war." The broad strategic goal was defined as the "defeat of Germany and her Allies," specifically including Italy. This, it was agreed, would remain the primary offensive objective even if Japan entered the war. Pursuant to this strategic policy, ABC–1 presented a tentative British-American basic war plan naming the specific military tasks to be performed; the naval, air, and ground forces available to perform them in each area; and a rough allocation between the two nations of primary strategic responsibility for directing projected military operations in various parts of the world.

The ABC–1 agreement served to harden the outlines of American military thinking. A month later the Joint Planning Committee presented Joint Basic War Plan—RAINBOW 5 for Joint Board consideration. The memorandum of transmittal was signed for the Army by General McNarney.[29] It explained that Joint RAINBOW 5 was based on the strategic concepts set forth in the report of ABC–1.[30] Secretaries Stimson and Knox approved both ABC–1 and Joint RAINBOW 5 and sent them to the President in June 1941.[31] President Roosevelt "familiarized

himself with the two papers," but did not approve them at the time, although he indicated his satisfaction by suggesting that they be returned for his approval in "case of war."[32] Given the political responsibilities of a government that was publicly committed to avoid war if possible, American military leaders had gone a long way toward preparing for the advent of hostilities, which was becoming more and more probable.

WPD planners were then able to turn back to the Army's RAINBOW 5 plan, work on which had been well under way before the British-American staff conversations. They finished War Department Operations Plan—RAINBOW 5 and War Department Concentration Plan—RAINBOW 5 in time to receive the Chief of Staff's approval on 19 August 1941. The planning wheel had then come full circle. Army ideas on strategy had filtered upward to interservice and international committees and conferences, where they were accepted, rejected, or integrated with other planning ideas. The approved strategic policy that resulted finally filtered down again to the Army, where, under the supervision of WPD, Army plans were drawn up and distributed to other Army agencies for elaboration in detail. This process was what "war planning"

---

[29] Promoted to brigadier general 7 April 1941.

[30] JB 325, ser 642–5, 30 Apr 41, sub: Jt Bsc War Plan—RAINBOW 5 and Rpt of US-British Stf Convs, Mar 27, 41.

[31] Ltr, SW and SN to President, 2 Jun 41, copy filed JB 325, ser 642–5, P&O rcds.

[32] Memo, Secy JB for CofS, 9 Jun 41, sub: JB 325, ser 642–5—Jt Army and Navy Bsc War Plan—RAINBOW 5 and Rpt of US-British Stf Convs—ABC–1, WPD 4175–18. The Chief of Staff stated that the President, although he had not approved RAINBOW 5, "is not disapproving it, and we can go ahead with our tentative arrangements." The British had similarly withheld approval of the US-British Commonwealth Joint Basic War Plan. Notes on Conferences in OSW, 10 Jun 41, Vol. I, WDCSA rcds.

Minor revisions in RAINBOW 5 were approved by the Joint Board on 19 November 1941 as set forth in JB 325, ser 642–5, Revision 1, 7 Nov 41, sub: Proposed Changes in Jt Army and Navy Bsc War Plan—RAINBOW 5.

meant in the period immediately preceding the outbreak of hostilities.

The difficulty of strategic planning in a period of world-wide insecurity, and the ramifications of staff work connected with it, appeared plainly in the work of WPD on the "Victory Program" estimate of September 1941. The needs of the U. S. Army for munitions conflicted with the requirements imposed on American industry initially by British (and briefly French) purchases and in 1941 by lend-lease allocations. The problem of calculating the Army's needs and fitting them into the national armaments production program had been under study for a long time by the War Department G–4 and the Office of the Under Secretary of War.[33] In the spring of 1941 various Army staffs were becoming aware of the urgent need for an integrated calculation of "Ultimate Munitions Production Essential to the Safety of America." [34] By this time WPD was taking an active interest in the problem of "Coordination of Planning and Supply." In May Lt. Col. Charles W. Bundy of the Plans Group informed his chief: "Confusion will reign until an agency for formulating a policy based on all strategic plans is designated." [35] On 21 May General Marshall directed WPD to take the lead in the General Staff in preparing a "clearcut strategic estimate of our situation from a ground, air, and naval viewpoint" in order to provide a "base of departure" for considering "increases and changes in armament." [36]

A few weeks later, in July 1941, President Roosevelt formally directed the initiation of studies on munitions requirements of the armed services with a view of formulating an integrated national industrial plan.[37] By this time General Gerow had a definite idea how this task should be approached, which he stated as follows: "We must first evolve a strategic concept of how to defeat our potential enemies and then determine the major military units (Air, Navy and Ground) required to carry out the strategic operations." This idea grew directly out of the experience of WPD in formulating strategic plans, and General Gerow felt very strongly that it indicated the only realistic way to go about setting up industrial objectives. The other main approach, depending on a calculation of the supply of American munitions necessary to add to the resources of potential allies in order to overbalance the production of potential enemies, General Gerow considered unsound. "It would be unwise to assume," he observed, "that we can defeat Germany by simply out-producing her," since production is only one factor determining the conduct of war. He added: "One hundred thousand airplanes would be of little value to us if these airplanes could not be used because of lack of trained personnel, lack of operating airdromes in the theater, and lack of shipping to maintain the air squadrons in the theater." [38] If, then, "ultimate production should not be adjusted to a capacity to ex-

[33] The rearmament program and the problem of foreign aid is treated in some detail in this series in Watson, *Chief of Staff: Prewar Plans and Preparations,* Chs. X and XI.

[34] Memo, USW R. P. Patterson for SW, 18 Apr 41, sub: Ultimate Mun Pdn Essential to Safety of America, WPD 4494.

[35] Memo, Lt Col Bundy for ACofS WPD, 20 May 41, sub: Coordination of Planning and Supply, WPD 4321–12.

[36] (1) WDCSA Notes on Conferences, 21 May 41, WDCSA Binder 15. (2) Memo, WPD for CofS, 7 Jun 41, sub: Ultimate Mun Pdn . . ., WPD 4494.

[37] Ltr, President to SW, 9 Jul 41, photostat copy filed WPD 4494–1.

[38] Memo, Brig Gen Gerow for ASW McCloy, 5 Aug 41, no sub, Tab G, Item 7, Exec 4.

ceed that of our potential enemies" but should be adjusted instead to a "strategic concept of how to defeat our potential enemies," the first step in setting up a "Victory Program" for the Army had to be taken by WPD. No other staff was in so good a position to estimate the strategic operations that would become necessary, and on that basis to calculate the major military units needed to carry them out.

Maj. Albert C. Wedemeyer, a new planning recruit, took the lead for WPD in conducting Army-wide researches on requirements in terms of men.[39] He also brought together estimates of the probable size and composition of task forces, the possible theaters of operation, and the probable dates at which forces would be committed. Thus did the War Department accomplish its part, an extremely critical part, in the initial Victory Program of September 1941, the starting point for all wartime calculations of munitions production.[40] To this extent the strategic planning of WPD, even in 1941, led the Division to take a primary part in major War Department planning regardless of whether or not it was strictly strategic in character.

Expansion of the Functions of GHQ

Shortly after GHQ had been activated in 1940 and given its training mission, WPD made a study of the responsibilities and authority which should be delegated to GHQ prior to active engagement in hostilities. The Division recommended that the responsibility of GHQ as laid down in 1940 be extended to include, in addition to training: (1) the preparation of plans and studies and the supervision of activities concerning actual operations in the theater of war and (2) consultation with WPD, G–3, and G–4 on major items of equipment and the organization or activation of combat or service units essential to prospective operations. WPD suggested that the special committee of planning officers working temporarily at the War College under the supervision of the Division be transferred to GHQ to form an Operations Section.[41]

In accordance with this general plan, in 1941 GHQ began to develop into an agency through which the Chief of Staff could command troops in the theaters of war. In May 1941, with discussion of sending U. S. Army troops to Iceland well under way, the Chief of Staff decided that it was time to "start certain designated staffs on working on an operations plan," as distinct from general strategic plans. General Marshall noted that this work ought to be started by GHQ

---

[39] (1) Memo, WPD for CofS, 19 Sep 41, sub: Resume of Conferences, etc., WPD 4494–12. (2) Cf. memo, WPD for CofS, 8 Dec 41, sub: Army and Navy Est of U. S. Over-All Pdn Reqmts, WPD 4494–21.

[40] JB 355, ser 707, 11 Sep 41, sub: JB Est, etc., Parts II and III of App. II. Since no Joint Board action on Serial 707 was ever taken, the papers remained simply the estimates of the Army and Navy. They had "already been acted upon by the Chief of Naval Operations and the Chief of Staff" in October 1941. See min of JB meetings, 22 Oct 41. For WPD background on the "Victory Program," see WPD 4494 file. JB Serial 707 is filed WPD 4494–13. App. II contains the Army estimate, Parts I and II being WPD's study, including Army Air Forces summary statistics, and Part III being a detailed study by the Army Air Forces, WPD.

[41] Memo, Actg ACofS WPD for CofS, 12 Aug 40, sub: Allocation of Responsibilities Between WPD and GHQ, WPD 3209–5.

This chapter presents only the aspects of the GHQ story that affected the status and work of WPD. For the full treatment of GHQ, see K. R. Greenfield and R. R. Palmer, "Origins of the Army Ground Forces: General Headquarters, United States Army, 1940–42," in *The Organization of Ground Combat Troops,* UNITED STATES ARMY IN WORLD WAR II (Washington, D. C., 1947). This study hereafter is cited as Greenfield and Palmer, "GHQ, US Army, 1940–42."

rather than by WPD.[42] On 17 June he and General Gerow worked out a policy transferring responsibility for the "organization and control of task forces and operations" to GHQ. General Gerow observed that "coordination and adjustment between WPD and GHQ" would be essential because WPD would have to "prepare the necessary plans and directives prescribing the units" while GHQ "would carry out the actual organization of units into task forces." [43] Two days later WPD recommended enlarging the functions of GHQ to make it a "command group designed to plan, initiate and control execution of such military operations as may be directed by the War Department." General Gerow's reasoning was: "Military operations in a number of relatively minor and widely separated theaters may be undertaken on short notice. The effective coordination, conduct, and control of such operations is an extremely difficult task and requires an executive organization capable of prompt decision and expeditious action. There is no agency of the War Department now organized to meet this requirement." [44]

After the Chief of Staff had approved the recommendation for enlarging the duties of GHQ, WPD prepared a new directive for GHQ which appeared 3 July 1941.[45] It provided that, in addition to training responsibilities, GHQ should have responsi-

bilities in planning and commanding operations in areas specifically allotted it by the War Department. General Marshall ordered Brig. Gen. Harry J. Malony, who was then chief of the WPD Plans Group, to take a small detachment of officers from WPD and, as Deputy Chief of Staff under General McNair, to exercise the new function of tactical planning and staff control of military operations in the new base and defense commands and in potential theaters of operations.[46] General McNair continued to be primarily concerned with the more immediate objective of training the new and steadily expanding Army.

General Malony's task was to make GHQ an organization that could develop tactical plans for military operations, issue orders to theater and task force commanders, systematically follow up receipt and execution of orders, and try to help the tactical commanders carry out assigned missions by securing for them the administrative, technical, and supply services they needed. Overseas operations by American troops called for detailed consideration of everything incident to the performance of a mission in the theater, from the development of cold-weather equipment to arrangements for pay of forces.[47]

The first assignment to GHQ under the new directive was the complex job of completing detailed plans for organizing, dispatching, and maintaining U. S. Army troops assigned to garrison duty in Iceland. The task was accomplished in accordance with general strategic plans made by WPD. In time all the Atlantic bases came under

---

[42] Informal memo, SGS for CofS, 1 May 41, WDCSA Binder 15.

[43] (1) Diary, Brig Gen Gerow, entry for 17 Jun 41, Item 1, Exec 10. (2) Note for rcd, Brig Gen Gerow, 17 Jun 41, WPD 3209–11.

[44] Memo, Actg ACofS WPD for CofS, 19 Jun 41, sub: Enlargement of Functions of GHQ, WPD 3209–10.

[45] (1) AG ltr, 3 Jul 41, sub: Enlargement of Functions of GHQ, AG 320.2 (6–19–41) MC–E-M. (2) Memo, WPD for TAG, 28 Jun 41, same sub, WPD 3209–10.

[46] (1) Diary, Brig Gen Gerow, entry for 15 Jun 41, Item 1, Exec 10. (2) Memo, WPD for G–1, 13 Jun 41, sub: Orders, WPD 3354–53. General Malony reported to GHQ 15 June 1941.

[47] For a full account of GHQ work, see Greenfield and Palmer, "GHQ, US Army, 1940–42."

command of GHQ, first Newfoundland, Greenland, and Bermuda, and, shortly after Pearl Harbor, the Caribbean Defense Command. The contribution of GHQ in managing the first pre-Pearl Harbor movement of troops in the Atlantic area, made in an atmosphere of uncertainty both administratively and policy-wise, paved the way for the later, much greater deployment. GHQ as an operations control center, though encountering steadily increasing difficulties in fulfilling its mission, was a going concern throughout the second half of 1941.[48]

Unfortunately, the tasks confronting the Army in mid-1941 did not lend themselves to any precise division into categories of responsibility that could be assigned definitely either to GHQ or to the War Department General Staff. Any newly established agency was sure to encounter many practical difficulties in maintaining its authority on staff problems on which older War Department agencies, particularly the General Staff, were already working. This process was especially difficult for GHQ as constituted in 1941. It had started its work in 1940 as a training agency rather than the high headquarters staff it was designed to become, and many of its staff officers continued to be preoccupied with the task of building up the ground combat forces. The feasibility of the GHQ concept also became more dubious as interservice and international staff planning became more decisive in Army affairs, and as WPD became more deeply involved in the intricate process. Increasingly, the Chief of Staff was working out his major military decisions in inter-

service and international committees, and WPD continued to be responsible for assisting him in this work. The staff agency that supported General Marshall in strategic deliberations on the highest plane of authority was obviously in a position to overshadow any other staff and in practice if not in theory become the Army's GHQ.

When WPD recommended the July 1941 increase in authority for GHQ, General Gerow had pointed out: "In this delegation of authority, however, the War Department should be careful to avoid the relinquishment of that control which is essential to the execution of its responsibility for the Army's function in the conduct of war."[49] The difficulty of determining what control should be relinquished soon became apparent. Operational command functions at the GHQ level and planning by the General Staff proved inextricably interrelated.[50] The world emergency was constantly shifting and constantly growing. The Chief of Staff could not conceivably finish a comprehensive war plan for operations and take his troops into the field to execute it. GHQ remained in Washington. To fulfill its mission as visualized in 1921, while remaining in Washington, it would have to be given power to co-ordinate overseas operations with zone of interior activities, particularly the allocation of equipment and supplies, and to bring them in line with the military operations it was planning to execute. Should military operations in defense of the continental United States begin, the four defensive

---

[48] For a brief administrative report of the most important of GHQ's early accomplishments, see memo, GHQ for CG Fld Forces, 15 Sep 41, sub: Quarterly Rpt of Planning and Opns Activities, GHQ, WPD 3209-14.

589727 O-61-6

[49] Memo, WPD for CofS, 19 Jun 41, sub: Enlargement of Functions of GHQ, WPD 3209-10.
[50] WPD chart approved by CofS, Jul 41, title: Opn of GHQ—Relation of GHQ to WD, copy atchd to memo, WPD for CofS, 21 Jul 41, sub: GHQ Functional Chart, WPD 3209-10. G-4 did not concur in this allocation of responsibilities.

Army air forces would also come under GHQ control.[51] With these powers GHQ would constitute a super-War Department as soon as hostilities broke out. The various War Department agencies, especially the new, autonomy-conscious Army Air Forces under General Arnold and the divisions of the General Staff, considered this development unwarranted.[52] Without full power GHQ experienced serious difficulties in doing its work, and its very existence further complicated the system of high-level control of the Army.

Thus in 1941 the General Staff, the Army Air Forces, and GHQ found themselves in the same place, Washington, working on many of the same problems. Efficient adjustment of responsibilities and authority among them proved to be arduous. In the field of operational planning, GHQ worked in a state of uncertainty as to what portion of the limited military resources available would be allotted it by other responsible Army agencies. GHQ had no authority to make the various staffs in the War Department work together to gear equipment and supply programs to the requirements of the theaters of operations. The G-4 Division of the General Staff controlled equipment and supply policies as such, following or disregarding GHQ recommendations as to operational needs. Moreover, the War Department never relinquished its direct control over certain areas, principally the Pacific bases. For the critical Hawaiian and Philippine Departments, WPD was General Marshall's only "command staff."[53] The operational control of GHQ

consequently was piecemeal, rather than uniform and a matter of established principle. In carrying out operations plans, GHQ soon became entangled in a series of issues concerning command, particularly with the Army Air Forces, which was legitimately occupied with its own tremendous expansion and training program just as GHQ was legitimately concerned with plans and resources for air operations in the Atlantic bases.

General McNair brought to General Marshall's attention some of the command difficulties that his operational control staff was meeting only a few weeks after the midsummer enlargement of the responsibilities of GHQ.[54] In the ensuing months the issue was clearly drawn. GHQ might be given control of all Army resources, including those ordinarily in the province of the War Department, that were essential to the mission of directing military operations on behalf of the Chief of Staff. Such a transfer of responsibility for "superior command," as General McNair expressed it, should be made only "on the basis that the War Department is not organized suitably for the expeditious action required." This line of reasoning followed the 1921 concept, which left unclear the relation between GHQ and the War Department, but which implied that GHQ was to be on an equal or superior plane. With inexorable logic, General McNair proceeded: "Unless GHQ can be freed from the complications of War Department organization, there is little advantage and some disadvantage in having a GHQ." If GHQ were not to be a headquarters with authority superior to that of the War Department and its General Staff, the War Department itself would have to be

---

[51] Memo for file, 30 Jun 41, WPD 4247-18.

[52] For Army Air Forces hostility to the GHQ system, see Chs. V and VI.

[53] Memo, G-4 for WPD, 24 Jan 42, sub: Coordination Between WPD; G-4, WDGS; GHQ and O'seas Theater Comdrs, WPD 3963-23.

[54] Memo, GHQ for CofS, 25 Jul 41, sub: Def Comds, WPD 4558, Tab. 1.

streamlined to exercise superior command directly for the Chief of Staff.[55]

The multiplicity of U. S. Army activities and interests in bases in the Atlantic as well as in the Pacific in the latter part of 1941 required WPD to supervise closely, by scrutinizing reports to the War Department from the tactical commanders concerned, many military matters that had little to do with high-level strategic planning. Planners had to understand what GHQ, the Army Air Forces, and other agencies were doing in order to take account of their work in strategic plans in the process of development. Within the General Staff, General Marshall turned to WPD for the "war measures, the war plans, the war advice to the Chief of Staff." [56] He had the privilege of using any of his staff advisers as he wished. As taught in the service schools, Army doctrine on staff organization and procedure in the late 1930's carried the qualification: "In actual practice the functioning of a commander and his staff and the method of organizing the staff departments will depend, to a great extent, on the personalities of the commander and the members of the staff." [57] The principal difficulty was that the Chief of Staff had no single staff to which he could turn for fully co-ordinated advice and assistance on all the issues. On any specific matter, he had to choose between one of the five General Staff Divisions and GHQ. He often turned to WPD in urgent cases, such as the broad question concerning the Iceland operation to which General Gerow referred in Novem-

ber 1941 when he said, "GHQ should handle this but the Chief of Staff wants us to take the lead." [58] By October 1941 WPD was so intimately concerned with plans for troop movements and actual troop shipments that it was given the responsibility of controlling centrally the assignment of code words for military plans and the movement of expeditionary forces.[59]

Aside from referring these special Army activities to its planners for review and recommendation as to strategic implications, WPD also had to examine projected enterprises in detail in terms of the local operational situation, particularly in terms of troop strength and supply. To be ready to deal with detailed matters of no broad planning significance, the Projects Group of WPD delegated to individual officers responsibility for intimate acquaintance with all the outlying bases (Hawaii, Philippines, and Alaska), the Caribbean Defense Command, the British-leased bases, and air ferrying operations.[60]

General Marshall often relied on WPD to draw on the other General Staff Divisions, in effect co-ordinating their work, in order to prepare staff studies, but he personally acted on every policy or command decision, often intervening in the process of drafting studies to make extremely detailed changes both in substance and language. WPD records, 1939–41, give conclusive

---

[55] Memo, GHQ for WPD, 2 Sep 41, sub: Functions, Responsibility, and Auth of GHQ, WPD 4558, Tab 10.

[56] *Pearl Harbor Attack: Hearings before the Joint Committee on the Investigation of the Pearl Harbor Attack*, Part 3, p. 1187.

[57] Foreword, Command and Staff Principles.

[58] Memo, Brig Gen Gerow for Col Bundy, 20 Nov 41, no sub, WPD 4493–174.

[59] AG ltr, 13 Oct 41, sub: Asgmt of Colors as Code Designations of WD Plans and Projects, AG 311.5 (9–29–41) MC–E–M.

[60] Projects Gp roster, with duties assigned to offs, 24 Sep 41, Paper 30, Item 2A, OPD Hist Unit file. One officer was designated as "WPD adviser on AA Artillery and AWS [Air Warning Service] matters," another, as "WPD adviser on Harbor Defense matters." One officer had "Miscellaneous" assigned to him as well as British Guiana, South American bases, St. Lucia, and Trinidad.

testimony to the tremendous burden which the General Staff system placed on the Chief of Staff and the energy with which he shouldered it. His handwriting is in evidence on drafts of nearly every important paper and on many comparatively unimportant ones. An early indication of the personal role General Marshall intended to take in staff work was given shortly after he became Chief of Staff. At a meeting on 23 October 1939, he had suggested that "studies would probably go through without change if a preliminary draft were sent up first for his once over before the final work was submitted." [61]

The WPD chief similarly carried a great work load that he did not consider himself authorized to delegate to other officers in the Division. The processing of correspondence in the Division followed very much the same channels at the end of 1941 that had been observed in previous years when the volume was infinitely smaller. All correspondence passed through the hands of the Division executive, who routed it to the proper group chief who in turn directed it to the proper section, where the section chief detailed an officer to take necessary action to dispose of the matter. Action might be merely reading and marking for file by the record room, it might require drafting a message to be dispatched by the Chief of Staff, or it might involve preparation of a long, complex study of the issue raised. In any case the action officer returned the paper to the executive with a disposition slip bearing his own initials, those of his section chief, and those of his

group chief, showing concurrence.[62] Although the executive might sign administrative memoranda, all policy papers were scrutinized or signed by the Division chief.

The pressure of work became so great in 1941 that General Gerow drafted a memorandum requesting permission to delegate final staff action on routine matters to his immediate assistants, the two WPD group chiefs. He pointed out: "The paper work in this Division has reached such proportions that the Assistant Chief of Staff finds that sufficient time for thorough consideration of problems of basic policy and matters of major importance is lacking." [63] The atmosphere created by General Staff tradition as of 1941 is indicated by the fact that General Gerow decided not to sign and dispatch this memorandum for fear that more strict regulations would be inforced.[64] Thus, with an increasing amount of work, WPD was turning into a hard-working and versatile planning staff, but was not the kind of staff General Marshall would need in his Washington command post if the United States engaged in open hostilities in World War II.

In recognition of this fact General Gerow consistently supported the policy of giving GHQ all the power it needed. Nevertheless some of the other officers in WPD in 1941 had developed a line of thought diverging from the conventional GHQ concept. They agreed in maintaining two propositions.

---

[61] Notes on Conferences in OCS, I, 12, WDCSA rcds. For an example of the detailed instructions General Marshall gave WPD concerning the preparation of important studies, see Notes on Conferences in OCS, II, 389–91.

[62] WPD adm memo, 16 May 41, sub: Orgn and Procedure, Paper 109, Item 2A, OPD Hist Unit file.

[63] WPD draft memo for CofS, sub: Delegation of Auth by Head of WPD, WPD 3963–20. This memorandum is undated but refers to the "Chiefs of Plans and Projects Groups," positions which existed May–December 1941.

[64] Note, Maj C. K. Gailey, Jr., Exec WPD for Brig Gen Gerow, n.d., atchd to WPD draft memo for CofS, sub: Delegation of Auth . . ., WPD 3963–20. After receiving Major Gailey's comment, General Gerow wrote on it: "No action at present, G."

First, the Army needed co-ordinated, central staff direction of military operations and, second, this direction had to come from somewhere in the War Department. General McNarney was one of the most outspoken advocates of these propositions at the time that transfer of operational responsibility to GHQ was being discussed. In April 1941, shortly before his departure for duty with the observer group in England, he recommended to General Gerow that WPD oppose the transfer of theater planning and operations functions to GHQ. He wrote: "It might be desirable and perhaps necessary, to set up in Washington a coordinating agency to tie together the Operations of Zone of the Interior with those of one or more theaters, but I doubt if this agency should be separated from the War Department." [65] This line of reasoning, with which General Gerow was familiar, remained beneath the surface of official WPD opinion while the Division tried in mid-1941 to make the GHQ system work in accordance with General Marshall's wishes. It emerged when critical study of the high command structure was authorized after GHQ began to meet tremendous difficulties in carrying out its operational planning mission.

When in July 1941 General McNair felt compelled to request clarification of conflicting command responsibilities for developing defenses in some of the outlying bases which had been placed under the control of GHQ, his memorandum was referred to WPD.[66] General Gerow informed the Chief of Staff that the problem raised by

General McNair affected "both the peace and war activities of almost every agency of the War Department—personnel, intelligence, organization, training, supply, planning, and responsibility of the Air Force." In other words, the dilemma of GHQ could be resolved only by treating it in the larger context of Army organization and functions. Accordingly WPD recommended that representatives of all those agencies make a formal study of the problems involved.[67] In mid-August the Chief of Staff directed General Gerow to form a committee representing the General Staff Divisions, the Air Forces, and GHQ and to proceed with the recommended study.[68]

The Army Air Forces Drive for Autonomy

The main drive to solve the GHQ problem by eliminating GHQ as it then existed came from the Army Air Forces, represented on the committee by Brig. Gen. Carl Spaatz, chief of General Arnold's Air Staff. At this point in Air history, the Army advocates of air power as an independent strategic weapon coequal with the ground forces were enjoying unprecedented freedom of action. In the Air Force Combat Command (former GHQ Air Force) they had their striking force. In the Air Corps they had their own procurement, technical service, and training agency. Through General Arnold's status as Deputy Chief of Staff, they were able to participate in command decisions. General Arnold also sat as a member of the Joint Board, the na-

---

[65] Memo, Brig Gen McNarney for ACofS WPD, 8 Apr 41, sub: Allocation of Responsibilities Between WPD and GHQ, WPD 3209-7.

[66] Memo, GHQ for CofS, 25 Jul 41, sub: Def Comds, WPD 4558, Tab 1. The specific bases in question were in Alaska, the Caribbean, and the North Atlantic.

[67] Memo, WPD for CofS, 11 Aug 41, sub: Activation of Alaskan and Caribbean Def Comds and North Atlantic Def Comd (Newfoundland, Greenland, and Iceland), WPD 4558, Tab 3.

[68] (1) Memo, OCS for WPD, G–1, G–2, G–3, G–4, AAF, and GHQ, 12 Aug 41, no sub, WPD 4558. (2) Memo, OCS for WPD, G–1, etc., 14 Aug 41, no sub, WPD 4558.

tional military high command. The main thing lacking to make the Army Air Forces virtually an autonomous arm of the service was a staff for General Arnold to make general strategic plans for the employment of air forces and to spell out that strategy in detail in operational plans controlling the employment of air units in combat. The existence of WPD blocked Army Air Forces from entering the strategic planning field, while the existence of GHQ similarly blocked it from operational or tactical planning.

The Army Regulation establishing the Army Air Forces [69] in June 1941 had in fact created a policy-formulating Air Staff for the chief of the new agency, but it did not free the Army Air Forces or the Air Staff from subordination to the General Staff, particularly to WPD, in regard to strategic planning or from subordination to GHQ in regard to control of tactical operations. The study of the GHQ issue coincided with an earnest Air Forces attempt to clarify or alter the regulation in the interests of air autonomy.[70]

The Air Staff interpreted the regulation as granting them the autonomy within the Army which they had long sought, either inside or outside the War Department. The regulation stated:

The Chief of the Army Air Forces, pursuant to policies, directives, and instructions from the Secretary of War, is charged with the following duties:

a. The control of the activities of the Air Force Combat Command and of the Air

Corps, the preparation of plans pertaining thereto, . . .[71]

The chief of the Air War Plans Division of the Air Staff, Col. Harold R. George, was trying, as late as October 1941, to get WPD to concur in the proposition that this phrasing meant that the "Air War Plans Division is the proper agency to formulate all plans for the allocation and employment of air units, and the services essential to such units, whether or not these air plans form a part of a larger plan involving combined (that is, ground and air) forces." [72] In other words, all plans for the employment of air forces, even when they constituted the Air part of joint strategic plans, would be written inside General Arnold's headquarters rather than in WPD.

WPD refused to concur in this interpretation, stating that the Division ought to work very closely with the Air Staff but that "it is fundamental that there must be one staff agency in the War Department responsible to the Chief of Staff for the soundness and adequateness of basic strategical plans governing the joint employment of Army ground and Army Air Forces. War Plans Division should be that agency." In these circumstances, the Air Staff would give technical assistance to WPD but would not actually participate in strategic planning at the higher levels. WPD went even further, adding that it would recommend a policy whereby "GHQ is responsible for the preparation of all tactical plans" based on strategic plans. This combination of views, if generally adopted, would leave the Air Staff out of operational planning al-

[69] AR 95–5, 20 Jun 41.

[70] See Craven and Cate, AAF I, Chs. 2 and 3 for developing Army Air Forces autonomy and Ch. 7, pp. 258–65, for the GHQ issue and the 1942 reorganization of the War Department. For parallel treatment of the GHQ issue, see Greenfield and Palmer, "GHQ, US Army, 1940–42," Chs. IX, X.

[71] AR 95–5, 20 Jun 41.

[72] Draft memo, AAF (AWPD) for CofS, n.d., sub: Allocation of Responsibilities Betwen WPD of GS and AWPD of AS, ASWA 320.2 (10–4–41). Notation on memorandum states "written 4 October 1941."

together, whether strategic or tactical. The WPD comment, passed informally to the Air Forces, called forth a marginal notation by Colonel George, "Where is our vaunted autonomy?" and a strong memorandum of complaint about the attitude of the General Staff, a copy of which was forwarded to the Assistant Secretary of War for Air.[73]

At this very time the Army Air Forces was trying to secure concurrence in a draft revision of Army Regulation 95–5 that would clearly support its position on Air planning. The proposed revision stated categorically that various sections of the Air Staff under the chief of the Army Air Forces, to be called "Air Divisions of the General Staff," should "prepare all plans for all air operations . . . and, after such plans have been approved by the Chief of Staff, to control and supervise their execution."[74] This project was dropped in November 1941 after WPD presented General Marshall with a long and careful analysis of the Air Forces plan. This analysis flatly rejected the idea of an Air division of the General Staff as constituting a component but autonomous part of the General Staff. The WPD study recommended that

the "Air Staff function as the staff of a commander subordinate to the War Department, and not as an element of the War Department General Staff," basing this conclusion on what it called "recognized military essentials of command relations," namely:

There must be a single military head (Chief of Staff) over all elements of the Army in order to coordinate their operations.

Because the Chief of Staff has not the time to perform the necessary research and detailed study for all matters which require his decision, he must have a staff.

The staff of the Chief of Staff must be a General Staff operating in the interests of the Army as a whole, not for part of the Army. This staff is an essential element of the unified command.[75]

After this last counterthrust from the General Staff, the Army Air Forces gave up its drive for control of strategic planning, at least for the time being. Instead it relied on its right to submit the strategic views of the Air War Plans Division to WPD for consideration. However much WPD might in practice indorse Air Forces planning ideas, this relationship indeed was not the "vaunted autonomy."

Engaged in fighting this losing battle, conducted quietly and rather informally by the Air Forces and WPD, the Army airmen were in no mood in the autumn of 1941 to temporize with GHQ. The latter agency's responsibility for tactical planning for ground and air operations not only interfered with the drive toward planning autonomy but also threatened to interfere with the allocation and use of the opera-

---

[73] (1) Draft memo, WPD for AAF, — Oct 41, sub: Allocation of Responsibilities . . ., ASWA 320.2 (10–4–41). No copy is in WPD files, the draft evidently having been handed informally to the Army Air Forces. (2) Memo, Lt Col K. N. Walker (AWPD) for CofAS, 14 Oct 41, sub: Allocation of Responsibilities . . ., ASWA 320.2 (10–4–41). Penciled note attached reads: "Think Mr. Lovett should see this as an example of Army Air Force autonomy and what part the General Staff thinks we play in the present organization. H. G."

[74] (1) Draft, AR 95–5, n.d., Tab Q, Item 7, Exec 4. This copy was circulated for concurrence. It differed from an earlier, 6 October, draft chiefly in designating the various parts of the Air Staff as "Air Divisions of the General Staff." (2) Cf. draft, AR 95–5, 6 Oct 41, Air Corps 300.3 AR 95–5, Air Corps 1941 files, Hist Rcds Sec, AG Rcds Br.

[75] Memo, WPD for CofS, 12 Nov 41, sub: Revision of AR 95–5, copies in WPD 3774–20 and Tab Q, Item 7, Exec 4. A note attached to the latter copy states that the action officer, Lt. Col. W. K. Harrison, drew up the study on the basis of comments by Colonels Bundy and Handy, Col. R. W. Crawford, and General Gerow.

tional air force for air defense of the continental United States and the Atlantic bases. The bases were already being placed under control of GHQ, and the continental defense commands would follow in the event of hostilities. The elimination of GHQ would free the Army Air Forces from an unwelcome competitor in one of the two main fields of disputed planning authority, even if WPD could not be dislodged from the other.

Early Proposals for Reorganization of the War Department

The members of the committee formed under the leadership of WPD in August to study the difficulties of GHQ quickly agreed that it was necessary to abandon hope of solving them within the terms of the GHQ concept and also agreed that a major reorganization of the War Department was necessary. The WPD representative, Lt. Col. William K. Harrison of the Plans Group, took the initiative in drafting an outline plan for readjusting the organization and functions of high-level staff work in support of an Army-wide command.[76] This study of August 1941 based its recommendations on the well-established distinction between the two major spheres of Army activities, "preparation and maintenance of the field forces for combat" and "combat operations" proper. Responsibility for the first task, a zone of interior function, Colonel Harrison proposed to assign to three large Army organizations set up as commands, dealing respectively with "air forces, ground forces, and service." Such a system would allow the General Staff to serve as the

[76] The action of the committee and General Marshall's position are described in memo, GHQ for DCofS, 21 Oct 41, sub: Functions, Responsibilities, and Auth of GHQ, WPD 4558, Tab 12.

"policy and planning agency for the Chief of Staff," delegating not only the actual work of the zone of interior but "supervision of the execution of plans and policies" as much as possible to "subordinate agencies—particularly the Commanding Generals, Services, Ground Forces, and Army Air Forces." This plan would limit the General Staff to an abstract, advisory plane and would make the new operating commands of the zone of interior directly responsible to the Chief of Staff for carrying out his general instructions, as formulated on the basis of General Staff ideas.[77]

The new element in Colonel Harrison's proposal and, from the point of view of WPD's future, the vital one, was a recommendation that an "Operations or Command Section should be organized on the General Staff to assist the Chief of Staff in exercising his command functions over

[77] Unused memo, WPD for CofS, n.d., sub: Orgn of Army High Comd, WPD 4618. The study bears no indication of author. Since this study was never officially dispatched to the Chief of Staff, it was stamped "NOT USED." In an interview with the author and Maj. D. H. Richards of the OPD History Unit, 15 October 1946, General Gerow stated that study of the reorganization problem was the work of Colonel Harrison, who represented WPD in all the later activities incident to the reorganization. General Gerow of course familiarized himself with the ideas in it (OPD Hist Unit Interv file). This unused WPD study clearly antedates official recommendation of the general plan by the Army Air Forces. The WPD draft memorandum is undated except for a stamped "November 1941," probably the filing date. The end limiting date for its composition was 30 September 1941 because the paper recommended appointment of a reorganization board to report "not later than September 30, 1941." In an interview with the author, 16 April 1947, General Harrison stated that he worked out the main ideas in the reorganization plan early in 1941 and drafted his unused study in August, when it was approved by the committee which resolved in favor of reorganizing the War Department as the only solution of the GHQ problem (OPD Hist Unit Interv file).

overseas departments and bases, defense commands, task forces, and theaters of operations." [78] This operational section proposed for the General Staff, whose supervisory function had never been stressed but rather inhibited, would be inside and not outside the War Department; it would thus be free from the handicaps of GHQ, which could hardly take any action without raising the question of whether its authority was superior or inferior to the older, well-established War Department agencies. At the very least an Operations or Command Section on the General Staff would not be considered inferior to any other agency. No specific mention of the name of WPD appeared in Colonel Harrison's study. Nevertheless, in view of its widely recognized priority of interest in overseas operations, above and beyond the general concern for zone of interior programs which it shared with the rest of the General Staff, no other existing agency of the War Department was likely to assume the role of the Chief of Staff's command post staff.

General Gerow, still trying to achieve a working solution in accord with his June understanding with General Marshall, refused to go along with the initial committee resolution of mid-August or to indorse the Harrison study. At this time General Marshall still wished to make GHQ work as an independent headquarters, and General Gerow was aware of the Chief of Staff's predisposition. Furthermore, General Gerow did not want to be an advocate of a plan that might lead to a great accretion of power to his own staff. Consequently the Harrison memorandum was never officially dispatched outside WPD. Instead the Division prepared and circulated for comment

a memorandum, dated 30 August 1941, proposing to continue GHQ substantially as then constituted. [79]

Although WPD did not take official action on Colonel Harrison's memorandum, the issues involved were aired in discussion in the committee formed to study the status of GHQ. Officers in other parts of the War Department were free to advance Colonel Harrison's proposal if they chose. Some of his ideas probably were already current elsewhere. In any case a number of them won official support from the Army Air Forces a few weeks later. On 24 October 1941 General Spaatz, as the Army Air Forces representative on the committee, formally submitted to General Gerow a suggestion for reorganizing the War Department much along the lines developed in Colonel Harrison's unofficial WPD study. He explained that Colonel Harrison's study had been prepared in harmony with Army Air Forces proposals and accepted in principle by the committee. The Army Air Forces wished to continue along this line. [80] This memorandum from Gen-

---

[78] Ibid.

[79] For official WPD proposal, see WPD draft memo for CofS, 30 Aug 41, sub: Functions, Responsibilities, and Auth of GHQ, WPD 4558.
In his October 1946 interview with the author and Major Richards, General Gerow stated that General Marshall had indicated that he still wished to keep his command post outside the War Department, as in the case of GHQ (OPD Hist Unit Interv file). In his April 1947 interview with the author, General Harrison stated that one of General Gerow's principal reasons for refusing to approve the Harrison reorganization plan officially was a feeling that it was inappropriate for him to recommend so great an increase in power and responsibility for his own Division (OPD Hist Unit Interv file).

[80] Memo, AAF for WPD, 24 Oct 41, sub: Functions . . ., WPD 4558, Tab 11. In his April interview with the author, General Harrison stated that he informally had urged Army Air Forces officers to take official action on this plan (OPD Hist Unit Interv file).

eral Spaatz went to WPD at about the same time that the Air Forces proposed the revision of AR 95–5. Thus, while Colonel Harrison was drafting for the Division a sharp memorandum of nonconcurrence with the idea of an Air division of the General Staff, General Gerow was trying to decide what to do with the Air Forces recommendation that Colonel Harrison's plan for reorganizing the War Wepartment should be carried out. It was also at this point that General McNair himself said that he was inclined to favor eliminating GHQ as then constituted and reorganizing the War Department.[81] Not many days later, 14 November 1941, just two days after WPD rejected the proposed revision of AR 95–5, the Air Forces refused to concur in the new, unequivocal directive which General Gerow had drawn up to clarify the position of GHQ.[82]

General Arnold at this juncture sent the Chief of Staff a plan for War Department reorganization, limiting GHQ to the mission of organizing and training ground combat forces and transferring its superior command and planning functions back to the War Department, itself to be reconstituted. The major specific recommendations were:

(1) That the ground combat forces be grouped together under a Commanding General, and that that General be provided a Ground General Staff. The present GHQ organization, supplemented by parts of the G–1, G–2, and G–3 Divisions of the present War Department General Staff might be utilized for this purpose.

(2) That the supply arms and services be grouped together under a Service Commander, and that that Service Commander be provided an adequate staff. This staff might be made up from members of the G–4 Division of the General Staff and the A–4 Division of the Air Staff, supplemented by officers from the Offices of the Chiefs of the supply Arms and Services.

(3) That the Chief of Staff function as the Commander of the military forces of the War Department, that he be provided a small General Staff, and that he exercise his control within the continental United States through the Ground, Service, and Air Force Commanders. This General Staff should be a small policy-making, war-planning, and coordinating staff, made up of equal representation from the Ground Forces and the Air Forces.[83]

The resemblance of General Arnold's plan to the basic ideas in Colonel Harrison's August study and in General Spaatz' October memorandum was unmistakable, though it was much less precise as to how the General Staff would exercise command functions on behalf of the Chief of Staff. General Gerow, to whom the November Air Forces plan was referred, promptly (18 November) informed General Marshall that WPD concurred in the "broad principles and the general organization of the War Department as set forth" in the plan, and recommended that it be developed in detail. In passing reference to the difference between this Air Forces proposal and the earlier idea of air divisions of the General Staff, he noted: "One General Staff, instead of two, is provided to assist the

---

[81] Memo, GHQ for DCofS, 21 Oct 41, sub: Functions . . ., WPD 4558, Tab 12. For General McNair's desire to "assist the War Department and facilitate operations," see particularly memo, GHQ for WPD, 2 Sep 41, sub: Functions . . ., WPD 4558, Tab 10.

[82] Memo, AAF for WPD, 14 Nov 41, sub: Proposed Revision of Directive to GHQ, etc., WPD 3209–10, Tab G.

[83] Memo, AAF for CofS, n.d., sub: Orgn of Armed Forces for War, WPD 4614. General Arnold's plan bears no date, but a chart attached to it as Tab A is dated 14 November. The second part of the memorandum dealt with the supra-War Department organization for national defense, a topic then coming to a deadlock in the Joint Board due to Army and Navy inability to agree.

Chief of Staff in coordinating the major activities of the Army." [84]

By this time General Marshall himself had become convinced that something had to be done to increase the efficiency of the War Department in directing the multitude of urgent Army activities carried on under its control. On 3 November, while discussing another matter, the Chief of Staff had explained his own ideas on staff work to General Gerow and Colonel Bundy. His remarks were recorded as follows:

The Chief of Staff pointed out that he was seriously concerned about recent command failures. He had been paralyzed to find that a shipment of bombs sent at the end of September would not get to Singapore until December 18. It is not only that delay occurs in matters of this sort, but that we do not know *why* it occurs. In this case, as in several others recently, it is evident that things have not been followed up as they should be. "We can have no more of this," General Marshall said. "This is the poorest command post in the Army and we must do something about it, although I do not yet know what we will do. . . ."

As General Marshall sees it, we have only begun when an order is issued. He does not want to pester commanders by checking up on them constantly, but there must be some means of knowing how things are progressing before a crisis develops, as in the case of bombs for Singapore.[85]

The comments of General Gerow and Colonel Bundy in reply to this criticism showed clearly how difficult it was to assign staff responsibility in the War Department as then organized:

General Gerow said that in the past when War Plans had indicated the desire of the Chief of Staff to have a certain thing go to the Philippines as rapidly as possible, it was assumed that G–4 or somebody else would see

that it got there. Colonel Bundy said that he had read carefully the directive regarding the bombs, and he had concluded it was necessary to specify that a certain agency was charged with the responsibility for following up the action directed. In this particular directive, it was nowhere stated that anybody had the specific responsibility for following through. Perhaps there should be a standard paragraph making this clear in each directive. In the case of the bombs, it was natural for the Air Force to follow up. General Marshall agreed that this seemed to be at least a temporary solution.[86]

Nevertheless, the Chief of Staff was not yet convinced that reorganization of the War Department and elimination of GHQ would solve the problem. In connection with his complaints on 3 November about his command post, he stated: "Careful consideration has been given to the idea of reorganizing the staff. This would virtually eliminate GHQ and provide a small staff, but it would still be an operational staff, and the Chief of Staff and the Deputies would still be troubled by pressure coming towards the top. While they would be freed of much detail, the proposed staff reorganization would not provide a complete solution." [87]

The "idea" to which the Chief of Staff was referring was clearly that of Colonel Harrison and General Spaatz, since General Arnold had not yet presented his plan. When that plan had come before him and WPD had indorsed its general outlines, the Chief of Staff for the first time indicated that he was willing to consider an alternative to the GHQ system. On 25 November he stated that he was "favorably impressed by the basic organization proposed" by General Arnold and formally charged WPD with studying it in detail.[88] The end of the GHQ experiment was in sight, but would not

[84] Memo, WPD for CofS, 18 Nov 41, sub: Orgn of Armed Forces for War, WPD 4614.

[85] Notes on Conferences in OCS, II, 424C, WDCSA rcds.

[86] *Ibid*, p. 424D.

[87] *Ibid*, p. 424C.

[88] Memo, SGS for WPD, 25 Nov 41, WPD 4614.

occur until the following March because development in detail of such a far-reaching plan for reorganization of the War Department was bound to take time. Furthermore, an agreed solution would have to be reached, the Chief of Staff and his civilian superiors must approve it, and necessary legislation must be secured to permit a departure from the provisions of the National Defense Act. Before further progress had been made in the direction of establishing a more efficient command post for the Chief of Staff, the problem was made easier from an administrative-legal point of view and more urgent from the point of view of command by the advent of open hostilities.

CHAPTER V

Transition Into War

The Japanese attack on Pearl Harbor abruptly upset the uneasy balance which had kept the United States poised between peace and war. The carrier-based air raid on Pearl Harbor and Hickam Field on the morning of 7 December 1941 was a violent shock to the U. S. Army as well as to the nation. In a certain sense the Army, in view of the overwhelming evidence long available that the Japanese might open hostilities by launching such an assault against American positions in the Pacific, including Hawaii, and in view of the virtual certainty that they would gain some initial success, was prepared to be fatalistic about the initial onslaught. But neither the Army nor the Navy had concentrated its attention on Hawaii, and the extent of the damage done, particularly the crippling of the U. S. Pacific Fleet, seriously compromised U. S. Army and Navy plans for wartime operations in the Pacific.

The Failure of Follow-Up

The larger issues of national defense involved in the Pearl Harbor episode, as well as the immediate sequence of events leading up to the attack, have been thoroughly studied in a series of official investigations, and individual writers have discussed at length the blame initially fixed on the Army and Navy commanders in Hawaii and subsequently shared with members of the higher military staffs in Washington.[1] Within the framework of the larger issues, Pearl Harbor had an aspect of special significance to the Chief of Staff and to the War Plans Division. In this vital instance the War Department General Staff failed to follow up and make sure of compliance with the Chief of Staff's operational instructions to the Army commander at the critical point, Hawaii.

The threat of a Japanese attack in the Pacific became increasingly apparent in the fall of 1941. It was imperative that, in threatened areas, the War Department keep commanders fully aware of the situation as it developed. The G-2 Division of the General Staff had the responsibility for dis-

---

[1] (1) The Joint Committee on the Investigation of the Pearl Harbor Attack, 1945–46, published extensive evidence about the Pearl Harbor episode, including the War Department documents in WPD files, the testimony of War Department officers, and the proceedings and reports of earlier investigations. The hearings before the committee and the exhibits submitted to it were published in thirty-nine parts: *Pearl Harbor Attack: Hearings before the Joint Committee on the Investigation of the Pearl Harbor Attack.* This document is hereafter referred to as *Hearings.* The one-volume report of the committee, summarizing the evidence and stating the conclusions of the committee, was published as *Investigation of the Pearl Harbor Attack: Report of the Joint Committee on the Investigation of the Pearl Harbor Attack,* S Doc 244, 79th Cong, 2d sess, and is cited hereafter as *Report.* (2) For a careful examination and interpretation of the Pearl Harbor evidence, see Walter Millis, *This is Pearl! The United States and Japan—1941* (New York, 1947). (3) For a briefer treatment in this series, see Watson, *Chief of Staff: Prewar Plans and Preparations,* Ch. XV.

semination of intelligence about the enemy and for specific warnings against the danger of subversive activities. The more important function of assisting the Chief of Staff in preparing and dispatching to the field orders that translated the current diplomatic situation into instructions governing military dispositions was WPD's responsibility, insofar as the Pacific area was concerned. WPD was therefore intimately connected with the transmission of the war warnings and operational directives that were sent to the Pacific commanders in November 1941.

Of the several war warnings which went out over the Chief of Staff's signature concerning the possibility of a Japanese attack in the Pacific, the most important was a message dispatched on 27 November 1941 to several commanders, including the commanding general of the Hawaiian Department. Progress in the protracted negotiations then being conducted between Japanese diplomatic representatives and the U. S. Department of State came to an end as of 27 November. Although no one at the time could be sure Japan would not resume the conversations, Secretary of State Hull informed Secretary of War Stimson on the morning of 27 November that the memorandum given the Japanese representatives on the preceding day had "broken the whole matter off." The President himself told Secretary Stimson that the "talks had been called off." [2]

Under these circumstances, it became necessary for the War Department to warn Pacific commands of the latest turn of diplomatic events. Secretary Stimson, in the temporary absence of General Marshall,[3]

discussed the problem with General Gerow and with the senior Deputy Chief of Staff, Maj. Gen. William Bryden. General Gerow reported the results of this early morning meeting with Secretary Stimson: "The Secretary . . . told me he had telephoned both Mr. Hull and the President this morning. Mr. Hull stated the conversations had been terminated with barest possibility of resumption. The President wanted a warning message sent to the Philippines. I told him I would consult Admiral Stark and prepare an appropriate cablegram." Such a warning message for the Philippines, the most exposed Pacific outpost, was formulated and approved at a second meeting on 27 November at which the Secretary of War, the Secretary of Navy, Admiral Stark, and General Gerow were present.[4] This draft "formed a basis for the preparation of other messages to the other three commanders in the Pacific area," that is, the Panama Canal Department, the Western Defense Command (which had responsibility for Alaska), and the Hawaiian Department. These three messages were drawn up in WPD, cleared with the Deputy Chief of Staff, and, together with the message for the Philippines, dispatched the same day over the name of General Marshall.[5]

The message which WPD thus came to prepare was carefully phrased to reflect the current diplomatic-military situation, and was intended to convey precise operational instructions based on a clear warning. This message (No. 472) read:

Negotiations with Japan appear to be terminated to all practical purposes with only the barest possibilities that the Japanese Government might come back and offer to continue.

---

[2] (1) *Report,* p. 46. (2) For an account of the negotiations with Japan and their termination, see *Report,* pp. 13–41.

[3] General Marshall was in North Carolina viewing Army maneuvers. *Report,* p. 199, n. 214.

[4] (1) *Hearings,* Part 3, p. 1020. (2) Memo, WPD for CofS, 27 Nov 41, sub: Far Eastern Situation, WPD 4544–13.

[5] *Hearings,* Part 3, pp. 1021–24.

Japanese future action unpredictable but hostile action possible at any moment. If hostilities cannot, repeat cannot, be avoided the United States desires that Japan commit the first overt act. This policy should not, repeat not, be construed as restricting you to a course of action that might jeopardize your defense. Prior to hostile Japanese action you are directed to undertake such reconnaissance and other measures as you deem necessary but these measures should be carried out so as not, repeat not, to alarm civil population or disclose intent. Report measures taken. Should hostilities occur you will carry out the tasks assigned in Rainbow Five so far as they pertain to Japan. Limit dissemination of this highly secret information to minimum essential officers. [Signed] MARSHALL.[6]

On the same day, 27 November, the G–2 Division sent a message (No. 473) to the G–2 of the Hawaiian Department, and to other Pacific and continental commands as well, which read:

Japanese negotiations have come to a practical stalemate. Hostilities may ensue. Subversive activities may be expected. Inform commanding general and Chief of Staff only.[7]

The warnings dispatched concerning the Japanese threat in the Pacific did not impress Lt. Gen. Walter C. Short, Commanding General, Hawaiian Department, sufficiently to induce his taking all the precautionary measures it was intended he should take. The nature of the measures that he did take was suggested if not clearly revealed in a report to the Chief of Staff sent in reply to the War Department's warning message No. 472, dated 27 November. It read: "Report Department alerted to prevent sabotage. Liaison with Navy reurad [Code: Reference your radio] 472 twenty-seventh. SHORT."[8] When this message was received, it was transmitted along with

other answers to the 27 November war warnings to the Office of the Chief of Staff. General Marshall probably saw it, and it was then passed on to Secretary of War Stimson, who certainly saw it. The message was then sent to WPD where, in accordance with normal procedure, it was first noted and initialed by Maj. Charles K. Gailey, Jr., the Division executive, and then shown to General Gerow, who also initialed it. Finally, General Short's message was referred to Colonel Bundy, chief of the Plans Group. During the following week General Gerow, as he subsequently testified, discussed it with no one, and there was no follow-up by WPD. The other commanders who received the 27 November warning message reported measures taken in sufficint detail to indicate clearly that they were complying fully with the intent of the order. Despite the marked contrast between General Short's reply and these other responses, it was not recognized at the time as inadequate by any one who saw it.[9]

The reasons for the failure of the War Department, and specifically of WPD, to recognize the inadequacy of General Short's reply of 27 November remain a matter of speculation. General Gerow subsequently testified that he had probably erroneously identified General Short's message as an answer to the G–2 message of 27 November.[10] Colonel Bundy, to whom the message was finally referred for any necessary action, was killed in an air accident while en route

---

[6] Hearings, Part 14, p. 1328.
[7] Hearings, Part 14, p. 1329.
[8] Hearings, Part 14, p. 1330.

[9] (1) Report, pp. 201–04. (2) Hearings, Part 3, pp. 1026–34.
[10] (1) Ibid. (2) General Gerow pointed out to the Congressional committee that the identifying number (472) cited in General Short's reply was meaningless at the time because "that number on the 27 November warning message was put on by the Signal Corps and it was not the number assigned to that particular document by the War Plans Division." Hearings, Part 3, p. 1031.

to Hawaii immediately after Pearl Harbor, and no clear evidence of his reactions to General Short's message has been discovered. The Plans Group was the agency of WPD which normally checked on compliance with operational instructions of the Chief of Staff. But the very name of this group, reflecting its primary function, points to a fact of administrative significance, namely, that there was no unit in WPD like the later OPD Theater Group, whose primary function was to follow up an operational order of the Chief of Staff and check in detail the adequacy of the measures reported as having been taken to execute it. Even when it was not specifically instructed to do so, WPD unquestionably had the responsibility for following up to see that the Chief of Staff's operational instructions were carried out whenever measures reported taken were recognized to be inadequate. In his testimony before the Congressional Pearl Harbor investigating committee, General Marshall said: "So far as the operations of the General Staff were concerned, the war measures, the war plans, the war advice to the Chief of Staff came directly from the War Plans Division." The Chief of Staff also expressed his belief that General Gerow, as Assistant Chief of Staff, WPD, had sufficient "operational authority to send a message that involved action," such as a query to General Short on his reply.[11] Accepting the fact that action should have been taken and that WPD was the staff that originally handled this case, General Gerow acknowledged responsibility for the failure of WPD to act. He stated to the committee:

In the light of subsequent events, I feel now that it might have been desirable to send such an inquiry, and had such an inquiry been sent

it would probably have developed the fact that the Commanding General in Hawaii was not at that time carrying out the directive in the message signed "MARSHALL." [12]

General Gerow also said:

If there was any responsibility to be attached to the War Department for any failure to send an inquiry to General Short, the responsibility must rest on War Plans Division, and I accept that responsibility as Chief of War Plans Division. . . . I was a staff advisor to the Chief of Staff, and I had a group of 48 officers to assist me. It was my responsibility to see that these messages were checked, and if an inquiry was necessary, the War Plans Division should have drafted such an inquiry and presented it to the Chief of Staff for approval.[13]

General Marshall testified that General Gerow had a direct responsibility and that he as Chief of Staff had full responsibility, in other words that the Chief of Staff was responsible for anything the General Staff did or did not do, just as General Gerow was responsible for all the work of his Division.[14]

Looming in the background of WPD's failure to take appropriate action on General's Short's report of 27 November was the unclear definition and the unsystematic assignment of Army responsibilities for controlling military operations. In November 1941 the Army high command had no single agency specifically charged with the task of promptly and carefully reviewing all reports concerning military operations received from the field. It had been intended that

---

[11] (1) *Hearings*, Part 3, p. 1187. (2) *Ibid.*, p. 1114.

[12] *Hearings*, Part 3, p. 1031.
[13] *Hearings*, Part 3, p. 1026.
[14] (1) *Hearings*, Part 3, pp. 1422–23. (2) The Congressional Pearl Harbor investigating committee drew this conclusion: "The War Plans Division of the War Department failed to discharge its direct responsibility to advise the commanding general [Marshall] he had not properly alerted the Hawaiian Department when the latter, pursuant to instructions, had reported action taken in a message that was not satisfactorily responsive to the original directive." *Report*, p. 252.

GHQ should become such an agency, but on the eve of Pearl Harbor responsibility for the Pacific areas had not yet been transferred from the General Staff to GHQ. The Pearl Harbor episode demonstrated the need for a clarification and reallocation of functions within the Army high command, a reallocation that would place squarely on a single agency properly organized to perform this function the responsibility under the Chief of Staff for directing all overseas operations and following up to see that his directives were executed.

WPD and Actual Operations

In one sense the transition from peace to war on 7 December 1941 was abrupt. Public opinion, particularly as presented in the press and in Congress, no longer was torn between fear of doing too much too quickly and fear of doing too little too late. The nation demanded that the President and the armed services should get things done. The President and his Army, Navy, and Army Air Forces advisers responded at once to the demand for military leadership. They set a high value on the assurance of the nation's wholehearted support, knowing how much it counted in winning a war.

Nevertheless, at first the armed services could work only with what they already had. General Marshall had to work with an Army still in process of mobilization and training, with neither the equipment needed to carry on large-scale operations in distant theaters nor the ships needed to transport the forces overseas. In directing what was not yet a wartime Army, he drew his assistance from what was not yet a wartime staff. The attack on Pearl Harbor, though it dramatized the shortcomings of the Army high command, obliged him to make use

of this command at once in order to get such results as he could from the Army as it was. In the process, the Army's high command began to act like the high command of an army at war, though the transition was comparatively slow.

GHQ, despite the difficulties it was encountering and despite the development of plans to eliminate it as a command headquarters, continued to have tremendous responsibilities after American entry into the war. From mid-December 1941 until the following March, GHQ controlled, under their temporary designation as theaters of operations, the Eastern and Western Defense Commands. It similarly directed operations in the Caribbean Defense Command and the base commands in the Atlantic area. It organized and controlled the first echelon of American forces sent to the British Isles. The War Department was using GHQ to control certain operations, but GHQ still was not authorized to act systematically and continuously as General Marshall's highest operational staff. Instructions issued on 11 December 1941 made it clear that GHQ was responsible for supervising the "execution and follow-up of troop movements and such operations as may from time to time be referred to GHQ by the War Department for action." [15] General Marshall, in issuing these instructions, attempted to resolve some of the administrative confusion about staff responsibility by directing that military orders within the jurisdiction of GHQ carry the clarifying an-

---

[15] AG ltr, 11 Dec 41, sub: Enlargement of Functions of GHQ, AG 320.2 (12–10–41) MO–C–M. Maj. Gen. R. C. Moore, Deputy Chief of Staff, and G–3 prepared the authorization for the AG letter as issued. WPD had drafted another letter, never issued, giving GHQ a broader grant of authority. See memo, WPD for TAG, 10 Dec 41, sub: Supervision of Execution of Opns, WPD 3209–15.

nouncement: "GHQ is charged with the execution of this order." [16]

In directing the first forced moves in the Pacific after the advent of hostilities, General Marshall depended on WPD, which retained its responsibility for acting on behalf of the Chief of Staff on all operational matters related to the Pacific bases. The Division rapidly assumed a form, adopted a procedure, and acquired a sense of responsibility for staff action that made it more and more like the new operational command staff visualized for General Marshall in the reorganization planning concurrently under way. Toward the end of January, while the final decision to reorganize the War Department was in the making, WPD, GHQ, and G–4 were still trying to find a practicable arrangement which would rationalize and co-ordinate their work. At that time General Marshall approved an agreement, based on mutual efforts at co-operation rather than any precise delimitation of duties, which governed the relations of GHQ and the General Staff until the reorganization in March 1942. [17]

Open hostilities, which brought theaters of operations into being, unequivocally gave WPD specific supervisory duties in the sphere of "actual operations in the theater of war." [18] On 10 December General Gerow informed the Chief of Staff that WPD had a section for operations and could act in close proximity to General Marshall on urgent matters. [19] On the same day, the Division inaugurated a seven-day week schedule of duty, and before the end of the month began to keep at least a skeleton staff at work throughout a twenty-four-hour day in order to meet the exigency of the situation. [20] In the direction of military operations in the Pacific theater WPD worked closely with General Marshall, adjusting strategic plans and Army operations to fit each other and to meet the rapidly developing military situation. General Gerow defined the responsibility of the Division in January 1942 when he informed a U. S. Navy officer: "War Plans Division (Army) acts as the War Department operating agency with respect to such of our foreign garrisons as have not yet, from a planning standpoint, been fully stabilized on a permanent basis. For the moment these foreign stations are those in the Pacific Ocean." [21] WPD also acted as General Marshall's staff for such theater operations as were international in scope. After an Australian-British-Dutch-American (ABDA) Command had been set up under Field Marshal Sir Archibald Wavell in January 1942 to attempt to defend the Netherlands East Indies area, General Marshall ordered that no message should be sent to the ABDA Command or to any officer of the United States in that command unless it had first been cleared

---

[16] Memo, Brig Gen Gerow for Col W. B. Smith, 10 Dec 41, sub: General Headquarters, WPD 3209–17.

[17] Memo, G–4 for WPD, 24 Jan 42, sub: Coordination Between WPD; G–4, WDGS; GHQ and O'seas Theater Comdrs, WPD 3963–23. General Gerow's comments at this time indicated his long-standing effort to make the GHQ system work by granting GHQ authority in its own sphere and by insuring co-operation between WPD, G–4, and GHQ. See memo, Col Handy for Brig Gen LeRoy Lutes, 18 Jan 42, sub: Coordination Between . . ., WPD 3963–23.

For General Marshall's approval of the co-ordination policy, see memo, G–4 for CofS, 18 Jan 42, sub: Coordination Between . . ., WDCSA, OCS 16374–47.

[18] AR 10–15, 18 Aug 36.

[19] Notes on Conferences in OCS, II, 447, WDCSA rcds.

[20] (1) WPD adm memo, 26 Dec 41, no sub, Paper 97, Item 2A, OPD Hist Unit file. (2) WPD adm memo, 17 Jan 42, sub: Sunday Dy, Paper 95, Item 2A, OPD Hist Unit file.

[21] Memo, WPD for Rear Admiral R. S. Edwards, 9 Jan 42, no sub, Book 2, Exec 8.

with WPD and then sent out over the Chief of Staff's signature.[22]

Immediately after Pearl Harbor WPD became the War Department center for current information concerning or affecting Army operations. Upon specific orders from the Chief of Staff, WPD undertook to report daily, for the benefit of the War Department and the President, the "operational decisions and actions of the War Department." For that purpose all other divisions of the General Staff and the Army Air Forces reported to WPD on their individual actions. The Daily Summary thus inaugurated, including the abridged form called the White House Summary, was prepared in much the same form throughout the war.[23] From its knowledge of strategic plans and from the detailed operational information made available by other Army agencies, WPD amassed a uniquely comprehensive understanding of current military issues, particularly the urgent ones under consideration by the Chief of Staff.

During this transition period WPD tried to harmonize staff actions of all kinds, including zone of interior functions clearly assigned to other War Department agencies, whenever the interests of military operations in the theater demanded it. Thus, for instance, when Maj. Gen. James E. Chaney, Commanding General, U. S. Army Forces in the British Isles, reported in January 1942 that his requests for personnel apparently were being ignored, WPD went into action. Col. Stephen H. Sherrill of the Atlantic Section, Operations Group, discovered that G–1 had sent instructions to The Adjutant General for action on General Chaney's request, but that "TAG (Major Daley) held up the action on telephone instructions from someone he does not now remember." Subsequently cables from General Chaney concerning this matter had been sent, by error, to the Air Forces, where no action was taken. At this juncture WPD received a message from General Chaney calling attention to the problem. Colonel Sherrill "secured necessary action by G–1," and the personnel got on their way to London. This staff work involved sending to Great Britain only eleven officers and twenty-three enlisted men, and it was a routine G–1 matter, but General Gerow ordered his officers to "follow-up on this and see that Chaney *gets* the personnel and information on his requests." [24]

In dispatching task forces to island bases on the Pacific line of communication, WPD became involved in the most detailed arrangements. In the case of the BOBCAT force (for Bora Bora Island in the South Pacific) a considerable staff effort was invested in arranging for the transfer of two privates, first class (one from Fort Bragg and the other from Fort Knox), that the Navy Department had requested because they were peculiarly qualified to assist in a special kind of construction work on Bora Bora.[25] Then WPD officers spent ten days in obtaining a Japanese interpreter for the same task force. At the request of the commanding officer of BOBCAT, Col. Charles D. Y. Ostrom, Gen-

---

[22] Notes on Conferences in OSW, 19 Jan 42, Vol. II, WDCSA rcds.

[23] A complete file of Daily Summary is in Current Group files, AGRcds Br. Also see: (1) memo, SGS for WPD, 8 Dec 41, no sub, WPD 4544–24; (2) memo, WPD for other GS Divs, 9 Dec 41, sub: Daily Summary of Decisions and Actions for SGS, WPD 4544–24; (3) memo, Exec WPD for Col Handy and Col C. A. Russell, 18 Dec 41, sub: Daily Summary for White House, WPD 4544–24. For the origins and development of the Daily Summary, see OPD Hist Unit Study G.

[24] Memo, Col. A. S. Nevins, WPD for Brig Gen Gerow, 17 Jan 42, sub: Gen Chaney's Cablegram 429, WPD 4402–147.

[25] D/F, WPD for G–1, 2 Feb 42, sub: Add Grs for BOBCAT Force, WPD 4571–24.

eral Gerow queried the G–2 Division, which reported that no interpreter was available in the zone of interior. However, G–2 recommended that WPD ask Lt. Gen. Delos C. Emmons, who had relieved General Short as Commanding General, Hawaiian Department on 16 December 1941, to furnish the interpreter. Accordingly General Gerow radioed: "In the event you consider it practicable and desirable to make available a Japanese speaking officer or enlisted man in your command, it is desired that you arrange for his transportation from Honolulu to Bobcat." [26] A few days later the Hawaiian Department advised WPD that an interpreter of unquestionable loyalty was not available at that time. The Division eventually located an officer on duty in the War Department who not only spoke Japanese but also was well acquainted with Bora Bora. By this time the convoy had sailed, so WPD asked the commanding general of the Panama Canal Department to pass this information on to Colonel Ostrom when his ship locked through the Canal about 2 February. The radio added that an attempt was being made to fly this officer to Panama to join the convoy en route, but failing in this, he would leave on the earliest transport for Bora Bora. [27] Finally, on 2 February, General Gerow was able to close the case by reporting that the interpreter would be flown to Balboa, Canal Zone, in time to join the Bobcat force. [28]

The premium put on follow-up and concrete results showed that the lesson of Pearl Harbor had been taken to heart and that WPD was learning to get things done as well as to plan. Other War Department agencies depended increasingly on WPD to act in urgent matters, even when it had no formal grant of authority to do so. Indicative of this attitude was a remark made by one of the senior civilian assistants of the Secretary of War in January 1942 concerning psychological warfare. He "suggested that it be taken away from G–2 and put under War Plans so that some use could be made of it." [29] A few weeks later General Eisenhower observed: "This psychological warfare business is going to fall right into the lap of WPD—principally for the reason that no one else will lead with his chin. We'll probably take it on." [30] The accuracy of this prediction was proved in the event. WPD and later the Operations Division furnished a member of the Psychological Warfare Committee set up in the Joint Chiefs of Staff system early in the war and continued permanently to have at least one officer specializing in developments in that field. [31]

For a brief period WPD took responsibility, along with G–2, for sending the commanding general of the Caribbean Defense Command intelligence based on decoded Japanese messages, called "Magic." On 29 December the Chief of Staff personally telephoned Col. Matthew B. Ridgway of the

---

[26] D/F, WPD for TAG, 20 Jan 42, sub: Japanese Intpr for Bobcat, WPD 4571–29.

[27] D/F, WPD for TAG, 31 Jan 42, sub: Asgmt 2d Lt Walter H. Pleiss, Ord Dept to Bobcat, WPD 4571–34.

[28] Memo, ACofS WPD for Rear Adm R. A. Turner, 2 Feb 42, sub: Asgmt 2d Lt Walter H. Pleiss . . ., WPD 4571–34.

[29] Notes on Conferences in OSW, 5 Jan 42, Vol. II, WDCSA rcds.

[30] Notations by Gen. D. D. Eisenhower, 24 Feb 42, Item 3, OPD Hist Unit file.

[31] Cf. memo, Capt C. E. Miller, Secy JUSSC for Brig Gen W. B. Smith, JCS secretariat, 6 Apr 42, sub: Lt Col E. E. Partridge, U. S. Army—Dtl of to [sic] Psychological Warfare Committee, OPD 210.3, 60. Psychological warfare, nearly always considered on a joint or combined level, was throughout World War II the special assignment of one or more officers in the Combined Subjects (later Policy) Section of Strategy & Policy Group.

WPD Latin American Section to assure himself that this type of intelligence was being sent and that the Caribbean Defense Command understood that it was not "merely 'authentic and from a reliable source' but was actual truth." He directed Colonel Ridgway to get in touch with the responsible G–2 officer, Col. Rufus S. Bratton, who stated that there was a "flexible arrangement whereby either War Plans or he himself transmitted this information." Only upon Colonel Ridgway's objection that such a division of responsibility "sooner or later would result in failure to transmit vital information in time for use," did Colonel Bratton agree to accept entire responsibility (including responsibility to inform GHQ as well as WPD of intelligence sent), if General Gerow approved, as he did.[32]

WPD's responsibility for staff action in the only active theaters of operations, together with its duties in interservice and international planning, now more vital than ever before, greatly enhanced its prestige and increased the scope of its activities after Pearl Harbor. Without any formal authority to do so, WPD officers were often able to resolve disagreements among representatives of the General Staff Divisions, provided they were not too bitter, simply by virtue of the readiness of most Army officers, other things being equal, to give precedence to a consideration affecting combat rather than one affecting administration or services in support of combat. It was mainly in this sense that WPD became the command post staff of the Chief of Staff during the first months of the war.

Strength, Personnel, and Organization of WPD

WPD continued in December 1941 and January and February 1942 to be organized around a nucleus of experienced officers, but it grew considerably in size. With the advent of war every attempt was made to achieve the Division's authorized ceiling strength, and two weeks after the Japanese attack it was at full strength with fifty-four officers, including the chief, on duty. Requests for officers continued to be by name, and selection continued to be based on first-hand knowledge by WPD officers of the record and ability of the officer under consideration.[33] Requests of a more wholesale, somewhat less carefully screened kind than before, became common in the emergency situation, when it was apparent that many officers sought would not be released by their superiors from their current assignments.[34] The Division also had to take steps to offset the unavoidable loss of some of its best officers to command assignments with troops. Consequently in January the Division sought and got permission from General Marshall to exceed its strength ceiling in order to begin training a number of promising young officers in junior grades, both Regular Army and Reserve, to fill the gaps when they appeared.[35] By 15 February 1942, the day General Gerow left the Division, the number of officers on duty in WPD had reached the total of sixty-four.

---

[32] Memo, Col Ridgway for Brig Gen Gerow, 29 Dec 41, no sub, Tab Misc, Book 1, Exec 8. The agreement is indorsed by General Gerow (initials) as recommended by Colonel Ridgway.

[33] For request for six Reserve officers by name, for example, see memo, WPD for TAG, 10 Dec 41, sub: Orders for Res Offs, Item 2, Exec 15.

[34] (1) WPD pers file, *passim*, WPD 3354. (2) Exec pers papers, Item 2, Exec 15.

[35] (1) Memo, WPD for G–1, 28 Jan 42, sub: Dtl of Offs, Item 2, Exec 15. (2) Memo, WPD for G–1, 31 Jan 42, sub: Dtl of Offs to WPD, Item 2, Exec 15.

Most of the twenty-five officers who joined the staff between 7 December 1941 and 15 February 1942 were junior in grade, and a number were in the Reserve. Among them were several who stayed to render valuable service in the Operations Division. From the point of view of OPD service, the most important recruit was General Eisenhower, who reported for work on 14 December. In all probability it was General Eisenhower's special knowledge of the Philippines and acquaintance with General MacArthur that caused the Chief of Staff to bring him to Washington as soon as hostilities broke out in the Far East. He became deputy chief of WPD for the Far East and Pacific area, and on 16 February 1942 succeeded General Gerow as chief of the Division.[36]

The basic organization of WPD followed the pattern set in 1941, though some minor alterations in structure and one significant change in terminology were made during the first three months of American participation in the war. The Division chief appointed two deputies, one for the Pacific theater and one for the Atlantic theater. General Eisenhower, Pacific area deputy, was specifically directed by the Chief of Staff to pay special attention to the Philippines, Hawaii, Australia, the Pacific Islands, and China.[37] Col. Robert W. Crawford (brigadier general 15 December 1941) moved up from his place as Projects Group

chief to occupy a similar position as deputy for the Atlantic area.

A new Executive Group was established under Major Gailey to handle the Division's administration, records, and correspondence. Of the many reforms for which there was evident need, one of the most urgent was in the handling of messages, particularly radiograms and cablegrams to and from overseas commands. At the outbreak of war, the Army faced the task of expanding a small but flexible peacetime radio network into a world-wide system of radio and wire communications.[38] While the Signal Corps was developing such a network, the War Department had to develop means of making fully efficient use of such facilities as there were. During the first few months after Pearl Harbor, War Department messages continued as before to be received and dispatched through the Adjutant General's Office. That office continued to distribute and file messages, which in peacetime had been relatively infrequent and rarely urgent, simply as correspondence. Messages which had been dispatched or received were not filed together serially, but scattered about with topically related material in subject files, in which they were extremely hard to locate.[39]

---

[36] (1) Memo, WPD for TAG, 19 Jan 42, sub: Mechanical Time Fuses for Philippine Department, WPD 4560–10. (2) Notations by Gen D. D. Eisenhower, 1 Jan 42, Item 3, OPD Hist Unit file. General Eisenhower noted: "I arrived in Wash. Dec. 14—41. Telephone call from office C/S." His official date of entering on duty was 20 December 1941. (3) Dwight D. Eisenhower, *Crusade in Europe* (New York, 1948), pp. 14–16. (4) See below, Ch. VIII.

[37] Notations by Gen D. D. Eisenhower, 1 Jan 42, Item 3, OPD Hist Unit file.

[38] In 1941 the Army Command and Administrative Communications Network (ACAN), installed and operated by the Signal Corps, consisted, in the main, of one-channel radio circuits, manually operated, connecting control station WAR at Washington with headquarters of corps areas in the continental United States, and with Panama, Hawaii, Puerto Rico, Iceland, Bermuda, and (by relay from San Francisco) the Philippines. Information supplied by Sig C Unit, Hist Div, SSUSA. See WD Sig C Sec, Army Comd Serv, Sig C Chronological Data Charts, 1940–45.

[39] For the prewar practice of AGO and the difficulties arising therefrom in 1940 and 1941, see Nelson, *National Security and The General Staff*, p. 332.

OFFICERS OF THE WAR PLANS DIVISION, *23 January 1942. Left to right: Col. W. K. Harrison, Col. Lee S. Gerow, Brig. Gen. Robert W. Crawford, Brig. Gen. Dwight D. Eisenhower, Brig. Gen. Leonard T. Gerow, Chief, Col. Thomas T. Handy, Col. Stephen H. Sherrill.*

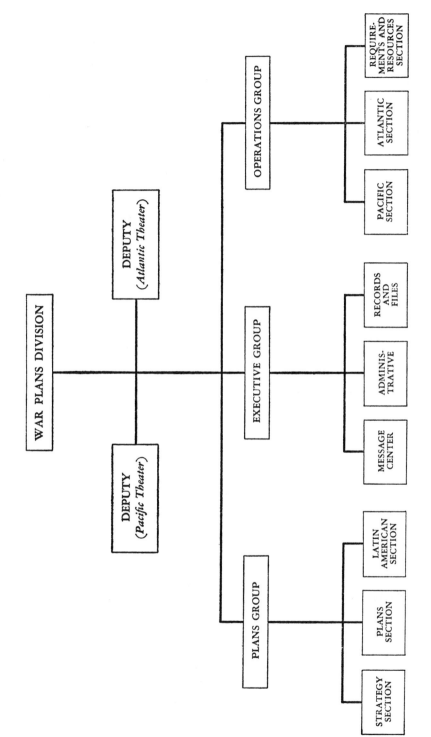

Source: OPD 312, 105.

Chart 2. War Plans Division, War Department General Staff: 21 December 1941

On the very day of the Pearl Harbor attack, WPD began to keep its own file, arranged by date and entirely separate from its other files, of incoming and outgoing operational messages which the Division, like the Adjutant General's Office, had hitherto treated for filing purposes like ordinary letters, staff memoranda, or studies.[40] The new WPD system, which was still imperfect for purposes of reference since there were separate numerical series of messages to and from each station, served the Division's needs during the first four months of American participation in the war. During this period the WPD message center staff was greatly enlarged, and continuous service on receiving and dispatching messages became available to officers in the Division. Through the service offered and the control exercised by the Division message center, the officers were able continuously to check reports from theaters of operations and overseas missions and thus to keep up with what was needed and to follow up systematically on compliance with War Department instructions. This activity was to remain the nucleus of the Operations Division's manifold activities throughout the war, the primary feature of its assistance to the Chief of Staff in the exercise of command over the operations of U. S. Army forces in the field.

The Plans Group made a small but important structural change to meet the post-Pearl Harbor situation, simplifying its make-up somewhat by transferring the Joint Requirements Section from the planning part of the organization of WPD. Both terminology and allocation of duties were also changed, the former Joint Policy & Plans Section being renamed the Strategy Section, while the Army Strategic Plans & Resources Section became the Plans Section. This shift involved some change in duties and accordingly some reshuffling of personnel. The Strategy Section devoted itself to the most general strategic thinking, that of estimating the strategic situation to determine ultimate military objectives and forces required to achieve them. The Plans Section, acting upon directives from the Strategy Section, prepared the actual war plans, both joint Army-Navy and War Department, and established priorities among Army forces and tasks. Its former duties involving the calculation of Army resources and the personnel occupied with them were transferred outside the group. Thus the principal concern of the whole WPD Plans Group in the post-Pearl Harbor period was the formulation of operational strategy governing military operations.

The principal formal change in the other main WPD group was in the name, Operations rather than Projects. It was still a section with miscellaneous duties that could be defined only negatively. Thus the Pacific and Atlantic Sections assumed WPD responsibilities for their respective areas insofar as the responsibilities were charged to the Operations Group. Both sections formally could be given only the function of liaison with GHQ in areas either already in the province of that headquarters or tentatively scheduled to be assigned to it in the future. In practice, particularly for the Pacific, the Operations Group provided a rudimentary command post for detailed

---

[40] (1) This serial message file, begun 7 December 1941, was continued through March 1942 and finally amounted to twenty volumes, collected as the WPD Message File. See it, together with its continuation, the OPD Message File, in Hist Rcds Sec, AG Rcds Br. (2) For procedure of dispatching and distributing messages, see OPD adm memo, 16 Dec 41, sub: Incoming and Outgoing Msgs, WPD, Paper 99, Item 2A, OPD Hist Unit file.

supervision and direction of operations such as WPD had lacked before Pearl Harbor.

In the Operations Group the old miscellaneous Current Section, renamed Requirements & Resources, assumed some new functions hitherto performed in the Plans Group. It carried the burden of recommending policy on munitions distribution to the associated powers. Immediately after Pearl Harbor the new section was designated the working agency for preparing War Department studies on allocation of munitions for submission by the Chief of Staff to higher authority.[41] For the benefit of the Army, especially for G–3 and G–4, its function was to translate into terms of troop units and equipment the strategic plans and operational enterprises being worked out by the rest of the Division. Finally it maintained an accounting of U. S. Army combat resources, current and projected, and advised the whole Division on the co-ordination therewith of munitions allocation and the use of American troops in task forces, overseas possessions, and defense commands.[42]

Among the most valuable post-Pearl Harbor contributions of the Requirements & Resources Section was a device for making available to the Division and other War Department agencies a simplified, integrated accounting of the Army's deployed strength in terms of personnel and aircraft. As the Army's size increased and as its deployment pattern became more complex,

the need was apparent for a rough, summary system of statistical control of U. S. Army resources. Such information was essential for operational decisions at every high command and staff level. Even before Pearl Harbor, WPD on occasion had produced maps presenting a tabulation of Army strength in the various overseas bases.[43] On 3 January 1942, the Resources & Requirements Section began regularly to issue a Weekly Status Map showing the current and projected deployment of personnel and aircraft overseas. The second status map, issued 8 January 1942, also listed major units and included the Western and Eastern Defense Commands, thus providing Army planners with a uniform tabulation of U. S. Army combat strength and deployment.[44] This information was essential to efficient staff integration of strategic plans and military operations.

The First Wartime International Conference

The important issues in strategic planning in this transition period were worked out on the interservice and international plans, primarily in the course of delibera-

---

[41] Memo, Col Donald Wilson for Exec WPD, 19 Dec 41, sub: Dys of Jt Reqmts Sec, Paper 98, Item 2A, OPD Hist Unit file.

[42] For its responsibility for troop unit calculations, designed to enable G–4 to plan equipment programs, see memo, WPD for G–4, 27 Dec 41, sub: Tr Basis for Victory Program, WPD 4494–26. Note states that the Troop Basis was filed in "Resources and Requirements."

[43] WPD map charts, 1 Aug 41 and 17 Oct 41, Tab C, Item 7, Exec 4. These charts showed present, projected as of "End 1941," and "After 1941" strength in terms of personnel and aircraft.

[44] WPD file copies of the Weekly Status Map, 3 Jan 42–9 Nov 44, AG 061 (4 Sep 45), 1. Attached to the Weekly Status Map, 26 Feb 42, is memo, Col L. S. Gerow for Sec Chiefs, Opns Gp, 3 Mar 42, no sub. The memorandum mentioned the "purpose of having uniformity," and explained that the Resources & Requirements Section produced the map, keeping its own "current strength reports and sailings," and drawing on the other sections of the Operations Group for projected strength of personnel and for both "present and projected number of airplanes." For continuation of this function, see p. 308.

tions at the ARCADIA Conference of 24 December 1941–14 January 1942, the first wartime meeting of the U. S. and British Chiefs of Staff. General Gerow and his planners labored prodigiously before the conference to provide General Marshall with ideas and information in support of the Army's position on Allied strategy, command structures, and deployment of troops. During the conference General Gerow or General Eisenhower, or both, attended all but one of the twelve formal ARCADIA sessions, assisting the Chief of Staff in presenting the Army's case on these problems. In this way WPD officers established a tradition of staff participation in preparations and deliberations connected with international military conferences, a tradition carried over into the OPD period and the great conferences of 1943 and later.[45]

While the British representatives, led by the Prime Minister, were still at sea aboard H.M.S. *Duke of York,* the British Chiefs of Staff sent ahead a brief message suggesting the agenda for the meetings. They proposed that the ARCADIA Conference should determine five main points, the "fundamental basis" of strategy, the "immediate military measures" to be taken, the allocation of forces necessary to carry out the basic strategy, a "long term programme" scheduling the raising and equipping of forces for victory, and some kind of British-American "machinery for implementing" all these de-

cisions when made.[46] To prepare studies, make recommendations, and draw up plans for ARCADIA were within WPD's recognized sphere of responsibility.

Immediately upon receipt of the proposed agenda General Gerow set the planning machinery of WPD in motion. By the following day, 19 December, the Division had prepared a tentative first draft study summarizing its conclusions about each of the five topics raised by the British. On that day and the next, WPD planners worked full speed. They prepared two complementary papers presenting information and comments on a variety of strategic questions raised by Secretary Stimson as relevant to the British agenda. They worked on full-length studies elaborating the position taken on fundamental strategy and immediate military measures in WPD's tentative first draft of 19 December. The elaborations of these two subjects formed the substance of a draft joint Army-Navy "Estimate of the Military Situation" as well as the first and second sections of the WPD Book compiled for use by the Chief of Staff and the Army planners at the conference.   In both forms these studies presented a strategic estimate and a list of specific military decisions necessary to meet the situation. A final, consolidated version was indorsed by Air and Navy planners as a sound "General Strategic Review." By 21 December WPD had supplemented its studies on these two basic subjects with other papers pursuing in detail the WPD conclusions of 19 December about the allocation of forces, the long-term program, and the creation of a Supreme Allied War Council. The five studies, with the 19 December tentative first draft summary as an

---

[45] For record of ARCADIA Conference and participants, see volume containing minutes of meetings and approved papers, entitled Proceedings of the American-British Joint Chiefs of Staff Conferences Held in Washington, D. C. on Twelve Occasions between December 24, 1941 and January 14, 1942, ABC 337 ARCADIA (24 Dec 41). Note that the term "joint" was still being used to mean international rather than interservice. The latter usage was recommended and adopted at this conference.

[46] Msg from British CsofS aboard H.M.S. *Duke of York,* 18 Dec 41, Item 5, Exec 10.

introduction, made up the WPD Book for ARCADIA.[47]

The strategic thinking that lay behind all these documentary preparations for ARCADIA was reviewed and in general terms accepted as the official American position to be developed in discussions and decisions at the conference. The Joint Board and the President, at two meetings on 21 December 1941, formally approved the strategic statements in WPD's tentative first draft study of 19 December. As approved, the study received the title of "Tentative U. S. Views on Subjects of British Memorandum, Dec. 18." The Joint Board and the President also agreed on the advisability of a number of "Broad Military Decisions" more or less as recommended by WPD and the Air and Navy planners as immediate military measures.[48] These views and decisions were scarcely a well-integrated grand strategy, as evident interservice differences of opinion all along the line were thinly disguised by very general language and passed by without formal notice in the troubled, hurried post-Pearl Harbor atmosphere. The actual measures indorsed by the President were specific military moves that did not necessarily reflect American commitment to any broad strategy or indeed to any particular operations, since the rather doubtful logistic feasibility of all the measures approved was largely ignored and no clear order of priority set for them. Partly as a result of these

facts, though much more because of the unforeseen rapidity of Japanese advances in the Pacific, the ARCADIA Conference as a whole was rather inconclusive except as a sound beginning of continuous, systematic British-American military planning in Washington. In any case, the views of WPD and of other service planners, especially the ones that were influential enough to determine decisions, constituted the basis for strategic recommendations by the American representatives at the ARCADIA Conference.

General Gerow, who had guided WPD during its period of tremendous expansion in size and activity, left the War Department for troop duty, on 15 February 1942. Under his leadership, WPD had done a good deal to help chart the course for winning the war, notably in emphasizing the principle of concentration of forces. Its staff work had helped to make Army-Navy and British-American co-ordination of military effort a fact rather than an aspiration. Above all, General Gerow had organized a staff of able, experienced officers capable of assuming greater responsibility under the Chief of Staff for directing military operations all over the globe, integrating these operations in a consistent grand strategy, and co-ordinating strategy and operations with the mobilization and munitions-producing capacity of the zone of interior. Despite WPD's accomplishments and its rapid development in the post-Pearl Harbor transition period, however, the Division still was far from being a satisfactory wartime staff. Only a reorganization of the Army high command could assure the development of a single agency under the Chief of Staff that could exercise responsibility for getting appropriate action within the Army on every kind of problem materially affecting the success of military operations.

---

[47] For a detailed study of the complicated documentary source material supporting the general statements made in the text about preparations for the ARCADIA Conference, see OPD Hist Unit Study H.

[48] (1) Draft paper, n.d., title: Broad Mil Decisions, WDCSA 381 (12–21–41) SS. (2) Min of JB meetings, 21 Dec 41. (3) Memo, SW, n.d., title: Memo of Decisions at White House, Sunday, Dec 21, 1941, copy in envelope with WPD 4402–136.

CHAPTER VI

Organizing the High Command for World War II

The limitations of the Army high command were sharply revealed by the failure to follow up the warning issued to the Hawaiian Department before the attack on Pearl Harbor. Two days after the attack General Marshall announced to his senior staff officers that he wanted the War Department to get away from the "routine of feeding out information without checking" even to see that it had been received where it was needed. It was necessary, he said, to "fight the fact that the War Department is a poor command post." [1] For the time being the Chief of Staff and his immediate subordinates in Washington were reluctant to take anything for granted. They personally directed defensive movements of troops and equipment, checking on every move that was made. But this kind of individual exertion could not indefinitely take the place of an effective staff system. At some time during the first few weeks of hostilities General Marshall reached the decision to proceed with the reorganization of the Army's high command. In March 1942 the reorganization was carried out in accordance with plans on which staff officers in the War Department had already begun working months before the Pearl Harbor attack. At the same time a new Army-Navy-Air (Army) staff system and a parallel British-American organization were taking definite shape. The U. S. Army made its strategic plans and conducted its operations during the rest of World War II on the basis of staff work done and decisions reached within the intricate structure of the national and international high command established in the first few months of 1942.

Reorganization of the War Department

Just before the Pearl Harbor attack, after General Marshall had stated that he was favorably impressed with the War Department reorganization plan which General Arnold had sent to him, WPD set to work to make a detailed study of the project. Colonel Harrison, whose own earlier plan was very similar to that proposed by the Air Forces, took charge of the reorganization study on behalf of WPD. He worked closely with Maj. Laurence S. Kuter, an Air Corps officer assigned to the task from the Office of the Chief of Staff.[2]

---

[1] Notes on Conferences in OCS, II, 441, WDCSA rcds.

[2] (1) See Ch. IV. (2) Memo, Exec WPD for SGS, 28 Nov 41, sub: Reorgn of WD, WPD 4614. (3) Testimony, Maj Gen McNarney, Brig Gen Kuter, and Col Harrison in Dept of Def Co-ordination and Control, 77th Cong, 2d sess, 6 Mar 42, *Hearing before the Committee on Military Affairs,* p. 1 (hereafter cited as McNarney, *Hearings,* 6 Mar 42). (4) Maj Kuter was promoted to the rank of Lt Col on 2 Jan 42 and Brig Gen on 2 Feb 42.

GEN. GEORGE C. MARSHALL AND LT. GEN. JOSEPH T. McNARNEY.
General McNarney was Deputy Chief of Staff, 9 March 1942–21 October 1944.

The third and senior member of the team eventually selected to take active measures in developing the organization outlined by General Arnold was General McNarney, whom the Chief of Staff had ordered home from England a few days before the beginning of hostilities.[3] General McNarney was an appropriate selection, because of his known abilities and experience and because he was familiar with and trusted by officers of both agencies sponsoring the reorganization scheme. A seasoned Air Corps officer, he had long served in WPD and was still officially assigned to duty with the Division.[4] General McNarney arrived in Washington about a week after American entry into the war, but for over a month he was busy as a member of the Roberts Commission, the first Pearl Harbor investigating board. He joined Colonels Harrison and Kuter in a study of the reorganization project about 25 January 1942, and they set to work with such speed that General McNarney was able to submit the final version of the reorganization plan to the Chief of Staff on 31 January.[5]

The recommendations submitted by General McNarney were as follows: (1) to free the General Staff from all activities except strategic direction and control of operations, determination of over-all military requirements, and determination of basic policies affecting the zone of interior; (2) creation of three commands, Army Air Forces, Army Ground Forces, and Services of Supply, to which the General Staff could delegate operating duties connected with administra-

tion, supply, organization, and training; (3) elimination of GHQ, the Air Force Combat Command, and the offices of the chiefs of Air Corps, Infantry, Field Artillery, Coast Artillery, and Cavalry as "unnecessary or obsolete headquarters"; and (4) creation of an "executive committee responsible only to the Chief of Staff" to put the reorganization into effect without giving "interested parties" a chance to record nonconcurrences and cause "interminable delay."

The fact that the first function of the General Staff, "strategic direction and control of operations," was to be performed by WPD was made plain in Tab 2, which provided: "GHQ will turn over to WPD its functions and records related to command and planning for theaters of operations, Defense Commands, Departments, Bases and Task Forces." Of the rest of the General Staff, G–2 was left to continue the collection and evaluation of information about the enemy. G–1, G–3, and G–4, which according to the memorandum were to be cut down to only "8 to 10 officers each," would advise the Chief of Staff of "basic decisions and policies" concerning the zone of interior activities being conducted by the three major commands and, presumably, co-operate with WPD in determining over-all requirements, which depended simultaneously on strategy and the Army programs of mobilization, training, and supply.[6]

The permanent structure of the War Department was established by law, and until after Pearl Harbor not even the President had the authority to redistribute power and responsibility within the War Department in the manner recommended in both Colonel Harrison's study of August 1941 and the November memorandum from the

---

[3] Gen Marshall's testimony in *Pearl Harbor Attack: Hearings . . .*, Part 3, pp. 1437–38.

[4] General McNarney had not actually been in WPD since May 1941, when he went to England with the Special Observers Group.

[5] Memo, Maj Gen McNarney for CofS, 31 Jan 42, sub: Reorgn of WD, Tabs 1, 2, and 3, OCS rcds, WDCSA 020 (1942).

[6] *Ibid.*

Army Air Forces. Congress, however, passed the First War Powers Act of 18 December 1941, conferring on the President the power necessary to reorganize the War Department, or other agencies, in order to "expedite the prosecution of the war effort." [7] The Chief of Staff thenceforth had an administrative recourse for solving his command and staff problems without entering into the long and trying process of getting legislation through Congress. Thus one important obstacle to a War Department reorganization had already been eliminated by the time that General McNarney submitted his recommendations to General Marshall.

A few days after receiving General Mc-Narney's memorandum, the Chief of Staff held a meeting of the officers he considered to be key personnel to explain the proposed reorganization. General McNair, General Gerow, General McNarney, General Eisenhower, and Colonel Harrison were among those present. General Marshall turned the meeting over to General McNarney, who consulted in turn all the officers present and found that they unanimously favored the plan. General McNair "enthusiastically approved" the reorganization proposal. General Gerow and General Eisenhower "were perfectly satisfied" with it.[8] General Eisenhower summed up the import of the changes involved by noting: "We are faced with a big reorganization of WD [the War Department]. We need it! The G. S. [General Staff] is all to be cut down, except WPD—

which now has all Joint and Combined work, all plans and all operations so far as active theaters are concerned!" [9]

On 11 February General McNarney received instructions to form an executive committee for putting the plan into effect as soon as it had been finally approved.[10] He mobilized his committee for a first meeting on 16 February and explained to its members that it was "not a voting committee . . . not a debating society . . . [but] a committee to draft the necessary directives" to put the new organization into effect.[11] Working out specific measures to be taken and drafting directives on them occupied the committee members only a few days. The Secretary of War approved the reorganization plan promptly and forwarded a draft executive order to the President. On 26 February President Roosevelt informed Secretary Stimson that he was "sure" the reorganization was a "good thing to do." Two days later Executive Order 9082 appeared directing that the reorganization be put into effect 9 March 1942.[12] War Department Circular 59 appeared 2 March 1942, ordering the necessary changes and presenting

---

[7] Memo, JAG for CofS, 2 Feb 42, sub: Reorgn of Army, and copy atchd of First War Powers Act, Pl 354 (H Res 6233), 18 Dec 41, "An Act to Expedite the Prosecution of the War Effort," WDCSA 020 (1942).

[8] Notes on Conferences in OCS, II, 459–63, WDCSA rcds. Representatives of the other General Staff Divisions and of the Army Air Forces were also present.

[9] Notations by Gen D. D. Eisenhower, 6 Feb 42, Item 3, OPD Hist Unit file.

[10] Memo, OCS for AAF, GHQ, WPD, G–1, G–2, G–3, G–4, SGS, TAG, TIG, and JAG, 11 Feb 42, WPD 4614.

[11] Min of Opening Session, Sp Com, Reorgn of WD, 16 Feb 42, WDCSA 020 (1942). Colonel Harrison represented WPD on the committee. General McNarney made it clear that the plan was designed to meet the emergency and not necessarily to be suitable for a peacetime Army. Lt. Col. O. L. Nelson, Jr., served as recorder for this executive committee.

[12] (1) Ltr, CofS to Dir Bureau of Budget, 20 Feb 42, WDCSA 020 (1942). (2) Ltr, SW to President, 20 Feb 42, WDCSA 020 (1942). (3) Notes on Conferences in OSW, 23 Feb 42, II, WDCSA rcds. (4) Ltr, President to SW, 26 Feb 42, WDCSA 020 (1942). (5) WD Bul 11, 3 Mar 42. This bulletin contains the text of EO 9082.

charts of the new organization.[13] On 9 March the reorganization was an official fact.

The "Streamlined" War Department

The 1942 reorganization of the War Department was designed, as General McNair had suggested, to streamline the Army for military action. The executive order from President Roosevelt, as well as subsequent War Department official circulars and regulations implementing it, clearly affirmed the paramount authority of the Chief of Staff under the President in the broad sphere of strategy, tactics, and operations, the most important functions of command. At the same time they dropped the Chief of Staff's additional title of Commanding General of the Field Forces. General Marshall lost no authority through the dropping of this title. Throughout World War II "Chief of Staff, U. S. Army" was for all practical purposes synonymous with "Commanding General, U. S. Army."

GHQ went out of existence and was replaced in the command structure by the Army Ground Forces. Keeping the training duties of GHQ the new organization absorbed the functions of the ground combat arms and proceeded with what had been the principal initial task of GHQ, the training of ground combat forces.

The Army Air Forces, though in some ways on a lower level of administrative authority than previously, had virtually complete control of the development of its own special weapon, the airplane. Having absorbed the duties of the Air Corps, the new

---

[13] (1) WD Cir 59, 2 Mar 42, sub: WD Reorgn. (2) AR 10–15, 13 Jul 42, sub: GS Orgn and Gen Dys.

Air Forces trained personnel and units to service and use the airplane. It organized and supported the combat air forces to be employed in theaters of operations. Finally, by advising the General Staff and participating in interservice deliberations, General Arnold's headquarters was able materially to influence, if it could not control, both strategic and operational planning.

The Services of Supply, more aptly named the Army Service Forces about a year later, assumed responsibility under the forceful leadership of Lt. Gen Brehon B. Somervell for the performance of administrative and technical services in the War Department, including the work of the two service arms (Engineers and Signal Corps). This new agency took over both the technical and administrative staff function of the services and service arms and their operating functions. It also assumed some of the procurement activities formerly carried out by the Under Secretary of War and such former General Staff tasks as handling personnel assignments (formerly G–1) and managing transportation outside theaters of operations (formerly G–4). A large, somewhat conglomerate organization, Services of Supply at least introduced an element of organized responsibility into what had been an odd assortment of independent agencies, rendering technical and administrative advice to the Chief of Staff and also engaging in the procurement and distribution of equipment and supplies, transporting troops and matériel overseas, and providing essential semimilitary services in support of the combat forces.

By setting up these zone of interior commands, the Chief of Staff rid himself of the great burden of dealing directly with a multitude of separate Army commands and staff chiefs.[14] An index of the need for consolidating the individual arms and services was the very fact that it had become necessary in 1940 and 1941 for the Chief of Staff to employ three deputies, each with itemized duties, responsibilities, and authority, to handle the ever-increasing press of business referred for decision to the General Staff.[15] After the tightening of lines of responsibility and the delegation of authority implicit in the reorganization, a single Deputy Chief of Staff remained, with duties (mainly in the fields of staff administration, budget, and legislation) and delegated authority essentially the same as originally had been prescribed for him in the period between the two world wars.[16] Moreover, the Secretary of the General Staff was able to restrict the range of his duties within much narrower limits than in the 1940–41 period. Then the secretary, with his several highly qualified assistants, had acted in a kind of executive capacity to co-ordinate the work of the General Staff in conformity with General Marshall's ideas. This function was delegated elsewhere in the reorganization, and the position of Secretary of the General Staff became practically that of assistant to the Deputy Chief of Staff.

The establishment of the three major commands not only enabled the Chief of Staff to delegate responsibility, it also permitted, in fact required, the General Staff to restrict its policy control of the zone of interior to those very general matters affecting all three commands. Within the sphere of their respective command responsibilities, the commanding generals of the Army Air Forces, Army Ground Forces, and Services of Supply made policy as well as carried out programs. Each of them had a sizable staff to assist in acquitting these responsibilities. The only remaining duties for the War Department G–1, G–3, and G–4 Divisions were to devise Army-wide policies governing personnel, unit organization, and supply, respectively.

The final contribution of the reorganization to the effectiveness of the Army's war-making machinery under the Chief of Staff was the provision for a central command post staff inside the War Department. The War Plans Division, soon renamed the Operations Division (OPD) in recognition of its altered status, was given this role. General McNarney and Colonel Harrison in explaining the reorganization emphasized the advantage of delegating administrative details to the three new responsible subordinate commands and restricting the General Staff to planning and policy making rather than operating.[17] They also made it clear that the Chief of Staff needed a high-level agency to take a positive, aggressive role in co-ordinating all Army efforts in support of military operations in the field. Accordingly the reorganization assigned to WPD those General Staff duties relating both to the "formulation of plans and the strategic di-

[14] According to General McNarney and Colonel Harrison, General Marshall had had to deal "personally or through his staff" with 40 large commands and "some 350 small" ones. See McNarney, *Hearings,* 6 Mar 42, p. 13.

[15] Memo, OCS for all GS Divs, TAG, and all Chiefs of Arms and Services, 30 Oct 40, sub: Apmt of Add DCofS, WPD 4382. See also Ch. I.

[16] Under the 1942 reorganization the Deputy Chief of Staff, besides acting for the Chief of Staff in his absence and "on all matters generally delegated to him by the Chief of Staff," was to exercise supervision over the General Staff and the three major commands and to deal with budgetary, legislative, and administrative questions. AR 10–15, par. 2, 13 Jul 42, sub: GS Orgn and Gen Dys. Compare parallel provisions in AR 10–15, 25 Nov 21 and 18 Aug 36.

[17] (1) McNarney, *Hearings,* 9 Mar 42, p. 2. (2) Memo, ASGS for TAG, 17 Mar 42, WDCSA 020 (1942).

rection of military forces in the theater of war." [18] As WPD's own representative, Colonel Harrison, explained it to the Senate Military Affairs Committee: "In this war, we are fighting on many fronts . . . we have the great question of the use of our means in different places. So that right here—under the Chief of Staff—we have to centralize the direction of operations so that this War Plans Division now, not only makes war plans, that is, future plans, but it necessarily must control and direct the operations under the Chief of Staff." [19]

In effect the reorganization gave General Marshall an additional deputy for planning and controlling military operations, and this deputy, the Assistant Chief of Staff, OPD, was given an adequate staff to carry out his broad responsibilities. OPD was WPD plus GHQ (without its training functions) plus the superior authority GHQ had lacked. Or, to put it another way, OPD was in itself a virtually complete general staff, tight-knit in a way the old War Department General Staff had not achieved at the time it was necessary, and definitely oriented toward operations in the field.

General McNarney carefully summarized the effects the new organization was designed to create. His statement accurately described the basic principles on which the U. S. Army and the War Department operated during World War II:

1. The War Department reorganization is intended to streamline the General Staff and subordinate elements of the Army in order to facilitate speedy and most effective control of mobilization and operations.

2. The magnitude of the Army and the nature of operations preclude adequate supervision by the Chief of Staff of the activities of the Army through the General Staff as now organized.

3. The major functions of the Army are two fold:

　　a. Mobilization and preparation of the forces for war.

　　b. Operations in the field.

4. Except for basic decisions which must be made by the Chief of Staff, the functions of mobilization and preparation of the forces for war are to be performed by three separate and autonomous commands, the Army Air Forces, the Army Ground Forces and the Services of Supply. Each of these commands will be under its own responsible and authoritative commanding general. The three will be coordinate in all respects. The primary function of the Services of Supply is to provide services and supplies for the Air and Ground Forces.

5. *Control of operations.* By the creation of the Air Forces, Ground Forces and SOS the Chief of Staff gains time to give most of his attention to war operations. The War Plans Division, WDGS, is the headquarters General Staff through which the Chief of Staff, plans, supervises and directs operations. His decisions are implemented by the Air Forces and Ground Forces who provide the trained forces, by the Service of Supply which provides supplies (except items peculiar to the Air Forces and provided by them) and moves them to the theaters of operations, and by the commanders of the various theaters of operations and task forces who actually control combat operations in their respective areas of responsibility.[20]

Thus OPD was provided a legal basis whereby it could exploit the high, central position of the War Department General Staff and yet be free from its procedural traditions. From then on it was able to work like a general staff in a field headquarters, issuing the Chief of Staff's orders and following up their execution in the theaters of operations.

---

[18] WD Cir 59, 2 Mar 42, sub: WD Reorgn. The phrase was incorporated unchanged in AR 10–15, 13 Jul 42.

[19] McNarney, *Hearings,* 6 Mar 42, p. 10.

[20] Memo, Maj Gen McNarney for Maj Gen A. D. Surles, 27 Feb 42, sub: Outline of Reorgn of WD, Tab Misc, Book 4, Exec 8.

National and International Planning

The first three months of American participation in World War II was a transition period in the sphere of national and international military affairs as well as in the sphere of U. S. Army organization. The successive slogans marking stages in American preparedness—"Hemisphere Defense," "Arsenal of Democracy," "Short of War"— gave way at once to "All-Out War Effort." It was in these months that the nation's productive efforts came under the leadership of Donald Nelson's War Production Board, which was given every legal and psychological sanction to help carry out its mission of industrial mobilization. Matters of conscripting, training, equipping, and employing American troops became merely technical problems instead of highly debatable national policy issues. Diplomatic and military relations with Great Britain and other anti-Axis nations, very friendly for some time, became far less reserved and cautious than had been necessary so long as Congress had not declared war. By January 1942 twenty-five nations at war with one or more of the Axis Powers, including the United Kingdom of Great Britain, the British Dominions, India, the USSR, and China, joined the United States in pledging to employ their full military and economic strength against Germany, Italy, and Japan. Thus national war policies had crystallized in more than a score of sovereign countries, coalitions had been formed, and the great conflict which had begun in Europe in 1939 had spread to every part of the globe.

The very fact that at last the U. S. Army could proceed to reach strategic and operational decisions within the framework of agreed national and international policy was an embarrassment as well as a liberation. Not all Army officers were ready to enter wholeheartedly into collaboration either with the Navy or with foreign powers, and such reluctance was unquestionably reciprocal. Nearly every issue that arose in regard to the deployment of forces, their command, and strategic plans for operations required the mutual adjustment of clashing views. The U. S. Navy, which had always been oriented toward the far reaches of the Pacific, and the U. S. Army, which had come to see its future mission tied up with the great land battles of Europe, could scarcely agree on a common course of military action without accepting compromises on the kind of operations each would like to conduct, the forces they would use in them, and the subordination of one component or the other in command. The Army Air Forces, nominally subordinate to the Army in these matters, actually had its own special strategic and operational projects that had to be harmonized with both ground and naval services. Similarly, on the international plane, the United States, Great Britain, the Soviet Union, and China plainly could not agree on any one way to conduct the war that would ideally meet the national needs of all four powers. Compromises had to be hammered out among the Allies as among their military services.

International collaboration during World War II continued to be achieved in negotiations between the heads of government and their diplomatic representatives, although the influence of military considerations and military advisers became increasingly compelling in the negotiations until victory was clearly in view. The United States, the strongest economically and the least threatened by the enemy, played a central role in liaison among the United Nations and especially among the "Big Four," the United States, Great Britain, the USSR, and China. The British Dominions had access to the U. S. Government through their diplomatic representatives but also participated indirectly through their British Empire connections in the more conclusive military co-ordination achieved between Great Britain and the United States. China, almost isolated geographically and by far the weakest of the Big Four politically and economically, depended a great deal on presenting its special needs through various political channels, including that maintained in Washington by Ambasador T. V. Soong with President Roosevelt and the State Department. Nevertheless, Chungking and Washington also exchanged high-ranking military representatives.

With the Soviet Union, which was geographically remote from the western Allies, which western minds only recently had transferred from the category of a near enemy to the category of an associated power, and which was completely preoccupied with the great land battle of eastern Europe, the United States maintained only comparatively formal diplomatic relations. These were conducted during the first part of the war primarily through the American ambassador in Moscow and the Soviet ambassador in Washington. Attempts to supplement this arrangement by establishing systematic military liaison met with indifferent success. The flow of lend-lease was the principal tie, and officials handling lend-lease aid were the principal agents that bound the USSR and its two western Allies together until the time when the armed forces of all three nations met in Germany and Austria.

By the time of Pearl Harbor the military objectives of the United States had already been co-ordinated with those of Great Britain, so far as was practicable on a hypo-thetical basis, and co-ordination thereafter became much closer and remained close during the rest of the war. The usual channels of negotiation between the United States and Great Britain were supplemented and for many purposes replaced by a military staff system that succeeded in bringing American and British conduct of the war into extraordinarily close accord. Moreover, the co-ordination of military plans achieved in the British-American staff system had two collateral effects of great importance.

First, British-American understandings arrived at for the conduct of the war in the Pacific (a primary concern of the United States), in the Middle East, which included part of Asia and Africa, in India and southeast Asia (all primary concerns of Great Britain), and in western Europe (of common interest) permitted co-ordinated military activity in most of the theaters of operations.[21] The only battle zones outside these areas were along the German-Soviet front in Europe and in the unoccupied territory of China. Military operations in China were subject to considerable influence by the United States because of the extremity of Chinese dependence on outside military assistance. Understandings between the United States and Great Britain concerning the areas which they controlled, reached after a long and careful interchange of ideas, provided a central point and a kind of arbitrary unity for less systematic, more formal negotiations with the Soviet Union and China regarding strategic issues of general concern. The Soviet military leaders never participated in the staff system set up by the United States and Great Britain in 1942. Nevertheless, it was possible to maintain the common front against the Axis

---

[21] For definitions of these geographical areas of strategic responsibility, see pp. 101–02.

and, on the basis of diplomatic understandings reached in the Moscow conference of October 1943, to bring representatives of the Soviet Union and China into the last international military conference of 1943 (SEXTANT-EUREKA: Cairo-Tehran). Soviet delegations subsequently participated in the semipolitical, semimilitary conferences of 1945, and British-American collaboration continually improved, but SEXTANT-EUREKA marked what probably was the high point of general co-ordination of Allied military plans during World War II.[22]

Development of the Joint and Combined Chiefs of Staff System [23]

The second correlative effect of the successful development in 1942 of a device for co-ordinating American and British military plans was that the U. S. Army, Navy, and Army Air Forces simultaneously formed an organization to co-ordinate their own views for presentation to the British military leaders. This organization sprang up almost accidentally to answer the practical need for a joint committee system that would fit the pattern of the well-established British arrangements for interservice collaboration. Thus the United States found itself with a more highly developed staff system than ever before for developing military plans on a level of authority below the President. Like the Joint Board system it was a committee system and as such worked perfectly only when there was no irreconcilable disagreement among representatives of the

separate armed services. It was not the unified high command that had long been discussed inside and outside the army,[24] but it did provide a mechanism whereby the Army, the Navy, and the Army Air Forces could reach clear agreements or acceptable compromises on nearly all military matters. The pressing problems raised when the United States entered the war gave a new incentive to compromise in the common interest. It was patently advisable in the critical months after Pearl Harbor to avoid referring minor issues to the President and to present a common recommendation to the President as often as possible on policies important enough to require his approval as Commander in Chief. In addition to this incentive to unity, much of the strength of the new organization, soon known as the Joint Chiefs of Staff (JCS), lay in the fact that, in contrast with the Joint Board, it had to present a common front to the British Chiefs of Staff on military plans affecting both nations.[25] In combination, the fact of war and the presence of Great Britain made this new staff system work well enough to meet the grave crises of 1942 and thereby to win the confidence and respect of President

---

[22] For SEXTANT, see Ch. XII. For Moscow conference and 1945 conferences, see Ch. XVI.

[23] Some of the developments reviewed in general under this heading are described in more detail, as they were related to the work of OPD, in several later chapters of this volume.

[24] For a brief analysis of "Early Proposals for Unification of the Armed Services of the United States," see OPD Hist Unit Study I.

[25] The only Army papers on the organization of the U. S. Joint Chiefs were: (1) memo, CofS for Admirals Stark and King, 17 Feb 42, sub: JB, U. S. CsofS, WPD 4402–159 (Colonel Handy drafted this memorandum, which still provided for the "Commanding General Field Forces" as well as the Chief of Staff); (2) WPD study, n.d., title: Proposed Combined (U. S.-British) CsofS Orgn, Tab "Collaboration," Book 3, Exec 8; (3) WPD study, n.d., title: Proposed Joint (U. S. Army-Navy-Air) CsofS Orgn, Tab "Collaboration," Book 3, Exec 8.

For indication that these two studies are by WPD, see atchd memo, WPD for CofS, n.d., no sub, Tab "Collaboration," Book 3, Exec 8.

Roosevelt, who placed great reliance in it thereafter.[26] The JCS began holding formal meetings on 9 February 1942.[27] No official charter or directive for the U. S. JCS committee ever appeared, but its effective authority, and the derived authority of the joint committees serving it, grew steadily and remained unchallenged, though undefined, throughout the war.[28]

The administrative character of the British-American staff system established in Washington in 1942 reflected in general outline the staff structure which already existed in Great Britain. Prime Minister Churchill, who was concurrently Minister of Defence, was the central directing figure in the British war effort just as President Roosevelt was in that of the United States. The Prime Minister had a more tightly knit administrative hierarchy to assist him than the President ever established. The highest executive authority in the government of the United Kingdom was the War Cabinet, presided over by the Prime Minister who, by virtue of his office as Minister of Defence, also presided over a defense committee

which included the Foreign Secretary, the Minister of Production, the three civilian Cabinet ministers in charge of the War Office, the Admiralty, and the Air Ministry, and the three military chiefs of the armed services, that is, the Chief of the Imperial General Staff (Army), the First Sea Lord and Chief of the Naval Staff, and the Chief of the Air Staff. These last three officers constituted the Chiefs of Staff Committee, a corporate authority for issuing unified strategic instructions for military operations in time of war. Thus the ultimate political responsibility for the conduct of the war in all its aspects and the senior military advisers and agents of the government were brought together in one organization under the Prime Minister, who gave unity and finality to War Cabinet Defence Committee decisions.

The degree of co-ordination achieved in this way depended in great part on the fact that the military members of the Defence Committee, that is, the Chiefs of Staff, were acting not only as representatives of independent agencies but also as a corporate authority with a special staff to assist them in reaching interservice command decisions just as each had a staff to assist him within his own organization. This staff was the British Joint Planning Staff. In addition to a Joint Intelligence Sub-Committee, it contained a Strategic Planning Section and an Executive Planning Section, the latter concerned primarily with getting prompt action on planned operations. The work of the Chiefs of Staff Committee and its staff planners was co-ordinated administratively with other war activities by the secretariat of the War Cabinet, headed by the Prime Minister's own chief staff officer, who sat as a secretary and in effect fourth member of

---

[26] For statement by Mr. Stimson that "Mr. Roosevelt learned to like the Joint Chiefs of Staff in 1942 . . .," see Stimson, *On Active Service in Peace and War*, p. 563.

[27] Min 1st meeting JCS, 9 Feb 42 [issued 14 Feb 42].

[28] A proposal to charter the JCS was made in 1943 in connection with the reorganization of the whole joint committee system, treated at length in Ch. XIII. See: (1) JCS 202/2, 25 Mar 43, title: JCS Orgn; (2) JCS Memo for Info 54, 9 Apr 43, same sub. In due course the JCS submitted to the President a charter which defined their duties, responsibilities, and functions, JCS 202/24/D, 15 Jun 43, title: Charter, JCS. The President, in a letter to Admiral Leahy, disapproved the proposal, saying that the issuance of an executive order approving the charter seemed superfluous at the time, and that instead of helping it might have a restrictive effect. The letter was circulated as JCS 415, 17 Jul 43, title: Jt Effort Regarding Supply.

the Chiefs of Staff Committee.[29] It was this system which the British Joint Staff Mission in Washington represented, and it was the British Chiefs of Staff themselves who came to Washington with the Prime Minister in December 1941 to attend the ARCADIA Conference.

At the 10 January 1942 session of the ARCADIA Conference the British Chiefs of Staff presented a paper which they called "Post-ARCADIA Collaboration." It stated that the British Chiefs of Staff proposed to leave representatives in Washington to hold regular meetings with the U. S. Chiefs of Staff. The British Chiefs of Staff, themselves, would of course return to their duties in London. This paper recommended the usage, thenceforth followed, of *Joint* as a term applying to interservice affairs in either country and *Combined* as a term for British-American collaboration. It also suggested that the Combined Chiefs of Staff committee thus constituted in Washington, with the help of a planning staff and other subordinate committees, should "settle the broad programme of requirements based on strategic policy," should "issue general directives laying down policy to govern the distribution of available weapons of war," and "settle the broad issues of priority of overseas movement." [30] This British proposal, somewhat revised in form but with basic recommendations unchanged, received approval by the U. S. as well as

British Chiefs of Staff at the last ARCADIA meeting, 14 January 1942.[31]

On 23 January 1942 the members of the Combined Chiefs of Staff (CCS) held their first meeting in the Public Health Building at Nineteenth Street and Constitution Avenue in Washington.[32] During the next three years they gradually assumed the greater part of the burden of strategic conduct of the Allied war effort. The British Chiefs of Staff in London of course kept in close touch with problems being discussed in Washington and instructed their representatives on co-ordinated British policy. When the U. S. Chiefs of Staff went to London or elsewhere for military discussions, as they did occasionally and somewhat informally in 1942 and were to do regularly in the formal international conferences of 1943–45, they dealt directly with the British Chiefs of Staff rather than their Washington counterparts. But the periodic conferences, especially the formal ones at which the heads of government were usually present were designed to reach final agreements on issues which had been thoroughly explored by the CCS. They were more nearly occasions for politico-military decisions than for the detailed work of military planning. The day-to-day deliberations of the CCS in Washington supplied the basic pattern for the strategic direction of American and British armed forces. On the basis of joint and combined resolutions, approved by the President and the Prime Minister whenever broad policy was involved, commands were

---

[29] For brief description of British joint planning system for World War II, see: (1) Maurice P. A. Hankey (Baron), *Government Control in War* (Cambridge, England, 1945), especially pp. 55–57, 60–65; (2) Central Organization for Defence (London, 1946), Cmd. 6923; (3) Organization of Joint Planning (London, 1942), Cmd. 6351.

[30] British Serial WW–8, title: Post-ARCADIA Collaboration, appended to min 8th meeting, 10 Jan 42, ARCADIA: Proceedings.

[31] Min 12th meeting, 14 Jan 42, p. 3, and U. S. Serial ABC–4/CS4, title: Post-ARCADIA Collaboration, ARCADIA: Proceedings.

[32] (1) Press release, 6 Feb 42, copy filed ABC 381 United Nations (23 Jan 42), 1. (2) Min 1st meeting CCS, 23 Jan 42.

established, troops deployed, munitions distributed, and operations undertaken.

The machinery was never expanded to include other national military staffs as regular members of the combined staff committees, but it became accepted procedure to arrange for consultation with representatives of all interested Allied nations in individual military matters under study by the U. S. and British Chiefs of Staff. Formal meetings of the "Military Representatives of Associated Powers" were held in Washington from time to time in 1942 and the first half of 1943.[33] As a result of this procedure and of the participation, beginning late in 1943, of China and the USSR in some of the important international conferences, the CCS system provided a center of strategic planning for all the United Nations.

This development of the British-American staff system, though it could hardly have been fully foreseen at the beginning of the ARCADIA Conference, soon received official approval by the United States. In early meetings the paper on Post-ARCADIA Collaboration underwent significant revision that made explicit CCS responsibility for the "formulation of policies and plans" related to the "strategic conduct of the war" in general as well as to munitions production, allocation, and priorities of overseas movements. On 21 April 1942 President Roosevelt approved a charter for the CCS system dedicated to all these broad objectives.[34]

In March 1942 the United States and Great Britain reached an understanding on the strategic control of operations through the staff committee system thus established. This working agreement was based on a division of the world into three major strategic spheres, marked out in a way that generally reflected the varying national interests of the two countries.

The United States assumed principal responsibility for conducting military operations in the entire Pacific area including Australia and, for diplomatic rather than geographical reasons, China. This responsibility, it was agreed, would be exercised through the U. S. Joint Chiefs of Staff, which would make minor strategic decisions and direct the conduct of all operations in the area assigned to the United States. The U. S. Navy was given the executive task of carrying out JCS decisions in most of the Pacific area, which was put under the unified command of Admiral Chester W. Nimitz, while the Army performed a similar function for the Australian and Southwest Pacific region, where Allied ground forces were concentrated in some numbers and where General MacArthur was placed in command. China continued to be treated as a comparatively independent theater under Generalissimo Chiang Kai-shek and his

---

[33] For principle of consulting representatives of Pacific powers, see min of conf at White House, 28 Jan 42, Notes on Informal Conferences Held During the Visit of the British Chiefs of Staff in Washington, WDCSA 334 (1–28–42).

See min 1st–9th meetings, 26 May 42–18 Jun 43, Military Representatives of Associated (Pacific) Powers, Misc S&P Files. This group was the military counterpart of the group of political representatives of Pacific nations usually termed the Pacific War Council. See Sherwood, *Roosevelt and Hopkins*, pp. 515–16.

[34] (1) CCS 9/1, 10 Feb 42, title: War Collaboration Between United Nations. (2) Cf. U. S. Serial ABC–4/CS4, title: Post-ARCADIA Collaboration, ARCADIA: Proceedings.

For President Roosevelt's approval, see memo, U. S. Secy CCS for Maj Gen E. M. Watson, 21 Apr 42. A photostat copy is filed in ABC 381 United Nations (23 Jan 42), 1. This memorandum has "OK, FDR" written on it. Apparently Prime Minister Churchill never gave formal approval to the CCS charter (see JCS Memo for Info 54, 9 Apr 43, sub: JCS Orgn).

American chief of staff, Lt. Gen. Joseph W. Stilwell. The British accepted the same kind of strategic responsibility, to be exercised by the British Chiefs of Staff in London, for the Middle and Far East areas except China.

The CCS in Washington undertook to exercise general jurisdiction over the grand strategy developing in both British and American zones and in addition to exercise direct strategic control of all operations in the Atlantic-European area. The CCS of course acted directly under and with the military authority of the President and the Prime Minister.[35] As a matter of practical convenience, the U. S. War Department accepted the task of communicating CCS instructions to combined headquarters conducting the main offensives in North Africa (1942) and Europe (1944), the command-

ing officer in both cases being General Eisenhower.[36]

The initial members of the CCS were four British officers, led by Field Marshal Sir John Dill, and four American officers, General Marshall, Admiral Stark, Admiral King, and General Arnold. Admiral Stark attended only the first few meetings, since he left Washington in March, and Admiral King assumed the dual title and office of Commander in Chief, U. S. Fleet, and Chief of Naval Operations.[37] Within a few months Admiral Leahy, acting as chief of staff for the President and presiding chairman at JCS meetings, joined the Army, Navy, and Army Air Forces chiefs to make up the thenceforth unchanging membership of the wartime JCS as well as of the American component of the CCS.[38]

In order for the combined system to function effectively, a hierarchy of subordinate British-American committees had to be established to prepare studies, render reports, and make investigations. The American members of these groups constituted the joint committees. At least partly because the British gave the Royal Air Force separate

---

[35] For definitions of strategic areas and system of executive conduct of the war, see: (1) JCS 19, 9 Mar 42, title: Strategic Responsibility of UK and U. S. (this JCS paper is a summary of suggestions made by the President in a conference at the White House 7 March 1942); (2) memo, Brig Gen Eisenhower for JCS, 8 Mar 42, same sub, Envelope 36, Exec 4; (3) JCS 19/1, 9 Mar 42, same title (with the exception of one sentence, this JCS paper was identical with General Eisenhower's memorandum of 8 March); (4) min 5th meeting JCS, 9 Mar 42, with CCS 56/1 in ABC 311.5 (1–30–42); (5) msg 46, Prime Minister to President, 18 Mar 42, with JCS 19/1 in ABC 371 (3–5–42); (6) msg 58, Prime Minister to President, 24 Mar 42, with CCS 56/1 in ABC 311.5 (1–30–42); (7) CCS 57/2, 24 Mar 42, title: Strategic Responsibility of UK and U. S.; (8) min 14th meeting JCS, 31 Mar 42; (9) memo, U. S. Secy JCS for Gen Marshall, 1 Apr 42, no sub, with CCS 57/2 in ABC 323.31 POA (1–29–42), 2; (10) memo, Gen Marshall and Admiral King for President, 30 Mar 42, no sub, and two incls, "Directive to the Commander in Chief of the Pacific Ocean Area" and "Directive to Supreme Commander in the Southwest Pacific Area," ABC 323.31 POA (1–29–42), 1–B (this memorandum has on it the penned notation, "Approved, Franklin D. Roosevelt").

[36] (1) Min 29th meeting JCS, 18 Aug 42, Item 10 and Annex I. (2) Memo, Brig Gen Wedemeyer for CofS, 18 Apr 43, sub: Responsibility for Implementation, or Channel for CCS Directives to CinC AEF, Paper 22, Item 2B, OPD Hist Unit file.

[37] (1) EO 9096, 12 Mar 42, title: Reorgn of Navy Dept and Naval Serv Affecting Office of Chief of Naval Opns. (2) Min of CCS meetings. Admiral Stark attended the 1st through 11th meetings, 29 January–10 March 1942.

[38] (1) Min of CCS meetings. (2) Rosters of CCS committees issued periodically, copies filed in ABC 381 United Nations (1–23–42), 6–A.

The British representatives changed fairly often. Sir John Dill remained in Washington until 1944 providing permanent leadership in the British group until his death. He was replaced early in 1945 by Field Marshal Sir Henry Maitland Wilson. Admiral Leahy attended first the 34th CCS meeting, 30 July 1942.

representation, the Army Air Forces always had its own spokesman in these American staff groups. The American committees studied, reported, and investigated military matters for the benefit of the U. S. JCS at the same time that they were representing the United States on the combined committees.

The JCS-CCS machinery became more and more comprehensive and more and more specialized as the war went on. In time there were combined committees for logistics, intelligence, transportation, communications, munitions allocation, meteorology, shipbuilding, and civil affairs (occupation and military government). From the point of view of Army operations, the most important of these were the committees dealing with the problem of allocating and moving munitions, troops, and supplies in conformity with operational plans. In addition, the joint and combined machinery throughout World War II contained the committees primarily responsible for assisting the Chiefs of Staff in planning the strategic conduct of the war—the Joint Staff Planners and Combined Staff Planners (JPS and CPS), and also, for the United States, a working subcommittee of the Joint Staff Planners.

The membership of the CPS consisted of three British officers, Army, Navy, and Air, and four American officers, Army, Navy, Army Air, and Navy Air, who constituted the U. S. JPS. Both the JPS and the CPS were central co-ordinating groups through which many policy papers prepared in other committees reached the JCS or the CCS. They received directives from the JCS and the CCS and often delegated work to other committees. Particularly during 1942, they were not exclusively strategic planners but also co-ordinators in all kinds of joint and combined matters that had a bearing on high policy. The U. S. Army planner on both the JPS and the CPS committees was originally the WPD chief, General Gerow. When General Eisenhower succeeded General Gerow as WPD chief in February 1942, he immediately delegated the position of Army planner to the chief of the Strategy & Policy Group, and thereafter left most of the routine of joint planning to him.[39] While the chief of the Division thus had no formal place in the JCS and CCS system, he exerted great influence in it through the Army planner and, indirectly, through the Chief of Staff.

The U. S. JPS drew heavily upon the services of its working war plans committee, which ranged in number at various times between eight and eighteen members. This committee originally was called the Joint U. S. Strategic Committee (JUSSC), and OPD supplied all of the three or four Army (including Army Air) representatives on it. The JUSSC concerned itself primarily with broad strategic planning on the joint level and related policy matters such as mobilization and use of manpower by the three services. The more technical task of drawing up joint strategic and operational plans and adjusting them in conformity to theater needs became increasingly important in the latter part of 1942, and the committee was reorganized as the Joint War Plans Committee (JWPC) early in 1943. The JWPC

[39] (1) U. S. Serial ABC–4/CS4, title: Post-Arcadia Collaboration, Arcadia: Proceedings. (2) Rosters of CCS committees, copies filed ABC 381 United Nations (1–23–42), 6–A. Initially General Handy was Army planner. When he succeeded General Eisenhower as chief of the Division in June 1942, General Wedemeyer became Army planner. OPD furnished two subsequent Army planners in World War II, Brig. Gens. F. N. Roberts and G. A. Lincoln. For joint planning later in the war, see Ch. XIII.

drafted studies and strategic plans covering every major joint or combined operation in World War II. Three or four OPD officers, constituting an administrative unit in the OPD organization, made up the Army section (at this time distinct from both the Navy and the Army Air Forces sections) of the JWPC.[40]

The fact that the JCS-JPS-JWPC hierarchy came into being as part of the Combined Chiefs of Staff system added tremendously to its effectiveness as interservice co-ordination machinery. At the same time this fact projected the whole JCS organization into the international field, where it acted concurrently as the American agent for British-American military co-operation. Its personnel, by virtue of their position and special knowledge, had to assume the responsibility of representing the United States at the international conferences which capped the United Nations planning with final decisions by heads of government. Thus from ARCADIA, the first British-American staff meeting in December 1941 and January 1942, through the British-American-Soviet meeting at Potsdam (TERMINAL) just before the end of the war, the American membership of the JCS-CCS system participated in top-level planning. The conference decisions, like the deliberations of the CCS, JCS, and other extra-War Department agencies forming the environment in which OPD worked, were of prime importance in all the work of the highest staff in the Washington command post of the Army.

---

[40] (1) Memo, Col R. T. Maddocks for Chief S&P Gp, 9 Jul 42, sub: Jt Strategic Com, ABC 020, OPD, WDGS (13 Jul 42), 3JA. (2) JWPC 401, 14 Aug 45. This paper is a note by Brig Gen. W. W. Bessell, Jr., sub: Jt War Plans Com. (3) Rosters of CCS Coms, copies filed ABC 381 United Nations (1–23–42), 6–A.

Military Planning and National Policy [41]

The machinery used by the American military services in co-ordinating their efforts in World War II, though scarcely all that could have been desired, was far more fully developed than any comparable system in the sphere of total national policy. While the President came to rely on the JCS for advice on the conduct of the war, he established no administrative machinery for integrating military planning with war production, war manpower control, or foreign policy objectives. The President himself co-ordinated these interrelated national enterprises by working in turn with his personal advisers (among whom Harry Hopkins continued to have unique influence), the executive agency chiefs, his cabinet secretaries, and the JCS. In contrast with the British Government, in which the War Cabinet Defence Committee brought all the major elements of national policy under the Prime Minister's personal supervision and direction, the various U. S. Government agencies had difficulty in making a well-articulated contribution to a balanced national policy or even in finding out the precise implications of national policy in their respective activities.

Secretary Stimson was conscientious about acting as a link between discussions on the cabinet level and the workings of the War Department staff. During the pre-Pearl Harbor and early wartime period he held regular meetings in his office, at which General Marshall was present, to discuss War Department policy matters and bring to bear on them governmental as well as serv-

---

[41] Some of the developments reviewed in general under this heading are described in more detail, as they were related to the work of OPD, in several later chapters of this volume, especially in Ch. XVI.

ice considerations.[42] Nevertheless the link thus created by Secretary Stimson could not add any strength to the elements it connected, and the lack of administrative organization on the cabinet level continued throughout World War II.[43]

Late in 1942 General Marshall drafted, though he never dispatched, a memorandum pointing out the awkwardness for the military leaders of having no systematic recording of Presidential instructions related to the war effort delivered to Cabinet members or to the Joint Chiefs of Staff individually or collectively. He said that "details supposedly decided on" were put into execution only by "impromptu coordination" and could easily be "left in the air or subject to varying interpretation." He contrasted this situation with the results of the "British coordinating system which works from the top . . . in the Cabinet meeting," and remarked that the JCS members themselves might "get into very serious difficulties in not knowing the nature of the President's revisions of the drafts of messages we submit to him." [44]

In 1943 and subsequent war years administrative co-ordination of national policy decisions improved by virtue of the great prestige of the JCS and the increasing extent to which Admiral Leahy, the President's chief of staff, was able to make the President's views a matter for day-to-day consideration by the JCS and the CCS.

The President's personal participation in the great international military conferences of the midwar period (Casablanca, January 1943; Washington, May 1943; Quebec, August 1943; Cairo and Teheran, November–December 1943) also contributed to the increasingly effective integration of national war policy.

Efforts were made comparatively late in the war to widen the area of administrative co-ordination among the various government agencies engaged in policy making on behalf of the President. Most important from the Army planners' point of view was the establishment, at the end of 1944, of a politico-military staff system patterned after and parallel with the JCS structure. It was designed to align foreign policy and military policy through formal staff deliberations among representatives of the State, War, and Navy Departments.[45] Somewhat earlier in mid-1943, the creation of the Office of War Mobilization under James F. Byrnes superimposed some unity of purpose upon the activities of the confusing welter of administrative agencies controlling the mobilization of the civilian economy for war. Mr. Byrnes came to occupy on the home front something like the position of the JCS in military affairs.[46]

Despite these advances toward integration in the fields of foreign policy, war mobilization, and military policy, the final step toward systematization was never taken. The President in his own person co-ordinated the work of his senior aides, and no

---

[42] Notes on Conferences in OSW, two volumes, WDCSA rcds. The meetings recorded cover the period 19 May 1942–24 February 1943.

[43] (1) Stimson, *On Active Service in Peace and War*, pp. 561–62. (2) Sherwood, *Roosevelt and Hopkins*. This entire book, describing the tremendous influence and responsibilities of Mr. Hopkins, is testimony of the personal way in which the President dealt with the many problems and agency chiefs he had to face during the war.

[44] Unused memo, Gen Marshall for Harry Hopkins, 4 Nov 42, WDCSA 381, 1 (SS).

[45] For the creation of this politico-military staff system, called the State-War-Navy Co-ordinating Committee (SWNCC), see Ch. XVI.

[46] For the establishment of the Office of War Mobilization 27 May 1943 and the general problem of "Coordinating the War Agencies," see *The United States at War: Development and Administration of the War Program by the Federal Government* (Washington, 1946), Ch. 12.

staff or secretariat was organized to assist him either in reaching his final policy decisions or in carrying them out. This situation was one which military leaders had no authority to remedy, and it frequently hampered their work. Shortly after the appointment of Mr. Byrnes as Director of War Mobilization, General Marshall hesitantly described the general problem to him:

The U. S. Chiefs of Staff have been aware for a long time of a serious disadvantage under which they labor in their dealings with the British Chiefs of Staff. Superficially, at least, the great advantage on the British side has been the fact that they are connected up with other branches of their Government through an elaborate but most closely knit Secretariat. On our side there is no such animal and we suffer accordingly. The British therefore present a solid front of all officials and committees. We cannot muster such strength.

More specifically he stated:

On the contrary, not only are our various agencies not carefully correlated but sometimes a day or more will elapse before the specific agency, the U. S. Chiefs of Staff, for example, is made aware of the important conclusions arrived at or the problem which is being considered and which deeply affects them. Important radios will sometimes be unknown to us for a considerable period of time because there is not an automatic procedure set up. Discussions with the British, officials or committees, bearing directly on Chiefs of Staff business, will take place here and there in Washington without correlation or later report of commitments.

There is also the continuing danger of misunderstandings. After Cabinet meetings Mr. Stimson invariably makes some pencil notes and dictates a memorandum which is circulated over here, with relation to any matters that may concern the War Department. Possibly Mr. Knox does the same thing in the Navy Department. However, we have had cases where their impressions varied as to just what the President desired.

Finally, he observed:

This is a rather delicate matter for me to discuss and to circulate in the form of a British paper [General Marshall sent Mr. Byrnes a paper on the British Secretariat system], because it could be charged that I was proposing not only a War Cabinet but a fundamental constitutional alteration in the matter of Cabinet responsibility to the Congress, etc., which is remote from my purpose. I am interested solely in some form of a Secretariat for keeping all these groups in Washington in an automatic relationship one with the other.[47]

This expression of criticism was the strongest ever made by General Marshall, for he was reluctant to step outside his own area of responsibility. The difficulties in reducing the civilian administrative agencies of the government to similar order, particularly while the war was going on, were almost insurmountable. From the Army's point of view, as General Marshall was careful to point out, no such drastic reorganization was necessary. The essential minimum objectives sought by the Army to improve the quality of its work in the highest policy sphere were in fact achieved by the personal abilities and efforts of the President and his principal advisers, such as General Marshall, along with extraordinary labors on the part of their individual staffs, such as OPD. In terms of administrative organization, the military problems confronting the United States in World War II were met by the national high command as organized in 1942.

---

[47] Memo, Gen Marshall for James F. Byrnes, 10 Jul 43, no sub, WDCSA 040.

CHAPTER VII

The New Army Command Post

The 9 March 1942 reorganization of the Army officially constituted the War Plans Division, formally redesignated the Operations Division on 23 March,[1] as General Marshall's staff for planning and for directing the execution of military operations. In exercising the Chief of Staff's authority for the conduct of Army activities in the theaters of operations, OPD was the Washington command post of the U. S. Army. Even within the Army, the implications of this new organization were fully understood by very few officers at the time it was undertaken. In their public explanation of the nature of the reorganization, General McNarney and his fellow committeemen had not dwelt on the special status to be occupied by OPD, but had emphasized instead the simplification of the command structure and the reinforcement, for the other General Staff divisions, of the traditional barrier between planning and operating. By not drawing attention to the consequences of giving to a single division of the General Staff all the functions of a command post staff in the field, General McNarney undoubtedly avoided a great deal of controversy as to the theoretical propriety of this aspect of the reorganization. The administrative rearrangements pursuant to War Department Circular 59

nevertheless insured that OPD's staff authority would be unique and that, abandoning the ambiguity of the traditional term "supervise," OPD would direct military operations insofar as necessary to carry out the orders of the Chief of Staff. During the tenure of General Eisenhower as Division chief (16 February–23 June 1942), the powers, duties, and organization of OPD were elaborated in a way that enabled the staff to meet the heavy demands made of it by General Marshall.

It was in recognition of the power centralized in the Division that General Marshall changed its name. At his suggestion a conference was held by General Eisenhower with his senior officers. The following conclusions were reached:

The name should, as nearly as possible, be indicative of the purpose of the office, that is, planning and operating. Effort was made to avoid laborious or hyphenated names. It was considered that the word "Command" included in the name of the office would be more nearly descriptive than any other of the functions you exercise through this office, since command implies not only planning and execution, but also responsibility for co-ordination with co-equals; i. e., the Navy, British, etc.

Many miscellaneous functions devolve upon this Division such as participation, for the War Department, in matters involving psychological warfare, economic warfare, allocation of material, State Department activity and etc. All of these involve phases of your responsibility as the Commander.

---

[1] (1) AG ltr, 23 Mar 42, sub: Redesignation of WPD, AG 020 (3–20–42) MB–F–M. (2) Memo, WPD for SGS, 25 Mar 42, sub: Change in Symbols Asgd to OPD of WDGS, OPD 320, 12.

The word "headquarters" was believed more applicable than "group", "division", "post", etc.

Consequently the term

a. "Command Headquarters" was selected as first choice. Others in order of preference were:

b. General Headquarters (GHQ). (2nd choice)

c. Command Group

d. Combat Headquarters [2]

There is no evidence that the Chief of Staff took exception to this emphasis on the "command" function, but he selected a name which indicated the single orientation which he expected his command post staff to give to all Army activities: "Operations." Working on the same principle General Marshall a few days later, in recommending General Eisenhower and his two principal group chiefs for promotion, avoided any reference to formal administrative positions on the General Staff. Instead he stated they were "involved with orderly organization for the control . . . of theaters of operations" and listed them as: Brig. Gen. Dwight D. Eisenhower, Chief of Operations for the United States Army, performing functions formerly assigned to General Headquarters; Colonel Thomas T. Handy, Field Artillery, Deputy Chief of Operations, United States Army, for the ground forces; Colonel St. Clair Streett, Air Corps, Deputy Chief of Operations, United States Army, for the air forces.[3]

---

[2] Memo, WPD for CofS, 15 Mar 42, sub: Redesignation of WPD, OPD 321.1, 4.

[3] (1) Memo, SW for President, 26 Mar 42, sub: Temp Promotions, AG 210.1 Gen Offs (1–13–42), 1. (2) Cf. atchd informal memo, GCM [Gen Marshall] for SW, n.d., no sub, AG 210.1 Gen Offs (1–13–42), 1. This note read: "I would like to have your approval for the attached," and is initialed "HLS" [Secretary Stimson] and carries the President's approval, "OK, FDR."

Functions of the Operations Division

War Department Circular 59 stated that "War Plans Division . . . is charged . . . with those duties of the War Department General Staff relating to the formulation of plans and the strategic direction of the military forces in the theater of war." To make these duties feasible, it specifically provided that "Commanding Generals, Army Air Forces, Army Ground Forces, and Services of Supply will, as soon as practicable after receipt, furnish War Plans Division, War Department General Staff, with a copy of all messages received by them from services outside the continental limits of the United States pertaining to current or projected combat operations. . . ." The functions granted to OPD meant that its planning and strategic direction of field operations were to dominate the World War II effort of the Army, since in wartime all activities were to be directed toward the development and operational employment of a "well-balanced and efficient military team." [4]

The extent of OPD's staff prerogatives and the intimate connection between its authority and that of the Chief of Staff was most explicitly indicated in a memorandum prepared in OPD and approved by the Deputy Chief of Staff, General McNarney, about three months after the reorganization. The tightly knit argument in this memorandum moved from two main premises, first, that the Chief of Staff had full power to issue or change "orders relating to strategy, tactics, or operations," and second, that OPD was the Chief of Staff's agency through which "orders relating to strategy, tactics, and operations will be issued." The fact was brought out that the OPD chief

---

[4] WD Cir 59, 2 Mar 42, sub: WD Reorgn.

referred only broad phases of plans or changes in plans to the Chief of Staff for approval by the President, while he could issue instructions in the name of the Chief of Staff "on matters to implement already approved plans or changes relating to strategy, tactics, and operations." Moreover, the memorandum indicated that in fact OPD group or section chiefs might sign the actual authentication of such orders, which would then have the full force of the authority of the Chief of Staff and the President:

Pursuant to your verbal request, the views of the Operations Division, with reference to the subject matter, are discussed below:

I. a. Broadly speaking, the Commander-in-Chief [the President] is responsible for plans relating to *strategy, tactics,* and *operations.* The Chief of Staff of the Army is the Commander-in-Chief's "Executive", for issuing or changing orders relating to strategy, tactics, or operations.

b. The Operations Division, WDGS, is considered the "Command Post" of the Chief of Staff and his agency through which orders relating to strategy, tactics, and operations will be issued.

Plans, or changes in plans, concerning the broad phases of *strategy, tactics,* and *operations* for which directives are desired, are presented to the Chief of Staff. After approval by the Chief of Staff, these directives are issued by direction of the Commander-in-Chief. It is believed that, in the interests of *consistency,* these directives should have the name and title of the Chief of Staff *typed* in. The "formal" directives are authenticated by the Assistant Chief of Staff, Operations Division, and are sent to The Adjutant General for reproduction and distribution. These directives go to The Adjutant General by a covering memorandum with the name and title of the Assistant Chief of Staff, OPD, typed in, and may be authenticated by a Group or Section Chief of the Operations Division.

c. The Chief of Staff, by virtue of his own office, has authority to direct any necessary action to *implement* already approved plans for strategy, tactics, and operations, including changes thereto.

d. In furtherance of c, above, and under paragraph 3 A, OCS memorandum of March 8, 1942, the Chief of Staff has authorized the Deputy Chief of Staff, and the Assistant Chiefs of Staff, on matters under their supervision, to issue instructions in the name of the Chief of Staff.

e. Therefore, under d, above, the Assistant Chief of Staff, OPD, may issue instructions, in the name of the Chief of Staff, on matters to implement already approved plans or changes relating to *strategy, tactics,* and *operations.* This would include troop movement; telegrams on operations, or strategy, to various theaters of operations; tactical changes in boundaries; activation of *already constituted* units, etc.[5]

The relative importance of OPD among the divisions of the General Staff after the reorganization was indicated by the allotment of personnel. From WPD's strength of 54 officers, as of 31 December 1941, the Division had increased to a total of 85 officers by 9 March 1942. Since more than 20 officers from the Air Corps and GHQ were assigned to the new command post pursuant to the reorganization, General Eisenhower received an initial allotment of 100 officers, including 3 brigadier generals, 22 colonels, 37 lieutenant colonels, and 31 majors. General Eisenhower noted that the higher ratio of colonels in the Strategy & Policy Group (S&P) was only "commensurate" with the "highly important duties" of "strategic planning, Joint and Combined" which made S&P the "co-ordinating agency with the Navy and the United Nations." When

---

[5] Memo, Col Gailey for Col O. L. Nelson, Jr., SGS, 17 Jun 42, sub: Functions and Procedures, OPD, WDGS, OPD 320, 30. This memorandum is stamped: "Approved By Order of the Secretary of War, Joseph T. McNarney, Deputy Chief of Staff," and signed in authentication by Colonel Nelson. For administrative instructions in "OCS memorandum of March 8, 1942," see p. 271.

new allotments were made on 1 April 1942, OPD received 107 positions in all, a figure in sharp contrast to the strengths allotted to G–1, 13 officers; G–2, 16 officers; G–3, 14 officers; and G–4, 12 officers. Before the reorganization (as of 1 March), General Staff strengths had been: G–1, 62 officers; G–3, 81 officers; G–4, 174 officers; and WPD, 80 officers.[6]

After four months' trial, the War Department issued revised permanent Army Regulations which described the reorganization as it had come into being during March, April, May, and June. These Army Regulations, 10–15 dated 13 July 1942, adopted the language concerning the Chief of Staff's position which President Roosevelt had asked Secretary Stimson to write in the executive order authorizing the reorganization. They read: "The Chief of Staff is the executive through whom the President of the United States, as Commander-in-Chief, exercises his functions in relation to strategy, tactics, and operations." In addition, they provided: "The Chief of Staff is the immediate adviser of the Secretary of War and is charged by him with the planning, development, and execution of the military program." Finally, they provided: "The Chief of Staff exercises general supervision

over the Army of the United States and the Military Establishment necessary thereto." [7]

This unequivocal grant of broad power over the whole Army and Military Establishment placed the Chief of Staff on the pinnacle toward which the successive incumbents of that office had been moving steadily since 1921. Inevitably, the power of the General Staff through which the Chief of Staff fulfilled this vast responsibility also increased. The 1942 regulations stated:

The War Department General Staff, under the direction of the Chief of Staff, plans and coordinates the development of the Army and assists the Chief of Staff in the direction of the field operations of the Army of the United States. It is specially charged with providing such broad basic plans and policies as will enable the Commanding Generals of the Army Ground Forces, Army Air Forces, Services of Supply, defense commands, task forces, and theaters of operation to prepare and execute detailed programs. The War Department General Staff supervises the execution of these detailed programs. In so doing, it does not engage in administrative duties or in operations for the performance of which an agency exists.

The grant of responsibilities to the General Staff taken in conjunction with the authorization for Assistant Chiefs of Staff, "on matters under their supervision, to issue instructions in the name of the Secretary of War and the Chief of Staff," was clearly as broad as the power of the Chief of Staff. In practice it resulted in a tremendous part of that power being vested in OPD. The traditional restraining clause on the General Staff—the injunction against engaging in "administrative duties or in operations for the performance of which an agency

---

[6] (1) For assignment of officers from Air Corps and GHQ, see memo, WPD for G–1, 3 Mar 42, sub: Dtl of Offs, OPD 210.3, 4. (2) For "initial reorganization" allotments, see memo, WPD for G–1, 3 Mar 42, sub: Revised Almts of Offs, for Dy with WD O'head (WPD), OPD 210.3, 5. (3) Table, 1 Apr 42, title: Almt for WDGS, OPD 210.3, 28. (4) WDGS Asgmts, Papers 1 and 7, Item 10, OPD Hist Unit file.

The pre-organization strength of G–2 (425) is not comparable to the reduced strength of 16 because the latter figure did not include a sizable working intelligence organization set up independently as the Military Intelligence Service, technically not part of the General Staff.

[7] The quotations in this paragraph and those which immediately follow are from AR 10–15, 13 Jul 42, sub: GS Orgn and Gen Dys.

exists"—applied to OPD in a way quite different from that in which it applied to the other General Staff Divisions. The three major commands, Army Ground Forces, Army Air Forces, and Services of Supply, were agencies for performing all administrative and operative duties in the zone of interior concerning personnel handling, mobilization, organization of units, training, equipment of forces, and service functions designed to deliver troops and supplies to the theaters of operations in an orderly fashion. Thus, G–1, G–3, and G–4 could only develop general policies applicable to all three commands, and in some cases to the theaters of operations. On the other hand, there was no Army agency below the General Staff for devising strategic plans and directives, transmitting them to the theaters of operations, and issuing supplementary instructions to all Army commands—either in the zone of interior or in the theaters of operations—to insure that military operations could and would proceed as planned and directed. These comprehensive duties were performed by OPD itself. OPD was necessarily an operating agency. Monitoring reports from the field and systematically checking them for indication that strategic directions were being followed was the heart of its method of operations control.

This situation was clearly revealed in the assignment of duties among the General Staff Divisions. G–1 was charged with "duties . . . which relate to the personnel of the Army as individuals"; G–3 with "duties . . . which relate to the mobilization, training, and organization of the military forces," and G–4 with "duties . . . which relate to the supply of the Army." G–2, a service staff performing a special function for the Army, was charged with "duties . . . which relate to the collection, evaluation, and dissemination of military information." In contrast to these narrowly delimited functional duties of the rest of the General Staff, OPD's assignment of responsibility stated: "The Operations Division is charged, in general, with those duties of the War Department General Staff which relate to formulation of plans and strategic direction of the military forces in the theater of war. In time of peace, it is charged with the preparation and supervision of war and mobilization plans. In time of war, it constitutes the command post for the strategic direction of the armed forces in the various theaters of operations." As if this broad sphere of responsibility were not clear enough to enable OPD to exercise its influence in any Army activity which affected operations, the Division was also "specifically charged with the preparation of plans and policies and supervision of activities" concerning the "strategic employment of the Army of the United States." [8]

Staff Procedure after the Reorganization

One of the primary purposes of the March reorganization was to lighten the burden of the Chief of Staff by giving greater discretionary powers to the chiefs of the General Staff Divisions as well as to the commanding generals of the new major zone of interior commands. At one of the

[8] The complete list of OPD's specific areas of responsibility included four very broadly phrased categories, of which the first three had been charged to WPD in similar form. They were: "(1) Location and armament of coast and land fortifications and bases. (2) Forces which may be required in the prosecution of the war or in furtherance of the national defense, and times and places at which they may be needed. (3) Testing of war plans by tactical exercises and maneuvers. (4) Strategic employment of the Army of the United States."

first meetings of the War Department General Council, on 17 March 1942, General McNarney clearly stated the principle that a considerable degree of delegated authority now rested with the Assistant Chiefs of Staff:

The purpose of the reorganization is to decentralize, giving officers in charge of activities greater powers of decision and responsibility in matters under their control. This principle, on the War Department General Staff level, means that the Assistant Chiefs of Staff will make the decisions on problems under their jurisdiction, and announce the decision. . . . This directive to take action on problems under your jurisdiction is a pretty broad statement, and it will probably take some time to work out the details so that there is understanding on the part of all concerned. The Deputy Chief of Staff indicated emphatically that the Assistant Chiefs of Staff should, if necessary, err on the side of taking final action on papers rather than to send everything up to the Office of the Chief of Staff for approval.[9]

In response to questioning about the "right of an Assistant Chief of Staff to change a policy that has previously been established by the Chief of Staff without referring the question to his office for approval," General McNarney indorsed the idea that it was appropriate for "an Assistant Chief of Staff to make exceptions to these policies where cases warrant it." He pointed out, however, that a "distinction should be made between exceptions granted without changing the policy and revision of policy." In reference to the latter case, the ruling stated: "On minor matters, and where there is general concurrence, the As-

sistant Chief of Staff may change policies and send up information copies. On major matters, General McNarney indicated that he desired to be consulted prior to their publication." [10] In elaboration of this last caveat, the Deputy Chief of Staff subsequently warned that he wanted "no policy forced on any division of the General Staff, or on any of the general commands. Where a policy will affect one of the general commands, he wants their concurrence. Where a nonconcurrence arises, the question should be brought up for the decision of the Deputy Chief of Staff." [11]

With special reference to OPD, General McNarney stated that he "believed that all War Department Staff officers understand as basic staff procedure the necessity of consulting and informing the Operations Division, WDGS on matters materially affecting or relating to the strategic direction of military forces in theaters of operations." He further observed that

. . . all papers which were to be referred to the Operations Division should have all action completed by the originating office before being sent to that division. The idea is to save the Operations Division as much paper work as possible. When the paper requires a directive to be written, it should not be left up to the Operations Division to write the directive but the study should have a proposed directive attached for the approval or disapproval of the Operations Division. All staff officers should bear in mind that it is most desirable to shield the Operations Division from all diversions that would distract it from its primary job of conducting the war as the command post of the Commander-in-Chief of the Field Forces.[12]

At a General Council meeting in early June, General McNarney observed, "All

[9] Min of Gen Council meetings, 17 Mar 42, DCofS rcds. The Assistant Chiefs of Staff were informally called the "Chiefs" of the General Staff Divisions (OPD, G-1, G-2, G-3, G-4). That is, "Chief of OPD" is equivalent to "Assistant Chief of Staff, OPD."

[10] Ibid.
[11] Ibid., 24 Mar 42.
[12] Ibid., 31 Mar 42.

papers coming from the three principal commands should be addressed to the Chief of Staff through the War Department General Staff Division which has primary interest in the subject involved. It will be the duty of this War Department General Staff Division to decide if the concurrences of other War Department General Staff Divisions are necessary." [13] The sweeping nature of OPD's responsibilities insured that nearly every problem relating to theaters of operations would be referred to that Division in the first instance and that it would determine the necessity of securing concurrences.

That General Marshall intended the reorganized General Staff to act with a new speed and dispatch was clear from the administrative instructions he issued on 8 March 1942. Though the old memorandum and concurrence system was left in force, the Chief of Staff directed that it be used only as a last resort. The 8 March instructions read in part:

Staff procedure will adhere to the following:

a. Where directives do not change established policies and where they relate to activities concerning only one division of the War Department General Staff, the Assistant Chief of Staff of the responsible division will issue the directive and furnish information copies to interested divisions of the War Department General Staff including the Secretariat.

b. Where directives do not change established policies but relate to activities concerning several staff divisions, the staff division with primary interest will obtain concurrences, by conferences preferably, from the interested divisions.

(1) If all concur, the division with primary interest will issue the directive. Copies will be sent to interested agencies.

(2) When there are non-concurrences, the division with primary interest will refer the conflicts to the Deputy Chief of Staff for decision.

c. Detailed staff studies will be made only when they are essential to directives initiating or changing important policies and when adequate understanding of the problem requires such a study.

d. When the facts upon which important decisions depend can be presented orally, the Assistant Chiefs of Staff or members of their division will present the matter to the Deputy Chief of Staff for decision. Whenever practicable, conferences and direct action will be utilized in lieu of written communications. All concerned are cautioned of the necessity to record and to issue information copies on actions or decisions arrived at orally.

Issuance of instructions and directives

a. The Deputy Chief of Staff, and the Assistant Chiefs of Staff are authorized, on matters under their supervision, to issue instructions in the name of the Secretary of War and the Chief of Staff.

b. Orders relating to strategy, tactics, and operations will be issued by order of the Commander in Chief; all others by order of the Secretary of War. [14]

The effect of these instructions was to permit OPD to proceed on its own initiative, issuing directives in the name of the Chief of Staff in the broad sphere of military operations. The other staff divisions had been interdicted from interference with the detailed performance of programs in which their primary interest lay. In contrast OPD had powers, duties, personnel, and facilities (that is, access to all operational messages) to follow up on compliance with its instructions. The Chief of Staff's injunction to the Assistant Chiefs of Staff to conduct their business informally and by direct action, amounted to giving OPD a clear field to take whatever steps were necessary to do its work. Moreover, as a result of the instruc-

---

[13] *Ibid.,* 9 Jun 42.

[14] Memo, SGS for G–1, G–2, G–3, G–4, and WPD (info copies to AGF, SOS, AAF, and TAG), 8 Mar 42, sub: Functions and Procedures, WDGS, OPD 320, 5.

tions to try to settle nonconcurrences informally and orally, OPD was free to employ this rapid way of co-ordinating all General Staff work related to military operations in combat zones.

OPD's Relations with Other War Department Agencies

Whereas OPD had never claimed anything but equal status with the four "G" Divisions of the War Department General Staff, the March reorganization put OPD on a different, if not necessarily superior, plane. The working relationships that evolved revealed this changed status. G–1 worked on personnel plans and policies, as distinct from administrative details, which comprised the duty of Services of Supply (SOS). However, when personnel handling made the theater commander's task more difficult or threatened to compromise actual operations, OPD intervened. G–2 handled enemy intelligence, but the principal demand for this information came from OPD, which was able to correlate it with information about American and Allied operations. G–3 worked on plans and policies for the organization and training of units, with OPD giving guidance in the light of operational needs and handling unorthodox or critical organizational problems when they arose in the theaters of operations. The activities and responsibilities pertaining to the movement of troops and control of operations, which in a general staff on a lower echelon are vested in G–3, were completely transferred to OPD. Finally, G–4 dealt with policies concerning supply and equipment, with much of the work in this field devolving on the Services of Supply, while OPD maintained its own logistics staff to furnish

guidance both in planning and directing overseas operations.

The secondary role in which the four "G" Divisions of the General Staff found themselves was promptly indicated by a 10 March memorandum from Col. Raymond G. Moses (brigadier general 11 March 1942) newly appointed G–4. He stated:

An officer from the G–4 Division will be detailed as a liaison officer with the WPD Future Operations Group, or groups designated for the study of areas for possible future action. This officer will spend as much time as practicable with the planning group in order to be fully informed of the development of plans and in order that he may provide from the G–4 Division any assistance which may be required.

When there is formed a Section in the Operations Group, WPD will request a representative from G–4 at the time representatives are required from SOS, Ground and Air Force Commands. The principal purpose of this officer being present during the planning of the Operations Section in WPD is to enable G–4 to prepare the broad policies and directives when necessary to coordinate the G–4 activities of the various Commands of the War Department. When the activities of the Operations Section, WPD pass into the control, rather than the planning stage, the G–4 representative will be withdrawn.

The G–4 Division is not large enough in itself to take on any extensive G–4 study but at any time WPD desires such a study G–4 will undertake to have it made.[15]

OPD consistently agreed in principle that G–4 ought to establish Army-wide supply policies that would correlate logistic activities throughout the three major commands and the overseas theaters. In practice the handful of officers in the G–4 Division could offer comparatively little assistance to the mammoth Services of Supply organization

---

[15] Memo, G–4 for Brig Gen R. W. Crawford, 10 Mar 42, sub: Proposed Method of Cooperation Between G–4 Div and WPD, OPD 320, 10.

or to the well-staffed OPD sections. Consequently G–4 tended to be squeezed out of an important part in logistic problems. Services of Supply proceeded to make its own policies in the course of performing day-to-day tasks delegated to it, and OPD often predetermined logistic policy by the nature of the demands it made in the interests of supporting specific combat operations.

By mid-1942 General Moses was calling attention to the consequences. He declared that his division found it difficult, as a result of the activities of SOS and OPD, to discharge its responsibility for the "preparation of such broad basic supply plans as are required by mobilization, training and strategic plans" and, even more operational in character, the development of "policies and directives necessary to coordinate among the various commands the distribution and movement of supply, technical, and labor troops not employed as combat units." General Moses stated:

It has been my observation since the reorganization of the War Department that in definite planning for operations conferences have been held between the Operations Division and the Services of Supply and Air Forces, on major issues involving matters of a G–4 nature, without a representative of the Supply Division present and in most cases without this Division being notified of plans officially for a considerable period of time.

At the same time, he continued:

I believe I am cognizant of the responsibilities of and the difficulties besetting the Operations Division and there is no thought of expanding unnecessarily the activities of the Supply Division or of reducing the responsibilities or activities of the Operations Division.[16]

Brig. Gen. St. Clair Streett, then chief of OPD's Theater Group, answered General Moses by stating: "This Division will render every possible assistance to secure the utmost coordination with G–4 with regard to both immediate and future planning." [17] Later in the year, General Wedemeyer, then chief planner, informed General Moses: "I have conferred with members of my Strategy and Policy Group who agree with me that much of the liaison contact maintained between the Operations Division and the S.O.S. should properly be with the G–4 Division." [18] Nevertheless, the steadily increasing power of General Somervell's Services of Supply organization in the whole logistic field and the recognized primary interest of OPD in regard to all matters affecting overseas operations continued to hedge in very closely G–4's actual area of decisive authority.[19]

The position of the other General Staff Divisions was very similar, though their work had less to do with OPD's direction of operations. G–1, like G–4, lost a great deal of its effective power to Services of Supply, which performed detailed personnel tasks and tended to establish policies in the process. G–3 fared somewhat better, but of course mobilization and training plans came to depend greatly on the ideas evolved in the actual training work being done by Army Ground Forces as well as on G–3 studies. For its part, OPD supplied the strategic and operational information on

---

[16] Memo, G–4 for OPD, 7 Aug 42, sub: Coordination with Supply Div, OPD 320, 25. General Moses remarked on the exceptional degree of cooperation from the "Future Operations Group, OPD, and from the head of the BOLERO Committee (General Hull)."

[17] Memo, Actg ACofS OPD for G–4, 18 Aug 42, sub: Co-ordination with Supply Div, OPD 320, 25.

[18] Memo, Brig Gen Wedemeyer for Brig Gen Moses, 6 Nov 42, no sub, OPD 320, 10.

[19] For General Somervell's suggestion that G–4 (and G–1) be abolished, and for OPD's transfer of some responsibilities for logistics to G–4 in the fall of 1943, see Ch. XIV.

which both personnel and mobilization policies had to be based. Beyond giving this guidance, OPD intervened only in a few G–1 and G–3 matters, such as assignment of high-ranking officers to combat theater commands or calculation of the over-all Army mobilization goal (Victory Program Troop Basis). In those matters its influence was usually decisive. With G–2, OPD's relationship was closer but more unilateral. G–2 provided OPD with its most carefully selected intelligence reports as a matter of routine and frequently furnished the various OPD sections with special intelligence reports for use in planning or directing overseas operations.[20] OPD officers normally drew on G–2 for information without bringing the intelligence officers fully into the long and complicated process of strategic planning. This practice tended to limit the capacity of G–2 to render relevant and timely advice to the planners. The G–2 officers frequently did not know and could not find out "what we had, where our divisions were, what we were doing, or what our next advance plan was for our own troops."[21] For their own purposes, however, on the "receiving end," OPD officers declared that they got very good intelligence from G–2 and testified that final decisions on plans were always made only after a complete analysis "from the G–2 standpoint."[22]

OPD's authority to plan and direct combat operations on behalf of the Chief of Staff was unquestioned by the major zone of interior commands. In accordance with the reorganization principle of delegating administrative detail to the new commands, OPD relied in large part on advice and assistance from the specialists in those organizations. The Division formally "requested, on all correspondence and allied papers referred to the War Plans Division for action, that comments, recommendations or technical advice be included" by Army Ground Forces, Army Air Forces, and Services of Supply.[23] The formula for the relationship with all three commands was much like that evolved in a conference with Air Forces representatives on 16 March 1942: "1. AF *will give* Expert Advice *toward workable directives* to Chief of Sections Concerned. 2. WPD will *issue* directives. 3. AF will carry them OUT."[24] This procedure applied regardless of whether the action resulted from decisions reached by the Chief of Staff, the JCS, or the CCS. While General Arnold and his planning representatives had a direct channel to and a special representation on the key strategic committees of the joint and combined staff system, OPD was recognized as having superior authority in direct-

[20] (1) For early request by OPD for regular receipt of several copies of G–2 report, title: Axis Situation and Capabilities of the Enemy, see memo, WPD for G–2, 16 Mar 42, sub: Est of Situation and Capabilities of Enemy, OPD 380 Axis, 3. (2) For assignment of G–2 liaison officers, see memo, SGS for G–2, 20 Mar 42, no sub, OPD 210.3, 16.

[21] Testimony of Brig Gen W. W. Bessell, Jr., 17 Nov 45, in Rpt of Com on Int Activities (Lovett Board), WDCSA 350.09 TS (1945). Cf. testimony of Col R. S. Bratton, 16 Nov 45, in the same report.

[22] Testimony of Lt Gen Hull, 17 Nov 45, in Rpt of Com on Int Activities (Lovett Board), WDCSA 350.09 TS (1945).

[23] (1) D/F, WPD for AGF, AAF, and SOS, 24 Mar 42, sub: Expediting Paper Work, OPD 312, 3. (2) Cf. D/F, WPD for AAF, 24 Mar 42, sub: Almt of Acft for Alaska, OPD 452 ADC, 1.

[24] Memo for rcd, 16 Mar 42, sub: Outline of Meeting Held Today, March 16, etc., OPD 320, 59. The main point of discussion was the "determination of where the responsibility rested for decisions and the issuances of directives in regard to air equipment outside the United States or between Theaters." The meeting agreed as first stated by Brig. Gen. M. S. Fairchild, senior Air Forces representative, that the "Army Air Forces as such had nothing to do with regard to decisions of movements and that they needed directives telling them what to do from WPD."

ing all Army overseas activities, including the commitment of air forces to theaters of operations.[25] In effect the Air Forces, as specialists in a critical sphere of Army activities, informally enjoyed a unique position as staff advisers on aircraft development and air operations. General Arnold's place in the joint and combined hierarchy was indicative of this fact. The old differences of opinion between the Army Air Forces and the War Department General Staff were also minimized by the assignment of a considerable number of Air officers to OPD and the other divisions of the General Staff.[26] The strategic direction of air units in the theaters of operations, a function legally transferred to OPD as of 9 March 1942, depended upon data and recommendations from General Arnold's staff to a degree far exceeding similar dependence of the Army Ground Forces staff.[27] OPD's responsibility in comparison with that of the Air Staff remained superior, in the sense that it was more inclusive, much as General Marshall's authority remained superior to General Arnold's. Despite the special privileges it enjoyed in influencing strategic plans and decisions, General Arnold's headquarters did not dispute the final authority of General Marshall's headquarters or the need for a joint air-ground staff to advise the Chief of Staff. The high priority accorded to the air arm in the wartime scramble for men and equipment reconciled the Army Air Forces to its

dominion status within the Army, the Air "autonomy" within the commonwealth of the Army that had been recognized in principle in 1941.

Since Army Ground Forces under General McNair was occupied with its tremendous job of mobilizing and training ground units, it had comparatively fewer contacts with OPD than either the Air Forces or the Service Forces. Most of them concerned the preparation for overseas movement of ground combat units and their service components. OPD issued general troop movement directives controlling schedules, preparations, and final movements to ports of embarkation. It worked closely with Army Ground Forces on these matters just as, in the case of air or service units, OPD worked with Army Air Forces and Services of Supply. Through G–1 and G–3 OPD kept in close touch with the manifold problems of procurement and training of ground combat troops, giving and receiving advice, but its staff intervention in these matters in the interests of overseas operations was seldom necessary.

The third major zone of interior command, General Somervell's Services of Supply, enjoyed a greater area of discretion than the Army Ground Forces, though less than that of the Army Air Forces, because so much of its work was of a technical character. In effect, General Somervell's organization was the logistic agency of the Army, controlling the movement of troops and matériel to the combat theaters, and the degree of responsibility which it assumed in that field rivaled OPD's responsibility for the operations themselves.[28] The Services of Supply contained all the technical and administrative staffs which had formerly ad-

---

[25] (1) AG ltr to CG AAF, 1 Jun 42, sub: WD Agency Charged with Publishing Official Commitments in Acft, AG 452.1 (5–27–42) MS–E. (2) Memo, OPD for CofS, 27 May 42, same sub, OPD 452.1, 24.

[26] The goal, never reached, was a general staff evenly divided between Ground and Air officers. See memo, SGS for CofS, 14 Feb 42, sub: Air Offs Recommended for New GS Set-Up, WDCSA 020.

[27] Memo, OPD for AAF, 16 Mar 42, sub: AAF Plans and Projects, OPD 580.4, 1.

[28] Interv, Gen D. D. Eisenhower with author, 11 Mar 47, OPD Hist Unit Interv file.

vised the Chief of Staff, normally through the General Staff. Under the new arrangement, they reported to General Somervell, who in turn reported directly to the Chief of Staff. The G–1 and G–4 Divisions attempted to supervise Army-wide policies and plans concerning manpower, production, and supply, but General Somervell's vast responsibilities and large staff made his headquarters virtually independent of control by G–1 and G–4. Only when logistic plans were closely related to theater affairs did General Somervell's programs undergo effective General Staff review. On those occasions OPD scrutinized policies and programs of first importance to Services of Supply and, if necessary, took action to secure their alteration to conform with approved strategy or to insure support for overseas operations.[29]

On the Army level, the principal tasks of OPD as the Chief of Staff's command post were, first, the translation of approved strategy and policy into Army directives, second, the organization of theater commands adequate to perform the operations called for, and third, the deployment of trained, equipped forces to the theaters. The rest of OPD's work was intermittent and special, arising from every kind of crisis which affected military operations and consequently was the business of OPD. Having discovered, by continuous monitoring of messages to and from the theaters, a shortage or a misunderstanding that threatened to interfere with scheduled operations, OPD used its strategic information gained in planning and its authority as the operations staff of the Chief of Staff to reach the most feasible solution to the problem without delay.

Thus the Chief of Staff, through his Washington command post, was able to project strategic and operational requirements across the whole field of Army activities and bring everything into line with combat needs. This emphasis on operations gave the whole War Department a single standard for organizing its efforts and a single staff for solving difficult day-to-day problems in the interests of the ultimate objective: success in battle. In this context OPD came to have a free hand in the War Department, and the OPD chief became a special kind of deputy to General Marshall, exercising his full authority in all cases that required command decisions in line with approved strategic plans and policies.

Unique Function of OPD

Besides this great source of strength in the nature of its Army-wide responsibilities, OPD had a unique asset in the information and authority it derived from participation in the principal committees of the joint and combined staff system. Actually the responsibility of representing the Army in interservice and international planning during the prewar and early post-Pearl Harbor period had been a prime factor in elevating WPD to a position of special eminence in the War Department. The prestige and power of the JCS and the CCS developed rapidly in 1942. Increasingly their deliberations and the work of the subordinate joint and combined committees determined the course of strategy. As the strategic planning staff for General Marshall in his capacity as both Chief of Staff of the Army and member of the JCS and the CCS, OPD helped lay down the foundations of strategy and military policy which, once approved by the Chief of Staff or the JCS or the CCS, provided a frame of reference for the guidance

---

[29] *Ibid.* For later specific assignment of responsibility for controlling the flow of personnel, units, and matériel to the theaters, see Ch. XIV.

of Army activities both in the theaters of operations and in the zone of interior. Having helped to formulate these interservice and international policies, OPD was the only Army agency that could issue Army directives designed to carry out joint and combined decisions. It assumed this responsibility and the corollary task of exercising General Staff supervision to insure that directives were being followed.

OPD's staff responsibility, thus firmly established, entailed the co-ordination of strategic planning for a world-wide war with actual operations in many theaters of combat and at the same time the co-ordination of the operations themselves with Army activities in the zone of interior. The extraordinary power and prestige of OPD derived simply from General Marshall's actual practice of relying heavily on it and from the ability of OPD officers to maintain his confidence by getting the results he wanted. Also, OPD had many things in its favor that made it hard for the Chief of Staff to put his greatest reliance elsewhere. Its responsibilities centered in operations in the theaters of actual combat, that is, in the end

product of all Army efforts in time of war. At the same time it was the main link connecting Army operations with joint and combined strategic plans and policies. This single staff was responsible to General Marshall for helping him in the JCS–CCS formulation of strategy, for conveying strategic instructions to commanders in the field, and for keeping informed of the efforts of Army commanders in the theaters to carry out the operations envisaged in those directions. Since the conduct of operations in the theaters depended directly on the military resources furnished from the zone of interior, this monitoring phase of OPD's work gave it a legitimate interest in the management of such enterprises in the zone of interior as affected theater operations in a critical way. The standard of operational necessity was one from which there was no appeal, and OPD was the Army's highest staff authority for applying it to Army policies and programs. Thus, in trying to insure that theater commanders could accomplish the missions assigned them, OPD in practice often co-ordinated the work of the whole War Department.

CHAPTER VIII

Inside OPD

Of the various changes brought about by the March reorganization, the innovation of an operations staff within the General Staff received the least attention outside the War Department. The Army and the interested public soon spoke familiarly of the Army Air Forces, the Army Ground Forces, and the Services of Supply, with some notion of the extent of the authority that had been delegated to General Arnold, General McNair, and General Somervell. Relatively few people knew of the existence of OPD, and fewer still appreciated General Marshall's need for such a staff. Inside the War Department the change was obvious if not well understood. OPD officers began to act under the extended grant of authority conferred on the Division. Their insistence upon speed and their readiness to assume responsibility produced hostile as well as favorable response from other Army officers with whom they dealt. These characteristics made the composite OPD officer of War Department legend a somewhat unamiable figure, but they began to produce the results for which General Marshall was looking. The basic practices adopted by OPD in the spring of 1942 soon became accepted as a matter of fact, if not necessarily applauded, by other Army agencies in Washington.

The Assistant Chief of Staff, OPD, provided General Marshall with what he had long needed, that is, one officer to whom he could turn for staff advice and staff action on any of the multitude of problems confronting the Chief of Staff as commander of the U. S. Army and its representative in joint and combined military negotiations. The OPD chief, like all staff officers, sometimes produced ideas that his immediate superior accepted and sometimes merely carried out instructions. Like most staff officers, he took decisive steps without referring them to his superior when he was confident that they were in conformity with approved objectives and policies. At other times he devised measures solely to support a policy decision by his superior. Never in the military history of the United States had a single staff officer been given so wide a range of responsibilities and such a clear authorization from the Chief of Staff to proceed aggressively in his work.

The first officer to fill this position in General Marshall's new command post was General Eisenhower, who succeeded General Gerow as Assistant Chief of Staff, WPD, on 16 February 1942 and remained as Assistant Chief of Staff, OPD, until 23 June 1942, when he departed for England to undertake the first of a series of high command assignments.[1] He was responsible for

---

[1] A Military Academy graduate in the class of 1915, 2d Lt. Dwight D. Eisenhower was promoted successively to reach the temporary rank of lieutenant colonel before the end of World War I. He never got to France, holding instead a variety of zone of interior command and instructor assignments, primarily with the new tank corps combat units. He progressed through the Army school system during the 1920's, served, 1929–33, in the Of-

setting up the staff in the new command post, for that purpose receiving broad grants of authority from the Chief of Staff and working out OPD's relations with other Army agencies as these grants required. But authority could have meant nothing had it not been paralleled by performance of assigned duties. General Eisenhower not only had to set up OPD but also had to make it work. He was able to discharge the extraordinary responsibility placed on him because he had under him a staff of carefully selected officers, organized efficiently to perform the specific tasks given them, and aided in their work by an appropriate delegation of the Division chief's authority. During his tenure in the War Department the internal organization of his Division crystallized in a form reflecting the WPD organization but designed to accommodate the new responsibility of continuous control of theater operations as well as strategic planning.

Through the decentralization of joint and combined planning inside the Division, General Eisenhower and subsequent chiefs

fice of the Assistant Secretary of War, and then in the Office of the Chief of Staff (General MacArthur), 1933–35. Still a major, he went to the Philippines for five years' service as assistant to General MacArthur, who had become Military Adviser, Commonwealth of the Philippine Islands. Upon returning to the United States as a lieutenant colonel in 1940, he held a series of assignments with increasingly larger troop units. His last post before Pearl Harbor was chief of staff of the Third Army, under the command of General Krueger. In this assignment he received his appointment as temporary brigadier general on 29 September 1941, at the age of fifty. In June 1942 General Eisenhower became commanding general in the European theater, and soon entered on his career as commander of American and British forces, first in North Africa and the Mediterranean, eventually in France and Germany. For General Eisenhower's own account of his work in the War Plans Division and the Operations Division, December 1941–June 1942, see his *Crusade in Europe*, Chs. 2–4.

of OPD who followed his precedent were enabled to act as co-ordinators of all planning and all Army operations in theaters without being personally engaged in detailed deliberations in either field. In this way the OPD chief kept the detachment and breadth of view he needed to advise General Marshall and, frequently, act for him in matters affecting strategic planning and strategic direction of the Army. General Eisenhower particularly relied on four men to whom heavy responsibilities were delegated.

The first of these was Colonel Handy, who became a brigadier general on 27 March. On the day General Eisenhower was made Assistant Chief of Staff, he designated Handy as Chief of the Strategy & Policy Group and made him the "representative of the Assistant Chief of Staff, War Plans Division, in all Joint and Combined Planning work." [2] Second, the officer to whom General Eisenhower delegated responsibilities for control of operations was the former WPD planner, Colonel Streett (brigadier general 27 March 1942). He was transferred to the Division from the discontinued Air Force Combat Command on 10 March 1942, and, upon the recommendation of General Marshall, took over the leadership of the Operations Group. [3] General Streett gave OPD an Air Forces representative at the highest level under General Eisenhower at a time of critical decisions as to the

[2] (1) Notations by Gen D. D. Eisenhower, 16 Feb 42, Item 3, OPD Hist Unit file. (2) WPD adm memo, 16 Feb 42, sub: Jt and Combined Planning, Paper 90, Item 2A, OPD Hist Unit file.
[3] (1) Memo, WPD for G–1, 3 Mar 42, sub: Dtl of Offs, OPD 210.3, 4. (2) Memo, Col Streett for Sec Chiefs, 7 Mar 42, no sub, OPD 312.11, 1. (3) Memo, CofS for Lt Gen H. H. Arnold, 20 Feb 42, no sub, WDCSA 020 (1942). General Marshall considered Colonel Streett of the caliber to qualify him to be OPD chief at some time.

deployment of air units. He remained group chief until December 1942, when he left to take command of the Third Air Force. Third, General Eisenhower relied heavily on his deputy, Brig. Gen. Robert W. Crawford, who stayed on in that capacity until 22 June. General Crawford handled special problems for the Division chief, particularly in the field of equipment and supply. In May 1942, for instance, General Eisenhower assigned him complete responsibility for following up on progress in the production of landing craft, already then beginning to be a critical factor in strategic planning.[4] Fourth, Colonel Gailey, General Eisenhower's executive officer, was responsible for organizing and maintaining administrative control over the expanding and widely diversified staff. He personally did much to set the tone adopted by action officers in OPD throughout World War II. He put a premium on speed and accuracy in every detail, demanding and frequently getting results that measured up to the exacting standards he set for OPD officers.[5]

The OPD chief, in view of the wide spread of Division responsibility for military matters affecting the work of the whole War Department had a general responsibility for giving other agencies the guidance

which participation in strategic planning and staff control of operations enabled him to give. Thus, immediately after the reorganization in 1942, General Eisenhower undertook to hold a series of conferences with officers in the Services of Supply, in which he would outline the strategic situation.[6] Even outside the War Department, the office of the Assistant Chief of Staff, OPD, acted as the official place of application for strategic or operational information. Thus, shortly after the constitution of OPD, Colonel Wedemeyer informed an officer of the British Joint Staff Mission in Washington: "Your Washington contact agency is now the Executive Officer, Operations Division, War Department General Staff. He will be able to refer you directly to the proper section for solution of any problems presented."[7]

At an early stage OPD began getting a variety of new assignments because of the special information available to its officers. General Eisenhower resisted this tendency as did his successors. Though the OPD chief was not unwilling to accept heavy responsibility, from the beginning he tried to direct every OPD effort toward one goal, channeling Army activities into direct support of military operations, and to delegate to other agencies as many of the tasks involved as they could perform. Thus, immediately upon reorganization of the War Department, OPD assumed "control of all missions," meaning the military missions set up in 1941 to expedite the flow of lend-lease munitions to such critical points as China

---

[4] Memo, Maj Gen Eisenhower for Col Gailey, 6 May 42, no sub, Book 5, Exec 8.

[5] Stories of Colonel Gailey's effective if sometimes somewhat autocratic control of the Division were given to the author by many persons, officers and civilians, on duty in the War Department during his tenure as executive. He is credited with successfully exploiting the command post responsibility in day-to-day staff work. Inside the Division some of the men who worked with Colonel Gailey were convinced that he always insisted on the impossible in order to get the nearly impossible done. In any case the working staff in the War Department for the most part considered the OPD executive office to be dedicated to arbitrariness, disagreeableness, and unreason.

[6] Memo, Hq SOS for CG SOS, etc., 24 Apr 42, sub: Conference, OPD 334.8, 2.

[7] Ltr, Col Wedemeyer to Maj E. H. Baume (Opns & Plans Div, British Jt Stf Mission), 15 Jun 42, OPD 334.8, 11.

and North Africa.[8] In less than a month, however, General Eisenhower accepted a proposal by General Somervell to transfer control of missions to the Services of Supply. Explaining his point of view, he wrote to General Somervell:

The primary interest of Operations Division, under current conditions, in missions is priority in the transfer of personnel and equipment to overseas stations. Subject to the proviso that no troops, either as units or large numbers of individuals, or equipment other than that involved in Lend-Lease agreements, will be shipped overseas without the prior approval of this Division, I will go along with you.[9]

In general, OPD was willing to divest itself of specific responsibilities whenever they could be effectively discharged by other agencies, provided that OPD could protect its own paramount interest, the conduct of military operations, by monitoring the actions taken by such agencies.

Group Organization and Duties

When recommending possible new names for WPD in mid-March, General Eisenhower listed the main elements of the administrative structure which the Division was building during these first months and which remained the basic components of OPD throughout the war: "No matter what name is given, major sub-divisions would be: *a*. Planning Division. *b*. Operations Group. *c* Resources and requirements group, to which will be assigned 'Missions.'

d. Administrative and Miscellaneous Section." [10]

The first move in grouping duties and personnel according to this scheme occurred before the effective date of the March reorganization of the whole War Department. General McNarney, in his executive committee meeting of 16 February, ordered the General Staff divisions, including WPD, to draft charts of proposed organization and present them to him by the morning of 18 February.[11]

In the intervening forty-eight hours WPD prepared a tentative chart dividing the division into four groups (Strategy & Policy, Resources & Requirements, Executive, and Operations) with a total of 140 officers.[12] General McNarney informally approved the plan but cut the number of officers to an even one hundred. The Division began converting to the new organization on 19 February 1942 and for most purposes was working in accordance with it by 21 February, though it took several weeks to complete administrative arrangements and section organization.[13]

---

[8] (1) Memo, Col Gailey for WPD and Home Offices of All Missions, 10 Mar 42, sub: Orgn of Home Offices of All Missions, Paper 84, Item 2B, OPD Hist Unit file. (2) Cf. WPD adm memo, 6 Mar 42, sub: Home Missions, Paper 88, Item 2B, OPD Hist Unit file.

[9] Memo, OPD for Lt Gen Somervell, 29 Mar 42, sub: Contl of Missions, OPD 210.684, 3.

589727 O-61—10

[10] Memo, OPD for CofS, 15 Mar 42, sub: Redesignation of WPD, OPD 321.1, 4.

[11] Min of Opening Sess, Sp Com, Reorgn of WD, 16 Feb 42, WDCSA 020 (1942). Cf. pp. 225–26.

[12] Early charts, including the one here referred to, used the name "Strategic & Policy Group," but for consistency the text in this volume uses the later, more common title, "Strategy & Policy Group."

[13] (1) WPD orgn chart, n.d., Paper 6, Item 2A, OPD Hist Unit file. Although undated, the chart was unquestionably prepared on 16 or 17 February 1942 in response to General McNarney's request. (2) For 19 February initiation of administrative procedure based on the new organization, see WPD cover sheet, 19 Feb 42, sub: Sailings of Vessels for INDIGO, MAGNET and "X," WPD 4497–37. The sections listed on this cover sheet conform in general with the draft chart of 16 or 17 February. (3) For official General Staff listing of OPD groups as of 9 March 1942, corresponding with the WPD chart

The only change in the designation of groups pursuant to the March reorganization was the elevation of Resources & Requirements to the group level, removing it from the Operations Group as constituted in the December–February transition period. Both as section and as group, it comprised a comparatively small number of officers, all dealing with logistics questions, including military requirements, resources, allocations, and priorities both in men and materials.

In contrast, the several groups themselves underwent internal changes of some significance. The Strategy & Policy Group retained its Strategy Section but delegated some of its responsibilities for joint and combined work to a new, separate section, called the Combined Subjects Section. Moreover, the officers assigned to the Joint U. S. Strategic Committee in the JCS system were established as a special section. Finally, instead of the old Plans Section, the Strategy & Policy Group had a Future Operations Section.

The Operations Group rapidly took on the character of an operational control center, organized in sections on a geographical basis. In addition to the old Atlantic and Pacific Sections, the new Operations Group had a Caribbean and Latin American Section (removed from its former position in the Plans Group); an ABDA Section for directing operations in the Australian-British-Dutch-American area, the Philippines, New Caledonia, and Australia; an Africa-Middle East Section; and a China-India

Section. A distribution of every base or operational area was made among these Operations Group sections, thus providing a specialized staff mechanism for continuous monitoring and control of all theater operations.

OPD's new group organization was set forth in the General Staff organization chart issued 2 March 1942. The chart carried a sweeping statement of duties of the Division as a whole. Its tasks included: "Preliminary studies, estimates, and plans for potential theaters of operations"; the "Preparation of directives to commanders of theaters or other task forces"; most "combined and joint planning," acting as "central control agency for operations" and as the "War Department Command Post for field operations," and the "coordination of all ground, air, and service activities required to effectuate War Department decisions pertaining to the organization and operations of task forces, theaters, defense commands, overseas possessions, and leased bases." This comprehensive list of responsibilities contrasts strongly with the vaguer list of duties assigned to WPD in similar General Staff charts of the previous fall. Particularly critical was the assignment to OPD of the great operational task of deploying troops to the theaters of operations, traditionally assigned to the G–3 Division of the War Department General Staff.

The intended relationship between the two principal groups in OPD was shown clearly in the General Staff chart of organization and duties issued on 2 March 1942. It indicated that general strategy affecting the allocation of forces to the various theaters of war and the issuance of strategic directives to theater or task forces was a Strategy & Policy matter, intimately associated with joint and combined planning.

---

of 16 or 17 February, see WDGS Orgn Chart, 2 Mar 42, OPD 320, 7.

Somewhat arbitrarily the author has selected 21 February 1942 as the date when most of the Division was working on the basis of the new organization. See OPD Hist Unit Study F. Actually the transition was gradual, beginning 19 February and ending 9 March.

The tasks of monitoring the theater commanders' activities in carrying out these directives, attempting to give them full and coordinated support of the War Department but at the same time keeping their strength and undertakings in line with approved strategy, was a function of the Operations Group. The chart specifically stated that OPD's Strategy & Policy "Branch" was responsible for making "preliminary studies, estimates, and plans for potential theaters of operations" and for preparing the "directive to commanders of theaters or other task forces." It provided, however, that "Officers charged with planning for a theater pass to the Operations Group when the commander selected for the theater joins WPD for the purpose of preparing his detailed theater plans."

The main innovation in OPD's organization between March and June 1942 affected the Operations Group. It was largely a change of name, one that reflected the new orientation of the Division, indicating an increasing awareness on the part of the Operations Group officers that their work would involve an additional unique aspect: to act in effect as the Washington rear echelon of the various theater headquarters in the field. The Operations Group itself was redesignated the Theater Group, and its sections were officially renamed "theaters." In practice the term "theater" was rarely used, and the components of the Theater Group continued to be called "theater sections." With these changes in nomenclature, General Streett realigned the theater sections to conform fairly closely with actual overseas commands.[14]

The volume of Theater Group business forced General Eisenhower to assign the largest single segment, about half, of Division personnel to General Streett. By mid-1942 this one group contained more than sixty officers. The strengths of the theater sections varied in accordance with the degree of operational activities in their respective areas, North American and Latin American being still the largest of the seven in June 1942. The officers assigned to the sections as chiefs carried heavy responsibilities on behalf of the Division. All in this period were Regular Army officers who had previous experience in WPD and all but one had been on duty before Pearl Harbor. The exception, the chief of the Asiatic Section, was chosen in January 1942 because of his specialized linguistic and geographical knowledge.

In addition to its area sections, the Theater Group contained throughout most of the war a section of specialists in the task of issuing clear, comprehensive, and timely orders for the movement of troops to the theaters of operations. Although no provision was made for such a section in the original March 1942 organization, the need was soon felt. As the Division plunged into the task of deployment to defensive bases in the Pacific and Australia, while planning even larger movements to the United Kingdom, it became clear that centralized control of troop movements was essential if co-ordinated management of the huge World War II army were to be maintained. OPD was made responsible for this task. The Theater Group was charged with this responsibility inside the Division since all of its duties cen-

---

[14] (1) Memo, Brig Gen Streett for G–2, 17 Apr 42, sub: Reorgn of Theatre Secs of Theatre Gp, etc., OPD 320, 14. (2) For initiation of the plan, see memo, Brig Gen Streett for Col K. N. Walker, Exec Theatre Gp, 6 Apr 42, sub: Preparation of Plan for Orgn and Opn of Theatre Gp, Paper 64, Item 2B, OPD Hist Unit file. (3) For section chiefs, see App. A.

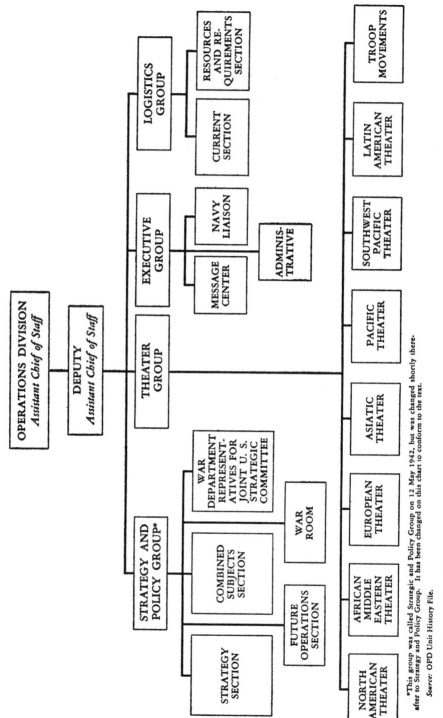

OPERATIONS DIVISION
Assistant Chief of Staff

DEPUTY
Assistant Chief of Staff

STRATEGY AND POLICY GROUP*

- STRATEGY SECTION
- FUTURE OPERATIONS SECTION
- COMBINED SUBJECTS SECTION
- WAR ROOM
- WAR DEPARTMENT REPRESENTATIVES FOR JOINT U. S. STRATEGIC COMMITTEE

THEATER GROUP

- NORTH AMERICAN THEATER
- AFRICAN MIDDLE EASTERN THEATER
- EUROPEAN THEATER
- ASIATIC THEATER
- PACIFIC THEATER
- SOUTHWEST PACIFIC THEATER
- LATIN AMERICAN THEATER
- TROOP MOVEMENTS

EXECUTIVE GROUP

- MESSAGE CENTER
- NAVY LIAISON
- ADMINISTRATIVE

LOGISTICS GROUP

- CURRENT SECTION
- RESOURCES AND REQUIREMENTS SECTION

*This group was called Strategic and Policy Group on 12 May 1942, but was changed shortly thereafter to Strategy and Policy Group. It has been changed on this chart to conform to the text.

Source: OPD Unit History File.

Chart 3. Operations Division, War Department General Staff: 12 May 1942

tered in dispatching units, trained and equipped for the purposes required by the theater commanders, to the theaters of operations. Consequently, immediately after the March 1942 reorganization, the following instructions were issued concerning "Overseas Movement":

1. For each movement, one order applicable to all of the Commands concerned will be issued through The Adjutant General.
2. The War Plans Division is responsible for the initiation, supervision and coordination of the preparation of the order.
3. Initially, War Plans Division will issue to the Commands concerned a basic directive for the movement.
4. Based on the War Plans Division directive, the Air Forces, Ground Forces, and Services of Supply will prepare so much of the draft of the movement order as pertains to their respective activities. As far as practicable, matters requiring coordination of the Commands will be arranged informally.
5. War Plans Division will be responsible for the final coordination of the portions of the draft applying to the Air Forces, Ground Forces, and Services of Supply.
6. The final draft will be transmitted to The Adjutant General, for publication in proper form.
7. Following transmittal of the draft to The Adjutant General, the Air Forces, Ground Forces, and Services of Supply may make changes in the order only after approval by War Plans Division.[15]

The Theater Group as a whole assumed responsibility for this duty, but the extreme decentralization of group work among the area sections made the task of co-ordination within the group almost as difficult as co-ordination between the three major zone of interior commands and the overseas theaters. Moreover, a considerable amount of co-ordinated, detailed information about

troops being moved had to be kept available in a systematic way. General McNarney, Deputy Chief of Staff, issued the following orders on 22 March 1942:

1. WPD must clear all movement orders with the Deputy Chief of Staff.
2. WPD must be able to present in connection with proposed movement orders:
    a. Whether troops are white or colored.
    b. Date of activation of unit.
    c. Amount of training (to include amount of actual firing of weapons).
    d. General efficiency rating of Commanding Officer.[16]

Accordingly, General McNarney announced a few days later that

The Operations Division prevailed upon him to approve the establishment of a troop movement section in that division . . . he had approved the establishment of a small three-officer section in the Operations Division so that it could be in close contact with all troop movements to see that no essential items have been omitted from their directives or the order moving the troops and so that exceptional items could be processed.[17]

Early in April this section was set up in the Theater Group with an allotment of three officers and with one of them, Lt. Col. Henry I. Hodes, on duty. Colonel Hodes had been loaned to the Division by G–3 previously and finally was assigned to duty in April as chief of the Troop Movements Section.[18] This section, which never had more than four officers assigned to the work, exercised a routine co-ordinating role

---

[15] Memo, TAG for WPD, 20 Mar 42, sub: Responsibility and Procedure for Preparation of O'seas Mvmt Order, OPD 370.5, 12.

[16] Memo, Exec OPD for ACofS OPD, 22 Mar 42, sub: Mvmt Orders, Tab Misc, Book 4, Exec 8.
[17] Min of Gen Council meetings, 31 Mar 42, DCofS rcds.
[18] (1) For establishment of Troop Movements Section, see memo, Brig Gen Streett for DCofS, 8 Apr 42, sub: Tr Mvmt Coordination Sec, OPD 210.3, 35. (2) For increased almt to OPD, see memo, OPD for Mil Pers Div SOS, 15 Apr 42, sub: Change in Almt of Grs to OPD, OPD 210.3, 40.

on the special problem central to most Theater Group action throughout the war. For this purpose the Troop Movements Section developed the Status Report system of central War Department control of the fitness of units for overseas movement, and established policies and issued instructions governing "Preparation for Overseas Movement" (POM) by all Army units.[19]

A unique feature and the most complicated aspect of this April–May organization of OPD was the interrelationship between the Future Operations Section of the Strategy & Policy Group and the European Theater Section of the Theater Group. Since the principal preoccupation of the officers in both these sections was the project for an early invasion of Europe from bases in the United Kingdom—the BOLERO plan written and vigorously advocated by OPD in March and April 1942—it was logical and most efficient that one man should be chief of both sections. In effect, there was only one section, with Col. John E. Hull as its chief and Lt. Col. Voris H. Connor as its executive officer and chief BOLERO planner. Three or four officers were assigned to planning for future operations other than European, and the rest of the personnel

worked on planning, troop movements, and theater control of the BOLERO project.[20] The intimate association of planning with deployment and control of operations by this dual section under Colonel Hull illustrated in miniature the principle on which OPD itself was built—the close proximity of plans and operations.

The basic problems of logistics, namely munitions production, distribution of equipment, military transportation of forces, and military supply in general, bulked very large among the factors determining strategic and operational decisions. For instance, the difficult problem of correlating the distribution of munitions and ammunition among the Allies and simultaneously equipping divisions of the United States occupied the War Department throughout the first half of 1942. Insofar as these issues intruded on strategy at the level of high command, which they often did while many critical items were in short supply, OPD handled the final staff work which enabled General Marshall to make decisions for the Army.[21] Yet, even when being considered as a factor in strategy, logistic matters required a degree of technical knowledge that staff planners would not normally possess. Similarly, if a transportation, equipment, or supply matter which could not be solved within the resources of any one area of operations should arise, OPD's theater sections were not organized to deal with the issue in its Army-wide context.

In order to acquire and draw on special logistic information in a systematic way, OPD continued to develop the former WPD

---

[19] (1) For Status Report System whereby Troop Movements Section received from the Army Ground Forces, Army Air Forces, or Services of Supply complete information on the fitness for its mission of each unit scheduled for overseas movement, see memo, OPD for AGF, AAF, and SOS, 1 Jul 42, sub: Status Rpts, OPD 370.5, 184. (2) For POM instructions, see study, n.d., title: Preparation for O'seas Mvmt, etc., incl with memo, OPD for TAG, 20 Jan 43, sub: Publication of "Preparation for O'seas Mvmt," OPD 370.5, 389/2. This document was issued by TAG, 1 February 1943, AG 370.5 (1–16–43) OB–S–E–GN–SPOT–M. It superseded instructions previously distributed as "Inclosure No. 1" with all overseas troop movement orders.

A complete file of troop movement orders, status reports, and associated papers is in the custody of Hist Rcds Sec, AG Rcds Br.

[20] (1) OPD adm memo, Col Hull, 17 May 42, no sub, OPD 321.19 OPD, 42. (2) Memo, Col Hull for Brig Gen Handy, 5 Jun 42, no sub, OPD 020.1, 7. (3) For BOLERO plan, see Ch. IX.

[21] Draft ltr, Gen Marshall to Sir John Dill, n.d., OPD 400, 1.

logistics unit, first having raised it to the status of a group. At first it was called Resources & Requirements, but by May 1942 had adopted the name of Logistics Group. The Logistics Group always had an advantage over other Army logistics agencies (G–4 and Services of Supply) because of its proximity to the OPD theater sections, which dealt with logistic factors as they affected operations in their individual areas, and because of its proximity to the Strategy & Policy planners, whose strategic calculations both determined and were influenced by the Army's logistic resources. The Logistics Group was reorganized in June 1942, and its main duties were divided between two sections. One, the Material Section, was officially described as a unit that:

1. Maintains a record for ready reference of production availability, and requirements of munitions and equipment in U. S.
2. Represents Operations Division on the following Committees:
   a. Defense Aid
   b. Munitions Allocation Board
   c. International Supply Committee
   d. War Materials Board
3. Establishes priorities for the distribution of ammunition and equipment between Army, Navy, Marines and Defense Aid recipients.[22]

The other, the Troop Section, was described as a part of OPD that:

1. Maintains a record for ready reference of:
   a. Status including strength, equipment and training of U. S. forces in, en route to, and projects for overseas theaters, bases, task and similar forces.
   b. Current statistical data required for operations and planning.
   c. Availability of forces in U. S.

2. Establishes priorities within the Army for the issue of items of equipment and equipment in which critical shortages exist.
3. Maintains a continued study of proper ratio of types of units required to maintain properly balanced forces.[23]

In addition to handling action papers for OPD when they dealt with matériel or other logistics problems and representing OPD on committees dealing with such technical matters as munitions allocations, the Troop Section of the Logistics Group produced several valuable periodical documents. One, the Weekly Status Map, which had been started in WPD's post-Pearl Harbor transition period, was continued after the reorganization until the fall of 1944, when most of the combat units were in the theaters of war.[24] A complementary tabulation, the Overseas Troop Basis, first circulated on 15 April 1942, was issued approximately monthly throughout the war, although OPD dropped the task of preparing it in mid-1944 shortly before it discontinued the issuance of the Status Map. The Overseas Troop Basis series of reports was designed primarily to give the Army Service Forces the basic data it needed for calculating Army overseas supply schedules.[25] These two documents, the Weekly Status Map showing total strength in troops and aircraft area by area, and the Overseas Troop Basis listing actual units by location or destination, provided General Marshall and the whole War De-

---

[22] OPD adm memo, 13 Jun 42, sub: Reorgn of Resources and Reqmts Sec, OPD 320, 29.

[23] *Ibid.*
[24] See Ch. V.
[25] For complete file of Overseas Troop Basis publications, 15 April 1942–1 June 1944, see Exec 101. This OPD publication was superseded by a publication called Troop List for Operations and Supply, issued by Strength Accounting and Reports Office, OCS.
For initiation of series, see: (1) memo, G–3 for WPD, 20 Mar 42, sub: Rpts on Status of O'seas Depts and Bases, OPD 320.2, 39; (2) D/F, WPD for G–3, 26 Mar 42, same sub, OPD 320.2, 39.

partment with its most reliable summary records of Army deployment.

The most important compilation prepared by the Logistics Group was the Victory Program Troop Basis. The first of these reports was prepared by the Resources & Requirements Section in December 1941 when it was still under WPD's Operations Group. It represented a necessary attempt to translate Army strategic and operational plans into terms of troop units so that munitions and supply production could be scheduled in conformity with ultimate Army needs. It took its name, like its point of departure in strategy, from the Victory Program estimate of requirements drafted in September 1941 by Major Wedemeyer.[26] The Victory Program Troop Basis determined the eventual over-all number of units to be contained in the Army, while the official War Department Troop Basis, prepared by G–3, governed the mobilization of units for the current year. The Victory Program Troop Basis not only gave G–3 a strategic guide for its calculations but also served as the standard strategic basis for the work of Army Service Forces and G–4 in the production and supply field. The Logistics Group brought out a revised Victory Program Troop Basis as of 25 May 1942 and continued to revise the estimate at approximately six-month intervals until November 1943, when production planning in general was less pressing and when OPD reorganized its Logistics Group, transferring this function to G–4.[27]

In its Logistics Group OPD had a microcosm of the vast zone of interior staffs and

agencies of the Army which were primarily concerned with supplying the two basic Army commodities, troops and matériel. Although the Logistics Group in OPD was not designed to carry on or even to supervise any of the work of procurement, training, transportation, and supply done by the Army Air Forces, the Army Ground Forces, or the Army Service Forces, its officers were expected to become sufficiently familiar with all of these programs to be able to calculate the resources of the Army in terms of troops and matériel for purposes of comparison with the calculation of Army requirements being made continuously by the other groups of OPD, the Strategy & Policy Group and the Theater Group. At the same time, in Army conferences and committees dealing with technical problems of organizing, training, equipping, transporting, and supplying troops, Logistics Group officers were qualified to talk the language of specialists and, in addition, bring to bear on these problems the knowledge of probable requirements and the operational orientation of the Chief of Staff's command post.

In addition to its planners, its theater control officers, and its logisticians, OPD contained still another category of specialists. They were specialists in collecting and disseminating the latest information available in OPD pertaining to operations, both the high-level decisions and War Department actions directly bearing on overseas operations and operational reports from overseas commands. The unit that provided OPD, the higher officials of the War Department, and the President with this service was set up as the Current Section of the Logistics Group. For some time before Pearl Harbor, WPD had found it necessary to include somewhere in its structure a unit (usually called "Current") to deal with miscellane-

<hr>

[26] See Ch. IV.

[27] Master file of Victory Program Troop Basis, December 1941–November 1943, envelope with OPD 400 WMP, 110. The series comprised seven issues: December 1941, 24 May 1942, 15 December 1942, 15 June 1943, 15 July 1943, 26 October 1943, and 22 November 1943.

ous staff problems so general or so unusual in nature that they did not fall within the province of any other unit. As WPD became larger in size, its duties more comprehensive, and its section organization better articulated, problems in this category became fewer. After Pearl Harbor the Current Section disappeared for a time, and when it reappeared in the March 1942 reorganization, its duties were still described negatively, simply as those not pertaining to any other part of OPD.[28]

The Current Section of course digested and circulated only a small part of the immense quantity of operational information received from overseas, reporting new items which deserved circulation on high levels in the War Department, and paying special attention to combat action. This work had very little to do with that of Logistics Group. As Col. Thomas D. Davis, Logistics Group chief, observed, the Current Section was "appended as an administrative fiction" and actually operated with complete independence of the group.[29] About the only continuous duty of Current Section at this time, one which it performed throughout the war, was assigning code names for the security of military operations, a task which OPD inherited from WPD.[30]

The direction in which Current Section was to develop was determined to a great extent by the officer designated as its chief in June 1942, Col. Thomas North. He had arrived in OPD in March 1942 and had been assigned as assistant to General Craw-

ford, OPD deputy chief. In this capacity he developed a staff enterprise that provided OPD with its most reliable summary record of Army activities on the War Department level during World War II. Toward the end of March 1942 General Eisenhower instructed Colonel North to prepare daily a brief summary of OPD actions, including major decisions by the JCS or the CCS.[31] On 29 March 1942 the first issue of the "1700 Report" appeared. It was written in the form of a letter, dated with the time of day (5:00 P. M.) from which its name developed, and addressed to the Assistant Chief of Staff, OPD, the Secretary of War, the Chief of Staff, the Deputy Chief of Staff, the Army Air Forces, and the Services of Supply. Subsequently, G–2 was added to the list of addresses. The Army Ground Forces never was put on the formal distribution list. The 1700 Report contained three sections: (1) Messages Received and Action Taken, (2) Other Action Taken, and (3) Plans. The last section consisted primarily of JCS and CCS actions.[32] It continued to be brought out until the end of the war, though it was renamed the OPD Diary and its form changed to present information by geographical area.[33]

When Colonel North became chief of the Current Section, he brought the task of

---

[28] (1) WPD orgn chart, n.d., Paper 6, Item 2A, OPD Hist Unit file. (2) OPD roster, 2 May 42, sub: Orgn of OPD, OPD Hist Adm file.

[29] Memo, Col Davis for ACofS OPD, 15 Sep 42, sub: Reduction of Commissioned Pers, Logistics Gp, OPD, OPD 210.3, 126.

[30] AG ltr, 10 Mar 42, sub: Code Words to Designate Plans, Projects, Localities, etc., AG 311.5 (3–10–42) MC–MD–M.

[31] OPD adm memo, 29 Mar 42, sub: Daily Rpt to CofS, OPD 319.1, 1.

[32] 1700 Report, 20 Mar 42–23 Apr 43, Current Gp files, AG Rcds Br.

[33] OPD Diary, 24 Apr 43–2 Sep 45, Current Gp files, AG Rcds Br.

The Current Section also produced a Situation Summary for fairly wide distribution in the War Department and (later) to the overseas theater headquarters. See: (1) War Department Daily Situation Summary, 11 Jun 42–3 Aug 43, OPD 350.05 (Fourteen Sections); (2) file of situation summaries, 5 Aug 43 through last issue, 18 Aug 45, in OPD 319.1; (3) for first issue in message form see msg, Col Handy for Theater Comdrs, 4 Aug. 43, CM-OUT 1174–1184.

preparing the 1700 Report with him. He also assumed the responsibility his predecessor had borne for screening incoming messages for the chief of the Division and getting important ones to him with minimum delay.[34] From these messages and other information available in OPD, his section prepared the War Department Daily Operational Summary and its modified version, the White House Summary. Upon the request of the Chief of Staff, WPD planners had begun to produce these two reports shortly after Pearl Harbor and had continued to do so on an *ad hoc* basis until Current Section took them over.[35] The concentration of all these informational activities in Colonel North's section made it into a special information service staff for OPD and the Army high command. It was the staff which gathered and disseminated current information about U. S. Army plans and operations, information available only in OPD. The Daily Operational Summary and the White House Summary were produced by Current Section for the rest of the war period.

The mechanics of organizing and maintaining administrative control over a large staff whose work was as diversified and decentralized as OPD's required an efficient service establishment. Its chief was the executive officer of the Division, Colonel Gailey. He and his principal assistant, who worked in the outer office through which passage to the private quarters of the Division chief was obtained, constituted the executive office proper. Duties there were always flexible, concerned with detailed matters, and primarily focused on procedure and administration.

The executive officer's first obligation was to protect the Assistant Chief of Staff from all interruptions that did not directly relate to the Division chief's task of supervising the integration of plans with operations. His second obligation was to see that the Division was run with maximum administrative efficiency. To this end he took on any responsibility that did not fit elsewhere.[36] Above all, the executive officer had to occupy himself with supervising in intimate detail the functioning of the complicated Executive Group machinery, which made it possible for the whole staff to attend to its business.

The principal components of this machinery were an Administrative Section comprising three officers, handling personnel management and miscellaneous paper work problems, the OPD message center, comprising six officers, and the OPD record room. In the new structure the former civilian administrative components were placed under military chiefs, although most of the individual civilian employees continued in their former work. In addition the Executive Group exercised general supervision over the registered documents room, established on 31 March 1940 to make easily available the use of registered, that is accountable, documents, particularly formal war plans, and at the same time establish central control over them. The actual or-

---

[34] OPD adm memo, 10 Jun 42, sub: Messages, OPD 311.23, 40.

[35] See Ch. V.

[36] Duties included establishing contact with and providing office services for task force officers detailed to temporary duty in OPD, arranging inoculations for OPD officers, and supervising over 200 enlisted male clerks on duty with the War Department General Staff. For example, see: (1) OPD adm memo, 20 Apr 42, no sub, OPD 210.3, 45; (2) memo, Maj James Stack for Col Gailey, 21 Oct 43, no sub, OPD 321.19 OPD, 27; (3) memo, OPD for Dir of Pers, SOS, 8 Dec 42, sub: Release of Under-Age Off and Asgmt of Over-Age Off, OPD 210.3, 14.

ganization and administration of the document collection was entrusted to Miss Alice M. Miller, veteran civilian clerk and Division research specialist, who served in this capacity as well as in that of chief clerk of the Combined Subjects Section, where joint and combined papers were filed.[37] This general organization and comparatively heavy staffing of the Executive Group remained intact throughout the war, reflecting the size of the Division, the press of work, and the urgency of prompt action on operational problems.[38]

Records, Procedures, and Personnel

Speed in handling correspondence, especially messages, had become critical to the control of every operation as soon as military operations had begun. The system of dispatching and receiving all correspondence through the Adjutant General's Office had several drawbacks, the most important of which was that the office did not act fast enough. As a result, War Department agencies tended either to bypass the Adjutant General's Office entirely or act on the basis of informal notification which the Adjutant General's Office would later formally corroborate.[39] The decisions of the General Staff and the headquarters of the three major zone of interior commands built up

their own unique records collections, referring to The Adjutant General only matters of routine or obsolete files for permanent record.

The problem of handling the message correspondence with overseas commands was particularly acute.[40] The War Department acted to improve the system in general as part of the March reorganization. On 1 April 1942 the War Department Classified Message Center (WDCMC) was set up. The sole responsibility of the new agency, directly under the Secretary of the General Staff, was the prompt receipt, distribution, and dispatch of classified messages. It established a single numbering system for all messages entering and all messages leaving the War Department. It made distribution of messages received from the field and dispatched messages prepared by the General Staff and the three major commands.[41] From 1 April 1942, all the classified messages which came into the War Department were filed serially by number (CM-IN series, with a new series beginning each month). All those dispatched by the War Department were filed serially by number (CM-OUT series, with a new series beginning each month). The numbers were assigned in chronological order so the file

---

[37] (1) OPD adm memo, 31 Mar 42, sub: Registered Documents Room, OPD, Paper 73, Item 2B, OPD Hist Unit file. (2) Cf. OPD adm memo, 13 Aug 43, sub: Registered Docs Room, OPD, OPD 311.5, 149.

[38] For a detailed description of paperwork procedure in OPD, see OPD Hist Unit Study M.

[39] (1) For regulations transferring the wartime functions of AGO in processing correspondence, see WD Cir 59, 2 Mar 42. (2) For a discussion of the prewar and wartime systems, including a step-by-step description of the handling of correspondence in OPD, see Nelson, *National Security and The General Staff*, pp. 470–80.

[40] The prize example of misfortune in sending military messages is that of the 7 December 1941 message to Pearl Harbor, which should have arrived before the attack but actually, by a series of accidents, was on its way to the offices of the commanders (ironically, in the hands of a messenger boy of Japanese descent) when the attack was launched. S Doc 244, 79th Cong, 1st sess, *Investigation of the Pearl Harbor Attack: Report of the Joint Committee on the Investigation of the Pearl Harbor Attack,* pp. 224–26.

[41] (1) AG ltr, 24 Mar 42, sub: WDCMC, AG 312.11 (3–20–42) MC–WD–M. (2) OPD adm memo, 6 Apr 42, sub: Messages, Paper 65, Item 2B, OPD Hist Unit file. (3) Cf. WD Cir 59, 2 Mar 42.

could be consulted either by date or number.[42]

OPD's message center, working in close liaison with the War Department Classified Message Center (messages were dispatched and received by pneumatic tube), was able to work much more efficiently under the new system. The OPD message center continued to receive incoming messages, sent to OPD either for action or information, distribute them to the proper sections of OPD, dispatch outgoing messages, and keep the Division's own serial file of messages for ready reference. The pace of work in the message center was fast and steady. Twenty-four-hour service was essential, and prompt and accurate handling of messages was demanded by the executive office and the theater sections, which received most of the messages requiring OPD action. During the first six months of operation of the new message system OPD handled, though it did not necessarily take staff action on, almost half of all the messages received or sent by the War Department.[43] Approximately three fourths were incoming messages, and one fourth outgoing. Normally about one fifth of the messages handled by the OPD message center required (in the case of incoming) or represented (in the case of outgoing) action by OPD.[44]

The official OPD records were maintained separately from the message files, although duplicate copies of messages were often inserted in the files and appropriate references were inserted in the records files whenever a message was part of the formal action relevant to a case recorded in the OPD files. The OPD record room file, started fresh on the War Department decimal system as of 1 March 1942, contained nearly all the official papers of the Division.[45] Outside it were the message file (in the message center), formal joint and combined papers (kept in Strategy & Policy Group), and the random collection of papers and Limited Distribution messages which were particularly important or which had to be kept particularly secure. The last collection continued to be kept in the executive office for the use of the Division chief and Colonel Gailey.[46]

The personnel in OPD expanded with the steadily increasing weight of World War II duties both in connection with strategic planning and with the direction of operations in the theaters. To bring the officers on duty to something like the number allotted in the reorganization and to help with the new duties incumbent on OPD, General Eisenhower selected 25 officers (15 from the Air Corps and 10 from GHQ) for addition to the Division "as a result of the new organization."[47] These officers (only one of General Eisenhower's list was not assigned) formally joined 10 March 1942, although some had been on duty a few days earlier.

Early in May the Division requested new officers again, citing as reasons the loss of a number of experienced officers, the necessity of having several key men always on "orientation and inspection trips to their respective theaters," the need to have of-

---

[42] (1) OPD Msg File, Hist Rcds Sec, AG Rcds Br. (2) For handling messages inside the Division, see WPD adm memo, 26 Feb 42, sub: Procedure for WPD Msg Cen, and All Secs of WPD, Paper 87, Item 2A, OPD Hist Unit file.

[43] Memo, Lt Col C. H. Muir for Exec OPD, 28 Oct 42, sub: Msg Cen Pers, OPD 320, 36.

[44] For work of OPD message center, see OPD Hist Unit Study L.

[45] For inauguration of the decimal system, see OPD adm memo, 1 Mar 42, no sub, Paper 85, Item 2A, OPD Hist Unit file.

[46] This "Exec" collection has been particularly valuable and is extensively cited in this history.

[47] Memo, OPD for G–1, 3 Mar 42, sub: Dtl of Offs, OPD 210.3, 4.

ficers on 24-hour duty in sections controlling active theaters, and the detail of several officers to work on the Canadian, Mexican, and Brazilian Defense Boards. Accordingly, as of 23 May 1942, OPD's allotment of officers was raised to a total of 157, exclusive of the 5 general officers then on duty in the Division. This strength proved to be a stable personnel ceiling for OPD for many months. On 23 June 1942, the official end date of General Eisenhower's incumbency as Assistant Chief of Staff, 140 officers were on duty in OPD. Personnel to fill the additional spaces were either under orders or had been requested for assignment.[48]

The clerical and stenographic assistance necessary for the dispatch of OPD's rapidly expanding operational correspondence required increases in the staff rendering this assistance roughly proportionate to increases in officer strength. Between February and June the number of civilian employees, clerks, and stenographers rose from about 85 to about 115.[49] This comparatively modest expansion of the civilian staff was far from being the whole story. Concurrently OPD added to its roster an enlisted detachment, considered appropriate for service in the Chief of Staff's command post despite the fact that the War Department General Staff never before had used the services of enlisted men. At the end of March 1942 the War Department activated the "Headquarters Detachment, GHQ," Washington, D. C., with a strength

of between 100 and 150.[50] This increase brought the clerical and stenographic staff, enlisted and civilian, to a little less than twice the size of the staff of commissioned officers, a ratio which proved adequate to the performance of Division duties.

The New Planning Process

The primary task of the Strategy & Policy Group in OPD was planning for the Army and representing the Army in the staff work which co-ordinated Army strategic ideas with those of other military agencies of the United States and the United Nations. The work of WPD in the same field had built up a strategic heritage of planning for S&P and in fact provided many of the experienced planners who carried on as what General Hull once called the "brain trust" of the Army.[51] Working in close proximity to theater section officers whose tasks concerned the immediate operational problems in the theaters of operations, the planners were able to base their plans on an up-to-date appraisal of theater needs in the light of Army-wide resources. At the same time the planners gave the operational control officers the framework of strategic assumptions required for building and readjusting the strength of the various overseas forces. Especially valuable was reliable information about the strategy being evolved in joint and combined deliberations, in which S&P offices participated. Thus S&P contributed

---

[48] (1) Memo, OPD for G–1, 2 May 42, sub: Dtl of Offs, OPD 210.61, 2. (2) Memo, TAG for OPD, 23 May 42, sub: Almt of Offs for Dy with OPD, WDGS, OPD 210.3, 68. (3) Memo, OPD for TAG, 12 Jun 42, sub: Offs on Dy in District of Columbia and Vicinity, Item 3, Exec 15.

[49] (1) WPD Civ Pers roster, 16 Feb 42, Paper 76, Item 2A, OPD Hist Unit file. (2) OPD roster of Div Employees, 13 May 42, Paper 53, Item 2B, OPD Hist Unit file.

[50] (1) Memo, OPD for TAG, 23 Mar 42, sub: Hq Det for Office of ACofS, WPD, OPD 220.3 Hq Det, GHQ, 1. (2) AG ltr to CO Hq Co, Washington Prov Brigade, 24 Mar 42, sub: Almts of Grs and Atzd Strs, AG 221 (3–18–42) EA–A. (3) AG ltr to CG Hq Det, GHQ, 7 Jul 42, sub: Almt of Grs and Atzd Str, DEML, to Hq Det, GHQ, Washington, D. C., AG 221 (7–2–42) EA–SD.

[51] Pers ltr, Maj Gen Hull to Lt Gen W. B. Smith, 23 Nov 44, Paper 1475, Book 24, Exec 9.

the general strategic information which, supplemented by precise operational information, gave OPD as a division an unequalled fund of knowledge about strategy and operations.

The chief of S&P, in addition to occupying one of the top positions of responsibility in OPD, acted as the Army planner on the main American and British-American strategic planning committees. The channel between the chief of S&P and the Chief of Staff on JCS and CCS matters was direct and unobstructed. The group ordinarily drafted notes, with recommendations, on every staff paper introduced in the joint and combined committees. On proposed actions involving a memorandum from the Chief of Staff for the JCS, the chief of S&P discussed the notes with the chief of OPD if he thought the matter important enough, and in any case dispatched them directly to the Chief of Staff's office. Copies were filed, with the pertinent papers, in the S&P record room and copies furnished the executive officer. On JCS and CCS papers to be taken up at formal meetings, the chief of S&P always briefed the chief of OPD and then went with him to brief the Chief of Staff orally, usually at the same time that the Air planner briefed General Arnold. Both OPD officers normally accompanied General Marshall, General Arnold, and the Air planner to JCS and CCS meetings.[52]

Besides the Army planner, several other officers from S&P worked in the joint and combined committee system throughout the war. They served as members of the Joint U. S. Strategic Committee, later known as the Joint War Plans Committee. In this capacity they took part in the detailed, preliminary discussion of a great many matters which had been referred by the JCS to the JPS, and helped to prepare drafts of papers for consideration by the JPS and—if approved by the JPS—on a higher level.[53] Studying future plans in administrative and intellectual proximity with the Strategy Section and the Combined Subjects (later renamed Policy) Section of S&P, the OPD officers working in the joint system were well qualified to represent the point of view of the Army on strategy, and they consulted frequently with their colleagues in S&P on the extent to which this point of view ought or had to be shifted in the interests of interservice compromise and adjusted to the demands of coalition warfare.

Thus, under the Army planner was a section (Strategy) for drafting strategic studies and reviewing joint and combined papers on strategy. There was also a section (Combined Subjects) for drafting and reviewing joint and combined policy proposals, initiating Army action designed to carry out joint and combined decisions, and following up to see that instructions had been received and understood. Finally, there was a full-time working committee (Army section of the JUSSC and, later, the JWPC) to draft joint plans and studies in collaboration with planners from the Navy and the Army Air Forces.

Thus, as far as the Army was concerned, there were two parallel chains of Administrative responsibility involving the same individual officers, one running from the working-level joint strategy planners through the JPS to the JCS, the other running from the working level in S&P, through the chief of S&P (and the chief of

---

[52] Memo, Brig Gen G. A. Lincoln for author, 3 Dec 47, sub: Hist of OPD, p. 16, OPD Hist Unit Comment file.

[53] For the reconstitution of the JUSSC in the spring of 1943 as the JWPC, for the work of the JWPC, and for OPD membership, see Ch. XIII.

OPD) to the Chief of Staff. The key position of the Army planner in both chains contributed greatly to the efficient co-ordination of Army planning.[54] The anonymity with which joint planning was carried on made it more and more difficult as the war went on to tell when a strategic idea stopped being merely an Army idea and started being a joint policy. In any case, the affinity of thought between OPD (S&P) and the Army's strategic planners in the joint committee system was usually pronounced, and it was OPD's policy to foster as close a relationship as possible.

The New Theater Orientation

The work of the Theater Group was usually more prosaic than that of the S&P planners, more voluminous, and more detailed. Nevertheless, the Theater Group chief was on a level with the S&P chief, and, like him, was responsible to the OPD chief for consistent, enlightened decisions reflecting both OPD's strategic and operational responsibilities. Thus, while the theater sections were positively oriented toward getting the resources their theaters needed, they operated in a framework that made their work realistic and amenable to the superior reasoning of strategic and logistic necessity. The close, day-to-day contact between officers working on strategic plans and officers performing the function of theater control meant that both tasks could be accomplished in harmony and could be performed on the basis of accurate information and realistic estimates of both strategic and operational situations. In the last analysis, it was always the Theater Group's control of

---

[54] The key position of the chief of S&P was reinforced late in the war by his position in the SWNCC system. See Ch. XVI.

deployment of troop units, the central core of all its work, that made strategic decisions binding on the theaters of operations.

The comprehensive scope of OPD's interest in Army activities affecting overseas theaters required Theater Group officers to work long and hard on the "pick and shovel" work prerequisite to solving operational problems arising in the theaters. A vast amount of legwork and informal telephonic co-ordination lay behind nearly all completed actions. It was the activities of these Theater Group officers, canvassing every agency of the War Department in the interests of their respective theaters, that earned for OPD the reputation of a supergeneral staff. Officers elsewhere in the War Department, whether willingly or reluctantly, came to realize that a lieutenant colonel in a theater section of OPD, using the lever of operational necessity and the special strategic information available only in OPD, could reach a decision which, assuming it was plausible enough to stand scrutiny by his superiors in OPD, was binding on the theater concerned, indirectly on all other theaters, on the three major zone of interior commands, and on the rest of the General Staff.

The Theater Group, as the staff agency for exercising the Chief of Staff's command function in each operational theater, had to maintain close working relationship with nearly every Army agency. Whereas other War Department agencies were responsible for individual or specially related Army activities, the Theater Group was responsible for the ultimate purpose of the whole activity—military operations. Its decisions prevailed in most cases of controversy. The Theater Group officers carried theater requests through with a minimum of conflict because, first, they had better sources of strategic and operational information, and second, they worked in constant and intimate relationship with the staffs of other Army agencies, particularly with the General Staff and the three major zone of interior commands.

Since OPD's Theater Group was responsible for supporting the commanding officers in theaters of operations, securing for them whatever kind of assistance they needed, its business proved to be everybody's business. For example, though not responsible for personnel policy or personnel assignment, matters which were handled by G–1 and the personnel division of Services of Supply, OPD issued instructions that all movements of individual officers to and from overseas garrisons had to be cleared, at least informally, with the OPD theater sections concerned if they involved: "(1) Officers in the grade of colonel and above. (2) Officers on special missions. (3) Officers relieved from or assigned to the General Staff Corps. (4) Officers below the grade of colonel who will relinquish command or who will assume command of separate posts, camps, detachments or special forces." [55] Generally comparable was the Theater Group's work in the special field of supply, normally the affair of G–4 and the Services of Supply. OPD theater sections followed closely the elaboration of supply and equipment programs, just as it followed G–3's work with troop unit organization, and monitored actual troop movements by Army Ground Forces, Army Air Forces, and Services of Supply. Liaison with G–2

was naturally more one-sided, with the Theater Group drawing on G–2 for information concerning enemy order of battle, terrain studies, and "conditions in Theater other than strictly military." Through informal liaison, OPD theater sections also tried to let G–2 know what it "might be expected to furnish in the future" in order to plan work accordingly.[56]

As an officer who worked in the Theater Group for three years pointed out, the group's problems were as broad as those of a normal general staff, time was pressing, and the premium was on immediate results:

The problems of the separate sections were, generally speaking, divided into the staff categories, G–1, G–2, G–3, and G–4. General Staff problems assigned to the various sections were solved by the officers in close liaison with all agencies of the War Department. They often worked under pressure against time. During early periods of the war, many actions were taken without prior precedent in the War Department. One of the foremost requirements seemed to be, "get a sound, workable solution" and apply the lessons learned in meeting subsequent problems of a like nature. Careful liaison was always maintained with overseas commanders in the interests of solving both current and future problems.[57]

In all of its work with the rest of the General Staff and the zone of interior commands, the Theater Group took the attitude that the theater commanders had to be given the resources they needed to carry out their missions or if that was impossible, advised fully why their needs could not be met. General Marshall himself was insistent on

---

[55] (1) Memo, OPD for Dir of Pers, SOS, 26 Jun 42, sub: Orders for Offs, OPD 210.3, 97. (2) Memo, Col H. A. Barber, Chief Latin American Sec, Theater Gp for ACofS OPD, 26 Jun 42, sub: Processing of Orders for Mvmt of Individual Offs to and from O'seas Garrisons, OPD 210.3, 97.

[56] Memo, Col A. D. Reid, Chief European Sec, Theater Gp, for Col C. W. McCarthy, Liaison Sec, 8 Feb 44, sub: Info Desired from and Recommendations Relative to Reorgn of MIS, OPD 320 WD, 20.

[57] Memo, Lt Col J. P. McKnight for Chief Theater Gp, 6 Sep 45, sub: Hist of OPD, OPD 321.19 OPD, 106/5.

this point.[58] One of the clearest indications of the systematic way in which OPD from the very beginning proposed to carry out its obligations to the theater commanders was the institution of the Ten-Day Summary in May 1942. By successive issue of this series throughout the war the theater sections reported regularly to their respective theater commanders the current status of War Department action on requests made by the theaters and current issues affecting them.[59] Through this kind of close relationship with all kinds of operational problems in the field, the Theater Group became the Washington headquarters of each theater commander. It was primarily responsible, on behalf of OPD and the Chief of Staff, for conveying to theater commanders the feeling, as one of them expressed it to General Marshall in a letter of appreciation for OPD's services, "that the utmost consideration was given to all recommendations submitted . . . and that the maximum assistance possible, consistent with other commitments of the War Department, would be rendered. . . ."[60]

Basic Administrative Practices

The chief of OPD of course could not follow in detail all the actions taken every day by each officer in his Division. Just as General Marshall delegated heavy responsibilities to him, the Assistant Chief of Staff, OPD, delegated his responsibilities as much as possible to his staff officers. He signed only the most important papers, permitting his group and section chiefs to issue them in his name if they fell within the area of responsibility assigned to them. The executive officer was permitted to sign routine correspondence not falling within the province of any particular group or section.[61] This delegation of authority was one of the basic procedures adopted by General Eisenhower and his successors in order to get the Division's work done.

As a result, the formal written concurrence virtually went by the board, and the staff co-ordination system was developed to a high pitch of efficiency. The individual action officer customarily bypassed the official lines of authority and instead informally consulted officers in other sections of OPD or in other agencies. He advised them of his proposed solution to the problem under consideration, that is, the action he thought OPD should take. On this informal basis criticisms and counterrecommendations could be freely and quickly exchanged. If the officers consulted gave their personal opinion that the action finally agreed on was satisfactory, the matter was said to have been co-ordinated with them. Their superior officers in positions of authority were not committed by a formal concurrence, but an opportunity had been provided for a special point of view to be brought to bear on the problem, serious oversights to be noted, and fresh ideas suggested.

By following this procedure OPD officers undoubtedly made some mistakes that could have been avoided in the course of the formal consideration that would have followed had the Assistant Chief of Staff,

---

[58] For example, see memo, CofS for WPD, 18 Mar 42, sub: Jt Army-Navy Plans for Alaska, OPD 381 Alaska, 6.

[59] OPD adm memo, 12 Jun 42, sub: Periodic Summaries, Paper 48, Item 2B, OPD Hist Unit file. Periodic summaries dispatched as messages are filed chronologically under a subfile heading for each theater in OPD 319.1 file. The first summaries were prepared in May 1942 for the Pacific commands.

[60] Ltr, Lt Gen M. F. Harmon to Gen Marshall, 26 Jul 44, Paper 1010, Book 21, Exec 9.

[61] OPD (Opns Gp) adm memo, 19 Mar 42, sub: Signature on Papers Initiated by Opns Gp, etc., Paper 77, Item 2B, OPD Hist Unit file.

OPD, sought written concurrences from the heads of all the agencies concerned. But decisions thus made often would have come too late to have any effect whatever, a consequence usually more disastrous than a wrong decision. By the procedure actually employed OPD gained the benefit of the knowledge and reflections of the rest of the War Department on staff actions and yet maintained the speed essential to most of OPD's work on behalf of the theaters of operations.[62]

This technique was all the more important because of the scope of OPD's duties. In almost every case up for action, some other War Department agency had a legitimate interest. In many cases the co-ordination was extensive. For example, in June 1942 the Division chief characteristically instructed his senior planner: "We will have to prepare an answer for the Chief of Staff's signature. You will have to consult the Theater Group and the Army Air Forces. On reduction of unescorted ship movements the SOS will have something to say." [63]

This co-ordination, especially important for tapping the special knowledge of officers in other agencies, also made it possible to tap the unique collection of information available in the various sections of OPD. Although OPD officers were encouraged to establish "informal direct contact with officers in other sections or groups for the purpose of exchanging information or securing informal concurrences," a formal administrative channel for routing papers between groups in OPD was evolved in order that the location and handling of papers might

be made a matter of record.[64] The action papers in OPD indicate the care usually taken by OPD officers in referring cases widely within the Division.

At the same time OPD never lost sight of the prime purpose of the co-ordination system, prompt arrival at a reasonable solution by the action officer who had been assigned a case. The spirit in which the Division worked from the beginning was exemplified in a note passed along by order of Colonel Harrison, an experienced plans officer, in sending an official memorandum for dispatch by General Crawford, Division deputy chief. Colonel Harrison left word that the "need for speed and the purely factual nature of the study prompted him to by-pass Gen. Handy," then chief of S&P.[65]

All this decentralization and emphasis on speed reflected the fact that OPD officers lived in the atmosphere of a real command post in the field. Overseas operations could not wait. General Marshall would not wait. Staff actions initiated in the Office of the Chief of Staff received priority treatment and were sent back for General Marshall's signature within twenty-four hours if any way possible.[66] It was reported at a General Council meeting in 1942: "Last week a letter was sent to the Operations Division for draft of reply for signature of the Chief of Staff. At the time the Chief was out

---

[62] Interv, Lt Gen Hull with author, 3 Jul 47, OPD Hist Unit Interv file.

[63] Memo, Brig Gen Handy for Col Wedemeyer, 22 June 42, no sub, Tab Misc, Book 5, Exec 8.

[64] Memo, Col C. W. Stewart, Exec Theater Gp for Theater Chiefs, 19 Sep 42, sub: Routing of Papers Through OPD, OPD 312, 29.

[65] Informal memo, Lt Col Godwin Ordway for Brig Gen Crawford, 9 Apr 42, atchd to memo, OPD for Secretariat JCS, 9 Apr 42, sub: Acft Allocations in Australia, OPD 452.1, 1.

[66] These papers for the Chief of Staff were called "Green Hornets" in reference to the green cardboard cover affixed to them for purposes of easy identification, to the speed with which they were supposed to "fly" through the office, and to the "sting" experienced from holding them too long.

of the office. When he returned in about an hour the draft of the reply was on its way. This is the ultimate to be desired." [67]

Despite the great emphasis which each Assistant Chief of Staff, OPD, put on decentralization of authority, he kept in intimate contact with the day-to-day work of the Division. He was able to become familiar with the main themes of the development of strategic plans and policies by frequent conferences with the chief of S&P and by attendance at the JCS and the CCS meetings. The diversified detailed work of the Theater Group was more difficult to follow. In order to keep the Division chief thoroughly informed in this field as well as aware of more miscellaneous issues being considered by the other groups of OPD, the Morning Meetings were instituted.

Daily the Division chief received a comprehensive report on current operations in the theaters. The theater sections of the Theater Group each had an officer select significant information from all messages and reports received from the field every day. Maps were prepared which outlined the situation in the various theaters. At 0800 the group chiefs, section chiefs, and officers designated to present the reports assembled in the office of the executive officer and proceeded to the office of the chief of OPD. For a period of about an hour the sections presented the operational situation in their respective theaters as of the previous twenty-four hours. In addition to covering the operational movements and location of units in the battle areas, the officers reported on the arrival and departure of troops, the enemy situation as known, and changes in command. Immediately after the presentation by the sections, group and section chiefs noted any special matters of interest in their current work. On the basis of this meeting the chief of OPD proceeded, with a summary report of the same kind, to the morning meeting of the Chief of Staff. [68] These meetings in General Marshall's office were originally private sessions attended only by the chiefs of OPD and G–2. Gradually they developed into more formal occasions attended by the commanding generals of the three major zone of interior commands, but presentations of information continued to come only from OPD and G–2. At this point the staff occupations of the chief of OPD were placed before General Marshall and his principal War Department subordinates. This procedure insured that the Chief of Staff was well informed about Army plans and operations, and it was one of the ways that the Assistant Chief of Staff, OPD, kept in close touch with General Marshall's major policy objectives. [69]

A device by which the Chief of Staff kept in touch not only with the Washington side of theater operations but also with conditions in the theaters themselves, was the continuous dispatch of OPD officers to the field. The successive chiefs of the Division themselves all took trips into the field for the Chief of Staff, beginning with an exploratory visit to the United Kingdom by General

[67] Min of Gen Council meetings, 12 Oct 42, DCofS rcds. In such cases OPD often went to work simply on oral instructions from the Chief of Staff or some one in his office. Often OPD kept only a very informal record of the action taken in the Division, particularly when the only action taken was to send the Chief of Staff a rough draft from which he could start preparing a communication to the President, Admiral King, or Sir John Dill. The record made of OPD action in such cases often consisted of filing a draft, bearing explanatory notes in pen or pencil, in the OPD executive office.

[68] Interv, Lt Col J. B. Morgan, Asst Exec OPD, with author, 1 Mar 46, OPD Hist Unit Interv file.

[69] Rpt [1945], title: Presentations, Item 2C, OPD Hist Unit file.

Eisenhower in May 1942.[70] They sent their group chiefs, section chiefs, and action officers into the field as often as they could, for the same reason—to help bring about and maintain close understanding between the overseas commands and the Washington command post. General Eisenhower inaugurated this policy of "sending staff officers for brief visits into the active theaters," in May 1942.[71] The trips also were expected to be helpful to theater commanders by virtue of the thorough acquaintance of OPD officers with War Department activities.[72] Headaches of the theater commanders, however small, became headaches of OPD. For instance, when one of OPD's officers sent to the South Pacific theater in mid-1942 reported his views on problems of the U. S. Army forces under General Patch in New Caledonia, a series of about a dozen interrelated staff actions resulted, dealing with everything from the activation of a new combat division to the dispatch of a mobile laundry unit.[73]

The closeness of the contact with combat thus being established by officers on trips for OPD was demonstrated by the fact that one officer, Lt. Col. Francis R. Stevens, lost his life in a combat flight over New Guinea in June 1942. He was the second officer from the Division to be killed on a trip to a theater during the war, the first, Colonel Bundy, having lost his life in an airplane accident while on his way to Hawaii immediately after Pearl Harbor. Before the end of the war the Division lost two more officers on observation trips, Col. Carl D. Silverthorne and Lt. Col. Frederick G. Terry, both killed in action on Saipan.

With its internal organization, its duties, and its basic practices worked out along these lines by mid-1942, OPD had become a working reality.[74] As of June, Colonel Gailey was able to report to General McNarney, Deputy Chief of Staff: "From the standpoint of the Operations Division the three months shakedown has resulted in an organization that is believed practical and efficient." [75] The Chief of Staff's Washington command post was in action.

---

[70] For General Eisenhower's trip to the United Kingdom in May 1942, see Ch. IX. General Handy made a trip to the United Kingdom in August 1942, for which see Ch. X. For subsequent trips by the chief of OPD, as well as many other officers, see Ch. XV.

[71] OPD adm memo, 4 May 42, sub: Visits to Theaters by Offs of OPD, OPD 331.1, 49.

[72] Min of Gen Council meetings, 4 May 42, DCofS rcds.

[73] For OPD's actions and Lt Col V. A. Lane's memo for record on the report, see copy of CM-IN

1698, 24 May 42, Lt Col F. R. Stevens for Gen Marshall, with atchd papers, OPD 381 New Caledonia, 29.

[74] For comprehensive administrative description of OPD, see OPD adm memo, 9 Jun 42, sub: OPD of WDGS, OPD 321.19 OPD, 4.

[75] Memo, OPD for DCofS, 16 Jun 42, sub: WD Orgn, OPD 320, 17.

CHAPTER IX

Case History: Drafting the BOLERO Plan

The staff work which OPD was doing in the spring of 1942 not only fixed the patterns of Division organization and procedures but also concentrated the attention of American and British military planners on the main strategic issue of World War II. That issue was whether, when, and on what scale the United States and Great Britain should carry the war directly to Germany by invading northwest Europe. General Marshall emphasized this critical question in April 1942 by presenting a specific plan for concentrating American forces in the United Kingdom in preparation for an early assault across the English Channel. The President and the Prime Minister in turn approved this plan, to which the code name BOLERO was thereupon assigned. It was basically a statement of a general course of military action, what Army officers later usually called a strategic concept, designed for the defeat of Germany. It dominated Army planning until July, when it was pushed into the background for the sake of action in 1942—the invasion of North Africa. Afterwards, it remained a point of departure for most American and British strategic planning for the defeat of Germany until troops actually landed in Normandy in 1944. OPD officers helped evolve the BOLERO outline plan of April 1942, aided the Chief of Staff in convincing the British of its sound-

ness, and took the lead in making concrete preparations to carry it out. Thereby they contributed a long-term unity and purposeful direction hitherto lacking in post-Pearl Harbor strategic planning and military operations. Aside from the importance which the plan for invading the Continent assumed in 1943 and 1944, the BOLERO episode in 1942 showed that General Marshall had found in OPD the staff he needed to assist him in thinking and acting on long-term as well as day-to-day problems of high command.

The Search for a Common Strategy

During the first six months of American participation in World War II, the immediate attention of the Army as well as the Navy was on the Pacific, where an aggressive enemy was making unexpectedly rapid gains. WPD and later OPD carried a heavy burden of staff work connected with setting up commands and deploying Army forces to help establish a defensive line in the Pacific and to help maintain sea and air communications with Australia.[1] The line, Midway-Fiji-New Caledonia-Australia, was defi-

---

[1] The designation WPD was changed to OPD during the period of the development of the BOLERO plan. In this chapter the names are used interchangeably, generally as they appear in the documents being described.

nitely established only in June 1942 and scarcely secure until after the Guadalcanal (Solomon Islands) and Papua (New Guinea) Campaigns of late 1942. Nevertheless, some of the Army strategists were planning in early 1942 for the eventual offensive against Germany.

The ARCADIA Conference of December 1941–January 1942, which had accomplished so much in setting up the British-American Combined Chiefs of Staff system, had accomplished little in the sphere of strategy except to confirm officially in wartime the general principles of ABC–1 and RAINBOW 5, mainly the "beat Germany first" idea. The President and the Prime Minister had directed that serious consideration be given to preparing for an offensive in North Africa, but the project was postponed and came to nothing during the first half of 1942 because the spectacular advances of the Japanese gave the Pacific area first call on American resources, particularly shipping. During the first few months of their common military effort, the United States and Great Britain were definitely on the defensive and were necessarily dealing with urgent military problems on a hand-to-mouth basis as these problems forced themselves one by one to the highest level for decision. In the critical fields of distribution and use of aircraft, troop deployment, and distribution of munitions, the Army in particular felt the need of a common standard by which to measure military enterprises against one another. In the frantic effort to build up Pacific defenses, the U. S. Navy recommended maximum reinforcement by Army units, especially Air units, in what the Navy had long considered to be its special area of responsibility. At the same time requests for lend-lease equipment came pouring in, particularly

from Great Britain, the USSR, and China, whose urgent needs could not be disregarded. To Army officers it therefore seemed altogether possible that American equipment might be irrevocably scattered, the American training program crippled, and the ABC–1 and RAINBOW 5 principle of concentrating strength for the defeat of Germany abandoned in practice without ever being repudiated in theory.[2]

Many American and British officers on the high staff or command level must have made the same diagnosis. It was up to General Marshall to prescribe a well-considered remedy, and, as a matter for staff action, it was up to the senior officers in WPD and OPD to offer him one. They were quick to do so, being acutely aware that the Army desperately needed some master plan that would channel efforts of every kind toward some major strategic goal. In fact Army officers had to solve most of their problems in relation to the deployment schedules, which answered the key question of where troop units were going to be used. If a unit went overseas its equipment went with it and its supplies had to follow. Necessary readjustments in mobilizing, training, and equipping new units and finding supplies for old ones had to be made in the zone of interior. Thus the co-ordination of Army activities depended upon developing a deployment program. A comparatively long-range deployment program was essential to daily staff work in WPD and OPD, yet it was bound to be a delusion unless it was based squarely on firm assumptions as to the main direction, scale, and timing of future military operations. The planners began very early in 1942 to search for a sound basis for

[2] For ABC–1 and RAINBOW 5, see Ch. IV. For ARCADIA Conference, see Ch. V.

their own staff work and to urge the general adoption of some common strategic plan.[3]

As General Gerow's deputy for Pacific and Far Eastern matters and, after 16 February 1942, as Division chief, General Eisenhower saw the problem clearly. In personal notes jotted down on 22 January 1942, he described it as follows:

The struggle to secure the adoption by all concerned of a common concept of strategical objectives is wearing me down. Everybody is too much engaged with small things of his own.

We've got to go to Europe and fight—and we've got to quit wasting resources all over the world—and still worse—wasting time. If we're to keep Russia in, save the Middle East, India and Burma; we've got to begin slugging with air at West Europe; to be followed by a land attack as soon as possible.[4]

----

[3] General Arnold and his staff were likewise dismayed by the piecemeal commitment of American forces as it affected the distribution of American Air strength. See memo, R. A. Lovett, ASW for Air, no addressee, 9 Mar 42, sub: Strategy of Scarcity, OPD 381, 4.

General Marshall and Secretary Stimson were also fully aware, of course, of the need for a common strategic goal, as they indicated by promptly becoming the stanchest advocates of the BOLERO outline plan which OPD evolved. In fact as time went on, OPD officers proved to be more inclined to deviate from the original BOLERO strategy, in view of later logistic and politico-military developments, than General Marshall and Secretary Stimson. See the latter's favorable presentation of the BOLERO plan in his *On Active Service in Peace and War*. On later thought some of the officers closely associated with drafting the initial plan were not so sure that it represented the wisest strategic course that could have been charted. Rather, as this chapter attempts to show, they strongly felt the need of *some* central strategy, and the BOLERO plan was their solution at the time. This chapter does not discuss the BOLERO plan as part of the developing pattern of strategy, but simply as a significant case history in staff planning.

[4] Notations by Gen Eisenhower, 22 Jan 42, Item 3, OPD Hist Unit file. At the bottom of this notation is an added sentence, dated 7 May 1942: "The above plan, which finally won official approval in Apr, is called BOLERO."

Two days later General Eisenhower indicated that Colonel Handy, WPD's Plans Group chief, shared this point of view and that General McNarney, who only recently had returned from England, supported it: "Tom Handy and I stick to our idea that we must win in Europe. Joe McNarney not only agrees—but was the first one to state that the French coast could be successfully attacked. . . . We can't win by . . . giving our stuff in driblets all over the world—with no theater getting enough." [5] The idea took more definite form a few weeks later, immediately after the fall of Singapore, when General Eisenhower had become Assistant Chief of Staff, WPD. He wrote: "We've got to go on a harassing defensive west of Hawaii; hold India and Ceylon; build up air and land forces in England, and when we're strong enough, go after Germany's vitals." [6] Again, three days later: "We've got to keep Russia in the war—and hold India!!! Then we can get ready to crack Germany through England." [7]

WPD's principal planning officers promptly began to put their personal opinions, such as those which General Eisenhower set down in writing at the time, into the form of staff recommendations urging the necessity of agreeing on a definitive strategic concept for winning the war. They proposed that this strategy should indorse the pre-Pearl Harbor ABC–1 and RAINBOW 5 concept of maintaining the strategic defensive in the Pacific and turning toward Europe as the decisive theater. But they recommended going beyond the general objective of preparing for an eventual offensive against the Axis Powers in Europe. Until there was agreement on a specific kind

----

[5] *Ibid.*, 24 Jan 42.
[6] *Ibid.*, 19 Feb 42.
[7] *Ibid.*, 22 Feb 42.

of operation in a specific area with a specific though tentative target date, agreement on an eventual offensive would not prevent the continued dissipation of troops and equipment for defensive purposes. Planning officers urged that the United States and Great Britain concentrate at once on a first-priority effort to build up resources in the United Kingdom for an early cross-Channel invasion of northern France. The name BOLERO which was adopted for this plan was also subsequently used by Army officers to refer to the whole drive for a central strategic concept—in the Army, in the JCS system, and in the high policy sphere of agreements between the heads of government of the United States and Great Britain, President Roosevelt and Prime Minister Churchill.

Insofar as officers in the strategic planning staff of the Army were directly involved, the general military idea eventually incorporated in the BOLERO plan first arose in connection with an immediate problem under discussion in the JCS system, namely deployment of forces in the Pacific. The very first directive given by the U. S. Joint Staff Planners to their working subcommittee, the Joint U. S. Strategic Committee, authorized a continuing study of priorities for the "Strategic Deployment of Land, Sea, and Air Forces of the United States." [8] This extensive project, initiated on 28 January, was hardly under way before it became apparent that Japanese advances were rendering obsolete most of the ARCADIA provisions for defense of the Southwest Pacific.[9]

Accordingly the Combined Chiefs of Staff called for a "comprehensive review of the strategical situation in the Japanese Theater of War (including the entire Pacific area) and the preparation of a combined plan for the forces of the United Nations in the area." [10] On 11 February the JUSSC, since it already was studying American aspects of the problem, received a directive to satisfy the CCS request by rendering an early report on over-all deployment by the United Nations in the Japanese theater of war.[11]

The imminent collapse of the first line of Australian-British-Dutch-American defenses in the Netherlands East Indies area, hastily erected as a result of decisions at the ARCADIA Conference, demanded prompt action. Nevertheless, the question of reinforcing the Pacific area could be settled only in the context of strategy and deployment policy of the United Nations all over the world. The JUSSC submitted a draft report, 18 February 1942, which proved to be only the first in a series of papers reflecting fundamental differences of strategic opinion among American planners. Essentially the issue was whether to concentrate forces in Europe or in the Pacific. Disagreement on basic policy marked the studies and discussions at every stage of planning. By the time the issue was presented to the JCS for decision, the basic papers consisted of several JUSSC studies plus a strong recommendation by the JPS that an early decision was essential.[12]

---

[8] JPS Directive 1 to JUSSC, 28 Jan 42, forwarded to JUSSC, 30 Jan 42, JPS 2. The first JUSSC meeting convened two days later, 30 January. See JUSSC Meetings, JCS rcds.

[9] President Roosevelt spoke of the obsolescence of ARCADIA plans in his Message 115 to the Prime Minister, 9 Mar 42, copy filed with CCS 56/1 in ABC 311.5 (1–30–42).

[10] Min 4th meeting CCS, 10 Feb 42. This CCS order resulted from consideration of a British paper on deploying air forces in the Far East, CCS 34, which the CCS forwarded to the CPS, 10 February 1942.

[11] (1) Min 13th meeting CPS, 11 Feb 42. (2) JPS directive to JUSSC, 11 Feb. 42, JPS 2/1.

[12] The issue was considered on the JCS level as JCS 23, 14 March 1942, title: Strategic Deployment of Land, Sea, and Air Forces of the U. S. JCS

Some of the language in the JUSSC studies indictated that invasion of Europe in 1942 was absolutely necessary to sustain Russia, was logistically possible, and should be launched at any cost to positions of the United Nations in the Pacific. The issue involved, in the first instance, the deployment of aircraft and the initiation of a major air offensive in Europe. The Air planner on the JUSSC, at this time Lt. Col. Haywood S. Hansell, Jr., was the principal spokesman for resolving the debate by attacking Germany as soon as possible.[13] At the opposite extreme some of the planners, principally the Navy representatives, urged that the Pacific area be strongly reinforced "at the expense of executing a vigorous offensive against Germany with United States Forces," thus abandoning the ABC–1 and RAINBOW 5 principle of concentrating strength in the European theater.[14] Colonel Handy, the Army planner on the JPS committee, and the WPD planning officers who made up the Army section (ground officers only until March, ground-air subsequently) of the JUSSC, Col. Ray T. Maddocks, Colonel Wedemeyer, and Lt. Col. Jesmond D. Balmer, took an intermediate position.

They recommended that reinforcements in the Pacific be restricted to the minimum calculated to be necessary for the defense of Australia and its Pacific lines of communications, and that the maximum effort be made to send troops to the United Kingdom for an early assault on Germany.[15]

While the JUSSC was still trying to resolve these differences of opinion among its own members, WPD undertook to consolidate its official view on the whole deployment issue in terms of strategic policy. By 28 February, six days before the JUSSC finally submitted its studies and recommendations to the Joint Staff Planners and two weeks before the whole problem was referred to the JCS, General Eisenhower prepared a formal study for the Chief of Staff setting forth WPD's conclusions and recommendations on world strategy as well as Pacific deployment. The argument followed the line which Colonel Maddocks and Colonel Wedemeyer were taking in the Joint U. S. Strategic Committee. The same argument, as well as a great deal of the language in this WPD study, reappeared again and again in basic planning papers of March and April 1942.

WPD's Recommendations on Strategy

The WPD study of 28 February 1942 presented an outline of world-wide strategic objectives from which a solution to strategic problems in the Southwest Pacific could be deduced. The views of the Division were set forth in three main postulates, all directly in line with strategic thought on which

---

23, which comprised all the previous studies, was submitted by the JPS to the JCS 14 March 1942. JCS 23 and all associated papers are filed in ABC 370 (1–28–42). In this chapter the citations of the complicated set of JCS 23 papers are as precisely descriptive of the individual studies in JCS 23 as possible, and the standard reference to JCS papers (number, date, and title) is not always employed.

[13] (1) JUSSC study (majority and minority reports) submitted to JPS, 18 Feb 42, JPS 2/2 and JPS 2/2 (A). (2) JUSSC study reconciling the two reports, submitted to JPS 6 Mar 42, JPS 2/5. (3) Min 4th meeting JUSSC, 3 Feb 42, JCS rcds.

[14] (1) JCS 23, 14 Mar 42, title: Strategic Deployment of Land, Sea, and Air Forces of the U. S. For the quoted phrase, see JPS conclusions added at the end of the JUSSC study (JPS 2/5). (2) Cf. min 6th meeting JUSSC, 5 Feb 42, JCS rcds.

[15] For evidence of the WPD point of view, see WPD notes on JCS 23, prepared for 6th meeting JCS, 16 Mar 42, filed with JCS 23 in ABC 370 (1–28–42). See also n. 23.

American and British planners had agreed since ABC–1 was evolved:

[1] In the event of a war involving both oceans, the U. S. should adopt the strategic defensive in the Pacific and devote its major offensive effort across the Atlantic.

[2] We must differentiate sharply and definitely between those things whose current accomplishment in the several theaters over the world is *necessary* to the ultimate defeat of the Axis Powers, as opposed to those which are merely *desirable* because of their effect in facilitating such defeat.

[3] The United States interest in maintaining contact with Australia and in preventing further Japanese expansion to the Southeastward is apparent . . . but . . . they are not immediately vital to the successful outcome of the war. The problem is one of determining what we can spare for the effort in that region, without seriously impairing performance of our mandatory task.

In developing the first of these three points the memorandum which General Eisenhower prepared for the Chief of Staff first set out to demolish an argument which might plausibly be advanced against the principle of concentrating strength in the European theater. The memorandum pointed out that the "strategic axiom" of attacking the weaker force of a divided enemy did not lead to the conclusion that forces should be concentrated in the Far East, even though the European Axis was "stronger in total combat power" than Japan. According to Eisenhower's reasoning, Japan was at the time "relatively stronger" than Germany and Italy because of her geographical position and the greater force that the United Nations could bring to bear in Europe, at least as long as the Soviet Union remained in the war. This condition obtained primarily because it took three to four times as many ships to transport and maintain a force in the Pacific as across the Atlantic.

Thus WPD's conclusion was that "logistic reasons, as well as strategic axiom, substantiate the soundness of the decision to concentrate against the European Axis."

Having asserted the second main postulate, the doctrine of the "necessary" as distinguished from the "desirable," General Eisenhower listed in his memorandum three objectives as "necessary"—always assuming that the "continental United States and Hawaii, the Caribbean area, and South America north of Natal" were secure:

a. Maintenance of the United Kingdom, which involves relative security of the North Atlantic sea lanes.

b. Retention of Russia in the war as an active enemy of Germany.

c. Maintenance of a position in the India-Middle East Area which will prevent physical junction of the two principal enemies, and will probably keep China in the war.

Next, he named as "things . . . highly desirable," even approaching the necessary:

a. Security of Alaska.

b. Holding of bases west and southwest of Hawaii.

c. Security of Burma, particularly because of its influence on future Chinese action.

d. Security of South America south of Natal.

e. Security of Australia.

f. Security of bases on West African coast and trans-African air route.

g. Other areas and bases useful in limiting hostile operations and facilitating our own.

Upon the basis of this memorandum, the WPD stand on minimum reinforcement of the Pacific and Far East inevitably followed. Its specific implications for the deployment of troops in the Southwest Pacific were developed at considerable length at the conclusion of the memorandum.

This presentation of long-established concepts led General Eisenhower to introduce the strategic idea which was even then claiming the attention of the JUSSC and which was to prove central to American wartime planning for many months. In elaborating on what was meant by the "task of keeping Russia in the war," WPD urged "immediate and definite action," first "by direct aid through lend-lease" and second "through the early initiation of operations that will draw off from the Russian front sizeable portions of the German Army, both air and ground." More specifically: "We should at once develop, in conjunction with the British, a definite plan for operations against Northwest Europe. It should be drawn up at once, in detail, and it should be sufficiently extensive in scale as to engage from the middle of May onward, an increasing portion of the German Air Force, and by late summer an increasing amount of his ground forces."

The choice of northwest Europe as the invasion point followed from the fact that another of the three essential objectives—protecting the United Kingdom and the North Atlantic sea lanes—could be achieved concurrently with building up resources in the British Isles for the cross-Channel assault. Greater shipping economy thus could be effected than if another " 'first priority' convoying" problem were created by establishing a "large force at any location other than the Northeast Atlantic." Indeed, WPD asserted, "The United Kingdom is not only our principal partner in this war; it offers the only point from which effective land and air operations against Germany may be attempted." [16]

The imprint of this line of reasoning was clear in subsequent JUSSC papers on troop deployment, particularly the two comprehensive reports submitted to the Joint Staff Planners on 6 March 1942. The studies from the first had emphasized the importance of supporting Russia as the only one of the United Nations "actively and aggressively operating against Germany." This assistance was taken to include a "supporting offensive in 1942," an operation which could be based only on the British Isles, though there was no unequivocal statement that such an offensive in 1942 was possible. Nevertheless, the Joint U. S. Strategic Committee asserted: "If the war is to be won in Europe, land forces must be developed and trained which are capable of landing on the continent and advancing under the support of an overwhelming air force." To concentrate strength for this effort, the planners recommended strict "economy of force in other theaters." [17]

The rather temperate statement of all these propositions reflected the middle-of-the-road policy which WPD had come to adopt as a result of further study and consideration on the part of its planners—a policy that broke away from earlier influences. Typifying the cautious stand of the Division, the Army Planner, Colonel Handy, explicitly refused to let emphasis on the critical importance of Soviet survival through 1942 lead to a flat declaration that "Germany would completely defeat Russia in 1942 unless we move all possible forces to the United Kingdom for an offensive this year." He also in effect

---

[16] All the foregoing is from memo, WPD for CofS, 28 Feb 42, sub: Strategic Conceptions and Their Application to Southwest Pacific, Envelope 35, Exec 4. General Eisenhower's initials appear in the action officer corner on this copy of the memorandum, indicating that he himself drafted at least the final version of the paper.

[17] JUSSC study, title: Review of Strategic Situation in Japanese Theater of War, submitted to JPS 6 Mar 42, and JUSSC study on strategic deployment also submitted to JPS 6 Mar 42, JPS 2/5 and JPS 2/6. JPS 2/5 superseded the JUSSC majority and minority reports, 18 Feb 42, JPS 2/2 and JPS 2/2 (A).

had warned against overvaluing the contribution which the United States could make to any operation in 1942, pointing out that the British would have to furnish the "bulk of the forces initially required for the land offensive" in 1942, and, consequently, that the movement of American troops to the United Kingdom would "influence the 1942 campaign only by permitting earlier employment of British Forces." [18] This sober reflection represented a major qualification of the 1942 orientation of both the earlier JUSSC papers and WPD's 28 February memorandum.

Consequently the specific recommendations by the Joint Strategic Committee, based on detailed statistical calculations of troop commitments and the amount of shipping available, did not mention any particular time for the major offensive. They were:

(a) Make secure the territory of North and South America and their coastal communication.

(b) In cooperation with the forces of the British Commonwealth make secure the trans-Atlantic sea and air routes.

(c) Secure Australia, the island positions between Australia and Hawaii, and their sea and air communications with the United States.

(d) Exert pressure against the Japanese by operations of naval and air forces. . . .

(e) Give limited air assistance to the defense of the India-Burma-China area.

(f) Having arranged for the accomplishment of the above courses of action with minimum forces, exert a maximum effort in cooperation with the British in offensive operations against Germany.[19]

The planners estimated that during 1942, to accomplish the recommended tasks which required overseas movement of troops, a total of about 416,000 forces of the United States would be needed to secure the entire Pacific area (including Australia). The bulk of these forces of course would have to be supplied by the Army. For the entire Pacific, the Army strength required for 1942 was set at about 235,000 ground forces and 115,000 air forces, equipped with approximately 1,650 aircraft.[20] To secure all other points outside the United States except Great Britain itself, forces totaling about 90,000, nearly all from U. S. Army ground or air units, were listed as necessary.

When these commitments had been met, the JUSSC originally calculated, shipping would be sufficient to move to the European theater:

By	Air Forces	(Aircraft)	Ground Forces
1 July 1942	50,000	(700)	51,000
1 October 1942	114,000	(1,400)	191,000
1 January 1943	183,000	(2,300)	252,000

Since it had been agreed at the outset that a force large enough to cause a material diversion of German forces from the Russian front would amount to about 600,000 ground troops, supported by some 6,500 planes, the study concluded that the American "force available for the European Theater is not adequate immediately for a major offensive." Nevertheless the American contribution, the planners asserted, would be "adequate to assist effectively in such an offensive in the fall of 1942. . . . Their prospective availability should enable the British

---

[18] WPD notes by Colonel Handy, on an early draft of JPS 2/5, filed with JPS 2/5 in ABC 370 (1–28–42). There is no indication of authorship, but the phrasing of the text suggests that the notes are intended as a guide from the Army planner to the Army section of the JUSSC. Much later (1947) General Handy was unable to say positively that he was the author of these notes, but thought that in all probability he had written them.

[19] JUSSC study, 6 Mar 42, JPS 2/6.

[20] This Pacific estimate included Alaska and Panama, plus the Caribbean Air Force.

to initiate an offensive even sooner." In fact, the JUSSC study had as an annex an outline plan for a British-American air offensive beginning in the last two weeks of July 1942, to be followed by an assault with ground forces six weeks later.[21]

Before the whole deployment issue reached the JCS, estimates of forces of the United States had to be revised in view of commitments made subsequent to the original JUSSC study. These commitments, involving the dispatch of two additional U. S. Army divisions to the Pacific and the diversion of ships for moving 40,000 British troops to the Middle East, materially reduced the number of American forces that could be moved to the United Kingdom, especially in mid-1942. Revised estimates were as follows:

By	Air Forces	Ground Forces
1 July 1942	40,000	. . . . .
1 October 1942	114,000	66,000
1 January 1943	183,000	207,000

However, these changes merely emphasized the wisdom of Colonel Handy's caution about overestimating the contribution which American troops could make to an invasion in 1942. The JUSSC did not alter its general strategic recommendations.[22]

WPD officially stood squarely behind the joint planning studies presented on 6 March, and continued to support them even after the revision of estimates of American forces that would be available in the European theater in 1942. The JUSSC, presumably in deference to WPD's reservations about the

idea, had refrained from stating in so many words that a 1942 invasion was either possible or necessary. The main point of their studies was to urge immediate action to build up strength in the United Kingdom.

WPD's strategists were perfectly willing to see the planning wheels start turning with a 1942 invasion as the objective ahead, even though they went on record as warning that conditions might well "preclude the actual accomplishment of this effort in 1942." At least the major point of concentrating maximum strength in the European area would have been won. In addition, air operations from the United Kingdom would create a "not inconsiderable diversion of German effort from the Russian front," and, "by 1943, the United Nations should be in a position to launch an offensive of such magnitude that the decision can be gained." Thus the WPD planners were tending toward agreement with the strategic timetable originally set up by Major Wedemeyer in the WPD Victory Program study of September 1941. With this ultimate objective in view, therefore, WPD recommended: "The plans and preparations for an offensive of this nature should certainly be laid now and efforts made to crystallize a decision for their execution. . . . It is the only alternative that has been suggested to inaction, dispersion, minor decision, and a scattering of effort in a secondary theater." [23]

---

[21] For all the foregoing, JUSSC study, 6 Mar 42, JPS 2/6. Annexes A through H present detailed statistics and description of operation planned. The outline plan is presented in Annex C.

[22] JUSSC study, prepared by direction of the JPS to revise estimates on troop deployment in the light of commitments made subsequent to the 6 March study, JPS 2/6, atchd as App. II of the JPS paper submitted to the JCS 14 Mar 42, JCS 23.

[23] All the foregoing concerning WPD's position is from WPD notes prepared for the Army planner's use at the 4th meeting JPS, 11 Mar 42, filed with JPS 2/6 in ABC 370 (1–28–42). There is no indication of the author.

For a clear indication that WPD at this very time did not take the 1942 possibility very seriously, see notations by Gen D. D. Eisenhower, 10 Mar 42, Item 3, OPD Hist Unit file:

Gradually some of the people with whom I have to deal are coming to agree with me that there are just three "musts" for the Allies this year—hold open the line to England and support her as nec-

JCS Decision on Deployment Policy

Since the Joint Staff Planners committee was able to agree only that "an immediate decision for a definite course of action" was essential, it forwarded the earlier studies and the strategic issue implicit in them to the JCS with a recommendation that the JCS "at once decide on a clear course of action, and execute this decision with the utmost vigor." The amalgamated paper comprising Joint U. S. Strategic Committee studies and Joint Staff Planners conclusions reached the JCS as JCS 23, "Strategic Deployment of Land, Sea, and Air Forces of the United States." [24]

The JPS reported the inability to reconcile differences of opinion among themselves and presented three mutually exclusive courses of action, each supported by some member of their committee. A middle-of-the-road course, which echoed General Eisenhower's 28 February study, was listed as the third of these alternatives. WPD planners had drafted the argument included in its support and recommended to General Marshall that it be approved by the JCS. [25]

The three alternatives were:

a. Ensure the security of the military position in the Pacific Theater by strong reinforcements . . . at the expense of executing a vigorous offensive against Germany with United States forces.

b. While Russia is still an effective ally, concentrate the mass of our forces for a vigorous offensive, initially from bases in England, with the objective of defeating Germany. Until Germany has been defeated, accept the possibility that the southwest Pacific may be lost.

c. Provide . . . forces in the South Pacific area considered by the Joint Strategic Committee as the minimum required for the defensive position and simultaneously begin to build up in the United Kingdom forces intended for offensive at the earliest practicable time. [26]

The issue of where the United Nations proposed to concentrate forces for its first major offensive was thus squarely presented. Implicit in any decision in favor of the third alternative, WPD's recommendation, was acceptance of the United Kingdom as the major offensive base. With very little recorded discussion the JCS agreed on 16 March 1942 that "of the courses of action available," it was "preferable" for the United States to restrict Pacific forces to the number allotted in current commitments and to "begin to build up forces in the United Kingdom." [27] This decision on JCS

essary; keep Russia in the war as an active participant; hold the India-Middle East buttress between Japs and Germans. All this assumes the safety from major attack of North America, Hawaii, and the Caribbean area.

For WPD's approval of the whole deployment study after the JUSSC had revised estimates on American forces in its study submitted to JCS, 14 Mar 42, as App. II of JCS 23, see WPD notes on JCS 23, prepared for the Chief of Staff's use at the 6th meeting JCS, 16 Mar 42, filed with JCS 23 in ABC 370 (1–28–42).

[24] (1) Min 4th meeting JPS, 11 Mar 42. (2) Min 5th meeting JPS, 14 Mar 42. At this second meeting of the JPS it was directed that a paper (JCS 23) be submitted to the JCS. (3) See n. 12 above.

[25] (1) JPS conclusions to JUSSC study on strategic deployment, JCS 23, basic paper, 14 Mar 42. (2) Cf. WPD notes on JCS 23, prepared for the Chief of Staff's use at the 6th meeting JCS, 16 Mar 42, filed with JCS 23 in ABC 370 (1–28–42). General Eisenhower had initialed a draft of the para-

graph in JCS 23 defending the point of view. See this draft and attached note indicating that the Army Air Forces members of the Joint Planners were by this time willing to go along with the WPD position, abandoning what was evidently an Army Air Forces argument in the JUSSC minority report of 18 February 1942, JPS 2/2 (A), filed with JCS 23 in ABC 370 (1–28–42).

[26] JPS conclusions to basic paper submitted to the JCS 14 Mar 42, JCS 23.

[27] Min 6th meeting JCS, 16 Mar 42. The members of the JCS recorded a general understanding that current commitments included one division in excess of JUSSC recommendations.

23 represented a clear preference for WPD's deployment policy in the Pacific, and, somewhat less conclusively, for the basic BOLERO concept of preparing an early offensive in Europe from the United Kingdom. The timing was still confused, and British agreement was yet to be won. But insistence on the need to concentrate forces for a large-scale offensive in Europe was beginning to act as a catalyst in forming a common British-American strategy for winning the war.

On the very day, 16 March 1942, on which the JCS approved the policy of limited deployment in the Pacific and concurrent preparation for a campaign in Europe, the British representatives in Washington presented for planning use a staff study that had been prepared in London in December 1941. It consisted of a tentative plan for landing British forces in the early summer of 1943 in the vicinity of Le Havre, France, "under conditions of severe deterioration of German military power." It flatly stated that the operations would have to be postponed unless the enemy already had been "weakened in strength and morale" before 1943.[28] At General Marshall's suggestion, the CCS directed the CPS to reconcile this very modest British approach to an operation on the Continent with JCS 23, which recommended, by implication, an invasion of the Continent, at least by British forces, in 1942. Specifically, the combined planners were to report on both the possibility of landing and maintaining ground forces on the Continent in 1942 and the possibility of an invasion early in 1943.[29] In effect this report would also serve as some kind of reconciliation between the early emphasis which WPD had been inclined to put on a 1942 invasion and WPD's later, more conservative emphasis on one in 1943. A CPS subcommittee, including the four OPD officers on the JUSSC, at once began work in an attempt to adjust the British-American differences on the timing of the European project.[30]

While this effort to reach an agreement on a plan to take the offensive in Europe was only beginning, OPD renewed its independent campaign to reach a "coordinated viewpoint" as to the major tasks of the war, particularly the task of building up an assault force in the United Kingdom. The Division drafted a study dated 25 March 1942 urging on the Chief of Staff the necessity of definitely deciding on the "theater in which the first major offensive of the United Powers must take place." Echoing the strategic ideas first expressed formally in General Eisenhower's study, OPD declared that the "principal target for our first major offensive should be Germany, to be attacked through western Europe." Only on the basis

---

[28] (1) British War Cabinet-Joint Planning Staff study, 9 Dec 41, title: Opns on Continent in Final Phase, copy filed before CPS 26/D, ABC 381 BOLERO (3-16-42), 1. (2) Ltr, Field Marshal Dill to Gen Marshall, 16 Mar 42, copy filed before CPS 26/D, ABC 381 BOLERO (3-16-42), 1. Field Marshal Dill simply turned this copy of the British study over to General Marshall personally "apropos of the offensive about which we spoke today." (3) Ltr, Gen Marshall to Field Marshal Dill, n.d., copy filed before CPS 26/D, ABC 381 BOLERO (3-16-42), 1. This British study of 9 December was marked as the second revised draft. The CPS used a later, almost identical draft, dated 28 December 1941 and bearing the name of ROUNDUP, for their studies. See CPS 26/1, 3 Apr 42. A copy of the 28 December study is in JCS rcds, CCS 381 (3-23-42), 1.

[29] (1) Min 7th meeting JCS, 23 Mar 42. (2) Min 13th meeting CCS, 24 Mar 42. (3) CPS 26/D, 25 Mar 42, title: Directive/Offensive Opns in Europe.
[30] Min 12th meeting CPS, 26 Mar 42. The CPS work coincided with but was largely negated by the final approval of the plan drafted in OPD. WPD was renamed OPD on 23 March 1942.

of general acceptance of this objective as the "principal target of all United Powers" could sound production and deployment decisions be reached.[31]

The choice of theater was supported by a long list of reasons, for the most part previously suggested in one way or another. Since the lines of communications to England had to be kept safe regardless of the areas in which forces of the United States were deployed, a theater in western Europe would not necessitate a dispersion of air and naval protective forces. By using the shortest possible sea route, a large force could be maintained with a minimum strain on shipping. The early build-up of air and ground forces in Great Britain would carry sufficient threat to prevent Germany from complete concentration against the USSR. This route represented the direct approach by superior land communications to the center of German might. The forward base in England already had the airfields from which a large air force could operate to secure the air superiority essential to a successful landing. A major portion of the British combat power could be used without stripping the home defenses of the United Kingdom. Finally, this plan provided for attempting an attack on Germany while she was engaged on a number of fronts.[32]

The success of the plan for taking the offensive, OPD pointed out, depended on securing complete agreement among the CCS that the attack against Germany through western Europe constituted the eventual task of the United Nations. With such a plan, training and production schedules could be adjusted, overwhelming air support built up, ample ships and landing craft found, and combat strength husbanded. OPD planners so strongly felt the necessity of having a "target on which to fix . . . [their] sights" that they declared: "Unless this plan is adopted as the eventual aim of all our efforts, we must turn our *backs* upon the Eastern Atlantic and go, full out, as quickly as possible, against Japan!" Above all, OPD emphasized the "tremendous importance of agreeing on some major objective" for "coordinated and intensive effort." [33]

The Bolero Plan

General Marshall needed no convincing on the desirability of securing a clear-cut strategic plan. He and Secretary Stimson immediately urged upon the President the project of concentrating forces for an invasion of Europe. The President approved the idea of developing a plan and clearing it directly with the British Chiefs of Staff in London.[34] Thus approval was gained on the highest policy level for completing a staff enterprise that had been under way in OPD for several weeks.

When Colonel Hull set up the Future Plans Section of S&P in February 1942, he had assigned a new officer, Colonel Connor, the task of drafting future strategic plans for Europe.[35] While Colonel Wedemeyer and his colleagues on the JUSSC were de-

---

[31] Memo, OPD for CofS, 25 Mar 42, sub: Critical Points in Development of Coordinated Viewpoint as to Maj Tasks of War, OPD 381 BOLERO, 6.

[32] *Ibid.*

[33] *Ibid.*

[34] The immediate use to which OPD's 25 March memorandum was put was for what Secretary Stimson called a "very fine presentation" of the issue at the White House 25 March 1942, attended by Secretary Stimson, General Marshall, General Arnold, Secretary Knox, Admiral King, and Harry Hopkins. For references to the meeting, see: (1) Stimson, *On Active Service in Peace and War,* pp. 416–17; (2) min of 7th meeting JCS, 23 Mar 42; (3) memo, Col J. R. Deane, OCS for Gen Arnold and Gen Eisenhower, n.d., Tab "Misc," Book 4, Exec 8.

[35] Interv, Lt Col Connor with author, 11 May 48, OPD Hist Unit Interv file.

bating the JCS 23 issue, Colonel Connor had discovered the conservative attitude Colonel Handy had adopted toward the possibility of an invasion of France in 1942. During the last week of March, while the subcommittee of the CPS was attempting to reconcile American and British ideas as to timing, Colonel Hull and Colonel Connor set the planning wheels in motion to assemble sufficiently detailed data to prepare the plan authorized by the President on 25 March. G–2 supplied estimates on British forces available for an invasion of the Continent and on the time of year for weather conditions favorable to a Channel crossing. G–3 and G–4 estimated the readiness for combat of major U. S. Army units, indicating the status of their equipment and training as of 15 September 1942 and 1 April 1943. Services of Supply submitted tables showing requirements and resources in shipping. Army Ground Forces listed the kind of units and total strength of a well-balanced ground component that could be made available for the offensive. Army Air Forces drafted their own outline plan for air operations in support of an attack to take place either on 15 September 1942 or on 1 April 1943.[36]

On the basis of all this information and in conformity with OPD's well-developed strategic ideas about an attack in western Europe, Colonel Hull and Colonel Connor drew up an invasion plan in outline, the first draft of which was ready on 27 March. Colonel Hull discussed it with Colonel Handy and General Eisenhower, the three officers weighing its merits as a concrete military project to carry out the strategy on

which they all agreed. On 1 April they presented the plan to General Marshall, who at once gave it his wholehearted support, though recommending substantial changes in language that General Eisenhower and his two staff assistants promptly incorporated.[37] Secretary Stimson and General Marshall took it to the President, who gave his prompt approval 1 April 1942.[38] A few days later, accompanied by Harry Hopkins, General Marshall set out for London as a Presidential envoy to secure British approval of the common strategy which OPD had recommended. In the Chief of Staff's party was Colonel Wedemeyer, who had figured prominently in the Joint U. S. Strategic Committee planning which pointed the way to the BOLERO plan and who had been working in the field of long-range strategy and logistics ever since he helped draft the Victory Program in 1941. The American delegation arrived in the United Kingdom on 8 April 1942.[39]

---

[36] (1) For responsibilities of Colonels Hull and Connor, see interv, Lt Gen Hull with author, 3 Jul 47, OPD Hist Unit Interv file. (2) For extra-OPD staff work, see papers in ABC 381 BOLERO (3–16–42), 4.

[37] (1) 1700 Report, 1 Apr 42, Current Gp files, AG Rcds Br. This is the only documentary record of OPD's submission of the BOLERO plan to the Chief of Staff. (2) Interv, Lt Gen Hull with author, 3 Jul 47, OPD Hist Unit Interv file.

[38] Three weeks previously the President had told the Prime Minister that he was "becoming more and more interested in the establishment of this new front this summer, certainly for air and raids." See msg 115, President for Prime Minister, 9 Mar 42, with memo, SW for CofS, 24 Mar 42, in ABC 371 (3–5–42). For Presidential approval, see: (1) Stimson, On Active Service in Peace and War, pp. 418–19 (Secretary Stimson says the plan was approved on 1 April); (2) cf. Sherwood, Roosevelt and Hopkins, pp. 519–21.

[39] (1) For reference to General Marshall's position as negotiator "in the name of the President," see memo, ACofS for SW, 12 Apr 42, sub: Review of Our Situation, OPD 381, 6. The memorandum was drafted by General Eisenhower. (2) For composition of delegation, see paper, n.d., title: Opn MODICUM, ABC 381 BOLERO (3–16–42), 5. In addition to Mr. Hopkins, General Marshall, and Colonel Wedemeyer, the party included Col. H. A. Craig, Air Forces planner, and a physician for Mr.

The Marshall Memorandum, as the British called the American plan, outlined the objective, the timing, the combat strength, and the strategic advantages of operations in western Europe.[40] First, it listed the principal reasons for launching the first British-American offensive in western Europe, the argument following the general lines WPD had drawn in its memoranda of 28 February and 25 March 1942. The selection of western Europe for invasion would "produce effective results" in less time than if any other theater were chosen. The "shortest route to the heart of Germany" passed through France. In this area alone could the necessary air superiority be achieved and the bulk of British air and ground forces be brought into action. The United States could "concentrate and maintain" a larger force in western Europe than any other area. There they could be employed in a concerted effort with British and Soviet combat forces. The western European front offered a "unique opportunity to establish an active

sector" in the summer of 1942 through air operations and raids or forays. Finally, an attack on Germany through western Europe would "afford the maximum possible support" for the Soviet Union, "whose continued participation in the war is essential to the defeat of Germany."

The plan then presented OPD's often reiterated contention that a decision as to the major effort had to be made at once so that the United Nations could co-ordinate all "production, special construction, training, troop movements and allocations" for one main objective. The American proposal was to harness all plans and preparations to the "single end" of "an attack, by combined forces of approximately 5,800 combat airplanes and 48 divisions against western Europe as soon as the necessary means can be accumulated in England—estimated at April 1, 1943."

Three main phases in the execution of the plan were listed:

> a. Preparation, involving:
> (1) Immediate coordination of procurement priorities, allocations of material and movements of troops and equipment.
> (2) Establishment of a preliminary active front.
> (3) Development of preparations for possible launching of an "emergency" offensive [in 1942].
> b. Cross-channel movement and seizure of beachheads between Le Havre and Boulogne.
> c. Consolidation and expansion of beachheads and beginning of general advance.

The preparatory phase constituted what shortly became known as BOLERO. The contingency mentioned as part three of the preparatory phase became known as SLEDGEHAMMER. The actual assault and consolidation, the second and third phases, became known as ROUNDUP.

In developing these ideas in detail, the OPD outline of operations stated that con-

---

Hopkins. Colonel Hull of OPD was not a member of the original MODICUM party although he was in England at the same time and took an active part in discussions of BOLERO with the British. The MODICUM party traveled under code names, General Marshall as Mr. Mell and Colonel Wedemeyer as Mr. White.

[40] The Marshall Memorandum or BOLERO plan is extant in a number of distinct versions, all similar in substance but varying considerably in language and order of presentation of points. Many copies are undated and the titles were changed on several occasions. Presumably for security, no formal file entry for the plan was ever made in either the regular OPD decimal file system or the files of the Office of the Chief of Staff. Even the President did not keep a copy. The plan itself was covered with a memorandum arguing the strategic propriety of the plan, and for that reason the British adopted the phrase Marshall Memorandum for the whole plan, then unnamed. The BOLERO/ROUNDUP/SLEDGE-HAMMER terminology came into use a few weeks later. For lengthy documentary references to the various versions of this plan, see OPD Hist Unit Study P.

centration on BOLERO rested on four assumptions: The Alaska-Hawaii-Samoa-Australia line would be held with an increase in Pacific garrisons from about 175,000 to about 300,000 total strength. The American commitments of ground and air forces to Australia, New Zealand, the Middle East, and the China-Burma-India theater would be met. The USSR would continue to contain the bulk of German forces. Axis strength in western Europe would remain approximately at the April 1942 level.

Under these conditions, the plan stated, the United States could furnish approximately one million men, including thirty divisions, and 3,250 combat aircraft for an invasion on 1 April 1943. If the British made available eighteen divisions and 2,550 combat aircraft, the combined force would be strong enough to establish air superiority and make a landing on a six-division front between Le Havre and Boulogne. One American airborne division and American and British parachute troops would be used to slow German reinforcements while strong armored forces, drawn from the six American and three British armored divisions assigned to ROUNDUP, "rushed in to break German resistance" and eventually to spearhead a general movement toward the port of Antwerp.

In indicating the strength necessary for the invasion, the plan noted that American troops would be equipped and trained in time for the operation but that shipping would be a critical factor requiring continuous attention to insure that troops reached the United Kingdom on schedule. It also called attention to the need for immediate "intensification of the construction program" to supply the 7,000 landing craft needed for the assault, a critical matter which had been occupying the attention of OPD for some time and which was to plague British-American planning throughout the rest of the war.[41]

Finally, the BOLERO plan provided in some detail a modified plan for the emergency invasion that might have to be launched in September or October 1942. This landing operation, SLEDGEHAMMER, would take place only if it should be absolutely necessary to prevent a collapse of Soviet resistance or if the German position in western Europe had become critically weakened.[42] Whatever forces could be transported across the Channel would be used if SLEDGEHAMMER were launched, but landing craft would be sufficient to sustain only about five divisions, half American and half British, at any time in the fall of 1942. In any case, only three and one-half American divisions, including the North Ireland (MAGNET) force, could be shipped to the United Kingdom by 15 September 1942, and only about 700 American combat aircraft would be available.

Despite the attention given the SLEDGEHAMMER contingency, the only operational activity definitely scheduled for 1942 in the BOLERO plan was the inauguration of air attacks and minor coastal raids. In addition to being of some help to the Soviet Union, these attacks would "make experienced

---

[41] Even after formal reference to the landing craft issue had been put in OPD's BOLERO plan and the plan approved, General Eisenhower noted: "This morning I attended a committee meeting on 'Landing Craft' at which were discussed questions on which I begged the answers last February. Who is responsible for bldg. landing crafts? What types are they bldg? Are they suitable for cross channel work? Will the number of each type be sufficient? etc? How . . . can we win this war unless we can crack some heads?" Notations by Gen D. D. Eisenhower, 6 May 42, Item 3, OPD Hist Unit file.

[42] Min of meeting, U. S. Representatives-British CsofS, London, 14 Apr 42, Tab E, ABC 381 BOLERO (3–16–42), 5.

veterans of the air and ground units." The plan dwelt on the advantage to be derived in the long preparatory phase by giving the troops in the United Kingdom intensive and specialized training from "fundamentals of technique in loading and unloading of boats" to "constant raiding of small task forces." The whole operational program presented in the BOLERO plan thus was pointed toward a major effort in 1943. The modified plan represented a concession to the earlier position, initially taken by the JUSSC and General Eisenhower, that a 1942 attack was possible and necessary. OPD did not alter the middle-of-the-road position it had subsequently adopted on this issue.

British Acceptance of the Marshall Memorandum

For almost a week, 9 through 14 April, the British Chiefs of Staff and planners and the representatives of the United States in London discussed OPD's plan for taking the offensive in Europe. In presenting and defending the plan, General Marshall was assisted by two OPD officers, Colonel Wedemeyer and Colonel Hull, who was present in London for most of the conferences although not a member of the official party. At the first meeting, 9 April 1942, General Marshall explained that the "reason for his visit was to reach a decision as to what the main British-American effort was to be, and when and where it should be made." [43] These decisions were linked with the acceptance or the rejection of the BOLERO/SLEDGEHAMMER plan. General Marshall emphasized the necessity of arriving at a decision in principle as quickly as

possible. Throughout the meeting the American representatives dwelt on the importance of maintaining the USSR as an effective fighting force in 1942 and of gaining combat experience for the U. S. Army. [44]

The American representatives explained that the flow of American troops and aircraft to the United Kingdom would not reach large proportions until the fall of 1942 because of shipping limitations and other American commitments. By 1943, however, considerable American forces would be available. Colonel Hull explained that cargo ships were a limiting factor in 1942, but he felt confident that their production would approach the level of personnel shipping by April 1943. He pointed out that in the main plan the American planners had mentioned 1 April 1943 as a possible target.

Colonel Hull explained that in the opinion of the American planners, the necessity of providing the ground forces with a fighter umbrella would limit the area for the assault to the French coast opposite southeast England. He added, however, that the planners wished to leave the detailed plan of operations to the commander of the invasion force. In his summary of the contemplated build-up of American forces he stated that the most the United States could provide within the time for execution of the main plan would be thirty divisions. [45] The American planners felt that about fifty divisions probably would be necessary to exploit fully the initial landing. [46]

---

[43] Min of meeting, U. S. Representatives-British CsofS, London, 9 Apr 42, Tab D, ABC 381 BOLERO (3–16–42), 5.

[44] Min of meeting, U. S.-British Planning Stfs, London, 11 Apr 42, Tab N, ABC 381 BOLERO (3–16–42), 5.

[45] Min of meeting, U. S.-British Planning Stfs, London, 13 Apr 42, Tab Q, ABC 381 BOLERO (3–16–42), 5.

[46] Min of meeting, U. S.-British Planning Stfs, London, 12 Apr 42, Tab O, ABC 381 BOLERO (3–16–42), 5.

In attempting to win British agreement to the BOLERO plan, the American representatives utilized the basic line of strategic argument developed during the previous two months. As Colonel Wedemeyer phrased it: "The United Nations must adhere to the broad concept of strategy, viz, that Germany is our principal enemy. . . . The dissipation of our combined resources . . . should be discontinued or at least held to a minimum in consonance with the accepted strategy of concentration on offensive operations in the European theater, with concurrently defensive operations in all others." [47] General Marshall summarized the U. S. Army planners' views that current American commitments to the Southwest Pacific, Middle East, and other theaters would be fulfilled but that calls for additional reinforcements would have to be carefully limited. He emphasized that it was essential for the United Nations to focus attention on the main project, offensive operations on the Continent, lest it be reduced to the status of a residuary legatee for which nothing was left.[48]

On 14 April 1942 the British Chiefs of Staff and the British Government formally accepted the Marshall Memorandum.[49]

They agreed with the American conception of concentration against the main enemy, Germany, as embodied in the plan, with one broad qualification.[50] This was that necessary measures be taken to hold Japan and prevent a junction of Japanese and German forces.[51] With this understanding, entirely consistent with the strategic ideas on which OPD had based the BOLERO plan, the British agreed that concerted planning should begin immediately for a major offensive in Europe in 1943 and, if necessary, an emergency attack in 1942.[52] The Prime Minister, in "cordially accepting the plan," predicted that the "two nations would march ahead together in a noble brotherhood of arms." [53]

Thus in mid-April 1942, the BOLERO plan became official British-American policy, designed to govern deployment and operations within the strategic framework established in ABC–1 and at ARCADIA. Planners could set to work at once on the BOLERO phase, the build-up of resources in the United Kingdom. As General Marshall pointed out, however, hewing closely to the BOLERO line and avoiding further dispersions would re-

---

[47] Min of meeting, U. S.-British Planning Stfs, London, 11 Apr 42, Tab N, ABC 381 BOLERO (3–16–42), 5.

[48] Min of meeting, U. S. Representatives-British CsofS, London, 14 Apr 42, Tab E, ABC 381 BOLERO (3–16–42), 5.

[49] (1) Msg, Gen Marshall for SW, 15 Apr 42, CM-IN 3939. (2) Min of meeting, U. S. Representatives-British War Cabinet Def Com, 14 Apr 42, WDCSA 381 (SS), 1. (3) Min of meeting, U. S. Representatives-British CsofS, London, 14 Apr 42, Tab E, ABC 381 BOLERO (3–16–42), 5. (4) British CsofS paper, title: Comments on Gen Marshall's Memo, COS (42) 97 (O), 13 Apr 42, Tab F, ABC 381 BOLERO (3–16–42), 5. (5) The Prime Minister had personally advised General Marshall of his acceptance of the plan 12 April 1942. Msg, Gen Marshall for Maj Gen McNarney, 12 Apr 42, CM-IN 3210.

[50] Msg 70, Prime Minister for President, 17 Apr 42, ABC 381 BOLERO (3–16–42), 4, Book 1.

[51] British CsofS paper, title: Comments on Gen Marshall's Memo . . ., Tab F, ABC 381 BOLERO (3–16–42), 5. The British qualification concerning the Middle East and India was premised on the belief that temporary diversion of British-American resources was necessary to stem the Japanese advance toward India and through the Indian Ocean and to prevent the Axis Powers from establishing a consolidated position from which even a concentrated attack against Germany would not dislodge them.

[52] (1) Min of meeting, U. S. Representatives-British CsofS, London, 14 Apr 42, Tab E, ABC 381 BOLERO (3–16–42), 5. (2) British CsofS paper, title: Comments on Gen Marshall's Memo . . ., Tab F, ABC 381 BOLERO (3–16–42), 5.

[53] Min of meeting, U. S. Representatives-British War Cabinet Def Com, 14 Apr 42, WDCSA (SS) 381, 1.

quire great firmness. The Chief of Staff reported: "Everyone agrees . . . in principle but many if not most hold reservations regarding this or that." [54]

Such reservations, some of them affecting fundamental elements in the BOLERO concept, were the subject of continuous discussion and debate by British and American strategists until the very day in June 1944 when troops actually landed on the shores of northwest Europe. It was almost two years from the date of initial agreement in principle before the time was finally set. Nevertheless, American staff officers at the time felt that the United States and Great Britain had reached a basic agreement on the way to win the war and that they could proceed directly from the Marshall Memorandum to concrete preparations for defeating Germany in northwest Europe. As General Eisenhower noted upon General Marshall's return from London: "At long last, and after months of struggle by this Div [WPD and OPD]—we are all definitely committed to one concept of fighting! If we can agree on major purposes and objectives, our efforts will begin to fall in line and we won't just be thrashing around in the dark." [55]

Machinery for Executing the Bolero Plan

Official approval of the BOLERO/ROUNDUP plan on 14 April 1942 enabled the Army planners to begin to carry out the basic strategic concept in day-to-day staff work. Army, joint, and combined administrative machinery for planning in detail the BOLERO build-up of men and resources in the United Kingdom soon began to function.

Even while General Marshall was still in London, OPD began to develop the BOLERO idea in terms of concrete U. S. Army preparations for the offensive. The production of landing craft and the deployment of American bomber forces to the United Kingdom were the two most critical elements in the whole scheme. Before the British accepted the BOLERO proposal, OPD had to relay detailed information on these subjects to General Marshall for use in convincing the British Chiefs of Staff of the feasibility of the plan. In response to instructions to "proceed vigorously in [the] matter of expediting and improvising landing craft," OPD informed General Marshall that Services of Supply was pressing for increased production, making arrangements through Navy procurement channels to meet estimated requirements of about 8,000 landing craft by April 1943. [56] OPD also concurred in General Arnold's transmittal to London of a tentative plan for moving Army Air Forces units to the United Kingdom. One heavy bombardment group with thirty-five B–17's, and two pursuit groups with eighty aircraft each, were scheduled for shipment about 15 May 1942, [57] thus beginning the Army Air Forces build-up for BOLERO.

On the same day that the British formally accepted the Marshall Memorandum, General Eisenhower proposed to General Handy (promoted from colonel as of 27

---

[54] Msg, Gen Marshall for Maj Gen McNarney, 13 Apr 42, CM-IN 3457.

[55] Notations by Gen D. D. Eisenhower, 20 Apr 42, Item 3, OPD Hist Unit file.

[56] (1) Msg, Gen Marshall for Maj Gen McNarney, 12 Apr 42, CM-IN 3210. (2) Memo, OPD for WDCMC, 13 Apr 42, sub: Landing Craft, Item 5, Exec 1. (3) Memo, SOS (Brig Gen W. D. Styer) for Maj Gen Eisenhower, 12 Apr 42, Item 5, Exec 1. The Navy estimated that one third of the required number of landing craft would be available by September 1942, the remainder by April 1943.

[57] (1) Msg, Lt Gen Arnold for Gen Marshall, 12 Apr 42, CM-OUT 2141. (2) Msg, Lt Gen Arnold for Gen Marshall, 14 Apr 42, CM-OUT 2433.

March) the idea of establishing a combined British-American master committee for detailed BOLERO planning.[58] Its main task would be to make the complicated arrangements and schedules, especially the troop-shipping programs, necessary to mount a major operation from the United Kingdom. On his return from England, General Marshall indorsed this and several other measures which would facilitate the building up of BOLERO forces. For example, several officers from OPD were to be sent to England, one at a time, to work with the British Joint Planners, and an American corps commander was to be selected to report with his staff to OPD, where he could be "given opportunity to familiarize himself with all details at this end." [59] General Handy suggested to the joint and combined committees that a master committee for BOLERO be established in Washington, and on 28 April the CCS directed the formation of a subcommittee of the Combined Staff Planners to develop the BOLERO plan.[60] This was called the BOLERO Combined Committee. It consisted of one U. S. Army Air Forces officer, two U. S. Navy officers, and one representative from each of the three British services,[61] with Colonel Hull of OPD acting as chairman.

The principal BOLERO committee task, as set forth in its directive, was to outline, co-ordinate, and supervise all British-American plans for moving, receiving, and maintaining American forces in the United Kingdom. This planning included estimates of requirements and availability of troops, equipment, and facilities; allocation of American and British components of the total force; and study of shipping, port facilities, concentration areas, communication systems, time schedules, and naval escort for the movement of American troops to the United Kingdom.[62] In order to facilitate the work of the BOLERO planners in Washington, a BOLERO committee was also set up in London to secure information and make administrative arrangements concerning port capacities and other accommodations for the reception and maintenance of American forces and supplies.[63] As Colonel Hull pointed out at its first meeting, the main objective of the new committee in Washington was to act as a shipping agency empowered to adjust the BOLERO troop unit and equipment program in accordance with the possibilities for actual movement to the United Kingdom. The committee did not attempt to dictate the strategical plans for employing troops, a function which it considered to belong to the commander of the ultimate operation on the European Continent.[64] But the initial mobilization and

[58] Memo, Maj Gen Eisenhower for Brig Gen Handy, 14 Apr 42, sub: BOLERO Planning, Book 1, ABC 381 BOLERO (3–16–42), 4.

[59] Memo for rcd, Maj Gen Eisenhower, 20 Apr 42, sub: Conf with Gen Marshall/Orgn for BOLERO Planning, Item 4, Exec 1.

[60] (1) For General Handy's suggestion, see min 13th meeting JPS, 22 Apr 42. (2) Forces directive, CPS 26/2/D, 28 Apr 42, title: Directive for Preparation of War Plan-BOLERO.

[61] (1) Memo, OPD for U. S. Secy CCS, 27 Apr 42, sub: U. S. Army Membership of BOLERO Combined Com, OPD 381 BOLERO, 8. (2) Min 1st meeting BOLERO Combined Com, 29 Apr 42, with CPS 26/2/D, ABC 381 BOLERO (3–16–42), 1.

[62] CPS 26/2/D, 28 Apr 42.

[63] (1) CPS 26/2/D, 28 Apr 42. (2) Min 17th meeting CCS, 28 Apr 42. (3) Memo, Secy JCS for ACofS OPD, 6 May 42, sub: BOLERO Combined Com in London, with CCS 69, ABC 381 BOLERO (3–16–42), 1.

[64] Min 1st meeting BOLERO Combined Com, 29 Apr 42, with CPS 26/2/D, ABC 381 BOLERO (3–16–42), 1. Although the original directive from the CCS (CPS 26/2/D) called for the preparation of a war plan, the committee confined its work to preparing troop movement and shipping schedules. No war plan BOLERO was ever prepared except the OPD BOLERO/ROUNDUP plan (Marshall Memorandum).

movement phase of taking the offensive began with the organization of the BOLERO Combined Committee under Colonel Hull.

While helping to set up a special agency for combined work on BOLERO, OPD reorganized its Theater Group to mount the European offensive. It was at this time, the last week of April, that the European Theater Section was formed under the leadership of Colonel Hull. Very soon, in the words of Colonel Hull, it was "handling everything in connection with the BOLERO movement and the MAGNET forces.[65] Colonel Hull and the officers under him worked in a dual capacity in OPD—serving for a time not only in the new section for controlling operational movements to the theater but also as planners in the Future Operations Section of S&P.[66] Since it was thus a unified plans and operations command post for the Army, OPD's European Theater Section was able to co-ordinate War Department work on BOLERO, mostly concerned with the organization, training, equipping, and transportation of ground and air units, and to provide a link between the Army and combined BOLERO activities. At the same time, OPD was trying to co-ordinate planning in the United States with planning in the United Kingdom. On 10 May Col. Arthur S. Nevins, chief of the Strategy Section, left for London for temporary duty with the British Joint Planners. Colonel Nevins was the first of a long series of OPD officers (most of them from the Strategy Section) to serve in this capacity.

The final contribution OPD made to BOLERO was the time and experience of its chief, General Eisenhower, in negotiations with the British during May and June. On 23 May General Eisenhower, accompanied by Generals Arnold, Somervell, and Mark W. Clark (Chief of Staff, Army Ground Forces, shortly thereafter designated corps commander for the BOLERO force), went to the United Kingdom on behalf of General Marshall specifically to see what progress was being made on BOLERO.[67] With General Chaney, then commanding general of the U. S. Army forces in the British Isles, General Eisenhower discussed such questions as the planning set-up for England, especially with respect to the tactical planning for the cross-Channel invasion assault, the composition of General Chaney's staff, consolidation of G-2 activities in England, and the timing of the arrival of the corps commander in England.[68] With officers of the Plans Section of General Chaney's staff, he discussed their conception of the invasion. He conferred with British commanders who were employing large landing craft, watched landing craft in operation, and attended a large field exercise by the British to test their new divisional organization.[69]

In addition to outlining to the British Chiefs of Staff the American position on the command organization for ROUNDUP, as ex-

---

[65] For Colonel Hull's description of the functioning of his new section, see pers ltr, Col Hull to Brig Gen C. T. Bolte (HQ USAFBI), 19 May 42, Tab 57, Book 2, ABC 381 BOLERO (3–16–42), 4.

[66] Chart on Future Opns and European Theater Secs appended to memo, Col Hull, no addressee, 17 May 42, OPD 321.19, 42.

[67] Notations by Gen D. D. Eisenhower, 21 May 42, Item 3, OPD Hist Unit file.

[68] (1) Maj Gen Eisenhower, Notes to Take to Great Britain, 22 May 42, Book 5, Exec 8. (2) Maj Gen Eisenhower's rpt, title: Account of "BOLERO Trip," 23–30 May 42, filed with CCS 72 in S&P rcds, ABC 381 BOLERO (3–16–42), 1.

[69] The director of these exercises was the British Army commander in the Southeast, General Sir Bernard L. Montgomery, who impressed General Eisenhower at this time as a "decisive type . . . extremely energetic and professionally able." Maj Gen Eisenhower's rpt, same title, filed with CCS 72 in S&P rcds, ABC 381 BOLERO (3–16–42), 1.

plained to him by General Marshall before he left Washington, General Eisenhower discussed the general plan of attack. He viewed the whole question of combined operations and the type and employment of landing craft necessary for the operation with Vice Admiral Lord Louis Mountbatten, British Chief of Combined Operations. General Eisenhower also took part in discussions with General Sir Bernard Paget, the British Commander of Home Forces, and talked with U. S. Army planners serving on General Paget's staff. He attempted to impress upon the British Chiefs of Staff General Chaney's complete authority to act for American forces in Europe and made arrangements concerning the special status of Colonel Nevins. Thus General Eisenhower made firsthand observations of the current status of the American and British military organization in the United Kingdom and of the current progress of planning for SLEDGEHAMMER/ROUNDUP, and became more familiar with British military commanders, planners, and Chiefs of Staff.

Upon his return to the United States on 3 June, General Eisenhower observed, without criticizing the ability of any of the officers in England: "It is necessary to get a punch behind the job or we'll never be ready by spring, 1943, to attack. We must get going!" [70] Within a week General Marshall had selected the chief of OPD to provide the punch in preparations for BOLERO.[71] General Eisenhower set out for London on 23 June 1942. His knowledge of General Marshall's views and his familiarity with concepts which had been embodied by OPD in the BOLERO plan were to prove useful to him as Commanding General, European Theater of Operations, in evolving the preparations and arrangements for SLEDGEHAMMER/ROUNDUP. Furthermore, as Commanding General, European Theater of Operations, he was able to exercise and put into effect some of the suggestions which he himself had advanced as a member of OPD. In a sense, therefore, General Eisenhower himself, the ex-Assistant Chief of Staff, OPD, provided one of the most important links between General Marshall's Washington command post and subsequent British-American military effort in the European area. There were major delays and many changes in strategic plans and operations before the BOLERO strategic concept reached its final fulfillment in the Normandy invasion of June 1944. Nevertheless OPD's span of activities in early BOLERO planning was indicative of the new role the Division was able to play in coordinating Army plans and Army operations as well as the contribution it could make to military planning and strategic decisions above its own and even above the Army's plane of authority.

---

[70] Notations by Gen D. D. Eisenhower, 4 Jun 42, Item 3, OPD Hist Unit file.

[71] *Ibid.,* 11 Jun 42.

CHAPTER X

The TORCH Period

The Army strategists in OPD had experienced the keenest satisfaction that can come to staff officers when they saw the BOLERO plan, which they regarded as their brain child, come to be the central feature in the strategy of the United States and Great Britain. In the second half of 1942 they had the trying experience of seeing this project for an early invasion of France pushed into the background by the decision to undertake an operation similar to the once-discarded project for the occupation of North Africa. The early enthusiasm for opening a second front in Europe in 1942, in which OPD had briefly joined, may have helped bring about the midyear deviation from the BOLERO line. In any event the President, like the Prime Minister, felt a compelling urgency to mount a major offensive before 1943. This urgency was less strictly military than psychological, affecting the American and British will to struggle, sacrifice, and win, as well as the international policies of neutral and allied states. In these matters, the importance of which Army planners did not belittle, the responsibility and the judgment of the President were final. His insistence upon action in 1942 and the strong case made by the Prime Minister for the North African venture led in June and July to a thorough reconsideration of strategy in that light. The unfeasibility of executing SLEDGEHAMMER (the project for a 1942 invasion) as a regular operation with calculable risks rather than as an emergency move, finally brought a decision by the British and American heads of government to attack northwest Africa in the autumn of 1942. General Eisenhower, already in the United Kingdom, was designated as Commander in Chief of the Allied (British-American) Expeditionary Force, the bulk of which sailed for North Africa from bases in the United Kingdom, and the rest of which left directly from the United States for the assault on Casablanca. The decision thus taken not only confused and darkened the prospects of invading France in 1943, but also once more plunged the long-range deployment schedules of the Army into chaos. While striving to restore order in strategic planning OPD had to turn its main efforts in the second half of 1942 to detailed preparations for the North African invasion, known as TORCH.[1]

---

[1] This brief summary gives only the high lights of the complex story which led to the adoption of TORCH and the postponement of BOLERO. For the President's insistence on action in 1942, see two key memoranda: (1) memo, President for SW, CofS, Gen Arnold, SN, Admiral King, Harry Hopkins, 6 May 42, no sub, WDCSA 381, 1; and (2) memo, President for Harry Hopkins, Gen Marshall, Admiral King, 16 Jul 42, sub: Instructions for London Conf, WDCSA 381, 1. For indication that Army planners were fully aware that considerations were involved in the BOLERO-TORCH decision other than the strictly military factors which it was their special business to weigh, see memo, Brig Gen Wedemeyer for Maj Gen Handy, 14 Jul 42, no sub, Tab 10, Item 1, Exec 5.

At the same time that TORCH was changing the tenor of military plans in the European area, OPD officers were observing uneasily the progress of the campaign on Guadalcanal in the South Pacific. The assault on Guadalcanal was predominantly a naval operation under U. S. Navy command, but it came to involve sizable Army air and ground forces. It was a tactical offensive originally conceived as staying well within the policy of a generally defensive strategy in the Pacific, on which the JCS had definitely decided as a prerequisite for the plan to concentrate strength in Europe, but it absorbed military resources of every kind considerably in excess of those originally allotted to it. These matters, and a host of related plans and policies, were debated thoroughly by Army spokesmen in the interservice and international staff committees as well as before the President. General Marshall himself, and consequently his strategists in OPD, had to accept command decisions that had a logic they could see but were contrary to the best military judgment they could bring to bear on the strategic problems at hand. Nevertheless, they went ahead to do their utmost in helping to carry out the very strategic decisions against which they had advised.[2]

The officer guiding OPD through the TORCH period was Brig. Gen. Thomas T. Handy, who succeeded General Eisenhower as Assistant Chief of Staff, OPD, on 24 June 1942. Two weeks later he was promoted to the rank of major general, which had been established for the post in March. He had vigor, stamina, and resolution, all demanded by General Marshall and all essential in any officer who assumed responsibility for co-ordinating the military operations of the U. S. Army with one another and with strategic plans. Through all the postponements and shifts that affected the planning of the invasion of France during the next two years, General Handy held this position in OPD, giving an element of continuity at a crucial point both in Army planning and control of Army operations. His personal experience encompassed the abstract if thorough Army planning of early WPD days, the achievements of 1941 and early 1942 when plans were being adjusted to meet the real circumstances of World War II, and the formative period dominated by BOLERO planning. General Handy, in the strenuous months following, there-

---

[2] During the TORCH period, General Handy had occasion to express the credo of the staff planner as he understood it in drafting for General Marshall an appropriate reply to an informal British suggestion that U. S. Army planners were not giving wholehearted support to the plan for invading North Africa. General Handy wrote:

Your planners have misconstrued the purpose of a frank exchange of ideas in open discussion and have interpreted the expressions of views by US Planners as a lack of adherence on the latter's part to a decision that has been made. The US Planners are at present concerned with planning and implementation of several operations, including TORCH, and therefore must consider the implications of each on the others.

Individuals charged with the execution of an operation must be imbued with full confidence in the success of the undertaking. It is equally true that those Planners who are responsible for the formulation of plans for projected operations, the assessment of their relative value to our war effort, and the integration of those plans with our overall strategy, must retain their intellectual integrity and view all military questions objectively. They must foresee and make provision to meet all difficulties involved in the execution of those plans. It is my opinion that we should demand absolute candor from our Planners when they discuss projected operations. Any weakness in our plans should be revealed through continued and frank discussion by our planning staffs rather than as a result of successful enemy action.

Draft ltr, Gen Marshall to Field Marshal Dill, n.d., Paper 11, ABC 381 (7–25–42), 4–B. This draft in the OPD files was initialed by General Handy.

fore, was able to bring General Marshall's plans and operations staff to an exceptionally high level of performance.[3]

General Handy did not make a formal appointment of a deputy to replace General Crawford, who left OPD on 22 June 1942. The primary function of a deputy, acting for the chief in his absence, was usually performed during General Handy's tenure by his Theater Group chief. Until 9 December, that officer was General Streett, who had served with General Handy several years in WPD in the late 1930's and who had worked in close association with him at a higher level of responsibility when both officers were group chiefs under General Eisenhower. On General Streett's departure General Hull, previously chief of the European Theater Section, became Theater Group chief. The other key post in OPD, that of Army planner in the JCS-CCS system and chief of S&P Group, General Handy assigned to Colonel Wedemeyer, who had been one of the Army members of the Joint U. S. Strategic Committee in February and March, member of the Combined Subjects Section from March to May,

and deputy group chief in May and June. He was officially appointed on 27 June to succeed General Handy both as chief of S&P and as Army planner, receiving a promotion to the rank of brigadier general on 7 July 1942.

In the smaller Logistics Group, whose functions were only gradually taking shape in the second half of 1942, Colonel Davis carried on as senior logistics specialist, becoming acting group chief on 25 June and permanent group chief on 1 August. He remained in that position until 4 December 1942. Colonel Gailey, Executive Group chief in charge of messages, records, and administration, and Colonel Davis afforded General Handy two additional officers to whom he could delegate the growing miscellany of logistics and administrative staff problems that did not properly fall within the sphere of the S&P or Theater Groups.

The firm status which General Handy and his staff in OPD had achieved by the middle of the TORCH period was reflected in a practical administrative way by its assignment of quarters in the tremendous new Pentagon Building erected across the Potomac southwest from Washington. OPD completed transferring its office from the old Munitions Building on Constitution Avenue on 15 November 1942, occupying what proved to be permanent quarters immediately adjacent to the Office of the Secretary of War and the Office of the Chief of Staff on the third floor of the Pentagon.[4]

Redefinition of Levels of Planning

The distinction between planners and operations control officers became much

---

[3] Educated at the Virginia Military Institute and commissioned in the Field Artillery in 1916, General Handy gained extensive experience in the American campaigns in France in 1918. Subsequently he went through the normal peacetime schooling of Regular Army officers, and also attended both the Army War College and the Naval War College. After a four-year tour of duty in WPD, 1936–40, he left the War Department to take command of the 78th Field Artillery Battalion at Fort Benning but was recalled to WPD in August 1941. His first tour of duty in WPD had given him a solid background in early Army strategic planning. His work under General Gerow at the ARCADIA Conference (December 1941–January 1942) was followed by four months' participation as Army planner in strategic planning in the JCS-CCS system. In this latter capacity he joined wholeheartedly in the struggle, led by General Marshall and promoted vigorously in OPD by Colonel Hull and Colonel Wedemeyer, to secure general approval of the BOLERO plan.

[4] For history of the physical location of WPD and OPD offices throughout the war, see OPD Hist Unit Study N.

MAJ. GEN. THOMAS T. HANDY, *Chief of the Operations Division, 24 June 1942–21 October 1944; Deputy Chief of Staff, 21 October 1944–1 September 1947.*

sharper than was originally intended when, in July, the Future Operations Section of the S&P Group was dropped from the Division. The rationale of this section had been that it provided a "connecting link between the S&P Group and the Theater Group"—between "broad phases of planning on many and varied projects" and immediate planning. The Future Operations Section was concerned with broad planning, but only on "projects, the implementation of which is intended in the near future." The principal concern of this section from the beginning had been the BOLERO movement to the United Kingdom. After initial approval of the BOLERO plan, this work became a task for theater implementation. In many ways the job was still planning, but it was planning of a more detailed kind than the formulation of strategy. Moreover, the build-up in the United Kingdom soon became entangled with the job of theater control of the North African task force. Accordingly, General Hull assumed the staff direction of BOLERO and of TORCH in his capacity as chief of the European Theater Section. The remaining functions of the Future Operations Section and three of its officers reverted to the Strategy Section.[5]

This transfer of the BOLERO and TORCH planners to the Theater Group was almost precisely the administrative process visualized when OPD was organized in March.

The officers who had drawn the plan in S&P took it with them to the Theater Group to put it into effect. From mid-1942 throughout the war, however, this simple system of the orderly movement of a plan, with its authors, from the level of grand strategy to the level of detailed operational planning did not prove to fit the actual facts of strategic planning. The BOLERO plan was not to be executed for a long time. Meanwhile the TORCH operation, which had been planned only in the most general outlines and not too clearly at that, was hastily launched.

Under these circumstances the European Theater Section found itself doing a lot of work on TORCH that resembled traditional Army planning on the highest level of strategy, while S&P continued to participate in joint and combined debates on some aspects both of BOLERO, which theoretically should have descended to the operational planning level once and for all, and of TORCH, an operation already being mounted. Just as in 1941, when the effort had been made to distinguish WPD's sphere of authority in such matters from GHQ's sphere, in the later months of 1942 and afterwards it proved to be impossible to draw a hard and fast distinction between general strategic planning and more detailed operational planning. The processes were so intermingled that they would not stay on different levels, even when both processes were carried on in one staff agency.

The result in administrative practice inside OPD was a new stratification of planning. It was achieved without much attempt at abstract definition by making a practical distinction between staff consideration of Army problems in the joint and combined committee system, usually involving world-wide strategy and policy, and

---

[5] (1) See chart No. 3, p. 126. (2) Memo, Col Elmer J. Rogers, Jr., for Col Wedemeyer, 29 Jun 42, sub: Remarks and Recommendations, etc., ABC 020 OPD, WDGS (13 July 1942), 3JA. (3) Memo, Brig Gen Wedemeyer for Exec OPD, 23 Jul 42, sub: Reorgn, S&P, Paper 44, Item 2B, OPD Hist Unit file. (4) Memo, Col A. C. Nevins for Chief S&P, 7 Jul 42, sub: Orgn of Strategy Sec, ABC 020 OPD, WDGS (13 July 1942), 3JA. (5) Colonel Hull was promoted to the rank of brigadier general on 7 July 1942.

Army problems, usually concerned with overseas operations, that could be handled between the theater commander and the Chief of Staff without reference to the interservice or international planning system. While strategy and theater operations might get mixed up on either side of the line drawn between these two levels of planning, it was at least clear which group in OPD would handle which problems. Thus, careful co-ordination between the groups in the Division was facilitated, and each group was free to develop in its officers, assigned for an indefinite period of time rather than until some specific strategic plan had been completed, as great a specialization in staff techniques as seemed profitable, in joint and combined planning on the one hand and in planning in conjunction with the theater commands on the other.

In effect in 1942 a new level of continuous, systematic planning had been established and superimposed on all previous levels of Army planning. It was the interservice and international level, where binding decisions had to be made in very general terms about a great many problems before the Army could proceed to plan at all. The kind of planning represented in the Army strategic plan of the 1930's had become simply a broad type of theater planning, whether strategic or operational by conventional definition. As such it could be handled most efficiently by the Theater Group, assisted increasingly by the Logistics Group. Later in the war the initiative in this kind of operational planning was taken over almost entirely by the growing overseas theater staffs. Throughout the war OPD's Theater Group officers studied the detailed calculations as to the units the overseas theaters needed for projected operations, monitored the movement overseas of forces in the numbers approved, and supervised the countless related arrangements that were essential to their use in the right place at the right time. In 1942 there were no large overseas staffs to carry on this kind of planning, and OPD's "pick and shovel" officers carried a heavy load, especially in making preparations for TORCH, working always, of course, under the direction of their group chief, the chief of OPD, and the Chief of Staff.

This process was the heart of planning for Army operations as such. In the prewar frame of reference, many of these decisions would have been considered high-level strategy. But by the end of 1942 it was obvious that they were being made below the highest level of staff work, and were hardly a matter of independent Army determination at all. For the most part they were settled within the pattern of interservice and international strategic agreements reached by the JCS and the CCS. In view of this fact, OPD tended to concentrate all kinds of planning that affected Army operations in the theaters in the hands of one group of expert staff officers, and reserve for another group, S&P, the kind of staff problem, whatever it might be, that in fact had to be settled in the joint and combined committee system.

The propriety of this pragmatic redefinition of planning levels toward the end of 1942 became clearer when it developed later that the Western Task Force of TORCH was the last major Army combat expedition launched from the United States under the direct supervision of OPD. In midwar there was comparatively little overlapping of staff work on grand strategy and strictly operational planning of the kind that had gone into the older Army strategic planning. The latter was being done almost altogether in the theaters of operations and merely monitored by OPD, chiefly by the Theater Group, on behalf of the Chief of Staff. Only insofar as impending decisions affecting the overseas theaters hinged on world-wide strategy being worked out in the JCS-CCS system were they of primary interest to S&P.

The redefinition of levels of planning along these lines served to stabilize OPD's internal organization and assignment of duties. There was no further evolution of the kind whereby Future Operations, S&P, had merged completely with the European Section, Theater Group. During the TORCH period and afterwards, S&P officers were mainly concerned with joint and combined planning, and theater section officers took care of every other problem referred to the Chief of Staff's command post. This system had the administrative virtues of stability and simplicity. It greatly facilitated the development of needed new techniques in joint planning in 1943, as well as the maintenance of close contacts with the huge overseas forces of the later war years.

Staff Work in the Joint Committee System

As a result of the shift in the focus of its work in the TORCH period, S&P began to develop its techniques for planning in the joint committee system. The Strategy Section provided the Army planner (the S&P chief) with a special staff for strategic study and advice. But the Army planner and the Chief of Staff, in their joint and combined capacities, had to face many policy problems being considered on the interservice and international level that were not strictly strategic and often were not strategic at all. These issues ranged from psychological warfare policy to systems of Army-Navy and Allied command. To make studies and recommendations on such miscellaneous

589727 O—61—13

matters was the function of the Combined Subjects Section. WPD had always dealt with Army-Navy problems for the War Department and from time to time had centralized this function in one of its planning sections. By mid-1942, however, the S&P Group had established a more systematic handling of joint and combined papers than had ever existed before. Whereas the Strategy Section reviewed studies on strategy, including joint and combined papers, and contributed ideas on strategy to these studies, the Combined Subjects Section had a more generalized responsibility of reviewing and making recommendations on any kind of paper which came under joint and combined consideration. Its officers prepared studies only on nonstrategic subjects, but the section co-ordinated all JCS-CCS paper work. It kept for reference and research the only comprehensive War Department file of joint and combined staff papers. While no clear line could be drawn between subjects properly classified as strategy and those that were not, close liaison between the sections made it possible for the group chief and his assistants to co-ordinate their work effectively.

The Combined Subjects Section in the latter part of 1942 not only had the task of studying and recommending appropriate action on matters under consideration or that ought to be considered in the JCS system, but also of initiating appropriate War Department action to carry into effect decisions reached by the JCS or the CCS. Ordinarily this implementation function, as it came to be called, was discharged by distributing JCS and CCS papers or directives based on JCS or CCS actions. A great deal of this work amounted merely to sending JCS directives to the Strategy Section or to the theater sections inside OPD, but on joint and combined matters outside the sphere of strategy and operational policy, the Combined Subjects Section dealt directly with other Army agencies and kept rather close watch over their compliance with instructions.

The importance of the Combined Subjects Section's implementation of JCS decisions increased immeasurably with the accretion of prestige and power to the JCS-CCS system. OPD had considered the Army bound by joint and combined decisions from the very beginning, despite the dubious legal status of the new organization, and this firm attitude as well as the efficient work of OPD officers in the system unquestionably contributed to the authority which joint and combined decisions had in the War Department. In this matter, of course, OPD was reflecting General Marshall's own strong conviction of the necessity of unified command on every level. The clearest exposition of this point of view had been presented in a memorandum drafted in April 1942 by General Eisenhower and Lt. Col. Kenneth N. Walker, General Streett's executive in the Theater Group. The Army Air Forces was encountering difficulties in meeting the JCS aircraft commitments for Hawaii. The memorandum stated that it was necessary to consider joint decisions as binding until reversed or amended by later joint action. It also made clear that OPD expected to play a central role in correlating all Army activities connected with joint and combined policies and decisions. General Eisenhower wrote:

It is the view of the Operations Division that any approved action by the Joint Chiefs of Staff must be taken as an authoritative directive unless and until modified by the same or higher authority. Any other view would imply a right to disregard decisions of the Joint Chiefs of Staff, which are either

specifically or by understanding approved by the Commander-in-Chief, and so create confusion and lack of coordination.

It is recognized that in certain instances commitments made for future operations cannot be completely executed, due to later developments. In such cases it appears that the logical course is to present the facts to this Division, which is charged not only with responsibility for initiating action for the War Department, involving operations, but for presenting to the Joint Chiefs of Staff, through channels, applicable data and recommendations in such matters.[6]

The Combined Subjects Section was the administrative embodiment of this policy. In the first six months of General Handy's tenure the contribution to unity of military effort which OPD was able to make through the work of the section became more and more apparent. Until September 1942, OPD performed the task of carrying out JCS directives primarily on the precedent of WPD's responsibility for similar initiation of action on Joint Board decisions. Finally, on 10 September, a formal assignment of this responsibility was made to OPD. Some such solution was necessary, since the JCS had no executive staff large enough both to issue directives and see that they were put into effect. Executive responsibility had to be taken independently by the Army—including the Army Air Forces—and the Navy. OPD was the only Army agency with the information necessary to do the job. To make this *de facto* situation *de jure,* the Chief of Staff assigned OPD the "duty, for the War Department, of implementing and following up directives and decisions of the Joint U. S. Chiefs of Staff and the Combined Chiefs of Staff," re-

---

[6] Memo, OPD for AAF, 27 Apr 42, sub: Reinforcement of Acft for Hawaiian Dept, Tab Misc, Book 5, Exec 8.

porting actions taken to the JCS secretariat, which had been "charged with the responsibility of following up directives issued to the Army and the Navy." [7]

On the following day this duty was formally delegated by the Assistant Chief of Staff, OPD, to the Combined Subjects Section. This section was charged with reviewing all joint and combined papers and initiating War Department action either by transferring them to another section of OPD authorized to issue the appropriate instructions or by preparing a supplementary directive to be issued formally by OPD to the Army agency which could appropriately take the necessary action.[8] This procedure was described in a directive distributed on 16 January 1943 throughout the War Department and to the JCS secretariat:

All joint and combined decisions requiring implementation by the War Department are sent to the Operations Division, WDGS. The Combined Subjects Section, OPD, either implements these decisions or forwards them with additional background, to the proper War Department agency for the necessary action. This Section also is charged with following up directives and decisions emanating from the Secretariat, Joint U. S. Chiefs of Staff, and also from the Secretary, Joint U. S. Communications Board. Periodic reports of War Department action are made to the several secretaries through the Office Chief of Staff.

Matters affecting both the Army and the Navy on which a decision is required by either the Joint U. S. Chiefs of Staff, or by the Joint U. S. Communications Board, will be prepared in the form of a brief memorandum for the Chief of Staff, through the Combined Subjects Section, OPD, which acts as a coordinating agency for the Chief of Staff in these matters.[9]

The second half of 1942, in comparison with the first half, was a period of uncertainty and diminished drive in joint planning. The change was largely a reflection of the confusion that had resulted from the collision of the BOLERO plan, never canceled, with the operational requirements of TORCH. This was especially apparent in joint planning below the level of the Army planner, who had plenty of joint decisions to consider, that is, at the level of the Joint U. S. Strategic Committee, which was supposed to help him study them in detail. Whereas in February and March the JUSSC had drafted the basic studies on Pacific deployment versus the BOLERO concentration in Europe, comparatively few of the major JCS decisions between June and December were based on studies prepared by the JUSSC. This change came about primarily because the major decisions concerning TORCH were worked out on the level of the CCS or heads of government, and Army-Navy debates over Pacific operations centered less in differences of strategic opinion than in disputes about command responsibilities as between General MacArthur's Southwest Pacific area and Admiral Nimitz's Pacific Ocean area, and the allocation of critical resources to operations in each area. Many of these matters could be settled only through personal dis-

---

[7] Ltr, SGS to G-1, G-2, G-3, G-4, OPD, AAF, AGF, SOS, and Secy JCS, 10 Sep 42, sub: Implementation of Decisions of JCS and CCS, WDCSA 334 JCS (1942).

[8] OPD adm memo, 11 Sep 42, sub: Implementation and Follow-up of U. S. JCS and CCS Directives, Paper 34, Item 2B, OPD Hist Unit file.

[9] (1) Ltr, SGS to WDGS Divs, AAF, AGF, SOS, Secy JCS, and Secy JCB, 16 Jan 43, sub: Submission of Papers to U. S. JCS or JCB, OPD 312, 40. (2) See also memo, Lt Col J. K. Woolnough for Combined Subjects Sec, 2 Apr 43, sub: Procedure for Implementing Action on JCS and CCS Papers, with JCS M/I 48, in ABC 381 United Nations (23 Jan 43), 2.

cussion and negotiation between the Chief of Staff and Admiral King, the Chief of Naval Operations. Under these circumstances the JUSSC, if it was to serve effectively, had to reorient its activities and during this period it was moving slowly toward a clarification of its own staff functions in the joint planning system.

In furthering this process Colonel Maddocks, senior Army member of the committee, took the initiative.[10] In July he recommended to General Wedemeyer that the JUSSC might well be constituted as a high-level advisory committee reporting directly to the JCS on the "coordination of the nation's strategic planning and the determination of the strategic direction of its war effort," a role which its name seemed to imply it was designed to fill. On the other hand it might be clearly designated as a working committee of the JPS and assigned the sole mission of "analyzing the effects of possible enemy courses of action and those of our own troops on our agreed concepts of strategy, and of preparing directives for the Joint Staff Planners to assist them in directing strategical planning in the planning groups of the War and Navy Departments." In any case, Colonel Maddocks inferred, the JUSSC should not be asked to work on the various kinds of administrative and operational problems which the JCS and the JPS had to deal with along with strictly strategic problems.[11]

In practice the JUSSC had tried to conform to all these possible conceptions of its functions. Its February and March studies connected with the early development of the BOLERO plan related directly to the top-level determination of strategy. Work on such problems as "Defense of the Island Bases" in the Pacific was the kind of joint planning under agreed strategy which Colonel Maddocks associated with a working committee of the JPS. Finally, JUSSC studies on the use of amphibious forces related more to the operational responsibilities of the JPS than to strategy proper.[12] With this assortment of precedents for the kind of staff activity it should be carrying on and in the absence of a ruling on one of the functions which Colonel Maddocks defined, the JUSSC in the second half of 1942 alternated between attempts to stay on the highest plane of strategy and efforts to assist the JPS decide what to do next about its operational responsibilities.[13] Usually the Joint Staff Planners, beset with a host of comparatively short-range issues that were semistrategic and semioperational, delegated its staff work to *ad hoc* subcommittees. JUSSC members were frequently selected as individuals to sit on these subcommittees, but other qualified Army and Navy officers were also appointed. The JUSSC as formally constituted was left with little to do in its own right, and its members were occupied with special studies for the JPS.

---

[10] The Army section of the JUSSC during the second half of 1942 contained four OPD officers: Colonel Maddocks, Col. E. E. Partridge, Col. R. E. Starr, and Lt. Col. W. R. Wolfinbarger, an Air Corps officer who joined OPD in March and JUSSC in August as replacement for Colonel Hansell. Colonel Maddocks was virtually an assistant Army planner for General Wedemeyer, attending most JPS meetings and sitting on nearly all the important subcommittees, especially those concerned with mobilization, equipment, and deployment of forces, which claimed more planning attention than strategy proper in this period.

[11] Memo, Col Maddocks for Chief S&P, 9 Jul 42, sub: Jt Strategic Com, ABC 020 OPD, WDGS (13 Jul 42), 3JA.

[12] *Ibid.*

[13] (1) For voluminous study of first type, see JPS 43, 8 Aug 42, title: Strategic Policy of United Nations and U. S. on Collapse of Russia. (2) For second type, see JPS 46, 21 Aug 42, sub: Mil Tunnel Under English Channel.

Although it was not to take effect until 1943, a clarification of JUSSC functions ultimately resulted from the JCS consideration of Colonel Maddocks' memorandum. In October, upon General Handy's recommendation, General Marshall referred to the JCS a formal proposal drafted on the basis of Colonel Maddocks' July paper. This proposal suggested reconstituting the JUSSC on the level of the Joint Staff Planners and giving it the mission of making "recommendations to insure that our basic strategical policy conforms to the developing situation, and upon the approval of such recommendations, to prepare the necessary strategical plans." In effect this proposal would clearly assign to the reconstituted JUSSC the two distinct functions of assisting in the determination of strategic policy and drafting strategic plans to carry it out, both of which Colonel Maddocks had described in his memorandum. At the same time it would free the JUSSC from nonstrategic problems and put it on a level where it could give strategic advice directly to the JCS.[14]

Discussion of this problem by the JCS ended in a decision to split the two functions between a new "Joint Orientation Committee composed of three senior officers" and the old JUSSC. The new committee undertook to keep the JCS "advised on the soundness of our basic strategic policy in the light of the developing situation, and on the strategy which should be adopted with respect to future operations." By implication the JUSSC, left as a group to which the Joint Staff Planners could "refer matters requiring detailed research," could best devote itself to the other function which the

Chief of Staff had suggested for it, that is, drafting Army-Navy strategic plans in accordance with approved strategy. The JCS agreed, however, merely to proceed with the establishment of the new committee and to let the change in JUSSC functions "be accomplished gradually by process of evolution."[15] The evolution lasted several months, until April 1943.

Meanwhile the high-level strategic group of three senior officers, named the Joint Strategic Survey Committee (JSSC), was set up on 7 November 1942. Composed of Lt. Gen. Stanley D. Embick, Maj. Gen. Muir S. Fairchild as Air Forces representative, and Vice Admiral Russell Willson, it continued throughout the war to make recommendations to the JCS on "global and theater strategy, rather than area strategy and campaign plans."[16] Or, as Admiral King had phrased it in discussing the new organization, the JSSC was an "independent group of so-called 'elder statesmen' to advise the Chiefs of Staff on national policy and world strategy."[17]

Shortly after the constitution of the JSSC, Colonel Maddocks prepared an informal paper which explained his conception of war planning as it then existed and which pointed the way to the role the old JUSSC was to assume in 1943. He wrote:

1. The following are considered to be the essential steps in military planning:
    a. Strategic concept.
    b. Strategic direction.
    c. Future operation planning.
    d. Operation planning.
2. The strategic concept is the basis for all military planning. The strategic concept must not only be developed but it must also be kept up to date in the light of developing and pre-

---

[14] (1) JCS 133, 19 Oct 42, title: Reconstitution of JUSSC. (2) Cf. memo, OPD for CofS, 18 Oct 42, same sub, OPD 334.8 Jt. Strategic Committee, 3.

[15] Min 40th meeting JCS, 3 Nov 42.
[16] JCS 149/D, 7 Nov 42, title: Charter of JUSSC.
[17] Min 40th meeting JCS, 3 Nov 42.

dictable situations. This is a function of the Joint Strategic Survey Committee.

3. Military planning must be coordinated and integrated with the strategic concept so that it will fit into the pattern of the whole. This is known as strategic direction. Without strategic direction, future operation planning will be haphazard and at random. . . .

5b. The study, coordinated with the strategic concept, of the strategic possibilities of projected and current operations provides a firm basis for the strategic direction of our military planning. The strategic possibilities which will result from projected operations and from the completion, partial completion, or failure of each operation now going on or ordered must be considered and a directive for future operation planning based on such possibilities must be issued. It is only in such a manner that our future operation planning will be realistic.

5c. One of the functions of the Joint Strategic Survey Committee is to provide strategic direction for the Joint Chiefs of Staff. The Joint Strategic Committee might perform this function for the Joint Staff Planners, if the Joint Strategic Committee is to be retained and to do strategic planning. . . .

6. Future operation plans can and should be developed in accordance with current and predictable situations. These plans when approved and ordered into effect become operations plans. At the present time, the Strategy Section of the War Department and the Future Planning Section of the Navy Department, without reference to each other, develop future operation plans. The Joint Staff Planners should issue directives for future operations plans.

7. Operation plans are the last step in planning and are completed by the Commander from approved future operations plans.[18]

It was to the special, technical task described in Paragraph 6 of Colonel Maddocks' memorandum—drafting joint strategic plans for future operations, particularly for the series of interrelated Pacific island campaigns—that the reorganized JUSSC turned during the following months.[19]

Theater Group Organization

The Theater Group went ahead in the second half of 1942 with the detailed work of controlling Army operations in the overseas theaters, a task as wide in its ramifications as Army activities. The section structure did not change, General Streett preserving the seven area units and the Troop Movements staff he had set up in April. In supervising and co-ordinating their work, the group chief devised a new system of executive control which gave him the assistance he needed and made it possible for the Theater Group to act with dispatch on varied Army issues which the sections were trying to solve. Shortly after Col. Charles W. Stewart became the group executive officer in July, a second executive officer, Lt. Col. Walter C. Sweeney, Jr., was brought into the group to co-ordinate its work on air matters. The precedent of having two executives, one representing the ground force interest and the other the air force interest, was followed thenceforth throughout the war. It was complemented after December 1942 by a system of Air and Ground deputies. Brig. Gen. John E. Upston, previously chief of the Africa-Middle East Section, became the first Air deputy. Brig. Gen. Carl A. Russell, formerly the only group deputy, continued to occupy the post of Ground deputy.

While the organization of the Theater Group into sections remained static during this period, the assignment of officers in and among the sections was kept flexible in order

[18] Draft JUSSC study (Col Maddocks), 7 Dec 42, title: Steps in Mil Planning, with JCS 149/D, in ABC 334.8 JSSC (11–3–42).

[19] See Ch. XIII.

to make strength correspond as closely as possible with the fluctuating requirements of overseas operations. Through the assignment and reassignment of personnel, the group was able to strike a balance between area specialization in the sections and group sensitivity to ever-changing overseas conditions.

A large proportion of Theater Group strength—nearly a third of the whole group—remained in the Western Hemisphere sections throughout this period. This proportion reflected the volume of Army activities associated with the initial defensive deployment in the United States and its defensive outposts. The growth of the Pacific sections in mid-1942 corresponded with the steady expansion of defensive garrisons throughout the Pacific and the inauguration of limited tactical defensives in New Guinea and on Guadalcanal, the latter of which developed into a fairly large-scale campaign by the end of the year. The smaller Asiatic Section struggled with complex problems. The geography of its area required particularly careful staff planning, and the line between military operations and national policy was very fine. The Asiatic Section found that the simplest military decisions were involved with American policy toward China, with Generalissimo Chiang Kai-shek's personal, political, and military interests, and with British policies as reflected both in India and in the Combined Chiefs of Staff system in Washington.

The most active element in the Theater Group during the first six months of General Handy's tenure as Division chief was contained in the two sections responsible for operations in the European and African areas. The expansion of U. S. Army activities in the Middle East, particularly in connection with the mounting of the British offensive in Egypt to support TORCH, led to a considerable enlargement of the Africa-Middle East Section. Even more notable was the development of the European Section upon its definite disassociation from the Strategy & Policy Group in July. Since TORCH was mounted from the United Kingdom and from the United States under General Eisenhower's command, the European Section carried the full load of detailed planning and staff supervision of activities connected with the operation. At the same time it proceeded with such minor phases of the BOLERO build-up in the United Kingdom as could be carried out simultaneously with TORCH.

Expansion of Logistics Group Activities

During the latter half of 1942, while members of the S&P and Theater Groups were adapting their activities to conform with actual experience in planning and mounting military operations, the officers of the Logistics Group were finding that wartime problems required them steadily to expand the area of their special staff activity inside OPD. They continued to act within OPD whenever necessary as specialists on munitions production and distribution, supply, and the organization, training, and availability of troops. Such problems came to the Logistics Group for action rather than to the Theater Group only when they transcended in scope the confines of individual theater planning. In the period of mounting TORCH, the overflow of technical problems requiring scrutiny by OPD's logisticians multiplied rapidly. The *ad hoc* character of these duties made it difficult for the group to describe and for others to grasp the rationale of its work. Nevertheless, there was always plenty of work for the dozen or so Logistics Group specialists to do merely in furnishing essential information on troops and material to the Theater and S&P Groups.

Under Colonel Davis' leadership the Logistics Group as a whole struggled to keep up with the miscellany of staff tasks which fell to it. In mid-September 1942 Colonel Davis informed General Handy that his logisticians were greatly overburdened:

I would consider myself remiss if I did not inform you of the seriousness of the situation. For example, the ammunition status is so vital that no *strategical decision can be made without accurate knowledge of the amount of ammunition we may or may not have*. Logistics Group apparently is the only agency that can provide this information. . . . The strategical "blitzes" of the Theatre Group and the logistic "blitzes" of the M. A. B. [Munitions Assignment Board] are becoming more frequent and each one hits the Logistics Group.[20]

During the second half of 1942 some of the activities of the Logistics Group were beginning to stand out as independent, valuable contributions to the accomplishment of OPD's staff mission, the planning and control of operations. In the first place, the Troop Section continued to prepare the Victory Program Troop Basis and the Overseas Troop Basis. Responsibility for compiling this data, basic to production and supply scheduling, brought to the officers concerned, through contacts with other War Department agencies, information and habits of thought conducive to integrated, long-range balancing of zone of interior resources with theater requirements. As authorities on the facts and figures of Army-wide production, supply, and deployment needs, Logistics Group representatives were

influential in determining Theater Group decisions depending on these factors, particularly when more than one theater was involved. As troops began to move overseas in considerable numbers in the second half of 1942, this function of the Logistics Group became more and more prominent and more and more distinct from the area-oriented efforts of the theater sections.

Colonel Davis' reference to the logistic "blitzes" of the Munitions Assignments Board indicated another plane on which the Logistics Group was carving out a small but increasingly important niche for itself. This plane was the one on which joint and combined decisions were taken concerning the distribution of munitions to the United Nations and to the theaters of war. The allocation of production capacity and armaments was the controlling factor in every major strategic decision, particularly during the wartime period of greatest scarcity of equipment, 1942. The translation of strategic policy into the mathematics of equipment and supply was an intricate and specialized task. For the most part it was being done in the relative obscurity of joint and combined deliberations, particularly by the Munitions Assignments Board and its subordinate committees.

The Munitions Assignments Board in Washington was subordinate to the CCS but enjoyed a special status that had been bestowed intentionally by the appointment of a trusted Presidential adviser, Harry Hopkins, as chairman. Co-ordinating its work with that of a similar board in London, the Munitions Assignments Board allocated the total stocks of finished war materials among the United Nations in accordance with strategic and operational decisions in force at the time the munitions were actually

---

[20] Memo, Col Davis for ACofS OPD, 15 Sep 42, sub: Reduction of Commissioned Pers, Logistics Gp, OPD 210.3, 126.

available for distribution.[21] The American representatives of the board were *de facto* the highest authority for similar allocation of the total American allotment among the three services, and a great deal of careful calculation of Army, Navy, and Army Air requirements entered into the formulation of the position taken by the American members of the munitions board.[22] Insofar as ground and air equipment was concerned, the mechanisms for providing this necessary calculation of Army and Army Air Forces interests were the War Department Munitions Assignments Committee (Ground) and the War Department Munitions Assignments Committee (Air).[23] The influence of OPD came to bear only in the ground committee, where General Crawford had represented WPD and OPD from February until his departure in June.

When it became necessary to find a replacement for General Crawford, who was the ranking equipment expert in OPD, Col. Patrick H. Tansey, chief of the Matériel Section of the Logistics Group, was chosen.[24] During the remainder of 1942 Colonel Tansey waged an aggressive campaign in support of distributing munitions among the United Nations and, on some items, among the three American services in accordance with the strategic and operational plans which other OPD officers were helping to develop. A continuing issue in 1942 was the delicate balancing of the combat needs of British and other Allied forces with the training requirements essential to American units if they were to be ready for employment as visualized in strategic plans. Even within the U. S. Army, critically scarce items of equipment had to be parceled out to units according to a priority determined by future plans. In these and similar areas of the munitions field where logistics blended into strategy, the OPD spokesman was able to bring special knowledge to bear. Within the Army, Logistics Group decisions on the assignment of ground force equipment, particularly ammunition, went out under the full authority of the signature of the Assistant Chief of Staff, OPD. The usefulness of OPD's logistic staff work in joint and combined logistic planning was little recognized during the 1942 period, but Colonel Tansey and the other Logistics Group officers were gaining experience for the much larger contributions in this field that were still to be made.

---

[21] For working agreement on principles of Munitions Assignments Board, see: (1) ltr, Maj Gen R. C. Moore, DCofS to Maj Gen G. N. Macready, Asst Chief, Imperial GS, 12 Jan 42, WPD 4651; (2) memo, Gen Macready for Brig L. C. Hollis, 7 Jan 42, sub: Allocation of Finished Mil Equip to Allies, copy in WPD 4651.
 This system was set up in January 1942 by the President and Prime Minister. See: (1) memo, DCofS for Chief, Air Corps, G-4 Def Aid Dir (Brig Gen H. S. Aurand), and WPD, 15 Jan 42, sub: Allocation Com, WPD 4651-1; (2) CCS 19/1, 4 Feb 42, title: Order Establishing MAB.
[22] The munitions assignment system was quite separate from the munitions procurement system, which was handled for the United States by the War Production Board and the Joint Army-Navy Munitions Board, both operating under Presidential direction outside the JCS system. Although JCS and Munitions Assignments Board decisions were reflected in procurement policies, the distribution of finished munitions (often a year or two after procurement contracts had been authorized) was the link between production and strategy.
[23] (1) Ltr, Harry Hopkins to SW, 9 Feb 42, AG 334 Mun Asgmts Bd (9 Feb 42), 2. (2) AG ltr, 21 Feb 42, sub: WD Mun Asgmts Com (Ground), AG 334.8 Mun Asgmts Board (2-11-42). (3) AG ltr, 21 Feb 42, sub: WD Mun Asgmts Com (Air), AG 334.8 Mun Asgmts Bd (2-11-42). (4) AG ltr, 16 Apr 42, sub: WD Mun Asgmts Com (Ground), AG 334.8 Mun Asgmts Bd (4-10-42) OF.

[24] AG ltr, 13 Jun 42, sub: Designation of Offs as Member and Alternate on WD Mun Asgmts Com, AG 334.8 Mun Asgmts Bd (6-12-42) OF-E.

Personnel and Personnel Problems

Despite the pressure of work in the TORCH period, the mid-1942 allotment to OPD of just over 150 officers below general officer rank met the needs of the Division. This ceiling in strength was confirmed in August by the official War Department authorization of officers for duty in Washington and vicinity—with sixteen Army Specialist Corps officer positions being substituted for Regular Army majors and captains.[25] By the time OPD moved to the Pentagon Building in November, the Division had actually present on duty 155 officers (including general officers), 1 warrant officer (head of the record room), 136 enlisted men, and 107 civilians. The growth of the Division leveled off at about this point and remained there for some time. At the end of the year officer strength was only 148, including general officers.

During this period the procurement of qualified personnel continued to be a major problem for the executive office, though decreasingly so as the allotment was completed. Every effort was made by G–1 and the Services of Supply to procure for OPD the kind of officers it requested.[26] Nevertheless the Division continued to lose valuable officers to field commands and continued to find them hard to replace. Although some were denied the chance to transfer, the Division usually released those of its officers who were selected for tactical assignments and particularly those of sufficient seniority to become eligible for promotion to the rank of brigadier general by accepting field duty.

The trend to the field was hard to stop because senior staff officers in responsible positions, both in Washington and in the theater headquarters, usually had to wait for promotion longer than associates of comparable experience who were on troop duty. General Marshall recognized the embarrassment this caused in large headquarters, including his own staff, but stated that he found great difficulty in getting such promotions for general officers through the White House.[27] OPD was comparatively fortunate in having its group chiefs classified as general officers and having a rather high allotment (20 percent of strength) of colonels. Nevertheless many of the older officers left the Division, thereby securing promotions. The younger ones were less restricted in chances for promotion by being on staff duty, and on the other hand found a great deal of compensation in the authority OPD delegated to them despite their rank. The executive office tried to keep the promotions in the lower field grades in balance with seniority in the Army as well as duty in the Division.[28]

An experiment in personnel procurement occurred in the second half of 1942 with the establishment of the Army Specialist Corps. This attempt to secure men with special training or knowledge for duty in uniform with the Army though on a Civil Service status was short-lived. In accordance with instructions from the Secretary of War, OPD set out toward the end of August to recruit fifteen specialists of the rank of major. To meet the corresponding reduction in the allotment of other officers to the Division in September OPD released three National Guard and four Reserve officers ac-

---

[25] Memo, OPD for G–1, 17 Aug 42, sub: Almt of Offs, OPD, OPD 210.3, 112.

[26] Memo, OPD for TAG, 13 Jun 42, sub: Offs on Dy in District of Columbia and Vicinity, Item 3, Exec 15. Colonel Gailey expressed complete satisfaction with G–1 and Services of Supply procurement methods.

[27] Ltr, Gen Marshall to Lt Gen D. C. Emmons, 1 Jun 42, WDCSA 210.2 Hawaii.

[28] E.g., see memo, Col Gailey for Maj Gen Handy, 10 Sep 42, sub: Pers, Item 3, Exec 15.

tually on duty. Nine Army Specialist Corps members joined the Division in October, one going to the Logistics Group, two to S&P, and the rest to the Theater Group. On 4 November the whole system was abolished. Thenceforth all appointments were made to commissions in the Army of the United States (AUS), and OPD recommended five of its nine Specialists for AUS commissions.[29] Three of these five were released at their own request. Two were commissioned and remained on duty in OPD through most of the war, Maj. Carleton Hunneman serving in the Logistics Group and Maj. H. D. M. Sherrerd in the European Section.

At the end of the year OPD was in the midst of a more difficult personnel problem. At that time the Secretary of War and the Deputy Chief of Staff were waging a campaign to reduce the number of combat-fit officers on duty in Washington. Instructions were issued for all agencies to manage their releases and replacements so that at least one third of their officers would be over the age for troop duty or would be physically qualified only for limited service, not more than one third would be under thirty-five years of age, and none would be under twenty-eight years of age.[30] This order represented a complete reversal of the personnel policy inaugurated by General Eisenhower, with the approval of the Chief of Staff, whereby comparatively young officers had been recruited. Colonel Gailey reported that as a result of this policy OPD had "built up and trained a corps of young, able officers" and was particularly vulnerable to the new policy. According to Colonel Gailey's calculations in December 1942, only 17 officers in the Division were over-age for troop duty, whereas the required one third of allotted strength would amount to 52 in that category. This meant an "influx of 35 over-age officers, 31 of whom would go into the operating theaters and sections."[31]

In view of the fact that the over-age officers whom G–1 recommended as qualified for service in OPD were nearly all colonels, their placement in the Division also posed a serious problem. Colonel Gailey observed: "They will be senior in age and grade to our present theater chiefs and very probably most of them will be older and hold a permanent grade higher than the group chiefs and their deputies. This is an unhealthy situation and might very well be detrimental to the morale of not only the over-age officer but the younger officer who is being dispossessed of his section." Finally, Colonel Gailey informed General Handy that the addition of a considerable number of older officers was a dubious project from the point of view of staff efficiency: "This is a fast moving organization—hitting on high at all times. Its members must be able to preserve an open-sound-agile mind in a healthy body to perform their assigned duties under the terrific strain of long hours . . . and pressure that

---

[29] (1) Memo, OPD for G–1, 18 Aug 42, sub: Procurement Objective, Army Specl Corps, OPD, Item 3, Exec 15. (2) Memo, OPD for G–1, 24 Aug 42, sub: Almt Army Specl Corps, Item 3, Exec 15. (3) Memo, OPD for Dir of Pers, SOS, 18 Sep 42, sub: Almt of Offs, Item 3, Exec 15. (4) WD (AGO) memo, 4 Nov 42, sub: Army Specls Corps Apmts in AUS, copy filed Item 3, Exec 15. (5) Memo, OPD for Army Specl Corps, 21 Nov 42, sub: Army Specl Corps Pers, OPD 210.3, 136.

[30] Memo, DCofS, no addressee, 5 Dec 42, sub: Offs on Dy in District of Columbia, copy filed Item 3, Exec 15. For the purposes of the directive, over-age for troop duty was listed as: colonels, 50 years plus; lieutenant colonels, 47 years plus; majors, 42 years plus; captains and lieutenants, 36 years plus.

[31] (1) Memo, Col Gailey for Maj Gen Handy, 27 Dec 42, sub: Over-Age Offs, Item 3, Exec 15. (2) Cf. memo, OPD for G–1, 1 Dec 42, sub: Over-Age Offs, Item 3, Exec 15.

must need be continually present to success-fully cope with war time conditions." [32]

Despite such misgivings, Colonel Gailey set about to comply with instructions. The morale problem was somewhat relieved by permission from G–1 to carry the over-age colonels as "surplus in grade," thereby avoiding the absolute block their presence otherwise would place on promotions of junior officers in the Division.[33] Twenty-four officers left OPD between mid-December and the effective end date for compli-ance with the order from the Deputy Chief of Staff, 31 January 1943. Of these, 7 were under twenty-eight, and nearly all were under thirty-five. During approximately the same period (9 December 1942–1 Febru-ary 1943) 19 officers entered on duty in OPD, and most of these were either in the over-age or limited service category. Al-though Colonel Gailey had counted some of these officers as on duty in his Decem-ber calculations, the net result was close enough to the required quota to escape official censure.

OPD's Role in Torch

After the President, in July 1942, had reached the decision to undertake the Torch operation, as the Prime Minister and the British Chiefs of Staff had been urging, OPD was responsible for seeing that it was carried out successfully. The Bolero movement of U. S. Army units, equipment, and supplies to the United Kingdom and the military resources of the continental United States had to be diverted to effect an immediate concentration of strength for the invasion of North Africa. While trying to keep alive the Bolero plan as a stra-tegic concept and an ultimate operational project, OPD turned its primary attention to the operation at hand.

Torch represented the first major Amer-ican operation against Germany, the first major British-American combined offen-sive, and the most ambitious Allied amphib-ious undertaking of the war thus far. The Army had to develop new procedures and practices, for instance, to facilitate and co-ordinate the complicated politico-military negotiations in which American representa-tives engaged with a view to securing a quick cessation of French resistance, there-by insuring the success of the landings and subsequent military operations in North Africa. Less novel but unprecedentedly complicated were the preparations required to build up a complete American task force in the zone of interior, three thousand miles away from the other two task forces and General Eisenhower's Allied Force Head-quarters in the United Kingdom, and to arrange for its convergence on North Africa simultaneously with the forces from the United Kingdom. Concurrently, OPD, as the Chief of Staff's command post with world-wide operational responsibilities, sought to weave together the activities of other theaters and areas in support of the major undertaking, Torch. In performing the latter function, OPD aimed not only at furnishing maximum support for the Torch operation but also at laying the groundwork for the subsequent exploitation of the success of Torch in the European-African area, whether from Mediterranean bases or from the United Kingdom.

Planning for Torch went on both in London and Washington. In mid-August General Handy took a trip to the United Kingdom to secure from General Eisen-hower and his planning staff firsthand

---

[32] *Ibid.*

[33] Memo, OPD for G–1, 18 Dec 42, sub: Almt of Over-Age Offs, Item 3, Exec 15.

knowledge of the factors on the scene at Allied Force Headquarters which had to be reckoned with in decisions about preparations for TORCH.[34] OPD officers played a leading part in organizing and preparing General Patton's Western Task Force (Casablanca), the only completely American task force in operation, acting as co-ordinating agency between General Patton's headquarters, temporarily established inside OPD, and Allied Force Headquarters. They also served as intermediaries between the overseas command and the zone of interior, weighing the needs of the Western Task Force and of the American forces in the operation as a whole in the light of the resources available and the requirements of the overseas commander.

An officer from OPD's European Theater Section spent his full time in duties as liaison officer with General Patton's Western Task Force headquarters.[35] Another from the same section worked at the New York Port of Embarkation, mainly supervising the loading of operational equipment in the big D plus 40 convoy carrying supplies for both the Western Task Force and the Center Task Force (Oran), the latter of which was sailing from bases in the United Kingdom. This officer was formally designated as authorized agent of the Center Task Force commander, whose operational requirements had to be balanced with those of General Patton's force.[36]

In the process of harmonizing and maintaining a balance between activities in the rear echelon in the United States and the requirements of American forces in TORCH, OPD constantly referred to the views of the commander in chief of the operation and sought to free him from every concern except the major strategic responsibilities of his command. With this philosophy, OPD found the area of its activities rapidly expanding. These activities quickly came to cover, for instance, political and diplomatic considerations completely outside the scope of conventional military planning. OPD leaders had recognized very early that success in TORCH was greatly dependent upon reactions of the governments, armed forces, and people in Spain, Vichy France, and French North Africa. OPD not only served as the vital link in the communications chain connecting General Eisenhower's headquarters in London with consular officials of the United States in North Africa, but also were active in co-ordinating arrangements for the clandestine negotiations between General Eisenhower's representatives (led by Brig. Gen. Mark W. Clark) and French supporters of Gen. Henri Giraud in Algeria shortly before the initial landings.[37]

Following the initial landings (8 November 1942), the Chief of Staff, relying on OPD to monitor correspondence and suggest appropriate action, continued to support General Eisenhower in his efforts to

---

[34] (1) Pers ltr, Lt Gen Eisenhower to Gen Marshall, 19 Aug 42, Paper 54, ABC 381 (7–25–42) 4–B. (2) Msg, Maj Gen Handy (in London) for Gen Marshall, 22 Aug 42, CM–IN 8444.

[35] Memo, Lt Col C. P. Smith for Brig Gen Hull, 20 Oct 42, sub: Suggestions for More Efficient Handling of Future Task Force Hq, OPD 320.2 Task Force, 79.

[36] Memo, OPD for TAG, 28 Nov 42, sub: Instructions Pertaining to Task Force "A" Shipts on D plus 40, OPD 370.5 Task Force, 126.

[37] For importance of communications link, North Africa via State Department channels to Washington, thence to OPD, thence to General Eisenhower's headquarters in London (briefly in Gibraltar) via military channels, see interv, Lt Gen Hull with author, 3 Jul 47, OPD Hist Unit Interv file.

For careful political briefing of General Eisenhower by OPD on behalf of General Marshall, see msg (originator OPD), Gen Marshall for Lt Gen Eisenhower, 17 Oct 42, CM–OUT 05682.

secure political equilibrium in North Africa so that he might be left undisturbed to pursue his major objective, the successful conclusion of the campaign in North Africa. In line with his consistent policy of giving overseas commanders great discretionary authority during the course of operations, General Marshall urged and secured Presidential approval for leaving General Eisenhower a free hand to deal with the Admiral of the Fleet J. L. F. Darlan and General Giraud immediately after the landings as the military situation required.[38] To the end of the year, OPD maintained close liaison with the State Department on the diplomatic problems related to TORCH, and kept General Eisenhower informed of the views of the President on politico-military negotiations and arrangements in progress.

OPD's efforts in support of the North African invasion reached into the theater of operations. Two Theater Group officers went to North Africa to secure firsthand observations and reports on TORCH. One of these, Maj. Alfred D. Starbird of the European Theater Section, was attached to the 1st Infantry Division as a War Department observer for the North African landings from 20 October until 23 November 1942.[39] The second was Lt. Col. Morris J.

Lee, also from the European Theater Section, who, at the end of 1942, was serving as OPD observer with Allied Force Headquarters in North Africa, gathering information on priority of the units to be prepared in the zone of interior for subsequent shipment to North Africa.[40] Throughout the campaign, by these devices as well as constant close monitoring of messages from overseas, OPD tried to keep abreast of the changing situation in North Africa and to keep other Army staffs and agencies in the zone of interior alive to the needs of the overseas commanders.

As soon as it was feasible, General Handy sought to add to OPD the leaven of experience that could be gained only in the field, particularly from participation in a large operation like TORCH. In November, as one direct approach to this end, he requested the assignment to OPD of Col. Claude B. Ferenbaugh, who had served both in the United Kingdom and North Africa and who was then on duty with Maj. Gen. Floyd R. Fredendall's II Corps. He reported for duty in mid-December as chief of the European Theater Section, which was still OPD's control center for TORCH.[41] General Hull, who had had intimate contact in OPD with the initial build-up for BOLERO in the United Kingdom and handled much of the detailed staff work on TORCH, moved up to the position of chief of

[38] (1) Msg, CINC for CCS via WD (OPD), 14 Nov 42, CM-IN 6267. (2) Draft memo, CofS for President, n.d., WDCSA Africa 1942. (3) Memo, Admiral Leahy for President, 15 Nov 42, WDCSA Africa 1942. (4) Msg (originator OPD), Gen Marshall for Lt Gen Eisenhower, 15 Nov 42, CM-OUT 4943.

[39] Memo, Maj Gen Hull for TAG, 15 Dec 44, sub: Promotion of RA Off in AUS, OPD file on Alfred D. Starbird, 27.

According to Col. Dan Gilmer, chief of European Theater Section, who at the time of the initial landings was secretary of the General Staff, Allied Force Headquarters, Major Starbird was the "one War Department representative who was present in the operation." See remarks of Colonel Gilmer in Rpt

of Proceedings of Bd of Offs, OPD, 16 Feb 45, OPD file on Alfred D. Starbird, 30.

[40] (1) Msg (originator OPD), Gen Marshall for Lt Gen Eisenhower, 13 Jan 43, CM-OUT 4319. See also appended note for record. (2) Ltr, TAG (thru CofS) to Lt Col Lee, 8 Dec 42, sub: Orders, OPD file on Morris J. Lee, 14.

[41] (1) Msg, OPD for USFOR, 20 Nov 42, Item 5, Exec 5. (2) Memo, Maj Gen Hull for AGO, Attn: WD Decoration Bd (through G-1), 26 Mar 44, sub: Recommendation for Award of DSM, OPD file on Claude B. Ferenbaugh.

the Theater Group, replacing General Streett, who returned to duty with the Army Air Forces.

In addition to co-ordinating arrangements of command and administration, movement of troops, equipment, and supplies, the conduct of politico-military negotiations, and all the other problems which arose in connection with TORCH, OPD served as a staff repository of the fund of experience accumulated in executing the TORCH operation. Accomplishments in supporting General Eisenhower's forces were the more remarkable because they not only reflected the overriding importance of the TORCH operation but also stemmed from a staff responsibility that required OPD simultaneously to render precisely the same kinds of service on a smaller scale to Army commanders in less spectacular spots everywhere from Panama to Alaska and China. The North African invasion provided a proving ground not only for American equipment, principles of command, military administration, troop training, supply, and tactics but also for the staff techniques of OPD and the rest of the War Department as well. To the close of the year OPD was acquainting Army agencies with evaluations, made both in the zone of interior and overseas, of various aspects of the American experience in TORCH.[42] Out of this experience gradually came principles, policies, and procedures to be followed in supporting all the overseas commands. These ideas and practices represented the results of the Army's first great effort to gear

preparations in the rear echelon in the United States to meet the specific needs of large-scale amphibious operations in a coalition war.

Case History in Confusion

There were no approved solutions for the problems the War Department faced in supporting overseas operations in 1942. The zone of interior commands insisted that they needed to be told long in advance exactly what they must provide, and when, and that schedules, once set up, must be frozen. The commanders in charge of the overseas operations undertaken in 1942 could not go even half way to meet such demands, however reasonable. They had to wait for the deliberations, which sometimes seemed interminable, of higher authorities who were trying to stretch their means to cover as many commitments as possible and who found it hard to agree finally on any major project. OPD, as the intermediary between the zone of interior staffs and the task force staffs, encountered this situation in its efforts to support every operation undertaken in 1942, notably those in the South and Southwest Pacific and in North Africa.

Operation TORCH was a classic example. Even the main outlines of the operation were not fixed until early in September, many weeks after the date that would have been acceptable to the zone of interior commands as the latest date for receiving final frozen schedules for the assembly and shipment of troops, equipment, and supplies. Although preparations had started in August in anticipation of a final decision on TORCH, a great deal of the process of adjusting operational requirements to the capacities of the zone of interior remained to be telescoped into a few weeks. The lack of

---

[42] (1) For example of study by an OPD officer, see memo, Lt Col C. P. Smith for Brig Gen Hull, 20 Oct 42, sub: Suggestions for More Efficient Handling of Future Task Force Hq, OPD 320.2 Task Force, 79. (2) Cf. memo (originator OPD), Gen Marshall for Lt Gen Eisenhower, 20 Dec 42, CM-OUT 7133.

time, especially as it hampered the work of the Services of Supply, was as acutely restrictive as the lack of shipping.

In the ensuing confusion, the function of OPD was to see to it that the zone of interior, at whatever expense to the orderliness, efficiency, and economy of its own operations, did everything possible to assemble the troops and equipment requested by the operations staff of General Eisenhower and General Patton. OPD continually advised them and their staffs on the readiness or unreadiness and availability or unavailability of units, insisted on their establishing priorities for filling various requests, and set deadlines for making or changing decisions. At the same time OPD tried to avoid making decisions for the overseas commands and set all deadlines as late as it dared. Fully realizing that postponements and changes entailed disorders that might seriously increase the risks being taken, OPD still held firmly to the theory that it was for General Eisenhower and General Patton and their staffs, not for the zone of interior commands, nor even for General Marshall and OPD, to calculate the risks to be run by the forces under their command.

In order to make sure that General Eisenhower and General Patton got what they wanted, insofar as it was humanly possible to give it to them, and in order to keep them constantly informed of what they could expect and what they had to decide, OPD followed preparations hour by hour and day by day, in great detail. The pressure of time forbade OPD to take anything for granted except, in a general way, the capacity of the zone of interior commands to adjust themselves somehow or other to the extraordinary demands being made on them. With every message sent and received, with every direc-tive issued, amended, or voided, with every telephone conversation and every hurried conference went the checking and rechecking of endless details, in the manner of field headquarters.

One of the many series of such transactions in which OPD became involved was one which dealt with a signal service unit which was shipped to the United Kingdom and then to North Africa to establish and maintain signal communications between the Center Task Force and Allied Force Headquarters and, if necessary, to relay signal communications between the Eastern Task Force (Algiers) and Allied Force Headquarters.[43]

On 11 August the Services of Supply listed among the signal units required by TORCH, with a high priority, the 829th Signal Service Company, and on 20 August the Signal Corps recommended its immediate activation, under the highest priority, with a strength of 13 officers and 238 enlisted men.

Meanwhile, on 15 August, General Eisenhower had requested at least a signal battalion, specially equipped, for the Oran force. OPD responded with the chief signal officer's list of signal units for TORCH headquarters and a skeleton services of supply organization, gave the exact composition of the signal company recommended therein for activation to perform the mission at Oran, and told in detail what would be done to meet his requests for auxiliary equipment. At the same time OPD went ahead to authorize the activation of the company.

---

[43] The textual narrative concerning the 829th Signal Service Battalion is based on extremely complicated documentary material. For a detailed treatment of the sources, primarily of interest as a guide to further research in the subjects discussed, see OPD Hist Unit Study O.

On 24 August General Eisenhower, with evident reluctance, fell in with the War Department plan. He emphasized that the mission was vital to the operation. He noted that men available in Great Britain were not highly enough trained, and insisted that the best trained personnel to be found in the United States be assigned to the company. He stated that the company as set up could carry out the mission only on the condition that all the radio personnel and most of the equipment should arrive at Oran with the assault convoy.

On 26 August Services of Supply headquarters set in motion the machinery for activating the 829th Signal Service Company, with an authorized strength of twenty men more than originally recommended. The orders authorized drawing upon specified units for an experienced cable operation section, pigeon platoon, and such radio operators and radio repairmen as the Signal Corps could not find elsewhere.

On 29 August when the machinery of activation had just begun working, the Signal Corps recommended, on the basis of "additional information just received" concerning its mission, further increasing the strength of the 829th Signal Service Company by 10 officers and 171 enlisted men. The added personnel were to operate the special equipment which General Eisenhower had requested on 15 August and which had not yet been provided for in setting up the 829th Signal Service Company. On 1 September OPD authorized the recommended increase, and the necessary orders to carry the increase into effect were issued on 7 September.

During the first week of September, Allied Force Headquarters recalculated its needs and listed for OPD still more signal equipment that would be needed at Oran.

The Signal Corps thereupon recommended that the 829th Signal Service Company be made into a battalion, with a total authorized strength of 40 officers and 626 enlisted men. This was a strength nearly three times that of the company projected in mid-August. Within three days, the recommendation was forwarded to OPD, it was approved, and the necessary orders were issued.

The orders for the last increase, like those for the previous increases, specified certain sources from which experienced personnel might be drawn. A specially noteworthy provision was the addition of experienced radio operators to be obtained from the Army Air Forces, to take care of the important Gibraltar-Oran air traffic. The carrying out of arrangements to effect their transfer also fell upon OPD. OPD approached Headquarters, Army Air Forces, which thereupon requested OPD to issue a directive instructing the First Air Force (Eastern Defense Command) and the Fourth Air Force (Western Defense Command) to assign specified numbers of high speed, fixed-radio operators to the 829th Signal Service Battalion, and to have them arrive by 13 September at Fort Dix, New Jersey. OPD issued such a directive to the Army Air Forces, authorizing travel by air for the men coming from the Western Defense Command.

Allied Force Headquarters continued to follow very closely the steps being taken in Washington to provide a unit equal to the Oran mission, until it was certain that the men and equipment had been found and would arrive in time, as they finally did. To describe such administrative tangles as the hasty organization and dispatch of the 829th Signal Service Battalion, the enlisted men and the junior officers of the Army, who seemed always to be feeling the effects without ever getting a glimmering of the cause for the confusion, coined the word "SNAFU," a term roughly equivalent to "Situation normal, all fouled up." As might have been anticipated from the circumstances of the 829th's departure, the confusion did not die at the water's edge. In December a report from theater headquarters in North Africa indicated that the 829th Signal Service Battalion had not performed altogether satisfactorily. General Somervell replied by recapitulating the measures taken in September to provide experienced technicians for the battalion:

In the time permitted between September 5th and September 28th, the date of sailing of the elements to the United Kingdom, every effort was made to provide the best available personnel. Radio repairmen were graduates of the Press Wireless School. Diesel mechanics and code clerks were taken from the 827th and 830th Service Companies and had been trained previously in the War Department Message Center. The 40 K. W. Radio Station team is one of the most highly trained units available in the United States Army on this type of equipment, having been thoroughly trained with the American Telephone and Telegraph Company and the Press Wireless and composed of men having previous commercial experience.

General Somervell observed in conclusion: "Obviously there was little or no time available for team training. The same difficulty had arisen with this unit as with other service units because of the difficulty in obtaining authorization for such units in adequate time to give them the necessary training." It was hard to blame anybody in particular for the SNAFU.

The case of the 829th Signal Service Battalion was only one of countless cases of acting on short notice to support overseas operations, a procedure which, everyone agreed, was dangerously inefficient. The zone of interior commands, in particular the Services of Supply, could point to such cases to demonstrate the advantages of acting on their advanced recommendations to organize special types of units against such contingencies, which they constantly tried to anticipate. OPD officers in advising on strategy emphasized, partly on the same grounds, the need to decide on operations far in advance and to adhere to the decisions once they were made. Their strong conviction on this point reflected, of course, General Marshall's own insistence on the importance of training and logistics.

Nevertheless, lacking a basis for longrange planning, OPD theater section officers were reluctant to authorize special types of units except as they had definite grounds for anticipating that such units would be used. Theater commanders similarly tended to postpone requests for special units until they had provided as well as they could expect for their needs for standard units and in particular for combat units. Then they began to see more and more special problems that could be solved only by having additional special units, service units in particular. OPD operations officers were then faced with the decision whether to direct a hurried activation, reorganization, or expansion which OPD had earlier refused to authorize, when proposed by a zone of interior command. Such cases could not be decided to anyone's satisfaction.

From the point of view of General Marshall, the important thing was that the representations of both the theater staffs and the zone of interior commands were taken into account in OPD and cases decided, for better or worse, in the light of policies which the Chief of Staff had approved. What was equally important, he could depend upon the fact that the decision taken, whatever it was, would be announced to all concerned and followed up. During the rest of the war the chief of OPD tried through his planning officers to prevent such situations from arising, and made sure through his operations officers that some positive action, however far from ideal, was taken at once to meet such situations when they arose.

CHAPTER XI

Transition to the Later War Years

The year 1943 introduced a new and promising era in the military fortunes of the United States and, therefore, of the entire coalition of associated powers. The German armies had failed to take Stalingrad, the key to the conquest of the Caucasus, and were facing heavy counterattacks from the Soviet forces, which had conclusively proved themselves equal to the task of defending the long Eastern front and the central homeland of the Soviet Union. In North Africa the United States and Great Britain had successfully launched their first major military operation and were making preparations to destroy the German forces there. In the Pacific the smaller, hard-fought campaigns in New Guinea and Guadalcanal were both nearing their final objectives. In the continental United States mobilization of the armed forces and the industrial strength to support them were far advanced. Military units of all kinds were being trained, equipped, and made ready for deployment in greater and greater numbers. Shortages of matériel, even the perennial shortage of shipping, though still chronic were becoming less acute.

The tide of war was at last turning. Germany, Italy, and Japan were losing the initiative in military operations. The Soviet Union, Great Britain, the United States, and all the powers associated with them in the war were determining strategy rather than reacting to strategic moves by the enemy. The military planning of American staffs in Washington became more complex but at the same time more rewarding in immediate results. The President and his senior military advisers entered into a series of British-American conferences with renewed confidence in victory. They could now stop making military moves to keep from losing the war and proceed in the course of the next two and one-half years to win it with greater economy in time and in human life.

The Army, sharing in the new strength and assurance of midwar, had to bring its organization and its procedures to a high level of efficiency. The scale of the military effort ahead was immense. General Marshall and his senior staff officers had to face the fact that it would place unprecedented strains on the Army, as on other government agencies participating in policy making in the national high command. Complex problems were bound to arise, demanding definite answers that would lead the nation toward its ultimate goal—the winning of the war. They could not be solved by the administrative device of assigning them to a single agency and granting it full authority to proceed with some, almost any, solution. The policies and programs recommended by various staffs and various agencies, for increasing the production of war matériel, for instance, or for strengthening the postwar international position of the United States, often conflicted with one another and did not always coincide with strictly military objectives. The President and, indirectly, the Congress were responsible for maintaining some balance among the legitimate concerns of all the government agencies and all the staffs in them, thus achieving a corresponding balance among the military, economic, and foreign policy aims of the United States. Since every national interest was at stake in winning World War II, it was an intricate and difficult task to decide precisely how to win it and assign specific duties connected with winning it.

Final determination of the balance to be established among the separate elements in national policy usually was left to the President. Nevertheless, he could work only on the basis of trial balances evolved on the staff level in the separate agencies whose chiefs, including Cabinet officers and the JCS, reported to the White House. For the most part his option was either to choose one or consolidate several of the programs passed on to him.[1] The more that individual programs showed a serious and responsible effort to frame recommendations in the light of the need for a balanced national policy, the easier was the President's task of final decision.

The War Department, and especially OPD, thus became more and more involved during the later war years in trying to evaluate from a military point of view all the elements of the national effort in a total war. Day after day the staff dealt with issues that were not conventionally considered part of the main military tasks of devising strategy and conducting operations. Yet military staff work could not proceed without making some tentative mutual adjustment of military and quasi-military is-

sues, as raised by staffs both inside and outside the Army. By making a careful, responsible effort in this direction, OPD greatly strengthened General Marshall's hand in getting approval of basic Army recommendations that were being considered by the JCS and the President.

Because they were complex, because they cut across so many jurisdictional interests, and above all because there were so many of them, the new staff problems that arose in 1943, 1944, and 1945 presented a special challenge. What they required was not so much the discovery of definitive solutions as the invention of techniques for getting some kind of compromise solutions that would permit positive, co-ordinated action. Policy decisions on the issues involved would affect the permanent relationships between the armed services of the United States, not only between the Army and the Navy but also between the quasi-independent Army Air Forces and the older services. They would affect the permanent status of component parts of the War Department, particularly the staffs made up of logistics specialists, who worked with civilian agencies to get the military optimum in war production from the civilian economy, and staffs made up of more traditional "field" soldiers, whose effort was directed mainly toward conducting successful military operations when necessary and with the resources then at hand. They would even affect the long-range political relations among nations, both the nations that were friendly with the United States and the enemy nations, which in time would become defeated, occupied countries. At these points the problems of war were coming once more to be major policy issues which had to be threshed out in the arena of national political controversy, an arena in which the Army leaders had not found it

---

[1] The President had no systematic staff work (in the Army sense of the term) done at his own level of authority except for the limited assistance offered by the Bureau of the Budget. See Chs. VI and XVI.

necessary to do much of their work since the trying years before Pearl Harbor.

In these circumstances, it was necessary for OPD to rely heavily upon committee work and informal liaison to get results which, while acceptable from a strictly military point of view, were not entirely unacceptable from any other point of view. The most notable achievement of the later war years was the development of techniques of co-operation among staffs rather than the assumption of responsibility by any single one. In this way, working with many other organizations and agencies, OPD helped to set the new pattern of military staff work in Washington in the later war years. Improvements were made in the machinery and process of joint strategic planning. Ways were found to preserve the delicate balance which had been created between air planning and the control of air operations by the Army Air Forces on the one hand, and OPD on the other. Both at the joint committee level and inside the Army a *modus vivendi* was established between strategists concerned with the determination of military objectives and logisticians concerned with the provision of men and matériel at the right place and the right time to carry out strategic plans. Similarly, OPD worked out methods for keeping in close touch with the combat soldiers and the military situations confronting them so that Washington staff work would reflect accurately the needs and capacities of the numerous, vastly expanded overseas theaters, as well as the more general strategic aims of the JCS committees and the President.

On the international plane, since decisions about military operations in the overseas theaters involved British, Soviet, and Chinese as well as American forces, a whole new code of procedures was elaborated for the great military staff conferences of midwar. These procedures were extremely valuable during the last year of hostilities, when the international conferences dealt less and less with military strategy and turned more and more toward the politico-military issues of the postwar world. In fact, OPD's staff work in the later conferences was a part of the increasing effort it was making on behalf of the Army to establish a mutually satisfactory relationship between military planning and foreign policy as interdependent elements in national policy.[2]

Staff officers in OPD, taking their cue from General Marshall, tried to resolve these new staff problems just as they resolved more familiar ones, by reference to the primary mission of the command post. Above all they tried to do whatever they could to help win the war quickly and with economy. Strictly military problems in strategy still had to be settled, and strictly operational decisions still had to be made. The command post went right on performing these conventional military tasks very much in the same way it had in 1942. Beyond that, the staff in OPD improvised as necessary to aid General Marshall in acquitting his responsibilities in the Army and in the national high command.

---

[2] The problems of staff organization and procedure that came up and the solutions that were adopted during the later war years are discussed at some length in the following chapters insofar as they affected the internal workings or the external relations of OPD. For a treatment of these problems and their solutions from the point of view of the General Staff as a whole, see Nelson, *National Security and The General Staff*. He cites or quotes a great many documents, not readily available elsewhere, which mark important administrative changes.

Staffing the Command Post (1943–45)

A military staff, like any other institution, can maintain its special identity and establish a record of consistency in its work only if it successfully adapts itself to changing situations of every kind. In time of war a military staff is doubly sensitive to changes in membership because its character and traditions exist primarily in the minds of its officers. If the same men do not carry on in the same jobs, the staff must insist on a comparable level of ability among new members and make appropriate experience a principal criterion for appointments to posts of responsibility when older officers depart. OPD probably was better able than any other Army staff to get and keep good officers. Even so, continuity was critically important for OPD. The Division had been built up to carry out a definite idea or principle in military staff work in support of the high command in Washington. Yet the idea itself was not too carefully articulated or very widely known in the Army even by the end of 1942. Many new situations were confronting the Division. The surest way to preserve the idea that made OPD what it was, whatever that might be in abstract terms, and to adapt the idea to meet the new problems of 1943 and later years, was to keep the same officers doing their work in the same general way they had set about it in 1942.

This solution to the personnel problem was not altogether practical, chiefly for two reasons. In the first place, the Army was gradually gaining new experience in combat, and it had to be taken into account in planning and directing operations from Washington. OPD needed to absorb a great deal of this experience, and one of the simplest ways to do so was to take in individual officers with experience in the overseas theaters. In the second place, the Army at large had a strong incentive to get capable officers overseas where actual battles were being fought. OPD was not only the largest unit of the War Department General Staff, but its officers also possessed knowledge of many War Department ways that officers in the overseas theaters would find it advantageous to know. Its members of longest standing had been assigned to WPD before Pearl Harbor, when duty on that staff was a high point in the career of fairly senior officers who were promising prospects for command in the field. As a result of the priority given to overseas service, both in Army tradition and in War Department personnel policy, OPD was subjected to a steady drain of its most experienced officers.

The continuing loss of personnel was impossible to stop, and OPD never attempted to restrict it more than enough to prevent it from crippling the remaining staff. It was clearly in the interests of OPD's work to have competent officers overseas. Moreover, with the loss of officers, however regrettable in the short run, the Division was acquiring replacements who more and more often had had World War II experience overseas. The policies set in practice in OPD concerning personnel, for the most part informal and sometimes not based on conscious administrative decisions at all, reflected an effort to maintain a close balance between loss of Washington experience and gain of overseas experience. In effect, this policy also established a rough balance between the needs of forces in the theaters and OPD's own need for continuity in planning and directing operations.

As a whole, Army leadership in Washington remained remarkably constant through this period of tremendous deployment of military manpower. Of basic importance to

OPD was the fact that General Marshall stayed on, relinquishing whatever aspirations he may have had for command in the field for the less conspicuous though equally arduous post of Chief of Staff.[3] The principal change among his senior subordinates, one which directly affected OPD, was occasioned by the appointment of the Deputy Chief of Staff, General McNarney, as Commanding General, U. S. Army, North African Theater of Operations. General Handy, who had served as chief of OPD since June 1942, moved up to become Deputy Chief of Staff on 21 October 1944. General Handy was succeeded in turn by his Theater Group chief, General Hull, who became Assistant Chief of Staff, OPD, on the same date.

General Handy's presence at the head of OPD until the fall of 1944 insured the consistency of the Division's staff work throughout the midwar period. During this same period a similar consistency in leadership was maintained within the smaller groups of the Division, Executive and Logistics. Colonel Gailey continued to head the executive office until December 1944, when he was succeeded by Col. Kenneth W. Treacy, who had been assistant executive since June 1944. The Logistics Group, which was to undergo major changes in duties during the midwar period, was led continuously until after V-E Day by Brig. Gen. Patrick H. Tansey, who left his post as Materiel Sec-

tion chief to become group chief in December 1942.[4]

The Theater Group remained from December 1942 until October 1944 under the direction of General Hull. As a planner and the European Theater Section chief, he had participated in nearly every aspect of OPD's 1942 work on BOLERO and TORCH. He thus probably had had more intimate experience in integrating strategy with overseas operational requirements and the resources of the zone of interior than any other Army officer in World War II. This experience, plus his responsibility for acting as General Handy's deputy in the latter's absence from Washington, enabled General Hull to assume a special role in the Division in tying together the many military factors which had to be synchronized by OPD.[5] The Theater Group under General Hull also enjoyed a considerable degree of stability in its internal leadership. Of the eight officers who were section chiefs in the Theater Group as of the beginning of 1943, six were still on duty at the beginning of 1944. There was a gradual replacement of section chiefs during the first nine months of 1944, but the new chiefs all had had some previous experience in their respective theater sections and most of them had been on duty since early 1942.

When General Hull moved into the chief's office in October 1944, he was succeeded as chief of the Theater Group by Maj. Gen. Howard A. Craig, the highest ranking officer brought into the Division during the war. General Craig was the Army Air Forces planning officer who, with Colonel Wedemeyer, had accompanied General Marshall to London in April 1942 to win British approval of the BOLERO plan.

---

[3] Originally most Army officers assumed and at one point, in the autumn of 1943, it seemed certain that General Marshall would become the Allied commander of the invasion of France, possibly of the whole European-Mediterranean area. The President finally decided to keep him in Washington rather than to bring General Eisenhower back to a new and exceedingly difficult job. See: (1) Stimson, *On Active Service in Peace and War,* pp. 437–42; (2) Sherwood, *Roosevelt and Hopkins,* pp. 802–03; and (3) Eisenhower, *Crusade in Europe,* pp. 196–209.

[4] See App. A.
[5] Memo, Brig Gen G. A. Lincoln for author, 3 Dec 47, sub: Hist of OPD, OPD Hist Unit Comments file.

LT. GEN. JOHN E. HULL, *Chief of the Operations Division, 21 October 1944– 2 September 1945.*

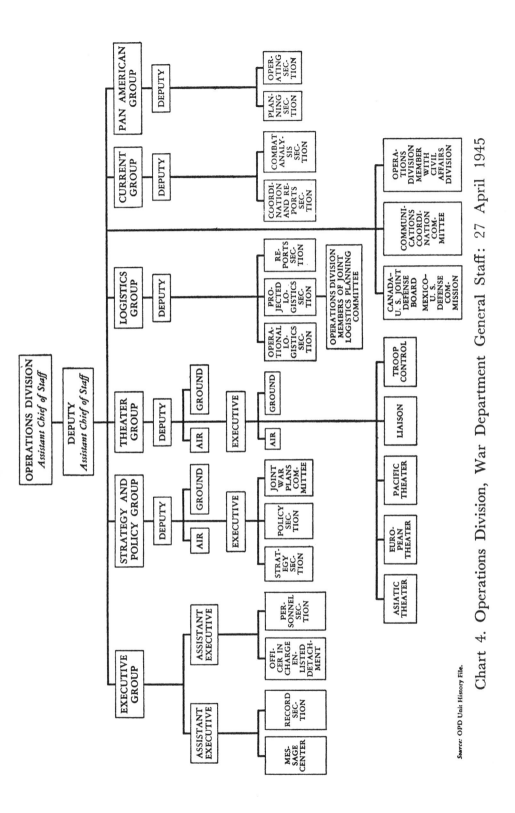

Chart 4. Operations Division, War Department General Staff: 27 April 1945

Source: OPD Unit History File.

After filling a succession of posts in the Allied Force Headquarters in the Mediterranean in 1942 and 1943, he had returned to Headquarters, Army Air Forces, from which he transferred to OPD on 23 October 1944. Shortly thereafter, General Craig lost the services of his Ground deputy, General Russell, as well as those of the latter's executive. Even though as chief of OPD General Hull could continue to keep closely in touch with the Theater Group, he thought it desirable, in expectation of the impending loss of General Russell, to bring into the group an officer thoroughly familiar with the Division.[6] For this purpose he gained special permission to delay Colonel Gailey's scheduled transfer overseas. Colonel Gailey became Ground deputy in the Theater Group on 16 December 1944, and remained at that post until after V-E Day.

Leadership of the S&P Group had much less continuity during this period. In late 1943 there was one complete change of principal officers. General Wedemeyer left in October to become deputy chief of staff of the new Allied command in Southeast Asia, soon drawing after him Colonel Maddocks, former chief of the Army Section of the JUSSC.[7] The loss of these two officers was offset by an administrative device adopted by General Wedemeyer early in 1943. At that time he reorganized the executive control system in the group, setting a pattern preserved throughout the war. Strictly administrative management was delegated to a single officer (the group executive), and two deputies were appointed, one a Ground officer and the other an Air officer. They, like the Theater Group deputies, were supposed to be able to substitute freely for the group chief in reaching decisions on any matter requiring action. Actually, the position of Ground deputy was a training post for the position of Army planner. The first Ground deputy chief under the new system was Col. Frank N. Roberts, who succeeded General Wedemeyer as group chief and Army planner upon the latter's departure in October 1943. Colonel Roberts was soon promoted to the rank of brigadier general, and served in his new position until November 1944, when he in turn was succeeded by his Ground deputy, Col. George A. Lincoln.

Two new, small, specialized groups whose work was subordinate or tangential to the main work of the Division carried on by the S&P and Theater Groups, were set up in OPD late in the war. The Current Group, established in February 1944, continued under General North to provide the information service for the Division which he had previously directed as head of Current Section (Logistics Group).[8] An American Theater Section was also established in February 1944 by consolidation of the Latin American and North American Sections.[9] It was superseded by the Pan-American Group in April 1945 under Brig. Gen. Kenner F. Hertford to handle hemisphere defense, which had previously been handled

---

[6] Pers ltr, Lt Gen Hull to Lt Gen Smith, 4 Dec 44, Paper 34, Item 9, Exec 2.
[7] Colonel Maddocks had been named special assistant to the chief of S&P during several months in mid-1943 when he was primarily engaged in committee work on several basic War Department policies of interest to OPD.

[8] For the main enterprises of Current Section and Current Group under General North, see Ch. VIII. For new duties in 1944 and 1945, see OPD Hist Unit Study Q.
[9] Memo, Lt Col James Stack, Asst Exec OPD for Gps & Secs, OPD, 31 Mar 45, sub: Establishment of Pan-American Gp, OPD, OPD 321.19 OPD, 86. For the significance of the organization of American Section and Pan-American Group see Ch. XVI.

in the Theater Group, and to carry on work of a politico-military character.

Officer Personnel (1943–45)

Even though its period of great expansion was over by the end of 1942 OPD still grew, slowly but steadily. This growth in itself required steady recruitment of officers from outside the Division as well as promotions and transfers within. The press of business in these years, as the tempo of operations in the theaters increased, brought a heavier and heavier work load on the action officers throughout the Division.[10] Nevertheless, increases in strength were justified solely on the grounds of specific new duties undertaken by OPD rather than on the grounds of increased volume of staff business already assigned.[11] As of 1 January 1943, with an allocation of 156 officers (excluding general officers), OPD was below ceiling strength with 148 officers, including six general officers, on duty. Not until June 1943 was it necessary to break the ceiling. Then, with 155 officers assigned,

OPD began to get small increments at irregular intervals. By the end of 1944 the authorized strength reached 190, where it remained until July 1945, when the ceiling was lifted to 193, its highest point.[12] Through the latter part of 1944 and all of 1945 until V-J Day the actual number of officers on duty was always around 200, reaching a peak of 205 on several occasions. As of 2 September 1945, officer strength in OPD totaled 198.[13]

There is no evidence in OPD records that the Division's officers ever believed that the strength of the Division was reaching a point at which the advantage of having more officers would be balanced by disadvantages resulting from an increase in the number of officers reporting to one officer, or from the addition of new levels of control. In fact the records contain almost nothing bearing on abstract questions of personnel management. Except for administrative detail, they are mostly filled with representations to the effect that the Division's officers were working to the very limit of their endurance and that their temporary absence was acutely felt, and frequent indications that the Division was finding it hard to secure acceptable officers. The individual officers in the Division appear to have been divided in mind between their feeling that

---

[10] The volume of business handled by the Theater Group corresponded fairly closely with the development and degree of activity of the overseas commands. Theater Group officers in 1944, OPD calculated, spent an average of 62 hours a week on the job, while S&P officers reported an average of 66, that is, eleven hours a day, six days a week. Memo, Exec OPD for Maj Gen Handy, 21 May 44, sub: Offs on Dy in Washington, OPD 210.3, 279. The Logistics Group simply informed its officers in 1943: "*Working Hours*—This group will function seven days a week. Officers will be available for duty twenty four hours a day." Memo, Exec Logistics Gp for All Sec Chiefs, Logistics Gp, 28 Apr 43, sub: SOP No. 1, OPD 321.19 OPD, 5. Cf. memo, Chief Logistics Gp for Exec OPD, 14 May 43, sub: 24 Hr Dy, OPD 321.19 OPD, 7.

[11] Detailed illustrations or evidence in support of generalizations about personnel and personnel policy are not included in this chapter. For such material, extensively documented, see OPD Hist Unit Study X.

[12] Pers Authorization 5, Chief Pers & Adm, OCS for OPD, 25 Aug 45, OPD 210.3, 152/27.

[13] OPD consistently had a larger staff than the other General Staff Divisions combined. For instance, in March 1944 OPD had an authorized strength of 179 commissioned officers while the combined G's (G–1, G–2, G–3, G–4) had 100. See memo, Maj James Stack for Col Gailey, 20 Mar 44, sub: Allocation of Commissioned Grs to OPD, Paper 418, Book 16, Exec 9. As of January 1945 OPD had 190 officers authorized, while the four G's were allotted 159. See Summary Sheet, Chief Pers & Adm, OCS for Col H. I. Hodes, 6 Jan 45, sub: Off Strength—Atzd & Actual, WDGS & WDSS, WDCSA 320.21, 66.

their sections needed more men and their realization that the men with whom they would be glad to work were scarce and badly needed wherever they were.

The steady growth of the Division, along with the steady loss of personnel, meant that OPD had to recruit officers constantly throughout the later war years. To achieve a net increase in strength of 50, it was necessary to bring 284 new members into the Division between 1 January 1943 and 2 September 1945. Division policy remained firm in requiring that most positions be held by able young professional officers in the field grades. While this policy could be justified by the great responsibility carried day in and day out by the action officer in OPD, it meant that the Division was trying to get the very officers whose experience, age, and grade made them sought after by every combat unit and overseas headquarters in the Army.

OPD used a high proportion of career officers, higher than that allotted to most units and commands of the wartime Army. Throughout the war it was always well over one half, and it rose slightly to about 70 percent of strength during 1945. A large proportion of the professional officers were graduates, with superior rating, of the command and General Staff School, but comparatively few had been far enough along in their military careers to complete their military education with attendance at the Army War College, which probably would have been more valuable training for S&P officers in particular. A good many of them had been instructors at branch schools, and several had taught at the Military Academy and at the Command and General Staff School. As in peacetime, most of the officers came from the ground combat branches, the Infantry, Cavalry, Field Artillery, and

Coast Artillery, or from the Air Corps. Those from the service branches came principally from the Corps of Engineers.

During the first half of 1943 War Department policy continued to require the General Staff, like other Army agencies in the zone of interior, to assimilate officers retired, over-age for duty with troops, or on limited service. In August 1943 the Deputy Chief of Staff relaxed the requirement for the General Staff and thereby ended the only formal limitation placed during World War II on OPD's selection of officers. Restrictions as to age continued, limiting the officers under thirty-five years old to one third of those on duty and prohibiting the assignment of any under twenty-eight, without specific authorization. In March 1944, however, the General Staff divisions were authorized to carry in excess of their quota officers under thirty-five who had had a tour of combat duty. Thenceforth restrictions on age level were no serious bar for OPD in its recruiting.

In fact the average age of officers in OPD during the period 1943–45 dropped from that of 1942. The 421 officers who served in the Division during these later war years averaged a little over 36 years of age on reporting for duty or, if already on duty, at the beginning of the period, 1 January 1943. The earlier average (for the period 9 March–31 December 1942), calculated in the same way, had been a little under 39 years. The similar average for the composite OPD officer, that is, the average man among the 475 who were on duty at various times between 9 March 1942 and 2 September 1945, was a little less than 37 years old. All of these age levels were lower by several years than in WPD days.

Restrictions on grades for its officers, in contrast with restrictions on age levels, was a problem from which OPD never became completely free, but eventually the Division was given considerable latitude in recruiting and promoting officers at the grades required in order to get and keep qualified personnel. By mid-1945 OPD was authorized 11 general officers, 69 colonels, 77 lieutenant colonels, 30 majors, and 6 captains. In other words, out of every ten officers in the Division, approximately four were colonels or general officers, four were lieutenant colonels, and only two were majors or company-grade officers.[14]

Promotion to general officer grades was based entirely on responsibility accompanying assignments. At no time during the war were there set allocations for the number of general officers assigned to the General Staff. Recommendations for promotions to general officer grades were made to G–1 or to the Chief of Staff personally and monitored by a general officer section of G–1,

which submitted final lists to the Chief of Staff for his approval. The final selections, of course, were cleared through the Secretary of War, presented to the President, and confirmed by Congress before promotions became effective. The number of general officer positions in OPD rose from five in March 1942 to a peak of eleven, and stood at ten at the end of hostilities. The ratio was always roughly one general for every twenty officers.

OPD's principal problem in recruitment and promotion, of course, did not concern general officers, nor even section chiefs, but the "rank and file" action officers. Promotions throughout the Army during and after 1941 left fewer and fewer officers in the grade of major who were considered to be qualified for work in OPD.[15] For this reason the percentage of majors in the Division was cut in half between 1943 and 1945, and the percentage of officers in the higher field grades increased correspondingly. The establishment of the grade of lieutenant colonel as the grade in which OPD normally could recruit or to which it could promote action officers also brought the grades of OPD Ground officers more nearly into line with those of OPD Air officers, who in July 1944 were appointed to the grades in the Army of the United States which they held in the Air Corps.[16]

---

[14] Statements about officer authorizations are based on information in the following table prepared from documents issued on the dates listed:

Percentages of Field Grades Allocated to OPD in Total Authorized Commissioned Officer Strength

	General Officers [a] and Colonels	Lieutenant Colonels	Majors	Total Authorized Strength [b]
	Percent	Percent	Percent	
(1) 1 Apr 42	24.3	37.3	30.8	107
(2) 17 Aug 42	22.8	35.8	32.7	162
(3) 21 Apr 43	24.0	35.1	37.0	162
(4) 20 Sep 43	28.3	42.7	26.5	173
(5) 15 Mar 44	28.4	43.0	26.2	179
(6) 21 Sep 44	38.2	40.3	18.3	191
(7) 5 Apr 45	38.9	39.4	18.9	190
(8) 25 Aug 45	41.4	39.8	15.5	193

[a] General officer grades were not usually included in allocations of officers prior to 1944. After the beginning of 1944, allotments of officers above the grade of lieutenant colonel were issued in a bulk allotment of colonels, and assignment of general officers correspondingly decreased the allocation of colonels.

[b] Total strength includes a few captains and lieutenants. Consequently, percentages in the field grades do not total 100 percent.

[15] For a statement to this effect, see memo, OPD for G–1, 21 Apr 43, sub: Readjustment in Almt of Offs, OPD 210.3, 152/3.

[16] After a promotion study made by G–1 in the summer of 1944, promotions in the AUS (Air Corps) under Public Law 455 were discontinued for all but exceptional cases, and officers holding rank in AUS (Air Corps) higher than Army of the United States were given equivalent AUS rank. To prevent a complete block in promotions for other than Army Air Forces officers, allocations were provided to the divisions to adjust these grades. This policy change gave OPD 17 colonel's positions in lieu of 8 lieutenant colonels, 8 majors, and 1 captain.

OPD ordinarily did not recruit officers above the grade of lieutenant colonel and did not promote to those grades except for positions of greater responsibility than those of action officers. The grade of colonel normally went only with the position of section chief, most of the positions on joint and combined committees, and some other positions that involved representing the Chief of Staff in dealings with other Army officers and with Navy or British officers of corresponding or higher grade.

The pressure to release officers from duty in OPD for overseas assignments increased at the same time that most officers qualified for work in the Division were themselves overseas, in units due to move overseas, or in jobs from which their superiors were reluctant to release them. From the outbreak of hostilities, the Division released very few officers to Army organizations in the United States other than combat units. OPD began sending officers to combat units and to overseas commands in 1942, many of them to newly activated divisions, and continued to lose them throughout the war. In all, departures from OPD during 1942 totalled 62 officers, while between 1 January 1943 and 2 September 1945, 234 officers left the Division.

OPD began getting some officers back from overseas very early, but during the period of rapid expansion in 1942 it secured most of its officers from various agencies in the continental United States. Only at the end of 1943, a year in which OPD lost fifty-five officers, did the Division face a serious personnel crisis because of anticipated losses and difficulty in finding replacements. The turnover in the General Staff as a whole had become so great that the Deputy Chief of Staff directed, 1 January 1944, the curtailment of "turnover of military personnel in important staff positions . . . in order to increase the continuity of past experience and efficiency." [17] It was easier to lay down this policy than to follow it, as officers themselves were eager to go overseas. Nevertheless the policy gave OPD firmer ground on which to stand in resisting demands for its most valuable officers. It was about this time that Colonel Gailey first articulated the Division's "two deep" policy, which called for keeping greater numbers of highly competent officers in the Theater Group than a roster of administrative posts seemed to warrant. He gave General Handy a note, saying:

> The Air Corps has requested either Colonel Ritchie or Colonel Todd. The question has been hanging fire for a couple of months. I recommend that Colonel Ritchie be given the opportunity.
> If Colonel Ritchie goes, this will directly affect a request for Colonel Reeder to command a regiment in the 10th Light Infantry Division. Colonel Baumann can run the section O. K., however, we should remain two deep in each theater. Therefore, we should keep Reeder as the top layer and Baumann as the second half.[18]

The general policy on releasing OPD officers was phrased clearly, though unofficially, in 1944:

> This Division has endeavored to maintain a policy that would insure continuity of past experience and efficiency and at the same time fill requests from theaters for officers for important command and staff positions and important command positions in the continental United States. A close study is continually being made of the situation with the

---

[17] Memo, Lt Gen McNarney, DCofS for G-1, G-3, G-4, OPD, and three major commands, 1 Jan 44, sub: Changes in Supply Procedure & Supply Levels, WDCSA 400 (1 Jan 44), 1.

[18] Memo, Col Gailey for Brig Gen Handy, 27 Dec 43, sub: Pers Matters, OPD 210.3, 224.

end in view of not jeopardizing an officer's career by keeping him on this duty for too protracted a length of time.[19]

OPD usually held out for an officer-for-officer exchange when it released personnel for overseas duty. General Handy and General Hull were constantly bartering with the theaters. These negotiations, while often lengthy, were facilitated by the consideration given OPD's needs by officers formerly on duty with the Division. The most conspicuous of these in positions of responsibility in the theaters in the later war years were Generals Eisenhower, Wedemeyer, and McNarney.

An even greater personnel crisis occurred in the fall of 1944, just after General Hull had taken over the Division. The Army Ground Forces was encountering great difficulty in furnishing sufficient numbers of regimental and battalion commanders of combat age (under forty-five years) with experience enough to permit them to step into immediate command in battle.[20] Consequently, the Deputy Chief of Staff approved a new policy on 16 August 1944, providing for the release upon request of all troop-age, Regular Army officers who were not serving with troop units in their basic arm or service. Moreover, Regular Army officers who had not served in an active overseas theater after 7 December 1941 would be released to the major commands automatically after completion of two years' service in staff assignments in the United States, and these officers normally would not

be reassigned to staff or similar positions in the United States.[21]

The announcement of this automatic two-year policy was a blow to OPD. It meant disruption in organization at a time of continued heavy responsibilities. A review of the status of officer personnel disclosed that twenty-nine Regular Army officers would have to be released by the end of the year, when they would have completed a two-year tour.[22] All of them held important positions in the Division. General Handy, in one of several similar letters offering the services of some of these officers to overseas theater commanders, presented OPD's problem:

I heartily agree in principle with this policy, but it is certainly going to raise hell with this Division unless we can secure suitable replacements.

It is highly desirable that replacements for these officers be Regulars who have proven themselves in active theaters. As a matter of fact, I see no satisfactory way of getting qualified replacements except by mutual swaps with theaters.[23]

By 1 January 1945, all but five of the twenty-nine officers scheduled to be relieved under the August 1944 policy had departed.

In all, between 16 August 1944 and 1 January 1945, fifty officers left OPD, only five fewer than left during the whole year 1943 and two fewer than left during 1944 prior to 16 August. Additions to the staff offset these losses and gradually increased Division strength. Sixty-three officers joined OPD between the announcement of the

---

[19] Draft memo, OPD for G-1, 10 Aug 44, sub: RA Fld Offs of Grd Arms Not Under AGF Jurisdiction, OPD 210.3, 315.

[20] For a statement of officer shortages in field grades experienced by the Army Ground Forces, see Palmer et al, The Procurement and Training of Ground Combat Troops, p. 133.

589727 O-61—15

[21] Memo, G-1 for CofS, 14 Aug 44, sub: Release of Offs to AGF, OPD 210.3, 315.

[22] (1) Memo, Col Gailey, Exec OPD for Brig Gens C. A. Russell, P. H. Tansey, F. N. Roberts, and Thomas North, 16 Aug 44, no sub, Paper 12, Item 9, Exec 2. (2) List, Roster of Offs, OPD, on Dy Two Yrs to 31 Dec 44, Paper 3, Item 9, Exec 2.

[23] Pers ltr, Maj Gen Handy to Lt Gen Devers, 30 Aug 44, Paper 22, Item 9, Exec 2.

two-year policy and the end of the year. During that period and especially in 1945, OPD received a great proportion of its new officers from overseas theaters. Altogether, between 1 January and 2 September 1945, seventy-eight officers were recruited. Nine of them were returning for a second tour of duty in the Division after duty overseas, and nearly all had theater experience to qualify them for their new posts. By postponing releases, by promoting or transferring within the Division, and by recruiting officers outside the Division, General Hull kept OPD at a strength commensurate with its duties.

The only major change in the composition of OPD during the later war years was in the experience of its officer personnel as a group. As time passed, more and more OPD officers had a chance to go on tours of temporary duty overseas. From the establishment of OPD in March 1942 until the end of General Handy's tour in 1944, at least a third of all the officers on duty in the Division at one time or another went on a tour of temporary duty in one of the active overseas theaters. A parallel increase of composite experience in OPD came from the acquisition of more and more officers from overseas command and staff assignments. By 1944 these officers began to constitute a significant proportion of the strength in the Division. In March 1944, thirty-nine officers in OPD had served overseas on permanent assignment as distinct from temporary duty. In May, two months later, the number had climbed to fifty-eight, approximately one third of the officers in the Division.[24] The proportion went on in-

creasing rapidly throughout the last year of hostilities, until practically all the officers in OPD had had some kind of experience overseas.

The composition of OPD also changed with respect to length of experience in the Division itself. The rapid initial expansion of the Division was so great that two thirds of the officers on duty in March 1942 had less than four months' experience in the Division. By the end of the year, however, over 75 percent of the officers had served between four months and a year in the Division. By the end of 1943 over 60 percent of the officers had served in the Division over a year, and another 30 percent had served from four months to a year. During 1944 there was little expansion but greatly increased turnover, especially as an effect of the two-year policy in the fall of the year. The number of officers with more than a year's experience decreased correspondingly, and the number with less than four months' service or with four to twelve months' service increased. In 1945, until V-E Day, fewer officers joined and left the Division than in 1944, and the level of experience rose. In the brief period between V-E Day and V-J Day, this tendency was reversed. In 1945 a number of officers had served in OPD for an exceptionally long time by wartime standards. The service of these officers, together with the retention of such men as General Hull and General Gailey in dominant positions, contributed an indispensable element of continuity to the Division's work through their personal knowledge of the techniques, accomplishments, and mistakes of the wartime high command in Washington.

---

[24] For statistics and names of officers, see: (1) List, OPD Offs Who Have Been Permanently Assigned to O'Seas Ts (14 Mar 44), Paper 401, Book 16, Exec 9; (2) memo, unsigned, for Col Gailey, 15 May 44, no sub, Paper 707, Book 18, Exec 9; (3) draft memo, OPD for G-1, 10 Aug 44, sub: RA Fld Offs of Grd Arms Not Under AGF Jurisdiction, OPD 210.3, 315.

The Secretariat

The decentralization of work to the separate sections, and, within the sections, to individual action officers, required a corresponding decentralization of administrative and clerical work. The civilians, warrant officers, and enlisted men and women who made up the Division secretariat were scattered about, working under the personal direction of officers, with relatively little supervision by senior clerks. Officers were absorbed in their current actions with rapidly approaching suspense dates, and their work schedules were full and unpredictable. Consequently they had little time for supervising and checking and almost none to spend waiting for memoranda to be typed and assembled or records to be compiled. They needed to be able to take for granted that papers would be drawn up quickly and correctly, circulated promptly to the proper people, and filed where they could be found at once. Individual members of the secretariat, like the officers for whom they worked, had to be willing and able to meet deadlines by working at top speed and serving long hours.

The ceilings set for the General Staff included figures covering the secretariat as well as commissioned officers, but Washington-wide shortages often resulted in the Division's having fewer clerks than it was authorized. By no means did every candidate for a job meet the requirements. The clerical and administrative staff was constantly handling highly classified papers, and as a result many of its members were acquainted with a great deal of highly classified information. OPD had to rely on their loyalty, after a thorough initial investigation, and trust their discretion as well as their willingness to share the strain that fell on everyone dealing with vital military matters. Moreover, it was essential to enlist their active co-operation in helping to enforce the elaborate and troublesome security regulations which were designed primarily to minimize the danger of unintentionally revealing valuable information to the enemy.

The difficulties the Division encountered in getting and keeping men and women who measured up to this work were much the same as in the case of officers. WPD had come into the war with a small secretariat, entirely made up of civilians, a few with long experience in the War Department. The enlisted detachment added to the Division secretariat in 1942 filled a need that could not well be met by civilians. In the first place, it was far more convenient to use enlisted personnel on the many jobs in the Division which might on short notice involve overtime work. Although throughout the war many of the civilians in the Division voluntarily stayed to work long extra hours, until early 1943 there was no authority to compensate them for this extra time, and until that time they could not be required to stay.[25] In the second place, the Division in wartime had many jobs that regularly involved night work. For these jobs, too, enlisted men and women were best suited, since their entire schedules were subject to arrangement at the convenience of the Army.

Even more important, qualified enlisted men were easier to obtain than qualified civilians. The War Department, using its own administrative machinery for locating specialists, could tap the large, steadily

---

[25] Civ Pers Br OCS, Civ Pers Instruction 5 A, 25 May 43, Compensatory Time Off in Lieu of O'time Pay for Civ Employees, OPD 230, 48.

growing Army. OPD was in a position to get promotions for enlisted personnel more rapidly than they could expect in the Army at large, whereas civilians could not expect particularly good appointments or rapid promotions.[26] Consequently, OPD came to rely mainly on military personnel to fill nearly all the new positions as the Division continued to expand. OPD's allotment of enlisted men reached its peak in April 1943, when General McNarney set a ceiling on the authorized enlisted strength of all Washington agencies and authorized OPD to employ 163 enlisted men.[27] Normally the number on duty was less than the ceiling but well over one hundred. The size of the civilian staff remained approximately at its early level, that is, slightly over one hundred employees, nearly equal to the enlisted detachment.[28]

In time OPD ran into difficulties in getting and keeping enlisted men. War Department policy demanded that able-bodied young enlisted men, like commissioned officers, should be replaced by men whose age or physical defect disqualified them for service overseas.[29] The War Department, like every other installation in the zone of interior, found it harder and harder to maintain high standards for its enlisted detachment. Toward the close of 1943 OPD was authorized to overcome its difficulties in staffing its secretariat by using enlisted women (Wacs) as well as enlisted men and civilians.[30] By recruiting increasing numbers of enlisted women, the Division added to the strength of its clerical staff and in general maintained its exacting standards of competence. By V-J Day enlisted women made up nearly one-third of the strength of the total Division secretariat, nearly equaling each of the other two components.[31] Early in 1942 the ratio between clerical staff and officers had been one to one. After the assignment of the first enlisted men in March 1942, the clerical and administrative staff, civilians, warrant officers, enlisted men, and enlisted women, outnumbered the officers by about seven to four.[32]

Army Planning and Control of Operations (1943–45)

The rationale and the processes of strategic planning and control of overseas op-

[26] The prospects of wartime appointees to clerical positions in the War Department and other "old line agencies" of the federal government were very limited since there was a tendency in these agencies to keep civil service grade ratings close to the familiar, prewar standards, whereas the shortage of good clerical personnel and recognition of the increasing cost of living in wartime Washington caused the newer war agencies to inflate job classifications in terms of permanent civil service grades to a level considerably higher than the prewar average.

[27] (1) Memo, Lt Gen McNarney, DCofS for ACofS OPD, 4 Apr 43, sub: Enl Men on Dy in WD, OPD 220.3 Hq Det, GHQ, 26. (2) Remarks of DCofS in min of Gen Council meetings, 29 Mar 43, DCofS rcds. Nineteen of these men were on duty in the Office of Chief of Staff but were supervised by OPD.

[28] (1) Pers charts, 1944–45, Paper 2, Item 2B, OPD Hist Unit file. (2) Cf. Civ Pers directory, 10 Jul 43, OPD 230, 54.

[29] The replacement of combat qualified enlisted men in OPD was not actually completed until July 1944. See memo, Maj James Stack, Asst Exec OPD for Maj H. H. Kidwell, 2 Jul 44, no sub, OPD 321.19 OPD, 52.

[30] (1) Handwritten memo, Maj James Stack for Exec OPD, 30 Jul 43, sub: WAC Det OPD, WDGS, OPD 220.3 WAC Det OPD, 1. (2) Memo, Col W. T. Sexton for Lt Gen McNarney, 2 Aug 43, no sub, WDCSA 291.9 (31 Jul 43).

[31] As of 31 August 1945, OPD's secretariat was made up of 109 enlisted women, 105 civilian employees, 123 enlisted men, and 17 warrant officers, a total of 354. See pers chart, 30 Aug 45, Paper 2, Item 2B, OPD Hist Unit file.

[32] These statements about the secretariat are approximate since no systematic reporting of strength for enlisted men, enlisted women, and civilians was made before June 1944.

erations, the main interests of the OPD staff, had become fairly well defined by 1943 and remained unchanged in the later war years. Although Army planners did more and more of their work as part of the joint committee system, or with the intention of influencing its work, the pattern of strategic planning as it developed inside OPD did not change materially.[33] The S&P Group kept the initiative in Army planning, and its chief continued to be the main link between the working echelons of the Army staff system and the joint and combined committee system. The duties involved in this task were redefined officially at the end of the midwar period, in October 1944, in words that showed how little change had taken place in the planning function. Substantially these same duties were charged to S&P throughout the period of hostilities.

The formal description of Strategy Section responsibilities was as follows:

Estimates the current war situation and initiates or reviews and coordinates strategic and operational plans. Specifically:

(1) Furnishes formal and informal strategic guidance to other agencies of the War Department General Staff and to agencies of the three major commands.

(2) In collaboration with G–2, maintains current estimate of the situation in theaters of operations to determine military objectives and possible lines of action.

(3) Initiates or reviews strategic plans and reviews operational plans for the Chief, Strategy and Policy Group and advises him on strategy matters.

(4) Reviews and coordinates plans of theater commanders and of General Staff divisions as they relate to strategy.

(5) Reviews, coordinates, and processes for the Chief of Staff all papers involving strategic plans submitted to the Joint or Combined Chiefs of Staff for decision.

(6) Reviews and advises on demobilization and post-war plans.

(7) The War Department General Staff member of the Joint Post-War Committee is assigned from this section.[34]

The Policy Section's duties read almost exactly as they had in 1942, though it was more clearly indicated that reviewing strategic plans under consideration by the JCS and the CCS was a duty of the Strategy Section, not of the Policy Section:

(1) Prepares staff studies on Joint and Combined policy matters.

(2) Initiates appropriate War Department implementing action on all decisions of the Joint and Combined Chiefs of Staff and their subordinate agencies and follows-up to insure that action is taken.

(3) Reviews all War Department papers to be referred to the Joint or Combined Chiefs of Staff by the Chief of Staff.

(4) Reviews, coordinates, and processes for the Chief of Staff all papers on subjects, other than strategic plans, submitted to the Joint or Combined Chiefs of Staff for decision.

(5) Provides the formal channel of communication between War Department agencies and Joint or Combined agencies through the appropriate Secretariat.

(6) Reviews and coordinates with other sections of Operations Division and with other War Department agencies, studies under consideration by the Joint or Combined Chiefs of Staff or their subordinate agencies.[35]

The services rendered by these sections, plus the work of the S&P officers sitting on the joint strategic planning committees, made it possible for OPD to integrate Army strategic planning at all levels. If a future operation was coming up for consideration by the United States and Great Britain, nor-

---

[33] For developments in joint strategic planning, see Ch. XIII.

[34] WDGS Cir 5–5, 4 Oct 44.

[35] *Ibid.* In May 1945 the S&P executive office became responsible for implementation, and in August the responsibilities for policy matters within S&P were divided between two sections, the Policy Section and a new politico-military section, the Strategic Policy Section. See Ch. XVI.

mal procedure was for OPD officers in the Strategy Section to prepare a study on it for the chief of S&P. He might introduce it to the Joint Staff Planners committee, of which he was Army member, or might suggest that a working subcommittee of the planners draft a plan for the same operation.[36] In the latter case OPD's Strategy Section would review the draft joint plan for the Army planner in his capacity as chief of S&P at the same time he was considering it in his capacity as a member of the JPS. If nonstrategic factors, such as psychological warfare, were important in the plan, the Policy Section might also review the plan and advise the chief of S&P on it.

If the Joint Staff Planners forwarded the plan in the joint system, the Army planner, as chief of S&P, advised the chief of OPD and the Chief of Staff when the matter appeared before the JCS, and possibly again if the JCS referred it to the CCS. If the JPS presented its views to the Combined Staff Planners, or if the combined committee undertook to prepare a study, the Army planner would be called upon to consider the matter as a member of the CPS and advise General Marshall when he considered it as a member of the CCS. The complex interrelationship of these dual and triple responsibilities made it extremely important that all these jobs be assigned to one officer, and that officer was the Army planner. It was his clear responsibility to General Marshall (through the chief of OPD) that induced an element of consistency into all these planning roles.

The continuity thus established by S&P in strategic planning ensured an adequate consideration of Army views in joint deliberations. General Wedemeyer in particular stressed the value of a comprehensive strategic studies program. In 1943, when the major strategic debates of World War II were being held, the Strategy Section built up a voluminous file of informal reports on every strategic aspect of military operations under consideration.[37] General Wedemeyer used these studies, sometimes formally, more often informally, as a basis of strategic discussions with General Handy and General Marshall. As time went on S&P had to deal more and more with complicated policy issues tangential to strategy and with operational problems arising in the theaters but requiring consideration from a general strategic point of view as well as normal study by the Theater Group.

Work on issues of policy as distinct from strategy was quite different from the rest of the work done in S&P. There was no standing joint committee on the working level to handle it until the spring of 1944, when the JCS established a committee to handle one increasingly important class of policy issues, postwar problems.[38] Even then there remained many miscellaneous problems of policy that could not conveniently be assigned to any joint committee on the working level. One result was that several members of S&P, mostly members of the Policy Section, were assigned to *ad hoc* joint committees to study such matters so frequently that they probably spent as much of their time on committee work as many of their colleagues assigned to standing joint com-

---

[36] This subcommittee might be *ad hoc* but usually was the Joint War Plans Committee, which replaced the old Joint Strategic Committee in April 1943. See Ch. XIII.

[37] ABC 381 Strategy Sec Papers (7 Jan 43). Besides the Strategy Section studies, S&P assembled "books" for ready reference during the international military conferences convened by the President and the Prime Minister. See Ch. XII.

[38] For joint study of postwar problems, see Ch. XVI.

mittees. Another result was that the Army planner, or even the Chief of Staff, was still apt to introduce for joint consideration, usually by the JPS, a paper on policy drawn up in S&P, whereas the basic papers on strategy in the late war period generally originated in the joint staff, usually in the Joint War Plans Committee.

Under the pressure of work on short-range problems and policy, long-range strategic planning suffered some neglect, and to a great extent OPD lived throughout the latter part of the war on an accumulation of such planning from the early midwar period.[39] There was a chronic shortage of the kind of personnel S&P needed, and the current operational planning had to have first priority on most of the time of most of the S&P officers. Moreover, the comparative difficulty of getting authoritative guidance on the political aspects of the most pressing military problems of 1944 and 1945 made the value of new strategic studies somewhat dubious. In any case, the accumulation of early strategic plans, some of which dated from the days of WPD, was sufficient to see the Army's strategists through the critical years. Only during the very last months of the war were they feverishly improvising plans, debating quasi-military policies such as surrender terms, and giving strategic guidance on pressing operational problems all at the same time.[40]

It was on the strength of its strategic planning, in whatever way it was being conducted, that OPD assumed the dominant

position that was widely recognized in the later war years. By 1944 the strategic guidance which the Assistant Chief of Staff, OPD, and his officers were able to give the Army as a whole had become so indispensable to the efficient operation of other War Department agencies that a War Department circular was issued to provide specifically that OPD and no other agency should give "official guidance or interpretations on future strategic or operational plans" to the War Department as a whole.[41] In carrying out this responsibility, the Division chief for-

---

[39] Memo, Brig Gen G. A. Lincoln for author, 3 Dec 47, sub: Hist of OPD, OPD Hist Unit Comments file. General Lincoln's careful generalizations on S&P have been extremely helpful in describing the work of this group, of which he was chief during the later part of the war. In every case they have been substantiated by research in the appropriate records.

[40] See Ch. XVI.

[41] WD Cir 134, 8 Apr 44, sub: WDGS OPD, Responsibility for Strategic and Operational Plans. The circular read:

1. In accordance with AR 10–15, the Operations Division, War Department General Staff, is charged, in general, with those duties of the War Department General Staff which relate to formulation of plans and strategic direction of the military forces in the theater(s) of war. It is specifically charged with the strategic employment of the Army of the United States.

2. In extension of these regulations, the Operations Division, War Department General Staff, will be the custodian of future strategic and operational plans involving the Army of the United States. It will be the responsibility of the Operations Division to develop and keep current these plans, when appropriate, in conjunction with the proper joint and combined agencies, and also to furnish the necessary guidance to all other agencies of the War Department, including other divisions of the General and Special Staff and the Army Ground Forces, Army Air Forces, and Army Service Forces, to enable them to conduct their future planning on the same common basis.

3. No agency of the War Department other than the Operations Division, War Department General Staff, is authorized to give official guidance or interpretations on future strategic or operational plans.

4. In order that a steady flow of essential operational planning information may be maintained between the Operations Division, War Department General Staff, and other major agencies of the War Department, these other agencies will maintain liaison with the Operations Division. Requests for information involving strategic guidance or interpretation, however, will be forwarded through channels. Such requests will be forwarded to the Operations Division by the heads of the staff divisions and of Army Ground Forces, Army Air Forces, and Army Service Forces only, who will be responsible for transmitting this guidance to their subordinate agencies.

mally assigned to S&P the task of providing strategic guidance to other agencies, accomplishing the "necessary coordination with other Groups and Sections of the Operations Division." For the special job of furnishing "logistical planning guidance," the Logistics Group assumed the responsibility, along with the responsibility of accomplishing the "necessary coordination with the Theater Group and/or the Theater Section involved." [42]

The general principles underlying the organization of the Theater Group remained unchanged throughout World War II. The object was simply to give the Chief of Staff a small general staff for each theater of operations and let it take such action as was necessary in Washington to carry out strategic decisions approved by the Chief of Staff. This theory of Theater Group functions presupposed occasional rearrangements of area assignments among the various theater sections to make them correspond with operational developments in the field. These rearrangements were made from time to time. New sections were created as military operations became more widespread, and old sections were consolidated as the several theater efforts converged against Germany and Japan late in the war. At the close of hostilities there were only three area sections, European, Pacific, and Asiatic, in the Theater Group. [43]

The first formal, detailed description of the Theater Group's duties appeared in October 1944. The scope of these duties required a great degree of authority, effective if not necessarily formal, not only over theaters of operations but also over operating agencies in the zone of interior and over the other General Staff divisions insofar as their work affected operations. The 1944 staff circular described the general duties of the Theater Group substantially as they were performed throughout World War II:

Serves as the operating command post for the Chief of Staff for all military operations beyond the continental limits of the United States and for defense commands. Receives from each theater of operations, defense command, and base command, requirements, requests, and recommendations pertaining to allocation of troops, supplies, equipment, and operational plans; investigates and determines the justification for such requests, and recommends priorities for personnel, matériel, and units. Prepares and publishes WD Troop Deployment and the Six Months Forecast of Unit Requirements and maintains individual troop basis for each theater of operations, defense and base command. Exercises control over documents governing overseas movements and redeployment of all U. S. Army Forces and directs and controls such movements. Maintains liaison for the Operational Division with the State Department, Navy Department, and other government agencies. [44]

Listing the various theater sections, the circular then set forth the broad sweep of duties exercised by all of them in their respective areas of responsibility:

Handles or monitors War Department action relating to the . . . Theater; keeps currently informed of plans, operations, supply status, and problems of the theater, and represents its interests in the War Department. Specifically:

---

[42] Memo, Maj Gen Handy for Gp Chiefs, 21 Apr 44, sub: WD Cir 134, Sec VII, dated 8 Apr 44, Paper 13, Item 2B, OPD Hist Unit file. This memorandum established the basic policy that "data relating to approved operational plans may be furnished orally and informally to designated liaison officers of other agencies in the War Department, whereas requests involving the opinion of the Operations Division on other than approved operations must be reduced to writing."

[43] (1) See Chart No. 4, p. 193. (2) For sectional reorganization within Theater Group, 1943–45, see OPD Hist Unit Study R.

[44] (1) WDGS Cir 5–5, 4 Oct 44. (2) For liaison activities, see Ch. XVI.

(1) Keeps the theater commander currently informed on War Department decisions, orders, regulations, policies, and actions, including information on status of units to be moved and unit movements.

(2) Reviews requests, recommendations, and reports of the theater commander, pertaining to operations, personnel, organization, training, supply, and other matters; determines their justification and modifies them when necessary to meet over-all War Department requirements; transmits such recommendations to War Department and other agencies for necessary action; and monitors action taken.

(3) Provides information and guidance to other groups of OPD and other War Department agencies on plans, operations, status, and other matters pertaining to the . . . Theater.

(4) Reviews and coordinates proposed War Department actions, plans, and programs affecting the . . . Theater, including—

  (a) troop basis and changes.

  (b) activation, inactivation, constitution, disbandment, TO and E's, TA's and TD's, and organization and reorganization of units.

  (c) disposition by transfer or inactivation of units declared excess.

  (d) overhead allotment for theater.

  (e) fillers and replacements.

  (f) rotation and leave policies and adjustments.

  (g) personnel and equipment priorities, allocations, and levels of supply.

  (h) unit requirements and availability of units and replacements.

  (i) unit movement orders and troop movements; shipping and water priorities.

  (j) availability of equipment and supplies for special units and operations.

  (k) air transportation, air tonnage allocations, and air priorities.

  (l) recommendations on the selection and promotion of general officers and assignment of other officers for special duties.

  (m) training of units, correction of training deficiencies, and special training.

  (n) civil affairs matters.

(5) Anticipates operational and logistical requirements in the . . . Theater to the extent required to permit ready solutions to problems arising from changes in the tactical situation.

(6) Reviews operations reports and intelligence reports for the . . . Theater; prepares periodic operations summaries and special intelligence studies; prepares situation maps and studies for current and future operations, and maintains statistical and historical records of operations, and current intelligence information as required.

(7) Provides members on boards and committees of the War Department and of Joint or Combined agencies, in connection with operations in the . . . Theater.

(8) Maintains direct contact on matters concerning the . . . Theater with other General Staff divisions, the major commands, the Navy Department, and other agencies.

(9) Makes arrangements on special matters involving the . . . Theater such as visits of Very Important Persons, Red Cross services, settlement of foreign claims, etc.

(10) Furnishes officers as observers for special operations and as exchange officers in the theater.[45]

To perform these duties, most of the theater sections had to organize along conventional general staff lines, with G–1, G–2, G–3, and G–4 units, plus sepecial officers for air matters.[46] This type of organization and the wide range of duties in the Theater Group indicated how far OPD had gone toward becoming a field-type general staff for the Chief of Staff.

As the volume of business increased, more elaborate precautions were necessary

---

[45] *Ibid.*

[46] OPD Theater Gp roster, 16 Mar 44, Paper 16, Item 2B, OPD Hist Unit file.

to protect the security of information flowing through the Division. Colonel Gailey, Colonel Treacy, and their representatives in the message center and record room made every effort to restrict access to Division files to those officers who required them in their work, and ordinarily each officer saw only the material related to his own field of staff interest. Representatives of other agencies and staffs had to prove to the executive office their need for operational information on the merits of each particular case.[47] To some extent the strict control of security matters was facilitated by the invention of new classifications in the midwar period. The papers on the big operation of 1942, TORCH, had been classified "Secret," the highest classification of the time, but were segregated from the rest of the files. Although this arrangement was administratively awkward, it pointed the way to a new procedure for isolating papers whose secrecy was vital from the many fairly routine documents that crept into the Secret files. As of January 1943, in accordance with a new War Department security procedure, OPD established a "Secret Security" classification under which papers were kept physically separated from the regular records although subdivided and numbered according to the system already in use. This practice was supposed to be applied only to those papers whose revelation to the enemy would jeopardize the safety of military forces, particularly those scheduled to take part in a major operation. This method of controlling the distribution of papers of highest secrecy remained in effect until March 1944, when it was superseded by the adoption of a similar classification, "Top Secret," by both the American and the British armed forces. Thereafter messages as well as correspondence were filed according to their designation as either "Secret" or "Top Secret."[48] Special measures were taken to limit the use of Top Secret material to key officers, as had been true previously in the case of Secret Security material. In OPD all current papers of this classification were covered by a red cardboard clearly indicating the care with which they should be handled, as well as the special importance that normally could be expected of the subject matter in them.

Even so, new devices were constantly being developed to govern the dissemination of highly classified material. Thus in mid-1942 a procedure was established whereby special messages from overseas began with the words, "For General Marshall's eyes alone." As these messages increased in numbers, they in effect constituted a special security classification, called "Eyes Only," which were meant for a limited distribution but were not actually restricted to the personal use of the Chief of Staff.[49] Similarly, messages dealing with plans for future military operations were marked, in accordance with British security

---

[47] Security consciousness in OPD was so well established by the end of the war that the author and associate historians, though explicitly authorized by the Chief of Staff and the OPD chief to see all War Department files, had many administrative battles with the executive office and the record room before officers in charge became convinced that the chief of OPD had really meant that anyone, particularly a civilian, should see everything in Division files. While the historians found most of the staff members extremely co-operative, the policy of tight security was very strong.

[48] (1) WD Cir 37, 20 Feb 43. (2) WD Cir 91, 29 Feb 44. The effective date for the new classifications was 15 March 1944. (3) The message center had established a separate file, later incorporated in the Top Secret OPD Message File, as early as May 1942 (19 April 1942 for CM-IN and 12 May 1942 for CM-OUT).

[49] For establishment of "Eyes Only" procedure, see book msg, Gen Marshall for comdrs, 24 Jul 42, CM-OUT 7028–7068.

measures, "Bigot" and were restricted in circulation to those officers working on the plans. This usage corresponded roughly with the Secret Security or Top Secret classification but in effect set up a special subcategory. It was widely employed at the time of the invasion of Sicily in mid-1943, when all Bigot correspondence originating in the War Department had to be co-ordinated with the North African Theater Section.[50] The working file of correspondence on Sicily (Husky) was kept in the OPD executive office rather than in the regular files.

The great bulk of correspondence with overseas commands was carried on by radio or cable. The old-fashioned staff memorandum was largely supplanted by a proposed draft of a message, with a cover sheet or memorandum for record indicating why it was necessary and how it met its problem, which probably had been presented by another message from overseas. In mid-1944 the message center in OPD, working at approximately its wartime peak, was handling more than 500 messages a day, and OPD took official action on about 100 messages every day. Practically all (about 98 percent in mid-1944) Top Secret or Limited Distribution messages received or dispatched by the War Department came to or went from OPD.[51]

New Patterns of Staff Work in OPD

During 1943 and later, the change in military staff work in Washington became more and more evident in OPD. In 1942 the Division often had been compelled to take virtually unilateral, frequently unprecedented staff action to get the results the Chief of Staff wanted. As the war went on, the Army and the interservice committee structure under the JCS worked more and more systematically. OPD increasingly played its part in the joint system as a starting mechanism or, in the Army, as a governing mechanism rather than as the main source of motive power. By the end of 1943 the whole military staff system was so well established and in such good running order that the critical problem was to monitor a thousand proposed military actions through the complicated Army and JCS organization without losing control of the thread of strategic and operational logic that tied them all together.

To a great extent this central thread was the Bolero strategic concept, which remained a basic part of Allied military policy in 1943 and 1944. The Roundup operation, intended to be an assault on northwest France in April 1943, was never launched, but it was succeeded in strategic planning by the Overlord operation, which was finally executed in Normandy in June 1944.[52] In the interim the success of Torch and of the co-ordinate British offensive in Libya had prepared the way for the invasion of Sicily and finally of Italy—in short, the large-scale offensive that the British had

---

[50] (1) Memo, Joint Security Contl for WD ACsofS, et al., 12 Mar 43, sub: Security Contl on "Bigot" Correspondence From and to CG, North African T of Opns, Case 32, Item 1A, Exec 3. (2) Bigot msg (originator OPD), Gen Marshall for Gen Eisenhower, 8 Mar 43, CM-OUT 2786, Item 12, Exec 3. (3) Bigot msg, Gen Eisenhower for AGWAR, 10 Mar 43, CM-IN 5209.

[51] (1) Memo, Lt Col L. E. Smith, Chief OPD Msg Cen, for Exec OPD, 16 Jun 44, no sub, OPD 210.3, 302. Colonel Smith was requesting an increase in personnel. (2) Cf. OPD Msg file. (3) Cf. Sp Rpt on Msg Cen, 48, Item 14, OPD Hist Unit file.

For OPD action cases as a whole, including messages as well as other correspondence, see table compiled by the P&O record room, Paper 4, Item 2B, OPD Hist Unit file.

[52] The assault phase of the 1944 operation was finally called Neptune, but the general plan remained under the name Overlord.

sought and General Marshall and his staff had hoped to forestall. OPD, particularly through its Theater Group, continued to concern itself in detail with the Army role in these operations exploiting the Allied position in the Mediterranean. At the same time, principally through its planners in the joint and combined committee system, OPD struggled to prevent these or any other military projects from interfering with OVERLORD.

In the Pacific the two lines of approach converging on the Philippines, which brought General MacArthur's forces through the New Guinea-New Britain-Solomon Islands region and Admiral Nimitz' forces from the Gilberts and the Marshalls to the Marianas, led to the last battles of the war with Japan, in the Philippines and on Okinawa. General Stilwell's long-planned campaign to reconquer North Burma opened the road to China in 1944, and made the defense of China during the next year a major task of the U. S. Army. Thus in the later war years, military operations in which the Army was involved were vast in size and world-wide in extent. Upon the first proposal for any commitment of Army forces, the attention of OPD officers was immediately engaged.

Much of the confusion in which task forces had been dispatched to garrison the principal bases of the Pacific early in 1942 and to join in the assault on North Africa in the autumn of 1942 disappeared later. Three factors largely accounted for the change. In the first place, most of the operations themselves were mounted from overseas rather than from the United States. After the North African operation the only large combat-loaded task force sailing directly from the zone of interior was the 45th Division, part of the Sicilian invasion

force. In the second place, the organization of the Army in the zone of interior had become more skilled in the mechanical business of readying troops and matériel and transporting them, either combat-loaded or in routine shipments, to the overseas theaters. Thus OPD's control over preparing the Western Task Force for TORCH had to be much more immediate and direct than its control over the preparation of the 45th Division, which was largely left to the Army Ground Forces.[53] In the third place, the tremendous growth of overseas theater headquarters staffs by midwar made it possible to determine requirements and carry on most of the detailed operational planning close to the scene of combat overseas. OPD consequently acted as monitor much more often than agent of the execution of the Chief of Staff's decisions as to Army operations.

Under these circumstances, Theater Group work became at the same time more fragmented and more systematic. It involved countless minor actions, usually inspired by a message from an overseas commander, designed to remedy specific difficulties encountered in carrying out a fairly well-established operational plan. Ordinarily these actions amounted to nothing more than securing agreement by an operating agency in the zone of interior to do whatever OPD considered necessary to meet the theater's requirements and dispatching a message to inform the overseas commander of what he could count on from the War Department. The "pick and shovel boys" worked their way through a pile of messages every day, stepping in to exercise OPD's authority only when co-ordination between the

---

[53] Palmer *et al, The Procurement and Training of Ground Combat Troops*, p. 580. The study here cited was written by Maj. B. I. Wiley.

theater and the zone of interior was required. The three major commands, Ground, Air, and Service Forces, did most of the work. The Theater Group, with some assistance from the Logistics Group, observed, monitored, supervised, and "followed up" throughout the rest of the war.

The exact character of the Logistics Group's assistance to the Theater Group is often difficult to trace in the written record, although there is no doubt that it was great. Most overseas messages went directly to the Theater Group for action. Many of these raised questions of supply and equipment. The action officer customarily consulted the appropriate specialist in the Logistics Group so that the solution reached would take into account the general logistic situation as well as area-oriented factors known best to the section officers of the Theater Group. If a Logistics Group officer could not answer a supply or equipment problem, he knew how to get the answer quickly. Informal conferences in the Logistics Group, with outside technical experts called in as needed, settled many important theater issues. Even when the determining factors were logistic, the Theater Group rather than the Logistics Group normally took the action. The very efficiency of this system tended to cloak in obscurity the Logistics Group's part in it.

The Chief of Staff continued to hold OPD responsible for the theaters getting what they needed. In the spring of 1943, for example, he took OPD severely to task for a delay in getting bazookas to the 16th Infantry in North Africa and for not seeing to it that the regiment had men trained to use the new weapons. He called General Handy's attention to the matter not only to find out what happened but also to show what he expected of OPD's theater sections. General Handy in turn observed to General Hull:

I believe that all of our theater groups [i. e., theater sections] should go actively into the question of equipment in their theaters, particularly new items. They should know exactly what is there; what is projected; and should make a special effort to see that Theater Commanders are informed of the availability of new items of equipment. The Chief of Staff mentioned, while Sutherland [General MacArthur's chief of staff] was here, about amphibious vehicles of various kinds for the Southwest Pacific.

I suggest that you go into this with the Theater Chiefs pretty thoroughly and not let us be caught on it again. The impetus, and it should be a strong one, should come from here and each Theater Chief should realize that it is his personal business to see that this is done.[54]

A sign of OPD's success in adjusting to the requirements of its task in the later war years was the extent to which its staff work less and less often resulted in laying down bold new lines of action. Instead of writing a BOLERO plan, as in 1942, OPD backed up General Marshall in CCS deliberations that finally resulted in a firm decision to invade France. Whereas in 1942 OPD had set up a new European Theater Section and virtually invented the BOLERO Combined Committee in order to get troops to the United Kingdom, in mid-1943, when the invasion decision was fairly firm, OPD simply arranged for the reconstitution of the BOLERO Combined Committee for assisting the experienced European Theater in the "handling of its business" connected with deploying forces for the operation.[55]

---

[54] (1) Informal memo, Maj Gen Handy for Brig Gen Hull, 7 Apr 43, Paper 52, Book 8, Exec 8. (2) Cf. memo, Maj Gen Handy, no addressee, 7 Apr 43, sub: Instructions From Gen Marshall Prior to Departure, Paper 51, Book 8, Exec 8.

[55] Memo, Brig Gen Hull for Col Roberts, 3 Jun 43, no sub, Paper 21, Book 10, Exec 9. General Hull remarked of the BOLERO Combined Committee: "It is somewhat different from a planning committee in that it spends all of its time on implementing things,

The patterns of strategic thought and of staff action were already laid down.

Under those circumstances, OPD could best serve the Chief of Staff by examining proposed actions thoroughly from the point of view of both strategy and theater operations. On major issues, formal internal staff co-ordination and continuous informal consultation between the S&P and Theater

---

finding out how to get more shipping and whether or not a British ACV [Auxiliary Aircraft Carrier] could be made available to transport some aircraft, and countless things of this nature." He further noted:

The European Theater Section itself will implement many of the agreed decisions. The British shipping member will implement many of them. A U. S. Navy member will also implement many of them. In some cases, and this is the exception to the rule in my opinion, the Combined Subjects Section will implement them; but if all of its business is transmitted through the Combined Subjects Section, it unnecessarily loads that section down with work which can be informally handled by the Chief of the European Theater Section. We must get away from the idea that this Committee is a high-level, formal-type committee.

Groups were matters of routine. The effect of this co-ordinated procedure in formulating policies was strengthened by the fact that OPD had the authority and the administrative machinery to insure that policies, once determined, were carried out in the Army.

The strength of OPD, as it worked in this way throughout the 1943–45 period of the war, was the strength of a single agency organized and staffed to bring into alignment all the military factors involved in any problem the Army faced. A policy reached or a recommendation made in OPD was bound to carry unusual weight in the deliberations of the many staffs and agencies which individual officers or sections from OPD were advising as well as of the dozens of committees on which OPD members were sitting. Thus in the full tide of World War II, the influence of OPD was less conspicuous on the surface but more permeating in the body of military affairs.

CHAPTER XII

Midwar International Military Conferences

The President and the Prime Minister convened four military conferences in 1943: in January at Casablanca, in May at Washington (TRIDENT), in August at Quebec (QUADRANT), and in November–December at Cairo and Tehran (SEXTANT–EUREKA).[1] The agreements reached at these conferences settled the order and scale of British and American operations in every part of the world. Like the earlier wartime meetings between the President and the Prime Minister, the 1943 conferences were primarily military.[2] The heads of government with their Chiefs of Staff met to decide on future military operations. They carried on their discussions on military grounds. Carefully agreed interpretation of the military decisions was made possible by increasingly effective military staff work done before the conferences, and the decisions were carried out after the conferences by the military staffs.

Although the staff techniques evolved for the 1943 conferences continued to be used subsequently, most of the critical questions that came up at the comparatively infrequent later meetings were more in the sphere of foreign policy than the sphere of strategy, and were handled mainly by the President and his civilian advisers rather than by the JCS.[3] It was in the midwar conferences that the major military decisions of World War II were approved. One of OPD's most pressing duties in 1943 was to help in preparing for the international conferences, through taking part in preliminary joint and combined committee work and in advising the Chief of Staff, upon whom always rested

---

[1] Code names were assigned by Allied authorities in advance of the conferences for reasons of security and convenience. The code names TRIDENT, QUADRANT, and SEXTANT-EUREKA were widely used. The Casablanca Conference also was given a less commonly used code name, SYMBOL. For use of the term SYMBOL see: (1) memo, Brig Gen Wedemeyer for Maj Gen Handy, 8 Jan 43, sub: SYMBOL, before Tab A in SYMBOL: Casablanca Book (8 Dec 42–Jan 43), Vol. I—Strategy and Plans, Exec 6 (the term SYMBOL Books was applied by OPD to the volumes which it prepared for the Casablanca Conference); (2) CCS 170/2, 23 Jan 43, title: SYMBOL—Final Rpt to President and Prime Minister Summarizing Decisions by CCS. OPD officers on occasion also used the term "ANFA" to signify the Casablanca Conference. This term was derived from the name of the Anfa Hotel, which served as headquarters for the conferees and for the Anfa Camp.

[2] In the course of congratulating the CCS on its work at the Casablanca Conference, the Prime Minister said it was the "first instance he knew of when military leaders had remained together so long, free from political considerations, and had devoted their full thought to the strategic aspects of the war. The President agreed to this. . . ." Min of ANFA 3d meeting CCS, President and Prime Minister, 23 Jan 43, Official Casablanca Conference Book.

[3] For staff techniques at the 1944–45 conferences, see Ch. XVI.

much of the burden of presenting American military views to the President and the Prime Minister.[4]

The predominant questions before the midwar conferences were the relation of cross-Channel to Mediterranean operations and the relation of European to Pacific and Far Eastern operations. These were at the same time matters of the first importance in the national policies, particularly in the foreign policies, of the United States and Great Britain. The President and the Prime Minister, in formulating their agreements, showed a tendency to bind themselves no further in advance than absolutely necessary, keeping it within their discretion as much as possible and as long as possible to readjust military agreements to suit current aims in the wider field of national policy. The uncertainty of future military operations thus continued to unsettle military planning. U. S. Army planners, still urging a maximum concentration of force for the invasion of France, became increasingly concerned with securing from the international conferences the long-range commitments which would make it possible to mount the OVERLORD operation and to organize other campaigns around the globe on the basis of a first-priority effort in northwest Europe.

The two previous conferences in Washington between the President and the Prime Minister, ARCADIA in December 1941–January 1942 and an impromptu White House meeting in June 1942, had been called on very short notice as a result of specific military crises. There was little opportunity either for a thorough analysis of American views or for the completion of detailed studies to establish their feasibility. The lack

of a carefully co-ordinated American case was also evident at the meetings in London of the Prime Minister and British Chiefs of Staff with General Marshall (in April 1942) and with Mr. Hopkins, General Marshall, and Admiral King (in July 1942). Most of the staff studies and memoranda had been drawn up in OPD for General Marshall and adopted or disregarded by the President, not always on the basis of clear-cut understandings with his military advisers.

Before the first conference of 1943, held in January at Casablanca, American staff officers had begun to appreciate the need for better preparation, and the conference greatly stimulated their appreciation of that need. Before each of the three conferences that followed during the year, they worked long and hard on a program to recommend to the President and did their best to anticipate the reasoning of the British Chiefs of Staff. In the face of British proposals worked out in great detail and evidently well co-ordinated with British foreign policy, American staff officers had to try to concert a program of British-American strategic aims at a time when the national policy of the United States was not always clear. Moreover, military proposals had to be presented in sufficient detail to avoid misunderstanding and yet in a form flexible enough to enable the President to work out with the Prime Minister acceptable compromises in matters that could be settled in the light of national policy. In short, military aims, conceived broadly and in detail, were subject to negotiation. The American military staff was in practice compelled to learn to apply, as the British staff so successfully applied, the methods of diplomacy to the development of military plans. This lesson in international planning techiques served OPD officers well, not only in the midwar conferences, but also in the comparable and simultaneous problem of joint strategic planning. In the end, also, it taught them how to make their military views heard in the 1945 conferences and in other areas of national planning late in the war, when nonmilitary issues were of great importance but when it was still necessary to conduct operations against the enemy.

The military conferences of 1943 thus received a great deal of attention in OPD. Decisions reached in them tended to govern staff work in the midwar period, planning officers dividing their time between alternating phases of preparation and performance. This rhythm regulated the closely associated work of the joint committee planning system and OPD's dealings with overseas commands.

Casablanca Conference: 14–23 January 1943 [5]

The Casablanca Conference was the first conference after June 1942 attended by both the President and the Prime Minister as well as the Chiefs of Staff. For several weeks before it was convened, there had been discussion of a high-level conference at which an agreement could be reached on the basis of the probable outcome of the North African campaign and the siege of Stalingrad.[6] By the time the Allied staffs and leaders were making final preparations for their departure to Casablanca, the tide of war definitely had begun to turn in Allied favor. Although the Ger-

mans were still east of Rostov, Soviet forces had successfully lifted the siege of Stalingrad in what proved to be the turning point in the Russo-German conflict, and had begun to wipe out the German salient in the Caucasus. Similarly, a hard struggle loomed in Tunisia, but most of North Africa was already in British and American possession. Even in the Pacific the enemy had lost the initiative, although the Guadalcanal and New Guinea campaigns showed how steadfastly the Japanese would defend the empire they had won so easily. The pressing question was what course of action the United States and Great Britain would follow in the Mediterranean area after the complete conquest of North Africa, the relation of that conquest to the projected cross-Channel offensive, and, less directly, its relation to operations in the Pacific and Far East.

To prepare for coming debates over these strategic issues OPD assembled a great deal of documentary material in loose-leaf volumes called SYMBOL or the Casablanca Book for use by the War Department representatives in the conference. Before putting these books into final form, General Wedemeyer reviewed the draft plans which officers in S&P had prepared and early in January submitted them to Generals Marshall, Handy, and Embick (JSSC) for comment.[7]

---

[5] The system followed in this chapter for dating the formal conferences of 1943 is simply to give the first and last meetings of the CCS at each conference.

[6] For early consideration of a high-level conference, see: (1) msg, Prime Minister for President, 4 Dec 42, Item 11, Exec 1; (2) msg, Prime Minister for President, 20 Dec 42, Item 63, Exec 10.

[7] (1) Memo, Brig Gen Wedemeyer for Gen Marshall, 2 Jan 43, no sub, with Paper 4 in ABC 016 (23 Jan 43), 2. (2) Memo, Brig Gen Wedemeyer for Lt Gen S. D. Embick, 2 Jan 43, no sub, Paper 4 in ABC 016 (23 Jan 43), 2.

For distribution of these books of staff papers, including the preparation of a book for the President, see: (1) memo, Brig Gen Wedemeyer for Maj Gen Handy, 8 Jan 43, sub: SYMBOL: Casablanca Book (Dec 42–Jan 43), Vol. I—Strategy and Plans, Exec 6; (2) memo, Col R. N. Young SGS for Capt J. L. McCrae, 9 Jan 43, no sub, WDCSA 381 (SS), 1.

The three volumes of the Casablanca Book covered a broad range of planning data. Volume I, "Strategy and Plans," contained current proposals of the British and U. S. Chiefs of Staff on the strategic concept for 1943, comments by the U. S. JSSC on British papers, S&P outlines of strategic plans for projected operations in the European, Mediterranean, and Pacific areas, reviews of the logistic feasibility of strategic plans, and views of the War Department G–2 and of British Intelligence on Axis strategy for 1943.[8] Volume II, "Command and Deployment," outlined the status of commands, the troop basis, schedules of troop movements, the shipping situation, and other miscellaneous current problems in the various theaters. For instance, in reference to the most crucial operational areas, it contained briefs on the status of Torch directives, the handling of civil affairs in North Africa, shortages of equipment in North Africa, handicaps to movement of troops, special supply problems, equipment of French troops in North Africa, the threat to the Allied line of communication in the Mediterranean from the possible closing of the Strait of Gibraltar, and the existing rate of build-up of American troops in the United Kingdom. It also summed up such political, economic, and social issues connected with operations in the European theater as the De Gaulle-Giraud rapprochement; exchange rates of franc, dollar, and pound; Jewish-Moslem conflicts; and the status of French citizens in the United States who wanted to volunteer for service in Africa.[9] Volume III, "Places and Personalities," simply contained short descriptions of leading foreign personages whom the American representatives might meet en route to Casablanca, important cities along the way, and a list of American military attachés and the commanding officers of American bases.[10]

In addition to compiling the Casablanca Book, OPD planners kept up with the interchange of views between the U. S. and British Chiefs of Staff on the proposed agenda for the conference.[11] They obtained for the Chief of Staff comments on the British proposals by War Department leaders, notably General Arnold and General Somervell.[12] Logically the next step to be performed by some staff, with more authority than OPD, would have been to secure agreement on both agenda and issues by the JCS and the President. This step was not taken, and the only high-level preparation for the conference was a meeting at the White House on 7 January 1943 with just the President, the four Chiefs of Staff, and the JCS secretary (Brig. Gen. John R. Deane) present. At this meeting the President gave the JCS free rein to follow the Bolero line of strategy at the forthcoming conference, although the Chiefs of Staff admitted that joint planning was not united in its support. The President

---

[8] Symbol: Casablanca Book (Dec 42–Jan 43), Vol. I—Strategy and Plans, Exec 6. For a special supplement of this volume prepared within OPD for the use of General Wedemeyer in connection with the preparations for Casablanca, see OPD study filed in ABC 016 (23 Jan 43), 3. This special supplement is divided into strategy, policy, intelligence, and miscellaneous subjects.

[9] See especially Tab "European Theater K" in Symbol: Casablanca Book (Dec 42–Jan 43), Vol. II—Command and Deployment, Exec 6.

[10] Symbol: Casablanca Book (Dec 42–Jan 43), Vol. III—Places and Personalities, Exec 6.

[11] Memo, Lt Col T. W. Hammond, Jr., JCS for Col R. N. Young, 9 Jan 43, sub: Symbol Agenda, WDCSA 334 JCS (JCS) SS.

[12] Memo, Maj Gen Handy for Gen Arnold and Gen Somervell, 7 Jan 43, sub: Proposed Agenda Submitted by British CsofS for (Symbol), with Paper 8 in ABC 016 (23 Jan 43), 2.

did not commit himself specifically to the BOLERO policy. He thus retained his freedom of action on the cross-Channel versus Mediterranean issue, which the JCS considered critical. Simultaneously he announced for the first time the unconditional surrender formula as the proper aim of the Allied war effort, a subject on which no real military staff work had been done at all. The President also spoke of certain political matters, such as disarmament after the war, which he and Mr. Churchill had to discuss and which neither he nor the Chiefs of Staff seemed to think were subjects for military staff consideration of any kind.[13]

General Marshall left for Casablanca on 9 January 1943. The U. S. Army delegation included three OPD officers, General Wedemeyer, General Hull, and Colonel Gailey, although the latter two were not present for the first few meetings. Meetings of the JCS at Casablanca began on 13 January, and the CCS conferences began the next day. General Wedemeyer, as Army planner, attended a number of meetings of the U. S. JCS as well as some of the meetings of the CCS. He was present at one of the two special meetings of the JCS at Anfa Camp, with the President presiding.[14] The British favored keeping up the momentum of the North African venture through further offensive action in the Mediterranean, but General Marshall and the other U. S. Chiefs of Staff reiterated their support of the BOLERO/ROUNDUP plan for invasion of western Europe in 1943. Sicily, Sardinia, or Corsica, and the eastern Mediterranean all were discussed as possible objectives. The American delegates questioned each one of these as something less than the second front which the Russians were seeking.[15]

The arrival of General Hull and Colonel Gailey, on the fourth day of the conference, gave General Wedemeyer some relief and assistance in his work as one-man Army planning staff at the conference.[16] In addition to assisting General Wedemeyer as much as possible and attending some of the JCS and CCS meetings, General Hull served on a combined subcommittee appointed to draft a summary of the conclusions of the conference for use in a message to Premier Joseph Stalin and a communiqué for the press.[17]

The conferees finally agreed to maintain the momentum of the North African campaign and invade Sicily (HUSKY) in July 1943 or, if possible, in June. While, as a consequence, prospects for the cross-Channel operation receded, the conferees gave a high priority to a combined bomber offensive against the Continent from the United Kingdom, one of the indispensable preliminaries to an invasion of France. With respect to other areas, Casablanca confirmed the policy of shipping military supplies to the USSR, of making a two-way advance through the Central Pacific and the Southwest Pacific toward the Philippine

---

[13] Min of White House meeting, 7 Jan 43, Item 45, Exec 10.

[14] Min sp meeting JCS-President, 16 Jan 43, in Official Casablanca Conference Book.

[15] For these CCS discussions on the issue of cross-Channel versus Mediterranean operations, see especially: (1) min 55th meeting CCS, 14 Jan 43; (2) min 58th meeting CCS, 16 Jan 43; (3) min 60th meeting CCS, 18 Jan 43.

[16] (1) Pers ltr, Brig Gen Wedemeyer to Maj Gen Handy, 22 Jan 43, Paper 5, Item 1A, Exec 3. (2) Msg, Brig Gen Wedemeyer to Col R. N. Young for Maj Gen Handy, 17 Jan 43, CM–IN 7912.

[17] For General Hull's appointment to this CCS subcommittee, see min 61st meeting CCS, 19 Jan 43. For the final decision of the President and Prime Minister concerning a communiqué for the press, see min 67th meeting CCS, 22 Jan 43.

area, and of building up U. S. Army air forces in the China-Burma-India area.[18] Just how, when, and with what these various operations, except for HUSKY and the combined bomber offensive, could or would be carried out, remained extremely vague, just as it had after similar 1942 conferences. Agreement in principle was still more impressive than agreement in operational detail. The most striking news of the conference released to the public reflected to some extent the general character of the results. The President announced that he and the Prime Minister had agreed that the aim of the war was the unconditional surrender of Germany, Italy, and Japan.[19] The Casablanca Conference marked the beginning of a series of British-American understandings on the military way to bring about those surrenders, but it was only a beginning.

The definite commitment to undertake a Mediterranean operation in 1943, in accordance with British urging, and the inability of the American delegation to secure an equally definite commitment to ROUNDUP, left the U. S. military representatives at the conference disappointed. Their attitude was reflected in a letter written by General Wedemeyer to General Handy, just before leaving Casablanca:

"We lost our shirts and . . . are now committed to a subterranean umbilicus operation in midsummer." General Wedemyer of course was referring to the phrase used earlier by the Prime Minister, the "soft underbelly of Europe." [20] He believed that the weak point in the position of the delegation from the United States was its staff work. The British delegation, he observed, had the American representatives on the defensive during almost the entire conference, and had plans worked out in detail to support all the British views. In trying to help General Marshall, General Wedemeyer said, he had depended a great deal on the antecedent preparations by S&P officers and, during the conference, on the work of General Hull and Colonel Gailey. This fact pointed to the desirability of having a great deal of staff assistance available before and during the next conference.[21]

General Wedemeyer took one of the most important steps in carrying out Casablanca decisions simply by making a trip around the world to tell senior American commanders and their staffs what had been agreed upon. In Washington, OPD began the paper work of implementation as soon as the conference was over, issuing instructions to zone of interior commands and exchanging messages almost daily with overseas commands. General Hull's Theater Group, which carried on most of this correspondence, also sent special representatives to North Africa to help untangle critical problems con-

---

[18] CCS 170/2, 23 Jan 43, title: SYMBOL—Final Rpt to President and Prime Minister Summarizing Decisions by CCS. In the pattern of Pacific operations which were outlined, the Aleutians were to be made as secure as possible, advances were to be made from Midway toward the line Truk-Guam and from the South and Southwest Pacific toward Rabaul. In regard to China, eventual reopening of the Burma Road was accepted as an objective, but not for the immediate future.

[19] For the announcement of agreement on the unconditional surrender concept, see *The New York Times*, January 27, 1943, quoted in *United States and Italy 1936–1946*, Dept of State Publication 2669, European Series 17, pp. 40–41.

[20] For the Prime Minister's use of the phrase, see copy msg 195, Prime Minister for President, 18 Nov 42. The message was included as part of JCS 153, 18 Nov 42, title: Plans and Opns in Mediterranean, Middle East and Near East.

[21] Pers ltr, Brig Gen Wedemeyer to Maj Gen Handy, 22 Jan 43, Paper 5, Item 1A, Exec 3. For the bearing of General Wedemeyer's remarks on joint strategic planning, see Ch. XIII.

nected with future operations in the Mediterranean.[22]

Trident: 12–25 May 1943

The American military staffs took to heart some of the lessons of Casablanca in preparing for the next conference, TRIDENT, held at Washington in May. It was just before TRIDENT that the JCS approved the major wartime reorganization of the joint committee system. One of the main purposes of the reorganization was to provide studies that would serve as a basis for agreement among the armed services, with the President, and, insofar as practicable, with the British.[23] General Marshall, speaking for the JCS, assured a Senate subcommittee that the members of the JCS, well aware that the British Chiefs of Staff worked very closely with the War Cabinet and the Prime Minister, were reorganizing their own staff to meet Great Britain on equal terms at the coming conference.[24]

In line with this reasoning, the JSSC had concluded that joint outline studies and plans on all "reasonable" courses of action subsequent to HUSKY had to be prepared for the JCS before the encounter with the "always well prepared British." [25] Upon receiving instruction to this effect from the JCS, the joint planning staff quickly produced a series of plans and suggested lines of action for consideration prior to TRIDENT.[26] The new Joint War Plans Committee did most of the work, preparing a proposed agenda and drafting over thirty studies, but time was short, and it drew extensively on plans and studies prepared by the separate service planning agencies. OPD contributed in this way, sifting into the joint committee system papers developed in the Strategy Section in the spring of 1943.[27] Furthermore, OPD went on briefing the Chief of Staff and the Army planner as usual and brought up to date the volumes of studies (SYMBOL) prepared for Casablanca.[28]

General Wedemeyer proposed to the JCS that the United States take the offensive at TRIDENT by asking the British to consider some of the papers agreed upon by the JCS so that the American representatives would not find themselves in the position of considering all British papers.[29] His suggestion, based on experience at Casablanca, was approved by General Marshall and General McNarney and accepted by the JCS on 10 May 1943.

In much the same spirit, General Hull recommended increasing the number of

---

[22] For trips to the theater, see Ch. XV.

[23] For the reorganization of the joint committee system, enacted by the chartering or rechartering of joint agencies in early May, see Ch. XIII. For a statement of the prevailing opinion within the American service planning agencies that the United States had been insufficiently prepared for the Casablanca Conference, see JPS 272, 26 Apr 43, title: Agenda for Next United Nations Conf.

[24] Min 79th meeting JCS, 10 May 43.

[25] OPD brief, title: Notes . . . 76th meeting JCS, 27 Apr 43, Opns Subsequent to "HUSKY" (JCS 271), with JCS 271 in ABC 384 Post HUSKY (14 May 43), 1.

[26] For JCS instructions to the JPS, see: (1) min 76th meeting JCS, 27 Apr 43; (2) memo, Capt F. B. Royal, USN, Deputy Secy for Secy JPS, 28 Apr 43, sub: Opns Subsequent to "HUSKY," with JPS 169/D in ABC 384 Post HUSKY (14 May 43), 1.

[27] For example of submission of an OPD plan to the JPS, see memo, Brig Gen Hull for Gen Marshall, 3 May 43, no sub, Item 15, Exec 3.

[28] TRIDENT Revision of SYMBOL: Casablanca Book (Dec 42–Jan 43), Vol. I—Strategy and Plans, Logistics and Command (1 May 43); Vol. II—Theaters: Command and Deployment (7 Apr 43); Vol. III—Theaters: Western Hemisphere and Pacific only (1 May 43), Exec 6. A revision of 7 April Vol. II was later put out by OPD under date of 25 May 1943, Exec 6.

[29] Min 79th meeting JCS, 10 May 43.

representatives in the American delegation, even though extra assistance would be on call from the War Department at any time since the conference was convening in Washington. General Marshall approved the idea, and the JCS made arrangements accordingly.[30] Shortly before the conference, General Hull informed General Handy, then on one of his visits to the overseas theaters, that the American planners and Chiefs of Staff would be well prepared for TRIDENT.[31]

When the conferees assembled in Washington for the first meeting on 12 May, the military situation on the Soviet front and in North Africa appeared even more favorable than at the time of Casablanca. The Soviet Army counteroffensive had overrun Kursk, Rostov, and the whole eastern shore of the Sea of Azov. All of North Africa was in British or American control except for a small area around Tunis, and on the following day, 13 May 1943, organized German resistance in North Africa ended. Although there had been no substantial change in the Pacific or Far East since Casablanca, a major conference was necessary to decide on the next step after Sicily (HUSKY). Again the critical decision was whether to continue with the Mediterranean campaign or to concentrate on the cross-Channel operation.

At TRIDENT the President came out unequivocally in favor of adhering to the principles of the BOLERO/ROUNDUP concept by planning for a cross-Channel operation in 1944. The JCS reaffirmed their support of this strategic policy. For the Mediterranean the JCS recommended undertaking only limited offensive operations after HUSKY lest a vacuum be created which would draw in the military resources necessary for the cross-Channel effort. The Prime Minister and the British Chiefs of Staff, on the other hand, stressed the importance of eliminating Italy from the war, classing it as the great prize and the first objective after HUSKY. They took the position that the end of Italian resistance would pave the way for a successful cross-Channel invasion and thus shorten the war. All agreed on the necessity of intensifying the combined bomber offensive from the United Kingdom, General Marshall in particular stressing the faith of American military leaders in its contribution to the cross-Channel operation.[32]

During the two weeks of the TRIDENT Conference the planners and other officers in OPD found themselves deeply involved in work connected with it.[33] General Wedemeyer went to nearly all the meetings of the CCS, though he did not attend the plenary sessions held at the White House in the presence of the President and the Prime Minister. The S&P Group continued to brief and analyze new or revised papers on conference issues for General Wede-

---

[30] (1) Memo, Brig Gen Hull for Brig Gen Wedemeyer, 5 May 43, no sub, with Paper 37, Book 9, Exec 8. (2) Penciled notation, Col Gailey, 5 May 43, appended to memo [Brig Gen J. R. Deane] for Admiral Leahy, Gen Marshall, Admiral King, and Gen Arnold, 4 May 43, sub: Conduct of Coming Conf, with Paper 37, Book 9, Exec 8.

[31] Msg (originator OPD), Brig Gen Hull to Gen Marshall to Gen Eisenhower for Maj Gen Handy, 7 May 43, CM-OUT 2928.

[32] For the discussions on British and American views on the cross-Channel versus Mediterranean issue at TRIDENT, see especially: (1) min 1st White House meeting, TRIDENT, 12 May 43, Official TRIDENT Conference Book; (2) min 83d meeting CCS, TRIDENT, 13 May 43; (3) min 84th meeting CCS, TRIDENT, 14 May 43; (4) min 85th meeting CCS, TRIDENT, 15 May 43.

[33] Ltr, Brig Gen Hull to Maj Gen W. C. Lee, 101st Div, Airborne Parachute, Fort Bragg, N.C., 20 May 43, Paper 78, Book 9, Exec 8.

meyer and the Chief of Staff.[34] S&P officers also briefed the minutes of the White House and CCS meetings, checking inconsistencies and incomplete statements in the American position and trying to anticipate arguments which the British might adopt. The Strategy Section, working under General Wedemeyer's personal direction, prepared studies on the strategic implications of British proposals for submission to the Chief of Staff. As the final agreement was being drafted, officers in both the Strategy Section and the Policy Section were constantly reviewing conference papers, offering suggestions in the interest of consistency and clarity in defining American policies, and accepting compromises with British views. In advising General Wedemeyer and General Marshall, OPD planners sought to supply the information on the basis of which the views of the President and the JCS could be harmonized.[35] Thus they emphasized the importance of using at the conference statistics prepared by the Army Service Forces or OPD's Logistics Group. They also continued to urge that the members of the JCS had to agree among themselves so they could strengthen their position in discussions with the British.[36] As General Marshall observed, the "Joint Chiefs of Staff must be a unit to determine our play." [37]

The results of the conference were much more satisfying to Army strategists than the Casablanca decisions had been. A major concession to British views was made in the form of a decision to plan further Mediterranean operations with a view to eliminating Italy from the war. At the same time the British approved continuing the combined bomber offensive from the United Kingdom on a large scale with the last stage to be completed by April 1944, designed to lead up to an invasion. Most important, they had agreed to assign a target date of 1 May 1944 for a cross-Channel operation intended to put twenty-nine divisions ashore on the Continent. Briefly called ROUNDHAMMER, this operation became OVERLORD, the central feature of all planning during the next year.[38]

The Army planners on the JWPC and other OPD officers who had helped in preparations for TRIDENT concluded that the

---

[34] Annex B, title: Analysis of Servs of the S&P Gp Preliminary to and During the TRIDENT Conf, atchd to memo, Lt Col L. J. Lincoln for Col Roberts, 15 Jun 43, sub: Working Stf to Accompany Planners to Next Combined Conf, with JPS 189, Tab 2, in ABC 337, 25 May 43.

[35] Memo, Brig Gen Wedemeyer for Gen Marshall [about 13 May 43], no sub, with Paper 72, Book 9, Exec 8.

[36] OPD brief, title: Notes . . . 83d meeting JCS, 17 May 43, with Tab 1, Folder 1, Item 10, Exec 5.

[37] Min 83d meeting JCS, 17 May 43.

[38] CCS 242/6, 25 May 43, title: Final Rpt to President and Prime Minister. The decision to eliminate Italy was to be reviewed in the summer of 1943 in the light of the progress at that time of the Sicily Campaign and the situation on the Russo-German front. At the close of the TRIDENT Conference, General Marshall accompanied Prime Minister Churchill to Algiers for a conference with General Eisenhower on post-HUSKY operations in the Mediterranean. Present at two of the meetings at General Eisenhower's villa in Algiers was General Handy, who had been on a tour of the theaters. At the Algiers conference, 29 May–3 June 1943, General Eisenhower was given broad latitude to determine the course of his advance in the Mediterranean after HUSKY for the purpose of eliminating Italy from the war. For the discussions at Algiers, see especially: (1) min of 1st meeting held at General Eisenhower's villa, Algiers, 29 May 43; (2) min 2d meeting, Eisenhower's villa, 31 May 43; (3) min 3d meeting, Eisenhower's villa, 3 Jun 43. All in Official TRIDENT Conference Book.

There was little change in Pacific and Far Eastern plans as a result of TRIDENT. In Burma minor land operations were scheduled as a first step toward opening the Burma Road. The capacity of the air route to China was to be increased. In the Pacific, operations were to be mounted against the Japanese in the Aleutians, the Marshall and Caroline Islands, the Solomons, Bismarcks, and Japanese-held New Guinea.

American staff had done much better than at Casablanca. They agreed that the United States should plan to send a large delegation to the next conference, due to be called within the next few months, and that all the members of it should work together beforehand. They advised settling well in advance what would be on the agenda, anticipating British arguments, and preparing the American case for the JCS thoroughly and in time for everyone to know exactly what it was. Above all, they wanted to be sure that the President and the JCS were willing to support the case as worked out in detail by the joint staff.[39]

As with all the major conferences, TRIDENT put a great strain on the OPD machinery after the conference was over. The Army command post had to inform Army commanders everywhere just what had been decided, and had to make arrangements for moving troops and supplies in conformity with the decisions. With so many decisions being made in the course of a few days, carrying them out involved careful co-ordination between the small joint and combined staffs on the one hand and the War Department and the Army's overseas commands on the other. S&P, the Army agency linking the Army with the joint committee system, laid great stress on close liaison with joint and combined agencies, including the joint and combined secretariats. It was responsible for implementing decisions already made, as well as for keeping in touch with joint and combined deliberations at every step in order to see that studies and decisions took into account the situation in the Army commands overseas.[40]

Quadrant: 14–24 August 1943

The preparation for the international conferences after TRIDENT became more and more centralized in the joint planning staff. Thus the studies drafted by the joint committees, especially the JWPC, superseded the books which OPD had prepared for Casablanca and revised for TRIDENT.[41] Nevertheless, the S&P Group, independently of the work of its representatives on the JWPC, went on making studies for submission to the Army planner and, through him, either to the JPS or to the Chief of Staff, on matters concurrently being considered by joint committees. The Strategy Section continued to advise the Army planner on the agenda of joint and combined meetings he was to attend.[42] OPD went on preparing papers for General Marshall on problems that would come before the next

---

[39] (1) JPS 189, 25 May 43, title: Preparations for Next U. S.-British Staff Conf. This paper was drawn up by the JWPC and submitted to the JPS for discussion. (2) SS 106 [25 May 43], title: Analysis of TRIDENT and ANFA Confs, ABC 381 Strategy Sec Papers 96–126/3 (7 Jan 43). (3) Memo, Brig Gen Wedemeyer for Gen Marshall, 8 Jun 43, no sub, Paper 68, Book 10, Exec 8.

[40] For implementation of TRIDENT, see: (1) min 63d meeting CPS, 27 May 43; (2) memo, Brig Gen Wedemeyer for Secretariat, JPS, 3 Jun 43, sub: Implementation of CCS 242/6, with CCS 242/6 in ABC 016 (5–21–43); (3) min 81st meeting JPS, 16 Jun 43; (4) Tab B, Supplemental Statement to Tab A, incl to memo, Lt Col L. J. Lincoln for Col Roberts, 19 Jun 43, sub: Working Stf to Accompany Planners to next Combined Conf, Tab 7 with JPS 189 in ABC 337 (25 May 43).

[41] For SEXTANT, OPD did put out an abbreviated version of the conference books, called a Condensed Information Book, for the use of the OPD chief. A different kind of book was prepared for the less strictly military conferences of 1945. See Ch. XVI.

[42] For examples of OPD briefs and analyses of JWPC proposals, see: (1) SS 93, 3 Aug 43, sub: Comments on Strategic Concept for Defeat of Axis in Europe (JWPC 48/3, Revised), Tab SS 93, ABC 381 Strategy Sec Papers (7 Jan 43). This paper was a Strategy Section analysis for the Army planner. (2) OPD brief on JWPC proposals, title: Notes . . . 102d meeting JCS, 9 Aug 43, Plans for Occupation of Italy and Her Possessions (JPS 247), with JPS 247 in ABC 384 Post HUSKY (14 May 1943), 2.

conference, especially in preparation for his meetings with the President prior to the international sessions.[43] In early August the Strategy Section summed up for General Marshall the various choices before the representatives of the United States at the coming conference, QUADRANT, to be held within the month at Quebec. Just prior to the opening of the conference, the Chief of Staff submitted to the President his conclusions, as drafted by the Strategy Section, on the main issue, which was the cost in time and resources of a failure to concentrate at once on a cross-Channel operation.[44]

The military situation in general had changed little since TRIDENT. In the Mediterranean, however, the campaign in Sicily (10 July–17 August 1943) had proved highly successful and was entering its final stages. The time had come to review the tentative TRIDENT decision to eliminate Italy from the war. Final decision on this point, the American delegation believed, would force a clear ruling on the familiar issue, whether the main effort would be made against northwest Europe or in the Mediterranean. The fighting forces were at an operational crossroads in the European war, and definite commitments of shipping, troops, and supplies could not long be postponed.

Among the American delegation sent to discuss these issues at QUADRANT were fifteen OPD officers.[45] General Handy and General Wedemeyer attended practically all the meetings of the CCS, except the plenary sessions with the President and the Prime Minister. Being well informed about day-to-day conference proceedings, they were able to take a useful part in analyzing British proposals and looking for ways to bolster the American position.[46] At one point General Handy submitted a paper written to counter British suggestions for qualifying the commitment to OVERLORD, and his study was accepted by the JCS and submitted to the CCS, where a final compromise was reached.[47] General Wedemeyer, as Army planner, briefed the Chief of Staff on all plans brought up for consideration at the conference. He also helped General Handy draft papers, as requested by the Chief of Staff, for submission to the JCS and via the JCS to the CCS.[48]

---

[43] OPD paper, title: Notes for Gen Marshall for Use in Conf with President [late July 43], Paper 1, Item 11, Exec 5.

[44] OPD draft [CofS for President], 8 Aug 43, sub: Conduct of European War, Paper 44 in ABC 381 (9-25-42), 7. The conclusions in this paper were those embodied in the OPD Strategy Section's study, SS 90, 8 Aug 43, title: Conduct of War in Europe, ABC 381 Strategy Sec Papers (7 Jan 43). A copy of SS 90 was distributed to all American officers who attended QUADRANT.

[45] Tel Directory, code title, Bosco. Filed in folder, annex to ABC 337 (25 May 43). The directory contains a list of the members of the American and British delegations present at QUADRANT.

[46] For examples of participation by General Handy and General Wedemeyer in work of JCS meetings at QUADRANT, see: (1) min 104th meeting JCS, QUADRANT, 15 Aug 43; (2) min 105th meeting JCS, QUADRANT, 16 Aug 43.

[47] For the discussion and acceptance by the JCS of General Handy's proposals, see min 105th meeting JCS, QUADRANT, 16 Aug 43. For a copy of the complete paper presented by General Handy to the JCS, see memo [16 Aug 43], no sub, Item 51, Exec 10. The memorandum begins: "The discussion in the Combined Chiefs of Staff meeting yesterday. . . ." For the incorporation of General Handy's proposals by the U. S. JCS in a memorandum for submission to the CCS, see: (1) CCS 303/1, 16 Aug 43, title: Strategic Concept for Defeat of Axis in Europe; (2) min 109th meeting CCS, QUADRANT, 16 Aug 43. For the compromise of U. S. and British Chiefs of Staff's views reached on these proposals, see: (1) CCS 303/3, 17 Aug 43, title: Strategic Concept for Defeat of Axis in Europe; (2) min 110th meeting CCS, QUADRANT, 17 Aug 43.

[48] Memo, Brig Gen Wedemeyer for Gen Marshall, 16 Aug 43, no sub, with CCS 320 in ABC 384 NW Europe (20 Aug 43), 1-A.

On the subordinate staff level at QUAD-RANT, as at TRIDENT, most of the activities of OPD officers revolved about General Wedemeyer. In studying proposals presented at the conference for consideration by the Chief of Staff, General Wedemeyer drew upon the advice of his S&P advisory planning staff and representatives of the OPD theater sections concerned. For discussion in meetings of the JPS and the CPS, he drew as well on the opinions of OPD officers assigned to the JWPC teams. Members of the entire OPD contingent, planners, logisticians, and theater section representatives, were present at planning meetings as required by the course of the discussions, and served on *ad hoc* committees from time to time.

During the course of the conference, the OPD team at Quebec was linked with the "home team" in Washington through telephone conversations and a constant exchange of messages between General Handy and General Hull.[49] To keep the Chief of Staff abreast of important activities in the overseas theaters and the reaction of his command post staff in Washington to them, General Handy prepared digests of significant cables with OPD comments on them.[50] General Handy also called upon General Hull for special studies, such as an analysis of the effect of moving divisions from one projected operation to another, to be presented to General Marshall.

All the American military spokesmen at QUADRANT pressed for a final commitment to OVERLORD, the plan for the cross-Channel

invasion developed by a combined British-American planning staff in London on the basis of the 1 May 1944 target date and twenty-nine division force accepted at TRIDENT. They were anxious to reach an agreement to give OVERLORD overriding priority above all other operations in the European-Mediterranean area in 1944.[51] The President again put the weight of his influence behind the cross-Channel operation, and the British representatives agreed that "OVERLORD should constitute the major offensive for 1944 and that Italian operations should be planned with this conception as a background." They argued, however, that the assignment of overriding priority to OVERLORD was too binding. In the ensuing discussions of measures to eliminate Italy from the war, including an operation in southern France in conjunction with OVERLORD, the American delegates, fearing lest Mediterranean ventures drain off vital strength from the cross-Channel operation, vigorously argued for a strict limitation of Mediterranean operations in accordance with the long-approved basic strategy for defeating Germany in western Europe.[52]

Although the QUADRANT conferees in the end came to a compromise phrasing which avoided the American term "overriding priority," they finally approved the outline plan for OVERLORD which had been studied at the conference, and classed the operation (target date still 1 May 1944) as the "primary U. S.-British ground and air

---

[49] For example, see tel conf, Washington, D.C. (Brig Gen Hull) with Quebec (Maj Gen Handy), 19 Aug 43, Paper 84, Book 11, Exec 9.

[50] For example, see memo, Maj Gen Handy for Gen Marshall, 15 Aug 43, sub: Digest of Cables Received from Stilwell: Reference: Burma Opn, Item 51, Exec 10.

[51] For phrase "overriding priority," see min 108th meeting CCS, QUADRANT, 15 Aug 43.

[52] For discussion of these issues at QUADRANT, and all the quoted phrases, see: (1) min 108th meeting CCS, QUADRANT, 15 Aug 43; (2) min 110th meeting CCS, QUADRANT, 17 Aug 43; (3) min 1st Citadel meeting, QUADRANT, 19 Aug 43, Official QUADRANT Conference Book; (4) min 2d Citadel meeting, QUADRANT, 23 Aug. 43, Official QUADRANT Conference Book.

operation" in Europe.[53] On the vital question of priority for resources, the final decision was ambiguous: "As between Operation OVERLORD and operations in the Mediterranean, where there is a shortage of resources, available resources will be distributed and employed with the main object of insuring the success of OVERLORD." The conferees interpreted this principle as not inconsistent with proceeding to eliminate Italy from the war and establishing bases at least as far north as Rome, seizing Sardinia and Corsica, and establishing a lodgment in southern France. All of these operations were approved, but the saving clause that reassured the American planners was the ruling that all of these Mediterranean operations would be "carried out with the forces allotted at TRIDENT."[54] Thus, after the long debate that had begun when General Marshall took the BOLERO/ROUNDUP outline plan to London in April 1942, the United States and Great Britain had agreed to allocate forces for the cross-Channel invasion of northwestern Europe and not to use them in other operations. With a plan for the operation written and approved, with a

definite restriction on the Mediterranean offensive, and with authorization for an extended combined bomber offensive in support of OVERLORD, general strategic planning for the campaign in Europe had crystallized in nearly final form.

QUADRANT, which thus was a decisive conference in the war against Germany, also marked the beginning of definite and constructive planning for large-scale offensives against Japan. The Pacific operations did not figure importantly in debates at any of the midwar conferences. The strategic responsibility of the United States and the commitment of American forces in the Pacific were so preponderant that the members of the JCS simply reported their plans, and the CCS normally approved them. At QUADRANT, operations were scheduled along both the Central Pacific and Southwest Pacific lines of advance to take deep bites into the Japanese defensive ring of islands. The Gilberts and Marshalls in the Central Pacific were marked out as the first big steps toward Truk, Guam, the Palaus, and the Marianas. In the Southwest Pacific "step-by-step airborne-water-borne advances" were approved to take or neutralize northern New Guinea as far west as Wewak, including the Admiralty Islands and the Bismarck Archipelago, while Rabaul, so long the main objective in the region, was to be neutralized rather than captured.

Similarly, the long-neglected China-Burma-India area received more definite commitments at QUADRANT than at previous conferences. In the first place, a beginning, at least, was made in reducing the command complexities that restricted cooperation among the British, American, and Chinese forces in the Burma combat zone. An Allied Southeast Asia Command (SEAC) was authorized with a British Su-

---

[53] In line with the decision at TRIDENT to plan for a cross-Channel operation with target date of 1 May 1944 and on the basis of twenty-nine British-American divisions assembled in the United Kingdom for the invasion by that date (ROUNDHAMMER), Lt. Gen. F. E. Morgan's combined planning staff (COSSAC planners) in the United Kingdom had developed between TRIDENT and QUADRANT a plan for an invasion of the Continent. The plan for this operation, given the code name OVERLORD, was developed with the same target date 1 May 1944 and on the basis of a maximum of thirty and a minimum of twenty-six divisions as likely to be available in the United Kingdom on that date and for follow-up shipments of three to five divisions per month. See Gordon A. Harrison, *Cross-Channel Attack* (Washington, D.C., 1951).

[54] This ruling on Mediterranean operations was qualified only by addition of the phrase, "except insofar as these [forces] may be varied by decision of the Combined Chiefs of Staff."

preme Commander, Admiral Lord Louis Mountbatten, and with an American Deputy Supreme Commander, General Stilwell. The American deputy retained his direct responsibilities to Generalissimo Chiang Kai-shek in the China theater, which was not included in the Allied Southeast Asia Command but left in its earlier nebulous state as part of the American area of strategic responsibility in the Pacific. He also exercised "operational control of the Chinese forces operating into Burma" as well as American air and ground forces committed to the Southeast Asia theater. The new command, though Allied, was put under the immediate jurisdiction of the British Chiefs of Staff in much the same way that the Southwest Pacific area was under the jurisdiction of the U. S. Joint Chiefs of Staff. The first operational assignment for the Southeast Asia Command was the long-planned, much postponed campaign in North Burma. It was scheduled once more, this time with a target date of February 1944, as a prerequisite for improving the air route and opening overland communications with China.[55]

OPD officers had set the stage for Army-wide implementation of these QUADRANT decisions even while they were still being discussed. In an effort to avoid the kind of delays encountered in starting the chain of actions necessary to carry out TRIDENT decisions, they prepared a master chart identifying CCS papers by number, subject, and date, listing the CCS meeting at which the paper was approved, and indicating the divisions of the War Department General Staff, theater sections of OPD, the major zone of interior commands (Army Air

Forces, Army Ground Forces, and Army Service Forces), and the overseas theater headquarters which needed copies of particular papers and minutes or extracts of them. The chart provided OPD with a convenient check list and running record of action taken to initiate Army execution of CCS decisions.[56] In addition, tighter administrative control of the whole process of carrying out QUADRANT plans was established by requesting every military agency concerned to send to OPD's Policy Section a brief résumé of the action proposed in line with the CCS papers supplied them.[57] This procedure, applied to international conference decisions for the first time, was a logical development from the follow-up technique OPD had long used in making certain that command decisions inside the Army were understood and carried out in the theaters of operations. In fact the two follow-up procedures tended to merge into one, since the Policy Section often simply furnished the appropriate OPD theater section with copies of the CCS papers sent to the overseas commands.[58]

Sextant: 22 November–7 December 1943

The next meeting, held partly at Cairo and partly at Tehran, in November and December 1943, brought Great Britain and the United States into military conference not only with each other but also with the

[55] For all the foregoing final QUADRANT decisions, see CCS 319/5, 24 Aug 43, title: Final Rpt to President and Prime Minister.

[56] (1) Chart, n.d., title: QUADRANT Implementation, ABC 319.1 (27 Aug 43), 1. (2) Memo, Brig Gen Wedemeyer for ACofS OPD, 27 Aug 43, sub: Implementation of QUADRANT Decisions, Tab 2 in ABC 319.1, 27 Aug 43.
[57] Note for rcd appended to memo, OPD [to G–1, G–2, etc.], 30 Aug 43, sub: QUADRANT Decisions, Tab 4 in ABC 319.1, 27 Aug 43.
[58] Memo, Lt Col J. K. Woolnough, Chief Policy Sec for Chief Theater Gp, 30 Aug 43, sub: QUADRANT Decisions, with Tab 4 in ABC 319.1, 27 Aug 43.

USSR and China.[59] The whole set of conversations were usually designated by the code name SEXTANT, although it properly applied only to the British-American-Chinese meetings at Cairo 22–26 November and 3–7 December. The discussions held at Tehran in the interim, 28–30 November, were given the special code name EUREKA. The composite conference, in any case, brought together the nations whose military efforts had just brought about the capitulation of the Italian Government (8 September) and the conquest of nearly half of Italy, the nation whose armies were sweeping German forces back from the Dnepr River in a huge winter counteroffensive, and the Asiatic nation whose hopes for survival after years of partial occupation by Japan depended on the offensives building up in the Pacific and Southeast Asia. The leaders of the Soviet Union had already indicated that they would eventually join in the war against Japan, and the War Department was aware of this confidential commitment.[60] In the view of Army planners, there was only one major military question to be settled by SEXTANT, and that was whether the Prime Minister and the British Chiefs of Staff would abide by the QUADRANT commitment to OVERLORD, which was nearly irrevocable—in short, whether they were at last going "to fish or cut bait." [61]

In reviewing conference procedure before SEXTANT, the JWPC concluded that the methods adopted at QUADRANT were sound, in particular early joint consideration of the American position, consultation with the President, limitation of the agenda, circumspect but continuous exchange of ideas with the British planners, taking the initiative in presenting papers, and continuously studying in detail at the conference the implications of British proposals. They criticized the performance in only two major respects, first because the American planners (JPS) still relied heavily on their own staffs rather than on the joint staff, and second because liaison between the JCS and the President was still imperfect.[62] Preparations for SEXTANT conformed in general with these principles. The joint staff took an increasingly large part in the preparations.[63] OPD continued, however, to advise the Army planner, the chief of OPD, and the Chief of Staff, much as before.[64]

---

[59] Memo, Gen Marshall for Admiral Leahy, 25 Oct 43, no sub, Paper 4, Item 12A, Exec 5. In this memorandum, drafted for him in OPD, the Chief of Staff suggested that consideration be given to Soviet participation in the forthcoming CCS conference meetings.

[60] Msg, Ambassador W. A. Harriman for Gen Marshall, 2 Nov 43, CM-IN 1946 (TS).

[61] (1) OPD draft memo [CofS for President], 29 Oct 43, sub: Conduct of European War, with Tab SS 90 in ABC 381 Strategy Sec Papers (7 Jan 43). (2) OPD draft memo [CofS for President], 8 Nov

43, with Tab 90 in ABC 381 Strategy Sec Papers (7 Jan 43). This draft memo contains the phrase "fish or cut bait."

[62] JWPC 85, 2 Sep 43, title: Lessons from QUADRANT. See also Chs. XIII and XVI.

[63] For reference to the role of the JPS, the JSSC, and the Joint Logistics Committee (JLC) in preparation for SEXTANT, see memo, Col C. H. Donnelly, Secy Planners Coms for JPS and JLC, 20 Oct 43, sub: Preparations for Next U. S.-British Stf Conf, with JCS 533 in ABC 337 (18 Oct 43), 1–A.

[64] In the course of briefing General Handy for his trip to SEXTANT, OPD assembled for him a variety of data in an abbreviated, more statistical version of the earlier conference books. This volume contained summaries by theaters of current estimates of the situation, plans for subsequent operations, existing troop dispositions and pending troop movements, and the current command set-up, as well as miscellaneous logistic data including the status of landing ships and craft and status and deployment of divisions. See OPD Condensed Information Book, 6 Nov 43, Exec 6. Much of the material gathered in this volume was drawn from the summaries and charts of the Logistics Group.

OPD sent a delegation of eleven officers to SEXTANT, including a number of the officers assigned to joint committee work. The roster was headed by General Handy and by General Roberts, who had succeeded General Wedemeyer as Army planner. Despite this comparatively large representation from OPD, the membership of the working staff as a whole at SEXTANT showed how far joint staff work had been regularized and had become the basis of the strategic and logistic arguments advanced at the conference.[65]

Preparation for SEXTANT continued aboard the USS *Iowa*, on which the President and the JCS party sailed en route to Cairo.[66] RANKIN (the plan for an emergency return to the Continent in the event of a collapse of German resistance), the projected occupation zones, the command of British and American forces operating against Germany, the possibility of Turkey's entrance into the war, and the projected strategic plan for the defeat of Japan were all under discussion on shipboard. The President and the JCS also presented their views on spheres of responsibility for the occupation of Germany, on postwar air bases, and on the agenda for discussions with Generalissimo Chiang Kai-shek and with Marshal Stalin.[67] The President's comments on such occasions afforded the best guidance on politico-military issues that the JCS could hope to get. General Handy and General Roberts attended the more strictly military meetings, and General Handy took an active part, continuing to press for agreement among the JCS and between the JCS and the President before the coming conference. He also laid emphasis on the operational need for some practical way of correlating Soviet advances in Europe with those projected by the United States and Great Britain.[68]

At Cairo, as always before, the Prime Minister and the British Chiefs of Staff emphasized the need for continuing the momentum of the Allied offensive in the Mediterranean, advocating an advance well beyond Rome to the Pisa–Rimini line, the seizure of Rhodes, a major supply operation for the benefit of Yugoslav guerrillas, and exploration of the feasibility of undertaking other eastern Mediterranean operations. As the Prime Minister phrased the British position: "OVERLORD remained top of the bill, but this operation should not be

---

[65] For list of officers present at SEXTANT, see Annex A, List of Offs Present at SEXTANT, incl with memo, Col C. H. Donnelly for Rear Admiral B. H. Bieri, etc., 5 Feb 44, sub: Attendance at Future U. S.-British Confs, with JPS 345/D in ABC 337 (7 Dec 43). Among the 66 American planning officers attending SEXTANT were 3 representatives of the JSSC; 4 members of the JPS; 2 JPS deputies; 12 members of JWPC teams (Senior, Red, Purple, Blue); 4 members of the Joint Logistics Committee; 8 Army and 5 Navy associates for logistics; and 5 Army and 2 Navy theater representatives. The presence of nine Army Air Forces planners and the liberal sprinkling of Army Service Forces representatives in the Joint Logistics Committee and among Army associates of the Joint Logistics Committee reflected the part played by the Army Air Forces and the Army Service Forces as Army agencies participating in joint planning.

[66] For the scheduled departure of the JCS party, including Generals Marshall, Handy, and Roberts, 10 November 1943, from the Washington Navy Yard, see JCS SEXTANT Info Bul 5, 8 Nov 43, Envelope 1, Item 15, Exec 5.

[67] For the discussions at an important special meeting on board ship en route to Egypt between President and the JCS, see min of JPS-President meeting beginning "Dakar" [19 Nov 43], and attached map with spheres of influence penciled by the President, Item 11, Exec 2. A partial record of these minutes is titled: Min of Meeting Between President and CsofS, Held on Board Ship in Admiral's Cabin, etc., with CCS 320 in ABC 384 N. W. Europe, 20 Aug 43, 1–A.

[68] (1) Min 123d meeting JCS, 15 Nov 43. (2) Min 124th meeting JCS, 17 Nov 43. (3) Min 125th meeting JCS, 18 Nov 43. (4) Min 126th meeting JCS (SEXTANT), 19 Nov 43.

a tyrant to rule out every other activity in the Mediterranean." Despite the Prime Minister's accompanying declaration that he "wished to remove any idea" that the British "had weakened, cooled, or were trying to get out of OVERLORD," the early discussions gave some promise of reviving the well-worn arguments over cross-Channel versus Mediterranean operations.[69]

At Tehran, where for the first time the President, the Prime Minister, and their top staff officers conferred with Marshal Stalin and his small staff, the situation changed completely.[70] Soviet leaders came out unequivocally in favor of making OVERLORD the main British-American effort for 1944 at the expense of any other operation, except a directly supporting invasion of southern France. This strong Soviet stand deflated any chance that might have existed for more ambitious eastern Mediterranean operations and cleared the way for concentration on OVERLORD and ANVIL (southern France). Back in Cairo after the Tehran meetings, the British-American staffs completed preparations to adjust the pattern of world-wide operations to fit the requirements of these undertakings for the defeat of Germany.

The final blueprints for Allied victory in Europe were quickly drawn. Marshal Stalin had promised that the Soviet forces would launch a large-scale offensive on the eastern front in conjunction with OVERLORD and ANVIL to contain German troops.[71] Other operations, including ANVIL, had to be assigned priorities and allocated resources in accordance with the operational needs of OVERLORD. To gain landing craft for ANVIL, the long-projected campaign against Burma was stripped of its phase calling for amphibious operations in the Bay of Bengal, and the date of the land campaign in North Burma was thereby made dubious once more. Plans approved for the Pacific remained far in advance of the operations that could be supported with available forces, already including the promising project of bombing Japan proper by very long-range bombers (B–29's) based in China and on the Mariana Islands.[72] The main outcome of the conference of significance for the Pacific and Far Eastern Commands was Marshal Stalin's definite commitment for the future that Soviet forces would enter the war against Japan as soon as Germany had been defeated.[73]

---

[69] Min 2d plenary meeting, SEXTANT, 24 Nov 43, Official SEXTANT Conference Book.

[70] After several inconclusive meetings in Cairo, 22–26 November, some of which were attended by Generalissimo Chiang Kai-shek and his staff, the President, the Prime Minister, and the CCS left for Tehran. Three plenary sessions at EUREKA, at which the CCS, President Roosevelt, Prime Minister Churchill, Marshal Stalin, Mr. Molotov, and Marshal Voroshilov were present, were held in the Russian Legation at Tehran, 28–30 November. A military conference between the CCS and the sole Soviet military adviser (Marshal Voroshilov) was held on 29 November at the Russian Legation in Tehran. On 30 November the CCS met by themselves in the British Legation, Tehran.

[71] Min 3d plenary meeting, EUREKA (SEXTANT), 30 Nov 43, Official SEXTANT Conference Book.

[72] (1) CCS 397, 3 Dec 43, title: Specific Opns for Defeat of Japan, 1944. This advance was to include the seizure of the Marshalls (January 1944) and the Marianas (October 1944) in the Central Pacific, and of New Britain (January 1944), Manus (April 1944), and Hollandia (June 1944) in the Southwest Pacific. (2) CCS 426/1, 6 Dec 43, title: Rpt to President and Prime Minister. (3) Draft msg, President and Prime Minister for Marshal Stalin [about 7 Dec 43], Case 7, Item 15, Exec 5.

Other decisions at SEXTANT included: (1) continuation of the assignment of the highest strategic priority to the bomber offensive against Germany; and (2) orders for increasing the production of landing craft in the United Kingdom and United States for the reinforcement of OVERLORD, and diversion of landing craft from the Pacific for the same purpose.

[73] Min 1st plenary meeting, EUREKA (SEXTANT), 28 Nov 43, Official SEXTANT Conference Book.

While these decisions were being reached at SEXTANT, General Handy, and General Roberts as Army planner, attended nearly all the meetings of the CCS but as usual were not present at plenary sessions with the Prime Minister and the President. In addition General Handy served as a link between the Washington command post and the Chief of Staff, keeping General Marshall abreast of current developments in the theaters. The other OPD representatives assisted General Handy and General Marshall as they were needed. For instance, for the benefit of General Handy, who went to Tehran, Colonel Ferenbaugh of the North African Section formulated a list of questions the Soviet delegates might ask.[74] General Tansey and Lt. Col. Edward B. Gallant of the Logistics Group briefed General Handy, after his return to Cairo, on the requirements and the availability of landing craft, critical in planning for the projected southern France operations in support of OVERLORD.[75]

At the JCS meetings held during SEXTANT, General Handy, General Roberts and his deputy, Col. Walter E. Todd, and General Tansey were in regular attendance, while OPD logisticians, area specialists, and joint planning staff members attended the sessions whenever their special knowledge was required.[76] General Marshall made free use of General Handy and his staff officers. At JPS and CPS meetings, the Army planner and his deputy, as well as technical and area specialists and members of the JWPC as required, were normally present, but the joint staff strategic planning teams carried the heaviest burden of preparing plans and papers.[77] The logistics specialists helped in the joint planning process, and the OPD theater specialists served on joint subcommittees dealing with problems relating to their theaters.[78]

At SEXTANT the fact that international conference technique was well advanced was manifest. From OPD's point of view it was equally important that the Washington command could keep up with its daily business while so many Division officers were away. General Hull, Acting Assistant Chief of Staff in General Handy's absence, reported to General Handy on 1 December that "Lincoln [Col. George A. Lincoln, S&P acting chief] and the entire 2nd Team doing grand job" and about two weeks later: "We have not had too difficult a time here, although it has been the usual grind. . . . Everything is running smoothly here, and there is nothing for you to worry about." [79] The system was in such smooth operation by this time that OPD continued to work on the "2nd Team" basis, while General Handy and a number of Division officers who had been at SEXTANT took extensive trips and, among other missions, ad-

---

[74] Memo, Col C. B. Ferenbaugh for Maj Gen Handy, 26 Nov 43, sub: A List of Questions Russians May Ask and Related Data, Envelope 3, Item 15, Exec 5.

[75] (1) Memo, Lt Col Gallant for Maj Gen Handy, 3 Dec 43, sub: Statistical Chart—Landing Ships and Craft, OPD Condensed Information Book, 6 Nov 43, Exec 6. (2) Memo, Brig Gen P. H. Tansey for Maj Gen Handy, 4 Dec 43, no sub, with Tab "Misc Papers (Drafts and Carbons)," Case 5, Folder 4, Item 15, Exec 5.

[76] For General Handy's participation in discussion at these meetings, see especially: (1) min 135th meeting JCS, SEXTANT, 5 Dec 43; (2) min 136th meeting JCS, SEXTANT, 6 Dec 43.

[77] For a reference to the "heavy load" on JWPC teams at SEXTANT, see min 115th meeting JPS, Mena House, Cairo, 24 Nov 43.

[78] For example of logistic planning, see min 114th meeting JPS, SEXTANT, 22 Nov 43.

[79] (1) Msg, Brig Gen Hull for Maj Gen Handy, 1 Dec 43, CM-OUT 729. (2) Cf. ltr, Brig Gen Hull to Maj Gen Handy, 17 Dec 43, Item 14, Exec 5.

vised Army commanders around the world of the results of the conference.[80]

The routine business of implementing SEXTANT decisions went on throughout December.[81] The S&P Group prepared a master implementation chart much like the one used in implementing QUADRANT decisions.[82] After its approval by General Hull, OPD proceeded to dispatch copies and extracts of SEXTANT papers and minutes to other War Department divisions, OPD theater sections, and the major zone of interior commands (Army Air Forces, Army Ground Forces, Army Service Forces), and the overseas theater headquarters concerned with each decision. OPD also continued the practice of following up the action taken by Army agencies on the SEXTANT decisions.

This last of the four great military conferences of 1943 marked the beginning of a major change in the character of the international meetings of World War II. The Prime Minister, who at best could have hoped only for concessions within the framework of what had appeared to be an irreversible QUADRANT decision in favor of OVERLORD, had yielded quickly in an unequal struggle when the American delegates were seconded by the Soviet military leaders. The great midwar debate on European military strategy was over after the SEXTANT Conference.

The very mechanics of the meeting reflected a consideration for diplomacy and affairs of state as much as for strategic planning. SEXTANT was procedurally complicated and geographically split for political reasons. Since the USSR and China were not technically allied in belligerency against any single enemy, diplomatic protocol required that discussions of military plans with the Chinese should take place apart from similar discussions with the Soviet representatives. The American and British delegations met the Chinese representatives in Cairo and the Soviet leaders in Tehran. The engineering of even an appearance of cooperation among the Great Powers fighting Germany and Japan was a triumph for the United Nations coalition. Coming after the successful conference of Foreign Secretaries at Moscow, 19–30 October, at which an international organization for peace and security had been indorsed by the United States, the USSR, Great Britain, and China, SEXTANT ended in a spirit of confidence and optimism.[83] The military course was set in Europe. It was being charted in the Far East. Already strictly military matters were becoming less pressing than plans for the political structure the world would adopt after the defeat of Germany and Japan. The changing situation was evidenced not only by the Moscow conference but also by the Chinese-British-American declaration at Cairo on policy concerning Far Eastern territorial settlements. Military leaders did not formally take these political matters under consideration at all on these later 1943 occasions, but the portents of increasing impor-

---

[80] For General Handy's trip, and other missions after SEXTANT, see Ch. XV.

[81] OPD worked closely with the JCS secretariat. Thus on 17 December the secretariat forwarded extracts of SEXTANT decisions requiring Army action and indicated that copies of key papers had already been furnished to General Handy. See memo, Secy JCS for ACofS OPD and Aide to CINC U. S. Fleet, 17 Dec 43, sub: Implementation of SEXTANT Decisions, with Case 3, ABC 337 18 Oct 43, 3.

[82] OPD chart, title: SEXTANT Implementation, 17 Dec 43, Case 1, ABC 337 18 Oct 43, 3.

[83] There were many indications of American optimism resulting from the Moscow conference and the subsequent SEXTANT-EUREKA meetings. For comment of an able, well-informed State Department specialist on Soviet affairs to the effect that the Soviets were "willing to play ball" in return for a "quick victory and postwar help," see msg, Brig Gen T. J. Betts to Maj Gen G. V. Strong for Gen Marshall, (WD G–2) 26 Nov 43, CM-IN 16026.

tance for foreign policy aims in future international deliberations of all kinds were clear. SEXTANT was the last of the great international military conferences of midwar.

Through Overlord

The political and military leaders of the United States and Great Britain, having at last committed themselves irrevocably to OVERLORD, could only await the outcome in mid-1944 before making further decisions on military strategy. Until OVERLORD had succeeded or failed, the military decisions to be made were tactical, logistic, or administrative rather than strategic. The Chiefs of Staff, relying primarily on the judgment of theater commanders, above all of General Eisenhower, made these decisions without referring them to more formal international deliberative processes than the CCS committees in Washington provided. The elaborately planned, full-dress conferences of 1943 had served their purpose. They were not resumed until after the invasion, and then under somewhat different circumstances, since the discussion of military matters on purely military grounds was rapidly becoming secondary in urgency to reaching international understandings on the postwar political world. In the meantime the only military conference that took place was a rather informal one held in the United Kingdom in June 1944, during the initial assault phase of the invasion of the Continent. It brought to a close, in a minor key, the midwar period of international military collaboration.

The British and American Chiefs of Staff arranged to be in session in the United Kingdom in the event that major military decisions were required at the time of launching OVERLORD. There were two possible developments which American military leaders and the President believed might require action by the CCS. First, an insecure hold on the beachhead might require a decision as to whether to withdraw or to continue the operation. Second, a German counterattack seven or eight days after D Day might pose the same difficult choice. The meetings were simply for discussion unless an emergency required a decision on the one critical subject of OVERLORD's chances of success. Since the American representatives did not bring the joint planning staff, they did not intend to consider any broad strategic issues.[84]

In addition to the four members of the JCS, General Handy and Admiral Cooke attended the London meetings. General Handy was accompanied by Colonel Lincoln and Lt. Col. Paul L. Freeman, Jr., of OPD. The whole military staff present was sufficient to permit the meetings, held on 10–15 June 1944, to broaden out to include not only current developments in the European theater but also current and projected operations in the Pacific.[85] General Handy attended some of the meetings and participated in some of the discussions, especially on the timing, forces, and equipment to carry out the ANVIL operation in southern France.[86] The most important development during the conference, however, was the

---

[84] Note for Conf with Field Marshal Sir Alan Brooke [May 44], Case 843, Book 19, Exec 9. This paper evidently was prepared by OPD. It was approved by the U. S. Chiefs of Staff and by the President on 26 May 1944.

[85] (1) Min 162d meeting CCS, 10 Jan 44. (2) Min 163d meeting CCS, 11 Jun 44. (3) Min 164th meeting CCS, 13 Jun 44. (4) Min 165th meeting CCS, 14 Jun 44. (5) Min 166th meeting CCS, 15 Jun 44.

[86] Informal notes of 163d meeting CCS, 11 Jun 44, Middlesex, England, prepared by U. S. Secy [of CCS], with Case 841, Book 19, Exec 9.

passage of time in which no action by the CCS was necessary. Neither of the contingencies arose that would have required an emergency decision. The last OVERLORD conference ended on 15 June without any action on the main subject on the agenda. This fact did not signify that the conference was a failure but that OVERLORD was a success. The era of the great international military conferences of midwar, all of which had dealt first and foremost with the cross-Channel invasion issue, had ended.

CHAPTER XIII

OPD and Joint Planning (1943–45)

The increase in the volume of inter-service and international staff work led in 1943 to some basic readjustments in the theory and practice of American joint planning. The practice of classifying as strategic planning all of the many kinds of problems that were referred for final solution to the JCS or the CCS accented the need for a careful analysis of the various functions performed by the joint committees as well as of the procedures the committees employed in their work. Officers in the S&P Group were of course intimately concerned with studying proposed readjustments in the JCS-CCS system, advising General Marshall on them, and conducting their own work according to the patterns finally approved. The operations officers in OPD also were affected, since the general framework of strategic policy within which they worked was established in the joint planning process.

The procedures adopted for joint strategic planning in 1942, however great an advance they may have marked beyond earlier achievements in the same direction, were not adequate for the midwar task of planning vast military operations involving the use of ground, air, and sea forces, often of two or more nations. Many military views had to be reconciled in every decision, and a process had to be evolved for reconciling them with sufficient formality and detail so that no time would have to be spent subsequently in debate over what had been decided or why something else had not been

the final decision. It had become increasingly evident that American strategy, if it were to be formulated clearly in joint deliberations and represented effectively in combined deliberations, would require a more elaborate strategic planning process in joint committees, better defined in its relation to other kinds of joint committee work.

In 1943 General Marshall lent his authority and prestige to the cause of reorganizing the agencies of the JCS and defining or redefining their duties in the complex process of reaching interservice and international agreement. His deputy, General McNarney, took an active part in working out the actual reforms made, and also controlled for General Marshall the requisite administrative adjustments within the War Department. He judged the extent to which various Army agencies had to be represented in various parts of the joint staff as reorganized and made certain, in particular, that OPD was adequately represented to accomplish the purposes for which it had been established.

OPD representatives on joint and combined committees very soon began to respond to the increasing need for reaching durable understandings with the Navy and with the British. They became adept in using the quasi-diplomatic techniques employed in drafting agreements, and they became more "joint-minded," although they remained in close touch with the operations officers in the Theater Group and never lost sight of the views and needs of Army commanders overseas. Operations officers in turn drew on the planning officers for knowledge and interpretation of joint and combined deliberations and agreements, upon which the Theater Group depended every day in carrying out its mission. OPD's work on strategic planning in the later war years thus went on almost entirely within the Army-Navy, British-American staff system and merged with the joint and combined planning process. Nevertheless, it remained characteristic of OPD's planners in these years, as in the early BOLERO period, that they attempted to set the course of Allied plans by constant reference to one fixed point in Allied strategy, the concept of an early assault in strength against the German forces in northwestern France.

Need for Better Joint Planning

Considerable dissatisfaction with the way the American joint planning committees functioned, particularly in contrast to the apparently smooth functioning of parallel British committees, began to appear during 1942. The basis for some of this dissatisfaction was simply the fact, apparent on the face of the record, that the formulation of joint (American) strategic directives as well as the negotiation of strategic agreements with the British went on at least as much outside the JCS-CCS system as inside it.

During 1942 compromise and agreement among the Army, the Army Air Forces, and the Navy on operations in the Pacific area usually came after extensive correspondence between Admiral King and General Marshall, with OPD performing most of the staff work necessary for drafting the Chief of Staff's memoranda in the series. The JCS took responsibility for command arrangements, operational policy, and troop deploy-

ments in both the Southwest Pacific, under General MacArthur, and the rest of the Pacific, under Admiral Nimitz. Yet deliberations on these questions in JCS meetings for the most part merely reflected the current status of the written negotiations between General Marshall and Admiral King. Thus in joint planning OPD officers exercised their main influence in 1942 through advice to General Marshall rather than through deliberations with their colleagues on the Joint Staff Planners or Joint U. S. Strategic Committee.

Strategic decisions in the Pacific usually represented a compromise between recommendations submitted by General MacArthur and proposals advanced by Admiral King. These recommendations and proposals frequently conflicted on questions of strategy, appropriate command arrangements, and the deployment of forces. They agreed on the need for Army forces in the Pacific over and above those which General Marshall (and General Arnold) thought it proper to divert from the major effort against Germany, but they disagreed on where forces allotted to the Pacific should be used. The extensive correspondence upon which General Marshall mainly relied in his efforts to reach an understanding with Admiral King on building up forces in either the Southwest or the Central Pacific region was phrased with great care, but in rather general terms. The formal joint agreements which embodied these understandings were also, therefore, very general. In view of the wide divergence in the opinions of Admiral King and those of General MacArthur, satisfactory compromise agreements on Pacific strategy clearly would have to be extremely circumstantial, setting forth exactly what forces would come under whose command for specified operations. Joint agreement on details as well as on principles would have to be reached on lower levels in Washington to make such strategic decisions possible on the JCS level.

Similarly, General Marshall, as Chief of Staff of the U. S. Army, rather than strictly as a member of the JCS, had taken the lead in 1942, first in recommending and later in defending Bolero in discussions with the British Chiefs of Staff. Two of the U. S. Chiefs of Staff, General Marshall and Admiral King, went to London in July with Harry Hopkins and agreed to the initial Torch paper, which was issued in the CCS document series. In fact they were negotiating with the British on behalf of the President in accordance with detailed instructions from him. They were not accompanied by joint staff planning representatives, as they were in all the subsequent international conferences. They finally accepted a strategic concept contrary to nearly everything that had been worked out either in the Army or in the JCS committees in Washington.[1] In the European area as in the Pacific, agreements in principle, divorced from the detailed staff work of the working-level plans committees, resulted in uncertainty as to precisely what had been decided and when it would take place. Thus, the most critical aspects of joint or combined strategy in 1942 evolved outside the planning system set up under the JCS. Insofar as OPD officers influenced planning, they did so chiefly as advisers and agents of General Marshall.

By 1943 the task of reconciling Army views with Navy views and American views with British views had become far too great to fall so heavily on one officer, General Marshall. The British-American staff conference held at Casablanca in January 1943 showed conclusively that the American staff, to be ready to argue its case before the President and the Prime Minister, must prepare it with the thoroughness of counsel for a large corporation, or simply accept the British case, which would have been so prepared. At the same time, the questions at issue had become far too complicated to be dealt with in formal CCS discussion. Military decisions on the level of the CCS and by the heads of government depended increasingly on the outcome of deliberations at the lower staff level, at which the delegation from the United States could not meet the British delegation on terms even approaching equality.

General Wedemeyer, the head of the OPD contingent at the Casablanca Conference and General Marshall's principal strategic adviser, observed—exaggerating the facts to make his serious point—that the story of the conference could be summed up in the words: "We came, we listened and we were conquered." He said that General Marshall, with his logic and candor, had done a magnificent job, but had been almost entirely on his own. The American delegation was in fact small and disorganized. The British delegation was large and well organized. Though disappointed, General Wedemeyer said he had the "greatest admiration for the way the British handled the entire show":

They swarmed down upon us like locusts with a plentiful supply of planners and various other assistants with prepared plans to insure

---

[1] (1) For the President's instructions to the delegation, see memo, President for Harry Hopkins, Gen Marshall, and Admiral King, 16 Jul 42, sub: Instructions for London Conf, WDCSA 381, 1. (2) For compromise paper resulting from the London conference, see CCS 94, 24 Jul 42, title: Opns in 1942–43. (3) For President's definite ruling that Torch was an approved operation, see memo, Brig Gen W. B. Smith for U. S. JCS, 1 Aug 42, sub: Notes of a Conf Held at White House at 8:30 P. M., 30 Jul 42, ABC 381 (7-25-42), 4–B, 79.

that they not only accomplished their purpose but did so in stride and with fair promise of continuing in their role of directing strategically the course of this war. I have the greatest admiration, as I indicated above, and if I were a Britisher I would feel very proud. However, as an American I wish that we might be more glib and better organized to cope with these super negotiators. From a worm's eye viewpoint it was apparent that we were confronted by generations and generations of experience in committee work and in rationalizing points of views. They had us on the defensive practically all the time.[2]

The moral was plain—that the military staffs of the United States, in preparing for later meetings, should not only emulate but also improve on British thoroughness and firmness in interservice agreement. An essential part of this preparation would be thorough realistic staff planning on a joint basis which would permit the JCS to arrive at timely, binding agreements on the military course to be followed in the Pacific and its proper relationship to combined operations under consideration in other areas.

Reorganization of the Joint Staff System

General McNarney hastened the process of development in joint planning techniques by proposing early in January 1943 an investigation of the JCS and all its subordinate agencies.[3] For all the prominence that had been given to interservice planning, little had been done in 1942 to define the existing terms of reference of the JCS and its committees. The key committees, the JCS and the JPS, did not even have charters.

The imperfect functioning of the joint committee system was particularly evident at the level of the JPS. The JCS secretariat listed the symptoms:

Their studies and recommendations have, perhaps, not always represented the best and most expert thought on the subject at hand.

At times they have become factional regarding the interests of their respective services as a cumulative result of attempting to compose disagreements.

They have sometimes entered on their deliberations with instructions from higher authority or with fixed and preconceived ideas.

The members who are authorized to come to an agreed recommendation have frequently been too busy to attend meetings. The result has been that the conclusions arrived at during such meetings have been nullified through the veto of a member who reviewed the paper following the regular session of the committee.

The general cause of these weaknesses lay in the effort by the JPS to do more than could be done by so small a committee, especially one whose members had many other responsibilities in their separate and distinct capacities as Army and Navy officers assigned to specific staffs in their respective services. As a result, the JPS had fallen far behind in its work and had acquired too many additional (nonvoting) members. The secretariat recommended that the JPS members should not themselves try to arrive at agreed solutions of the manifold problems that came before them but instead merely review solutions as submitted by subordinate working committees and either transmit them to the JCS or agree to recommit the problem to the working committees.[4]

---

[2] Pers ltr, Brig Gen Wedemeyer to Maj Gen Handy, 22 Jan 43, Paper 5, Item 1A, Exec 3.

[3] JCS 202, 16 Jan 43, title: War Planning Agencies.

[4] Annex B, JCS 202, 16 Jan 43, title: Draft Proposal Prepared by JCS Secretariat Suggesting that it be Referred to JCS by CofS, U. S. Army, 16 Jan 43. General Wedemeyer at the same time presented recommendations toward the same end. See memo, Brig Gen Wedemeyer for CofS, 7 Jan 43, sub: Reconstitution of Supporting Planning Agencies of JCS, Annex C, JCS 202, 16 Jan 43. Cf. OPD paper, Miss Alice Miller and Maj D. C. Fahey, Jr., 22 Oct

General McNarney's action in reopening consideration of joint organization led to the appointment of a special committee, representing the Joint Deputy Chiefs of Staff and the JCS secretariat, to study the workings of the entire joint system with a view to regularization. Colonel Roberts (Strategy Section, OPD) was appointed to represent General McNarney.[5] The committee studied the various directives and understandings, written and unwritten, which served to authorize and guide joint deliberations. Toward the end of March it made a report, which included draft charters for all joint agencies, including the JCS and the JPS. In most respects, the reorganization was carried out according to the committee's recommendations and remained in effect throughout the period of hostilities.

The principal achievement of the reorganization was a reduction in the range and the number of issues upon which the JPS committee attempted to work out joint agreements. Even though some time-consuming studies had been assigned to the Joint Strategic Survey Committee since its establishment late in 1942, the JPS had been trying to advise the JCS in the general field of logistics and to pass upon many special military questions which had to be decided in conformity with strategy but which did not bear on the development of strategy. Some relief for the JPS was arranged by dividing the labor with another joint committee, initially called the Joint Administrative Committee, and subsequently the Joint Logistics Committee (JLC). The establishment of this new committee was a revolutionary step in the conduct of joint (and combined) planning for procurement, allocation, and transportation of supplies and equipment.

The Army and Air members of the JPS (and their advisers) initially viewed with some suspicion the Joint Administrative Committee and its successor, the JLC. They anticipated that the new committee might reach conclusions concerning logistic capabilities that would amount to basic recommendations on strategy. They feared that in case the JPS did not agree to recommend corresponding adjustments in strategy, the new committee would appeal its case directly to the JCS, setting itself up in effect as a second, competing committee in the field of joint strategy. They urged that the JPS must continue to be the central or pivotal planning committee of the JCS, in accordance with their belief that strategic planning must be the central or pivotal planning activity. This view was upheld and formally approved in the late summer of 1943. They therefore continued throughout the war to consider all joint planning as within their province, and the JPS committee remained the channel through which most important joint papers passed to the JCS for decision.

The JCS had to establish all kinds of military policies to govern the joint activities of the armed services in fields ranging as far from strategy, narrowly defined, as the ship construction program, the exchange of

42 [revised as of 12 Jan 43], title: Background, Existing Auth, Functions, Orgns and Membership of CCS and their Supporting Agencies, folder filed with ABC 381 United Nations (23 Jan 43), 2. General Wedemeyer had this paper prepared for new planning officers. For the fact that the JPS, as of early 1943, was not operating under any charter or directive, see JPS 123, 2 Feb 43, sub: Proposed Charter of JPS. This paper, prepared by the Army members of JPS, pointed out that the only basis for the JPS was a phrase in CCS 9/1, defining the functions of the CPS. "By implication," then, "the Joint Staff Planners have a parallel relationship to the Joint Chiefs of Staff."

[5] JCS 202/1/D, 20 Jan 43, title: War Planning Agencies.

intelligence missions with foreign governments, the administration of civil affairs in occupied countries, and the definition of surrender terms for defeated enemies. There were special joint committees to study problems in some of these fields, but the JPS had to review the issues involved, whatever they were, from a strategic point of view, since in fact nearly everything the JCS might decide would have strategic implications.[6] Under these circumstances, in order to deal with the main current questions of strategy and closely related military policy, the members of the JPS were more than willing to leave to other committees much of the work in fields like logistics planning. They mainly concerned themselves with reviewing, either collectively or individually, all important papers under consideration by the JCS, thereby making certain that the central thread of joint strategy was running through and tying together all the various kinds of joint planning.

By working along these lines, the four members of the reorganized JPS were able to deal with a host of problems as diverse as ever, but at the same time to reduce sharply the number of issues which had to be threshed out in the first instance in JPS committee meetings.[7] It was increasingly necessary for the members of the JPS to trust one another and their junior staff members because the job of planning the war had become so big and so urgent that they no longer could take time to study in detail and to argue at length matters which only a few months before had been their intimate personal business, the outline of operational plans and deployment schedules. In order to guide the entire effort of the joint committee system and keep it in harmony with the commitments, intentions, and expectations of the JCS, they had to learn to regard military strategy as simply one of several specialized fields of planning. Though it remained for them the most important field, it was also for them and for their subordinates the most familiar field with comparatively firm standards of achievement. Particularly with respect to Pacific strategy, they came to delegate most of their planning in this field to the subordinate Joint War Plans Committee.[8]

The Joint War Plans Committee

The need of the JPS for timely, detailed, agreed studies on deployment and future operations was one of the main points made in the report on the joint committee system. It found that there was no agency charged with the "preparations of joint plans of a lesser scope than that of broad strategy." Such plans, termed war plans, had been prepared by independent planning staffs of the Army and Navy without the benefit of joint action. Only rarely, and then by temporary subcommittees, had a synthesis been made of the war plans prepared by the two

---

[6] The continuing concern of the Army planner with many kinds of joint planning was shown by the fact that the Policy Section had about as much staff work to do for the chief of S&P as the Strategy Section did.

[7] From the late spring of 1943 throughout the rest of the period of hostilities, membership on the JPS regularly went with four staff positions in the services. The Army planner was chief of S&P, OPD. The Army Air planner was Assistant Chief of Staff, Plans, Air Staff. The Navy planner was Assistant Chief of Staff, Plans, Office of the Commander in Chief, U. S. Fleet (COMINCH). The second Navy member, who brought the Army-Navy strength into balance, normally (beginning in June 1943) was his immediate subordinate, the Assistant Planning Officer (Air), Plans, COMINCH.

[8] The planners individually went on using their own staffs, of course. They also continued to appoint ad hoc subcommittees, mainly to deal with questions of policy, many of which did not fall within the scope of any of the standing subcommittees in the JCS system.

service staffs working separately. This separation was not only administrative but also physical after the removal of the Army to the Pentagon in November 1942. The committee believed that "all studies of combined action and joint war planning should be undertaken by joint action from the time the studies or war plans are initiated." To do this job, the committee proposed setting up a Joint War Plans Committee, to consist of the "Joint U. S. Strategic Committee and members of the existing planning sections of the individual Joint Staff Planners." The additional members were to be detailed as necessary, and organized in working groups or teams.[9]

The proposed Joint War Plans Committee would operate directly under the JPS. A group roughly equivalent to the old JUSSC would be responsible for its work. This senior planning team of the new, larger committee had the task of assigning work to the additional members, called planning teams, reviewing their work, and presenting it to the JPS. The senior planning team, answerable only to the JPS committee, would assume to some extent the functions of the chiefs of the separate strategic planning sections under the Army, Navy, and Air planners.

Anticipating that the JCS would approve these recommendations, the JPS set up the Joint War Plans Committee on 24 April 1943, just in time to undertake the task of preparing joint studies for the American delegation to use at the coming conference in Washington (TRIDENT). Early in May it received from the JCS a charter, nearly the same as that earlier recommended by the investigating committee.[10]

Colonel Maddocks, who had been the first to recommend the reconstitution of the JUSSC, did not continue as a member of the new committee, which in many ways was the embodiment of the kind of joint planning he had defined in 1942. Besides serving on the JUSSC, he had served as General Wedemeyer's representative in JPS meetings and (during General Wedemeyer's absence from January through mid-March) as General Wedemeyer's deputy in S&P. He represented the very close association that joint planning in 1942 had with executive duties in S&P and with personal responsibility to the Army planner. His expected departure for duty with troops was the occasion of a dissociation of these functions.

Col. William W. Bessell, Jr., of the OPD Strategy Section was named as senior Army member of the JWPC, in effect succeeding Colonel Maddocks in his capacity as principal joint planner under the Army planner. Six other OPD officers were named to the JWPC as members of the planning teams. All had had considerable experience in planning and in committee work. Three of them were Air officers. As soon as replacements could be found for them in OPD, they were transferred to the Army Air Forces, to be carried as members of the Army Air Forces planning staff. This change gave the Air Forces a voice in joint strategic deliberations on the working level as well as on the JCS and the JPS.[11] Thirteen

---

[9] JCS 202/2, 25 Mar 43, title: War Planning Agencies.

[10] (1) Memo, OPD for CofS, 27 Apr 43, sub: Representation on War Planning Agencies of JCS,

ABC 381 United Nations (23 Jan 42), 2. (2) JCS 202/14/D, 11 May 43, title: Charter/JWPC.

[11] This administrative change, though not accomplished until the beginning of June, was contemplated at the time of setting up the JWPC. See memo, OPD for DCofS, 27 Apr 43, sub: Representation on War Planning Agencies of JCS, ABC 381 United Nations (23 Jan 42), 2. This change being accomplished, there were four members (including Colonel Bessell) from OPD, and four from the Air

OPD officers (excluding Air officers) served on the JWPC during the period up to and including V-J Day, all of them but one having had at least a few months previous experience in strategic planning in OPD. The only one to serve in the JWPC throughout the entire period was Colonel Bessell (brigadier general 27 May 1944). He remained the senior Army member until after the defeat of Japan.

The three senior JWPC planners, or directors as they came to be called, representing the Army, the Navy, and the Army Air Forces, controlled the workings of the JWPC. The charter provided, though a little ambiguously, for equal representation from the Army and the Navy, with the Army section absorbing Army Air membership, as on the JPS. The JWPC actually conducted most of its business on the principle that there were three separate spheres of special knowledge, as represented by the three directors. Usually the Army officers (including Army Air) enjoyed a slight superiority in numbers on the whole committee. The detailed staff work of the JWPC was divided up as far as possible according to major areas of the world, among three planning teams—one for the Pacific and Far East (Red Team), one for the European-Mediterranean area (Blue Team) and one for other areas (White Team). There was also a RAINBOW team, mainly concerned with interservice Air plans, on which OPD was not regularly represented. The individual teams did not follow any set pattern of representation from the three services.[12]

By the end of 1943 the JWPC had put joint strategic planning on a solid footing,

and it continued to work in much the same way throughout the rest of the war. From its establishment in April 1943 until the surrender of Japan, nearly twenty-eight months later, the JWPC prepared over a thousand studies. They included recommendations on every major strategic decision, outline plans for all operations under consideration by the JCS, and independent analyses of a great many special joint problems, in particular on the future strategic deployment of American forces, the size of occupation forces in Europe, special equipment and training for amphibious operations in the Pacific, and the establishment of a postwar joint general staff.[13]

In 1942, when Colonel Maddocks was attempting to define joint planning, he had identified three main elements, first, formulating the broad strategic concept and coordinating staff work in accordance with it, second, planning in outline a number of future operations that might be selected to carry out the strategy, and third, planning in detail each specific operation scheduled for execution.[14] The JWPC did not formulate its function on any precise distinction of this kind. It simply prepared any studies which the JPS needed. If there was no special joint committee to which to refer special, nonstrategic issues under consideration, the JWPC very commonly became involved in studying them on behalf of the JPS just as the JPS was involved on behalf of the JCS. Even in the general field of strategic planning, the range of JWPC activities was broad. It comprehended all three of the ele-

---

Forces. The fourth Air Forces member was from the Air Plans Division.

[12] For membership of the JWPC and specific assignments from OPD to the JWPC through V-J Day, see OPD Hist Unit Study T.

[13] JWPC 401, 14 Aug 45, title: JWPC. For lists of plans, studies, and other papers prepared by the JWPC, see: (1) JWPC Memo for Info 22, 24 Apr 44; (2) JWPC Memo for Info 30, 3 Jul 44; (3) JWPC Memo for Info 36, 22 Jan 45; (4) JWPC Memo for Info 39, 24 Apr 45.

[14] See pp. 173–74 above.

ments of joint strategic planning defined by Colonel Maddocks. Thus, in formulating policy statements for the use of the JCS at international conferences, it dealt with matters of broad strategy. Very often, however, the JCS, advised by the JSSC and the JPS, handled such issues, and they were not referred to the JWPC. On the other hand, in developing detailed operational directives for the Pacific campaigns, the JWPC often came very close to planning specific operations. But the main burden of operational planning fell on the overseas theater staffs, guided by the plans drafted in the JWPC and assisted by central headquarters staffs in the individual services (OPD in the Army). Thus the main function of the JWPC was developing outline joint plans for future operations. As a result of the accomplishments of the JWPC in this field, the JCS made more solid decisions on the actual execution of projected operations. Moreover, task force or theater commanders had the benefit of detailed joint studies of the difficulties involved, and frequently had a broad area of joint agreement to base their work on when they proceeded to plan still further and mount the operation.

In all the aspects of joint planning in which it participated, the JWPC was an instrument for translating Army, Navy, and Air views into joint war plans. Close liaison with the agencies responsible for formulating the official views of the individual services was therefore essential. OPD's Strategy Section and, in regard to detailed problems of overseas operations, the OPD theater sections carefully scrutinized every plan formulated in the JCS system.

The real value of joint war planning conducted in this way, as was observed at the time when establishment of the JWPC was being worked out, was that the outline plans for future operations gave theater commanders a "starting point" and saved them "much necessary labor" in drafting more detailed operational plans. In addition they were indispensable to the formulation of broad strategy, which could not be "on firm ground" unless someone examined all projected operations with care. The members of the junior planning teams were the ones who initiated the whole "exasperating process" of working out details, adjusting differences of opinion, and getting consent from all concerned on higher levels of authority. Above all, this kind of planning was literally and thoroughly joint in character: "The very act of taking the preliminary draft to the Departments achieves a most useful purpose for it helps the Army and Navy Departments to understand each other's points of view." The JWPC did in fact turn out to be a "good liaison mision between the War and Navy Departments." [15]

Army Versus Joint Advice for the Army Planner

Gradually during the later war years the Army members of the JWPC established an effective working relationship with their colleagues in OPD. Once the need for detailed joint war planning had been satisfied by the creation of the JWPC, no further basic development in the strategic planning system occurred. The problem confronting OPD after mid-1943, particularly its members on the JWPC, was to devise ways of harmonizing or at least maintaining a balance between Army views and

---

[15] The foregoing quotation, describing what could be expected from the proposed JWPC, is from an informal British paper, no author indicated, 19 Feb 43, title: Orgn for Joint Stf Planning, with Memo for Info 48 in ABC 381 United Nations (23 Jan 42), 2.

joint views in strategic plans. For the most part, the techniques employed were simply various ways of strengthening liaison between the JWPC and other Army planning officers.

The question of the proper roles of the Army members of the JWPC and the other officers in S&P promptly arose in connection with the international conferences of mid-1943. JWPC members had all they could do to prepare the studies required for TRIDENT in the short time between the establishment of the committee (24 April) and the beginning of the conference (12 May). As at previous conferences, the Army planner relied on other officers in S&P to supply him with information and advice concerning issues with which he and General Marshall would have to deal in JPS and JCS meetings.[16] Looking forward to the next conference, the Combined Subjects (Policy) Section suggested in June that the Army planner again would need the full-time services of at least two S&P officers to help him with the many duties he performed for the chief of OPD and the Chief of Staff.[17] Colonel Bessell initially entered a strong dissent, seeing these advisers simply as competitors in the field which the JWPC properly should monopolize:

Do *not* concur. This is exactly what is *wrong* with Joint Planning *right* now. The Planners at a *combined* conference certainly do not need to have prepared for them any papers for their own individual Chief (e. g. Cooke for King). The papers should be *joint* papers at least and that is exactly what JWPC is set up to prepare. I intend to fight for this principle to the last cartridge. The practice of our individual Planners preparing papers on joint subjects for their individual chiefs may be condoned to some extent in inter-conference periods, but certainly *not* for a combined conference. We must continue to impress on the Planners the necessity for their *getting* together and *using* their joint agencies or soon we will have JWPC and JIC working without direction, coordination and in an atmosphere of vacuity.[18]

The Combined Subjects Section rejoined that its proposal did not envisage the preparation of joint papers in competition with the JWPC, but simply the provision of an "analysis staff which would keep abreast of all conference matters and assist the WDGS [Army, as distinguished from Army Air] planner with the discharge of his responsibility." The dual responsibility of the WDGS planner was in fact the point at issue. Advice from the JWPC to the JPS was strictly joint, that is, from one committee as a whole to another committee. The Combined Subjects Section held it to be unrealistic to object to having the planners individually advised by their own staffs. The unification of the armed services, however desirable, was not an accomplished fact, and the planners were obliged to think and act accordingly.[19] General Marshall on occasion looked to the Army planner and his subordinates in S&P for a first draft of a paper for introduction directly into the

---

[16] Annex B, title: Analysis of Servs of S&P Preliminary to and During TRIDENT Conf, incl with memo, Lt Col L. J. Lincoln for Col Roberts, 15 Jun 43, sub: Working Stf to Accompany Planners to Next Combined Conf, Tab 2, correspondence filed with JPS 189 in ABC 337 (25 May 43).

[17] Memo, Lt Col L. J. Lincoln for Col Roberts, 15 Jun 43, sub: Working Stf . . ., Tab 2, correspondence filed with JPS 189 in ABC 337 (25 May 43).

[18] Memo, Col Bessell for Col Roberts, 17 Jun 43, sub: Working Stf . . ., Tab 4, correspondence filed with JPS 189 in ABC 337 (25 May 43).

[19] Memo, Lt Col L. J. Lincoln for Col Roberts, 19 June 43, sub: Working Stf . . ., Tab 7 in correspondence filed with JPS 189 in ABC 337 (5 May 43).

JCS.[20] Some of these papers dealt with matters outside the province of the JWPC and required careful tailoring to fit and to express clearly General Marshall's own views. This job was not joint committee work in any sense. Consequently, General Marshall still expected his staff at all times to advise him and, paying close attention to his ideas, to draft papers for him. Thus, the daily work of the Army planner in S&P gave him an intimate knowledge of what the Chief of Staff thought on important issues, even though General Marshall did not believe in binding his joint staff officers by specific instruction. Many of these issues were settled in JCS and CCS sessions, not infrequently in closed sessions, rather than in joint planning papers, and the Army planner therefore had a conference role apart from his role in JPS and JWPC matters.

Throughout the later war years both the Strategy Section of S&P and the JWPC continued to advise the Army planner on strategic plans. No clear division of labor was possible, and the effectiveness of this dual staff work in support of the Army planner depended on working liaison between the Army officers in both sections. The Strategy Section continued to originate plans and studies, on its own initiative and at the direction of the chief of S&P. Its officers did not invariably discuss such papers with the JWPC before passing them to their chief, and the JWPC did not invariably discuss its papers with the Strategy Section before passing them up to the JPS.[21] On the whole a close relationship, not without minor frictions, was established and preserved.

Frequently the members of the Army section of the JWPC used their connection with the Strategy Section to sound out Army opinion on matters at issue in joint planning. For instance in mid-1944 the Army section of the JWPC prepared a study on the then controversial subject of operations against Kyushu, working entirely apart from the Navy members of the committee. The study went as a Strategy Section paper directly to General Marshall, who had it reviewed by General Somervell

---

[20] For example, after the CCS meeting on 20 October 1944, General Marshall notified Generals Handy and Hull that he had been requested, on the basis of discussion at the meeting, to propose a directive regarding the use of the proximity fuze, "which should be in the form of expressing a general policy, and which would govern the Combined Chiefs of Staff as well as General Eisenhower." See memo, Gen Marshall for Lt Gen Handy and Maj Gen Hull, 20 Oct 44, no sub, with SS 316 in ABC 381 Strategy Sec Papers (7 Jan 43). Under SS 316 are filed the drafts prepared in the Strategy Section, and subsequent drafts, including that submitted by General Marshall to the JCS. General Marshall made very great changes, and the chief of the Strategy Section called them to the attention of his officers, remarking that they gave a good idea of what the Chief of Staff wanted, and that the officers should look them over carefully "with a view of familiarizing ourselves with this and other matters of like nature which we may expect from time to time." See memo, Col J. J. Billo for All Offs of Strategy Sec, 23 Oct 44, no sub, with SS 316 in ABC 381 Strategy Sec Papers (7 Jan 43).

[21] The Strategy Section studies (in numbered series, identified by the initials SS), are filed under ABC 381 Strategy Section Papers (7 Jan 43). This file (of which there are more than twenty volumes in the period of World War II hostilities) runs from SS 2 (7 Jan 43) to SS 395 (26 Jul 45). Many papers of the series are lacking. For procedure in preparing Strategy Section studies, see Strategy Sec Memo 1, 29 Mar 43, with SS 45 in ABC 381 Strategy Sec Papers (7 Jan 43). Besides this file, the other regular source of Strategy Section opinion is the series of briefs (entitled Notes on Meetings) prepared for the use of the Army planner. These are in the ABC files with the subject JWPC papers.

For an example of simultaneous study, see memo, R.J.W. [Col Wood] for Lt Cols C. E. Hutchin, Jr., J. A. Bassett, and A. J. Goodpaster, Jr., 19 Jan 45, no sub, with JWPC Memo for Info 35 in ABC 384 Pacific (1–17–43), 7.

and, finally, by Admiral Leahy, without introducing it in joint planning channels.[22] Normally, however, the Army section of the JWPC worked within the JCS committee system and thereby unquestionably relieved the Strategy Section, in turn the Army planner, and ultimately the Chief of Staff, of much of the burden of detailed exploratory conversations with the Navy. The results, to be sure, often were in the nature of compromises, but it was realized in S&P, as in the JWPC, that compromise in the interests of joint action was necessary. The process was slow, probably slower than it had been in 1942, but for the most part it was taking the time of junior officers who had no other duties, rather than of their colleagues and superiors with heavy service responsibilities.

By being assigned to the JWPC, with offices in the JCS-CCS building rather than in the Pentagon, Army officers tended to lose their intimate acquaintance with current operational problems, the very thing which had been achieved by combining the tasks of strategic planning and control of operations in one Army staff. The effect of this loss in joint planning greatly concerned Colonel Bessell and the other responsible officers in OPD. All of them were striving to maintain the closest possible connection between all Army plans, including Air Forces plans, and the daily developments in overseas commands. Colonel Todd, deputy chief of S&P at the time, raised this point in August 1943, writing to Colonel Bessell that the senior Army member on the JWPC was "charged with seeing to it that the appro-

priate representative or representatives of the Theater Group are called into consultation in the planning of any operations in their respective theaters." Colonel Todd explained that he did not mean to imply that the members of the JWPC should be guided in their judgments by these representatives, but only to make it clear that the JWPC should "carefully consider" not only the Theater Group views but also, and more especially, the information its officers could furnish.[23]

On occasion the JWPC worked very closely with OPD, as it did, for example, in preparing to study the requirements for operations in the Pacific and Far East.[24] Nevertheless, General Roberts, after he had succeeded General Wedemeyer as chief of S&P, noted early in 1944 what he considered to be a "growing tendency—right or wrong—to view the JWPC as an organization apart, one which has its head in the clouds and its feet completely off the ground." He informed Colonel Bessell that the Army members of the JWPC, while acting independently, must still represent the Army point of view, and therefore must keep in touch with the planning and operating (theater) sections in OPD to "learn for themselves existing conditions or current trends of thought."[25] In replying, Colonel Bessell made it plain that he did not regard the Army section of the JWPC as bound to represent the Army point of view except insofar as the phrase meant that the members

---

[22] Papers filed with SS 265 in ABC 381 Strategy Sec Papers (7 Jan 43), including the following: (1) memo, Col C. S. Babcock for Col T. D. Roberts, 20 Jul 44, no sub; (2) memo, Lt Gen Somervell for CofS, 24 Jun 44, sub: Opns Against KYUSHU; (3) memo, Lt Gen Somervell, 17 Jul 44, sub: Opns Against KYUSHU; (4) memo, Maj Gen Handy for Admiral Leahy, 2 Sep 44, no sub.

[23] Memo, Col Todd for Col Bessell, 30 Aug 43, sub: OPD Theater Gp Liaison with JWPC, with JCS 202/14/D in ABC 334.8 JUSSC (10–19–42).
[24] Memo, Secys JWPC for ACofS (Plans), Hq COMINCH and ACofS OPD, 6 Oct 43, sub: Reqmts for Pacific-Far East Opns, 1943–44. See Ch. XVII.
[25] Memo, Brig Gen Roberts for Col Bessell, 11 Jan 44, no sub, with JCS 202/14/D in ABC 334.8 JUSSC (10–19–42).

must keep informed about Army views. He referred to the fact that the JWPC charter required the committee members to reach joint solutions unhampered by instructions from any source except the whole JPS committee. At the same time, he agreed with the need to keep in touch with Army and OPD thought.[26]

In order to promote closer working relationships between the Army members of the JWPC and OPD, visits were formally scheduled, beginning early in 1944, to the JWPC each Monday and Thursday by some Strategy Section officer, and by JWPC members to OPD on Tuesdays. On Saturday mornings Colonel Bessell conferred with the chief of the Strategy Section.[27] These regular visits back and forth remained standing operating procedure. During the first year following the establishment of the JWPC, it was in any event necessary to keep in touch with S&P officers in order to have access to important messages of which there was very limited distribution. In April 1944 the JWPC brought the matter to the attention of the JPS and succeeded in obtaining assurances of distribution to the JWPC in the future.[28] But because it was

impracticable to duplicate OPD's facilities for keeping up with overseas operations and difficult to get operational data through Navy channels comparable with that available from OPD, the visits remained a principal source of up-to-date information for JWPC throughout the war.[29]

In general the Army staffs in the overseas theaters of operations, particularly in the Pacific, were not familiar with the workings of the joint committee system, which was unlike anything in their experience. More intimate knowledge of the work of the JWPC, based mainly on trips by planners to the theaters and on the use in the theaters of JWPC plans and studies, greatly improved relations between the JWPC and the theater headquarters staffs. In early 1945, for example, Maj. Gen. Richard K. Sutherland, General MacArthur's chief of staff, expressed his appreciation of its work. Colonel Freeman, OPD member of the JWPC, reported after a trip to the Southwest Pacific area:

The General spoke of the Joint War Plans Committee plans—a copy of the Hainan plan being on his desk at the time. He stated that these plans were of immense value to the planners in the Theater; that they contained sound ideas and a mass of information which oftentimes is not available in the Theater.

---

[26] (1) Memo, Col Bessell for Chief S&P, 13 Jan 44, sub: Coordination, Army Sec, JWPC, with Other Agencies of OPD. (2) Memo, Senior Army member [Col Bessell] for Offs of Army Sec, JWPC, 13 Jan 44, sub: Regular Scd of Visits to Strategy Sec and Theater Secs, OPD, with JCS 202/14/D in ABC 334.8 JUSSC (10–19–42).

[27] Memo, Col J. J. Billo for Col Bessell, 14 Jan 44, no sub, with JCS 202/14/D in ABC 334.8 JUSSC (10–19–42).

[28] Min 143d meeting JPS, Item 12, 5 Apr 44. Colonel Bessell at this meeting explained that there had been:

numerous cases in which the Joint War Plans Committee have been asked to conduct studies, as a matter of urgency, and have found that information contained in War and Navy Department dispatches had not been brought to their attention because of its highly secret nature and special distribution.

The ensuing delay meant that either the information contained in these dispatches was not taken into consideration during the preparation of the report, or that completion of the report had to be delayed until the messages became available.

The JPS also discussed, but did not agree to, the dissemination of such information to other JCS working committees, the Joint Logistics Committee and the Joint Intelligence Committee.

[29] Colonel Bessell afterwards wryly observed: "Perhaps the greatest single difficulty of the JWPC in performing its mission of staying ahead of the war was keeping up with it." See summary, Col Bessell, for use of OPD Hist Unit, Feb 48, title: JWPC, OPD Hist Unit Comments file. Many of the points made in the text correspond to points made by Colonel Bessell in this analysis.

In conclusion, General Sutherland stated that he was well satisfied with the way Theater affairs were handled in Washington. He knew that all the backing possible was being given, and that he had no complaints or suggestions to make.[30]

This testimony from the area where interservice difficulties were the greatest afforded persuasive evidence that the JWPC had justified the faith of its members in the joint planning process. More and more in the later war years joint planning was producing some basis or other for interservice agreements, which were essential not only for effective operations in the Pacific but also for the conduct of the entire war.

Joint Strategic Preparation for CCS Discussions

The success of the JWPC in exploring and insofar as possible in ironing out interservice disagreements, not only helped the JCS to adopt a carefully phrased, fully developed outline of strategy and future operations in the Pacific, the principal area of American strategic responsibility, but also made it much easier to develop a solid planning program for world-wide operations. To a great extent the interest of American officers in improving their joint planning machinery had sprung from a recognition of the need for establishing a common and firmly based front in dealing with British staffs. The achievements of the JWPC thus strengthened the JCS and the JPS in deliberations at the CCS level in Washington and the formal international military conferences. At every stage in this process OPD officers were joining in the common effort, and with the results at every stage

the Army as a whole was earnestly concerned.

General Wedemeyer's reflections after the Casablanca Conference of January 1943 were characteristic of the mixed admiration and exasperation with which the American planners continued to observe the British performance during 1943. The need to match as well as to collaborate with the British greatly intensified the whole drive toward general improvement in joint planning. It involved emulating British methods not only in interservice planning, which required techniques of collaboration, but also in combined planning, with its techniques of negotiation.

General Marshall himself drew attention to the skill with which the British planners had worked at Casablanca, recalling how prompt they had been in producing staff papers for action. He credited a great deal of this skill to observance of a distinction between furnishing data and information as requested to support a policy which had already been established, and making independent recommendations or comments on policy issues not yet determined. In the latter case, General Marshall felt strongly that it was important for the planners to enjoy freedom of action, without limiting instructions from higher authority, so that they would avoid deadlocks and reach compromises among themselves. He remarked that:

What was wanted by the Chiefs of Staff was the best product the Planners could produce—for the approval or disapproval by the Chiefs of Staff. . . . When our planners are instructed they present a paper in which, in effect, they are carrying out a policy which sometimes had not yet been established. . . . In almost every case the British had a finished paper and a better paper at Casablanca, largely because their Planners were unin-

---

[30] Memo, Col Freeman for Maj Gen Hull, 13 Feb 45, sub: Interv with Gen Sutherland, with JWPC M/I in ABC 384 Pacific (1-17-43), 7.

structed and allowed to present their own individual opinions.

It was noted by the JCS that the British had roughly ten times as many planners as the United States at Casablanca, and furthermore that since their planners did not attend the meetings, they were free to devote their entire time to planning. General Marshall did not consider being outnumbered a real handicap for the American planners. Instead he emphasized that what they mainly needed was to "be *together* and *ahead* of them." [31]

In order to settle on detailed agreements that would stand up as a basis for long-range calculations, American military planners had to learn to make preparations well in advance, go into the conference agreed among themselves, and (by preconference agreements with the British) limit as far as possible the number of issues to be taken up at the conference. In addition, they became convinced that it was desirable to take the initiative if possible and, whenever the initiative lay with the British, to have a prepared line of defense on which to fall back. The Strategy Section observed:

Strategic aims at these conferences are determined to some degree by elements of national policy which are other than military. This fact must be accepted and we must also accept that the aims of national policy vital to Great Britain do not always coincide with those of the United States and may in certain cases conflict. This situation should be accepted as a fact and should not excite recrimination. The U. S. Planners should, in their preparation, establish completely self-sufficient cases not only for the position which to us is the optimum but also for each succeeding defensible position back to the minimum which we can possibly accept. The British have obviously adopted this technique in negotiation. It is perhaps true that we have been weak in preparing for only the position which we consider the optimum and when defeated upon that line have no plans and no recourse but to accept the British carefully prepared first line position. [32]

The least answerable question that arose was how much frankness should be exhibited toward the British in discussing issues on the planning level, in exchanging information on internal disagreements and uncertainties at the staff level and above, and in revealing in full the contents of papers prepared to rebut British proposals. Among the suggestions advanced by the JWPC in the course of their analysis of the TRIDENT Conference was one for much closer collaboration between JWPC teams and their British opposites:

Now that we have developed a system for *joint planning* which proved its worth during the TRIDENT conferences and which will further improve with experience, steps should be taken to improve *combined planning*. A system should be developed wherein information, ideas, and studies are continually interchanged between the U. S. and British planners without commitment of the Chiefs of Staff of either nation. In this way *many* of the differences of opinion and interpretation of data, and *all* of the misunderstandings of the others' viewpoints, could be eliminated prior to the conference. This would assist in avoiding our Chiefs of Staff receiving a British paper during the conference with no advance information and little time in which to give it the analysis and study it deserves. [33]

A very different view was promptly expressed by an officer in OPD's Strategy Section:

I disagree with this optimism. If we run true to form, our "honesty" will require that we give all our ideas to them; they will *never* do

---

[31] Min 72d meeting JCS, 6 Apr 43.

[32] OPD brief, Notes . . . 98th meeting JCS, with CCS 288 in ABC 337 (25 May 43).

[33] JPS 189, 25 May 43, title: Preparation for Next U. S.-British Stf Conf.

that for us. They will have our papers, know what we are thinking, will plan on how they can get us to do what they want. Far from assisting "in avoiding our Chiefs receiving a British paper . . . with no advance information," etc., it would result in our Chiefs receiving the same shotgun proposal but vastly better prepared on the British side.[34]

The ambivalence reflected in these statements continued throughout the war to characterize American planning in conjunction with the British. The senior planners and Chiefs of Staff of both nations (Combined Staff Planners and CCS) worked in an atmosphere of comparative "frankness and openness," but at the same time the U. S. Joint Staff Planners had at hand studies prepared by their independent war plans committee solely from the point of view of American strategic policy. Studies of this kind were exchanged with the British only occasionally. The compromise represented in this procedure reflected the uncertainty of most members of the American staff, especially the junior members, about national policy as it might bear on military decisions in the making. At least the OPD officers engaged in this kind of planning remained a little reluctant to deal altogether openly with their British opposites before the President and the JCS had made their positions clear. The process actually followed was a compromise between two divergent tendencies, one toward simply representing national interests and views and the other toward insuring close British-American co-operation in winning the war. Both tendencies were part and parcel of the unprecedentedly intimate military association between the United States and Great Britain. The balance struck between them in the CCS committee system preserved Anglo-American harmony and at the same time met the requirements of World War II.

Planning With Army Air Forces

In the joint committee system as organized in 1943, the Army Air Forces held separate representation almost as a matter of course. It followed logically from the quasi autonomy of the Army Air Forces in the War Department. Administratively, General Arnold's special position in the JCS and the CCS justified the position, co-ordinate with the representatives of the War Department General Staff, that members of his own staff at Headquarters, Army Air Forces, held on the key agencies under the JCS, and therefore on those under the CCS. This *ad hoc* arrangement could not but have some implications for the permanent organization of the armed forces, but it was established with a minimum of formal debate. The desirability of parallelism with British organization was in itself a sufficient reason for granting not only to General Arnold but also to his staff a quasi-independent status in interservice relations. This independent position of the Army Air Forces had been carved out largely at the expense of OPD, which still was formally responsible for planning and directing all overseas operations by Army forces, in the air as well as on the ground. It was clearly in the interests of the common military effort, as it was clearly the intent of General Marshall, to preserve the system whereby the Army Air Forces exercised great influence in determining the way in which U. S. Army air units were employed but whereby OPD monitored Air plans and operational orders in the interest of the ground-air team as a whole.

[34] Penciled note atchd to copy of JPS 189 in ABC 337 (25 May 43).

The wide acceptance of the Army Air Forces as an armed service virtually equal with the Army and Navy was evident in the joint reorganization, especially in the draft charters and the actual membership of the joint committees. Representation for the Army Air Forces was provided or promptly granted in setting up every committee.[35] This procedure was not new, merely reflecting the system already in being. It did not become an issue for debate, either at the time of the reorganization or during the rest of the period of hostilities. The membership of the JWPC in particular represented a new and important recognition of the independent status of the Air Forces since the Air representatives on it were not assigned from OPD, as the Air representatives on the JUSSC had been, but from the Air Forces. Having his own subordinates on the working plans committee, the Air planner himself was in a stronger position as a member of the Joint Staff Planners.

Since unanimity, not a majority, was required for joint action, Army-Navy parity in joint committees was not a matter of voting strength but simply a matter of form. It operated primarily as a tacit notice of reservation of official judgment on any claims that the Army Air Forces might ultimately make to coequal status with the older services, or any general propositions relating to the employment of air power as a separate strategic entity, co-ordinate with land and sea power. Nevertheless, the representation granted the Army Air Forces in the joint and combined system made it possible for General Arnold's headquarters to exert an increasing influence on decisions concerning the employment of air forces in World War II. As General Arnold observed in June 1943: "The AAF are being directly controlled by the Joint Chiefs of Staff and the Combined Chiefs of Staff more and more each day. Consequently AAF representation in the joint and combined planning staffs has become a position of paramount importance to me." [36]

During the first year of the existence of the JWPC the Air Forces members were the same officers who had worked as planners in OPD. This fact helped in reconciling Army Air Forces views on strategy with those of OPD, as did the continued practice of assigning a considerable number of Air Forces officers to OPD to work on Air problems. As one of the Army planners later noted, OPD, with its air-ground staff, was "probably the only completely integrated joint headquarters we had during the war." [37] Recognizing that the Army Air Forces, if not entirely independent, properly constituted an *imperium in imperio,* OPD officers consciously strove to accommodate Air Forces designs within the broader framework of Army and joint strategy and policy.

The status of the Army Air Forces within the joint planning system received further formal recognition in the autumn of 1943. The Air Staff was granted the right to use its own channel to introduce papers for consideration in the JCS committee system instead of going through OPD (Policy Section, S&P), which remained the normal channel for Army memoranda dealing with

---

[35] See comment from the Army Service Forces in memo, Lt Gen Somervell for CofS, 27 Mar 43, sub: Reorgn of Supporting Agencies for JCS, JCS 202/2, with JCS 202/3 in ABC 381 (12–19–42), 1.

[36] Msg, Gen Arnold for Maj Gen I. C. Eaker, 19 Jun 43, CM-OUT 8090. General Arnold also noted with reference to the JPS: "The Navy side is represented by two able rear admirals, and the Army is represented by an outstanding general officer, who has a large section of OPD as his staff."

[37] Memo, Brig Gen Lincoln for author, 3 Dec 47, sub: Hist of OPD, OPD Hist Unit Comments file.

"matters affecting both the Army and the Navy on which a decision is required by the Joint U. S. Chiefs of Staff." [38] Planners in Headquarters, Army Air Forces, had objected to going through OPD to bring Air problems before the JCS, arguing that such a procedure was inconsistent with General Arnold's position as a member of the JCS in his own right.   In October 1943 General Marshall, upon recommendation from OPD, formally authorized the Army Air Forces to place matters before the JCS "which the Commanding General, Army Air Forces desires to transmit directly to the Joint Chiefs of Staff in his capacity as a member of that commitee." [39] The Army Air Forces still often consulted OPD, at least informally, on actions to be taken in the joint committees. For example, General Arnold sent an informal note to General Handy in the summer of 1944 concerning an Air matter which involved the Navy:

The question now comes up as to what we should do next.
(a) C.G.A.A.F. to CofS to King
or
(b) C.G.A.A.F. to OPD to CofS
or
(c) C.G.A.A.F. to JCS
or
You tell me.
Obviously something must be done. What is your advice. [40]

Collaboration between the Army Air Forces and OPD throughout the later war years operated on the principle of opportunistic exploitation of any and all channels leading to joint decisions.

As agencies of the JCS became more important in drafting joint plans and making preparations for combined deliberations, the main function of OPD in relation to joint decisions on Air matters became what Division officers called "implementation." OPD remained the implementing agency within the Army for JCS and CCS decisions. [41] In this capacity it continued to direct and advise theater commanders, answer their questions, act on their requests, and make sure that the complicated machinery of the zone of interior was working to supply the theater commands with the resources for carrying out their missions. Since General Arnold and his staff took part at every stage of the process of reaching joint and combined decisions, they were in a position to pass them on directly to Air commanders in the theaters, and occasionally did so. OPD at times tried to discourage the Army Air Forces from bypassing the War Department General Staff in regard to overseas Air operations, insisting that confusion was bound to result from using more than one Army channel to communicate joint or combined decisions to theater commanders. At the end of March 1944, OPD's Policy Section chief, responsible for implementation in OPD, noted:

It is my opinion that we *must* reach an understanding with the Air Forces as to the responsibility for implementing decisions of the Joint and Combined Chiefs of Staff.   In this connection it is believed that communications to subordinate commanders in the field must be restricted to technical matters. What occurred Saturday is only minor compared to what may happen if these decisions continue to be implemented independently by two

---

[38] Ltr, OCofS to WDGS, AAF, AGF, and ASF, 23 Oct 43, sub: Submission of Papers to Jt U. S. CsofS, OPD 312, 40.

[39] (1) Memo for rcd, JKW [Lt Col Woolnough], 25 Oct 43, OPD 312, 40. (2) Memo, OCofS for CG AAF, 26 Oct 43, sub: Submission of Papers to Joint U. S. CsofS, OPD 312, 40.

[40] Informal memo, Gen Arnold for Maj Gen Handy, 14 Jul 44, Paper 935, Book 21, Exec 9.

[41] Ltr, OCofS to WDGS, AAF, AGF, and ASF, 23 Oct 43, sub: Submission of papers to Jt U. S. CsofS, OPD 312, 40. See p. 171 above.

agencies, particularly in view of the fact that the AAF has never coordinated any of these messages with us and often inform subordinate commanders directly. In view of the fact that the Air Forces' messages are usually sent at the personal direction of General Arnold, I believe the "understanding" will eventually have to be between General Handy or possibly even General Marshall and General Arnold.[42]

Headquarters, Army Air Forces, also was inclined to issue orders for the movement of Air units overseas without co-ordination with OPD. In August 1943 OPD formally directed the Army Air Forces not to act independently: "It is desired that in the future all orders for overseas movements of Army Air Force units be processed through normal channels in order to avoid confusion, prevent movement of units not cleared, and insure compliance with WD Circular 102, 1943, which requires War Department authority for movement of units beyond the continental limits of the United States."[43] For a long time in 1943 and 1944 delays in getting JCS approval of the basic data required for publishing new authorizations for commitments of Army air units to overseas commands prevented OPD from discharging its full responsibility. The Army Air Forces consequently had to "proceed on its own authority to deploy AAF units to meet strategic requirements."[44] In this situation as in other Air plans issues, OPD and the Army Air Forces had to find compromises and *ad hoc* solutions, frequently unstable but at worst capable of averting military disaster.

Control of Army Air Operations Overseas

Most of the difficulties concerning Washington control of Air operations arose as a result of the effort of the Army Air Forces to establish the closest possible relations with air commands overseas. Until late in the war, the duties formally assigned to the Air Forces in connection with operations overseas were so limited as to overlap hardly at all with those assigned to OPD. General Arnold's responsibilities, like those of General Somervell, were for "world-wide service activities," strictly technical work which could be directed from Washington without interfering with the essential prerogatives of theater commanders.[45] However, current thinking in the Air Forces clearly anticipated air operations independent of control by area ground commands, that is, directly under the Army Air Forces just as ground operations were under the War Department and naval operations were under the Navy Department. Conflicts of opinion on the propriety and effectiveness of such direct Air Forces control of operations were of long standing, many of them deriving from the prewar period.

As the tempo of air operations in the theaters gradually accelerated, the Army Air Forces followed more and more closely the results achieved, as well as the techniques

---

[42] Informal memo, JKW [Col Woolnough] for Brig Gen Roberts, 28 Mar 44, with CCS 520/2 in ABC 381 (22 Jan 43), 2.
[43] Memo, OPD for AAF, 7 Aug 43, sub: Issuance of O'seas Mvmt Orders, OPD 370.5, 555.
[44] Memo, JKW for Brig Gen Roberts, 2 Jan 44, sub: Sixth Revision of OPD Chart, Cur Commitments of AAF, Item 11, Exec 2.

[45] The responsibilities of the Army Air Forces and the Army Service Forces for overseas activities were defined in: (1) memo, DCofS for AAF and ASF, 24 Apr 43, sub: Opns Outside Continental Limits of U. S. by Three Maj Comds, OPD 320, 45; (2) AG memo [W850-39-43], no addressee, 12 Aug 43, sub: Responsibilities of CG, ASF, in Connection with Opns Outside Continental U. S., OPD 320, 45; (3) AG memo [W95-15-43], no addressee, 22 Jun 43, title: Responsibilities of CG, AAF. . . . For reference to a "growing tendency" on the part of the Air Forces (as well as the Service Forces) to become involved in overseas operations, see min of Gen Council meetings, 26 Apr 43, DCofS rcds.

employed, in this first wartime test of American strategic air power. Communications between General Arnold and the Air commanders were direct and often personal. In this way the Air Forces exercised informal but effective control of air operations, especially long-range strategic bombing, which cut across the boundaries of ground theaters. OPD, following the lead of the Chief of Staff, recognized the value of the airplane as a strategic weapon and that its employment raised special organizational and doctrinal problems. For the most part OPD was willing to go along with Air Forces solutions to these problems if they did not jeopardize unity in the theater commands, another vital objective in General Marshall's military philosophy. In addition, in all the *ad hoc* arrangements into which it entered with the Army Air Forces, OPD sought to protect the interests of the theater commanders and of other Army agencies, particularly the Army Service Forces, which had to help support all overseas operations, both ground and air.

The success of the makeshift arrangements balancing the staff interests of OPD and the Army Air Forces so they could get on with the war did not conceal the ultimate importance in future national defense of arriving at a clear-cut definition of the functions and status of the Air Forces in relation to both the Navy and the rest of the Army. In particular, a definition of basic strategic missions was needed. The Army Air Forces was sending its long-range bombers across oceans and continents, and the Navy was increasingly centering all its operations around the fast carrier task force and its aircraft. It was impossible to reconcile the Air Forces claim to control the operations of all long-range air striking forces, whether employed over land or sea, with the Navy's claim that

it was appropriate for naval commanders to employ any kind of weapon needed in operations in, on, or over the sea.[46]

In general OPD supported the case for making long-range air operations exclusively an Air Forces responsibility, transcending the area limitations of ground theaters as well as of naval theaters. Early in 1943, OPD had indorsed as sound doctrine the thesis that "land power and air power are co-equal and interdependent forces." What OPD insisted on, in addition, was unity of command of all forces:

The Operations Division is of the opinion that command and control of air, ground and sea forces in any theater must be invested in the theater commander charged with the actual conduct of operations in the theater; the superior commander should normally exercise command through the senior officer of each of the services included in his command; in all cases the *direct* command of Army Air Forces must be exercised by the Army Air Forces Commander.[47]

By the end of 1943, Air Forces officers were speaking openly, to OPD planners at least, of the advantages to be derived from setting up "Strategic Air Forces out from under the control of the Theater Commander," although recognizing that this procedure would be a "radical departure

---

[46] For 1943–44 record of inability of Army and Navy to agree on combat roles, particularly of their respective air forces, see: (1) memo, Brig Gen F. A. Keating, Brig Gen B. E. Gates, and Col Maddocks for JSSC, 21 Aug 43, sub: Missions or Roles of Army and Navy, ABC 062.2 Jt. Action (8–7–42), 1; (2) memo, Rear Admiral B. H. Bieri for JSSC, 18 Oct 43, sub: Missions of Army and Navy, ABC 062.2 Jt. Action (8–7–42), 1; (3) memo for rcd, Lt Col D. C. Fahey, Jr., 25 Jan 44, sub: Revision of Joint Action, ABC 062.2 Jt. Action (8–7–42), 1.

[47] OPD draft memo, CofS for ACofS G–3 [29 Apr 43], sub: Revision of Tng Literature, incl to memo, Brig Gen Hull for CofS, 29 Apr 43, sub: Gen Montgomery's Notes on "High Command in War," Paper 43, Book 9, Exec 8.

from the present chain of command." [48] In January 1944 a command called the U. S. Strategic Air Forces in Europe was established under General Spaatz to direct the long-range strikes of the Eighth Air Force, based in the United Kingdom, and the Fifteenth Air Force, based in Italy. The CCS exercised direct strategic control over this new air command, initially employing as executive agent the chief of the Air Staff, Royal Air Force. From 14 April until 14 September the new command was subordinated to the British-American theater headquarters, that is to General Eisenhower and SHAEF, for direct support of the Normandy invasion. In September it reverted to something like its original status, but at that time executive control under the CCS was vested jointly in the chief of the Air Staff, Royal Air Force, and the Commanding General, Army Air Forces. Thus General Arnold's quasi-independent position in the JCS-CCS system finally had led to establishing a direct channel from CCS to the Army Air Forces in controlling American air operations overseas. [49]

Even before General Arnold was thus formally introduced into the chain of command, the model of the U. S. Strategic Air Forces in Europe had been followed in establishing an independent air command to control the use of the new very long-range (VLR) bombers (B–29's) in the war against Japan. The Army Air Forces had been active since mid-1943 in urging joint and combined consideration of plans for use of the B–29 from advance bases in China and in the Pacific. [50] The Twentieth Air Force, set up to carry out this objective, was activated 4 April 1944 under the immediate command of General Arnold. The JCS, by informal action, designated Commanding General, Army Air Forces, as the "executive agent of the Joint Chiefs of Staff in implementing their directives" on the employment of the new, long-range air weapon. [51] In this way Army Air Forces gained equal status with the ground and sea forces in the Pacific, the area in which Army-Navy command relationships proved most difficult to adjust throughout the war and in which, therefore, the limitations of unified joint command were least restrictive. At the same time the Twentieth Air Force, like the U. S. Strategic Air Forces in Europe, made the formal, legal position of Army Air Forces vis-à-vis OPD, especially in joint planning, virtually obsolete. Only the exercise of mutual discretion could henceforth preserve smooth working of an anomalous administrative situation.

OPD promptly arranged for the amendment of War Department instructions governing Air Forces activities outside the zone of interior to include authorization for the Commanding General, Army Air Forces,

---

[48] (1) Memo, AAF for OPD, 12 Aug 43, sub: Proposed Combined Contl of Long Range Bmrs in European-North African Theaters, OPD 381 Sec, 113. (2) Informal memo, Gen Marshall for Gen Arnold, 5 Nov 43, OPD 381 Sec, 113. (3) Cf. Memo, ACofS OPD for CG AAF, 7 Jan 43, sub: Employment of Air Forces, Paper 50, Book 7, Exec 8.
[49] CCS 520/6, 14 Sep 44, title: Contl of Strategic Bmr Forces in Europe Following Establishment of Allied Forces on Continent.

[50] (1) CCS 323, 20 Aug 43, title: Air Plan for Defeat of Japan. (2) JPS 288, 4 Oct 43, title: Plans for Defeat of Japan Within 12 Months After Defeat of Germany.
[51] (1) Min 155th meeting JCS, 28 Mar 44. (2) JCS 742/5, 1 Apr 44, title: Comd and Contl of VLR Bmr Forces in War Against Japan. This paper consisted of a memorandum submitted by the Commanding General, Army Air Forces, defining his authority as Commanding General, Twentieth Air Force, and recognizing the problem of co-ordination with the theater commanders, but containing nothing on co-ordination within the War Department. (3) Min of Gen Council meetings, 10 Apr 44, DCofS rcds.

to "implement and execute major decisions of the Joint Chiefs of Staff relative to deployment and missions, including objectives, of the Twentieth Air Force." Specifically, General Arnold was authorized to transfer very long-range bombardment units between theaters in accordance with JCS directives, to communicate directly with commanders of very long-range bombardment units in the field, and to co-ordinate Army Air Forces activities in support of the Twentieth Air Force with the work of other War Department agencies.[52] At the same time OPD and the Air Forces got together to arrange for the movement and logistic support of VLR bomber units which were to go to the Central Pacific.[53] In this way the Army Air Forces on the one hand and OPD and the theater commands on the other could co-ordinate their actions, particularly with respect to service support of the air offensive against Japan and other military operations in the Pacific.[54] As an OPD theater section chief observed, the air campaign was bound to compete with "other requirements within the theater, full details of which are known to OPD only." [55]

The Twentieth Air Force directive approved by the JCS, which had been prepared in General Arnold's headquarters, recognized what it called the "problem of local coordination" in the theater, but did not allude to the existence of a similar problem in Washington, between the staff of General Arnold (promptly reorganized to handle its dual functions), and the staffs of General Marshall and Admiral King, who were the executive agents of the JCS responsible for instructing General MacArthur and Admiral Nimitz and supporting their operations.

The Army planner very soon brought this Washington problem to the attention of his opposite number in the Army Air Forces. Whereas Air Forces officers seemed, General Roberts said, to want to act on every aspect of the VLR effort, including such Army-wide matters as shipping, logistic support, and local defenses, General Roberts believed that the JCS decision related only to the operational command of units actually assigned to the Twentieth Air Force. Legally, he pointed out, implementation of agreed JCS action was initiated under the authority vested in the Secretary of War or the Chief of Staff by the National Defense Act, and as further delegated by them. The authority to effect co-ordination within the War Department as a whole had not been delegated to any of the three major commands. It plainly remained a function of the War Department General Staff, specifically a responsibility assigned to OPD. General Roberts maintained that the Commanding General, Twentieth Air Force, had no control over stations, bases, units, and personnel not directly assigned to him, and none over shipping and other logistic support essential to the operation of the VLR forces. In all these matters he believed Army-wide co-

---

[52] (1) D/F, OPD for CG AAF, 4 Apr 44, sub: Comd and Contl of VLR Bmr Forces . . ., OPD 384 TS, 35. (2) Cf. OPD memo for rcd [4 Apr 44], same sub, OPD 384 TS, 35.

[53] (1) OPD memo for rcd, 18 Apr 44, sub: Plans for Mvmt of VLR Units, OPD 384 TS, 35. (2) Memo, Deputy Secy JCS [Capt E. D. Graves, Jr., USN] for CG 20 AF, Aide to COMINCH, ACofS OPD, 13 Oct 44, sub: Logistical Spt of Air Forces in Future Pacific Opns, OPD 381 TS, 442/10.

[54] Memo, Col J. DeF. Barker, Deputy Chief Theater Gp for Chief S&P, 25 Mar 44, sub: Deployment of Very Hv Bomb Acft, with JCS 742/3 in ABC 384.5 Japan (9 Nov 43) 1–A.

[55] Memo, Brig Gen T. S. Timberman for Brig Gen Roberts, 2 Mar 44, sub: Atchd Directive on VLR Bmrs, with CCS 501 in ABC 384.5 Japan (9 Nov 43), 2–A.

ordination to be a specific responsibility of the War Department General Staff.[56]

OPD recommended solving the administrative difficulties inherent in this situation by dispatching JCS directives to the Commanding General, Twentieth Air Force, through OPD, which could concurrently arrange for necessary Army action outside the province of the Army Air Forces. This procedure came to be followed as a general rule, but the JCS secretariat from time to time continued to send joint directives regarding the Twentieth Air Force directly to General Arnold.[57] OPD proceeded in these cases, as in earlier ones, to reach understandings with General Arnold and his staff according to individual circumstances and the needs of the time. To the end of the period of hostilities, OPD drew upon its detailed knowledge of theater problems and their interrelation with the work of various Army agencies to monitor and, if necessary, modify Army Air Forces activities in the theaters.

On 29 May 1945 the JCS agreed to transfer Headquarters, Twentieth Air Force, from Washington to the Pacific, initially to Guam, as of 1 July 1945. The Twentieth Air Force, along with a second B–29 command to be formed by moving

the Eighth Air Force from England, was redesignated the U. S. Army Strategic Air Forces (USASTAF). General Spaatz was placed in command of the new organization.[58] Strategic control of the B–29 fleet remained with the JCS and, in a certain sense, with General Arnold as the latter's agent.

OPD recommended leaving the B–29 force for strategic bombardment of Japan under the JCS until shortly before D Day, when it would come under General MacArthur's control, just as the strategic air forces in the European theater had passed to General Eisenhower's control for a few weeks prior to the Normandy landing. OPD also recommended, with hearty support from the Army Service Forces, that logistic responsibility for all Army units in the Pacific, including USASTAF, be assigned to General MacArthur, who could make any necessary arrangements with Admiral Nimitz for Navy assistance. While USASTAF ought to have representation on all joint logistic agencies in the Pacific, its logistic needs had to be considered in the light of all Army needs in the theater, which could be judged only by General MacArthur.[59] As the Army planner, General Lincoln, informed the Army Air Forces, OPD's effort was simply to "get something acceptable to the Logistics people which will, at the same time assure adequate sup-

---

[56] (1) Memo, Brig Gen Roberts for Col R. C. Lindsay, 4 Jun 44, sub: Comd and Contl of VLR Bmr Forces . . ., with CCS 501/6 in ABC 384.5 Japan (9 Nov 43) 2–A. (2) Informal penned notation, Lt Col J. K. Woolnough for Brig Gen Roberts [about 4 Jun 44], no sub, with CCS 501/6 in ABC 384.5 Japan (9 Nov 43) 2–A. (3) Informal penciled notation, Brig Gen Roberts for Maj Gen Hull [about 4 Jun 44], with CCS 501/6 in ABC 384.5 Japan (9 Nov 43) 2–A.

[57] See, for example, JCS 823/5, 7 Oct 44, and thereon, OPD memo for rcd, B. B. [Lt Col Buttles], 14 Oct 44, OPD 381 TS 442/10. Colonel Buttles noted that JCS 823/5 (par. 11) provided for implementation through Commanding General, Twentieth Air Force, and that the secretary, JCS, had "handled directly."

[58] For action to establish USASTAF, see: (1) JCS 742/10, 31 May 45, title: Establishment of USASTAF in Pacific; (2) msg (originator JCS) for CINC AF Pacific, CINC Pacific Ocean Area, 1 Jun 45, CM–OUT 10463, ABC 384.5 Japan (9 Nov 43) 2–B; (3) draft memo, OPD for CofS, 8 Jun 45, sub: Redesignation of 20th AF, ABC 384.5 Japan (9 Nov 43) 2–B (this draft memo is the clearest explanation of irregular JCS procedure of USASTAF).

[59] Memo, Brig Gen Lincoln for Col Dan Gilmer, 5 Jun 45, sub: AAF Problems to be Settled with CINCAFPAC, ABC 384.5 Japan (9 Nov 43) 2–B.

port for the Twentieth Air Force." [60] Furthermore, the Army planner and S&P in general tried to follow informal procedures that would get issues involving the Air Forces and OPD "buttoned up" on the working staff level and keep the "difference of opinion, if any, within the Army," where it would not "embarrass the Chief of Staff by making him pull out the matter in a green [JCS] paper in front of the Navy." [61]

The time during which these arrangements were tested was short. One of the early enterprises of USASTAF was dropping atomic bombs on Hiroshima and Nagasaki, and hostilities ended shortly thereafter. In the last months of the war against Japan, OPD continued to assist the Army Air Forces in its staff work, especially in co-ordinating proposed actions on JCS and intragovernmental levels, where OPD had had long and often bitter experience. Probably as much harmony existed between the views of OPD and the Army Air Forces as the fact of the quasi independence of the Army Air Forces and the fact of OPD's staff responsibility permitted. Under these circumstances, the difficult problem of authoritatively defining the basic missions of the armed services, particularly of their respective combat air forces, remained simply a troublesome legacy for postwar military leaders. Nevertheless, the working relationship between OPD and the Air Forces, preserved until after the defeat of Japan, made it possible to employ both the ground and air components of the Army in a co-ordinated war against a common objective.

Joint Logistic Planning

The reorganization of 1943 made even more radical changes in joint logistic planning than in strategic planning or in planning with the Army Air Forces. In many ways the strengthening of the JPS committee and the achievements of the JWPC were made possible by drawing a line beween strategic planning proper and other kinds of joint committee work. The delimitation was not always clear, and the JPS continued to consider a great many problems that were only vaguely strategic in character but which could not be assigned to any other particular sphere of joint committee work. The special field of logistic planning, however, was marked out with some clarity, and primary responsibility for joint staff work in it was assigned outside the JPS committee. Joint committee work on logistics progressed strikingly, coming into its own as a distinct and vital type of military planning.

During World War II the much-used term logistics most often was taken to include every activity in which the Army (or any armed service) engaged in order to carry out its strategic plans. [62] Logistic

---

[60] Memo, Brig Gen Lincoln for Col A. L. Johnson, AAF, 30 May 45, no sub, ABC 384.5 Japan (9 Nov 43) 2–B.

[61] (1) Informal memo, Brig Gen Lincoln for Strategy Sec, 25 May 45, no sub, ABC 384.5 Japan (9 Nov 43) 2–B. (2) Memo, Brig Gen Lincoln for Col J. B. Cary (Info Strategy Sec), 14 Jun 45, no sub, with JCS 1357/1 in ABC 323.31 Pac Ocean Area (1–29–42) 3–B.

[62] Memo, Col J. C. Daly, Actg Chief Logistics Gp for Maj Gen Hull, 7 May 45, sub: Membership of G–4 on Jt Stf Com Which Deal with Logistics, OPD 334.8 Jt Logistics Plans Comm, 9. Colonel Daly noted: "During the present war the word logistics has been applied as an all-embracing term to the overall support of the execution of strategy." Cf. introduction (p. viii) to Logistics in World War II, final Report of the Army Service Forces, submitted to the Under Secretary of War and the CofS by the Director of SS&P WDGS, Lt Gen LeRoy Lutes, 1 July 47. The introduction states:

As the word is used in the following pages, its meaning . . . embraces all military activities not included in the terms "strategy" and "tactics." In this sense, logistics includes procurement, storage,

factors, understood in this sense, entered into every formulation of strategy. At the beginning of the war, strategic decisions had been reached on the basis of comparatively simple logistic calculations. But it quickly became a major Army staff activity to simplify the complex logistic calculations of total war so they would give a firm basis for reaching Army and joint strategic decisions, and to translate the decisions, once made, into technical terms which could be used to guide the specialized, interrelated efforts of millions of soldiers and civilian workers engaged in equipping, supplying, transporting, and otherwise serving an Army of eight million men. It was a staff problem that had thrust itself into the field of OPD's interests very quickly and completely occupied the attention of a number of OPD officers during the later war years.

The War Department reorganization of 1942 had provided a staff within the Army—Headquarters, Services of Supply (redesignated the Army Service Forces in 1943)—to direct procurement and supply in the zone of interior. In order to do so, it engaged increasingly in the collection and simplification of logistic data. The last stages in simplifying logistic data to be used in strategic decisions and the first stages in translating strategic decisions into logistic plans proved to be virtually inseparable from the preparation of strategic plans and from strategic direction of operations. These latter two staff activities had been assigned to OPD, not to General Somervell's headquarters, in the 1942 reorganization. Furthermore, G–1, G–3, and G–4 of the War

---

and distribution of equipment and supplies; transport of troops and cargo by land, sea and air; construction and maintenance of facilities; communication by wire, radio and the mails; care of the sick and wounded; and the induction, classification, assignment, welfare, and separation of personnel.

Department General Staff remained formally responsible for formulating Army-wide policies on personnel, troop unit organization, and supply. While no duplication of functions had been intended in the 1942 reorganization, in practice the work of Army Service Forces Headquarters, of OPD, and of G–1, G–3, and G–4 overlapped. In practice also, OPD tended to determine logistic policy by taking action without reference to G–1, G–3, and G–4, dealing directly with the Army Service Forces (ASF) which had the information necessary to provide advice, as well as the staff and the command authority to carry out directives.

The influence of the Army Service Forces inside the Army became steadily greater as the scale of the war increased and as the planning of great military operations involved more and more elaborate long-range planning in the zone of interior. The Army Service Forces was in effect the Army's agent, or in some cases its buffer, for contact with the civilian economy, which was under strain as a result of being geared by civilian agencies under the direction of the President to support the greatest military effort the United States had ever made. Thus General Somervell spoke with great authority in the Army as to what could be achieved in the way of production, supply, and related matters. At the same time, he was the man who had to fight the confusion that resulted, both inside and outside the Army, when strategic decisions were made without taking account of or allowing time for necessary adjustments in zone of interior programs. The experience of 1942, particularly in preparing for BOLERO and TORCH, confirmed the importance of establishing a harmony between strategy and logistics.

Despite the role of the work of the Service Forces in determining the feasibility of Army plans, General Somervell had not been made a member of the JCS, and his headquarters was not represented in the joint strategic planning committees. The British planning system likewise did not assign to specialists in the field of logistics any part of the task of working out strategic plans. British officers were quick to acknowledge the importance of logistic (in British terminology "administrative") factors but, as General Wedemeyer, who agreed with them, pointed out, they thought experts on logistics should not participate in planning strategy but simply should "be consulted just as intelligence experts, for example, are consulted." [63]

The joint and combined planners tended to regard war as so risky and unpredictable as to preclude a very accurate computation of future requirements. They received information and often asked for advice from logistics specialists. Nevertheless, they saw little to be gained by undertaking to convince the logisticians, while strategy was in the planning stage, that contemplated operations actually could be carried out. The strategic planners went ahead on the premise that major decisions, based on their rough calculations, had to be made before technical planning staffs could profitably undertake detailed calculations and the effort to adjust resources to objectives. They themselves were eager, therefore, to get major decisions made well in advance, and careful to leave a broad margin for error in making their recommendations. The President noted this caution on various occasions, as when he told General Marshall that the "Planners were always conservative and saw all the difficulties, and that more could usually be done than they were willing to admit." [64]

Even the Chief of Staff, although strongly convinced of the advantages of thorough preparation, at times found the JPS too cautious. On one such occasion, drawing upon his experience in World War I, he talked at some length on the perennial need to weigh logistic factors in the balance with the other factors to be considered by the commander, the need "to decide the relation between urgency and perfection." He said that he considered it to be the duty of the JCS to make such decisions, and he concluded his remarks by declaring that as the Allies gained the initiative, "it was increasingly necessary to resist any inclination to delay operations in order to achieve perfection." [65]

It was not how important the facts of logistics were in strategic planning, but who should interpret them, that was in question in 1943. As early as September 1942 General Somervell had recommended giving the JCS and the CCS specialist advisers on procurement, supply, transportation, and related logistic problems, rather than relying on the JPS or the CPS, whose members, in his opinion, were incompetent to deal with them. Since it was not the business of the planners and their staffs to direct the procurement and movement of supplies and equipment, he observed, the "views which they express must therefore be those of others, with a consequent delay in formu-

---

[63] Paper [Brig Gen A. C. Wedemeyer], n.d., title: Comments on Gen Somervell's Memo to CofS Pertaining to Supporting Agencies of JCS (JCS 202/2), atchd to memo, Lt Col J. K. Woolnough for Col O. L. Nelson, Jr., 5 Apr 43, with JCS 202/3 in ABC 381 (1–29–42), 1.

[64] Informal memo, G.C.M. [Gen Marshall] for Maj Gen Handy, 9 Aug 43, with SS 90 in ABC 381 Strategy (7 Jan 43), 1.
[65] Supplementary min 121st meeting JCS, 2 Nov 43.

lating their opinions, or else their own opinions which are predicated neither on knowledge nor experience." [66] General Handy, in a memorandum for the Chief of Staff, objected that General Somervell took for granted what was really the point at issue: whether in practice matters like supply could be distinguished from questions of strategy and treated separately. General Handy observed that he believed the distinction could not be drawn. Although the matter was dropped without further action, by these contrary expressions of opinion an issue of primary significance had forced itself to the surface. [67]

The March 1943 report of the reorganization committee was the starting point of a long controversy over Army Service Forces representation in joint and combined agencies, as well as the closely related question of responsibility within the War Department for planning logistic activities, including management of personnel, activation of units, procurement, supply, transportation, and related activities. Among the proposals made by the committee with a view to preventing the accumulation of unsettled questions on the agenda of the JPS, were two that would critically affect relations between the Army Service Forces and OPD both in the joint planning system and inside the Army. The first one was the limitation of membership on the JPS to four members— the Army planner (from OPD), the Air planner, and a Navy planner and his assist-

ant. The second was the creation of a new three-man committee to be called, in accordance with British terminology, the Joint Administrative Committee to take over from the JPS all matters "not primarily concerned with war plans." According to these recommendations, the Army Service Forces should not be represented on either committee and therefore would be excluded from participation in joint (and therefore in combined) planning of a general or strategic character, as distinguished from the specialized or technical kind of planning done by such committees as the Joint Military Transportation Committee (JMTC), the Joint Communications Board (JCB), the Munitions Assignments Board (USMBW), and the Army-Navy Petroleum Board (ANPB), on each of which the headquarters of Army Service Forces or one of the component branches in the Army Service Forces was represented.

General Somervell wrote a long memorandum to General Marshall, vigorously protesting the exclusion of the Army Service Forces from general or strategic planning. He rested his case on what he considered to be the inevitable incompetence of the Army planner, or anyone else from OPD, to do justice to the logistic aspects of strategic planning, arguing—"Unless you are represented on the Planners by an able officer who KNOWS supply, its ramifications, requirements, adaptability, production, availability, etc. and our capabilities in transportation, and moreover by one who has intimate touch with all sources of information, you will be badly served, the Army will suffer, the war will suffer, and America will suffer." Similarly, he termed "another glaring error" the proposed constitution of the Joint Administrative Committee, observing:

---

[66] Memo, Lt Gen Somervell for CofS, 9 Sep 42, no sub, WDCSA 334 JCS.

[67] Memo, OPD for CofS, 27 Sep 42, sub: Standing Com for Handling Supply Matters, WDCSA 334 JCS. (2) Cf. OPD draft memo [CofS for Lt Gen Somervell], same sub, WDCSA 334 JCS. Not used. (3) For temporary shelving of General Somervell's recommendations, see memo, GCM for Lt Gen Somervell, 26 Oct 42, no sub, WDCSA 334 JCS.

The Navy is properly represented on this committee by some one who knows something about the subject, whereas the Army has a representative from O. P. D. which, above all things, should not concern itself with administration. The Air Force is also represented. The only logical arrangement on this committee would seem to be to have you represented by an officer from your Administrative Services, the Army Service Forces.[68]

It was certainly true that the Army planner and the other officers in S&P did not pretend to "have time to become experts on shipping, landing craft, naval matters, and the like."[69] They did not question the need for data from the Army Service Forces but simply denied that officers outside the Army Service Forces were incapable of assimilating such data sufficiently to formulate strategy. General Wedemeyer prepared a study for the Chief of Staff, dealing one by one with General Somervell's objections to the committee's report. On the latter's remarks about the incompetence of the Army planner this study observed: "The implication in these statements is that no one else in the Army recognizes the importance of or has knowledge of logistics except members of the ASF. Further, the statement that 'the premises on which plans are based were incorrect,' is unfortunate because the logistic information and data required for such plans were invariably obtained from the ASF." Similarly, with reference to his remarks on the proposed membership of the Joint Administrative Committee, it noted:

The OPD representative proposed is the logistics expert within the OPD organization and as such, is the logistics advisor to the AC/S, OPD. He handles not only logistics matters but also is responsible to the Chief of the Operations Division for appropriate recommendations and counsel pertaining to personnel, organization, troop basis, requirements, production supplies, and matériel. Obviously he is well equipped to accomplish the tasks assigned in the Charter of the Joint Administrative Committee.[70]

The disagreements within the Army over logistic aspects of the proposed reorganization, after they had been restudied and discussed at some length in JCS meetings, were resolved for practical administrative purposes by a compromise. The JCS satisfied several of General Somervell's demands, including one of the two demands that particularly concerned the Army planner and OPD: Although General Somervell's headquarters did not acquire membership on the JPS, a representative did replace the proposed OPD representative on the Joint Administrative Committee, which was formally chartered on 15 May 1943.[71]

The creation of the Joint Administrative Committee ended a phase in the debate, but it left unresolved the main issue of the relation of joint logistic with joint strategic planning. In a very real sense, the difficulty was not administrative and could not be remedied by committee appointments. Logistic planning could proceed only a step at a time and in no way could advance faster than strategic planning. Dependable estimates of how many units and how much

---

[68] Memo, Lt Gen Somervell for CofS, 27 Mar 43, sub: Reorgn of Supporting Agencies for JCS, JCS 202/2, WDCSA 334 JCS (Vol. II).

[69] Memo, Col Roberts, no addressee, 3 Apr 43, no sub, with JCS Memo for Info 48 in ABC 381 United Nations (23 Jan 42), 2.

[70] Paper, title: Comments on Gen Somervell's Memo to CofS Pertaining to Supporting Agencies of JCS (JCS 202/2). Original filed with memo, Brig Gen Wedemeyer for CofS, 5 Mar [sic, but certainly 5 Apr] 43, WDCSA 334 JCS (Vol. II). Copies of these papers are filed also with JCS 202/3 in ABC 381 (1–29–42), 1, with memo, Lt Col J. K. Woolnough for Col O. L. Nelson, Jr., 5 Apr 43.

[71] Memo, DCofS for Secretariat, JCS, 5 May 43, sub: Army Representatives on Jt Adm Com, copies with JCS 202/10/D in ABC 334.8 JAdC (5 May 43), 1–A.

equipment would be needed in different theaters could go no further into the future than decisions on the main outlines of future operations. Such firm decisions could not be made until the initiative had passed to the United States and the other nations of its coalition, as it finally did in 1943.

General Wedemeyer pointed to the relationship between long-range strategic decisions and long-range logistic plans in reviewing the history of wartime planning and dwelling on the opportunism of British-American planning up to April 1943 and the need for "adoption of a long-range concept for the defeat of the European Axis." Once such a concept had been firmly established, he concluded, "long-range planning for organizational and equipment requirements can be initiated." [72] Colonel Ferenbaugh, chief of the European Theater Section, which had been mainly responsible for passing on requirements for operations in Europe and the Mediterranean, agreed, reiterating:

It is desired especially to stress the difficulty in making necessary strategic forecasts due to the lack of a definite and consistent long-range strategic concept of operations in the European Theater. The apparently irreconcilable divergence between the British and American viewpoint and the lack of definite decision between the two, prevents the formulation of a sound plan both as regards troop basis and the types of equipment necessary for operations in Europe or adjacent areas.[73]

These particular memoranda, written for General McNarney, were held up in OPD

pending the outcome of the international conference (TRIDENT) in Washington in May.[74] In forwarding them to General McNarney after the conference, General Hull observed that it was still not possible to foresee just how far American plans might have to be changed to allow for further operations in the Mediterranean, in the Balkans for example. Nevertheless, he said, the conference had given much greater assurance than had existed previously both on cross-Channel operations and on the strategy to be used against Japan, making it possible to "put our planning on a much firmer basis, with respect to both the European-Mediterranean and Pacific-Far Eastern areas." [75] Just as the uncertainty about future strategy that followed the Casablanca Conference had affected the course of joint planning through April 1943, the confidence that followed on TRIDENT strengthened the conviction that it was at last becoming possible to plan on a long-range basis for providing the resources to win the war. Conversely, the uncertainties that continued into the later war years kept responsible officers still cautious about settling planning problems both in the joint system and in the War Department.

Creation of the Joint Logistics Committee

The occasion for reopening the question of joint logistics planning was a communication from the President in July, stating that he wished to provide for joint (and combined) planning in the field of logistics to run parallel with planning in the field of strategy, "to the end that there shall be one

---

[72] Memo, Brig Gen Wedemeyer for DCofS, 28 Apr 43, sub: Rpt of Mission Headed by Gen Devers, OPD 381 Sec, 118.

[73] (1) Memo, Col Ferenbaugh for DCofS, 30 Apr 43, sub: Rpt of Mission Headed by Gen Devers, OPD 381 Sec, 118. (2) Cf. memo, G–4 for DCofS, 20 Mar 43, sub: Memo of March 5, 1943, from Gen Shugg to Gen McNarney, OPD 381 Sec, 118.

[74] Memo, Col Godwin Ordway, Jr., for All Concerned, 27 May 43, no sub, OPD 381 Sec, 118.

[75] Memo, Brig Gen Hull for DCofS, 29 May 43, sub: Rpt of Mission Headed by Lt Gen Devers, OPD 381 Sec, 118.

unified and balanced supply program consistent with up-to-date strategic concepts." [76]

General Somervell recommended telling the President that the various supply programs were in an "excellent state of balance at present" and also that the JCS, in setting up the Joint Administrative Committee, had provided a joint agency "charged solely with logistical planning and with the integration of such planning with strategic planning." The JCS approved a reply substantially as suggested by General Somervell. [77]

Some of the S&P officers in OPD promptly pointed out, quite correctly, that it was a misstatement to say that the Joint Administrative Committee was chartered to integrate logistic planning with strategic planning. If the JCS letter to the President in fact corresponded to the intentions of the JCS, these planners concluded, the charter of the Joint Administrative Committee should be revised accordingly. [78] A recommendation to this effect had already been made by the JWPC in a report on "Phases of Joint War Planning" which it submitted to the JPS very soon after the President's initial statement about the need for more effective co-ordination of logistic and strategic planning. The JWPC observed that there was no joint agency charged "specifically with the preparation and revision of broad long-range programs for mobilization, deployment, troop bases, training, equipment and supply, and transportation," and that the Joint Administrative Committee was best fitted to perform this function. [79]

The Joint Administrative Committee itself went to work at once to draft a new charter charging it with the functions ascribed to it in the JCS reply to the President and renaming it, more appropriately, the Joint Logistics Committee. Early in August it submitted such a proposal to the JCS (JCS 450) with a provision that the Army and Navy components each should be increased from two or three, and that one Army Service Forces officer be added, making the total Army membership two Army Service Forces officers and one Army Air Forces officer. [80] General Tansey, OPD's Logistics Group chief, heard of the proposal while it was still under consideration by the Joint Administrative Committee and recommended that he, rather than another Army Service Forces officer, should be added to the committee. He listed the subjects that had been referred to the Joint Administrative Committee since its establishment, and said that over half of these subjects were of "direct interest" to OPD. General Handy agreed, and sent the recommendation forward to General McNarney. [81]

---

[76] JCS 415, 17 Jul 43, title: Joint Effort Regarding Supply. JCS 415 consists of ltr, President to Admiral Leahy, n.d., no sub.

[77] (1) Draft ltr [JCS (Admiral Leahy) to President], incl with memo, Lt Gen Somervell for CofS, 19 Jul 43, no sub, with JCS 415/1 in ABC 334.8 JAdC (5 May 43), 1–A. (2) Min 97th meeting JCS, 20 Jul 43. (3) JCS 415/1, 21 Jul 43, title: Jt Effort Regarding Supply.

[78] (1) OPD brief, 20 Jul 43, title: Add Discussion on JCS 415, with JCS 415 in ABC 334.8 JAdC (5 May 43), 1–A. (2) Draft memo [OPD for CofS], 23 Jul 43, sub: Balanced Supply Program Consistent with Cur Strategic Concept, (JCS 415, 415/1) with JCS 415/1 in ABC 334.8 JAdC (5 May 43), 1–A.

[79] JPS 227, 19 Jul 43, title: Phases of Jt War Planning.

[80] (1) Min 99th meeting JCS, 3 Aug 43. (2) JCS 450, 8 Aug 43, title: Adjustments in JAdC.

[81] (1) Memo, Brig Gen P. H. Tansey for Maj Gen Handy, 31 Jul 43, sub: Representation of OPD WDGS, on JAdC, with inclosed memo, unsigned, for Col V. J. Esposito [29] Jul 43, sub: Work of JAdC, OPD 334.8 JAdC, 2. (2) Memo, OPD for DCofS, 3 Aug 43, sub: Representation of OPD . . ., OPD 334.8 JAdC, 2.

The principal objections to JCS 450 came from the Army planner and the Air planner. Their objections were shared by their staffs in the Army Air Forces and OPD, the Strategy Section being very strongly opposed.[82] The common theme of all the criticisms was that it was unsound for the proposed JLC to share on an equal basis with the JPS, as provided in the proposed charter, responsibility for the "integration of logistics with strategy in the preparation of joint war plans." [83] The clause in question had provided in the charter proposed by the Joint Administrative Committee, that the Joint Logistics Committee should "act in coordination with the Joint Staff Planners in the consideration and preparation of Joint War Plans as necessary to insure the logistic feasibility of such plans." As phrased in the final report to the JCS, the provision stated that the Joint Logistics Committee should "advise the Joint Staff Planners in the consideration and preparation of joint war plans as to the logistics aspects of such plans, in order that the Joint Staff Planners may ensure the integration of logistics with strategy in the preparation of joint war plans." [84] With this phrasing incorporated, the Army planner and the Air planner agreed to the charter and also to the related proposal to set up a working subcommittee, the Joint Logistics Plans Committee (JLPC), which would serve the new committee much as the JWPC served the JPS.[85]

The Joint Logistics Committee was formally chartered on 13 October as the "primary logistics advisory and planning agency of the Joint Chiefs of Staff." It still had to study miscellaneous "matters under the jurisdiction of the Joint Chiefs of Staff not assigned to other agencies thereof," but its main function was to systematize logistic planning by furnishing advice and information on logistics to the JCS and to other government agencies. Its duties, with reference to the JPS, were defined in the way that Army planners had urged:

Advise the Joint Staff Planners in the consideration and preparation of joint war plans as to the logistic aspects of such plans in order that the Joint Staff Planners may insure the integration of logistics with strategy in the preparation of joint war plans:
Prepare logistic plans for implementing the war plans prepared by the Joint Staff Planners.
Advise the Joint Chiefs of Staff and the Joint Staff Planners concerning the logistics implications of proposed U. S. commitments relating to joint and combined operations.[86]

In accordance with OPD's recommendations the three Army memberships were divided among the Army Service Forces, the Army Air Forces, and OPD.

The position of the JLC and the influence, therefore, of joint logistic planning, were further strengthened by the establishment of the Joint Logistics Plans Committee. The clear enunciation of the principle that the JPS would remain responsible for integrating logistics with strategy implicitly covered the work of the JWPC in relation to that of the JLPC. The charter of the working subcommittee provided for a control group of six members, to be assisted by

[82] (1) Incl with OPD brief, title: Notes . . . JPS 95th Meeting, 18 Aug 43, with JPS 279/D in ABC 334.8 JAdC (5 May 43), 1–A. (2) Min 95th meeting JPS, 18 Aug 43. (3) Incl with memo, Col J. C. Blizzard, Jr., for Rear Admiral B. H. Bieri, 18 Aug 43, sub: Adjustments in JAdC (JPS 279/D), with JPS 279/D in ABC 334.8 JAdC (5 May 43), 1–A. (4) Min 98th meeting JPS, 1 Sep 43. (5) Min 99th meeting JPS, 8 Sep 43. (6) JCS 450/2, 13 Sep 43, title: Adjustments in JAdC.
[83] JCS 450/2, 13 Sep 43, title: Adjustments in JAdC.
[84] JCS 450/3, 14 Sep 43.

[85] Min 100th meeting JPS, 14 Sep 43.
[86] JCS 202/29/D, 13 Oct 43, title: Charter JLC.

associate members designated as required. The control group was analogous to the senior planning team of the JWPC, being composed of members whose work with the JLPC was their primary (though not their only) duty. The three Army members of the control group were to come from OPD, the Army Service Forces, and the Army Air Forces. No provision was made for organizing the associate members in teams, or for relieving them from regularly assigned duties. They were to be on call, individually, to "assist the permanent members in the solution of problems on which they have special knowledge." To insure their continuing usefulness as experts, they were to remain on duty in the various Army and Navy staff sections dealing with logistics. Their usefulness would thus differ from that of members of the JWPC planning teams, who were trying to detach themselves to a great extent from the point of view of staff work in the individual armed services. Nevertheless, like their colleagues on the JWPC, the members of the JLPC were enjoined to follow no instructions except the ones they received through joint committee channels. Thus the JLPC, despite differences, occupied a position in the field of logistic planning comparable to that of the JWPC in the field of strategic planning, just as the JLC was roughly parallel with the JPS committee.

OPD and Joint Logistic Planning

These changes in the joint logistic planning system were accompanied by adjustments in OPD. The Logistics Group in its own field of specialization came to acquire a position comparable to that of S&P.[87] In both cases the OPD group chief represented the War Department General Staff in the joint and combined committee system. General McNarney promptly named the chief of OPD's Logistics Group as the third Army member of the JLC.[88] Another Logistics Group officer served on the control group of the JLPC. This assignment was his primary duty, though he also remained chief of the Projected Logistics Section (formerly Plans & Assignment Section) of Logistics Group. His position thus differed from that of OPD's senior member of the JWPC, who did not have any corresponding duties within S&P. As a consequence the task of co-ordinating JLPC work with that of OPD's Logistics Group was not comparable to the JWPC-Strategy Section problem.[89]

Initially, working members of the JLPC were not assigned on a full-time basis. There were over eighty of them, drawn from various agencies of the War Department. Fifteen were from OPD. Of these, eight represented the various sections of the Theater Group and seven came from the Logistics Group.[90] The OPD associate members of the JLPC thus represented two types of specialization, one by areas, as in the theater sections, and one by subject, such as communications or shipping, from Logistics Group. By the end of the war, Logistics Group itself was furnishing subject specialists and some of the area specialists in such varied fields as levels of supply, signal com-

---

[87] Memo, Col V. J. Esposito for author, 2 Jan 47, sub: Comments on Draft Manuscript "The Way OPD Worked," OPD Hist Unit Comments file.

[88] (1) D/F, OPD for TAG, 16 Oct 43, sub: Request for Orders, OPD 334.8 Jt Ad Comte, 3. See memo for rcd thereon. (2) Memo for rcd, CKG [Col Gailey], 16 Oct 43, sub: Decisions Reached at Conf, Gen McNarney's Office, 14 Oct 43, etc., OPD 320 WD, 14.

[89] (1) Memo, Brig Gen P. H. Tansey for ACofS OPD, 10 Nov 43, sub: Apmt to JLPC, OPD 334.8 JLPC, 1. (2) Memo, OPD for Secy JCS, 13 Nov 43, sub: Apmt to JLPC, OPD 334.8 JLPC, 1.

[90] JLC Memo for Info 2, 4 Dec 43, title: JLPC/ Associate Members.

munications, deployment, shipping, quartermaster and engineer equipment, motor transport, artillery, ammunition levels, Army Air Forces supply, tanks and armored vehicles, and civil affairs. Thus OPD was prepared to furnish members for joint committee work on logistic studies of any kind directly bearing on overseas operations.[91]

The JLPC found by experience that officers with heavy duties in individual service staffs could not handle all the work which fell to the joint logistic planning staff. Not being regularly associated with joint planning and having other regular duties, they could not fill one of the most important functions of the JLPC, which was to provide on short notice agreed critiques of the studies continually being turned out by the comparatively large full-time staff of the JWPC. The JLC therefore suggested in the spring of 1944 that a few associate members should be assigned to the JLPC on a primary duty status, as the JWPC had originally recommended. In advocating this action, the JLC declared that it was out of the question for the six permanent members of the JLPC control group, with the help of associate consultants, to keep up with the demands of the JWPC, with approximately twenty permanent members: "By its nature, logistical planning requires exhaustive and detailed investigations which are usually matters of high urgency resulting in heavy peak loads. To meet such demands it is necessary that an adequate and trained group be available for such work." [92] The JLC recommendation was approved on 19 April 1944, and twenty permanent associate members were appointed, eleven of them

Army officers. From that time on three members were assigned to this duty from OPD's Logistics Group, additional strength being allocated to OPD for the purpose.[93]

The permanent associate members assigned to primary duty with the JLPC had a position not very different from that of the members of the JWPC planning teams. The three OPD officers (from the Logistics Group) serving in that capacity dealt specifically with only two categories of problems—units and personnel, and logistic analysis. Officers from appropriate agencies of the War Department dealt with the other categories defined by the JLPC as of immediate interest to the Army—shipping and transportation, air logistics, petroleum, oil, and lubricants, and construction. The single OPD member dealing with units and personnel was paired with a representative from G–4 (as well as two Navy representatives). The two OPD members classified as logistics analysts were part of a group to which the Army Air Forces and the Army Service Forces (as well as the Navy) each furnished one representative.[94]

Joint logistic plans, even more than joint war plans, depended primarily on the work and the opinions of the operating agencies in the War and Navy Departments, which had up-to-date, detailed information. The function of OPD representatives, greatly outnumbered on all the logistic committees,

---

[91] For the list of OPD associate members (part-time duty status) on the JLPC near the end of the war, see JLC Memo for Info 10, 26 Jul 45, title: JLPC/Associate Members.

[92] JCS 810, 8 Apr 44, title: Membership, JLPC.

[93] (1) Memo, JCS Secretariat [Capt E. D. Graves, Jr., Deputy Secy JCS] for OPD and for Aide COMINCH, 21 Apr 44, sub: Membership, JLPC, with JCS 810 in ABC 334.8 JAdC (5 May 43), 2. (2) Memo, Brig Gen P. H. Tansey for Exec OPD, 27 Apr 44, sub: Increase in Off Almt for WD Agencies (Membership, JLPC), OPD 334.8 JLPC, 2.

[94] (1) JLC Memo for Info 4, 25 Jul 44, title: JLPC Membership. (2) JLC Memo for Info 8, 31 Aug 44, title: JLPC Membership. (3) JLC Memo for Info 9, 29 Jan 45, title: JLPC Membership.

was to bring to bear on problems under discussion their appreciation of current and future requirements in the overseas theaters. Representatives of other War Department agencies, notably of the Army Air Forces and the Army Service Forces, also had ideas about strategy and were in a position to influence strategic planning indirectly by their selection and presentation of information regarding their programs in the zone of interior. No organization, procedure, or policy could entirely alter the fact that the logistic information synthesized in joint planning was accumulated by several staffs, each influenced by the policies of the particular agency of which it was a part. OPD membership merely insured that OPD's point of view would be represented at every stage of joint logistic planning.

It was not easy to establish full understanding between the staff officers concerned with future operations, who were well informed of developments in strategy, and those occupied with logistics. Throughout the war, officers concentrating on logistic matters tended to feel that they needed to know more than they were told about current strategy and operations. In the summer of 1944 the JLC called attention to the fact that it was working without the latest theater plans and estimates, although the JWPC occasionally made some of them available for a quick reading. The JLC therefore recommended that the JPS furnish them to JLC and the JLPC on the same basis on which they were furnished to the JWPC, and also asked for the minutes of JPS meetings.[95] The JPS did not agree to distribute minutes of meetings, plans, reports, or messages to the logistics planners.

Their position was that the minutes of the meetings were brief and, taken by themselves, easily misinterpreted, while the circulation of plans, reports, and messages were limited by security regulations. The effect was simply that logistics specialists were not to be allowed to participate fully in the day-to-day work of strategic planning.[96]

From the point of view of the joint logistics planners, the situation remained unsatisfactory throughout the war.[97] Strategic planners were likewise dissatisfied, since they felt that the logistics planners in the Army Service Forces were still making assumptions of their own regarding strategy, as a basis for logistic planning, which deviated from the assumptions adopted in joint strategic planning.[98] Strategic planners distinguished between the tentative estimates that were used as a basis for reaching strategic decisions and the calculations that controlled carrying out decisions, which were the basis for more and more detailed breakdowns. Calculations of the latter sort, which ultimately governed the physical movement of troops and equipment, were necessarily the affair of the responsible

---

[95] Memo, JLC for JPS, 28 Jul 44, no sub, with JLC Memo for Info 4 in ABC 334.8 JAdC (5 May 43), 2.

[96] (1) Draft memo, Col C. H. Donnelly [Secy JPS] for JLC, n.d., sub: Basis for Revision of Logistical Studies. Forwarded with memo, Col Donnelly for members JPS, 29 Jul 44, sub: Request by J.L.C. . . ., with JLC Memo for Info 4 in ABC 334.8 JAdC (5 May 43), 2. (2) Min 163d meeting JPS, 16 Aug 44. (3) Memo, JPS for JLC, 16 Aug 44, sub: Basis for Revision . . ., ABC 334.8 JAdC (5 May 43), 1–A.

[97] JPS 715/M, 6 Jul 45, title: T Plans and Policies for Use in Logistical Studies.

[98] On one occasion General Somervell frankly admitted that he objected to a study on grounds of strategy. The study in question was SS 265. See: (1) memo, Lt Gen Somervell for CofS, 24 Jun 44, sub: Opns against KYUSHU, with SS 265 in ABC 381 Strategy Sec Papers (7 Jan 43); (2) memo, Lt Col R. V. Boyle, British G.S. for Chief Strategy Sec, 27 Jun 44, sub: ASF Paper "Operations Against KYUSHU," with SS 265 in ABC 381 Strategy Sec Papers (7 Jan 43).

operations officers and logistics experts. But the tentative estimates represented merely an "educated guess" as to what would be needed and what could be made available. Its accuracy depended to a great extent on the ability of the planners to anticipate enemy reactions and to gauge the risks the high command would be willing to run and the sacrifices it would be willing to make in order to attain specified military objectives. The strategic planners, especially OPD members of the joint committees, were very insistent on the distinction between these two ways of using information about needs and resources, and they were inclined to be jealous of their prerogative to draw up the estimates used in future planning. These estimates, in the words of one of the members of the JPS, were "used as a strategic guide and form a part of creative planning; therefore they should be originated as a planning and not as a logistic function." [99]

As a result of apprehensions and misapprehensions on both sides, OPD members of the joint logistic committees were in a

position to perform a very useful quasi-liaison function. They could secure informally in OPD the current information on plans and operations that was essential for keeping joint logistic plans in harmony with parallel developments in strategic thinking. At the same time, they could keep other OPD officers aware of logistic realities. Thus OPD Logistics Group helped to weld together the strategic or operational planning with logistic planning in the joint staff in Washington.[100] In the later war years, when many of the main lines of strategy had hardened, the little-advertised contribution of OPD in helping tailor logistic preparations to fit planned operations probably was fully as valuable as the continuing development of strategic ideas.

---

[99] Min 152d meeting JPS, 17 May 44.

[100] The control of deployment and of redeployment was for OPD the essential responsibility through the exercise of which it could harmonize strategic planning and logistic planning within the Army, and on the basis of which OPD officers in the joint staff could effectively represent the Army in harmonizing strategic planning and logistic planning on a joint (and combined) basis. See: (1) min 143d meeting JPS, 4 Apr 45; (2) correspondence filed as SS 247 in ABC 381 Strategy Sec Papers (7 Jan 43).

CHAPTER XIV

Controlling Troops and Matériel

The changes in the JCS committee system in 1943 involved administrative readjustments to balance the War Department's internal organization and procedure with its way of conducting its external affairs. The main issue that arose was the proper assignment inside the War Department of responsibility for making certain that the flow of Army troops and matériel to the overseas theaters was in harmony with strategic plans. This question was hotly debated by the Army agencies concerned at the same time that the parallel problem of the relationship between strategic and logistic planning was being discussed in the joint committee system. In the War Department distinct but necessarily interlaced problems were attacked concurrently, often by the same officers, sometimes by the same committees, and usually in the same memoranda and reports. One problem involved the relations between the Army Service Forces and the War Department General Staff as a whole. The second involved the relations between OPD, particularly the Logistics Group, and the rest of the General Staff. The third concerned the administrative organization inside OPD for carrying out the responsibilities of the Division in controlling the flow of troops and matériel to the theaters of operations.

The adjustment of zone of interior programs to overseas operations was the con-

cern of the whole War Department, not exclusively of the Army Service Forces and the General Staff. The Army Air and the Army Ground Forces were vitally affected, as was the Army Service Forces, by the allocation of manpower, the procurement of equipment, and the scheduling of overseas movements. But the controversy over War Department control of the flow of troops and material to the theaters directly involved only the Army Service Forces and the divisions of the General Staff. General Arnold and the Air Staff had a great deal of influence on War Department policies governing the wartime expansion and employment of air forces, and took no formal action to remove the vestiges of General Staff control. General McNair and his staff did not seek to circumvent or limit General Staff control, although they vigorously protested War Department policies that compromised their program for training ground combat forces.[1] General Somervell and his staff, on the other hand, not only protested specific War Department policies that affected the procurement of supplies and equipment and the organization and training of service troops, but also attacked the very principle

---

[1] For an indication of the mixed exasperation, resignation, and understanding with which the Army Ground Forces regarded OPD's direction of the movement of units overseas, see memo, AGF for OPD (Attn: Maj Gen Handy), 6 Aug 43, no sub, OPD 370.5, 556.

of control over these matters by the War Department General Staff.

The General Staff and the Army Service Forces

Early in April 1943 General Somervell recommended eliminating logistic planning altogether from the activities of the War Department General Staff and reassigning it to the Army Service Forces (and, as appropriate, to the Army Air Forces). To this end, he proposed abolishing G–1, G–4, and the Logistics Group of OPD, transferring their "personnel, equipment, records, facilities, functions, duties, responsibilities, and authority" to General Somervell's headquarters (or to General Arnold's headquarters). "In matters of supply and administration," General Somervell argued, "it is highly impracticable, if not impossible to separate policy and operations. The enforcement of the policy inevitably tends to become the actual operation of that policy with all of the extra administrative detail and personnel required for an additional agency to do the work of another." He therefore concluded that General Staff logisticians were unnecessary:

The need for an Operations Division and a Military Intelligence Division is apparent, one to plan and coordinate operations, and the other to collect, evaluate, and disseminate military intelligence data. There is no other agency provided in the organization of the War Department to perform these functions. It is believed that the Chief of Staff, and the War Department, have been satisfactorily served by these two divisions, and that they have performed essential functions. G–3 may or may not be more effective as a part of OPD.

With respect to the G–1 and G–4 Divisions, it is believed that an analysis of their duties, responsibilities, and the contribution which they make to the activities of the War Department will indicate that they duplicate largely the work which must perforce be carried out by the Army Service Forces and by the Army Air Forces for supplies and equipment peculiar to those forces.[2]

General Somervell's proposal to abandon the General Staff principle entirely in regard to zone of interior affairs showed to what a great extent the Army Service Forces in fact had taken over the traditional duties of G–1 and G–4. General Somervell's headquarters staff had succeeded in supervising, co-ordinating, and in fact dominating the work of the administrative and technical staffs, the old "bureaus," in a way the General Staff had never done. By 1943 the Army Service Forces was asserting on its own behalf the claim for independence from the General Staff that its several component agencies had long asserted for themselves in their respective fields of special administrative and technical competence. The net effect of General Somervell's proposals would have been to recognize the Army Service Forces as the proper staff to give the broadest kind of logistic advice to the Chief of Staff as well as the command in the zone of interior to carry out approved policies based on that advice. In its own sphere the Army Service Forces would then have been equivalent to OPD plus the tactical commands overseas in the separate sphere of military operations. The Chief of Staff would have a second command post in the War Department, one to deal with logistics, in addition to his operational command post. Moreover, one officer, General Somervell, would have been at the head of the staff in the logistic command post and at the head of the operating logistic command.

---

[2] Memo, ASF for CofS, 3 Apr 43, sub: Suggested Changes in Orgn of WD, copy filed OPD 320 WD, 1.

Such a concentration of power in the Army Service Forces certainly would have challenged and probably would have surpassed the authority wielded by OPD at that time. OPD's position might have been magnified to some extent by the absorption of G–3, but at the expense of the continued existence of the General Staff. The abandonment of the General Staff idea would abrogate the principle from which OPD's prerogatives had sprung, that is, the principle of high-level staff co-ordination of all Army activities that affected military operations.

General Marshall referred the document to General Handy for his reaction, and General Handy responded to General Somervell's proposal with a strong indorsement of the General Staff concept. He said that he was inclined to believe that the error of the past year lay in taking away from G–1 and G–4 too many operating responsibilities rather than in limiting the authority of the Army Service Forces to determine policy. General Handy went on to observe that the entire General Staff should be permitted to engage in "operating" insofar as necessary to insure that its plans and policies actually governed and met the practical operating, administrative, or executive problems of the Army. General Handy categorically stated his own views:

My belief is that the General Staff has a very distinct function and that it should not be abolished. We would be going back to pre-World War [I] setup. The experience of every Army in the world has shown the necessity for a planning, policy making, and coordinating group. A move to abolish it would be a distinct step backwards. . . . My idea is that G–1 should not be abolished but extended to include an operating function as to personnel similar to that now exercised by the Director of Military Personnel in the Army Service Forces. The idea that the General Staff never

operates is not sound. I never saw an effective staff that did not to a certain extent operate. It is my impression that many of the proper functions of G–4 have already been absorbed in the Army Service Forces. Some of these undoubtedly should have been. But I am of the opinion that the Chief of Staff needs a coordinating and policy making agency on supply matters. A very definite need exists for this coordination.

General Handy likewise defended G–3, which, in his opinion, was doing a big job and doing it very well. He saw no reason for OPD's taking the job over, as General Somervell had suggested. For these reasons General Handy advised against making OPD virtually the sole remnant of the General Staff, and against giving the Army Service Forces a monopoly on making plans and policies governing personnel, supply, and other technical matters, as well as performing the operating or administrative duties in those areas of Army activity. In conclusion General Handy stated: "My impression is that the present organization is working fairly well. It has accomplished what was a crying need in the War Department, namely decentralization. The danger in too great a decentralization is uncoordinated action. There must be a coordinating agency, and I know of nothing better to accomplish this than the General Staff." [3]

The Logistics Group was the center of the particular activities of OPD which conflicted with those of the Army Service Forces and in addition tended to minimize the functions of the other divisions of the General Staff. By mid-1943 General Tansey had developed his Logistics Group into a small but very influential staff for studying all matters of logistics, supply, and equipment as such, as distinguished from such matters

---

[3] (1) Note, GCM for Maj Gen Handy, OPD 320 WD, 1. (2) Memo, Maj Gen Handy for Gen Marshall, 6 Apr 43, no sub, OPD 320 WD, 1.

in any specific theater. It dealt with nearly every aspect of the mobilization and assignment (i.e. allocation) of Army troops and matériel, the paramount interests of the Army Service Forces. The Logistics Group thus was directly involved in the long controversy, set off by General Somervell's memorandum, concerning the role of the General Staff in logistic planning and in controlling the movement of troops and matériel. General Somervell had observed:

There appears also to be some duplication of effort between the Army Service Forces and the Army Air Forces and the Logistics Section which has been established in the Operations Division, W.D.G.S. This appears to be a straight and unnecessary duplication of effort. . . . It would seem highly desirable therefore for this duplication to be eliminated, the personnel released and the duties absorbed in the appropriate agencies of the Army Air Forces and the Army Service Forces.[4]

General Somervell wanted to abolish the Logistics Group not only on the grounds that also applied to G–1 and G–4, but in addition because, he felt, the members of the Logistics Group were not competent to advise and assist the rest of OPD, the Chief of Staff, or the JCS. He explained his point of view to the Army planner about the same time, urging that advice from the Army Service Forces should be taken most seriously, since the Service Forces was continuously studying supply problems in all their ramifications, that is, the "logistics of total war." He believed that the Logistics Group was getting beyond its depth in offering advice except on "supply requirements for specific overseas operations," and doubted whether it should undertake even that much, asserting: "Even in this field, the data must be developed in my staff and

technical divisions and much duplication of effort and possibilities of confusion would be eliminated if the Operations Division called on the Army Service Forces for all of its logistical studies. In any event, this section should not be permitted to wander without a guide in the deep forests of war economy." [5]

In commenting on General Somervell's April memorandum, General Handy explained with regard to the special problem of the Logistics Group:

I doubt very much if General Somervell understands what the so-called Logistics Group of this Division does. Its real purpose is to let our theater and planning people know what forces and material are available for operations. Probably the use of the term "Logistics Group" is unfortunate. The information selected and made available by this group concerns many other things besides supply; for example, readiness of troops, organization, troop bases, etc. You will recall that the Victory Program study was guided by the War Plans Division. We are continually called upon for opinions on such matters as the organization and composition of the Army, on policies as to equipping French and other forces. It was with the idea of having an agency to study these questions and to keep up-to-date data on availability of troops, supplies and equipment that this group was organized. My opinion is that something of the kind will always be necessary even though it is called by some other name.[6]

No administrative action resulted from General Somervell's memorandum, and later in the spring he repeated his proposal.[7]

---

[4] Memo, ASF for CofS, 3 Apr 43, sub: Suggested Changes in Orgn of WD, copy filed OPD 320 WD, 1.

[5] Memo, Lt Gen Somervell for Brig Gen Wedemeyer, 23 May 43, sub: Memo on Shipts Required for Opns in India, Paper 1, Book 10, Exec 8.
[6] Memo, OPD for CofS, 6 Apr 43, no sub, OPD 320 WD, 1.
[7] Memo, ASF for CofS, 1 Jun 43, sub: Reorgn of Serv Activities, G–4 020, Vol. I. With this memorandum General Somervell submitted two inclosures, one of which reproduced most of the 3 April memorandum under the title, "Proposed Organization of the War Department." Chart VII at-

A draft study prepared in OPD on this occasion called attention to the long-run implications, which recalled the old "bureau" versus General Staff struggle, of General Somervell's proposal. It concluded:

I believe that, although we should organize primarily for war, we should not forget the after-the-war period and the effects of any organization adopted now on the post-war Army. . . . In peace time all our experience shows a tendency to build up and increase the power of the services as opposed to the combat element. The present setup, with one of these commanders [i.e., the CG, ASF] controlling funds, allotments, and, to a certain extent, personnel, would result in this commander practically running the Army in peacetime. We should not forget what a struggle it was for the Chief of Staff to get control of the Army. No system should be started that may well result in the breaking down of that control.[8]

The Army Ground Forces likewise opposed doing away with the General Staff as then organized. When General Somervell repeated his proposal, General McNair wrote a highly personal comment. He first took note of the argument that the proposed reorganization would make for economy, as follows: "I note that your staff, exclusive of Chiefs, aggregates over 20,000, while G–1 and G–4 of the War Department aggregates 90. If there is duplication of personnel and effort, it is in your house. In general, the modern headquarters is a fearful and wonderful thing." He abruptly dismissed General Somervell's reasons against the General Staff's "operating," declaring the question to be "quite irrelevant" since the distinction could not be clearly drawn between determining policy and "operating." He then came to his main point of disagreement: "The fundamental fallacy of your proposal lies in the fact that you are trying to create an administrative commander, breaking down the functions of the over-all commander and violating the fundamental principle of unity of command." He concluded with a statement of his own views:

I believe in your A.S.F., because you are essentially the commander of the zone of the interior. The former set-up whereby the War Department attempted to command both the theaters and the zone of the interior, was impracticable in war. But I do not admit that you are responsible for logistic operations in the War Department or in overseas theaters. G–4 is the proper adviser of the Chief of Staff in logistic policies, even though such is not the case today due to the force of your personality.[9]

The Chief of Staff, probably in view of the strong opposition from these and other quarters, never took formal action on General Somervell's plan. Logistic policy making in theory at least remained a function of the General Staff. Nevertheless, some thought had to be given to the fact, to which General Somervell drew attention, that the Army Service Forces with its immense staff and OPD with its broad powers between them tended in practice to decide the questions which traditionally belonged to G–1, G–3, and G–4. An alternative solution to that proposed by General Somervell was, as General Handy indicated, to strengthen the G–1 and G–4 Divisions of the General Staff by increasing their responsibilities in their own fields by explicitly recognizing

---

tached (though placed separately in the same file) showed that he proposed a General Staff composed of G–2 and OPD, with Planning, Training, and Operations Branches.

[8] Draft study, 26 Jun 43, title: Notes on Proposed Orgn of Serv Activities, OPD 320, 53. This study bears General Handy's initial.

[9] Memo, Lt Gen McNair for Lt Gen Somervell, 24 Jun 43, sub: Your Proposed Reorgn of Serv Activities, Hq, ASF, AGF file (1943–1944), Hist Rcds Sec, AG Rcds Br.

their authority to "operate." For its part, OPD was clearly in favor of avoiding all kinds of work that was not inextricably entangled with its own duties and consequently was ready to recommend increasing the responsibilities of the other General Staff Divisions.[10] Such a step, however, required a very careful examination into the means by which OPD would continue to exercise its superior authority and broad jurisdiction within the General Staff and thereby avoid reverting to the painfully slow method of concurrences, which the 1942 reorganization virtually had eliminated.

Logistics Inside the General Staff

The question of the distribution of responsibilities as among OPD, G–1, G–3, and G–4, and the related question of Army Service Forces aspirations to control all logistic planning, had to be settled in close connection with the substantive questions of mobilization and deployment of forces. The issue was taken up first by a Special Army Committee organized in mid-1943 to study the troop mobilization program.[11] In a special report on the subject of General Staff organization, the committee emphasized the need for a strong General Staff but

recommended the elimination of the Logistics Group, OPD, in order to avoid duplicating or ignoring the efforts of G–1, G–3, and G–4 and proposed that the theater sections of OPD take up theater requests for personnel, units, and supplies with the appropriate General Staff Divisions. This arrangement would have left OPD entirely dependent on logistic advice from outside the Division. In other words General Handy would have no logistics specialists responsible directly to him for evaluating the very factors that, in many cases, determined the course of strategy or operational policy being formulated by S&P or the Theater Group.[12] The report did not remark on the fact that in some ways the Logistics Group was a kind of composite G–1, G–3, and G–4 unit in OPD, and that consequently the presence of such a unit might be exploited to advantage without basically changing the S&P-Theater Group system.[13]

The problem was neither solved nor dropped after this report, but passed on for further study by a committee of G–1, G–3, G–4, and OPD officers. It was instructed to find "policies and procedures which will restrict the present uneconomical flow of unnecessary individuals, units and materiel to the several theaters." Plainly, designation of the agent for establishing such policies and procedures was part of the problem.[14]

---

[10] For recognition in G–4 that General Staff Divisions, except for OPD, did not have the necessary authority to get things done, see: (1) memo, Capt J. C. Cross for ACofS G–4, 20 Mar 43, sub: Activities of G–4 Div WDGS, G–4 020, Vol. I; (2) memo, Lt Col James McCormack for Brig Gen R. C. Moses, 16 Apr 43, sub: Reorgn of WD, G–4 020, Vol. I.

[11] See OPD Hist Unit Study U, "Maddocks Committee Report on Revision of the Current Military Program," for discussion of this report, extremely important in the history of the mobilization of the Army. The committee members were Col. R. T. Maddocks of S&P, Col. E. W. Chamberlain of G–3, and Lt. Col. M. S. Carter of the Logistics Group. Cf. R. R. Palmer, "Mobilization of the Ground Army," in *The Organization of Ground Combat Troops*, p. 226.

[12] Rpt circulated as Tab D with memo, Col O. L. Nelson, Jr., [for DCofS], 6 Jul 43, sub: Info Supplementing Directives Implementing Revision of Cur Mil Program, OPD 320.2, 891.

[13] The chief of the Logistics Group promptly pointed out the potentialities of his staff for the task at hand. See memo, Brig Gen P. H. Tansey for Maj Gen Handy, 15 Jul 43, sub: OPD Secs for Coordination of Pers, Tr and Materiel Matters, OPD 320 WD, 7.

[14] Memo, Col O. L. Nelson, Jr., 1 Jul 43, sub: Mvmts to Theaters, OPD 370.5, 551. General McNarney instructed G–1, G–3, G–4, and OPD to submit a joint report by 1 August.

It was precisely in regard to transportation and supply that the Army Service Forces, lacking systematic supervision by the General Staff, was in most cases the final authority. It was the extraordinary influence it exercised in these fields that had led General Somervell to argue that G–1 and G–4 were useless staff agencies. Any remedy of this situation that augmented General Staff control of the movement of troops and matériel overseas would destroy the possibility of the virtually autonomous logistic command then still being urged upon the Chief of Staff by General Somervell.

The General Staff committee appointed to study this problem, without even considering an alternative, recommended strengthening General Staff machinery for controlling the flow of troops and matériel to the theaters. Colonel Maddocks, OPD member of the committee, drafted the initial committee report, circulated for adoption by all four General Staff Divisions represented. It stated that it was necessary, in view of dwindling American resources in manpower and material, to abandon the current system whereby the General Staff exercised only very loose control over the flow of military resources to the theaters. The report pointed out that a great deal of the previous difficulty lay in the way OPD worked. The individual theater sections, representing their respective theater commanders, made a strenuous effort toward "supplying theaters with individuals, units, and material" as requested by the theater commanders without much systematic study of the effect this had on the logistic problems of the zone of interior. Colonel Maddocks proposed that OPD "establish an agency to review and correlate operational and supply plans, including troop bases, submitted by the several theater

commanders, and, by coordination with the Personnel, Organization and Training, and Supply Divisions, War Department General Staff, to balance the operational demands of these plans with each other and with those of the war as a whole." [15]

This proposal offered a solution to the problem of logistic-operational balance by placing the responsibility squarely on the General Staff and setting up a special agency in OPD to discharge it. It offered no solace to Headquarters, Army Service Forces, whose interests would be challenged just as much or more by an OPD thus strengthened as by a reinvigorated G–1 and G–4. Unlike the earlier recommendation of the Special Army Committee, it was a practical way to strengthen General Staff performance of logistic staff functions as an alternative to relinquishing them to the Army Service Forces. It did not require a complete reorientation of G–1 and G–4 but instead merely a grant of authority and a minor reorganization inside OPD.

The Issue of Staff Authority

The ensuing staff discussion of Colonel Maddocks' proposal for a new agency in OPD to integrate operational and supply planning, centered first and foremost around what its relations with G–1, G–3, G–4, and (by implication) the Army Services Forces, would be like. No other issue could be resolved until there had been a definite ruling on the issue of authority.

[15] Rpt, n.d., no title, attchd to memo, Col Maddocks for ACofS OPD, 11 Jul 43, sub: Mvmts to Ts, OPD, 370.5, 551. This draft report might well be called the second Maddocks report of mid-1943, the first being the June report on the troop program. Since there was still a third in August, on internal OPD organization, the terms "Maddocks Report" and "Maddocks Committee" have been avoided in this case for the sake of clarity in reference.

Comments by Theater Group officers on the draft report mentioned specifically that it ought to state clearly that OPD would have superior authority in working with the rest of the General Staff and with the other logistic agencies of the War Department. As the Pacific Theater Section chief put it: "This reorganization is believed to be completely sound and workable, provided Operations Division is fully authorized *to direct* and control all action by the supply and service agencies to the extent such is necessary." [16]

As a result of divergent comments on Colonel Maddocks' draft, the General Staff committee submitted two versions of its report to the Deputy Chief of Staff. One, approved by OPD and G–4, followed the initial draft fairly closely but plainly subordinated the activities of the other General Staff Divisions to the work of OPD on controlling the flow of troops and matériel to the theaters. It provided:

> The Operations Division, War Department General Staff, acting with the assistance and advice of the Personnel, Organization and Training, and Supply Divisions, War Department General Staff, will review and correlate the operational and administrative plans, including troop bases, submitted by the several theater commanders, and will balance the operational demands of these plans within themselves, with each other, with those of the war as a whole and with the means available.
>
> The Operations Division, War Department General Staff, will take the necessary action to implement approved operational and administrative plans, including troop bases, of the several theater commanders.

An alternate version of this part of the report, approved by G–1 and G–3, equally acceptable with the other draft to G–4, but not acceptable to OPD, inserted the provision: "Prior to final approval of the administrative and operational plans, the Personnel, Organization and Training, Supply, and Operations Divisions of the War Department General Staff, acting jointly, will determine that the total means proposed for the several theaters are not in excess of the means that are available or can be made available." [17]

Commenting on these alternate versions, General Handy objected strongly to the provision for concurrent action by all General Staff Divisions:

> It provides for a return to the old system of concurrence between the several War Department General Staff divisions, which necessitated the present War Department General Staff Organization. The Operations Division, subject to the direction of the Chief of Staff, must be held responsible for balancing the operational demands of the several theaters with the means available, and for the approval or disapproval of requests of the theater commanders concerned. It is the only General Staff division which is fully cognizant of all the factors affecting the employment of U. S. Forces. The Operations Division should not be required to obtain concurrences from other General Staff divisions since such a procedure would seriously slow down the war effort. At the same time, however, the Operations Division should utilize the advice and assistance of the other General Staff divisions in solving these problems. [18]

Within a few days, on 5 August 1943, General McNarney resolved the controversy insofar as it related to the distribution of staff authority in logistic matters, categorically indorsing General Handy's point of view:

---

[16] (1) Memo, Col. C. D. Silverthorne for Chief Theater Gp, 14 Jul 43, OPD 370.5, 551. (2) Cf. memo, Brig Gen Hull for Exec OPD, 15 Jul 43, sub: Mvmts to Ts, OPD 370.5, 551.

[17] Alternate versions of p. 4 of rpt submitted with memo, OPD for DCofS, 31 Jul 43, sub: Mvmt to Ts, OPD 370.5, 551.

[18] Memo, OPD for DCofS, 31 Jul 43, sub: Mvmt to Ts, OPD 370.5, 551.

The Operations Division, War Department General Staff will scrutinize the requirements of the several theaters, will balance the requirements against the means available, and will determine the priority and time when they are to be made available. The Operations Division will then inform the theater commander and the Assistant Chiefs of Staff, G–1, G–3, and G–4 what units, individuals and material are to be furnished and when they will be made available.

Each theater commander will be furnished with that portion of his estimated requirements which the Operations Division has determined necessary and consistent with over-all requirements balanced against available means. Priorities will be established in accordance with approved directives. Where units are requested which are not included in the Troop Basis, the Operations Division, War Department General Staff will determine the necessity therefor.

The Operations Division, War Department General Staff has primary interest in all matters involving overseas operations. Where these problems involve functions and policies which are primarily the responsibility of other War Department General Staff Divisions, the Operations Division will consult with the War Department General Staff division having primary interest. The Assistant Chief of Staffs, G–1, G–3, and G–4 will designate a section officer, or officers, through whom coordination may be effected. Formal concurrences will be eliminated whenever possible.[19]

By definitely assigning staff authority to OPD, General McNarney settled the central issue of OPD's position vis-à-vis the rest of the General Staff and, since the General Staff's authority over the three major zone of interior commands was left unaltered, vis-à-vis the Army Service Forces. The principle General McNarney was affirming was that the strategic and operational interests

of the Army, as determined within OPD on behalf of the Chief of Staff, took precedence in case of conflict with other matters normally of primary interest to the other divisions of the General Staff. Correlation of logistic policy with strategic policy inside the War Department was to be a function of the General Staff, mainly a function of OPD. The fact that deliberations on strategy or operational policy might critically affect logistic programs, which ordinarily were within the province of the other General Staff Divisions or of the three zone of interior commands, did not limit the right of OPD to take staff action looking toward a solution of the problem at hand. In these cases OPD proceeded either to reach a decision or to recommend one to the Chief of Staff. The basis of such staff action was a general evaluation of the logistic situation, viewed in conjunction with a detailed appreciation of strategic operational requirements in the theaters. Thus Logistics Group officers joined with S&P and Theater Group officers to give balanced study to the most difficult kind of issues that came before the chief of the division and the Chief of Staff. Like General Marshall, OPD officers continued throughout the war to pay a great deal of attention not only to logistic information from General Somervell and his headquarters, but also to Army Service Forces recommendations and policies.[20] Nevertheless it was clear henceforth in the Army that

---

[19] Memo, DCofS for G–1, G–3, G–4, and OPD, 5 Aug 43, sub: Mvmts to Ts, OPD 370.5, 551. The copy signed by General McNarney is erroneously stamped "not used" but bears notation by Colonel Gailey: "This was used. C.K.G."

[20] For one example of OPD's healthy respect for Service Forces influence, see memo, CKG for Brig Gen Hull, 3 Dec 43, no sub, Paper 6, Book 14, Exec 9. Colonel Gailey observed: "If the conference [on Victory Program Troop Basis] decides against the Army Service Forces, they are going to take it up with General McNarney anyhow. Therefore I recommend seeing General McNarney first and getting his definite ideas prior to holding the conference. We can then . . . know just how far to go with the appeasement."

the strategists in OPD, not the logisticians outside it, would control staff action whenever logistics and strategy were both involved in a military problem affecting overseas operations.

The Issue of Staff Organization in OPD

Although it settled the debate over authority for the rest of World War II, General McNarney's 5 August ruling left open the whole question of staff machinery appropriate to carry out the staff responsibility which it unequivocally placed on OPD. The Division had already been studying the administrative problem of internal staff organization while participating in the rest of the debate over the place of logistics in the War Department.[21] General Hull, as chief of the Theater Group, had recommended that a Troop Section be established within Theater Group and that this section be charged with the control and coordination of all troop matters over which the Operations Division has responsibility, and that this Troop Section be formed by augmenting the present Troop Movements Section of the Theater Group, with personnel from the present Troop Section, Logistics Group, and such additional personnel as may be necessary from other sections of the Theater Group.[22]

With regard to the related matter of supply, General Hull expressed a willingness to let the Logistics Group act as OPD's coordinating agency.

This device would preserve OPD's orientation to the theaters, characterized by decentralization of the Chief of Staff's powers to staff officers in the individual theater sections. These officers had detailed knowledge of the area concerned, and their decisions were checked only by the Theater Group chief and his deputies for conformity with world-wide operational policy, by reference to S&P, or, in the last analysis, to the Assistant Chief of Staff, OPD, for conformity to grand strategy. What General Hull was proposing in fact was that the Theater Group check its own tendency to too much decentralization by strengthening the Troop Movements Section and giving it the job of co-ordinating the deployment of troops as suggested by the individual theater sections. Thus the Theater Group would retain the function that had always been the core of its work, namely, troop deployment to the theaters of operations. Provided this function was left intact, General Hull was willing to refer the closely connected problems of supply and equipment, insofar as they required co-ordination outside a single theater section, to supply specialists in another part of OPD, namely the Logistics Group.

A week after General McNarney's 5 August ruling, General Handy and Colonel Gailey worked out a solution on the issue of staff organization in OPD.[23] It was only an interim solution since the whole logistic problem was reconsidered within two months. Nevertheless, most of the features of internal reorganization and reassignment of duties in OPD as chartered in this compromise became firmly fixed elements of the Division's logistic control machinery. Its

[21] (1) Memo, OPD for Col H. I. Hodes, etc., 17 Jun 43, no sub, OPD 320 WD, 7. (2) Memo, Col H. I. Hodes, etc., for ACofS OPD, 1 Jul 43, sub: OPD Secs for Coordination of Pers Tr and Materiel Matters, envelope with OPD 320 WD, 7. Note inclosures, including chart of proposed reorganizations.
[22] Memo, Brig Gen Hull for ACofS OPD, 19 Jul 43, no sub, OPD 320 WD, 7.

[23] Note, CKG for Brig Gen Hull, n.d., atchd to draft memo, Col Gailey for Chiefs, Theater, Logistics, and S&P Gps, 11 Aug 43, sub: OPD Coordination of Pers, Tr and Materiel Matters, OPD 320 WD, 7.

effect was to establish an expanded Troop Movements Section in the Theater Group as General Hull had suggested. Under the direction and with the authority of the chief of the Theater Group, it would co-ordinate all troop movements to conform with its own determination of theater-wide requirements. The only function that General Hull had wanted for the Theater Group which was assigned to the Logistics Group was the task of maintaining information concerning the availability of troops.[24]

Nevertheless, the Logistics Group retained its previous duties and in fact gained authority. It was explicitly assigned responsibility for furnishing information on the availability of troops "as directed by the Theater Group," thus keeping a hand in the development of the troop program in general though not in the specific task of deploying troop units. In addition, the Logistics Group was responsible for estimating "future planning" in regard to "individuals, units and material," the task stressed by S&P as essential to strategic planning. It was solely responsible for all OPD action connected with the War Department (G–3) Troop Basis, the Overseas Troop Basis (for the use of supply agencies), and the Victory Program Troop Basis (for the use of procurement agencies). Finally, the Logistics Group was assigned the duty of co-ordinating "within Operations Division" all matters of supply handled by the individual theater sections. These duties, along with the Logistics Group's accustomed tasks of monitoring general supply problems, especially as they affected theaters of operations, and rendering logistic planning assistance

to S&P and to joint and combined agencies, gave the Logistics Group broad responsibilities. At the same time the Theater Group in its own right kept the powers it needed to co-ordinate troop movements.[25]

Final changes in assignment of tasks in OPD were initiated at once after the interim agreement of 12 August. They were not completed until after one more careful re-examination by OPD of the whole logistic problem, including both the matters of organization inside the Division and the proper distribution of duties between OPD and the rest of the General Staff. At the request of General Hull, Acting Assistant Chief of Staff at the time, Colonel Maddocks prepared for General Handy a new study on the "duties now being performed by the Operations Division which might be assigned to other General Staff Divisions." In drawing up this report, Colonel Maddocks worked independently and not, as in June and July, as a member of a committee.

The point of departure for Colonel Maddocks' inquiry into the subject assigned him was a distinction between the two major functions of the War Department General Staff. He stated them as follows:

The War Department General Staff is performing two general functions, as follows:
(1) Mobilization, organization, training, equipping, and supplying the Army.
(2) Formulation of plans for employment of the Army, the allocation and movement of available individuals, units and materiel to the several theaters of operations and the strategic reserve based upon approved plans and the shipping situation, and the direction of the field forces in the various theaters of operations.[26]

---

[24] (1) Memo, OPD for Chiefs, Theater, Logistics, and S&P Gps, 12 Aug 43, sub: OPD Coordination . . ., OPD 320 WD, 7. (2) Draft memo atchd to memo, Brig Gen Hull for ACofS OPD, 19 Jul 43, no sub, OPD 320 WD, 7.

[25] Memo, OPD for Chiefs, Theater, Logistics, and S&P Gps, 12 Aug 43, sub: OPD Coordination . . ., OPD 320 WD, 7.
[26] Rpt, n.d., no title, atchd to memo, Col Maddocks for ACofS OPD, 31 Aug 43, sub: Duties of WDGS Divs, Paper 120, Book 11, Exec 9.

In general, Colonel Maddocks argued, it was sound to "charge the G1, G–3, and G–4 Divisions with the function of providing the means for conducting the war and the Operations Division with the function of directing the employment of the means provided." Since the "two functions are so closely interrelated that they can not be sharply separated," Colonel Maddocks considered it necessary for OPD to "perform every duty which is essential for the efficient discharge" of its responsibility for the "direction of field operations of the Army." Conversely, any duty OPD was performing which was "not essential to its work should be accomplished by the other General Staff Divisions."

This principle of transferring all work concerning "mobilization, organization, training, equipping, and supply of the Army" to G–1, G–3, and G–4 whenever it did not vitally affect OPD's discharge of its basic responsibility for operations, echoed a long-standing practice in OPD. It helped explain General Handy's negative reply to General Somervell's April 1943 proposal for the absorption of G–3. To some extent it vindicated OPD from charges that it was trying to make itself a complete General Staff. As Colonel Maddocks understood it, this self-denying principle rested on the following reasoning:

> The Operations Division should discharge its responsibility by acting with the assistance and advice of the other General Staff Divisions in their respective fields. It is only by so doing that the Operations Division will be able to function efficiently unless it establishes agencies to perform the duties normally accomplished by G–1, G–3, and G–4 Divisions. Two general staffs would either have considerable overlap and duplication or one staff would overpower and swallow the other.

In borderline cases, where OPD was either overlapping the activities of other General Staff Divisions or threatening to absorb them entirely, Colonel Maddocks proposed the following criterion:

> The Operations Division should perform all duties, under the supervision of the Chief of Staff, which are essential for the direction of the field operations of the Army and it should contain such agencies and assemble such data as is needed for the efficient discharge of this responsibility.

> The other General Staff Divisions should perform all other General Staff duties, under the supervision of the Chief of Staff, that are not essential to the Operations Division.

So far, Colonel Maddocks' study proceeded in complete conformity with General McNarney's 5 August ruling on staff authority. In fact it was the classic wartime statement by an OPD officer on the authority of General Marshall's operations staff.

The administrative question, however, still had to be answered. Did OPD, in order to discharge its staff responsibilities, need a special logistic control agency primarily concerned with the general coordination of G–1, G–3, and G–4 activities? Colonel Maddocks personally considered that OPD did not need such an agency except insofar as the Theater Group already controlled troops and matériel. In support of his contention, he submitted an analysis of the thirty-six duties assigned to the Theater Group and the Logistics Group by the 12 August memorandum.[27] From it he concluded that "every duty now assigned to the Logistics Group can be performed logically by remaining groups of the Operations Division and the other General Staff Divisions." To summarize his analysis supporting this conclusion, Colonel Maddocks listed the duties of Logistics Group in six "general categories":

---

[27] Colonel Maddocks listed these duties as thirty-four instead of thirty-six by combining three duties as one.

(1) *Future planning.*—This is logically a function of the Strategy and Policy Group to which logistic planners might be added, if desired.

(2) *Troop Basis.*—All matters with respect to the troop basis of theaters are logically the responsibility of the Theater Group, in which the assistance and advice of the other General Staff Divisions would be utilized, as necessary, and all matters with respect to the troop basis under development in the United States are logically the responsibility of the G–3 Division. The troop basis under development is based upon the needs of the Operations Division.

(3) *Materiel.*—All matters with respect to materiel in theaters are logically the responsibility of the Theater Group in which the assistance and advice of the G–4 Division would be utilized, as necessary, and all matters with respect to materiel being produced in the United States are logically the responsibility of the G–4 Division. The materiel being produced is based upon the needs of the Operations Division.

(4) *Availability of individuals, units and material.*—The G–3 Division is responsible for the organization and training of individuals and units in the United States, and should be required to keep the Operations Division informed on the status of training of such individuals and units, and the availability of individuals and units for operations. Likewise the G–4 Division is responsible for the supply of the Army and should be required to keep the Operations Division informed on the availability of equipment, supplies and materiel in the United States. The Operations Division should obtain required reports from the G–3 and G–4 Divisions, and should assemble such data therefrom as it needs for efficient performance of its work.

(5) *Victory Program.*—The G–4 Division, based upon the approved plans and operational demands of the Operations Division, is the logical agency to prepare and keep up to date the Victory Program.

(6) *War Department Representative on the Munitions Assignment Committee and other Committees.*—Since most of these committees deal with supply or matters related thereto, G–4 is the logical officer to represent

the War Department. The needs and desires of the Operations Division, however, should be obtained in all matters affecting that division.[28]

This proposal to eliminate the Logistics Group was not easy to refute logically, but it presented grave administrative difficulties as of mid-1943. In the first place, most of the officers in S&P and the Theater Group, including General Hull, had always recognized in practice as well as principle that logistics (particularly supply) was a specialized field in which neither planners nor operations control officers were necessarily expert. Thus the practice has developed of letting the Logistics Group do the work on future planning, so far as logistic factors were concerned. General Hull had accepted the idea of referring intertheater operational problems involving matériel to the Logistics Group for Army-wide co-ordination while insisting that actions concerning troop deployment be referred to his new Troop Movements Section for Army-wide co-ordination. While Colonel Maddocks was correct in saying that both S&P and the Theater Group should perform the logistic or matériel aspect of their work, in practice both had left that aspect to the Logistics Group. To assume the duties connected with the logistic side of planning and operations control, both the Theater Group and S&P would have to attach their own specialist logistics officers and reorganize their work

---

[28] Rpt, n.d., no title, atchd to memo, Col Maddocks for ACofS OPD, 31 Aug 43, sub: Duties of WDGS Divs, Paper 120, Book 11, Exec 9. Annex A is a large table showing the "duties of Theater and Logistics Groups insofar as individuals, units, and materiel are concerned and proposed reassignment of these duties to the Operations and the other General Staff Divisions." The terminology follows that in the 12 August 1943 memorandum cited in note 24. Logistics Group duties are well summarized in the memorandum as quoted above.

to fit in with that of the other officers in each group.

In the second place, Colonel Maddocks' proposal raised the question of how OPD would secure its logistic information as promptly as necessary and with reasonable assurance of its reliability. Colonel Maddocks only hinted at one mechanical aspect of this problem when he pointed out that the other General Staff Divisions would have to start working on a 24-hour day, like OPD, so that "information vitally needed by the Operations Division" could be promptly obtained at all times. This difficulty so far had been avoided by having in OPD one officer, with his own group of assistants, responsible to the Division chief for meeting any and all of OPD's needs for logistic staff information or advice.

For both these reasons, the officers responsible for the main bulk of work in OPD were reluctant to make the readjustments necessary to carry on without the Logistics Group. Colonel Gailey summarized for General Handy the views of General Hull, Colonel Roberts (by then acting chief of S&P), and General Tansey, to all of whom Colonel Maddocks' August report had been referred for comment.[29] General Hull reported that he was "in general agreement" with the Maddocks report, but that the Theater Group would require additional personnel for "liaison on materiel matters," strengthening his Troop Movements Section by the "transfer of officers from the Logistics Group." General Tansey strongly advised against any dismemberment of the Logistics

Group, recommending, if Colonel Maddocks' suggestions were to be followed, that the "bulk of his Group be transferred to G–4 and that G–4 be directed to perform aggressively the duties" reserved for it in General Staff regulations. Colonel Roberts reiterated the point of view of S&P, which was that the "Logistics Group should be retained as an agency of Operations Division" in order that it could represent OPD on "Joint and Combined Committees or agencies concerned with personnel, supply, assignment of munitions or other administrative matters" and be "made responsible for interpreting approved future plans and translating them into terms of supply requirements."

After analyzing the original report and these comments, Colonel Gailey recommended against the reassignment of Logistics Group functions. His decision rested on the need of OPD to have a unit specializing in information on logistics in its broadest aspects, that is, information on all zone of interior resources:

The Operations Division must be prepared at all times to have sufficient data on hand in order that it may advise the Chief of Staff on strategical and operational questions, with the least practicable delay. Quite naturally it can do this more effectively and efficiently if it has in its own organization a group that can furnish this information on moment's notice and be reasonably sure that the information is correct. If some of the functions of this group are reassigned to other divisions of the General Staff, the Chief of the Operations Division must be able to get from them such information as he desires, when he desires it and in what form he desires it. I am afraid this will be hard to attain. . . . Even before the reorganization the old War Plans Division recognized the necessity for some sort of Group that would keep information up to the minute and in the form desired. After the reorganization, this need was more acute and the Logis-

---

[29] For reference to Colonel Maddocks' study to group chiefs for comments, see memo, Brig Gen Hull for Chiefs, Logistics, S&P, and Theater Gps, 5 Sep 43, sub: Study on Possible Reasgmt of Functions, OPD 320 WD, 13.

tics Group was expanded to its present organization.[30]

General Handy indorsed this point of view, neatly phrasing it as the gist of his comments to General McNarney:

I discussed the proposed transfer of Logistics Group or a part thereof, to G–4 with General McNarney this morning. I indicated my views briefly as follows:
a. That the functions of this Group could be transferred to G–3, G–4 and to other Groups in Operations Division but that, in my opinion this would slow down our work.
b. That the Chief of Staff could not be reorganized, and we would be in a hell of a fix if we continued to get a great many of the papers and matters to act on that come to us.
c. That the question actually was much larger than a transfer of the Logistics Group. That to really build up G–4 would require a reassignment of functions and some changes as far as the Army Service Forces were concerned. I also pointed out to General McNarney that if we got satisfactory results out of G–4, they would have to change their entire tempo of doing business.[31]

The point about the difficulty of "reorganizing" the Chief of Staff was compelling. If General Marshall chose to use the staff of his command post in such a way as to require its chief to have logistics staff officers, General Handy had to make the necessary administrative arrangements to perform the services required of him. By the very logic set forth so clearly by Colonel Maddocks, whereby OPD had to do whatever work it found necessary to discharge its general responsibility for operations, OPD needed logisticians. As long as the Logistics Group met General Handy's requirements, there was little advantage and some disadvantage in redistributing the work in the Division.

After a preliminary discussion with General Hull, General Tansey, Colonel Roberts, Colonel Maddocks, and Colonel Gailey, General McNarney held a conference on 14 October and issued his instructions with reference to the questions raised in Colonel Maddocks' study. Though he issued no "formal directive," General McNarney indicated that his decisions were "final." [32] His ruling was fairly close to OPD's interim solution of 12 August, but it made some reduction of Logistics Group duties. Duties in the field of troop basis planning and procurement and supply scheduling, fields which by this time were no longer first priority problems either in strategic planning or operational control, were removed from Logistics Group and transferred to G–3 and G–4. Otherwise the duties of the Logistics Group, and in all respects the OPD group organization, remained precisely as agreed in August.

Of the long list of twenty-five responsibilities given the Logistics Group in Colonel Gailey's 12 August 1943 memorandum, General McNarney left all but eight. The elimination of these eight in effect took the Logistics Group out of the planning of munitions production and munitions assignment, both in the Army and in joint and combined committees, and made clear that its interest in troop basis calculations did not imply a "primary interest" in the War Department Troop Basis or in the determination of training requirements, both of which were duties belonging to G–3. Responsibility for the Victory Program estimates for the computation of the Army procurement

<hr>

[30] Memo, Col Gailey for Maj Gen Handy, 26 Sep 43, sub: Study on Possible . . . , Paper 95, Book 12, Exec 9.

[31] Memo, Maj Gen Handy for Brig Gen Hull, etc., 3 Oct 43, no sub, OPD 320 WD, 13.

[32] Memo, Col Gailey for Chiefs, Theater, Logistics, and S&P Gps, 29 Oct 43, sub: Decisions Reached at Conf, Gen McNarney's Office, 14 Oct 43, etc., OPD 320 WD, 14.

and supply program was turned over to G–4, as well as that of representing the War Department on all joint and combined boards and committees dealing with munitions assignments, production and resources, and communications. Although this transfer of duties did not go so far toward strengthening G–4 as had been suggested from time to time during the debate over logistic planning, it marked the beginning of a gradual rise in the volume of staff business done by G–4.

After General McNarney's October ruling, the Logistics Group still had a broad roster of duties, all of which fell into two main categories.[33] Henceforth it did all kinds of logistic planning for the benefit of S&P, particularly on the joint and combined levels. Consequently General Tansey sat on the JLC and provided representatives for the JLPC, although he no longer did any work on the munitions assignments committees. By reviewing the work of the individual theater sections, the Logistics Group continued, in addition, its Army-wide co-ordination of operational activities related to matériel. In other words, the Logistics Group was responsible for G–4 kinds of work in OPD, both in the form of planning and in the form of operational control. It was the agent or adviser of S&P and the Theater Group for logistic matters. Through the specialized knowledge thus available, OPD was able to make educated guesses about the semistrategic, semilogistic issues that constantly required a decision by the Chief of Staff or by someone in his command post staff. As General Handy observed in 1944, in discussing an OPD ruling

on the procurement of a special kind of radio set:

Almost all planning, procurement, and even operating agencies must have some assumptions or bases to work on. We have "stuck our necks out" continually in arriving at and giving out such assumptions or bases. Many of these will certainly, and all of them may, prove to be wrong. Some agency, however, must try to give answers and we happen to be in the position where we can't pass these questions on, much as we would like to do so.[34]

The final resolution of the long 1943 debate on War Department General Staff logistic planning and control of the movement of troops and materiel to the theaters permitted the Logistics Group and the Troop Movements Section of the Theater Group to adjust their organization and assignment of duties to conform to the final ruling. The change was not a radical one for the Logistics Group, merely simplifying its structure and clarifying the categories into which its work fell. The Troop Movements Section, on the other hand, rapidly expanded in size and continued for some time to increase the scope of its responsibilities as the Theater Group agency for co-ordination of the world-wide deployment of Army troops. Both the logistics and troop movement specialists in OPD were able to proceed throughout the rest of the period of hostilities with the orderly development of their activities in conformity with the general understanding achieved at the end of the August–October discussions.

Logistics and Troop Movements (October 1943–September 1945)

In its status as OPD's agency for logistic planning (Army, joint, and combined) and

---

[33] Memo for rcd, CKG, 16 Oct 43, sub: Decisions Reached at Conf, Gen McNarney's Office, 14 Oct 43, Reference Annex A to Col Maddocks' Study on Reasgmt of Duties of Logistics Gp of OPD to OPD and other GS Divs, OPD 320 WD, 14.

[34] Memo, OPD for Lt Gen McNair, 4 Apr 44, sub: Development and Procurement of New Radar, Paper 514, Book 17, Exec 9.

for operational control of supply on an Army-wide basis, the Logistics Group performed a host of interrelated tasks. Many of them were concurrences on behalf of OPD, such as clearing actions of G–4 or other agencies for conformity to strategy and operational control policy, or committee work, in which the Logistics Group represented the special OPD point of view in joint and combined deliberations even on logistic matters so indirectly related to Army plans and operations as allocation of oil and food resources among the United Nations.

In January 1944 General Tansey formally reassigned duties in the group to mirror its duties after the October ruling. Henceforth throughout the war the Logistics Group was divided organizationally into an Operational (Theater Group type) Section and a Projected (Planning or S&P type) Section.[35]

The primary job of the Operational Logistics Section was the allocation of critical items of equipment among the several theaters. The Projected Logistics Section was the future planning part of the Logistics Group. It studied and made recommendations on joint and combined logistic issues and, in the Army, screened and passed on the allotment of equipment and supplies to future operational projects submitted by theater commanders for War Department approval.[36] It supported the work of its chief and the group chief in joint and combined logistic deliberations. Also it continued informally to advise and assist other War Department agencies on all kinds of logistic matters, since the knowledge of its officers with regard to operational requirements and future plans was invaluable.[37] Logistics Group duties were greater in volume after its divestment of some of its responsibility in October 1943 than before, since the group still had to advise or act for OPD on the multitude of logistic issues referred to the Division for concurrence and since the rapid development of joint logistic planning brought a flood of new work.[38]

Like the Theater Group, the Logistics Group carried on much of its work in 1944 and 1945 merely by monitoring and taking staff responsibility for being certain of the fact of accomplishment of essential duties by the Army Service Forces or the Army Air Forces, the latter of which handled its own services. For instance an "operational projects" system was set up in the War Department to secure approval for supply and equipment to carry out enterprises planned by theater commanders. The Logistics Group kept a file with a card for each project "showing action taken and date dispatched from OPD." At set intervals Logistics Group officers reviewed the file to determine whether or not the Army Service Forces or the Army Air Forces had taken appropriate action and had notified the appropriate theater.[39] If not, of course, OPD turned its attention to the project again as if it were a matter of current business.

In April 1944 the Logistics Group was assigned the special task of acting for OPD in the "assembly and coordination of information pertaining to the future strategic deployment of the Army of the United States."[40] The group was well equipped to

[35] Memo, Col E. C. Bomar [Exec Logistics Gp] for Exec OPD, 17 Jan 44, sub: Reorgn—Logistics Gp, OPD 321.19 OPD, 34.

[36] WD Cir 220, par. 13, 20 Sep 43, sub: Supply of O'seas Comds.

[37] Memo, Col V. J. Esposito for author, 2 Jan 47, sub: Comments on Draft Manuscript "The Way OPD Worked," OPD Hist Unit Comments file.

[38] WDGS Cir 5–5, 12 Jun 45.

[39] Memo, Brig Gen Tansey for Maj Gen Hull, 1 Jun 44, sub: Follow-Up on Projects, Item 2B, OPD Hist Unit file.

[40] WD Cir 134, 8 Apr 44.

discharge this responsibility, which included supplying information for deployment studies conducted by joint planning agencies, since it had been furnishing the same information to the other groups in OPD for about two years. Specifically designed to convey deployment information were two monthly tables, which the Logistics Group had issued since June 1943. One of them showed systematically the current deployment of all Allied ground combat divisions, and the other showed the status of U. S. Army divisions with respect to training, date of deployment overseas, operational experience, casualties, and current locations.[41] The Logistics Group prepared these publications throughout the period of hostilities and represented OPD in strategic deployment planning until March 1945 when the duty passed to the Theater Group.[42]

Elimination of the apparent overlapping of Logistics, G–4, and Army Service Forces functions, demanded in the 1943 controversy, was discussed again toward the end of hostilities. OPD's position, based on its pragmatic concern with its immediate objective of carrying out its wartime responsibilities to the Chief of Staff, was clearly and finally stated by General Hull in May 1945:

Primarily because of the magnitude and tempo of the war, new logistic agencies have arisen and old ones developed considerably to meet the demands for speedy action. Within

OPD itself I find it necessary to maintain a small logistics group to assist in the rapid conduct of work and to render prompt service to the Chief of Staff and Deputy Chief of Staff. Any material disturbance or realignment of logistic agencies within the War Department now or during the period of active operations would, in my opinion, affect adversely the expeditious prosecution of the war.[43]

One result of the interim solution of the August–October debate in OPD was the assignment of new duties to the Troop Movements Section, and a corollary was the rapid expansion of its staff. After August 1943, instead of merely checking and coordinating all troop movement orders for technical correctness, Troop Movements began to advise the Theater Group as a whole on the availability of troops and to pass approval on their allocation to the theaters by the individual theater sections. Its functions were described as follows:

(1) To perform the operational duties of G–1 and G–3 for the Theater Group insofar as is practicable.

(2) To relieve Theater Sections of the necessity for searching for means to fill their requirements.

(3) To determine for the Theater Group Chief the justification for all requirements and approve or disapprove all requirements.

Its orientation with regard to theater sections was explicitly set forth:

The Troop Movement Section will actually operate in all matters relating to contacts with the three major commands and with other interested agencies of the W. D. concerning overseas troop requirements and allocations insofar as available means are concerned. . . .

The Troop Movement Section will normally *not* deal direct with theater command-

---

[41] (1) OPD Book, 15 Jun 43–31 Aug 45, title: Deployment of Allied Divs, separate envelope with OPD 320.2 TS 15/18. (2) OPD Book, Jun 43–15 Nov 45, title: Estimated Status of Divs, separate envelope with OPD 320.2 TS, 15/18, This book contains a chart showing "genealogy" of U. S. Army divisions.

[42] (1) Memo, OPD for Gp Chiefs, 17 Jun 44, sub: Cir 134, Sec VII, 8 Apr 44, OPD 400, 313. (2) OPD adm memo, Col K. W. Treacy for Gp Chiefs, 24 Mar 45, sub: WD Cir 134, etc., OPD 400, 313.

[43] Summary Sheet, OPD for DCofS, 5 May 45, sub: Integration of Logistical Agencies, OPD 320 WD, 27. Colonel Esposito was the action officer in this case.

ers but will furnish theater *section chiefs* with appropriate information copies of all *actions*.

The Troop Movement Section (Requirements and Allocations Branch) will obtain through the Theater Sections' chiefs such information as is necessary to

(1) Issue movement directives.

(2) Determine priorities.

(3) Maintain Troop Basis, present and projected.

(4) Maintain *firm* commitments for the ensuing three months.

Theater Sections will normally have no reason to contact the three major commands or other W.D. agencies concerning troops.[44]

Thus for troop matters common to all the theater sections, the Troop Movements Section acted for the Theater Group, clearing all theater section actions on theater requirements for troop units and replacements before their submission to the Theater Group chief for approval.[45] In Troop Movements, OPD had its equivalent of G–3 for matters of theater-wide or Army-wide concern. The rest of the Theater Group still provided specialist staffs thoroughly acquainted with all problems of each theater and able to direct operations on a day-to-day basis, while Troop Movements after its expansion served to redress the balance of theater section decentralization.

This organization and assignment of duties in the Troop Movements Section lasted until the fall of 1944, when the section was renamed the Troop Control Section and augmented to act as a central War

Department agency for co-ordinating and controlling the redeployment of the Army upon the defeat of Germany. This problem, along with the interrelated problems of concurrent partial demobilization and eventual full demobilization, was the responsibility of the Special Planning Division of the War Department Special Staff set up for the purpose. Nevertheless, redeployment was a matter of vital concern to operations and therefore to OPD. General Handy recommended that "overall fundamental policies and procedures be adopted and announced, in order that War Department agencies, the three principal commands, and overseas commanders may act on a sound and common basis," and General McNarney, 11 September 1944, directed: "The Operations Division, War Department General Staff is charged with the responsibility of insuring coordination of all matters pertaining to redeployment." [46]

General Hull already had informed General Handy:

My view is that there should be a control section. The Operations Division must run this redeployment if it is to be done effectively. Therefore, the control section should be in the Operations Division. I feel that the responsibility should rest with the Theater Group, and do not feel that another group should be established for this purpose. A control section within, or closely connected with the Troop Movements Section of the Theater Group is the best solution.[47]

---

[44] Tr Mvmts Sec adm memo, 16 Aug 43, sub: Orgn, Functions and Procedures, Paper 79, Book 11, Exec 9.

[45] Memo, Exec OPD for Gp Chiefs, 28 Oct 43, sub: Procedure to be Followed in Activation of Units, Paper 59, Book 13, Exec 9. The actual directive was to be initiated and issued to the Army Air Forces, the Army Ground Forces, or the Army Service Forces by the "appropriate Theater Section."

[46] (1) Memo, OPD for CofS, 7 Sep 44, sub: Redeployment of U. S. Army Forces Upon Defeat of Germany, OPD 370.9, 44/1. The memo is stamped "Approved" by DCofS, 11 September 1944. Tab A of this memorandum is a statement of "Policies and Procedures Governing the Redeployment of the Army upon the Cessation of Hostilities in Europe," containing the assignment of full responsibility for redeployment "coordination" to OPD. (2) Cf. min of Gen Council meetings, App. D, 11 Sep 44.

[47] Memo, JEH [Maj Gen Hull] for Lt Gen Handy, 7 Sep 44, no sub, OPD 370.9, 44/1. Colonel Gailey penned the notation, "I concur."

General Handy instructed General Hull to set up any organization he considered necessary to assume for OPD the responsibility for "coordination of all matters concerning redeployment." [48] On the same day, General Handy informed General McNarney that a Troop Control Section was being set up in the Theater Group, "utilizing as a basis the present Troop Movements Section, to discharge OPD's responsibilities for redeployment." [49] The Troop Control Section was officially established 1 October 1944 with twenty-one officers including all of the Troop Movements Section personnel. [50]

Throughout the last two years of hostilities, the Troop (Movements) Control Section produced two valuable new documents in addition to carrying on its day-to-day work. In the first place, on the basis of its close collaboration with G–3 in preparing the War Department Troop Basis, it produced the OPD complement to it, the War Department Troop Deployment, the only War Department document showing in detail the planned future distribution of units and strength of the Army by theaters. It was produced quarterly during 1944 indicating deployment as of the dates used in the current War Department Troop Basis. Beginning with the 1 July 1944 publication, it indicated the planned deployment of the Army by quarter-year through 30 June 1945. Beginning in December 1944, after a special trial issue of 1 October 1944, it was published monthly. [51]

The second document issued by the Troop (Movements) Control Section was the Six Months List or Six Months Forecast. [52] Initially, during 1943, the individual theater sections compiled this document, which simply indicated the units earmarked for movement to each theater during each of the six months following publication. Published approximately monthly after the first issue, 12 January 1943, the Six Months Forecast assisted all War Department agencies, particularly the three major zone of interior commands, to meet commitments in forces and equipment by advance planning. When Troop Movements took over the Six Months Forecast in the fall of 1943 as part of its intertheater troop co-ordination job, the document became more reliable since its commitments to each theater were then made with close reference to one another and to total availability from the three major commands. It continued to be published through the 27th Revision, 6 May 1945. Thereupon it was replaced by putting into effect the Redeployment Forecast, de-

[48] Memo, Lt Gen Handy for Chief Theater Gp, 26 Sep 44, sub: Redeployment of U. S. Armed Forces, OPD 321.19 OPD, 58.

[49] Memo, OPD for DCofS, 26 Sep 44, sub: Redeployment of U. S. Army Forces, OPD 210.3, 357. This memorandum requested four additional commissioned officers for Troop Control, a request approved 27 September 1944.

[50] Theater Gp adm memo, 29 Sep 44, sub: Orgn or Tr Contl Sec, OPD 321.19 OPD, 58.

[51] The War Department Troop Deployment first appeared in February 1944, geared to the War Department Troop Basis for the calendar year 1944. See: (1) study, n.d., title: OPD–WDGS Deployment of Tr Basis with ltr, OPD, no addressee, 8 Feb 44, sub: OPD Deployment of 1944 Tr Basis, envelope with OPD 320.2 TS, 275; (2) cf. memo, Brig Gen C. A. Russell for Maj Gen Handy, 20 Feb 44, sub: OPD Deployment . . ., OPD 320.2 TS, 275; (3) see also other papers in OPD 320.2 TS, 275.

[52] A complete set of Six Months Lists and Forecasts from the original, 12 January 1943, through the 27th Revision, 6 May 1945, is filed in Current Group Files, AG Rcds Br. For first Six Months List, cf. memo, OPD for AGF, ASF, 12 Jan 43, sub: Orgn, Tng and Equip of Units for O'seas Serv, OPD 370.5 TS, 34.

veloped by the Troop Control Section pursuant to its being charged with co-ordinating redeployment.[53] The Redeployment Forecast was a detailed schedule for moving units, theater by theater, from the Atlantic to the Pacific. It was the master plan that was just going into operation when the Japanese surrender ended hostilities.

[53] A complete set of Redeployment Forecasts is filed in Current Group Files, AG Rcds Br. It consists of First Edition, Atlantic (20 February 1945) and Pacific (5 March 1945); Second Edition, Atlantic (15 May 1945) and Pacific (23 May 1945); and Third Edition, covering all areas (19 July 1945).

CHAPTER XV

Links With the Overseas Theaters

As the war moved into the period of maximum effort on the part of American forces, the Army command system stretched out from Washington to encompass theaters of operations in every part of the world. Most of the time during the later war years the Army system of tactical organization included at least a half-dozen major overseas headquarters reporting directly to the Chief of Staff. The overseas commanders and their staffs, faced with practical military problems on the spot, were called upon to play an ever greater part in planning and in advising the Chief of Staff and the JCS in the strategic direction of the war. The growth of the overseas theater headquarters in size and influence was one of the two main developments of the later war years that affected OPD's work, ranking in this respect with the expansion of the JCS-CCS committee system.

The growth of theater headquarters meant that there was an ever-increasing amount of military business to be conducted between Washington and overseas, and more and more it was necessary to reckon with political and economic consequences of military action. A great many Army organizations had to fit into the intricate combined (Allied) headquarters and theaters such as the North African (later the Mediterranean) Theater of Operations, the Supreme Headquarters, Allied Expeditionary Force (SHAEF), the Southwest Pacific Area Command (which reported to the U. S. JCS but was an Allied headquarters), and the Southeast Asia Command. Others had to participate in joint American theater headquarters staffs, in some of which, as in the Pacific Ocean Area, a Navy officer was in superior command.[1] Collaboration between OPD and each of these theaters necessarily went on within the framework of joint and combined staff deliberations, which were being conducted simultaneously and in which OPD officers were participating. In this situation, with military operations so widespread and the machinery for directing them so intricate, it was more important than ever that OPD keep in touch with actual conditions in the theaters of combat, where the war had to be won.

The military staffs in Washington, and particularly OPD, used every available means of establishing close working relations with their theater counterparts. Above all, they depended on the elaborate wartime system of signal communications, both radio and cable, including facilities for direct group discussion in overseas "conferences."[2] In addition they made extensive use of officer couriers, by whom they could send papers of the highest classification as well as personal letters commenting frankly on

---

[1] For major American commands and commanders during World War II, see App. B.

[2] For the initiation of the completely secure "radio telephone" overseas conference system, see AG ltr, 9 Jul 43, sub: Operating Procedure for O'seas Tel System, AG 676.1 (8 Jul 43) CB-S-F.

their problems. But even the most modern methods of communication could not take the place of personal visits and informal face-to-face talks. A meeting of the individual men who were planning and fighting created a bond of common experience with the problems encountered at each stage of waging war that went far toward insuring agreement on the business of military operations. Fortunately, with the development of a world-wide system of air transport, it was possible for staff officers to travel back and forth between Washington, London, and the various other headquarters with considerable frequency.

Officers from War Department agencies during their trips overseas (and theater officers while present in Washington) were able to take up many questions which were too debatable, too complicated, or too delicate to settle promptly and satisfactorily by means of formal correspondence. Personal association of officers from the War Department, particularly from OPD, with theater commanders and their staffs hastened the work of planning and the process of reaching decisions, and reduced the accumulation of erroneous impressions with regard to the what, why, and how of actions taken outside the immediate field of vision of any single command or staff.

The need for personal visits back and forth had been great from the beginning of hostilities because so few officers had had wartime service both in Washington and in the field. As operations became larger and more complex, the need made itself felt more and more. Agency chiefs in Washington tried to get officers for their staffs with overseas experience as they became available, and in exchange assigned their own officers overseas. This rotation of assignments, which in peacetime had been the principal means of bringing about a general correspondence between views in the field and in Washington, could not take effect rapidly enough to produce uniform results until late in the war. Commanders were reluctant to weaken their newly formed and still expanding staffs by releasing their most experienced officers. Yet the military situation was everywhere changing so fast that exchange of personnel was far more necessary than in peacetime.

It was some help to familiarize officers with current War Department views, plans, and procedures before they went overseas, as was done in OPD, for example, in the briefing of commanders and officers with special missions, and in the orientation of junior officers in a staff school conducted by OPD.[3] Effective liaison with the theaters, however, depended a great deal on personal association among officers with closely related jobs. All of OPD's general officers and a great many of its field-grade officers were sent overseas for short periods to teach and be taught, as well as to settle a wide variety of specific issues. The principal interest of OPD officers on such trips was the development of greater understanding and cooperation between the theaters and Washington, particularly in regard to strategic and tactical operations. They were not supposed to adopt the attitudes or perform the duties of War Department inspectors or investigators.

The Assistant Chief of Staff, OPD, and his group chiefs usually visited overseas theaters on their way to or from international or interservice conferences, partly to discuss conference agenda with the theater commanders and their staffs, and partly

---

[3] For the Task Force Officers School set up in Current Section, OPD, at General Marshall's request, see OPD Hist Unit Study V.

to get firsthand impressions of local situations. Occasionally they went on trips to talk over the myriad matters of concern to the Army—problems of internal organization, appointment of American officers to important posts, and deployment and employment of American forces. They also, of course, were very much interested in theater plans for future operations.

OPD junior officers very often took part in planning and carrying out operations in the theaters, "earning their way" while they gained invaluable experience to bring back to their work in Washington. They went in various capacities, singly or in groups, by themselves or accompanying senior officers. Sometimes they went as mere assistants or observers but more often either to serve on overseas staffs or to complete some particularly urgent piece of business. Even though theater commanders preferred to deal with senior officers who could commit themselves, rather than with subordinates who on their return could only report impressions and make recommendations, they acknowledged that visits by junior officers from the OPD sections did help to get things done and to avoid misunderstandings. The visits undoubtedly contributed to a better understanding in the theaters of the extent to which wartime Washington staff work, both in plans and in operations, depended upon the initiative and discretion of field-grade officers.

Even the junior officers sent on such missions had duties in OPD or in the joint planning system which gave them an exceptionally broad view of the war and required them to express their opinions freely and at length. Their visits were therefore useful not only for what they accomplished and what they gained in practical experience but also for the frank statement of

their views to overseas staffs and commanders, and their outspoken reporting of their impressions when they returned to Washington. OPD set a high value on such frankness in its junior members as a necessary condition of effective interservice and international planning, as well as a protection against the accumulation of erroneous impressions at higher levels. Given so much freedom to think and speak for themselves, OPD officers felt morally obliged to do so, even though they realized that they might sometimes cause trouble for themselves.

OPD had sent section officers into the field since the beginning of the war, but it was not until mid-1943 that the practice finally became systematized, mainly as a result of recognition of its value in North Africa.[4] On the basis of this experience, General Eisenhower informed the War Department in June 1943 that he could temporarily place fifteen or twenty majors or lieutenant colonels in key planning positions. He recommended that, if possible, a few officers be sent from the Theater Group.[5] On 20 June General Handy announced the inauguration of a continuing policy of exchange with all the theaters, whereby at all times at least one officer from each OPD theater section would be serving overseas.[6] Pursuant to this policy, the War Department sent overseas several groups of officers, including a considerable number from War Department agencies other than OPD, to get firsthand experience with battle conditions. The need for such trips ulti-

---

[4] Msg, Gen Eisenhower to OPD for Maj Gen Handy, 25 May 43, CM-IN 16329, Item 7, Exec 3.
[5] Msg, AFHQ (NATO) for WD, 3 Jul 43, CM-IN 1794 [TS], Action: OPD.
[6] (1) Memo, Maj Gen Handy for DCofS, 20 Jun 43, sub: Increase in Almt of Commissioned Pers, Item 3, Exec 15. (2) Msg, Gen Eisenhower for Gen Marshall, 24 Jun 43, CM-IN 15160, Action: OPD, Item 7, Exec 3.

mately was reduced by the normal turnover in the War Department. By the end of 1944 the composition of OPD began to be affected visibly as a result of the assignment of more and more officers with firsthand experience in combat. Nevertheless a great many trips were made in 1945, some of them in connection with important phases of the war against Japan. Liaison between Washington and the combat theaters was essential until the last shot had been fired, and OPD continued to try to help supply it for the Army.

Special Trip for the Chief of Staff, 1943

There were some confidential missions to the theaters which only officers in important positions were well qualified to undertake. While the Chief of Staff placed great confidence in his theater commanders and left them a broad area of authority and independence in their respective theaters, he wished to maintain close personal contact with them. Since he could not leave Washington for extended periods, the next best thing was to designate one of his staff assistants to make the circuit of the theaters for him. These trips not only served to strengthen the informal relationships between the Chief of Staff and the theater commanders but also provided an opportunity for exchange of informed opinion by general officers in positions of authority on such matters as the appointment or relief of officers holding key positions in the theaters, the practical workings of international and interservice commands, and the employment of U. S. Army troops in joint or combined operations. The Chief of Staff did not want to leave questions connected with these matters entirely up to the theater commanders, yet could not or would not settle them in Washington. On several

occasions General Marshall used the Assistant Chief of Staff, OPD, his subordinate most concerned with such questions, to transmit his opinions, form impressions for him, and make recommendations to him concerning them. General Eisenhower, as Assistant Chief of Staff, had gone to the United Kingdom in May 1942 on such an errand. General Handy had made a short, exploratory visit there in August 1942 at the most critical stage of planning for TORCH, while preparations were still very much up in the air. In the spring of 1943 General Handy made his most extended trip overseas during his tenure as OPD chief, going to the United Kingdom, North Africa, the Middle East, India, and China. He traveled in the company of Maj. Gen. George E. Stratemeyer, Chief of Air Staff, Army Air Forces, who represented General Arnold in much the same way in which General Handy represented the Chief of Staff. The record of the conversation he had with General Marshall before going, and the reports he made while he was away, provide a glimpse of the part General Handy played in maintaining personal contact with Army commanders overseas.

General Marshall did not issue detailed instructions for the 1943 trip, on the specific grounds that General Handy was "familiar with his views" and knew "how he felt about things." General Marshall did say what he thought on a few questions about which he was especially troubled, beginning with the North African theater. He was afraid that General Eisenhower might, "to make things go smoothly [with the British], be going too far in agreeing to disruption of American command and organization." He did not want General Eisenhower to "lower himself to make too many explanations" of decisions made, such as on the celebrated Darlan episode of the previous autumn, believing that he should "simply listen and smile, taking the attitude 'I am the Commander; I did it and that is the end of it.' " General Marshall went on to various other matters, involving persons or policies, for General Handy to take up very informally with General Eisenhower, Lt. Gen. Frank M. Andrews (Commanding General, U. S. Army Forces in the European Theater), General Stilwell (Commanding General, U. S. Army Forces in China, India, and Burma), Maj. Gen. Lewis H. Brereton (Commanding General, U. S. Army Forces in the Middle East), and Maj. Gen. Donald H. Connolly (Commanding General, Persian Gulf Service Command).[7]

General Handy and General Stratemeyer left the United States on 8 April 1943 and arrived in the United Kingdom on 15 April.[8] General Handy found waiting for him additional instructions, cabled by OPD. The British staff in London had reopened the question, raised in January at Casablanca and settled early in March, of setting up a new staff (COSSAC) to plan for an emergency operation across the English Channel, suggesting that it might be just as well not to set up a large planning staff to begin with, since there was such a shortage of qualified planning officers and since American forces were not being concentrated in the United Kingdom as rapidly as had been expected. According to an S&P officer just back from a tour of duty in London with the British planners, the Prime Minister was responsible for reopening the question. General Wedemeyer and his planning staff were dismayed, fearing that any reconsideration of the matter would prejudice the invasion in the spring of 1944. Accordingly General Marshall urged General Handy to make sure that General Andrews understood that the President and the JCS wanted to do nothing to compromise the American position.[9]

General Handy remained in England until 26 April, conferring with General Andrews on this question and the other questions of command and organization that General Marshall had discussed with him in Washington. These included the question of the prospects as a corps commander of General Gerow, one of General Handy's colleagues of WPD days.[10] He also observed units and installations of American forces in the United Kingdom.

From the United Kingdom General Handy and General Stratemeyer went to Algiers. In North Africa, General Handy spent some time in trying to give General Eisenhower a clear impression of General Marshall's views on organization and com-

---

[7] Memo [for rcd, Maj Gen Handy], 7 Apr 43, sub: Instructions from Gen Marshall Prior to Departure, Paper 51, Book 8, Exec 8. Among other things, General Handy was to find out General Andrews' ideas on filling certain corps and division commands. He was to tell General Connolly to make reports suitable in form to be sent to the President concerning the operation of the Iranian railroad and covering relations with British and Soviet representatives. Finally, he was to discuss with General Stilwell the reasons and possible arrangements for his making a return visit to the United States. As usual in such cases, General Handy's travel orders did not indicate where he was to go nor how long he was to be away, though they did indicate that he would leave on or about 6 April. See AG ltr to Maj Gen Handy, 1 Apr 43, sub: Temp Dy, AG 201 Handy, Thomas T. (3–31–43), PO–A–E.

[8] Citation of voluminous documentary evidence concerning arrivals, departures, itineraries, and similar details of the trips is not included in this chapter. They may be consulted in a more detailed study of trips by OPD officers, OPD Hist Unit Study W.

[9] Msg (originator OPD), Gen Marshall to Lt Gen Andrews for Maj Gen Handy (Eyes Only), 14 Apr 43, CM–OUT 5710.

[10] Msg, Maj Gen Handy (signed Andrews) for Gen Marshall (Eyes Only), 26 Apr 43, CM–IN 15693 [TS], Action: OPD.

mand of American forces, but spent most of his time with the II Corps at the front. His visit came during the closing stages of the North African campaign. He observed the operations and morale of American troops, formed impressions of the efficiency of American commanders, and watched the progress of HUSKY (Sicily) planning. He wrote to General Marshall that in his visit to the front he had seen a good deal of Maj. Gen. Omar N. Bradley, of division commanders, and of several regimental and battalion commanders, and had had a chance to watch the operations of American troops "rather closely" for a few days. In his opinion, the 1st, 9th, and 34th Infantry Divisions and the 1st Armored Division had become seasoned divisions. He reported that General Bradley was doing a "wonderful job" and enjoyed the best of relations with the British, who regarded him highly. He also praised the work of Maj. Gen. Terry Allen of the 1st Division, and of Brig. Gen. Theodore Roosevelt, his assistant commander.[11]

The notes on which this letter was based, taken on the back of a mimeographed itinerary for one of his visits of inspection in Great Britain, showed even more plainly the main interests of General Handy and General Marshall:

Spent 5 days with II Corps. Had a chance to talk to all Div Comdrs, several Rgt and some Bn Comdrs. Morale high but troops tired. Some in since Dec—short combat inf strength—We can feel sure of the Divs in line—There had been some doubt as to 34th Div—But while I was there this Div took Hill 609 which was really the key point of German position. Its capture was followed by general withdrawal—This apparently made the Div. They now believe they are good & Bradley used them for main effort in May 5 attack.

Believe Div Comdrs are all OK.

There has been some trouble re air support and some unfortunate messages have been sent. However it appears to be on way to solution—Discussed it with Spaatz, Kuter, Alex, Anderson & Cunningham.

General opinion US Troops has changed most markedly since moved to North—not much expected as terrain extremely difficult but they did [advance] and are advancing— The fact that 8th Army was stopped by same type of terrain has tended to raise very much the opinion of all concerned re our troops—

Husky plan accepted then changed on Montgomerys rec.[12]

In addition to his discussions with General Eisenhower and his observations in the field, General Handy acted on a War Department request to investigate what troops ought to be sent to North Africa after HUSKY in case a large-scale cross-Channel invasion should be launched from the United Kingdom in 1944. He was able to make his recommendations on the basis of observation in both theaters.[13]

Prior to his departure from North Africa in early May, General Handy wrote to General Marshall that the trip was taking longer than he had expected but that it had been, in his opinion, altogether worth taking. He said that he would go on unless he received instructions to cut the trip short.[14] General Handy made no further formal report during the rest of his trip. The principal question with which he had expected to deal, that of General Stilwell's returning to Washington, had already been settled, General

---

[11] Pers ltr, Maj Gen Handy to Gen Marshall, 7 May 43, Paper 61, Book 9, Exec 8. General Handy sent this letter by Maj. Gen. W. B. Smith, General Eisenhower's chief of staff, who was leaving for Washington on temporary duty.

[12] Notes, 20 Apr 43, issued by Hq Eastern Base Sec SOS ETO, Envelope 2, Item 15, Exec 5.

[13] BIGOT HUSKY msg, Maj Gen Handy (signed Eisenhower) for Gen Marshall, 8 May 43, CM-IN 4894 [TS].

[14] Pers ltr, Maj Gen Handy to Gen Marshall, 7 May 43, Paper 61, Book 9, Exec 8.

Stilwell having arrived in the United States at the end of April. However, General Handy went on with General Stratemeyer, stopping at Cairo, Tehran, Karachi, New Delhi, and going as far as Chungking, where they arrived on 21 May. There on 22 May they met Generalissimo Chiang Kai-shek. On 28 May General Handy was back in Africa, at Eritrea, whence he planned to proceed to Accra, but he was instructed to go on to Algiers to take part in a conference with the Prime Minister, General Marshall, and General Eisenhower on the next move to be made in the Mediterranean after the HUSKY operation. After taking part in meetings of this conference, 31 May and 3 June, General Handy returned to his desk in Washington, from which he had been absent two months.[15]

Preview of Amphibious Assault

In mid-1943, during and after General Handy's long, world-survey trip on behalf of General Marshall, OPD was following with special attention the progress of the North African operation and the preparations for invading Sicily. Members of the Division made a number of trips directly and exclusively to the North African theater, the first proving ground of a major combined British-American offensive. The campaign required continuing large-scale support from the zone of interior, and the situation in North Africa was a major factor in the strategic planning for subsequent operations with which OPD was preoccupied. By sending out officers to the North African theater, sometimes several at a time,

OPD tried to maintain all the way down the line an approximation of the close understanding which had always existed between General Eisenhower and General Marshall.

Senior officers in OPD were particularly interested in the invasion of Sicily for the precedents it might establish and the practice it would afford as a forerunner of a more important amphibious operation, the invasion of the Continent. The Division had long held as something of an article of faith that the early invasion of the Continent, by way of the English Channel, was both practicable and necessary. But in order to reach a firm agreement with the British and carry it out, the American planners had to examine in detail the methods of conducting an amphibious operation on such a scale, against such opposition as might be expected to develop, and to show how it could be done while continuing major campaigns on other widely separated fronts. The S&P chief and Army planner, although his duties were as heavy and as vital as any in the Division, did not always have continuous, day-to-day operating responsibilities comparable with those of the Division chief or the Theater Group chief. Accordingly, in the summer of 1943, General Marshall was able to send General Wedemeyer on extended temporary duty in North Africa with the staff of Lt. Gen. George S. Patton, Jr. His aim was to become acquainted with lower echelon planning, particularly for landing operations and to gain actual experience in the coming amphibious assault. He was instructed to come back to the United States only when he had learned everything that would serve him as the "Head War Department Planner."[16]

---

[15] (1) Msg, Maj Gen Handy for Brig Gen Hull, 28 May 43, CM-IN 17957 [TS], Action: OPD. (2) Msg, Brig Gen Hull for Maj Gen Handy, 28 May 43, CM-OUT 11888 [TS].

[16] (1) BIGOT HUSKY msg (originator OPD), Gen Marshall for Gen Eisenhower, 11 Jun 43, CM-OUT 4430. (2) Msg (originator OPD), Gen Marshall

General Wedemeyer arrived at Algiers on 12 June. He joined General Patton's staff and on General Patton's request analyzed the entire operational plan for Husky. He reported the plan to be weak in two respects, namely that it provided neither direct air support nor a tangible diversionary movement or feint. He took issue with the air leaders in the theater (General Spaatz, Air Chief Marshal Sir Arthur Tedder, and Air Vice Marshal Sir Arthur Coningham) who believed that air power should be used in direct support of troops only when enemy air forces had been neutralized. With General Patton's support, General Wedemeyer argued that this doctrine was unsound when applied to the situation expected in Sicily, where the defenders would be numerically stronger and would have the advantage of prepared fortifications. As it happened, Gen. Sir Harold Alexander, General Eisenhower's British deputy, was also concerned over the lack of direct air support, and so were a number of British ground and sea officers, as became evident in a final conference of commanders. General Alexander directed the Husky air commanders to provide for direct air support. Nothing was done on General Wedemeyer's suggestion for providing a diversionary effort, probably because General Patton himself did not actively support the idea.

Besides entering into the staff preparations for Husky, General Wedemeyer was busy, during his first three weeks in the theater, in what he called "strenuous observation" and "innocuous participation" in amphibious exercises "from Tunis to Oran" involving all the American units due to take part in Husky. At times he went with the units on landing craft. At times he hiked along the beaches to watch the debarkation and advance inland. He went inland with the landing units to see how they handled themselves, and once he found a cub plane from which to observe the landing operations as a whole. Although he confessed, writing to General Handy shortly before the operation came off, that he had been a "little vague" about what he was to do in the theater, he had tried, he said, to see everything that went on from top to bottom without getting in the way, and he had tried to be useful.[17] At the end of this period of familiarization, General Patton wrote back to General Handy: "We are delighted to have him [General Wedemeyer] and have given him a complete run of our staff, and have also sent him to see several of the divisions and to watch three landing operations. At the moment he is learning what he can (if anything) around AFHQ and will come aboard this ship the night we sail."[18]

Soon after the landings on Sicily, General Wedemeyer asked to be reduced in rank to a colonel so that he might take over a regimental combat team. The Army command at once accepted his offer of service (without reducing him), and he commanded a regiment of the 45th Division during part of the early fighting in Husky. General Patton in a letter to General Marshall described the offer itself as "very inspiring," and testified that General Wedemeyer, while in command, "by his courage, in-

for Gen Eisenhower, 7 Jun 43, CM-OUT 2634 [TS]. (3) Msg (originator OPD), Gen Marshall for Gen Eisenhower, 8 Jun 43, CM-OUT 3271 [TS].

[17] Pers ltr, Brig Gen Wedemeyer to Maj Gen Handy, 4 Jul 43, with Tab 16 in ABC 381 Husky (1943), 1–B.
[18] Pers ltr, Lt Gen Patton to Maj Gen Handy, 5 Jul 43, OPD file on A. C. Wedemeyer, Sec. 4.

telligence and enthusiasm helped materially to correct a confused situation." [19]

On 22 July, after almost a month and a half of duty in the North African theater, General Wedemeyer started home, by way of Fifth Army Headquarters (at the invitation of Lt. Gen. Mark W. Clark) and the United Kingdom. General Handy suggested that General Wedemeyer make his stop in London short, not over two days, and bring back with him all he could find out from the British planners on their preparations for the coming Quebec conference (QUADRANT). He spent four days in London (26–29 July) talking with the British planners and with the other principal British and American officers in London, and was able to report in some detail on their various attitudes, notably on operations in Burma (ANAKIM) and on OVERLORD (the cross-Channel invasion). On the latter he said the British planners appeared divided while the Prime Minister seemed to be "seeking every honorable avenue" of escape. General Wedemeyer was back in Washington early in August.[20]

As General Eisenhower had anticipated, General Wedemeyer brought the War Department a great deal of useful information.[21] The long informal report which he had sent to General Handy on 4 July expressed his views not only on the conduct of amphibious operations but also on the organization of American forces in a theater, training of American commanders in the field, and the use of War Department staff officers as working members of overseas staffs. He concluded that in getting ready for future operations employing air, ground, and sea forces, responsible representatives of the commander of each of these forces should be brought together early in the planning and should remain together on the staff of the force commander. He had observed that it was only with great difficulty that General Patton's staff had been able to get in touch with authorized representatives of air and naval commanders in planning for HUSKY. He had suggested to Admiral Henry K. Hewitt, in command of American naval forces in the Mediterranean, that it might be a good idea to move his staff, or send a few of his trusted subordinates, to a place near General Patton, but Admiral Hewitt apparently did not see the need for it, preferring to remain near General Eisenhower. General Wedemeyer also recommended that the military resources, the "means" for carrying out an operation, should be made available early and then "frozen," and that the commander should have, besides this security, complete control over the training, movement, discipline, morale, and employment of all forces under him.

On the basis of his own experience, General Wedemeyer became thoroughly convinced of the value of observing overseas preparations and operations. He stated that it would have been a good thing to send

[19] (1) Pers ltr, Lt Gen Patton to Gen Marshall, 18 Jul 43, with Tab 16 in ABC 381 HUSKY (1943), 1–B. (2) Pers ltr, Gen Eisenhower to Gen Marshall, 21 Jul 43, Paper 38, Book 11, Exec 9. (3) Memo, Brig Gen Wedemeyer for CofS, 2 Aug 43, no sub, with Tab 16 in ABC 381 HUSKY (1943), 1–B. This memorandum is a summary of daily events from D Day to D plus 7.

[20] (1) Msg, Brig Gen Wedemeyer (signed Eisenhower) for Maj Gen Handy, 21 Jul 43, CM-IN 14792. (2) Msg (originator OPD) Maj Gen Handy (signed Marshall) for Brig Gen Wedemeyer (Eyes Only), 22 Jul 43, CM-OUT 8885. (3) Ltr, Lt Gen Patton to Brig Gen Wedemeyer, 1 Aug 43, OPD 381 ETO, 77. (4) App. A, title: Observations of British-American Stf Planning, incl with memo, Brig Gen Wedemeyer for CofS, 24 Aug 43, sub: Obsrs' Rpt, OPD file on A. C. Wedemeyer, Sec. 5.

[21] Pers ltr, Gen Eisenhower to Gen Marshall, 21 Jul 43, Paper 38, Book 11, Exec 9.

division commanders from the United States to see how divisions worked in the final phases of training and in combat, and suggested that in the future the War Department should send not only staff officers but also division commanders or even potential division commanders.[22] General Patton, for his part, said of General Wedemeyer: "I believe that we derived as much benefit from him as he did from us."[23] In strategic planning in Washington, General Marshall at once made use of General Wedemeyer's experience. Early in August, during JCS discussion of the outline plan for OVERLORD just received, the Chief of Staff called upon General Wedemeyer to say whether, on the basis of his experience in HUSKY, he considered the OVERLORD operation practicable. General Wedemeyer replied that he was "very optimistic" about the prospects of success, was greatly impressed by the Navy's efficiency in HUSKY, and was convinced that the difficulties foreseen relative to maintenance over the beaches could be surmounted in OVERLORD.[24] He had paid particular attention to this problem and had helped in preparing a long report on it, submitted to General Patton by a British observer, Col. W. E. V. Abraham, with whom General Wedemeyer had previously worked in Washington.[25] The confidence gained

---

[22] Pers ltr, Brig Gen Wedemeyer to Maj Gen Handy, 4 Jul 43, with Tab 16 in ABC 381 HUSKY (1943), 1–B.

[23] Pers ltr, Lt Gen Patton to Maj Gen Handy, 27 Sep 43, OPD 381 ETO, 126.

[24] Min 100th meeting JCS, 6 Aug 43.

[25] (1) Paper, Col Abraham, 14 Jul 43, title: Notes on Visit to Seventh Army, 12 Jul 43, with Tab 16 in ABC 381 HUSKY (1943), 1–B. (2) Paper, Col Abraham, 23 Jul 43, title: Note on Working of Sicilian Beaches, with Tab 16 in ABC 381 HUSKY (1943), 1–B. (3) Paper [Brig Gen Wedemeyer, early Aug 43], title: Notes Covering Obsns Prior to and During HUSKY Opns, Paper 35, Book 11, Exec 9.

by General Wedemeyer in his HUSKY trip strengthened the American stand at the first Quebec conference, at which a firm commitment to OVERLORD was made.

The Overlord Period and After

The successful invasion of Normandy in June 1944 by British and American troops was an occasion long anticipated by OPD officers. OVERLORD was finally an accomplished fact rather than a future plan. During the preceding six months of uncertainty, the principal officers in OPD for the most part had stayed close to Washington. General Handy and General Tansey had taken a brief tour in December 1943, returning home from the Cairo-Teheran conferences by way of the Far East and the Pacific. Similarly at the end of February 1944, General Hull and Colonel Lincoln, then Ground deputy chief of S&P, joined U.S. Navy planners in informal British-American conferences in London. These sessions dealt primarily with the availability of landing craft, particularly for the invasion of southern France (ANVIL) and helped a great deal to support American strategic arguments with respect to the feasibility of ANVIL.

With the successful launching of OVERLORD, the strain of debating and waiting was over, and none of the great anxieties of the present and future could obscure the consciousness of accomplishment on the part of everyone who had worked on the operation, above all, those officers who saw their convictions of 1942 translated into action. General Handy expressed the feeling of the "old hands" among OPD planners after a visit to the front. Late in May he went to London with Rear Admiral Charles M. Cooke, Jr., and Maj. Gen. Laurence S. Kuter, as an advance party for the American Chiefs of Staff, who participated in the brief conference of the CCS in London at the time of OVERLORD. Colonel Lincoln and Colonel Freeman from OPD also went to London and, with General Handy, saw the final preparations for the assault.

General Handy was much impressed with the initial obstacles to be overcome and with the "quiet, confident attitudes" of the commanders who appeared to fear only the weather. On D Day General Handy and Admiral Cooke went into the Channel on the invasion flagship, moved to a fire-support destroyer, and went ashore on Omaha Beach. D plus 1 they spent on Utah Beach, and inland, going both to Maj. Gen. J. Lawton Collins' (VII Corps) headquarters and to the position of the 4th Division. They spent D plus 2 making a round of the beaches. The following week they spent a day in the American sector between Isigny and Trévières, and at General Bradley's (First Army) headquarters. General Handy noted the work of some of his personal friends, among whom were several former members of the Division, particularly General Gerow, who commanded the V Corps in its assault on Omaha Beach. General Handy, upon his return, described the high points of the first days' fighting in a letter to General Wedemeyer, who, with General Handy, felt a kind of paternal pride in the invasion.

General Handy recalled that the OPD planners had been told, in 1942, when they were talking of only three divisions for the assault, that every beach in southern England would have to be used for loading. Actually, he observed, only three port areas and the Bristol Channel had been used, and the job was done "without any great difficulty." He noted the encouraging lack of fighter opposition, stating that he had become "convinced from what happened during the attack and particularly afterwards, when there were literally miles of ships at anchor in restricted areas, that the German Air Force is pretty well whipped down." He spoke of the fine work of divisions then for the first time in action. The order and efficiency shown, in the midst of such danger and confusion, particularly impressed him, and he admitted that he could not "but think back to our Tennessee maneuvers in 1941 and note the difference." In conclusion, he reflected:

It really was a great undertaking. During the day before it there was, of course, a tense feeling that permeated from the highest to the lowest. However, we did not take the chances here that we did in TORCH. I doubt if we ever have one where there are as many uncertainties as there were in that operation. Events, I believe, have established conclusively that our ideas basically were sound from the beginning on this operation, and I want to tell you again that you would have had a great feeling of satisfaction and pride in the performance of our commanders and our troops.[26]

During the summer and autumn of 1944 the problems confronting OPD began to be very different from those of the OVERLORD period. It was still necessary to follow closely the progress of operations in Europe, but OPD was more and more concerned with preparing for a new series of decisions, primarily on occupation policy in Europe, and on the timing and direction of operations in the Pacific.

Soon after General Handy's return from Europe, General Hull took a long trip to talk to U. S. Army commanders about re-

---

[26] Pers ltr, Maj Gen Handy to Maj Gen Wedemeyer, 16 Jul 44, OPD file on A. C. Wedemeyer [TS], 14.

adjustments due to be made in the immediate post-OVERLORD period. Of General Handy's immediate subordinates in OPD in midwar, General Hull was the one whose responsibilities most nearly corresponded in extent with those of General Handy. He was not only chief of Theater Group but also General Handy's deputy. To use General Hull's own words, he was captain of the "second team" in OPD, taking over when the "first team" was busy preparing for and attending major conferences or, alternately, going to the conferences while General Handy stayed in Washington.[27] When he went overseas, as when he remained in Washington, he was General Handy's representative, but he had a more specific interest than General Handy in the operational details of deployment of forces and support of overseas theaters, his special concern as chief of Theater Group. General Hull had been away from Washington only once since attending the Casablanca Conference of January 1943, and that was when he had gone to London more than a year later for the informal landing craft conference. On his summer trip in 1944 General Hull went around the world, stopping in Italy, the Middle East, Australia, and Hawaii. He was away from Washington for nearly six weeks, from mid-July to the end of August.

General Hull traveled with a party which included Lt. Gen. Barney M. Giles (Chief of Air Staff) and Maj. Gen. Wilhelm D. Styer (Chief of Staff and Deputy Commander, Army Service Forces), although he had misgivings that it would be an "inconvenience to the people in the theaters for a large mob of brass hats to

drop in on them all at once." [28] The party made its first main stop in Italy, to which nearly all of Allied Force Headquarters had by then been moved. Although the party stayed only three days in Italy, General Hull had a chance to talk with General Clark, spend a day with the 88th Division, visit the Fifteenth Air Force, and attend conferences at Lt. Gen. Jacob L. Devers' (NATO) and General Patch's (Seventh Army) headquarters. He reported his impressions of these conferences, and in particular detail discussed the possibility of moving the Fifth Army out of Italy, as well as the projected organization of Sixth Army Group headquarters in France (General Devers).

From Italy the party went to Cairo and, after a short stop there, to Jerusalem, Baghdad, Tehran, and Basra. At Cairo, General Hull got the "distinct impression" that there were more American troops in the Middle East garrison than were any longer necessary. On the basis of his admittedly superficial observation, he suggested that the War Department ask the American commander what effect it would have if about 3,000 men were withdrawn. In Iran, on the other hand, General Hull felt that the American command had its hands full and was working very efficiently, and therefore he "seriously doubted" that it was yet time to cut down the forces of the Persian Gulf Command. Nevertheless, he observed that it was easy in that area to get "localitis" and recommended, with the concurrence of General Styer, that General Connolly, Commanding General of the Persian Gulf Command, be ordered home to tell officers in the War Department how things

---

[27] For quoted phrases, see msg, Brig Gen Hull for Maj Gen Handy, 1 Dec 43, CM-OUT 0429.

[28] Pers ltr, Maj Gen Hull [Cairo] to Maj Gen Handy, 19 Jul 44, Paper 965, Book 21, Exec 9.

looked to him and to see how things looked from Washington.[29]

After their hurried trip through the Middle East, which lasted only about four days, the party went on to India, across to Burma, up to Chungking, and back to Calcutta. Admiral Lord Louis Mountbatten was out of India, and at Chungking they failed to see Generalissimo Chiang Kai-shek. Otherwise they talked to most of the military leaders in India and China. General Hull saw Maj. Gen. Daniel I. Sultan, General Stilwell, and General Wedemeyer, visited the front at Myitkyina in Burma, and sent back various observations on policies and personalities—the confusion of responsibilities, the failure of the Chinese to make use of planes assigned them, and the apparent effectiveness of the Services of Supply in the theater in setting up communications from Calcutta to Assam. He again observed that he had seen too little to have firm opinions and that General Wedemeyer might well disagree but gave it as his impression that the War Department might have been "unduly harsh" in handling General Stilwell, who seemed to him to have the "patience of Job." [30]

Leaving India at the end of July, the party went on to Ceylon and Australia, being met at Exmouth Gulf by Col. William L. Ritchie, deputy chief (Air), S&P, who had arrived in the Southwest Pacific to take part in conferences with General McArthur and his staff. General McArthur had just returned from Hawaii, where the President, accompanied by Admiral Leahy, had discussed with him and Admiral Nimitz (26–29 July 1944) the next move to be made

in the Pacific, particularly whether to go from Mindanao to Luzon or, instead, to Formosa, and the future role of the British in the war against Japan.[31]

When General Hull arrived at SWPA headquarters, it was urgent to get General MacArthur's views on future operations in the Pacific beyond the Palaus. As General Marshall had informed General MacArthur, directives were being held up to give General MacArthur a chance to go over everything with General Hull who had received "all the available data on the present status of studies of operations in the Pacific." [32] On 7 August General MacArthur held a conference, attended by his principal subordinates (Lt. Gen. George C. Kenney, Lt. Gen. Richard K. Sutherland, and Maj. Gen. Richard J. Marshall), by Generals Giles, Hull, and Styer, and by Colonel Ritchie. General MacArthur summarized the Pearl Harbor conference with the President and then went on to answer General Hull's numerous questions on what was best to do, what was possible, and what additional military resources were necessary. General MacArthur explained his views on joint planning for coming operations, Army-Navy relations, and command arrangements, and General Giles, General Kenney, and General MacArthur discussed Air operations.[33] On the same day General Hull and Colonel Ritchie conferred with the SWPA planners on operations in the

---

[29] Pers ltr, Maj Gen Hull to Maj Gen Handy, 24 Jul 44, Paper 991, Book 2, Exec 9.

[30] Pers ltr, Maj Gen Hull [Brisbane] to Maj Gen Handy, 8 Aug 44, OPD file on J. E. Hull [TS], 2.

[31] For a summary of the discussions at Hawaii, as given by General MacArthur to Colonel Ritchie, see paper [unsigned, n.d.], title: Notes for Discussion with Gen Marshall, Paper 1120, Book 22, Exec 9.

[32] Msg (originator OPD), Gen Marshall for Gen MacArthur (Eyes Only), 4 Aug 44, CM-OUT 75632.

[33] Paper [unsigned, Col Ritchie], 16 Aug 44, title: Notes on Conf Aug 7 at GHQ, SWPA, filed at top of ABC 384 Pacific (1–17–43), 5.

Philippines.[34] General Hull had a long "overseas conference" that day with General Handy, reporting on the results of the discussions and attempting to answer questions that Colonel Ritchie had brought out with him from Washington.[35]

After the Australian visit, the party proceeded to the Marianas, primarily to study the feasibility of locating VLR bomber bases in that area. They arrived in Hawaii on 18 August. During the three days spent there before returning to the United States, General Hull discussed future operations with Lt. Gen. Robert C. Richardson, Jr., as well as the eternal question of Army-Navy relations in the Pacific.[36] To General Richardson's chief of staff, General Hull expressed the opinion that "too many formal letters were being written by the two commanders and that if they and their staffs would confer together more often and on an informal basis, they would not only get along better with each other, but would accomplish a great deal more." [37]

General Hull, who became chief of OPD not long after his return from this long trip, did not leave Washington again until he attended the international conferences of January–February 1945 at Malta and Yalta (ARGONAUT). After these conferences were over, General Hull accompanied the party

of the Chief of Staff to Allied Force Headquarters at Caserta and went on to France to confer with General Eisenhower on projected operations (beginning with the Roer crossing), returning to the United States on 19 February.

Liaison With Commands in the Pacific and Far East

The work of OPD in midwar was less closely related to plans and operations in the Pacific and Far East than to plans and operations in the European area. Until the attainment of the first objective of Allied strategy, the defeat of Germany, was in sight, plans for the defeat of Japan were of necessity largely exploratory, and the theater headquarters in the Pacific and the Far East had to solve current operational problems within allotted means. A good many officers in OPD were always completely occupied with Army operations against Japan, and the peculiar difficulties of their work were fully appreciated in the Division and, ultimately, by the theater commanders directly concerned. But the provision of adequate means for prosecuting the war in the Pacific was contingent on the defeat of Germany. Only the availability of such means could bring the Washington staff as a whole close to the daily work of the theater staffs and relieve the long-existing tensions among the proponents of divergent views on strategy and command in the war against Japan. Even then the much greater distances between the United States and the fighting fronts were bound to make for a slower readjustment in Washington to changes in the theaters, and to leave the theater commanders and their staffs more on their own.

The result was that OPD officers, in dealing with Army commanders and staffs in the Pacific and the Far East, spent more of their

---

[34] Paper [unsigned, Col Ritchie, n.d.], title: Notes on Conf with SWPA Planners 7 Aug 44, filed at top of ABC 384 Pacific (1–17–43), 5.

[35] Tel conf, Washington, D. C. (Maj Gen Handy and others) with Brisbane (Lt Gen Giles and others), 7 Aug 44, WD–TC 797.

[36] (1) Tel conf, Washington, D. C. (Maj Gen Kuter and others) with Honolulu (Lt Gen M. F. Harmon and others), 21 Aug 44, WD–TC 849. (2) Memo, Maj Gen Handy for CofS, 30 Aug 44, no sub, Paper 1238, Book 23, Exec 9.

[37] (1) Informal memo, J. E. H. [General Hull] for Maj Gen Handy, 26 Aug 44, filed with Paper 1238, Book 23, Exec 9. (2) Memo, Maj Gen Handy for CofS, 30 Aug 44, no sub, same file as (1).

time trying to improve relations with them and less in "getting things done" than was necessary in similar dealings with Army commanders and staffs in the European area. It was their main business to listen, to understand, and, when they could, to do something about the grievances of the Army headquarters in the Pacific and Far East, as well as to try to explain what was going on in Washington and to reassure theater commanders that their time would come. This work tied in closely with the major conferences of the President and the Prime Minister with the CCS, and with the major staff conferences at which the Pacific commanders (or their representatives) presented, and partially reconciled, their plans. OPD officers handled for General Marshall the preparations for the two Pacific commanders' conferences held in Washington, one in March 1943 and the other in February and March 1944, and kept the Chief of Staff in touch with the joint conferences held at Pearl Harbor in January 1944, at Hollandia in November 1944, in Guam at the end of February 1945, and in Manila in July 1945.

From the beginning of the war OPD had benefited from the firsthand experience of several officers recruited from the Pacific, and in turn had released a number of officers for assignments in the Pacific. In addition, since the spring of 1942, OPD regularly had sent out observers to headquarters in Hawaii, New Caledonia, and Austrialia, to see what the Army forces in the Pacific were doing and what they needed, and especially to explain the policy of limiting the deployment of Army forces to the Pacific as a necessary corollary of the policy to concentrate Army forces against Germany.

The officers who went to the Pacific carried on the tradition of taking an active part in operations. During the early sum-

mer of 1943 two officers from the Pacific Section, Col. Charles S. Miller and Maj. William R. Frederick, Jr., were sent to the South Pacific to accompany the force seizing New Georgia. The force commander commended these officers for what they had done:

Both accompanied the expedition to New Georgia and in addition to making observations which will prove of benefit to themselves and to your division they were of much help to my headquarters. They visited all parts of the area occupied by our troops, including the front lines, and closely observed our activities.

Soon after landing in New Georgia our G–2 became a temporary casualty and Col. Miller took over and handled the assignment in a highly satisfactory manner. Major Frederick proved of value in assisting the G–3 division. Both were most cooperative and it was a pleasure to have them with us.[38]

Lt. Col. Russell P. Reeder, Jr., SWPA Section, was sent to the South and Southwest Pacific as an observer early in October. On his return he wrote an account of his interviews with soldiers who had been in the bloody fighting on Guadalcanal, later published and widely circulated throughout the Army. General Marshall was much struck with the value of this pamphlet as a means of bringing home to troops in training the realities of jungle warfare.[39] Observers were also sent to Alaska, and accompanied forces that seized Amchitka (December 1942–January 1943) and those landing on Attu (11–31 May 1943).[40]

---

[38] Memo, Col Godwin Ordway, Jr., for Col Miller and Maj Frederick, 30 Aug 43, with extract from ltr by Maj Gen J. H. Hester, force commander, Paper 217, Item 4, Exec 15.
[39] Interv, Col W. A. Walker with author, 8 Aug 47, OPD Hist Unit Interv file.
[40] (1) Msg (originator OPD), Gen Marshall for Lt Gen J. L. DeWitt to relay to ADC for Col J. K. Tully, 12 Jan 43, CM-OUT 4492. (2) Ltr, Col Reeder to Maj Gen Sutherland, 2 Jun 43, OPD 381

An indication of the range of OPD's interests, and the range of its officers' interests when they were in the theater, was given by Col. Godwin Ordway, Jr., assistant executive officer, who took a month's trip to the South and Central Pacific in the fall of 1943. His mission was to check performance by zone of interior agencies on theater requests, and he had a great many details to take up with War Department staffs on his return. Among them were a request for two ships to send troops on leave to New Zealand, the need in jungle fighting for an abnormal proportion of 81-mm. mortar ammunition of the heavy type, complaints on a new Table of Organization for ordnance companies, a project for establishing an engineer pool in the South Pacific, the theft of desirable components of rations before they reached troops at the front, a shortage of parachutes for dropping food, the reclassification of officers, measures for improving the morale of infantry troops, objections to War Department training pamphlets, revision of censorship regulations, slowness in getting service troops and replacements, increase in number of regimental aid stations, and of course, Army-Navy relations.[41]

Again and again OPD officers on trips tried to explain to theater commanders the strategic background for the limitations imposed by the War Department on their operations, principally through the allocation of units, critical equipment, and shipping. A full and personal explanation of the reasons behind these allocations was of practical value, both to the theater commanders and their staffs as well as to the War Department. OPD officers had frequent occasion to make such explanations, not only in the earlier but also in the later stages of the war, when the Division was busy with what the War Department called "rolling up" the less active theaters.

To explain, as well as to learn, as always, several officers visited the China-Burma-India theater, which was the most difficult of all to supply, to direct, and to understand. General Marshall indicated the extent to which he relied on such visits in a letter to General Stilwell in October 1942, sent with Col. Thomas S. Timberman, chief of OPD's Asiatic Section. He began by saying that since Colonel Timberman was going out to the theater, he did not think it would be "necessary for me to elaborate on the state of affairs at this end of the line," Colonel Timberman being "completely familiar with all the circumstances." After a short statement of his views on relations with Generalissimo Chiang Kai-shek and with the British, and the hope of sending air reinforcements to Burma, he concluded: "Timberman can talk over all these things with you. About all I can say is to develop more of patience and tolerance than is ordinarily expected of a man and much more than is your constitutional portion. You have had an almost overwhelming task to perform, with little aid from us, and we are deeply aware of what you have accomplished and the extreme difficulties of your present position."[42] When Colonel Timberman came back to Washington, General Stilwell sent with him a letter to General Marshall. He expressed the hope that when Colonel

ADC, 71. (3) Memo, Lt Col R. W. Meals for Maj Gen Handy, 21 Jun 43, sub: Obsers' Rpt on Northern Landing Force, Attu, OPD 381 ADC, 73.

[41] Memo, Col Ordway for Brig Gen Hull, 16 Nov 43, sub: Comments of South and Central Pacific Offs Made to Undersigned During Period 20 Sep to 23 Oct 1943, Paper 105, Book 13, Exec 9.

[42] Pers ltr, Gen Marshall to Lt Gen Stilwell, 6 Oct 42, Book 6, Exec 8.

Timberman reported he would "not dwell on . . . troubles" of the CBI area "because I know you have plenty of your own." Nevertheless, he emphasized how important it was to him to be sure that General Marshall knew what he was up against and did not "expect miracles." [43]

The service that trusted intermediaries could perform between the Chief of Staff and the commanders and staff officers representing the Army in the Far East, was particularly great and particularly useful to OPD before General Wedemeyer and his planning assistants from OPD were assigned to the Southeast Asia Command in the fall of 1943. Only in 1944, after the invasion of Normandy, was the Division in a position to exchange staff officers with the Far Eastern theaters as frequently as it had with other headquarters. [44]

The most frequent and most important occasions for seeing and explaining in person, despite the multiplicity of problems in China and Southeast Asia, arose in connection with operations in the Southwest Pacific. Of the various officers sent to the Southwest Pacific at one time or another, the one who established particularly close relations with General MacArthur was Colonel Ritchie. [45] In 1945 General MacArthur voiced his "appreciation that the Chief of Staff would send a staff officer to give complete and frank answers to his questions about matters in Washington and

the war in other theaters." [46] Similar expressions of appreciation were in many instances given to other officers who served to link the Chief of Staff's command post with the firing lines everywhere.

Strategic Planning Liaison

Strategic planning officers in OPD, interested primarily in the processes and results of theater planning, as well as theater section representatives who were more concerned with operations, played an important part in keeping in touch with overseas staffs, particularly with the British Joint Planners (the interservice staff of the British Chiefs of Staff) and with other planners, American and British, in London. OPD sent a steady succession of officers to the United Kingdom to work with the British Joint Planners, beginning early in 1942. Their absence from Washington on this duty lasted from two to three months, and with the overlapping of their tours in London, frequent extensions to go to North Africa and the Middle East, and the time taken in coming and going, two of them were absent much of the time. [47]

The Division attached a high value to the experience gained by planning officers overseas, not only the value to the officers themselves and to the theaters but also to the War Department. General Handy emphasized the point in a message of January 1944 to General Eisenhower, who had requested the assignment to Supreme Headquarters, Allied Expeditionary Force, of Lt. Col. William H. Baumer, Jr. This officer, a

---

[43] Pers ltr, Lt Gen Stilwell to Gen Marshall [Nov 42], Book 6, Exec 8. Cf. entries for 27 September, 18 October, and 16 November in *The Stilwell Papers*, pp. 152, 163, 169.

[44] Msg, Maj Gen Handy (signed Marshall) to Maj Gen Sultan for Maj Gen Wedemeyer, 28 Apr 44, CM-OUT 29556.

[45] Colonel Ritchie visited the Southwest Pacific in September – October 1942, September – October 1943, January 1944, and July–August 1944.

[46] Informal memo, G. A. L. [Brig Gen Lincoln] for CofS, 8 Mar 45, OPD 381 [TS] 77.

[47] The practice of sending a planning officer from OPD to London to work with the British Joint Staff Planners was started as a means of facilitating BOLERO staff work.

member of the Strategy Section with several months' experience in the JWPC, had been in London working on future plans, and was then given an assignment to temporary duty in the Soviet Union as a member of Maj. Gen. John R. Deane's staff. General Handy told General Eisenhower that Colonel Baumer could not be released and explained that his tour of duty overseas had been as extended as it already was, not because OPD could well spare him but merely to supplement his already extensive experience and thereby fit him for further work in Washington.[48]

One of the most ambitious strategic planning trips taken by OPD officers was a world-wide tour in February and March 1945. A group of Washington planning officers attending the ARGONAUT Conference continued around the world at the conclusion of the conference. The party included Admiral Cooke (Chief of Staff, COMINCH), the three directors of the JWPC, three officers from the Air Staff, and two OPD officers, Brig. Gen. George A. Lincoln (Army planner and S&P chief) and Col. Vincent J. Esposito (chief of Projected Logistics Section, Logistics Group, and senior Army member of the JLPC). The purpose of the trip was to confer with the principal American officers along the way, in particular with the commanders in India, China, and the Pacific, on the results of the conference, especially as they bore on the war against Japan. The party left the Crimea on 10 February.[49] General Lincoln made his first report from India on 17 February, covering a conference that he and Admiral Cooke had that day at

Bhamo, Burma, with Admiral Mountbatten and General Sultan, Commanding General, India-Burma Theater of Operations. The conference dealt with short-range tactical plans, theater needs in transport aircraft and naval lift and especially landing craft, and long-range expectations, such as Admiral Mountbatten's plan to take Rangoon by 1 June.[50]

For the rest of the trip, the movements of the Washington planners were co-ordinated with those of a party (headed by Ambassador Patrick Hurley and General Wedemeyer, then Commanding General, U. S. Army Forces in China) scheduled to confer with General MacArthur and Admiral Nimitz on the enormously complex problems of the war against Japan.[51] Before leaving the Crimea, General Lincoln had received instructions from General Marshall to talk to General MacArthur specifically about "oil in north Borneo, the Chusan-Ningpo operation, and the entry of Russia into the Pacific War."[52] Admiral Cooke and General Lincoln had a long conference with General MacArthur on 25 February, in which they discussed Iwo Jima, the Philippine campaign, command in the Pacific, oil in Borneo, ending resistance in the Southwest Pacific, and plans for turning over to the British responsibility for operations in the Netherlands East Indies and New Guinea. Later, General MacArthur talked with his chief of staff, General Sutherland, and General Lincoln, mainly on command in the Pacific, empha-

---

[48] Msg, Maj Gen Handy [signed Marshall] for Gen Eisenhower, 30 Jan 44, CM-OUT 12165.

[49] Lincoln's promotion to brigadier general dated from 16 January 1945, though not approved by the Senate until after his return to Washington.

[50] Msg, Brig Gen Lincoln [signed Stratemeyer] to Gen Marshall for Maj Gen Hull, 17 Feb 45, CM-IN 17886 [TS].

[51] Msg, Lt Gen Wedemeyer for Gen Marshall (Eyes Only), 17 Feb 45, CM-IN 17566 [TS], Action: Gen Hull.

[52] Informal memo, G. A. L. for CofS, 8 Mar 45, OPD 381 TS, 77.

sizing his opposition to giving the Navy supreme command of the final operations against Japan. General MacArthur spoke of the strength of the opposition to be expected in invading the Japanese home islands. He declared that planning should start at once, that heavy fire power would be needed to cover the beachheads, and that as many Japanese divisions as possible should first be pinned down on the mainland, principally by Soviet forces.[53]

After these conferences the planners' group and the party with Ambassador Hurley and General Wedemeyer went on at once to Guam, the advance headquarters of Admiral Nimitz, where they arrived the following day.[54] The conference held at Guam brought to light a major difference of opinion, the Navy officers there wishing to proceed against Korea while the Army officers preferred an attack against Kyushu, the southernmost of the Japanese home islands. The conferences completed, the Washington planners left for the United States, with only a brief stop at Hawaii. In reporting the substance of the Guam meetings from Hawaii on 2 March, General Lincoln directed Col. Thomas D. Roberts in OPD to get to work at once studying the timing for various courses of action against Japan, in particular as affected by the date of cessation of hostilities in Europe. Finally, he declared, OPD should start making logistic studies to cover whatever proposals CINCPAC, through COMINCH, would

be making shortly to JCS.[55] Soon after arriving in Washington, the first week in March, General Lincoln completed his long and comprehensive mission by reporting fully on it to the Chief of Staff.[56]

The last long planning trip to the Pacific came in the early summer of 1945. The original party of seven, which left Washington near the end of June, was headed by General Ferenbaugh, newly appointed chief of the Troop Control Section of OPD, and included two other OPD officers, Lt. Col. Fred C. Smith, also of the Troop Control Section, and Lt. Col. Andrew J. Goodpaster, Jr., of the Strategy Section. Several other officers joined the party en route to Manila, including two OPD officers, Col. Kenneth B. Hobson of the Pacific Section and Lt. Col. Paul J. Long of the Troop Control Section, who joined the party at Hawaii. The main party spent nearly two weeks in Manila, discussing redeployment, command, personnel, co-ordination among Army, Navy, and Army Air Forces, movement and storage of supplies, relations between the War Department and theater headquarters, artificial harbors for the invasion of Japan, British and French participation, and standardized loading of cargo shipping. On the party's return to Washington, Colonel Goodpaster wrote a report, beginning with a classic statement of the purposes of any such trip:

To reach a closer understanding with the theater on redeployment.

To obtain first-hand information on important theater problems.

To obtain information on future plans currently being developed by the theater.

---

[53] (1) Msg, Brig Gen Lincoln to Gen Marshall for Maj Gen Hull, 25 Feb 45, CM-IN 25948 [TS]. (2) Informal memo, G.A.L. for CofS, 8 Mar 45, OPD 381 TS, 77.

[54] Navy msg, CINCPAC Adv Hq to COMINCH, 26 Feb 45, CM-IN 27411 [TS].

[55] Msg, Brig Gen Lincoln (signed Richardson) to Gen Marshall for Maj Gen Hull, 2 Mar 45, CM-IN 1622 [TS].

The Strategy Section promptly initiated the directed study. See memo for rcd, J.A.B. [Col Blizzard], 3 Mar 45, OPD 381 TS, 71.

[56] Memo, G.A.L. for CofS, 8 Mar 45, OPD 381 TS, 77.

To observe the scale and progress of preparations for future operations, including those for the reception of redeployed units and the mounting out and support of expeditionary forces.

To become acquainted with the officers who are developing the plans and directives for the theaters' operations.

Colonel Goodpaster ended with a reminder of the principles that should guide the Division in dealing with overseas commands— to give "every consideration" to theater requests for trained personnel and other stated needs, to "avoid arguments over generalities," and, if correspondence failed to "get down to specific cases on a complicated subject," to send out a party of staff officers to talk things over "before blood pressures begin to rise." The experience of the Division throughout the war testified to the wisdom of this final prescription.[57]

Attitudes of the Theater Commanders

OPD thought highly of what its representatives learned overseas, highly enough in fact to try always to have them report back in person, even though they were to be permanently assigned overseas. The Division took special pains to explain in each case to the theater commanders and staffs why officers were sent out, whether to gain experience, to observe, or to handle some special mission. In the beginning, theater commanders doubted the value of sending comparatively junior officers, as distinguished from group chiefs and the Division chief. Lt. Gen. Millard F. Harmon's chief of staff, Brig. Gen. Allison J. Barnett, said

as much in a letter to General Hull in reference to the activities of an OPD officer in the South Pacific in the spring of 1943. General Barnett began by declaring that he understood that the Division was trying to be helpful: "As to your statement that the Operations Division is not trying to find fault with people in the field, but is sending people out here with the sole purpose of finding out how you can assist the troops, this area has not one complaint to make with your Division. As a matter of fact, the Operations Division has gone much further than might be expected, in co-operating with us." He observed, nevertheless, that first impressions by visitors were very often unreliable, and went on: "There is usually a reason for every condition. Most assuredly we are not entirely satisfied with the set-up at this time, but the kinks are being ironed out with regularity." He explained that his headquarters made an "honest effort" to help the War Department by "showing people around who are ordered over here in order to get a picture of the set-up," but noted that he preferred visits by "heads of sections and departments rather than the secondary assistants who are unable to be of any help to us." He strongly urged visits by General Handy, by General Hull himself, and by "high-calibred assistants." [58]

General Eisenhower wrote General Marshall to much the same effect in the summer of 1943. He said that he encouraged "all military visitors to report to the War Department fully and frankly whatever they have seen, the bad as well as the good," but that he doubted the value, from the theater point of view, of trips by junior officers. His words were: "I remain of the conviction that visits to an active theater by officers

---

[57] Memo, Lt Col Goodpaster for Chief S&P, 19 Jul 45, sub: Rpt on Trip to GHQ, AFPAC, with CCS 893 in ABC 384 Pacific (1–17–43), 9. Filed in the same place is a preliminary rpt, memo, Lt Col Goodpaster for Col Roberts, 18 Jul 45, sub: Interim Rpt on Trip to GHQ, AFPAC.

[58] Pers ltr, Brig Gen Barnett to Brig Gen Hull, 4 Apr 43, Paper 14, Book 9, Exec 8.

of influence and energy and in responsible positions cannot fail to have a beneficial effect in our war effort—the only thing that is really trying is a visit by an ordinary sightseer or by a junior staff officer whose influence at home cannot compare to that of a division commander or a branch chief." [59]

General MacArthur also distinguished between visits by senior and by junior officers. An officer from OPD who talked with him early in 1945 reported that General MacArthur was disturbed that "except for a brief visit of General Marshall and General Hull to the Theater, no persons other than those in the lower level had ever visited the Theater to inquire as to the difficulties, problems, and plans." [60] On the other hand the theater commanders and their staffs appreciated the value of exchanging staff officers with Washington for temporary duty, whatever reservations they may have had about visits from junior officers for strictly observation purposes. It became increasingly evident that OPD officers were really anxious to understand the theater's needs as seen in the theater, making allowances for the inevitable "localitis," which they realized no one could escape if stationed long in any theater headquarters. OPD officers themselves, including the senior officers, repeatedly emphasized that they went out principally to learn. Just after returning from the Pacific in the summer of 1944, General Hull told General Sutherland, in a radio conference: "We had a marvelous ten days with you. It was an education. It was of immense benefit to us. . . . We don't know all the answers,

of course, we don't even say that we do, but we do have a little better appreciation of your problem." [61]

In time statements of appreciation began to come in from the theaters. For example, Maj. Gen. Ray W. Barker (senior U. S. Army officer in the early OVERLORD planning headquarters in London, called COSSAC), wrote to General Handy about the "helpful attitude of everyone in O.P. D." He went on: "I have told all and sundry hereabouts that if they do not in future get what they want from you, one of two things is wrong: Either they haven't got a good case, or they haven't stated it clearly." [62] Such recognition came most readily, of course, from commanders who themselves had served in Washington during the war. General Harmon, for example, wrote to General Handy soon after he had taken command of U. S. Army Forces in the South Pacific in 1942 to explain that he held to his original estimate of forces required: "What goes to U.K. cannot influence the determination of our *needs* here. I can only tell you what we believe to be our requirements in this area to accomplish the mission. My experience in Washington makes it easy for me to understand the difficulties confronting you in making these requirements available." [63] Much later, reviewing his experience as Commanding General, USAFISPA, General Harmon wrote to General Marshall about his relations with the War Department:

There never was a time during this entire period in which I did not feel that the utmost consideration was given to all recommenda-

---

[59] Pers ltr, Gen Eisenhower to Gen Marshall, 21 Jul 43, Paper 38, Book 11, Exec 9.

[60] Ltr, Col P. L. Freeman, Jr., to Gen Marshall and Maj Gen Hull, 13 Feb 45, sub: Summary of an Hour and a Half Conv with Gen MacArthur, Item 11, Exec 2.

[61] Tel conf, Washington, D. C. (Maj Gen Hull) with Brisbane (Maj Gen Sutherland), 25 Aug 44, WD–TC 871.

[62] Pers ltr, Maj Gen Barker to Maj Gen Handy, 19 Sep 43, Paper 72, Book 12, Exec 9.

[63] Pers ltr, Maj Gen Harmon to Brig Gen Handy, 20 Aug 42, OPD 381 PTO, 91.

tions submitted by me and that the maximum assistance possible, consistent with other commitments of the War Department, would be rendered to the South Pacific Forces. General Handy's attitude in these respects was reflected throughout the echelons of the Operations Division, and contributed in great measure to the effectiveness of the operations of Army Forces under my jurisdiction.[64]

In the Southwest Pacific, likewise, theater officers came to appreciate the value of frequent trips back and forth, as was shown by General MacArthur's acknowledgement of the value of what he had learned directly from Colonel Ritchie about other theaters and Washington problems. Overseas headquarters officers in general came to realize that visits to the theater by officers from the War Department were the best possible assurance that theater views would be presented effectively and taken seriously in Washington, whether in connection with relatively trivial matters or in connection with the most important decisions. In February 1945 General Sutherland told Colonel Freeman, OPD member of the JWPC then visiting General MacArthur's headquarters, that visiting officers were always welcome: "He [Sutherland] wished many visitors from Washington would come to the Theater and spend as much time as possible. They would be shown everything that they desired, would be taken into full confidence, and he was sure the education of the individuals would prove of great value not only to the Theater but to their home offices." [65]

The overseas trips helped OPD make itself literally the Washington headquarters of every theater commander. The trips themselves were only interludes in the liaison between OPD and the staffs overseas, normally maintained by an enormous and varied correspondence carried by high-speed transmission messages. The personal link between Washington and the combat theaters helped to build up confidence in all quarters that OPD, especially its theater section officers, sympathetically studied and faithfully represented theater needs, even when they could not be met within the framework of current strategic policy and military resources. In this way OPD succeeded in maintaining its orientation toward military operations in the theaters through the whole war, while at the same time intergrating theater plans with world-wide strategy.

---

[64] Pers ltr, Lt Gen Harmon to Gen Marshall, 26 Jul 44, Paper 1010, Book 21, Exec 9.

[65] Memo, Col Freeman for Maj Gen Hull, 13 Feb 45, sub: Interv with Gen Sutherland, with JWPC M/I/35 in ABC 384 Pacific (1-17-43), 7.

CHAPTER XVI

Military Planning and Foreign Affairs

Among the many elements in national policy, foreign affairs most immediately affected military planning in the later war years and especially affected OPD's staff work on the last phases of the war against Japan. OPD officers, trying to calculate future deployment and to guide overseas commanders on their current operational problems, needed continual guidance as to the main objectives of the United States in its foreign relations. At the same time it became more and more important to them to make sure, from day to day, that the authorities responsible for formulating foreign policy aims were aware of the military implications of their proposals and actions. For these reasons, OPD attached increasing importance to the maintenance and improvement of effective liaison with the White House and the State Department.

Liaison with the White House

As soon as the United States entered the war, American staff officers had begun their education in the methods of conducting a great war within a coalition of great powers. They quickly learned that the President, like the Prime Minister, could not determine military strategy, even in wartime, solely upon the basis of advice from professional officers. The President also had to take into consideration many other matters, on which he had advice from many sources and took action through many nonmilitary channels. While Army officers appreciated this situation, it was only gradually that they came to recognize the need for continuous collaboration with the White House and the State Department. Very little in their previous training or experience prepared them for the circumstances under which they had to work. Those who had served longest in the War Department, though experienced in the ways of government, were themselves extremely circumspect, being unwilling that discussion or action on military questions should be entangled unnecessarily with discussion or action on other matters of national policy. They had fresh in their memories the bitter contention concerning the policy of the United States in the years before Pearl Harbor. Experience in those days had re-emphasized the advantages of the discipline in which they had been schooled, that is, of proceeding on the assumption that the formulation and execution of the military plans of the United States could be segregated in administrative practice from staff work on other aspects of national policy. For all purposes of the record, at least, their code was that the Army, when asked, would advise "how" to achieve stated military objectives, but would not otherwise influence decision about "what" to do.[1]

During the early part of the war the President helped his military advisers to maintain their reticence on other than "strictly" military questions by making it understood, as a basis for dealing with them, that it was the administration's aim to win the war in the way most efficient from a strictly military point of view.[2] But as Army forces began going overseas, it became increasingly impracticable for military planners to avoid taking foreign affairs into their military calculations. Almost all early deployment was influenced by political as well as by military considerations, and Army commanders, once they had arrived overseas, faced political as well as military problems. The public clamor over the negotiations which General Eisenhower conducted with Admiral Jean Darlan in his effort to end the resistance of French forces in North Africa, dramatically illustrated the fact that the Army, even in executing military plans as ordered, and in making decisions on grounds of military necessity could not avoid becoming involved in the most controversial questions of foreign policy.

In 1943 the long-range interaction of military operations with American foreign policy began insistently to force itself on the attention of the Army. General Wedemeyer observed, in the spring of 1943, that American military opinion would "have to be reinforced by the full weight of national policy

as opposed to that of the British" to get the British military staff to support a cross-Channel invasion.[3] The fact that the armed forces, even in trying to follow the quickest, easiest road to victory, had to watch with care the development of foreign policy, was well enough established by the spring of 1943 for General Marshal to make an official statement on the subject. Shortly before the TRIDENT Conference and speaking on behalf of the JCS he assured a subcommittee of the Senate Committee on Foreign Relations that the U. S. Chiefs of Staff had not discussed political matters at Casablanca, but that the "thought of political matters" was of course continuously on their minds. He emphasized that the British Chiefs of Staff, through their secretariat, were closely bound with the War Cabinet and the Prime Minister and that the U. S. Chiefs of Staff were alert to the British "united front" methods and would be able to match the British performance. In concluding his statement, General Marshall took his stand on the ground that military strategy had to be decisive in the conduct of a great war.[4] In that sense, military strategy was the principal expression of wartime national policy, and the co-ordination of staff work on military planning was the principal administrative problem of the government for the time being. Better co-ordination of military staff work in support of the JCS and closer collaboration between the JCS and the President answered the most critical need for greater coherence and realism in American national policy in the midwar period.

General Marshall recognized that the British planned and carried out national

---

[1] See Ch. III.

[2] The assumption that the President would support this position, as opposed to the assumed position of the British Government, often considered to be seeking postwar political advantages, underlay American strategic planning for World War II. See informal paper, 25 Jul 43, title: Effects of Changes in Strategy for Winning War in Europe, OPD 381 Sec, 218.

[3] Memo, Brig Gen Wedemeyer for DCofS, 28 Apr 43, sub: Rpt of Mission Headed by Gen Devers, OPD 381 Sec, 118.

[4] Min 79th meeting JCS, 10 May 43.

policies on a much broader basis of co-ordinated interdepartmental committee work. The British Chiefs of Staff were better advised on matters of foreign and domestic policy than were the U. S. Chiefs of Staff, who had to depend to a large extent on the President himself for such advice, since he kept such matters largely in his own hands and had no executive secretariat to supervise the orderly flow of such information from his study. Until the President told them what he thought, the U. S. Chiefs of Staff were often on very uncertain ground, and even after he took a position, and informed them of it, usually through Admiral Leahy, they were not always thoroughly acquainted with the background of the decision and frequently were not at all certain of its detailed implications for related military plans and operations. It was in reference to this situation that General Marshall in mid-1943, departing from his usual scrupulous practice of dealing only with administrative questions affecting his own department, confidentially informed James F. Byrnes, who as Director of Economic Stabilization had become a kind of "Assistant President," that the need was great for some secretariat agency for "keeping all these groups in Washington in an automatic relationship one with the other." [5]

This weakness was evident on the level of the staff committees on which the JCS depended so much in making their recommendations and decisions. The American military planners were at a serious disadvantage at every step in drawing up military agreements with the British because they lacked continuous guidance from men fully informed, both in general and in detail, on the foreign policies of the United States. A great part of their difficulty probably lay in the absence of clearly articulated national policy, but part was due to the lack of systematic dissemination downward of such policy as there was. As an officer in OPD's Strategy Section observed, the British joint planners had less to do with "matters of an economic, sociological or administrative nature" than their American counterparts. These matters were being dealt with authoritatively by other British agencies in the light of the same national policy that guided the military planners while nonmilitary policy decisions, especially foreign policies, were brought into harmony with military planning on the highest level. This OPD officer observed that at least one of the British military planners in Washington "didn't even know how some of the subjects handled by our planners were dealt with in the U.K." The "greater play of partisan politics in our government," he went on to state, "militates strongly against greater integration between our services and other departments except the State Department," and even the methods of coordinating military plans with the State Department left much to be desired. [6]

Liaison between the military staffs and the White House was carried on almost entirely by a few high officials, who could not begin to handle the volume of staff business requiring co-ordination. They were the Chiefs of Staff (individually and collectively, directly and through Admiral Leahy), the civilian secretaries and undersecretaries, Harry Hopkins, and (after mid-

[5] Memo, Gen Marshall for James F. Byrnes, 10 Jul 43, no sub, WDCSA 040. See pp. 105–06.

[6] Paper, Col H. D. Kehm, n.d., title: Comparison Between British and American Jt Planning, part of SS 161 in ABC 381 Strategy Sec Papers (7 Jan 43).

1943) Mr. Byrnes.[7] Senior staff officers sometimes had a chance to talk with Mr. Hopkins, who was actively interested in military strategy, but not so often as they probably would have liked. General Wedemeyer wrote a note to Mr. Hopkins after the Washington conference of May 1943, inclosing summaries of the decisions and maps illustrating them, to "help you and the President to retain a comprehensive grasp of the entire TRIDENT." He also expressed his regrets that he had not had a chance to talk with Mr. Hopkins, explaining that he had "wanted to discuss projected operations so that you would know how we envisage developments subsequent to a firm lodgment on the continent."[8] The problem of liaison with the White House, inherently difficult, was made more complicated by unsystematic organization within the White House staff.[9]

In this situation the War Department could be sure that the President received a professional interpretation of current military operations only when he specifically asked for one or on the occasions when General Marshall felt obliged to submit one, even without being asked. OPD, besides drafting the papers sent on such occasions, prepared for the White House a War Department Daily Operational Summary which gave the President in a page or two the simple facts of current operations.[10] The senior Army officer on duty in the White House Map Room was in a position sometimes to explain to the President and his staff the latest reports, and thus to check the circulation of vague ideas and misconceptions concerning matters of fact. The officers who served in this capacity during the latter part of the war were well qualified to perform this task, two of them having been in charge of theater sections in OPD previously and the other having served on the Joint Intelligence Committee.[11] But though they could help keep the White House informed about military operations and help keep the military staff in touch with developments at the White House, these officers and other staff officers in daily contact with the White House could not compensate for the fact that during most of the war the President formed his impressions and made his decisions on military matters, as on others, without the benefit of fully systematic interdepartmental staff work.

Symptomatic of the lack of co-ordinated staff action in general was the difficulty of keeping up with the President's day-to-day activities even in the field of military strategy. The President often had someone on his staff prepare a message on military operations, or revise a draft message prepared either in the joint staff or by one of the service staffs. The phrasing of such a message could often involve important changes in American military plans, and General Marshall, Admiral King, and General Arnold were very anxious to see the final draft before it was dispatched so that, when necessary, they could call attention to the military consequences.

On one such occasion, Admiral Leahy himself drafted such a message (to Mar-

[7] The best single source of information about the way the President and White House advisers conducted executive business is Sherwood, *Roosevelt and Hopkins.*

[8] Pers ltr, Brig Gen Wedemeyer to Harry Hopkins, 28 May 43, OPD 381 Sec, 141.

[9] Memo, Col C. W. McCarthy for SGS, 5 Mar 43, sub: Lack of Adequate Representation at White House, Paper 2, Book 8, Exec 8.

[10] For War Department Daily Operational Summary, and White House Summary, see Ch. V.

[11] The White House Map Room was operated jointly throughout the war by Army and Navy officers serving under the Military and Naval Aides to the President.

shal Stalin) at the President's direction. General Deane, secretary to the JCS, after talking with Admiral Leahy about it, came away with the impression that the message might indicate a willingness to do something not hitherto considered, against which the military staffs would strongly advise. He therefore got in touch with General Handy and told him that General Marshall probably should talk with Admiral Leahy about it. Apparently as a result of General Handy's suggestion, General Arnold took up the matter with Admiral Leahy and, as General Arnold noted, a "satisfactory cable" finally was sent.[12] Only the next day did OPD manage to get a copy of the message for the War Department from an officer on the President's staff, via an intermediary in the JCS secretariat.[13] Under the circumstances, informal procedure of this kind was about the only solution to the problem of "following up" on the fate of messages drafted for the President.

Another symptom of the difficulties in maintaining liaison with the White House was the fact that the War Department was frequently indebted to the British Joint Staff Mission for copies of correspondence between the President and the Prime Minister dealing with future military operations or related matters. Field Marshal Sir John Dill, head of the mission during most of the war, was aware that liaison between the White House and the JCS was often rather haphazard and recognized that Gen-

eral Marshall needed to know at once about such correspondence, which the British military staff in Washington received as a matter of course. He therefore frequently sent copies, on a strictly personal basis, to General Marshall, who normally turned them over to OPD, still in strictest confidence, for information, action, or comment. OPD's normal channel for getting such information was through the Office of the Chief of Staff, particularly through the Secretary of the General Staff.

General Marshall made it a regular practice to pass on to OPD any and all information that might be useful in study or action. The flow of documents into the Division files steadily increased, and by the end of the war they included an extensive though incomplete record of the President's correspondence with the Prime Minister. OPD in fact drafted a great many of the messages on the President's side of this exchange of views, as well as many other memoranda for the President, either for his information or for his signature and dispatch.[14] By mid-1944 the executive office was sufficiently uninhibited to start a file called "Information from the White House," consisting mostly of messages the President actually dispatched to the Prime Minister or Marshal Stalin in connection with problems in which OPD was involved. All of this correspondence was kept in the special executive office file, along with the highest security military information of the whole war period, and excluded from the regular files of the Division. Above and beyond following the dictates of a well-trained sense of respect for military security, OPD officers realized that they had moved into fields

---

[12] (1) Penned note, Brig Gen Deane for Gen Marshall, 16 Dec 42, on copy of msg, CsofS for Jt Stf Mission, 16 Dec 42, Item 11, Exec 1. (2) Informal memo, Maj Gen Handy for CofS, 16 Dec 42, Item 11, Exec 1.

[13] Memo, Secy to Lt Col T. W. Hammond, Jr. for Col Gailey or Col Ordway, 17 Dec 42, sub: Atchd Copy of Draft of Msg Sent by President to Stalin, 12–16–42, Item 11, Exec 1.

[14] Msgs and papers of war period, in Items 62, 63A, 63B, and 63C, Exec 10; Item 70, Exec 10; and Items 53, 54, and 55, Exec 10.

of national policy in which their presence might be criticized, however much they needed to be there in the interests of doing their own work well. Hence the Division adopted an extremely strict policy on access to its records, even by officers in OPD, who were entitled to know everything available only about those subjects to which their staff actions related. In this guarded way, quite informally, OPD maintained essential liaison with the White House throughout World War II.

Liaison with the State Department

OPD also tried to meet the need for staff co-ordination on questions of foreign policy through informal liaison with the State Department. On certain kinds of problems, especially those related to foreign affairs, the War Department dealt directly with the State Department because such matters were legally and traditionally the business of the Secretary of War and the Secretary of the Navy rather than of the Chiefs of Staff, either individually or in their collective capacity as the JCS. While the status of the JCS committees in negotiations with the State Department was in doubt, the position of OPD in the War Department permitted the Division to establish contacts with foreign policy staffs that were extremely useful in both Army and joint staff military planning. In the midwar period this informal liaison with the State Department was the chief resource of Army planners for checking their work against the foreign affairs element in national policy.

Staff officers were well aware of the need for liaison between the joint staff and the State Department, but nothing was done in

midwar to guarantee systematic co-ordination. Late in May 1943 the JWPC, then recently established, recommended that the State Department name a part-time representative to advise the joint committees on drafting important papers since it was "impossible entirely to divorce political considerations from strategic planning." [15] The Strategy Section of OPD agreed that it was "becoming increasingly evident that State Department advice and assistance during the planning period is not only desirable but necessary," and called attention to the fact that the Policy Section was then preparing a paper for joint consideration recommending "closer relationship between the war planning agencies and the State Department" in "emulation" of the relationship existing between the British Foreign Office and British military authorities.[16]

General Wedemeyer, of the same opinion, recommended to General Marshall that something should be done to "provide closer coordination" with the State Department, perhaps by making a State Department representative an associate member of the Joint Staff Planners or by inviting one to attend JCS meetings "when papers concerned with national and foreign policies are on the agenda." He observed in explanation:

The JCS frequently require information and advice as to how their military decisions will affect our foreign and national policies, or as to whether the decisions are in conformity with international law, or as to what effect, if any, their decisions will have on our national interests. Some solution will be necessary if we are to achieve that unity of na-

---

[15] JPS 191, 26 May 43, title: Jt War Planning Agencies.

[16] OPD brief, Notes . . . JPS 77th meeting, 9 June 43, with JPS 191 in ABC 381 United Nations (23 Jan 42), 2.

tional effort which is so well exemplified in the British organization.[17]

Those recommendations produced no immediate result, and by the end of the summer of 1943, the JWPC tacitly recognized that there was no use repeating them for the time being. They began to put even more emphasis than before on the utility of close relations between the JCS and the President, through which the planners could find out what the State Department was doing as well as what the President and the Prime Minister were considering in their almost continuous correspondence, so far as it might "influence our strategy." [18] No provision was made for formal, regular consultation with representatives of the State Department until 1944.

The closest liaison between OPD and the State Department had to do only with Western Hemisphere matters. Since before Pearl Harbor the Division had handled this kind of liaison for the War Department, mainly through the Latin American Section and, later and to a lesser extent, through the parallel North American Section. Early in 1944 a single American section was set up under Col. Kenner F. Hertford, amalgamating the North American and Latin American Sections. Most of the problems dealt with by both these sections were not strictly military in character but instead concerned the interrelation of minor Army operational decisions with national policies of the United States concerning relations with other American governments, and with public opinion in the continental United States.

The staff work which the Division had long supplied in support of the inter-American (Canada, Brazil, and Mexico) defense boards and commissions was characteristic of this kind of quasi-military action. In recognition of the broad significance of questions of policy in this kind of work, Colonel Hertford divided the American Section into two units, one called Operations and the other specifically called Policy.

Colonel Hertford left the Division in May 1944 to become Deputy Commander, U. S. Army Forces, South Atlantic, in which capacity he was promoted to brigadier general on 5 September 1944. At the end of 1944 he was recalled to Washington on temporary duty to serve on a committee preparing for the conference of "American Republics Cooperating in the War Effort," held in Mexico City.[19] It was then proposed that General Hertford stay in Washington to set up in OPD a single agency to handle all War Department action that concerned Latin America. The State Department responded very favorably, promising to give General Hertford every facility for knowing the State Department's views.[20] Accordingly, at the end of March 1945 General Hertford returned to OPD to form the Pan-American Group, of which he was chief for the duration of hostilities. Designed to be a central co-ordinating agency for all politico-military affairs of the United States involving Latin America, it performed those functions of the former American Section pertaining to South America, the Caribbean

---

[17] Memo, Brig Gen Wedemeyer for Gen Marshall, 8 Jun 43, no sub, Paper 68, Book 10, Exec 8.

[18] (1) JPS 191/1, 14 Jun 43. (2) For the JWPC's increased emphasis on close relations between the JCS and the President, for the sake of keeping up with what was going on, see JWPC 85, 2 Sep 43, title: Lessons from QUADRANT.

[19] (1) Memo, Maj Gen Hull for Lt Gen Handy, 1 Jan 45, no sub, Paper 1518, Book 24, Exec 9. (2) App. B to SANAC Memo for Info 113, 21 Jan 48.

[20] Pers ltr, Nelson Rockefeller to Gen Marshall, 5 Jan 45, no sub, atchd to memo, OPD for DCofS, 19 Mar 45, sub: Gen Agency in WDGS for Latin American Affairs, OPD 320 WD, 21.

Defense Command, and the U. S. Army Forces, South Atlantic. [21]

The elevation of Pan-American affairs to the group level reflected the fact that late in the war OPD's interest in Latin America was more a matter of planning and policy making than of theater operations. The Pan-American Group operated as both a planning and operating staff, a specialized OPD within OPD for Latin American affairs. Co-ordination between its work and that of S&P was especially close.

A great many liaison relations with other agencies in Washington had to be established in order to secure for OPD information that did not fall within the range of knowledge of any of the sections in the Division, not even the broadly diversified Policy Section or the Western Hemisphere units. At first these matters were handled through the OPD executive office, and as the number involving liaison with the State Department grew, by a specially qualified member of the Division, recruited for the purpose, Lt. Col. Harry A. McBride, formerly an assistant to Secretary of State Cordell Hull. Colonel McBride came on active duty in the Division in November 1942 "to be used for handling all our OPD contacts with the State Department." [22] He served in this capacity for approximately sixteen months, most of them with inactive duty status without pay, necessary because of legal requirements of another, permanent government position.

The advantages to OPD of having this special channel to the State Department were soon apparent. By early 1943 General Hull, on behalf of the Theater Group, reached an understanding with a high-ranking State Department officer, who asserted: "I'm going to take on myself to tell a great many thing to Harry [McBride] that he'll get across to you . . . for whatever value they have to you in the military effort." General Hull's observation, in accordance with military doctrine, was: "General Marshall felt, and I think there are certain reasons for it, that although he's [General Marshall is] not the man to decide whether you do these things or not, that any move in a global war has military implications." [23] Soon OPD was getting copies of State Department messages of the "highest secrecy" that other Army agencies, even the War Department G–2 Division, did not see, and important military messages, in return, were furnished to the State Department. [24]

The importance of the liaison thus established was recognized administratively in February 1943 when a special Liaison Section was set up in the Theater Group to maintain the flow of information, not only from the State Department but also from the Navy Department and other government agencies, to the working staff in OPD. Colonel McBride became a member of this new section, which grew to comprise about a half-dozen officers. The function of the Liaison Section was pri-

[21] (1) OPD adm memo, 31 Mar 42, sub: Establishment of Pan-American Gp, OPD, OPD 321.19 OPD, 86. (2) Cf. pers ltr, Nelson Rockefeller to Gen Marshall, 5 Jan 45, and other papers atchd to memo, OPD for DCofS, 19 Mar 45, sub: Gen Agency in WDGS . . ., OPD 320 WD, 21.
[22] Memo, Brig Gen St. Clair Streett for Maj Gen Handy, 7 Nov 42, sub: Lt Col H. H. McBride, AUS, OPD file on H. H. McBride, 9.

[23] Tel conf, 23 Apr 43, Paper 6, Book 9, Exec 8.
[24] (1) OPD adm memo, 26 Dec 44, sub: Info Received from State Dept, Paper 1522, Book 24, Exec 9. (2) Memo, Lt Col C. P. Light, Jr. for Brig Gen Hull, 18 Aug 43, no sub, Paper 82, Book 11, Exec 9. (3) Memo for rcd, no signature, 5 Apr 44, Paper 510, Book 17, Exec 9.

marily to secure and transmit information needed in OPD.[25] Much of this information was not hard to discover nor difficult to distribute appropriately, but in view of the security content of the documents with which the Liaison Section worked, understanding of the issues involved and a high sense of staff responsibility were essential to satisfactory performance.

Although for such purposes informal liaison worked very well, it did not solve the problem of getting information on policy decisions. The lack of an organized staff to co-ordinate Presidential decisions with the staff work of the various government departments could be remedied only by improvised techniques. In special cases, and more frequently as the war went on, staff officers went directly to some high official in the State Department who had the authority to give them the information they needed.[26] But though such meetings were helpful, they, too, were far from filling the need for regular information. The midwar techniques of interdepartmental liaison evidently needed improvement, which came only later in the war after a striking object lesson had been given the War Department by its experience in handling civil affairs.

[25] WDGS Cir 5–5, 4 Oct 44. With slight changes in phrasing, the same provisions went into WDGS Cir 5–5, 12 June 1945, with the addition of a provision giving the Liaison Section, in effect, Theater Group responsibilities for commands within the continental United States, for the Western Hemsphere base commands, and for forces in Canada (formerly belonging to the North American Section).

[26] For example, see memo, Col G. A. Lincoln, no addressee, 23 Nov 43, sub: Conf with Secy State, Paper 12, Folder 3, Item 15, Exec 5. For Secretary Hull's narrative of the developments in American foreign policy during his long period of service, including his own dealings with military leaders and military problems, see Cordell Hull, *Memoirs* (New York, 1948).

Early Politico-Military Committee Work

The administration of civil affairs was the first major staff problem involving Army commands and Army operations overseas that was clearly a critical matter both in military planning and foreign affairs. The invasion of North Africa and subsequent operations in the Mediterranean and in Europe brought American commanders a great deal of responsibility for administering civil affairs in liberated and occupied territories. They exercised their responsibility in close collaboration with their British colleagues and with the advice and help of representatives of both British and American civil agencies. The governments of the United States and Great Britain encouraged interdepartmental and international collaboration within the theater commander's staff. But a theater staff, in dealing with politico-military problems as in dealing with strictly military problems, could proceed efficiently and with confidence only on the basis of clear agreements reached in Washington and London on important questions of policy. Similarly an overseas commander could meet new developments quickly and decisively only if he had channels through which to get prompt advice, instructions, and support from Washington and London.

General Eisenhower, as an Allied commander responsible for civil affairs, as well as commander of U. S. Army forces, constantly had to appeal to the War Department when he wanted to find out something from Washington, or get something done in Washington about his civil affairs problems. For several months after the landings in North Africa a considerable part of OPD's work in supporting operations in North Africa related to the administration of civil affairs. Through the spring of 1943 the Chief of Staff consulted daily with General Handy and General Hull on these matters, which remained a very important factor in planning military operations in the Mediterranean area.[27] These officers in Washington shared General Eisenhower's view that interim political arrangements, temporary fiscal measures, emergency police regulations, and early economic rehabilitation should all be designed to fit in with the immediate objective of the military forces, the defeat of the enemy. They had in fact very little else to guide them except operational requirements, since the United States had no well-defined political aims of its own in the Mediterranean or in Europe, and the President and the State Department did not take a definite stand with reference to British political aims there.

Under these circumstances, the War Department proceeded to set up an agency of its own to handle civil affairs on a military basis, dealing directly with other Washington agencies concerned. General Marshall and General Handy decided that a separate agency was necessary to relieve the Chief of Staff, General Handy, and General Hull, as well as the Theater and Logistics Group officers who did the "pick and shovel" work, of the burden of political and diplomatic problems they had been carrying. In addition, General Marshall argued that a staff with officers giving full attention to questions of civil significance in occupied areas would improve the co-ordination between the many military and civilian agencies interested or involved in civil affairs.[28] The Secretary of War was in full agreement, and

OPD drafted a charter for a Civil Affairs Division, which was established on 1 March 1943 as a special staff under the Chief of Staff.[29] The primary function of the Civil Affairs Division, as outlined in the War Department directive establishing it, was to inform and advise the Secretary of War about all civil matters within the scope and province of the War Department in areas occupied as a result of military operations.[30] To insure that the Civil Affairs Division carried on its work in harmony with the regular military business of the War Department, the directive provided that all communications between the Civil Affairs Division and a commander in the field were to be cleared through OPD. The Policy Section of S&P assumed the responsibility inside the Division. Furthermore, OPD, following instructions, detailed one officer to the Civil Affairs Divisions as a "working member."[31]

For most purposes civil affairs continued to be handled in Theater Group, OPD, until the end of the campaign in North Africa.[32] Thereafter the Civil Affairs Division gradually took over most of the work and became, under Maj. Gen. John H. Hilldring, an independent and extremely influential part of the Washington military staff.

---

[27] Min 72d meeting JCS, Item 5, 6 Apr 43.

[28] (1) Min 75th meeting JCS, 20 Apr 43. (2) Ltr, Gen Handy to author, 2 Jan 48, OPD Hist Unit Comments file.

[29] (1) Memo, TAG for Col J. H. F. Haskell, 1 Mar 43, sub: Civil Affairs Division, Paper 100, Book 7, Exec 8. (2) Testimony of General Hull, in Rpt of Proceedings of Board of Offs, 19 Oct 44, OPD file on J. H. F. Haskell.

[30] Memo, TAG for Col J. H. F. Haskell, 1 Mar 43, sub: Civil Affairs Division, Paper 100, Book 7, Exec 8.

[31] This officer was Col John H. F. Haskell, who initially was acting director of the Civil Affairs Division and became deputy chief in April 1943, as soon as a permanent Director of Civil Affairs, Maj. Gen. J. H. Hilldring, had been appointed. See CAD office memo, 27 Apr 43, sub: Tentative Dy Asgmts CAD, Paper 20, Book 9, Exec 8.

[32] Ltr, Lt Gen Handy to author, 2 Jan 48, OPD Hist Unit Comments file.

The JCS officially noted that the War Department had recently established a Civil Affairs Division, "closely related to OPD," and agreed that it seemed to be the logical agency to plan and co-ordinate advance planning and the administration of civil affairs in "nearly all" occupied countries. The Secretaries of War and Navy quickly approved the JCS recommendation.[33] As a result the Civil Affairs Division of the War Department became in effect a joint Army-Navy agency for civil affairs policy planning.

OPD continued to keep a liaison officer in the Civil Affairs Division until after V-J Day. The Policy Section also kept up with civil affairs policy, especially joint and combined deliberations, for the purpose of advising Assistant Secretary of War John J. McCloy, as well as the Army planner, the Division chief, and the Chief of Staff on proposals that affected strategic planning or command relations. In the spring and summer of 1943, for example, S&P spent a great deal of time analyzing for the Army planner the various proposed versions of a debated provision then under combined discussion for control of civil affairs policies in recaptured territory of Great Britain, the British Dominions, or the United States.[34] From the middle of 1944 to the end of hostilities S&P intervened on several occasions in discussion of joint committee work on civil affairs and also criticized papers prepared by the Civil Affairs Division to establish specific administrative policies.

But normally OPD avoided interposing formally in the work of the Civil Affairs Division or its representatives on joint, combined, and interdepartmental committees, even during the closing months of hostilities, when OPD officers were busy with staff work on military problems involving nearly every aspect of foreign policy.

In most fields, at least as far as OPD was affected, the formulation of foreign policy began to enter a new phase of relationship with military planning toward the end of 1943. At that time the State Department began furnishing the JCS with guidance in foreign affairs, thereby establishing what came to be called the "politico-military" field of Washington staff work.[35] The initial, somewhat haphazard efforts in this direction came after the October 1943 conference of foreign secretaries in Moscow. At these meetings British, American, and Soviet representatives considered a number of pending political issues that were clearly outside the competence of military leaders, although many of them had been created by the military situation, and their final settlement would vitally affect future military plans. In particular, they agreed to require the "unconditional surrender" of Germany, and they indorsed the proposal to set up a world organization for peace and security.[36] This Moscow conference, in some phases of which Chinese representatives participated, marked the beginning of a new period of the war in international collaboration, during which military plans gradually became less urgent matters than

---

[33] (1) Min 72d meeting JCS, Item 5, 6 Apr 43. (2) JCS 250/3, 17 Apr 43, title: Planning for Handling of Civil Affairs in Enemy Occupied Areas Which May Become Ts of Opns.

[34] (1) Memo, Lt Col Woolnough for Col Nelson, 4 Jun 43, sub: Planning for Handling of Civil Affairs . . ., following CCS 227 in ABC 014 (11–27–42), 1. (2) Memo for rcd, Lt Col L. J. Lincoln, 12 Jul 43, sub: CCS 190/6/D, with CCS 190/6/D in ABC 014 (11–27–42), 1.

[35] The compound adjective "politico-military" came into official use late in the war to characterize problems, policies, and actions requiring consultation and preferably agreement between the State Department and the armed services.

[36] JCS Memo for Info 146, 13 Nov 43, title: Tripartite Conf, Moscow, 19th to 30th Oct 43.

the politico-military terms on which the great powers winning the war could agree to co-operate. As a result of tentative understandings looking toward long-term British-American-Soviet co-operation in Europe, the European Advisory Commission was set up in London to "study and make joint recommendations to the three Governments upon European questions connected with the termination of hostilities which the three Governments may consider appropriate to refer to it." One of the first duties of the commission was to "make detailed recommendations to them [the three governments] upon the terms of surrender to be imposed upon each of the European States with which any of the three powers are at war, and upon the machinery required to ensure the fulfillment of those terms." [37]

At the turn of the year the European Advisory Commission began its sessions. Ambassador John G. Winant headed the American delegation, which included representatives of the State, War, and Navy Departments. To serve the American delegation there was a great need for a system in Washington whereby the State, War, and Navy Departments could give prompt, concurrent guidance on matters of importance from both political and military points of view. As a step toward meeting this need, the State Department set up in December 1943 a special committee, called the Working Security Committee, to clear communications to the European Advisory Commission. In accordance with the wishes of the

State Department, the War and Navy Departments appointed representatives to sit on this committee. The Army member came from the Civil Affairs Division, the Navy member from the parallel Navy staff section (the Naval Office for Occupied Areas). Committee communications that had military implications were referred through the Army and Navy members for clearance by the War and Navy Departments. [38]

Under this procedure, the formulation of American policy on disarmament, demobilization, and demilitarization of Germany went on largely without reference to the JCS. Not until June 1944 did the JCS establish a new joint committee, called the Joint Post-War Committee (JPWC), and instruct it to study all "post-war military problems of interest to the Joint Chiefs of Staff," excluding only permanent organization for national defense and civil affairs. The JPWC was to "work in close liaison" with the Joint Staff Planners and the Joint Strategic Survey Committee, in particular with the latter, through which it was to present its reports to the JCS and to which it was to refer its disagreements. The functions of the JPWC were defined in its charter:

a. Be responsible for preparing studies and recommendations concerning post-war military plans, problems and policies on their initiative or on reference to them by the Joint Chiefs of Staff or the Joint Strategic Survey Committee.

b. Assist and cooperate with agencies of the State and other Departments, as may be appropriate, in matters concerning post-war military problems of interest to the Joint Chiefs of Staff, including instructions to the United States representatives on European

---

[37] Annex to Secret Protocol of Conf, circulated as Annex 2 to incl A of JCS Memo for Info 146, 13 Nov 43. OPD was represented at the conference only by its liaison specialists, Col. H. A. McBride and Col. C. W. McCarthy. See Min of Tripartite Conf, Moscow, 20 Oct 43, Tab 20, Item 12, Exec 5.

[38] Army and Navy representation on the Working Security Committee was arranged on an informal basis. See JCS 624/1, 29 Dec 43, title: Mil and Naval Advisors for European Advisory Commission.

Advisory Commission on military matters pertaining to Axis surrender terms.[39]

The senior Army representative on the JPWC was Maj. Gen. George V. Strong, who had served two tours before the war in WPD, the second (October 1938–December 1940) as head of the Division, and a wartime tour (June 1942–February 1944) as War Department G–2. There were initially two other Army officers serving on the JPWC, one, Col. Stanley J. Donovan, from OPD.[40] Colonel Donovan was an Air Corps officer who had come into the Division in August 1943 after combat service in the Mediterranean, and who, as a member of the Strategy Section, had served on several important special committees, most recently on a joint subcommittee for studying postwar bases, which was absorbed by the JPWC. He served on the JPWC until within a few days of V-J Day.[41]

The most urgent business of the JPWC for several months was the work it was doing, in close connection with the interdepartmental Working Security Committee, to facilitate the negotiations of the European Advisory Commission on the disarmament, demobilization, and demilitarization of Germany. The Working Security Committee was a very cautious experiment in recon-

ciling and synthesizing at the staff level the views of the State, War, and Navy Departments on politico-military issues. The status of the committee was somewhat obscure since it was a working committee, not a policy-making committee, and the State Department had organized it on a very informal basis. Varying numbers of State Department officials in varying positions of authority attended its meetings, together with three military representatives, a lieutenant colonel from the Civil Affairs Division, a Navy lieutenant representing Navy interests in military government, and Colonel Donovan from OPD, present as the JPWC representative. Through his work with the JPWC and the Working Security Committee during the second half of 1944, Colonel Donovan became the first OPD officer to specialize in joint and interdepartmental study of politico-military issues.[42]

The setting up of the JPWC did not simplify, but rather complicated the process through which the Working Security Committee was supposed to clear papers to guide the American delegation on the European Advisory Commission. On questions pertaining to military affairs, the Working Security Committee had to get comments from the State, War, and Navy Departments, the JPWC, the Civil Affairs Division, and any other interested Washington agency. It then prepared papers incorporating these and its own comments and circulated them either to the JPWC, in cases involving primarily military problems, or to the Civil Affairs Division, in cases involving civil affairs. These agencies could then prepare papers for the JCS,

[39] JCS 786/2/D, 7 Jun 44, title: JPWC.
For the study and discussion that led to the proposal to set up the JPWC, see: (1) SS 273 series in ABC 381 Strategy Sec Papers (7 Jan 43); (2) JPS 786/1, 27 May 44, title: Disarmament, Demobilization, and Demilitarization of Axis Countries.
[40] (1) JCS Memo for Info 248, title: JPWC. (2) OPD brief, Notes, n.d., title: Disarmament, Demobilization . . ., with JCS 786/1 in ABC 334.8 Jt Post-War Committee (7 Jun 44). In the spring of 1945 the JPWC was reorganized with two Army "members" (General Strong and Maj. Gen. J. B. Brooks, an Air officer), and all other officers were assigned "for duty with" the committee. See JCS 202/34/D, 5 Apr 45.
[41] See entire file, OPD file on S. J. Donovan.

[42] Memo, Brig Gen F. N. Roberts for Lt Gen Handy, 29 Sep 44, sub: Meeting in ASW's Office at 1100, Saturday 30 Sep 44, etc., with JCS 624/4 in ABC 334.8 European Advisory Comm (13 Nov 43), 1.

and the JCS could refer those acceptable from a military point of view back to the State Department. The State Department then, if it wished, could give its final approval to such papers and send them to Ambassador Winant as a basis for negotiations in the European Advisory Commission.[43]

This first attempt to organize interdepartmental staff work on a basis that would include the JCS committees and the State Department was clumsy and slow. At the end of April 1945, after the JPWC had been at work for over ten months, the Army planner criticized the slowness of the JPWC. He observed that, except for OPD's representative, JPWC members tended to sit in an "ivory tower" and produce "little themselves and that very slowly." The papers they did produce, he went on to say, were "often so discoordinated that we have to work them over again here."[44] The task of the Working Security Committee in getting co-ordinated military opinion was impeded not only by the slowness of the JPWC but also by the very complexity of the interlocked Army and JCS staff system. Thus Working Security Committee papers on civil affairs did not get to the JPWC but

were cleared by the Civil Affairs Division, which acted for the War Department and in a joint Army-Navy capacity. Even then, the chief of OPD's S&P Group and his Policy Section might feel obliged to slow the process down at the last moment when reviewing papers that had reached the JCS level. Since OPD had a liaison officer on duty with the Civil Affairs Division, as well as a member on both the JPWC and the Working Security Committee, and since it assumed responsibility for getting co-ordinated action on JPWC and Civil Affairs Division matters as well as other policy issues, the Working Security Committee system did work as far as the Army was concerned, but at best it did not work very well.

In the autumn of 1944, while criticisms of Washington politico-military planning multiplied, it became increasingly urgent to start getting policy papers cleared in order that Ambassador Winant and his colleagues could get ahead with their negotiations in the European Advisory Commission.[45] With military operations on the Continent moving rapidly, the collapse or surrender of Germany before the end of the year was a distinct possibility. Yet high State Department officials, being themselves uncertain about American foreign policy as applied to the surrender and occupation of Germany, could give the Working Security Committee very little to go on. At the same time, after more than two years without systematic co-ordination of foreign policy with military planning, the State Department was very hesitant about asking for JCS views on matters obviously having military significance, while the JCS, espe-

---

[43] For this simplified statement of the way in which the Washington staff functioned, or at least was supposed to function, see notes, unsigned, 24 Oct 44, no sub, on a talk given by General Strong to the Policy Section of S&P, with CCS Memo for Info 251 in ABC 381 UN (25 Jan 42), 3–A.

[44] Informal memo, Brig Gen G. A. Lincoln for Maj Gen Hull, 28 Apr 45, sub: Asgmt of an Add Off for Dy With JPWC, with JCS 786/7 in ABC 334.8 Jt Post-War Committee (7 Jun 44). He remarked on the volume of JPWC work: "We have in the Planners and the Logistics Committee demonstration that joint planning can be made to work providing it is tied to the Department . . . . S&P probably writes one Planners' paper a day on the average. On the other hand the JPWC, with the same number of members as the JWPC, produces only ten papers during a month."

[45] For criticisms from Ambassador Winant, see summary of msg (COMEA 108), Ambassador Winant to State Dept, 7 Oct 44, with CCS Memo for Info 244 in ABC 381 UN (23 Jan 42), 3–A.

cially Admiral Leahy, hesitated to offer opinions on matters that affected foreign relations. While special exertions by State and War Department representatives finally got action on the papers most urgently needed, the system itself was inadequate to meet the severe strains put on it.

State-War-Navy Coordinating Committee

The crisis in Washington staff work on German surrender and occupation pointed the way to the major development of World War II in administrative procedures for handling politico-military affairs, the creation of the State-War-Navy Coordinating Committee (SWNCC). This committee, with its standing subcommittees for particular areas and important topics, finally provided a basis for interdepartmental staff work that brought foreign policy formulation into close connection with joint committee work and JCS deliberations.[46] In the latter part of November 1944 Secretary of State Edward R. Stettinius, Jr., after exploratory conversations with members of the three departments, recommended setting up a committee of highly placed State, War, and Navy Department officials to consider politico-military questions. The need was evident, and in December 1944 the State-War-Navy Coordinating Committee was set up. The three members were civilians, each holding the position of Assistant Secretary in his own agency. John J. McCloy represented the War Department.[47] The function of these men, as originally described, was to assist their chiefs in handling "politico-military matters" and

"coordinating the views of the three departments on matters in which all have a common interest, particularly those involving foreign policy and relations with foreign nations."[48]

The principal subcommittees of the SWNCC were established in January 1945, including one for Europe (absorbing and superseding the Working Security Committee), one for Latin America, one for the Far East, and one for the Near and Middle East. During the succeeding months, until V-J Day, OPD was represented on two of these committees, those for Latin America and for the Far East. OPD's liaison officer in the Civil Affairs Division served as working representative of General Hilldring, whom the War Department designated as special member for civil affairs on the Far Eastern subcommittee.[49] In addition to the work done by OPD officers who directly participated in the work of SWNCC subcommittees, and the assistance furnished them by their colleagues or subordinates, especially in S&P, the activities of the SWNCC made a great deal of difference in the work of OPD, particularly in that of the Policy Section, which took the main responsibility for handling SWNCC papers. With the approach of victory, a material part of S&P's staff work had some relationship to SWNCC deliberations and decisions.

In the many cases in which strictly military operations would be a factor of prime

---

[46] D/F, OPD for TAG, 12 Feb 45, sub: Procedure JCS and SWNCC, OPD 334.8 SWNCC, 5.

[47] SANACC (State-Army-Navy-Air Force Coordinating Committee) Memo for Info 113, 21 Jan 48, sub: Brief History, etc.

[48] (1) JCS 1224, 7 Jan 45, title: Procedure—JCS and SWNCC. (2) Cf. SWNCC 12/4, 26 Oct 45, title: Signed Statement by Secys State, War, and Navy, 16 Oct 45.

[49] (1) SANACC Memo for Info 113, 21 Jan 48, sub: Brief History, etc. (2) Memo, DCofS [Lt Gen Handy] for John J. McCloy, 26 Jan 45, no sub, OPD 334.8 SWNCC, 3. (3) Memo, Maj Gen Hilldring for Maj Gen Strong, 30 Jan 45, sub: Pacific-Asiatic Ad Hoc Com of SWNCC, OPD 334.8 SWNCC, 3.

importance in a politico-military situation, SWNCC papers were referred to the JCS. On the whole the SWNCC system meshed very well with the JCS system. OPD officers, who had felt the need for it since 1943, welcomed the development of a staff system that could begin to bring the State Department and the armed forces together in something like the way the joint staff had brought the armed forces together. In this way the military staffs could force consideration of some of the issues in national policy on which they lacked authoritative guidance. In March 1945 Mr. McCloy had occasion to remark that any new agency dealing with politico-military affairs should come within the orbit of the SWNCC so it would not "break up the general co-ordination machinery with the armed services into too many separate organizations . . . and disturb our now well established relationship with the Joint Chiefs of Staff." General Lincoln indorsed this idea of preserving or strengthening the SWNCC.[50]

A very important independent committee of high officials, Informal Policy Committee on Germany (IPCOG), was in fact established in April 1945, on the President's initiative, to determine policy for Germany in the period immediately following the German surrender, and functioned until the end of August. The Informal Policy Committee, which included Treasury Department representation, in effect superseded the SWNCC in the period of the defeat and early occupation of Germany.[51] The Far East was a

different matter. The SWNCC and its subcommittees played the dominant part in formulating Japanese surrender terms, and in the period after V-J Day became the main channel for co-ordinating Washington staff work on occupation policy, first in Japan and eventually in Europe.

Staff Action by OPD

Questions of foreign policy directly concerned most of the senior officers in OPD in one way or another, but the synthesis of military policy with foreign policy was the special interest of the Army planner. At every new stage of the war a greater amount of the time of the S&P officers under him had to be devoted to staff work in this field. As they had begun to point out in 1943, they could not do their proper work without continuous support and guidance from the State Department. When Army and Navy representatives finally began sitting with State Department officials on the Working Security Committee in 1944, OPD officers found it helpful in their work to have some kind of regular channel for staff discussion of interdepartmental politico-military problems. OPD's Policy Section in particular benefited from the establishment of the Working Security Committee and the SWNCC, since Policy Section officers had to study and recommend action on questions of policy (as distinguished, rather vaguely, from strategy) that came up in joint and combined deliberations. Previously, no normal, regular staff procedure had existed whereby the Policy Section could make sure that the State Department was aware of impending decisions by the armed forces and did not object to their implications in foreign relations. For instance, in March 1944 when the chief of Policy Section tried to clear with the State Department a tech-

---

[50] (1) Ltr, ASW to Asst Secy State [W. L. Clayton], 27 Mar 45, with JCS 1192/2 in ABC 334.8 Jt Post-War Committee (7 Jun 44). (2) Informal note, Brig Gen G. A. Lincoln for "Tick" [Col. C. H. Bonesteel, III], n.d., with JCS 1192/2 in ABC 334.8 Jt Post-War Committee (7 Jun 44).

[51] For Informal Policy Committee on Germany, see SANACC Memo for Info 113, 21 Jan 48, sub: Brief History, etc.

nical paper on communications, the State Department official who read the paper went no further than to say that the "State Department had no concern" if the paper confined itself to strictly military matters, but that "they would like the paper to be formally referred for their consideration in case political implications were involved." This observation was no help to the OPD officer, who thought the paper had "definite political implications" and wanted quick, informal staff guidance or clearance comparable to the informal concurrence he normally could get by working-level staff co-ordination in the Army.[52]

The growth of joint and interdepartmental study of politico-military questions in the later war years, while it facilitated, also added to the work of the Army planner, S&P generally, and the Policy Section particularly. During 1944 the staff interests of Policy Section began to acquire a new and more definitely delimited character rather than pertaining simply to nonstrategic issues. The orientation of the section became increasingly political. As papers began to pass between the State Department and the JCS, the Policy Section had to study them and formulate recommendations on them for the Chief of Staff. The increasing frequency and importance of questions affecting foreign policy as well as military plans and overseas operations, made it imperative that the civilian officials of the War Department be aware of pending JCS actions relating to their work. Policy Section from the beginning referred politico-military papers to the Secretary, Under Secretary, or Assistant Secretaries of War for information and comment whenever the

issue under consideration fell within their respective spheres of responsibility.[53]

The SWNCC and its subcommittees, as they got into operation early in 1945, gradually brought more order into politico-military staff work. One result was the formal assignment of responsibility to OPD (and within OPD) for staff co-ordination of War Department action on SWNCC papers. The Policy Section began drafting staff papers for the benefit of the Army member, Assistant Secretary of War Mc-Cloy, on matters up for formal action by the SWNCC as soon as the committee's work got under way, just as it formulated recommendations for the Chief of Staff on similar JCS papers. At Mr. McCloy's request, in April 1945, the Deputy Chief of Staff made OPD responsible for securing, considering, and putting together the "coordinated views of the War Department" on all issues before the SWNCC and for carrying out SWNCC (and IPCOG) decisions within the War Department. Inside OPD, the work was delegated to S&P, and there it was carried on almost mechanically in accordance with the procedures set up by Policy Section for JCS and CCS papers.[54]

---

[53] (1) Memo, Maj Gen Hilldring for Maj Gen Hull, 28 Jun 44, sub: Reference of Political Questions to JCS, with JWPC Memo for Info 28 in ABC 381 United Nations (23 Jan 42), 3–A. (2) Memo, Maj Gen Hull [action in Policy Sec] for Maj Gen Hilldring, 2 Jul 44, same sub, with JWPC Memo for Info 28 in ABC 381 United Nations (23 Jan 42), 3–A. (3) Memo for rcd, Maj J. C. Streett, 2 Jul 44, same sub, with JWPC Memo for Info 28 in ABC 381 United Nations (23 Jan 42), 3–A.

[54] For OPD action on SWNCC (and IPCOG) papers, see: (1) memo, ASW McCloy for DCofS, 25 Mar 45, sub: WD Procedure in Handling SWNCC Papers, OPD 334.8 SWNCC, 5/4 (OPD already was briefing Mr. McCloy on papers before the SWNCC for formal action; Mr. McCloy wanted the procedure to be routine and to include informal action); (2) S/S, OPD for DCofS, 29 Mar 45, same sub, OPD 334.8 SWNCC, 5/4; (3) S/S, OPD for DCofS, 1 May 45, same sub, OPD

---

[52] Memo, Lt Col J. K. Woolnough for Brig Gen F. N. Roberts, 14 Mar 44, sub; Security of Allied Communications, with JCS 725/1 in ABC 311.5 (25 Jan 44).

In June 1945 responsibility for Army staff action in this field was incorporated into the formal administrative regulations by the addition of a new item to the list of the duties of the Policy Section: "Reviews and coordinates for the Assistant Secretary of War all papers submitted for decision to the State-War-Navy Coordinating Committee." [55]

The final, formal administrative adjustment within OPD to the steady increase of politico-military planning came after the end of hostilities. General Lincoln then established in S&P a new unit, called the Strategic Policy Section, to work exclusively in the field of politico-military problems.[56] Initially it contained six officers, including the chief, Col. Charles H. Bonesteel, III, who had been a member of the Policy Section since October 1944 and its chief during July and August 1945. The small group of officers associated with him in S&P already had made themselves OPD's specialists in politico-military affairs while working as a subsection of the Policy Section for several months in the spring and early summer of 1945. Colonel Bonesteel, like his immediate superior, General Lincoln, was

a former Rhodes Scholar, as were two of his colleagues, Col. James McCormack, Jr., and Col. Dean Rusk, the latter having been in addition a political scientist of good standing in the academic world. All the members of the new section enjoyed a reputation in the War Department for being exceptionally well-educated members of the military profession.[57]

The decision to set up a separate unit designated the Strategic Policy Section marked the end rather than the beginning of a stage in the development of OPD's philosophy of staff responsibility. For several months, without the name, Colonel Bonesteel and the Policy Section officers had been doing the same kind of staff work. General Lincoln was referring particularly to their work and to the circumstances in which they did it when he remarked: "Our problem goes beyond the normal one of working out the answer to a message or paper with a suspense date on it; we are constantly being forced into a precipitate determination concerning long-range projects and objectives." [58] Especially in the hectic days of the unexpected surrender of

---

334.8 SWNCC, 5/5; (4) memo, Exec OPD for Chief S&P, 1 May 45, sub: Procedure for Advising ASW on SWNCC Matters and on Implementing Decisions of that Com, OPD 334.8 SWNCC, 5/5; (5) memo, Col T. D. Roberts for Gen Handy, 12 Jul 45, sub: Implementation of SWNCC and IPCOG Papers, OPD 334.8 SWNCC, 5/6.

The task of "implementation," long a Policy Section responsibility, was transferred to the S&P executive office a few months before the end of hostilities. The mechanical work of disseminating the papers was done, of course, in accordance with well-established S&P policies and procedures. See memo, OPD for Secy JCS and Secy SWNCC, 8 May 45, sub: Implementation of Decisions of Jt and Combined CsofS and of SWNCC, OPD 319.12, 59.

[55] WDGS Cir 5–5, 12 Jun 45.

[56] S&P orgn chart, 4 Sep 45, Paper 6, Item 2B, OPD Hist Unit file.

[57] Memo, ASW [J. J. McCloy] for OPD, 14 Nov 45, sub: Commendation, OPD file on S. J. Donovan. In this memorandum Mr. McCloy expressed his appreciation to General Hull for the "superb services" of the officers in S&P, referring particularly to the "important politico-military work to which they have made such a vital contribution during this critical period." He characterized the S&P officers as follows: "They exhibit balanced judgment and keen powers of analysis. They are the sort who would disabuse anybody of the impression that Army officers lack flexibility of mind and capacity to deal with new problems imaginatively." For these reasons, Mr. McCloy said, "I always have a comfortable sense that the background of a problem has been pretty well exhausted when I act in the State-War-Navy Coordinating Committee upon a briefing by your division."

[58] Memo, Brig Gen G. A. Lincoln for Lt Gen Hull, 3 Oct 45, sub: Pers Situation, OPD 321.19, 127.

Japan, they were struggling in every way they could devise to bring about what General Lincoln called the "official marriage of political and military policy of the State Department and the War Department." [59]

The International Conferences of 1944 and 1945

The ever greater importance of political and diplomatic considerations in the national policy of the United States in the later war years was reflected in the international conferences just as in day-to-day staff work in Washington. The year of military decisions had been 1943, at least with respect to the major theater of operations in Europe. Although in the four major conferences of that year the U. S. Joint Chiefs of Staff had been faced with more and more problems that they recognized as quasi military, they had dealt with them in connection with the major problem of how to defeat Germany. In contrast, 1944 was a year of military action in Europe, and operations against Japan were still only getting well under way by the end of the year. [60] There were no major conferences until the second Quebec meeting (OCTAGON) in September 1944. At that conference, and much more at the Malta-Yalta meetings (ARGONAUT) in January and February 1945 and at the Potsdam (TERMINAL) meetings in shattered Berlin in July 1945, the military issues were being crowded out by semimilitary or plainly political problems of first importance to the United States. While the JCS did not deal directly with these nonmilitary issues, their own

work had to take into account agreements being reached and commitments being made by the President on the basis of his knowledge of both diplomatic and military plans.

The changing tone of the international conferences in the late war period was reflected somewhat in the military representation at them. The mechanics of staff attendance had been worked out very carefully in 1943 and early 1944. Thus for OCTAGON (12–16 September) the JCS decided upon a staff attendance that included fifteen "key" conferees (4 JCS, 2 JSSC, 4 JPS, 3 "Chiefs of Operations," which included General Handy, and 2 JCS secretaries) and 22 other planning officers. [61] Most of the military issues raised at OCTAGON were not nearly so far-reaching as one distinctly politico-military item on the agenda, the problem of the "Occupation of Germany, its satellites, and Axis-occupied countries." [62]

At ARGONAUT (30 January–9 February 1945) about twenty American military representatives attended the opening meetings, although a number of specialists (mainly shipping experts) were brought in before the sessions ended. [63] As the President ob-

---

[59] Rpt of Proceedings of Bd of Offs, 6 Nov 45, copy in OPD file on S. J. Donovan.

[60] For the military side of the later international conferences, primarily concerning the war against Japan, see Ch. XVII.

[61] List, 29 Aug 44, title: Pers to Attend Octant [sic], Item 16, Exec 5.

[62] (1) JCS 729/2, 22 Aug 44, title: Preparation for Next Allied Stf Conf. (2) Official OCTAGON Conference Book.

[63] (1) Memo, CofS for Admiral Leahy, 29 Dec 44, no sub, Item 17, Exec 5. (2) Memo, Admiral Leahy for Gen Marshall and Admiral King, 28 Dec 44, no sub, Item 7, Exec 5.
ARGONAUT, like SEXTANT, was held in two places. The principal part, MAGNETO (4–9 February 1945), was a tripartite meeting in the Crimea at Yalta, while preliminary British-American discussions, CRICKET (30 January–2 February 1945), took place at Malta. The dates given for ARGONAUT are not assigned entirely in conformity with the practice in Ch. XII, where first and last CCS meetings are used as terminal dates for the conference at

served before the conference, ARGONAUT would require discussion of "Poland, Greece, the World Security Organization, Palestine, Indo-China, Latin America, and the general administration and control of Germany." [64] In preparing the voluminous dossier of documents that OPD always collected for the use of the Army conferees, S&P included, along with exhaustive briefs of many military problems ranging from "Operational Plans on Western Front" to "Lend Lease Protocol with Soviets," a paper on "Political Questions Which May Possibly Be Involved in Military Discussions." It merely raised a number of questions without trying to present information or recommend solutions in the way that the accompanying papers on military problems did. There were seventeen questions, all rather similar to one of the key queries: "What is the Government's view on Soviet participation in War against Japan if further negotiations indicate that little military contribution can be expected from the Soviets and the result of their participation would be to give them a greater voice in the Pacific settlement and the possible absorption of North China if the Kuomintang disintegrates?"

The cautious attitude with which the military staffs were turning to such issues in early 1945 was carefully stated in a preface to the list of questions formulated in S&P:

The war is now entering the phase where many military decisions will have broad political effect and since the Joint Chiefs responsibility is to concern itself with military matters only it is necessary to consider the political

questions involved in, or the political effect of, military decisions. Although political questions should not be persuasive to the Joint Chiefs of Staff in determining the purely military view it is important that they recognize such questions immediately and it would be helpful if they could know the government's position on such questions in advance of military discussions.[65]

As a result of this basic caution, the military proceedings at ARGONAUT did not include formal consideration of any of the critical semistrategic problems in which the President and his foreign policy advisers were immersed.

By July, after Germany had surrendered and when the military effort was turning toward Japan, OPD's staff experience with the SWNCC, together with the bare fact of inseparable admixture of postwar political problems in Europe with current strategic planning for the Pacific, had overcome all scruples on the part of OPD about getting into matters that traditionally were none of the Army's business. Maj. Gen. Howard A. Craig, General Hull's Theater Group chief, had noted a few months earlier: "The time has come when, whether we like it or not, the War Department must face the fact that it has a real interest in political matters of varying categories." [66] The work of the politico-military specialists in S&P was being openly recognized and commended. The voluminous compilation of papers on subjects for use by the comparatively few Army participants in discussions at TERMINAL (16–24 July 1945), the last international conference, in-

---

Yalta. Tripartite meetings were held before the first CCS meeting (6 February 1945) and the earlier date is used here. See Official ARGONAUT Conference Book.

[64] Memo, Gen Marshall for Lt Gen Handy, 23 Jan 45, no sub, Item 17, Exec 5.

[65] OPD Book, title: Compilation . . . Relating to Subs of Possible Discussion at ARGONAUT, ABC 337 (11 Jan 45), 1–B.

[66] Draft memo, Maj Gen Craig for Lt Gen Handy, 3 Feb 45, sub: WD Participation in Political Affairs, Paper 1562, Book 25, Exec 9.

cluded briefs and recommendations on such frankly politico-military issues as: "U.S. Intentions with Regard to General Soviet Intentions Towards Expansion," "U.S. Policy with Regard to Indo-China," "Terms of Japanese Surrender," and "Military Staff Committee, United Nations Organization." In all, eighty-six topics were carefully studied and briefed. Considerably less than half were concerned primarily with military operations.[67] While the military conferees as usual played no formal part in determining policy on such matters, at TERMINAL they and their staffs were finally beginning to organize their thoughts in the broader context of national instead of strictly military policy.

By the time of TERMINAL a great change had come about in international military planning proper as a result of the defeat of Germany. The United States, Great Brit-

ain, and the Soviet Union had achieved the major military objective of equal interest to all three nations. The many unanswered questions about Germany were henceforth topics for discussion primarily on a political basis, among experts on foreign policy, even though the military forces of occupation in Europe remained for the time being the chief instrument of foreign policy. The operations against Japan still to be launched were the common military concern of all three powers to a far lesser extent than the operations that had brought the defeat of Germany. The war in the Pacific had long been an American war, and American resources were bound to remain preponderant in it. A great part of the military planning for operations against Japan had always taken place, not on an international level, but within the JCS, and between the JCS and the American commands in the Pacific, which brought about the defeat and occupation of Japan at the very time that the plans for it were being written and debated on higher planes of authority. This military planning, carried on amid the confusions and cross-purposes of the late war period, was the last wartime test of the Army's Washington command post.

[67] OPD Book, title: Compilation of Subs for Possible Discussion at TERMINAL, Item 21, Exec 5. For dates of TERMINAL, see Official TERMINAL Conference Book. There was a special meeting between American and Soviet military leaders, concerning operational collaboration in the war against Japan, after the CCS and plenary meetings, 26 July 1945. OPD officers present at TERMINAL were General Hull, Assistant Chief of Staff; Brig. Gen. G. A. Lincoln, S&P chief and Army planner; Brig. Gen. V. J. Esposito, Logistics Group chief; and Col J. B. Cary, S&P deputy chief (Air).

CHAPTER XVII

Case History: Planning the End of the War Against Japan

Military planning in OPD during the later war years, particularly in the last six months of hostilities, reflected the many adjustments the command post had made to the new problems of 1943, 1944, and 1945. Aside from pursuing the BOLERO/OVERLORD issue to the very end, Army planners during this period had to face the most momentous question still unanswered in World War II strategy, that is, how to defeat Japan. Fundamentally the situation was the same one that had engendered the original BOLERO plan in 1942. A powerful enemy had become firmly entrenched in a vast area. The war in Europe, at least until Germany had been defeated, required the husbanding of limited resources. The utmost efforts of many agencies in several nations had to be geared together in the interest of speed and economy. In these circumstances, OPD began to press for a decision that would permit the concentration of forces for an early, decisive attack on Japan. Just as in 1942, OPD's strategists and operations officers collaborated in the later war years to make planning consistent and yet imaginative as well as both practical and timely. OPD had to work through the committee and conference network toward some kind of strategic plan acceptable to General Marshall and to the Army commanders in the field. OPD also had to direct the deployment of U. S. Army troops to the theaters months before operations could begin.

The techniques of military planning in the later war years, unlike its objectives, had changed since 1942, and OPD's staff work showed it. In the first place, in 1944 and 1945 the Joint War Plans Committee was initiating many of the new studies on military operations, while the overseas theater headquarters staffs, whose ideas on projected operations were based on steadily accumulating experience, had an increasing amount of influence. In the second place, the Army Air Forces more and more often were advancing independent views in joint discussions, even though these usually had been threshed out in advance with OPD, and it was coming to exercise more direct control over Air operations. In the third place, American planners on all the higher staffs and committees, above all in OPD, had learned to feel out the position of their British "opposite numbers" in an effort to anticipate and minimize the difficulties in the way of firm agreement. In the fourth place, these same planners could turn to qualified staffs and standing committees in the field of logistics for critical analysis of strategic studies, and recognized the need for doing so. In the fifth place, finally, the planners recognized that wartime military strategy had to be tailored to fit the rest of national policy, especially foreign policy.

The military plans for the end of the war against Japan took shape very slowly. Most of them were drafted during the last twelve months of hostilities and were ground out by the complicated Washington planning machinery that had been set up by that time. OPD officers continued to have influence in military planning, but the Division usually expressed its point of view indirectly through the JLC, the JPS, or the JCS. This procedure was the logical development of planning in a joint coalition war. The new machinery produced results, but it tended to produce them slowly, not so much because of its own weaknesses as because of the magnitude and complexity of the problems. In addition to the normal uncertainties in planning, there were such basic factors limiting progress as the unknown date of the end of the European campaigns and the delicacy of trying to achieve a compromise or resolution of the Army-Navy (SWPA-POA) deadlock on operations north of the Philippines. Only a staff with interests as broad and authority as great as OPD's could attempt to tie all the elements of military planning together and call the result strategy or policy.

What OPD was able to do was to participate in nearly every phase of Washington staff preparations for redeployment to the Pacific after the defeat of Germany, draft the outline plans for the guidance of theater staffs in planning final operations in the Pacific, and hurriedly improvise the first plans for the surrender and occupation of Japan. Much of this planning was never tested by operations in the way that the strategy OPD recommended in 1942 had been tested. Much of it was altered materially, or entirely superseded by the events which followed in rapid sequence after the

experimental use of the atomic bomb at Los Alamos, New Mexico, in mid-July 1945. The first of these was the Potsdam decision to use the atomic bomb, the second, the bombing of Hiroshimo and Nagasaki (6 and 9 August, Japanese time), and the third, the surrender of Japan (14 August, Eastern Standard time).

Initial American Strategy [1]

American strategy in the war against Japan necessarily remained shapeless and vague long after the crystallization of the main lines of thought about defeating Germany. Through 1942 and early in 1943 long-range strategic planning for Pacific and Far Eastern operations was compounded of approximately equal parts of tactical opportunism and abstract geopolitical theory. At the beginning of 1943 the tactical opportunism, operating for the most part within the limitations of a general defensive strategy in the Pacific, had brought about the campaigns in New Guinea and the Solomon Islands. At that time Admiral King at Casablanca restated the geopolitical abstraction which constituted the main justification in military terms for keeping China in the war and for establishing an American command in the China-Burma-India area: "In the European theater Russia was most advantageously placed for dealing with Germany in view of her geographical position and manpower; in the Pacific, China bore a similar relation to the Japanese. It should be our basic policy

---

[1] Except for documents quoted for illustrative purposes, the materials on which the following summary of early Pacific and Far Eastern strategy is based are not cited. The summary is designed as a simple introduction to the case history of 1945 staff action. A detailed account of the development of Pacific strategy will be presented in subsequent volumes of this series.

to provide the manpower resources of Russia and China with the necessary equipment to enable them to fight." [2] Beyond this point, there were as many theories about future strategy as there were separate staffs in Washington and separate commands in the Pacific and Far East. Official approved strategy as of early 1943 went no further.

During 1943, without any clear repudiation of the previous trend of planning, a new strategic concept gradually emerged in Washington planning. Planning officers in OPD and on the JWPC began urging a "firm decision" and an "early decision" about "an over-all plan of campaign against Japan." [3] The character of the over-all plan developed slowly in response to a number of interdependent factors. The most complicated political and administrative situation in which the U. S. Army operated in World War II was prolonging interminably the organization of Allied ground forces for campaigns in Burma or China. Early island operations in the Pacific, together with the beginning of the gradual reorganization of American fleets around the new, fast aircraft carriers, attracted attention to the naval route to Japan through the island chains of the central Pacific. The new VLR bomber, the B–29, proved to be capable of operating at a range that would let it strike at the Japanese home islands from bases in the Marianas as well as from China, where the bases were originally planned. The British Chiefs of Staff and the Prime Minister continued to be reluctant to schedule major operations in Burma, the overland road to China, but instead favored throwing the weight of their effort in the Far East toward the Netherlands East Indies and Singapore.

Planning for American operations against Japan gradually came to center east of Singapore, to include the Marianas in one main line of approach, and to converge on what was usually called the Formosa-Luzon area. An air campaign in China was approved by President Roosevelt and Generalissimo Chiang Kai-shek. A ground campaign in China was not definitely ruled out. Some kind of operation in Burma remained on the planning schedule. The American advance from the Southwest Pacific was to continue until it brought General Mac-Arthur's forces to within striking distance of the Formosa-Luzon objective. A great many questions about the ultimate defeat of Japan were left unanswered, but by the end of 1943 American planners favored and the CCS had approved in principle as a basis for future planning that the main avenue of approach to Japan would be across the Pacific Ocean rather than from the Asiatic mainland.[4] General Handy advised General Marshall in December 1943, a few days before the CCS approved the over-all plan for the defeat of Japan:

This paper in effect agrees to put the main effort of the war against Japan in the Pacific. It does not attempt to establish at this time any long range main effort within the Pacific area. A great advantage of the plan is its flexibility in allowing the Joint Chiefs at any time to create a main effort by the commitment of forces to one or the other axis. It also, of course, allows the Joint Chiefs of Staff to take advantage of the situation as it develops. By accepting this paper, we leave all discussions of the merits of the Central and Southwest Pacific to the Joint Chiefs of Staff.[5]

---

[2] Min 58th meeting CCS, 16 Jan 43.

[3] Memo, Brig Gen Hull for Maj Gen Handy, 17 Jul 43, no sub, with Tab SS 111 in ABC 381 Strategy Sec Papers (7 Jan 43).

[4] (1) CCS 417/2, 23 Dec 43, title: Over-All Plan for Defeat of Japan. (2) Min 137th meeting CCS, SEXTANT, 6 Dec 43.

[5] Memo, Maj Gen Handy for Gen Marshall, 3 Dec 43, no sub, Paper 21, Item 15, Exec 5.

Underlying the decision in favor of the Pacific approach to Japan was an assumption that forced American planners to push their strategic thinking one step further in 1944. It had been implicit in CCS decisions on the Pacific war since the Casablanca Conference, and it was stated explicitly in QUADRANT, when the President, the Prime Minister, and the CCS agreed: "From every point of view operations should be framed to force the defeat of Japan as soon as possible after the defeat of Germany. Planning should be on the basis of accomplishing this within twelve months of that event." [6] Both determination and hope to defeat Japan quickly received a powerful reinforcement shortly afterwards by the Soviet commitment at SEXTANT to join in the war in the Far East.

The necessity of planning for a speedy conquest of Japan, with speed defined in terms of months rather than years, made it imperative for staff officers to come to grips with the question of how to end the war against Japan. Earlier in the war, with limited forces a great distance from Tokyo, a hedging statement would suffice. Thus the JCS presented and the CCS "noted" at Casablanca the following convictions:

The ultimate defeat of Japan proper will be accomplished by measures which greatly resemble those which would be effective against the British Isles—blockade (attack on ships and shipping), bombing (attack on forces, defenses, industries, and morale), and assault (attack via the sea). Of these measures, attacks on ships and shipping along enemy lines of communications are inherent in all offensive operations; it is our purpose during 1943 to work toward positions from which Japan

can be attacked by land based air; assault on Japan is remote and may well not be found necessary. [7]

Once the CCS had approved plans for an advance to the Formosa-Luzon area and had clipped the Pacific timetable to fit a target end date of twelve months after the collapse of Germany, concrete planning for the decisive operation was in order. [8] OPD officers in particular, since they would have to redeploy and organize assault forces long in advance of any full-scale attack, had to get a ruling on whether or not invasion of the Japanese home islands would be necessary.

During 1944 the Washington planners threshed out this last major issue in Pacific strategy. By March the JCS had issued definite instructions to the Pacific commands for the dual advance, with General MacArthur's forces moving to the southern Philippines and Admiral Nimitz' forces moving to the Marianas and Palaus, to culminate in a major operation somewhere in the Formosa-Luzon area by February 1945. [9] Every American military agency had good reason to want to know what that major operation would be and where it would lead. The Army Air Forces in particular had an urgent practical need to proceed at once to a decision on the projected employment of air and ground forces in the ultimate defeat of Japan. [10] As a re-

---

[6] (1) CCS 319/2, 21 Aug 43, title: Progress Rpt to President and Prime Minister. (2) Memo, JPS for JCS, 17 Aug 43, sub: Appreciation and Plan for Defeat of Japan (CPS 83), with CPS 83 in ABC 381 Japan (27 Aug 42), 3. (3) CPS 83, 8 Aug 43, title: Appreciation and Plan. . . .

[7] (1) CCS 168, 22 Jan 43, title: Conduct of War in Pacific Theater in 1943. (2) Min 67th meeting CCS, 22 Jan 43.
[8] The late 1943 estimate—for planning purposes, not a prediction—was that Germany would be defeated by 1 October 1944. See CPS 86/D, 26 Aug 43, title: Preparation of Studies on Defeat of Japan.
[9] JCS 713/4, 12 Mar 44, title: Future Opns in Pacific.
[10] JCS 751, 8 Mar 44, title: Bsc Decisions which Will Give Strategic Guidance for Conduct of War in Pacific.

sult of General Arnold's urging, the wheels of the joint planning machinery began to turn. The JWPC and the JSSC began studying the issue of where to go in the Formosa-Luzon area, and where to go from there.[11]

As early as April 1944 OPD's Strategy Section had formulated the basic stand which, after a number of adjustments and refinements in subsidiary recommendations, the Army adopted in joint discussions. In the simplest terms, as originally phrased in the Strategy Section, it was: "*a.* The collapse of Japan as a result of blockade and air bombardment alone is very doubtful. *b.* The collapse of Japan can be assured only by invasion of Japan proper." [12] Some of the Army Air Forces staff officers reacted to this statement of Strategy Section views promptly, vigorously, and adversely. Among many pointed criticisms of the paper, these critics stated most emphatically, first, that it made insufficient allowance for the possible effects of strategic blockade, and bombardment, and second, that JCS and CCS strategy so far had been directed at bringing about the collapse of Japan "by other means than invasion, while preparing for invasion as an ultimate alternative requirement." [13] The comment on previous strategy was correct, but OPD officers presented two reasons why that strategy was no longer practicable under the twelve-month victory assumption:

The fact that future operations beyond Formosa must be planned and resources for them gathered. This probably will require six months.

The increasing pressure by the British to be allowed to participate in the planning for the Pacific war. It is mandatory that the United States determine the strategy and plan the operations as soon as possible so that its position is settled before the next United States-British conference.[14]

While this exchange of ideas did not reflect any basic disagreement between General Marshall and General Arnold or between the Army planner and the Air planner, it called attention to the fact that it was becoming more and more urgent either to decide that blockade and bombardment definitely would bring about the collapse of Japan or to begin preparing for an invasion of the home islands.

Early in June the JWPC finished its inquiry into Pacific strategy and issued a comprehensive study, JPS 476, entitled "Operations Against Japan, Subsequent to Formosa." [15] It incorporated the essential point made by OPD's Strategy Section officers about the necessity to develop plans for an early invasion of Japan proper. In fact it proceeded well beyond the Strategy Section's original position and came out with a detailed strategic study outlining a series of campaigns leading to an assault on the Tokyo Plain by the end of 1945. The study as a whole was a compromise, incorporating recommendations and suggestions made by Ground, Air, and Navy.

The JWPC pointed out in JPS 476 that the present and projected rate of advance of the increasingly strong American forces

---

[11] (1) JPS 418/1, 23 Mar 44, title: Bsc Decisions . . . . (2) JCS 751/3, 4 Apr 44, title: Bsc Decisions . . . . (3) JPS 418/2/D, 11 Apr 44, title: Strategic Plan for War in Asia.

[12] SS 282, 24 Apr 44, title: Opns in Pacific, ABC 381 Strategy Sec Papers (7 Jan 43).

[13] AAF brief, Lt Col F. S. Wildman [Chief, Strategy Sec of Combined & Joint Stf Div of Air Planner's Stf] for Air planner, 17 May 44, sub: Opns in Pacific/SS 282, with SS 282 in ABC 381 Strategy Sec Papers (7 Jan 43).

[14] Memo, Col J. J. Billo [Chief Strategy Sec] for Chief S&P, 6 May 44, sub: Opns in Pacific, with SS 282 in ABC 381 Strategy Sec Papers (7 Jan 43).

[15] JPS 476, 6 Jun 44, sub: Opns Against Japan, Subsequent to Formosa.

in the Pacific gave solid grounds for expecting to reach the "Inner Zone defense of Japan" by the spring of 1945. In the light of this fact, the JWPC concluded that the over-all strategy approved by the CCS at SEXTANT, extending only to the perimeter of the Formosa-Luzon area, was inadequate. The committee observed, in reference to this strategy:

It reflects the fact that we were a long distance from Japan at that time and that our future operational plans were somewhat vague. It implies that it is quite possible to defeat Japan without an invasion. We consider this to be an overly optimistic attitude. While the bombing and blockade of Japan will have a considerable effect upon Japanese morale and their ability to continue the war, there is little reason to believe that such action alone is certain to result in the early unconditional surrender of Japan.

While taking pains to recognize that it might be possible to "defeat Japan by aerial bombing and blockade, accompanied by destruction of her sea and air forces," the JWPC concluded that this strategy "probably would involve an unacceptable delay in forcing unconditional surrender" and therefore recommended that "our concept of operations against Japan, subsequent to a lodgment in Formosa, should envisage an invasion of the industrial heart of Japan." Restated in JPS 476 accordingly, the concept would then be:

To force the unconditional surrender of Japan by:
(1) Lowering Japanese ability and will to resist by establishing sea and air blockades, conducting intensive air bombardment, and destroying Japanese air and naval strength.
(2) Invading and seizing objectives in the industrial heart of Japan.

The JWPC further recommended, irrespective of CCS approval of this restatement of the over-all objective, that the JCS

approve it "as a basis for planning by agencies of the Joint Chiefs of Staff, and War and Navy Departments."

The JWPC also proposed a schedule of operations in harmony with this new strategic concept. Operations striking directly at the Japanese home islands in 1945 were outlined in three phases. In the first (1 April–30 June 1945), American forces would seize the Bonins and the Ryukyus and launch an assault on the central China coast in the Ningpo (Hangchow Bay) area. The second phase (30 June–30 September 1945) would be occupied with consolidation and initial exploitation of these positions, and the third phase (30 September–31 December 1945) would bring American forces ashore on Kyushu, 1 October, and on the Tokyo Plain (Honshu), 31 December.

After committee discussion, during which Brig. Gen. William W. Bessell, Jr., the senior Army member of the JWPC, explained that the selection of Kyushu as the first target in the home islands was tentative, and emphasized the need to orient operations toward the final attack on the Tokyo Plain by giving "theater commanders an idea of the diminishing importance of the China coast," the Joint Staff Planners approved JPS 476 for submission to the JCS.[16]

As the Joint Staff Planners noted in forwarding the study, the joint staff was examining the possibility of accelerated operations bypassing Formosa entirely and moving directly to Japan proper.[17] On the basis of the JWPC study and the Joint Staff Planners recommendation, the JCS proposed to the CCS, 11 July 1944, to revise

---

[16] Min 157th meetings JPS, 28 Jun 44.
[17] (1) JCS 924, 30 Jun 44, title: Opns Against Japan. . . . (2) Min 157th meeting JPS, 28 Jun 44.

the over-all objective, on the following basis:

Our successes to date, our present superiority in air and sea forces, and the prospective availability of forces following the defeat of Germany, lead us to believe that our concept of operations against Japan following Formosa should envisage an invasion into the industrial heart of Japan. While it may be possible to defeat Japan by sustained aerial bombardment and the destruction of her sea and air forces, this would probably involve an unacceptable delay.[18]

As General Marshall explained, during initial CCS discussion of the proposal:

It was now clear to the U. S. Chiefs of Staff that, in order to finish the war with the Japanese quickly, it will be necessary to invade the industrial heart of Japan. The means for this action were not available when the over-all concept had been originally discussed. It is now, however, within our power to do this and and the U. S. Chiefs of Staff feel that our intention to undertake it should be appropriately indicated.[19]

The initial success of the OVERLORD assault was encouraging hopes of rapid progress of the war in Europe while the JCS was considering the new strategic plan. By the time the British Chiefs of Staff were ready to act at the end of July, the battle for Saint-Lô was over and American forces were beginning their great break-through in Normandy. The British chiefs, through their representatives in Washington, accepted the JCS view on 29 July 1944, subject to assurance that the change in Pacific strategy would not affect existing agreements giving priority to operations in Europe nor con-

stitute implied authorization for specific operations in the Pacific not already approved by the CCS.[20] Finally, at OCTAGON in September, the CCS formally incorporated in combined strategy the new definition of the over-all objective of the war against Japan and, at the same time, approved for planning purposes a new schedule of operations incorporating the 1945 campaigns ending with Kyushu in October and the Tokyo Plain in December.[21]

At the end of 1944, then, although many critical and controversial problems remained to be solved within the general pattern, the main lines of strategy in the Pacific were fixed. The military staff could turn attention to the many related issues, ranging from logistic preparations for the assault to politico-military terms on which the war might be brought to end within the limits of the unconditional surrender policy. Army officers were very much aware that the task of inflicting a decisive defeat on Japan, whose army was believed to be stronger than at the outset of the War, was not easy. OPD emphasized this point, even while urging the necessity of invading Japan, and also emphasized the importance of economizing life and resources. A long study written at the end of September 1944 for the Under Secretary of War, at his request, on the implications of the new broad strategy of the war against Japan, concluded:

Summing up, we find that the problem of attacking Japan with forces based in China presents logistic problems far greater than

---

[18] CCS 417/3, 11 Jul 44, title: Over-All Objective in War Against Japan. The JCS acted informally to approve the recommendations of JCS 924, JCS unnumbered paper, 11 Jul 44, title: Decision Amending JCS 924, with JCS 924 in ABC 384 Pacific (1-17-43), 4.

[19] Min 167th meeting CCS, 14 Jul 44.

[20] (1) CCS 417/4, 29 Jul 44. (2) CCS 417/5, 4 Aug 44.

[21] (1) CCS 417/8, 9 Sep 44, title: Opn for Defeat of Japan. (2) CCS 417/9, OCTAGON, 11 Sep 44, title: Over-All Objective in War Against Japan. (3) Min 173d meeting CCS, 13 Sep 44.

anything yet attempted in this war. To attack Japan from the sea with an amphibious force means transporting hundreds of thousands of men and vast quantities of supplies some thousands of miles across the Pacific Ocean with only small islands at which staging or mounting can be effected. To those who vividly remember the difficulty of landing on the Normandy beaches, only some fifty miles across the Channel from the base in Britain, the magnitude of this problem is apparent.[22]

Planning for a Prolonged Pacific War

The late 1944 period of optimism about the early collapse of German resistance, in which planning for the early invasion of Japan took place, diminished at the end of September when the Allied airborne army failed to hold a bridgehead across the lower Rhine, and definitely ended with the German counteroffensive in the Ardennes in December. The S&P compilation of papers for use by planners and the Chief of Staff at ARGONAUT advanced the same plans for the defeat of Japan that had been drawn up in September 1944, but pointed out that the critical operations, Kyushu and Tokyo Plain, had not been approved except for planning purposes and that because of the "estimated lengthening of the war in Europe, it is anticipated that the tempo of operations in the Pacific will have to be decreased." [23] At ARGONAUT General Marshall and Admiral King reported that plans were ready for an attack on Kyushu and Honshu in 1945, but that these plans depended on redeployment from Europe,

which would require from four to six months.[24]

The CCS and the heads of government approved a policy designed, "upon the defeat of Germany," to "bring about at the earliest possible date the unconditional surrender of Japan." They also approved as one of the basic undertakings related to this strategy the continuation of operations leading to the "earliest practicable invasion of Japan." Their common emphasis on a speedy defeat of Japan was tempered by a conservative official estimate of the time at which it would come. They recommended that for planning purposes the date for the end of the war against Japan be eighteen months after the defeat of Germany which they set at sometime after 1 July 1945. These dates of course were conservatively selected to provide a safe yardstick for logistic planning and were in no sense predictions. Finally, they took note of the strategic ideas about the Pacific war, evolved during the previous six months and amalgamated in a single ARGONAUT paper.[25]

This ARGONAUT planning paper stated that the agreed objective in the war against Japan was to force unconditional surrender, first, by lowering Japanese ability and will to resist by establishing sea and air blockades, conducting intensive air bombardment, and destroying Japanese air and naval strength; and second, by invading and seizing objectives in the industrial heart of Japan. The paper then reported that the JCS, which had primary strategic responsibility for Pacific operations, had adopted a plan of operations against Japan. First, intensification of the blockade and air bom-

---

[22] Study, Col J. J. Billo, submitted with memo, OPD for USW, 28 Sep 44, sub: Info on Broad Strategy to be Used Against Japan, with CCS 417/8 in ABC 381 Japan (8–27–42), 7.

[23] Tab 5, Tab B, S&P Book, n.d., title: Papers for Discussion at ARGONAUT, ABC 337 (11 Jan 45), 1–B.

[24] Min 184th meeting CCS, ARGONAUT, 1 Feb 45.

[25] CCS 776/3, 9 Feb 45, title: Rpt to President and Prime Minister. The amalgamated study on the war against Japan was CCS 417/11, ARGONAUT, 22 Jan 45, title: Opns for Defeat of Japan.

bardment of Japan would create a situation favorable to an assault on Kyushu; second, the Kyushu operation would further reduce Japanese capabilities and further intensify blockade and air bombardment, thus establishing a tactical condition favorable to the decisive invasion of the industrial heart of Japan through the Tokyo Plain.

At the last ARGONAUT meeting Prime Minister Churchill suggested that after the defeat of Germany an ultimatum should be issued to Japan directing them to surrender unconditionally. He suggested that some mitigation in the Allied attitude toward Japan "would be worth while if it led to the saving of a year and a half of a war in which so much blood and treasure would be poured out." However, he hastened to add, "Great Britain would not press for any mitigation but would be content to abide by the judgment of the United States." President Roosevelt agreed that an ultimatum should be considered, but declared that he "doubted whether the ultimatum would have much effect on the Japanese, who did not seem to realize what was going on in the world outside, and still seemed to think that they might get a satisfactory compromise." [26] Despite the President's skepticism about the results of an ultimatum and the clear implication of the statements of both the Prime Minister and the President that mitigation did not mean a compromise peace satisfactory to the Japanese, the whole problem of the possibility of Japanese surrender received a great deal of attention in the following months.

The Army planning staff continued to emphasize the need for being prepared at any time to reorient American plans without delay toward the Pacific, even though 1 July 1945 had been adopted by the CCS as a date to be used in making logistic preparations. The Army planner, General Lincoln, left special instructions on this point, before departing on the round-the-world planning survey in February 1945, for Col. Thomas D. Roberts, who was to represent him on the Joint Staff Planners during his absence:

At the JCS meeting today Admiral King made a comment on the CCS decision to accept 1 July as a planning date which is the earliest the war is likely to end. His remark indicated that in his mind we would now consider that the Pacific War would be planned on the basis of the European War lasting until 1 July or thereafter.

The fallacy is, of course, evident to you. These planning dates for the end of the war were selected at the request of the British for use of their civilian and logistical people and administrative purposes.

You may find it necessary in the Planners before I get back to edit papers rigidly with a view to maintaining our stand that we must be prepared to switch at once to the Pacific any day from today forward since there is a possibility, increasing with every week, that this war in Europe may fold up ahead of 1 July.[27]

Nevertheless, the planners, while recognizing the need for flexibility, began to readjust their scheduling of operations to take account of the unexpected duration of the war against Germany. The Kyushu and Honshu operations clearly had to be postponed. Notes prepared in S&P pointed out that the "continuation of the war in Europe made the planning dates for Kyushu and Honshu unrealistic." These notes warned: "We may thus be forced from our 'invasion' strategy into a 'blockade' strategy, at least temporarily, by our inability to assemble

---

[26] Min 2d plenary meeting, ARGONAUT, 9 Feb 45, Official ARGONAUT Conference Book.

[27] Memo, Brig Gen Lincoln for Col Roberts, 7 Feb 45, no sub, with JWPC Memo for Info 35 in ABC 384 Pacific (1–17–43), 7.

forces required." [28] In March OPD drafted a message for General MacArthur succinctly summarizing the new planning schedule then being worked out as a result of the necessity of decelerating in the Pacific: "Coronet [Tokyo Plain] will be the decisive operation against Japan and will be concurrently supported and assisted by continuation of Olympic [Kyushu]. . . . Based on assumption the European war ends by 1 July 1945, planning is aimed at making possible target dates for Olympic and Coronet of 1 December 1945 and 1 March 1946 respectively." [29]

In mid-March 1945 OPD's senior representative on the JWPC noted: "It seems at last to be acknowledged that the ultimate defeat of Japan will require the invasion of Japan proper and the defeat of her ground forces there." [30] Nevertheless, some of the American planners were still inclined to prolong the period of time before the decisive invasion in order to give the Japanese a chance to feel the effect of the sea-air blockade. [31] At this time the inference was less that the Japanese would surrender under the influence of the air-sea blockade than that the ground forces should not be sent ashore before the full weight of the naval and aerial campaign had been brought to bear. No one clearly went on record in formal discussions as believing that any method of attack would end the

war very quickly, although the Army Air Forces and Navy air planners almost certainly retained more optimistic private views about the effects of bombardment than the ground force officers held. Thus the detailed operational planning that later brought about the concentrated and coordinated bombardment of the Japanese home islands by Army Air Forces B–29's and naval fast carrier task groups began in March, but the language used indicated merely that the bombardment should be conceived as undertaken "in order to create the most favorable situation in the shortest possible time for an amphibious assault against Japan proper." [32]

Similarly, American planners who were busy evaluating the degree of possibility of Japanese surrender before a "decisive invasion" of the home islands showed no conviction that there was any probability requiring immediate preparations. [33] In February 1945 Col. Robert J. Wood of OPD had raised the possibility that the Japanese might conceivably collapse or surrender about V–E Day and that no advance planning to take care of such an eventuality had been done. [34] However, his own group in OPD, in considering some "proposals respecting surrender documents for Japan" drawn up by the State-War-Navy Coordinating Committee about that time, declared that urgency was not apparent. [35]

[28] OPD notes for 190th meeting JPS, 21 Feb 45, filed with JCS 924/11 in ABC 381 Japan (8–27–42), 7.

[29] Msg, Gen Marshall for Gen MacArthur, 23 Mar 45, CM–OUT 57902. OPD drafted the message.

[30] Memo, Brig Gen Bessell and Brig Gen F. F. Everest for Army and Air planners, 16 Mar 45, sub: Reorgn and Future Opns in Pacific Theater, OPD 384 TS, 1/9.

[31] (1) Memo, Brig Gen Lincoln for Maj Gen Hull, 26 Mar 45, no sub. (2) Msg, Gen Marshall for Gen MacArthur, 4 Apr 45, OPD 384 TS, 1/12, CM–OUT 63196.

[32] JWPC 325/M, 8 Mar 45, title: Jt Bmr Offensive Against Japan.

[33] (1) JIS 141/M, 6 Apr 45, title: Defeat of Japan by Blockade and Bomb. (2) JIS 143/M, 7 Apr 45, title: Unconditional Surr of Japan.

[34] Memo, Col Wood for Chief S&P, 11 Feb 45, sub: Collapse of Japanese Govt on or About V–E Day, filed with JWPC 264/D in ABC 384.1 Japan (22 Aug 44).

[35] OPD Memo for Asst Secy WDGS, 4 Mar 45, sub: Unconditional Surr of Japan (JCS 1275/1), filed with JCS 1275/1 in ABC 387 Japan (15 Feb 45), 1–A.

The limits of such disagreement as existed about the possibility of Japanese surrender were defined in a Joint Intelligence Committee paper on the war in the Pacific. It developed at length the idea that a "clarification of Allied intentions with regard to the Japanese nation might bring nearer the possibility of unconditional surrender [and that] . . . there is a possibility that some constitutional Japanese central government, backed by the Emperor, may seek and accept a rationalized version of unconditional surrender before the end of 1945." This date, the end of 1945, was the extreme range of optimism officially expressed at this time. This fact gave momentum to the effort to find a formula which would be acceptable to the Allies and yet cause Japan to surrender before the invasion of Japan proper. The paper went on to say, in connection with this optimistic interpretation of the time factor: "For planning purposes, however, it is obviously impossible to count upon such a development, and it is more probable that unconditional surrender could not be forced upon the Japanese before the middle of the latter part of 1946, if then, as a result of air-sea blockade and air attacks alone." The contribution of this paper to the resolution of differences of opinion about the results of the air-sea blockade and air attacks was a clear-cut intelligence estimate of the time factor:

> The Japanese "will" to continue the war may be expected to weaken progressively. Entirely apart from the physical results obtained by air-sea blockade combined with strategic bombing, the psychological effects upon the Japanese people as a whole will be most detrimental and will progressively undermine their confidence in victory or even confidence in the hope of avoiding complete and inevitable defeat. Thus we believe that under the full impact of air-sea blockade combined with

strategic bombing, Japan's "will" to continue the war can be broken.

> It does not follow that such air-sea blockades and air attacks upon Japan Proper, without actual invasion of the home islands, will force unconditional surrender within a reasonable length of time. On this point there is a wide divergence of informed opinion. . . . Estimates with regard to the time element vary from a few months to a great many years.[36]

The general philosophy of the possibility of Japanese surrender changed very little in official pronouncements after April. By the end of April the Army planner, General Lincoln, had become convinced that some thinking should be done on "what we do if Japan decides to surrender on VE-Day," as he provocatively phrased it.[37] Even though the prospect of an early surrender of Japan began to get a little consideration from Washington staffs in April and May, much more attention was being concentrated on issuing a directive for operation OLYMPIC, scheduled for 1 November 1945. There was no disagreement about the necessity of preparing to launch this initial invasion of the home islands. The directive to Pacific commanders finally was approved on 25 May 1945, although its precise meaning continued to be debated hotly until well into the latter part of June.[38] Somewhat earlier, on 5 May, the JWPC produced an outline plan for the invasion of Tokyo Plain. The generally conservative planning approach then current prevented a categoric statement that even this

---

[36] JIC 266/1, 18 Apr 45, title: Defeat of Japan by Blockade and Bomb.

[37] Memo, Brig Gen Lincoln for Strategy and Army Secs, JWPC, 28 Apr 45, no sub, filed with JIC 268/1 in ABC 387 Japan (15 Feb 45), 1–A.

[38] JCS 1331/3, 25 May 45, title: Directive for Opn "OLYMPIC," Kyushu (4 Jul 44) dispatched as msg, JCS for Gen MacArthur, Gen Arnold, and Admiral Nimitz, 25 May 45, CM-OUT 87938 (TS).

operation scheduled for March 1946 would be decisive. The outline plan cautiously stated:

> The invasion of the Kanto [Tokyo] Plain may prove to be the decisive operation in the campaign to bring about the unconditional surrender of Japan through domination of her home islands. The over-all objectives of this operation are therefore considered to be to inflict a decisive defeat upon the Japanese Army in the heart of the Empire and, in the event this campaign does not in itself bring about unconditional surrender and achieve full military control of the main islands, to obtain positions from which to continue air, ground and amphibious operations in the main islands.[39]

After completing the outline for the operation against the Tokyo Plain, the JWPC produced its first two studies on military operations in the event of sudden Japanese surrender. They discussed "strategic positions selected for operation upon Japanese withdrawal, collapse or surrender" and the "forces required for the occupation."[40] OPD planners revealed their attitude toward the possibility of surrender in commenting on these JWPC papers for the benefit of the Army planner and the Division chief. The comment combined a general emphasis on preparedness to meet all military contingencies with explicit skepticism about the chances of an early Japanese surrender. OPD recommended merely that JWPC studies be furnished the commanders in the Pacific and that the JCS

instruct those commanders to plan specifically for a contingency such as collapse or surrender. OPD's recommendations were approved all the way up the line to the Joint Chiefs of Staff. On 14 June a directive went out to General MacArthur, Admiral Nimitz, and General Arnold. It followed the basically conservative language used in the original OPD draft: "Although there is at present no evidence that sudden collapse or surrender of Japan is likely, the Joint Chiefs of Staff direct that plans be made to take immediate advantage of favorble circumstances, such as a sudden collapse or surrender, to effect an entry into Japan proper for occupational purposes."[41]

The clearest statements of OPD's attitude on the subject of surrender and the desirability of developing a precise formula for unconditional surrender, appeared in two studies prepared in early June at the request of the Secretary of War. The first study concluded:

> The point in our military progress at which the Japanese will accept defeat and agree to our terms is unpredictable. . . . Like the Germans, their protracted resistance is based upon the hope of achieving a conditional surrender. Presumably, only the conviction that their position is completely hopeless will persuade them to give up their holdings in Asia. Probably it will take Russian entry into the war, coupled with a landing, or imminent threat of landing, on Japan proper by us, to convince them of the hopelessness of their position.[42]

The second study on the same subject dwelt more specifically with the surrender formula:

---

[39] JWPC 263/4, 5 May 45, title: An Outline Plan for Invasion of Kanto (Tokyo) Plain.

[40] (1) JWPC 264/1, 16 May 45, title: Strategic Positions Selected for Occupation Upon Japanese Withdrawal, Collapse, or Surr. (2) JWPC 264/2, 16 May 45, title: Forces Required for Occupation of Strategic Positions in Japan Proper. (3) Memo, Brig Gen Lincoln for JPS, 28 May 45, no sub, and atchd note, Brig Gen Lincoln for Col T. D. Roberts, n.d., no sub, JWPC 264/2 in ABC 384.1 Japan (22 Aug 44).

[41] (1) Msg, JCS for Gen MacArthur, Gen Arnold, and Admiral Nimitz, 14 Jun 45, CM-OUT 17064. (2) JCS 1331/4, 8 Jun 45, title: Occupation of Strategic Areas in Japan Proper in Event of Collapse or Surr.

[42] S&P study, Brig Gen Lincoln, 4 Jun 45, no sub, incl to OPD draft memo, CofS for SW, n.d., no sub, OPD 336 TS, 119.

The proposal of a public declaration of war aims, in effect giving definition to "unconditional surrender" has definite merit.

We must make certain our military operations and preparations continue with undiminished pressure, even though we bring increasing political and psychological pressure on the Japanese to persuade them to capitulate.[43]

Evolution of the Terminal Surrender Formula

The latter half of June saw the formulation of the surrender ultimatum issued from Potsdam. It was an example of characteristic Washington staff work in the last months of the war. Secretary Stimson and Assistant Secretary McCloy took the lead in working out the formula all had agreed might hasten Japanese surrender or at least increase the psychological strain under which the Japanese continued to resist. Representatives of the State Department, the Navy Department, the Army Air Forces, G–2, the Civil Affairs Division, and the Operations Division worked on the proposed proclamation. General Lincoln, as S&P chief, took a hand in fashioning the ultimatum, as did Colonel Bonesteel and his politico-military specialists in the Policy Section. In addition, OPD prepared the supporting memorandum on timing. On 2 July 1945 Secretary Stimson sent the net result of all this work to the President as "background for . . . discussions at the forthcoming conference," the Potsdam (TERMINAL) international staff meeting of 16–26 July 1945.[44] As OPD officers put it in one of the

papers prepared in S&P for the Potsdam Conference, the proclamation was "intended to induce the surrender of Japan and thus avoid the heavy casualties which would result from a fight to the finish." [45]

Just before the Army delegation departed for Potsdam in July 1945, OPD completed its "Compilation of Subjects for Discussion at TERMINAL," the War Department's summary book of operational fact, military doctrine, and planning opinion as of 12 July 1945. In addition to recommending that the planners adhere to the planned sequence of operations—invasion of Kyushu on 1 November 1945 and invasion of Honshu on 1 March 1946—OPD declared:

There is much to be gained by defining as completely as possible, the detailed U. S. war aims in Japan. . . .

Japanese surrender would be advantageous for the U. S., both because of the enormous reduction in the cost of the war and because it would give us a better chance to settle the affairs of the Western Pacific before too many of our allies are committed there and have made substantial contributions towards the defeat of Japan. . . .

The present stand of the War Department is that Japanese surrender is just possible and is attractive enough to the U. S. to justify us in making any concession which might be attractive to the Japanese, so long as our realis-

---

[43] (1) S&P study, Brig Gen Lincoln, n.d., no sub, incl to OPD draft memo, CofS for SW, 15 Jun 45, no sub, OPD 387.4 TS, 17. (2) Memo, OPD for CofS [17 Jun 45], sub: Amplifying Comments on Planners' Paper for Presentation to President, OPD 381 TS, 135/27.

[44] Ltr, SW to President, 2 Jul 45, no sub, filed with JCS 1340/2 in ABC 387 Japan (15 Feb 45),

1–B. For reports on the various conferences and several draft papers, see draft memo, SW for President, 27 Jun 45, sub: Proposed Program for Japan, ABC 336 Russia (22 Aug 43), 3. See also the following papers, filed with JCS 1340/2 in ABC 387 Japan (15 Feb 45), 1–B: (1) memo, Col Bonesteel for Brig Gen Lincoln, 27 Jun 45, sub: Immediate Demand for Japanese Surr; (2) memo, Brig Gen Lincoln for Lt Gen Hull, 28 Jun 45, no sub; (3) memo, Brig Gen Lincoln for Lt Gen Hull, 29 Jun 45, sub: Demand for Japanese Surr; (4) memo, Brig Gen Lincoln for Lt Gen Hull, 29 Jun 45, no sub; (5) memo, Brig Gen Lincoln for Lt Gen Hull, 30 Jun 45, sub: Demand for Japanese Surr.

[45] Memo, OPD for Lt Gen Hull [in Potsdam], 14 Jul 45, sub: JSSC Comments on Proclamation Regarding Unconditional Surr of Japan, OPD 387.4 TS (14 Jul 45), 10/7.

tic aims for peace in the Pacific are not adversely affected.[46]

The TERMINAL Conference reaffirmed every principle of previous military planning for the defeat of Japan. American plans for the Kyushu and Honshu operations were noted, and the preparations of Great Britain and the USSR to join in the defeat of Japan were carefully and favorably considered. The over-all objective announced in the agreed summary of conclusions of the conference brought out the emphasis on the time factor, the intention of attacking Japanese will to resist by every device, and concentration on the main effort of invading the Japanese home islands. Thus the "over-all strategic concept for the prosecution of the war" was set forth:

In cooperation with other Allies to bring about at the earliest possible date the defeat of Japan by: lowering Japanese ability and will to resist by establishing sea and air blockades, conducting intensive air bombardment, and destroying Japanese air and naval strength; invading and seizing objectives in the Japanese home islands as the main effort. . . .
The invasion of Japan and operations directly connected therewith are the supreme operations in the war against Japan.[47]

The conservative logistic planning date of 15 November 1946 for the end of organized Japanese resistance was accepted.[48] The Potsdam Ultimatum was issued on 26 July 1945 as a calculated effort to lower Japanese

will to resist while military pressures were building up.[49]

At Potsdam, General Arnold, in describing the long-range plans for the use of B–29's (full strength to be reached in March 1946), read into the record a statement representing the most optimistic point of view, that of the Army Air Forces, on a date when the Japanese might be forced to surrender. General Arnold foresaw a possibility of cracking Japan's resistance by a month before the invasion of Japan, that is during October 1945:

In the employment of these forces in the Ryukyus supplementing the present forces in the Marianas, we expect to achieve the disruption of the Japanese military, industrial and economic systems. . . . We estimate that this can be done with our forces available in the month prior to the invasion of Japan. Japan, in fact, will become a nation without cities, with her transportation disrupted and will have tremendous difficulty in holding her people together for continued resistance to our terms of unconditional surrender.[50]

The Atomic Bomb

At the same time that these well-established planning tenets for the war against Japan were being reaffirmed, the decision concerning the use of the atomic bomb was in the making. The Los Alamos experiment, proving the destructive power of the bomb, had taken place on 16 July 1945, the first day of the conference. Also there were many indications that the Japanese were interested in getting out of the war, though under what conditions no one could

---

[46] OPD Book, title: Compilation of Subs for Possible Discussion at TERMINAL, Tabs 39 and 62, Item 21, Exec 5.

[47] CCS 900/3, TERMINAL, 24 Jul 45, title: Rpt to President and Prime Minister.

[48] (1) OPD memo for rcd, 28 Jun 45, no sub, with JPS 708 in ABC 387 Japan (15 Feb 45), 2. (2) JPS 708, 25 Jun 45, title: Planning Date for End of War Against Japan. (3) CCS 880/8, 7 Jul 45, title: Planning Date for End of Organized Resistance by Japan. (4) CCS 900/3, TERMINAL, 24 Jul 45, title: Rpt to President and Prime Minister.

[49] The text of the Potsdam declaration in the names of the heads of government of the United States, China, and Great Britain, is reprinted as App. 1, *Activities of the Far Eastern Commission* (Washington, D. C., 1947).

[50] CCS 894, TERMINAL, 16 Jul 45, title: Rpt on Army Air Opns in War Against Japan.

positively say. At the end of June the War Department G–2 had prepared an "Estimate of the Enemy Situation" at the request of OPD, emphasizing that the possibility of surrender hinged on the terms which the United Nations would grant:

The Japanese believe . . . that unconditional surrender would be the equivalent of national extinction, and there are as yet no indications that they are ready to accept such terms. . . . The surrender of the Japanese government might occur at any time from now until the end of the complete destruction of all Japanese power of resistance, depending upon the conditions of surrender which the Allies might accept.[51]

On 30 July the Potsdam Ultimatum of 26 July 1945 was publicly rejected by Premier Kantaro Suzuki. At this juncture, after approval of planning on the necessity of invading Japan, President Truman decided, with the concurrence of the British and Soviet heads of government, that it was necessary to use the atomic bomb.

In the War Department the decision to use the bomb played no part in orthodox military staff work. Only the faintest suggestion of the existence of the bomb appeared in OPD records before 6 August 1945. On 5 April an officer from MANHATTAN DISTRICT consulted Col. William A. Walker, Current Group deputy chief, and secured a "code word for a TOP SECRET operation overseas, which was discussed . . . with the Chief of Staff and the Secretary of War this morning." Contrary to usual procedure, the meaning of this code word was not filed in OPD, and

Colonel Walker who assigned it had no inkling of the nature of the project.[52]

Sometime in July 1945 while General Marshall was at Potsdam, General Craig drafted a letter, for signature by General Handy as Acting Chief of Staff, giving Maj. Gen. Leslie R. Groves of MANHATTAN DISTRICT and General Spaatz of the new U. S. Army Strategic Air Forces authority to waive security regulations about permitting the flight of personnel with specialized military knowledge over enemy territory. The letter made special reference to the 509th Composite Group, which carried the bomb, but only the rough draft was kept in OPD, and it was put in the special executive office file.[53]

Previously a few OPD officers had seen a JCS message addressed to General MacArthur, Admiral Nimitz, and General Arnold ordering that Kyoto, Hiroshima, Kokura, and Niigata should not be attacked in ordinary bombing raids under any circumstances. Knowledge of this list of cities was extremely limited, and only a rough draft of the message was put in the executive office file.[54] OPD's planning went on virtually as if the atomic bomb did not exist.[55]

---

[51] Memo, G–2 for ACofS OPD, 30 Jun 45, sub: Estimate of Enemy Situation, filed in ABC 384 Pacific—Far East (26 July 1943). The memo incloses an estimate in response to an OPD request of 25 Jun 1945. Attached is memo, Lt Gen Hull for Brig Gen John Weckerling of G–2, 4 Jul 45, saying, "This is a very fine estimate."

[52] Memo, Maj Gen L. R. Groves for ACofS OPD, 5 Apr 45, no sub, OPD 311.5 TS, 1, 24.

[53] Draft ltr, Gen Handy to Maj Gen L. R. Groves, n.d., sub: Waiver of Provisions of Secret Ltr, AGO, 6 Aug 45, Item 11, Exec 2.

[54] Msg, JCS to CINCAFPAC, CG AAF, 3 Jul 45, draft filed Item 11, Exec 2.

[55] In performing their assigned duties under the Chief of Staff and the Secretary of War, both of whom had a part in national policy making related to the atomic energy project, the three chief officers of OPD inevitably gained some knowledge of the MANHATTAN DISTRICT work. These officers were General Hull, Assistant Chief of Staff, OPD, General Craig, deputy chief of the Division, and General Lincoln, Army planner on joint and combined planning staffs. No other OPD officer knew anything about the atomic bomb. A brigadier general then in OPD told the author that, after some extracurricular scientific reflection in the early

Toward the end of July a new note sounded by officers at Potsdam, including General Hull and General Lincoln, turned the attention of military planners in Washington to the possibility of early Japanese surrender. On 20 July the JWPC began, "as a matter of priority," a report on the steps that would be necessary to "facilitate prompt allied action in the event of a Japanese collapse or surrender in the immediate future." [56] During the next three weeks preparations to deal with a Japanese surrender steadily gathered momentum. A whole series of OPD papers was drafted, and most of them reflected a new seriousness in the approach to the problem of a sudden end of Japanese resistance. Even at Potsdam OPD officers were working on a study called "Japanese Capitulation," which General Marshall could use to call to President Truman's attention the many national problems that the sudden end of the war would bring. In it OPD planners

spoke of the possibility that the Japanese might "capitulate unexpectedly in the next few weeks." The insertion of the word "unexpectedly" revealed a great deal about the background of conservative military planning against which the War Department staffs were attacking this particular problem. [57]

Information available to some of the military men at Potsdam made the situation seem different. The JCS sent a message from TERMINAL informing General MacArthur that there were increasing indications that it might "prove necessary to take action within the near future on the basis of Japanese capitulation, possibly before Russian entry." [58] On 25 July 1945, General Hull sent a message to General Craig who was acting for him in OPD: "Forward immediately gist of available information on MacArthur's plans for occupation of Japan and Japanese held areas in event of Japanese collapse or surrender in immediate future." [59] General Craig replied the same day that an OPD officer had studied MacArthur's plan for occupation in draft form at Manila on 11 July, that General MacArthur would be prepared to impose surrender terms at any time after 15 July, that occupation forces would be prepared for landings against moderate opposition, and that the initial landings were scheduled to follow twelve days after collapse or surrender. [60] On the following day, 26 July, the

---

spring of 1945, he conceived the idea that the release of atomic energy for military purposes might be practical. He said he innocently aired the suggestion in the War Department that the Japanese might be working on such a weapon and wondered if the United States should not be doing something about it. He was considerably surprised at the intensive security check to which he was suddenly subjected. The fact that OPD officers in general had no idea of what was in the immediate future is indicated by their consternation when a project for construction of an artificial harbor for use in the March 1946 attack on Japan was approved with "priority above all military and naval programs except MANHATTAN project." See msg, JCS (from TERMINAL) for AGWAR (info to MacArthur and Nimitz) 20 Jul 45, CM-IN 20314. OPD officers told the author that they could not guess nor discover what the mysterious MANHATTAN was and doubted that it could be more important than the harbor for 1946. One S&P officer said he received oral orders from General Hull to quit trying to find out anything about MANHATTAN.
[56] JWPC 390/D, 20 Jul 45, title: Planning for Initial Japanese Occupation Period. The JWPC study was in response to suggestions from Potsdam.

[57] Memo, CofS for President, 25 Jul 45, inclosing OPD study, "Japanese Capitulation," OPD 370.9 TS, 17/8.

[58] Draft msg, JCS for Gen MacArthur, 21 Jul 45, Item 11, Exec 2. Russian entry was then anticipated on 15 August 1945.

[59] Msg, Lt Gen Hull at TERMINAL for Maj Gen Craig, 25 Jul 45, CM-IN 25078.

[60] Msg, Maj Gen Craig for Lt Gen Hull at TERMINAL, 25 Jul 45, CM-OUT 38262.

JCS dispatched a message to General Mac-Arthur and Admiral Nimitz that began: "Coordination of plans for the procedure to be followed in the event of Japanese governmental surrender is now a pressing necessity." [61]

After the first clear indication from Potsdam that surrender was a distinct possibility, S&P undertook a planning review and prepared a "paper outlining the steps necessary to be taken in planning for an early surrender." [62] An intensive program thereupon began. On 30 July General Craig gave General Handy, then Acting Chief of Staff, a memorandum outlining the steps necessary to produce a "final, integrated War Department plan to be implemented upon a sudden surrender of Japan." Provision was made for a "War Department Interim Outline Plan," to be produced at once. Military (JCS) and other national policy decisions necessary to a final plan were listed. A draft directive was presented, ordering an operation to occupy Japan "in the event of Japanese capitulation prior to OLYMPIC." Finally, in order to produce the War Department Interim Outline Plan, General Craig recommended a meeting of the chiefs of staff divisions concerned.[63] On 3 August General Craig forwarded to General Handy a final draft of a paper OPD had been working on for several days, supplying, particularly in regard to redeployment and production, "interim instructions to all concerned in preparing and planning for a sudden collapse or surrender by the Japanese Government prior to completion of the present readjustment and redeployment of the Army." [64]

The dropping of the atomic bomb on Hiroshima on 6 August, the long-awaited entry of the USSR in the war against Japan on 8 August Eastern Standard time, and the public offer to surrender broadcast by the Japanese Government on 10 August Eastern Standard time, speeded staff work and the decision-making process. OPD's draft plan was submitted to the chiefs of the major War Department agencies on 8 August for comments prior to 9 August, so that a coordinated study could be presented to the Chief of Staff on 10 August. With Japan's public declaration of intent to surrender, the Chief of Staff hastily approved OPD's interim plan for instant dispatch. At 1015, 10 August, General Hull sent out a message in the name of General Marshall to the three zone of interior Army commands, all War Department General and Special Staff Divisions, the Defense Commands, the Alaskan Department, and U. S. Army forces in Central Canada, the South Atlantic, the European theater, the Pacific, the Mid-Pacific, and China, and the U. S. Strategic Air Forces on Guam. Conveying all the instructions in the OPD interim plan, the message began: "The following interim instructions will become effective when you are formally notified by War Department

---

[61] JCS 1331/6, 30 Jul 45, title: Occupation of Strategic Areas in Japan Proper in Event of Collapse or Surr.

[62] Memo, Col T. D. Roberts for Maj Gen Craig, 31 Jul 45, Gen Lincoln file, S&P Exec Office rcds.

[63] Memo, OPD for Gen Handy, 30 Jul 45, sub: Planning for Early Surr of Japan, OPD 370.9 TS, 17. Symbolic of the confusion during the last two weeks of the war is the filing of various copies of this important memorandum. Parts of it are filed under several different files, and the original paper carries a somewhat misleading memorandum for record, saying "it has now been overtaken by events." Actually, it supplied the chief immediate frame of reference for dealing with the events that had overtaken all planning.

[64] Memo, Maj Gen Craig for Gen Handy, 3 Aug 45, Item 11, Exec 2. For draft of 31 July 1945, see OPD 370.9 TS, 17/3.

of formal capitulation of Japan." [65] Formal notification of the capitulation came only four days later, on 14 August 1945.[66]

Surrender Documents and Occupation Plans

Much had to be done in the feverish last few days of the war, particularly in the politico-military field. As Colonel Bonesteel, Policy Section chief, pointed out to General Lincoln on 9 August: "For your convenience a check list indicating unfinished business re early surrender of Japan is attached. First and foremost is the *fact* that there is *no* approved surrender document, surrender proclamation, or General Orders No. 1 in existence." [67] These basic documents for the surrender were finished and approved by President Truman just in time for their use. Only the existence of the State-War-Navy Coordinating Committee and the experience of staffs like Colonel Bonesteel's politico-military group in the Policy Section made such speed possible. The Instrument of Surrender, the Directive to the Supreme Commander for the Allied Powers, and the Proclamation by the Emperor of Japan ending hostilities under the provisions of the Potsdam declaration, were finished on 13 August 1945 and forwarded to General MacArthur, who thenceforth was the Supreme Commander for the Allied Powers.[68] General Order 1, designed as one of the four basic surrender documents, was not completed until a few days later.[69] In fact, less than a week before the date of the actual signature of the surrender in Tokyo Bay, OPD had to inform General MacArthur: "Time does not permit provision of a properly engrossed document." [70]

Meanwhile, the JWPC and the Joint Staff Planners were hastening to complete the "early surrender" work begun some months before. The JWPC had produced a study, 10 July 1945, which presented a plan for occupying Japan either prior to OLYMPIC or prior to CORONET, which dates were taken to mean about 15 August 1945 or 15 January 1946.[71] On 30 July, in response to the suggestions received from Potsdam, the JWPC brought out a study on the steps necessary to "facilitate prompt allied action in the event of a Japanese collapse or surrender in the immediate future." It stated flatly: "Until recently an early surrender by the Japanese was considered improbable. As a consequence the procedures and plans to be followed in the event of an immediate Japanese surrender are indistinct." [72] In reference to this study, OPD commented on 3 August: "This paper is a good planning paper. It was originated at the same time as all the other sudden actions on Japanese surrender and occupation." [73]

---

[65] Msg, Gen Marshall for Army comds, 10 Aug 45, CM-OUT 47214.

[66] Msg, Gen Marshall for Army comds, 14 Aug 45, MC-OUT 49583. The MC designation meant that the message was not classified.

[67] Memo, Col Bonesteel for Brig Gen Lincoln, 9 Aug 45, no sub, filed with SWNCC 149/1 in ABC 387 Japan (15 Feb 45), 1–B.

[68] (1) JCS 1467, 13 Aug 45, title: Instruments for Surr of Japan. (2) Memo, OPD for Lt Gen R. K. Sutherland, 13 Aug 45, no sub, Item 11, Exec 2.

[69] (1) JCS 1467/2, 17 Aug 45, title: Instruments for Surr of Japan, General Order No. 1. (2) Msg, JCS for Gen MacArthur, 15 Aug 45, CM-OUT 49961.

[70] Msg, OPD for USAFPAC, 25 Aug 45, CM-OUT 55055.

[71] (1) JPS 722/D, 3 Aug 45, title: BLACKLIST Plan. (2) JWPC 264/7/D, 4 Aug 45, title: Over-All Exam of Planning for Occupation of Japan.

[72] JWPC 390/1, 30 Jul 45, title: Planning for Initial Japanese Occupation Period.

[73] OPD note, Col T. D. Roberts, 3 Aug 45, sub: JWPC 390/1, filed with JWPC 390/1 in ABC 014 Japan (13 Apr 44), 18–A.

Despite the tardiness of the planning, enough had been done both in Washington and in the theater headquarters to take care of the situation at hand. On 3 August the Joint Staff Planners sent General MacArthur's plan (BLACKLIST) for the early occupation of Japan to the JWPC for briefing, comment, and recommendation in the light of their own studies, particularly that of 10 July (JWPC 264/6) and the basic surrender directive, Victory 357.[74] The JWPC produced a study on 10 August 1945, the critical date, proposing a recon-

cilement of General MacArthur's BLACKLIST plan with the parallel plan, CAMPUS, drafted by Admiral Nimitz. With *ad hoc* modifications, BLACKLIST was ready and went into operation just in time.[75] Hostilities ended formally on 2 September 1945 with the signing of the surrender document aboard the USS *Missouri* in Tokyo Bay. The last great series of staff actions in World War II had achieved its purpose. The Washington planning machinery, in which OPD officers were carrying a full load, had not worked with any remarkable efficiency in the hectic, complicated preparations for the end of the war against Japan, but it had worked.

---

[74] (1) JPS 722/D, 3 Aug 45, title: BLACKLIST Plan. (2) JWPC 264/7/D, 4 Aug 45, title: Over-All Exam of Planning for Occupation of Japan. (3) JCS 1331/6, 30 Jul 45, title: Occupation of Strategic Areas in Japan Proper in Event of Collapse or Surr.

[75] (1) Msg, JCS for Gen MacArthur, 11 Aug 45, CM-OUT 47945. (2) Msg, Gen MacArthur for subordinate comds, 15 Aug 45, CM-IN 14771.

CHAPTER XVIII

After OPD

The sudden end of hostilities in World War II, formally concluded on 2 September 1945, did not immediately reduce the press of military staff work or dispose of the grave issues in national military organization that had come to stand out in high relief in the later war years but had been fended off by improvisation rather than finally settled. Washington agencies and staffs worked feverishly on the occupation of Germany and Japan, the unsnarling of deployed and redeployed forces, and demobilization. In contrast to the years just past, all these tremendous undertakings, which materially affected urgent military tasks and long-range responsibilities, were carried out in the midst of national debate, both in Congress and in the press. Above all, looming in the background, was the general problem of the postwar structure of the armed services of the United States, a matter of professional and personal interest to every Army and Navy officer.

The precedents of World War II were cited, interpreted, reinterpreted, recommended, and condemned, particularly the performances of the high command and the higher staffs in Washington. Those precedents would be the point of departure for discussions and debate for years to come. It was clearly desirable for the Army insofar as possible to sift out permanent principles of organization and procedure from other less tangible and controllable factors in success-

ful performances, such as personal qualities of leadership and the energy and talent of wartime personnel. In the first two years after the Japanese surrender, a number of major organizational changes were made in the national defense system affecting staff work in support of the high command and therefore affecting the methods and traditions OPD had established. The direction and implications of these changes is not yet altogether clear, and the permanent usefulness in the Army of the idea that OPD represented is uncertain. This concluding chapter is a kind of epilogue to the institutional biography of OPD, tracing the influence of its subject as it reached out into the future. On the other hand, it may be more nearly an epitaph, memorializing the gone and soon to be forgotten. In any case, it describes in a very summary form the issues in military policy that arose and the major reorganizations that took place between September 1945 and the passage of the National Security Act in July 1947, relating these issues in passing to the history of OPD in World War II.

Postwar Study of Army Organization

OPD, like the rest of the Army, continued to work at full speed for some time after the Japanese surrender. The Troop Control Section of the Theater Group, built up to handle the redeployment of forces from

Europe to the Pacific, guided the post-hostilities deployment homewards for the hasty demobilization that followed as a consequence of national public demand rather than military decision. A large volume of politico-military staff work, particularly the part of it concerned with defining occupation policy and sketching plans for the postwar military establishment of the United States, was handled in S&P, especially in the new section organized under Colonel Bonesteel after the end of hostilities. Accordingly, General Hull directed that the September 1945 organization of OPD be continued, with maximum economy of personnel being effected as duties diminished, pending a major decision as to the permanent postwar organization of the War Department.[1] What OPD was to become was worked out in the course of ensuing months as part of the larger problem of what the entire high command and staff of the Army would be like and how it would fit into a national defense organization embracing ground, air, and naval forces.

For the purpose of proposing an "organization appropriate for peacetime adoption," a board of officers under Lt. Gen. Alexander M. Patch was constituted on 30 August 1945 to "examine into the present organization of the War Department."[2] The board conducted inquiries for several weeks, submitted its report to the Chief of Staff on 18 October 1945, and was dissolved two days later. The Patch Board report was circulated for comment or con-

currence by the General and Special Staff Divisions, and to major commands in the zone of interior and overseas.[3]

The Patch Board professed to have based its report on World War II experience, and many of its provisions were designed to carry into permanent effect the arrangements worked out pursuant to the 1942 reorganization. Thus it recommended abolishing the positions and offices of the Chiefs of Infantry, Field Artillery, Cavalry, and Coast Artillery, in abeyance since 1942, and keeping the Army Ground Forces to control ground combat training. It also proposed that the Army Air Forces retain its World War II status with as much autonomy as possible so that it could be separated easily from the War Department in case an independent air establishment should be set up by law, a project which the Army had been fostering as part of its plan for creating a single Department of Defense containing ground, air, and naval arms.[4]

In the area of high command and the General Staff, also, the Patch Board very consciously attempted to apply the lessons of World War II. It set forth as a vital principle that the "top organization of the War Department must be capable of car-

---

[1] Memo, Lt Gen Hull for Maj Gen Craig [Chairman of Sp Committee], 11 Sep 45, no sub, OPD 321.19 OPD, 126/2.

[2] For constitution of board of officers, see memo, Brig Gen H. I. Hodes, Asst DCofS for Lt Gen Patch, etc., 30 Aug 45, sub: Reorgn of WD, copy filed OPD 320 War Department, 31.

[3] Memo, Asst DCofS for WDGS, WDSS, AAF, AGF, ASF, Maj O'seas Comds, EDC, and WDC, 19 Oct 45, sub: Rpt of Bd of Offs on Reorgn of WD, with incl, memo, Lt Gen Patch for CofS, 18 Oct 45, same sub, OPD 320 War Department, 31/5.

[4] For Army initiation of the long struggle for unification, see: (1) OPD Hist Unit Study J, "Wartime Study of Unification of the Armed Services"; (2) OPD Hist Unit Study I, "Early Proposals for Unification of the Armed Services of the United States"; (3) most of the information in these studies was published, without documentation, in an article by Ray S. Cline and Maurice Matloff, "Development of War Department Views on Unification," in *Military Affairs*, 1949, Vol. XIII, No. 2, pp. 65–74.

rying out the Chief of Staff's orders quickly and effectively and must also have the means and the authority to supervise and direct the actual execution of such orders." Deprecating the "much quoted statement that 'a General Staff should be restricted to matters of high policy and planning and must not operate,' " the board recorded its belief that "while the General Staff must be the agency to deal with matters of high policy and high-level planning, it must also operate and direct, to the end that orders and directives are issued and supervised to the necessary degree in their execution." It noted the "devitalization of the General Staff during wartime" with the exception of G–2 and OPD. It also recommended that the staff should be organized "with a minimum of individuals reporting directly to the Chief of Staff or his Deputy." Finally, the Patch Board urged the "aggressive application of the principle of decentralization," stating that "no functions should be performed at the staff level of the War Department which can be decentralized to the Major Commands or the Services without loss of adequate control of operations by the Staff."

Nearly all of these principles reflected accurately the experience of the War Department in World War II, particularly the experience of OPD. The emphasis on "carrying out the Chief of Staff's orders quickly and effectively," without regard to abstract restrictions on staff activities, plus the policy of decentralization of duties, was the essence of OPD's philosophy. The Patch Board did, however, use the term "operate" somewhat loosely in recommending that the General Staff "operate and direct." A more correct way of expressing the wartime philosophy of OPD would have been to say that a staff should *direct* operating agencies suffi-

ciently to insure that orders were being executed, not permitting fear of becoming involved in *operating* to prevent the performance of the duty. OPD did not "operate" as a matter of principle but rather refused to let any arbitrary or abstract limitation on staff authority stand in the way of what it considered necessary for discharging in full the staff function of issuing commands and observing that they were executed.

The Patch Board proposed, in line with its emphasis on staff direction of Army activities, that the chiefs of General Staff Divisions should adopt the title of "Director" and should "have the authority to plan, direct and supervise the execution of operations within the confines of his sphere of action." This idea was even further spelled out:

The old theory that a staff must limit itself to broad policy and planning activities has been proved unsound in this war. . . . Unless a staff officer is able to assist his commander in getting things done, in addition to coordinating, planning and policy-making, he is not serving his full usefulness. In short a staff is a commander's principal means for determining that his orders, instructions, and directions are being carried out as he intended.

Pursuant to this concept, the Patch Board recommended allocating the "operating" functions of the Army Service Forces, an organization which it did not propose to perpetuate, among the General Staff Divisions, each supervising the work of the administrative and technical services insofar as they fell within their respective spheres of functional responsibility. This arrangement plainly put the weight of responsibility for the execution of orders on the General Staff. It went considerably farther than giving the General Staff directors permission to "operate" if necessity arose. It made them take "operating" responsibility for the work of the "operating" agencies of the Army. How this procedure could in practice be reconciled with the principle of decentralization was open to question.

In one important respect the Patch Board proposed to depart from World War II precedents. It recommended returning control of military operations in the overseas commands to G–3, which would be redesignated the Operations and Training Division of the General Staff. OPD's Theater Group would be absorbed in the new G–3 Division. Since the Logistics Group was to be transferred to G–4, only one of the wartime groups in OPD would remain. It would be S&P, which would constitute a Plans Division of the General Staff performing much the same function as WPD before Pearl Harbor.

OPD officers reacted to the Patch Board report with mixed approval and dismay. Most of them found generally acceptable the procedures and principles recommended by the Patch Board with a view to strengthening the General Staff as a whole, but all of them protested against separating strategic planning from control of operations. General Hull drew on the content and language of comments by his group chiefs in drafting a detailed commentary on the Patch Board report. His main criticism concerned the failure to preserve intact the dual staff responsibility that had fallen to OPD during the war. General Hull observed:

Plans and Operations should be combined and the Training Section should be charged with organization and training. This consolidation of plans and operations under one head appears necessary to achieve essential coordination. The experience of the Operations Division in World War II has indicated that such is a vital necessity. An aspect of the problem which dictates the above is the relation of political with operational matters. Political considerations are strong factors in wartime;

they will be stronger in peacetime and perhaps predominant, and the Chief of Staff and Secretary of War as well as the JCS organization, the Secretary of State and SWNCC, will look to one office for the marriage of the political and military.This will logically be the responsibility of the officer in charge of planning and policy even though the pressing military-politico problems will often be classified as operational. It must further be recognized that U. S. relations are so complicated that no matter how effective a long-range plans organization becomes we will, at least for several years, still be writing important plans and policy on short notice from the operational cables.

He further recommended:

Change title to Director of Operations and Plans. The Director of Operations and Plans should be charged with the over-all supervision of military operations as well as the preparation of strategic plans. During the recent war effort, the Operations Division, WDGS, was most successful in effecting close coordination and control. This proven agency should be retained.

To carry out these recommendations in detail, General Hull suggested the addition of three extremely important duties besides general strategic planning to the listed responsibilities of the Director of Plans [and Operations]:

He will exercise supervision and direction of matters relating to overseas commands.
Advise the Assistant Secretary of War on all military-politico matters. . . .
Review, and after coordination with other interested War Department agencies, recommend action to the Chief of Staff on action papers of the Joint or Combined Chiefs of Staff.[5]

The board of officers for studying reorganization was reconstituted, effective 6 December 1945, with Lt. Gen. William H.

---

[5] Memo, OPD for DCofS, 5 Nov 45, sub: Rpt of Board of Offs on Orgn of WD, OPD 320 War Department, 31/6.

Simpson as president in the place of General Patch, who died on 21 November. Its mission was to consider comments on the original Patch Board report, make any warranted revisions, and draft appropriate orders for putting the reorganization into effect. The new board worked rapidly and submitted its report on 28 December 1945.[6]

In most respects the provisions of the Patch Board report were retained as sound recommendations. The major changes introduced were those recommended by General Hull, whereby the Director of Operations and Training (revitalized G–3) became the Director of Organization and Training, and his responsibility for "supervision and direction of matters relating to overseas commands" was transferred to the Director of Plans. The latter officer thereby became the Director of Plans and Operations, with responsibility for developing "strategic and operational plans" and in addition for "assisting the Chief of Staff in preparing the Army for war and in the strategic direction of the military forces in the theaters of war."

The Simpson Board report, as revised 18 January 1946, was promptly "approved for planning purposes" by the Chief of Staff, then General Eisenhower. In this form it represented to a considerable extent the principles of War Department organization and procedure embodied in OPD's wartime practices. In particular the acceptance of the idea of a combined plans and operations staff left the successor to OPD with comprehensive powers. In some ways the Simpson Board report, especially where it deviated from the Patch Board report, gave an appearance of being an OPD-contrived

study. The original Patch Board report had gone far, perhaps too far, in recommending OPD's techniques to the rest of the General Staff, but had deliberately recommended going back to the pre-Pearl Harbor division of duties among the five divisions of the War Department General Staff. In the interim the Assistant Chief of Staff, OPD (General Hull), had suggested changes to the Deputy Chief of Staff (General Handy, his predecessor in OPD). The Deputy Chief of Staff instructed the board to consider these comments, most of which were incorporated, and the final report was then approved by the Chief of Staff (General Eisenhower, General Handy's predecessor in OPD).

Nevertheless, the Simpson Board reorganization continued to contain two provisions contrary in spirit if not in the letter to OPD's experience. In the first place, the General Staff directors were made responsible for "operating" duties rather than made free to supervise in as much detail as necessary the execution of such duties by "operating" agencies in conformity with General Staff instructions. This strong emphasis on "operating" achieved the desired result as far as supervision of execution of orders was concerned, but it also made the General Staff directly responsible for the performance of duties that were bound to pre-empt a great deal of General Staff time and were likely to interfere with the formulation of general plans and policies. It tended to run counter to the injunction to decentralize duties and it overlooked the extent to which OPD had depended on merely monitoring the activities of Army agencies to pick the critical points for staff action rather than engaging in routine duties.

In the second place, although the Plans and Operations Division was left with a

[6] Simpson Board rpt, 28 Dec 45, title: Rpt of Bd of Offs on Orgn of WD, P&O 020 War Department, 2. This report contains revisions as of 18 January 1946.

formidable concentration of powers, it was not made superior in any way to the other General Staff Divisions. OPD had never enjoyed any special status on paper, but its size and responsibilities, in contrast to the small and limited G–1, G–3, and G–4 Divisions of the General Staff, had made its influence paramount. OPD officers on the working staff level had drawn on the information and ideas of their colleagues in many other agencies bringing it all together in one place, OPD, where one officer, the Assistant Chief of Staff at the head of the Division, had authority to make decisions on any matter affecting military operations and where the same officer had competent specialists to advise him on strategic plans, logistic plans, and actual operations. In peacetime, without the urgency of military operations in process, and with "operating" responsibilities assigned to much larger G–1, G–3, and G–4 Divisions than had existed during World War II, the co-ordination that OPD had been able to bring about informally was not going to be easy to achieve.

Some future Chief of Staff in the period of transition from peace to a possible future war probably would need co-ordinated advice just as much as General Marshall had needed it in 1942. That advice, to be most effective, would have to tie strategic planning and military operations to the mobilization, training, and equipment and supply programs of the zone of interior. The Chief of Staff himself would find it hard to absorb and evaluate the mass of details necessary for such co-ordination. He would need a staff. Under the Simpson Board scheme, the staff best fitted to co-ordinate all these kinds of planning on behalf of the Chief of Staff was likely to be the Plans and Operations Division. Prompt and efficient co-ordination, however, might prove as difficult between five coequal "operat-

ing" staff divisions as it had between five coequal "nonoperating" staff divisions in 1941. The integration of all planning on the basis of detailed information and after co-ordination of the various points of view would not clearly be the function of any one staff. The Chief of Staff, with such help as his deputy could give, still would have to try to bring about this final co-ordination himself.

While co-ordination of Army plans and policies by the Chief of Staff alone might have been feasible in peacetime like the "peacetime" of the 1920's, it was far from certain after World War II that one man, even if assisted by one or two or a half-dozen deputies, could give proper weight to all the detailed considerations in a long sequence of interrelated Army activities dependent on a single policy decision. In effect, during World War II General Marshall had had about two hundred officers, including strategists, operations officers, and logisticians, all working for him on the co-ordination of Army affairs that had a bearing on military operations. In a sense, the Assistant Chief of Staff, OPD, was a special deputy for the Chief of Staff and had at his elbow the information, the judgment, and the staff services of about two hundred subdeputies.

Designating a single staff like OPD and finding a single standard of value like success in actual operations admittedly were more difficult in peacetime than in the emergency of 1942. Yet a report on permanent staff organization might profitably have touched on this problem at least in passing, and indicated how that permanent organization would adapt itself to the approach of war. On this problem the Simpson Board report, like the Patch Board report, was silent.

Reorganization in 1946

Temporary "authorizations for personnel to govern upon reorganization of the War Department" were issued on 1 April 1946 in order to give a finite quality to the advance planning. The personnel allotment revealed how heavily the General Staff Divisions were going to be burdened with activities formerly carried on by other agencies, particularly by the Army Service Forces. While the Plans and Operations was authorized 82 officers, a considerable reduction from OPD's peak size, the other divisions were comparatively large organizations. Service, Supply and Procurement (S,S&P, formerly G–4) was allotted 200 officers; Personnel and Administration (P&A, formerly G–1), 100 officers; and Intelligence Division (ID, formerly G–2), 250 officers. Only Organization and Training (O&T, formerly G–3) was smaller than Plans and Operations, with 60 officers.

During April, while the Simpson Board reorganization was shaping up for final approval, General Eisenhower and his deputy, General Handy, were required to comment on some of the central features of the new organization in justifying it to the Bureau of the Budget. The time-honored issue of General Staff "operating" had to be dealt with, and General Eisenhower tried to explain the "follow-up" function of the staff:

In commenting upon the fear that the new organization implies an intention to engage the General Staff in *operation,* I can only say that this is most emphatically not the case. Long experience has shown that the process of investigating, and informing the Secretary of War requires a degree of "follow-up" that is essential to efficiency but which, if abused, inevitably leads into operation and unwarranted interference. There is no specific organization that will eliminate this tendency. Only proper indoctrination and careful policing by the head of the organization will keep true General Staff functions separated from those of the operating services. The new organization retains the old operating services and charges these, and appropriate commanders, with the responsibility of operating the whole.[7]

Similarly, General Handy observed that it was unfortunate that General Simpson's report had used the phrase "operate and direct," and that the wording had already been changed in the War Department circular in preparation "omitting the word 'operate' and substituting 'direct and supervise'" therefor. In conclusion, General Handy asserted, "there is no intention of permitting the General Staff to 'operate' in the sense that a command or a service 'operates.' The General Staff directs, co-ordinates and supervises (follows up)."[8] Both of these explanations accurately reflected OPD's experience. The provisions of the Simpson Board report did not distinguish so clearly between operating and following up, and it was far from certain that staff officers trying to work under the terms of the Simpson Board reorganization would be able to observe the distinction in practice.

Presidential approval for the reorganization finally came on 13 May 1946. War Department Circular 138, containing the official instructions governing the reorganization, was distributed on 14 May, and the reorganization became effective 11 June 1946.[9] Circular 138 embodied the principles and used the language of the final

---

[7] Memo, CofS for Dir of Bureau of Budget, 16 Apr 46, no sub, WDCSA 020 (2).

[8] Ltr, Gen Handy for Dir of Bureau of Budget, 29 Apr 46, WDCSA 020 (2).

[9] (1) WD Cir 138, 14 May 46, sub: WD Reorgn. (2) Memo, OCS (Asst DCofS) for AAF, AGF, ASF, and WD Stf Divs, 14 May 46, no sub, P&O 020 War Department 2/12. (3) EO 9722, 13 May 46, sub: Reasgmt of Functions of SOS Comd and CG SOS. This order merely amended EO 9082, 28 Feb 42.

Simpson Board report. It made two major administrative changes in the Army as a whole. First, it established the Army Ground Forces as the headquarters through which the Chief of Staff commanded the six armies concurrently established and assigned to six army areas in the continental United States. These permanent elements of the ground Army replaced the old field force organization and the corps areas. Second, the new circular abolished Headquarters, Army Service Forces, bringing back as quasi-independent War Department agencies the administrative and technical services.

Insofar as the General Staff was concerned, the abolition of the Army Service Forces brought two important changes. First, the Director of Personnel and Administration (G–1) absorbed the functions and staff of the Army Service Forces Military Personnel Division, the agency that had controlled the assignment of military personnel during the war. Although the Director of P&A was authorized to reassign parts of this function to The Adjutant General, P&A was brought intimately into the task of procuring, allocating, and managing military manpower.

Second, the Service, Supply, and Procurement Division (G–4) assumed complete responsibility with respect to "service, supply, and procurement activities," although by official fiat the "command functions" which the Army Service Forces had exercised in connection with these activities were abolished and thereby somehow transformed to staff functions. In addition, S,S&P absorbed the functions and personnel of the Logistics Group, OPD. As a result of this reorientation, S,S&P became a large organization deeply involved in equipping, supplying, and providing services for the Army. A new General Staff

Division, Research and Development, was also temporarily established in the reorganization of 1946. This was merged in December 1947 with S,S&P, which subsequently was renamed the Logistics Division.

The Organization and Training Division (G–3) found its status almost unaffected by the reorganization, continuing to be concerned primarily with Tables of Organization and training policies. The Army Ground Forces remained in existence as headquarters for the six Army areas in the zone of interior, and Plans and Operations controlled the overseas commands. Plans and Operations carried on the activities of OPD minus those of the Logistics Group, which it lost to S,S&P. Finally, the Intelligence Division (G–2) did much the same work as always.

The way these divisions were expected to work and the authority they exercised on behalf of the Chief of Staff were set forth unequivocally in the circular. The Chief of Staff's command of all Army forces was specifically affirmed, and something like the staff technique followed by OPD during the war was prescribed for the whole General Staff. The propriety of this technique for managing the detailed work of zone of interior programs was not examined, but the language and instructions plainly presumed that the problems were analogous. The circular read:

The Chief of Staff is the principal military adviser to the President and to the Secretary of War on the conduct of war and the principal military adviser and executive to the Secretary of War on the activities of the Military Establishment. The Chief of Staff has command of all components of the Army of the United States and of the operating forces comprising the Army Ground Forces, the Army Air Forces, the army areas, oversea departments, task forces, base commands, defense commands, commands in theaters of operations, and all other commands, and the related supply and service establishments of the Army, and is responsible to the Secretary of War for their use in war and plans and preparations for their readiness for war. The Chief of Staff, under the direction of the Secretary of War, is responsible for the co-ordination and direction of the War Department General and Special Staffs and the administrative and technical services. . . .

The War Department General Staff, under the direction of the Chief of Staff, will be responsible for the development of the Army and will insure the existence of a well-balanced and efficient military team. It is specifically charged with the duty of providing such broad basic policies and plans as will enable the Commanding Generals of the Army Ground Forces, the Army Air Forces, task forces, theaters of operations, oversea commands, and such other commands as may be established, and the heads of the administrative and technical services, to prepare and execute detailed programs. In addition, the General Staff assists the Chief of Staff by issuing in the name of the Secretary of War and the Chief of Staff, necessary directives to implement such plans and policies and supervises the execution of these directives. In performing its duties the General Staff follows the principle of decentralization to the fullest degree. No function will be performed at the general or special staff level of the War Department which can be decentralized to the major commands, the army areas, or the administrative and technical services without loss of adequate control of operations by the General and Special Staffs. The War Department General Staff will include six divisions, each under the immediate control of a director. Each director will plan, direct, and supervise the execution of operations within the confines of his sphere of action. In carrying out their duties, the Directors of the six General Staff Divisions will be guided by the following general principles:

a. They will *plan, direct, coordinate,* and *supervise.* They will assist the Chief of Staff in *getting things done,* in addition to coordinating, planning, and policy-making on an Army-wide level.

b. They will, by means of direct contact with troops, determine that orders, instruc-

tions, and directions are being carried out as the Chief of Staff intended.

c. *They will follow the principle of decentralization to the fullest degree.* The War Department General Staff will concern itself primarily only with matters which must be considered on a War Department or Army-wide level. All other matters will be decentralized down to the proper echelons of command for action or decision. In order for this to be done properly, adequate authority will be delegated to responsible commanders and the heads of the administrative and technical services. Each director will take necessary action to indoctrinate each officer of his division with a thorough understanding of the duties, functions, responsibility, and authority of the various echelons of command in the Army.[10]

In addition to a General Staff organized along these lines, the War Department as set up in 1946 contained ten "Special Staff" divisions reporting to the Deputy Chief of Staff on such special fields of activity as public relations, military history, and budget. Most of them had been established during World War II to perform their special functions for the Secretary of War or the Chief of Staff. Finally, there were five "administrative services" and eight "technical services," the former working primarily under the supervision of P&A, and the latter under the supervision of S,S&P. The circular specifically indicated the dual nature of the services as operating agencies (with command functions) and administrative and technical staffs serving the Secretary of War and Chief of Staff. It enunciated the principle that the "two functions of staff and command, although vested in a single individual, are separate and distinct in that each involves different responsibilities and duties, and the exercise of one is not to be confused with nor permitted to interfere with the exercise of the other." [11]

---

[10] WD Cir 138, 14 May 46, sub: WD Reorgn.
[11] *Ibid.*

All of these arrangements, plus the establishment of two or three special offices or committees and the organization of the Army Air Forces on a virtually autonomous basis, gave the reorganized Army an extraordinarily complex structure at the War Department level. The chart showed twenty-nine individual staffs reporting directly either to the Chief of Staff or his deputy.

National Security Act

Minor changes in the basic Army organization and terminology of Circular 138 came about as a result of the passage of the National Security Act of 1947 (Public Law 253, 80th Congress), approved 26 July 1947. This act reorganized the National Military Establishment by creating a U. S. Air Force on an independent basis, legalizing the JCS committee system, and grouping all three service departments (Army, Navy, and Air Force) under a Secretary of Defense. The latter official was designated "principal assistant to the President in all matters relating to the national security," exercising "general direction, authority, and control" over the three departments of the National Military Establishment. The legislation also provided for a National Security Council, composed of the President, the Secretary of State, the Secretary of Defense and his three immediate subordinates, and the Chairman of the National Security Resources Board, a new agency created concurrently to "advise the President concerning the coordination of military, industrial, and civilian mobilization." [12] The contemporary Secretary of the Navy, James V. Forrestal, became first

---

[12] National Security Act of 1947, distributed in the Army as War Department Bulletin 11, 31 July 1947.

U. S. Secretary of Defense and thenceforth attempted to co-ordinate the civilian control exercised over the military services by the civilian heads of the three services.

A great many of the ideas that Army planners had long advocated were embodied in the National Security Act, for which the Army fought vigorously. Some compromises with what the Army had wanted were made, notably in the failure to provide for a Chief of Staff of the armed services to co-ordinate military plans and operations for the Secretary of Defense and the President. The committee of the Chiefs of Staff remained the highest professional military authority in the nation. Its status changed primarily by virtue of the creation of a small, independent working staff, assigned directly to the JCS system rather than delegated from some particular staff in one of the three services. The Department of the Army (as the War Department was renamed) could anticipate that many of the functions that OPD had performed informally and sometimes with misgivings would be handled in a more systematic way within the framework of the new national security structure. While Plans and Operations might in a future war play the role of OPD inside the Army, its planners would presumably never have such a dominant influence in formulating national strategy as OPD representatives, acting for the Chief of Staff, had exercised in the joint and combined staff system. The awkward element in the position of Plans and Operations, and that of the Army as a whole, was uncertainty as to how long a transition period the new machinery would require before it became reliably efficient.

The whole system as finally worked out on the basis of Circular 138 of 1946 and the National Security Act of 1947 appeared strangely similar to the 1941 structure. The Chief of Staff still had command of a huge, complicated organization. He still needed well-organized, comprehensive staff work to assist him in formulating decisions and carrying them out. The Department of the Army had plenty of staffs, as the War Department had in 1941, but it did not reflect very clearly any particular philosophy of staff support of the high command in Washington. Whatever may be the way Army staff organization and practice develop from the 1947 pattern, it is unlikely to follow exactly the precedents of World War II. New tasks and new difficulties demand new ideas and new techniques. Nevertheless, the meaning of staff assistance in the exercise of command is something that officers in the U. S. Army will always have to try to understand intimately and fully. The experience of OPD in World War II will always shed some light on this basic military problem, as well as on the perennial problem of any living institution, that is, keeping organization and principles of conduct in line with mission and functions.

Appendix A

DIVISION, GROUP, AND SECTION CHIEFS IN OPD
21 FEBRUARY 1942–2 SEPTEMBER 1945 [1]

Name	Rank [2]	Serial Number	Period of Assignment	Age [3]	Component	Branch	Graduated		
							USMA	C & GS	AWC
DIVISION CHIEFS AND DEPUTIES									
Assistant Chief of Staff									
Eisenhower, D. D............	MG	O3822	16 Feb 42–23 Jun 42	51	RA	Inf	1915	1926	1928
Handy, T. T.[4]............	LG	O4665	24 Jun 42–21 Oct 44	50	RA	FA	......	1927	1935
Hull, J. E.................	LG	O7377	21 Oct 44– 2 Sep 45	49	RA	Inf	......	1936	1938
Deputy Assistant Chief of Staff[5]:									
Crawford, R. W.............	BG	O3667	21 Feb 42–22 Jun 42	50	RA	CE	1914	1929	1936
Craig, H. A.[7]............	MG	O11264	25 Nov 44– 2 Sep 45	46	RA	AC	......	1936	......
EXECUTIVE GROUP									
Executive Officer									
Gailey, C. K., Jr.........	Col	O12782	21 Feb 42–16 Dec 44	40	RA	Inf	1920	1937	......
Treacy, K. W..............	Col	O16052	16 Dec 44– 2 Sep 45	41	RA	FA	1925	1941	......
Section Chiefs:									
Record Room									
Bond, V. W................	Capt	O925953	26 Aug 44– 2 Sep 45	33	AUS	AGD	......	......	......
Message Center									
Jacobs, R. C., Jr.........	Col	O10908	21 Feb 42–12 May 42	53	RA	Inf	......	......	......
Muir, C. H., Jr..........	Lt Col	O215977	13 May 42– 1 Feb 44	38	Res	Inf	......	......	......
Smith, L. E..............	Lt Col	O271612	1 Feb 44–12 Jul 44	41	Res	Cav	......	......	......
McDonald, J. A............	Maj	O1284001	12 Jul 44– 2 Sep 45	39	AUS	Inf	......	......	......
Current [6]									
Frederick, R. T...........	Lt Col	O17196	21 Feb 42– 9 Mar 42	34	RA	CAC	1928	1939	......

(Footnotes at end of table)

DIVISION, GROUP, AND SECTION CHIEFS IN OPD
21 FEBRUARY 1942–2 SEPTEMBER 1945 [1]—Continued

Name	Rank[2]	Serial Number	Period of Assignment	Age[3]	Component	Branch	USMA	C&GS	AWC
THEATER (OPERATIONS) GROUP									
Chief									
Gerow, L. S........	Col	O4681	21 Feb 42– 9 Mar 42	50	RA	Inf	......	1931	1939
Streett, St. C.[4]......	MG	O9619	9 Mar 42– 9 Dec 42	48	RA	AC	......	1934	1935
Hull, J. E........	MG	O7377	9 Dec 42–21 Oct 44	47	RA	Inf	......	1936	1938
Craig, H. A.[7]......	MG	O11264	23 Oct 44– 2 Sep 45	46	RA	AC	......	1936	......
Deputy Chief									
Russell, C. A........	BG	O5144	27 Apr 42–16 Dec 42	50	RA	Inf	......	1931	1936
Deputy Chief (Ground)									
Russell, C. A........	BG	O5144	16 Dec 42–28 Nov 44	50	RA	Inf	......	1931	1936
Stewart, C. W., Jr.....	Col	O15124	29 Nov 44–10 Dec 44	44	RA	CE	1923	1938	......
Gailey, C. K., Jr.....	BG	O12782	16 Dec 44–28 Jun 45	43	RA	Inf	1920	1937	......
Tandy, F. S........	Col	O15521	5 Jul 45– 2 Sep 45	44	RA	CE	1924	......	......
Deputy Chief (Air)									
Upston, J. E........	BG	O10595	16 Dec 42–27 Feb 44	52	RA	AC	......	1937	1939
Barker, J. DeF.[7]...	BG	O11416	27 Feb 44– 2 Sep 45	46	RA	AC	......	1936	1938
Executive Officer									
Walker, K. N........	BG	O12510	10 Mar 42– 1 Jul 42	43	RA	AC	......	1935	......
Executive (Ground)									
Stewart, C. W., Jr.....	Col	O15124	1 Jul 42–29 Nov 44	42	RA	CE	1923	1938	......
Darby, W. O........	Col	O19133	29 Nov 44–27 Apr 45	33	RA	FA	1933	......	......
Tandy, F. S........	Col	O15521	27 Apr 45– 5 Jul 45	44	RA	CE	1924	......	......
Mather, G. R.[4]....	Col	O18696	5 Jul 45– 2 Sep 45	34	RA	Cav	1932	......	......
Executive (Air)									
Sweeney, W. C., Jr....	Lt Col[2]	O18080	19 Jul 42–21 Jan 44	32	RA	AC	1930	......	......
Briggs, J. E........	Col	O17103	21 Jan 44–15 Feb 45	37	RA	AC	1928	......	......
Hipps, W. G........	Col	O20787	15 Feb 45– 4 Jun 45	32	RA	AC	1937	......	......
Picher, O. S........	Col	O18009	4 Jun 45– 2 Sep 45	40	RA	AC	......	......	......

	Rank	Serial No.	Dates	Age	Comp.	Branch			
Section Chiefs:									
ABDA (ANZAB)									
Irvine, W. W.	Col	O5838	21 Feb 42–17 Apr 42	49	RA	CAC	......	1928	1936
Stevens, F. R.	Lt Col	O15779	17 Apr 42–27 Apr 42	39	RA	Inf	1924	1939	......
Southwest Pacific									
Stevens, F. R.	Lt Col	O15779	27 Apr 42– 8 Jun 42	39	RA	Inf	1924	1939	1936
Ritchie, W. L.	Col	O16059	8 Jun 42– 4 May 44	40	RA	AC	1925	1940	1936
Baumann, J. H.	Col	O16326	4 May 44– 7 Apr 45	42	RA	FA	......	1940	......
Pacific									
Russell, C. A.	Col	O5144	21 Feb 42– 9 Mar 42	49	RA	Inf	......	1931	1936
McKee, J. L.	Col	O5613	9 Mar 42–20 Aug 42	47	RA	Inf	......	1932	1936
Silverthorne, C. D.	Col	O15225	20 Aug 42–26 Jun 44	43	RA	Cav	1923	......	......
Johnson, H. C.	Col	O15345	27 Jun 44– 7 Apr 45	42	RA	Inf	1923	1938	......
Baumann, J. H.	Col	O16326	7 Apr 45–15 May 45	43	RA	FA	......	1940	......
Johnson, H. C.	Col	O15345	15 May 45–29 Jun 45	43	RA	Inf	1923	1938	......
Gilmer, D.	Col	O18876	2 Jul 45– 2 Sep 45	35	RA	Inf	1932	1941	......
Atlantic									
Sherrill, S. H.	Col	O5258	21 Feb 42–27 Apr 42	48	RA	Sig C	1917	1932	1939
North American									
Sherrill, S. H.	Col	O5258	27 Apr 42–12 Aug 42	49	RA	Sig C	1917	1932	1939
Barber, H. A., Jr.	Col	O8576	12 Aug 42–16 May 43	46	RA	Inf	1917	1935	1937
Goode, P. R.	Col	O8651	16 May 43–24 Jan 44	50	RA	Inf	1917	1936	1939
Caribbean & Latin America									
Barber, H. A., Jr.	Col	O8576	21 Feb 42–27 Apr 42	45	RA	Inf	1917	1935	1937
Latin American									
Barber, H. A., Jr.	Col	O8576	27 Apr 42–12 Aug 42	45	RA	Inf	1917	1935	1937
Mathewson, L.	Col	O14980	12 Aug 42–20 Oct 43	43	RA	FA	1922	1939	......
Hertford, K. F.[8]	Col	O15120	21 Oct 43–31 Jan 44	43	RA	CE	1923	......	......
American [9]									
Hertford, K. F.[8]	Col	O15120	1 Feb 44–19 May 44	43	RA	CE	1923	......	......
Edwards, P. W.	Col	O16775	19 May 44–31 Mar 45	39	RA	CAC	1927	......	......
African-Middle East									
MacKelvie, J. W.	Col	O5476	21 Feb 42– 9 Mar 42	51	RA	FA	......	1932	1936
Upston, J. E.	BG	O10595	9 Mar 42–16 Dec 42	51	RA	AC	......	1937	1937
Johnson, D. V.	Col	O15072	16 Dec 42– 8 Feb 43	42	RA	FA	1929	1939	1939
Middle East-Central African									
Johnson, D. V.	Col	O15072	9 Feb 43–10 Aug 44	42	RA	FA	......	1939	......
Chaffee, F. H.	Col	O17524	11 Aug 44–15 Sep 44	37	RA	FA	1929	1942	......

(Footnotes at end of table)

DIVISION, GROUP, AND SECTION CHIEFS IN OPD
21 FEBRUARY 1942–2 SEPTEMBER 1945 ¹—Continued

Name	Rank²	Serial Number	Period of Assignment	Age³	Component	Branch	Graduated		
							USMA	C & GS	AWC
European (European-North African)									
Hull, J. E.⁷	BG	O7377	26 Apr 42– 9 Dec 42	46	RA	Inf	......	1936	1938
Brown, W. D.	Col	O12260	9 Dec 42–14 Dec 42	43	RA	FA	1918	1937	......
Ferenbaugh, C. B.⁸	Col	O12479	14 Dec 42–30 Jun 43	43	RA	Inf	1918	1937	1940
Reid, A. D.⁸	Col	O15234	1 Jul 43–10 Aug 44	42	RA	Inf	1923	1940	......
Gilmer, D.	Col	O18876	11 Aug 44– 1 Jul 45	34	RA	Inf	1932	1941	......
Starbird, A. D.⁴	Col	O18961	2 Jul 45– 2 Sep 45	33	RA	CE	1933	......	......
North African									
Ferenbaugh, C. B.⁸	Col	O12479	1 Jul 43–26 Jan 44	44	RA	Inf	1918	1937	1940
Connor, V. H.	Col	O15405	27 Jan 44–14 Sep 44	42	RA	FA	......	1941	......
Mediterranean									
Connor, V. H.	Col	O15405	15 Sep 44–14 Nov 44	42	RA	FA	......	1941	......
Bowen, J. W.	Col	O18904	15 Nov 44–27 Apr 45	34	RA	Inf	1932	......	......
China-India (Burma)									
Timberman, T. S.	Lt Col	O15328	21 Feb 42–27 Apr 42	41	RA	Inf	1923	1940	......
Asiatic									
Timberman, T. S.	BG	O15328	27 Apr 42– 3 Feb 44	42	RA	Inf	1923	1940	......
Wood, W. H.	Col	O16135	3 Feb 44–31 Aug 44	43	RA	Cav	1925	1938	......
Lincoln, L. J.⁴	Col	O18968	1 Sep 44– 2 Sep 45	35	RA	CE	1933	......	......
Troop Movements									
Hodes, H. I.	Col	O12845	8 Apr 42–24 Jan 44	43	RA	Cav	1920	1937	1940
Rehmann, E. J.	Col	O5060	3 Feb 44–30 Sep 44	59	RA	Inf	......	1930	......
Troop Control									
Rehmann, E. J.	Col	O5060	1 Oct 44– 9 May 45	60	RA	Inf	......	1930	......
Barker, J. DeF.⁷	BG	O11416	10 May 45–28 May 45	48	RA	AC	......	1936	1938
Ferenbaugh, C. B.⁴	BG	O12479	29 May 45– 2 Sep 45	46	RA	Inf	1918	1937	1940

	Rank	Serial No.	Dates	Age	Comp	Arm				
Liaison										
McCarthy, C. W.	Col	O16667	9 Feb 43–12 May 44	40	RA	Inf	......	......	......	......
Maddux, H. R.	Col	O19086	13 May 44–13 May 45	35	RA	AC	1933	......	......	......
Divine, D., II.	Col	O19088	13 May 45–17 Jul 45	34	RA	AC	1933	......	......	......
Reid, A. D.[4]	Col	O15234	17 Jul 45– 2 Sep 45	44	RA	Inf	1923	1940	......	......
PAN-AMERICAN GROUP[9]										
Chief										
Hertford, K. F.[4]	BG	O15120	1 Apr 45– 2 Sep 45	44	RA	CE	1923	......	......	......
Deputy Chief										
Edwards, P. W.	Col	O16775	1 Apr 45–26 Jul 45	39	RA	CAC	1927	......	......	......
Ericson, R. A.	Col	O12117	27 Jul 45– 2 Sep 45	50	RA	CAC	1918	1939	......	......
Section Chiefs:										
Operating										
Lewis, M.	Col	O18163	1 Apr 45–26 Jul 45	39	RA	AC	1930	......	......	......
Edwards, P. W.	Col	O16775	27 Jul 45–27 Aug 45	40	RA	CAC	1927	......	......	......
Divine, D., II.	Col	O19088	27 Aug 45– 2 Sep 45	34	RA	AC	1933	......	......	......
Planning										
Blaine, M. D.	Col	O21500	1 Apr 45– 2 Sep 45	35	RA	AC	......	......	......	......
STRATEGY & POLICY GROUP										
Chief										
Handy, T. T.[4]	BG	O4665	16 Feb 42–23 Jun 42	49	RA	FA	......	1927	1935	......
Wedemeyer, A. C.	BG	O12484	27 Jun 42–10 Sep 43	45	RA	Inf	1918	1936	......	......
Roberts, F. N.[8]	BG	O12734	11 Sep 43–30 Nov 44	45	RA	Inf	1920	1940	......	......
Lincoln, G. A.	BG	O17497	30 Nov 44– 2 Sep 45	37	RA	CE	1929	......	......	......
Special Assistant										
Maddocks, R. T.	BG	O7291	24 May 43–15 Nov 43	47	RA	Cav	......	1938	......	......
Deputy Chief										
Harrison, W. K., Jr.	Col	O5279	21 Feb 42–20 May 42	46	RA	Cav	1917	1934	1938	......
Wedemeyer, A. C.	Col	O12484	20 May 42–26 Jun 42	45	RA	Inf	1918	1936	......	......
Nevins, A. S.	Col	O7110	27 Jun 42–31 Jul 42	51	RA	Inf	......	1933	1936	......
Rogers, E. J., Jr	Lt Col[2]	O16622	1 Aug 42– 5 Jan 43	38	RA	AC	1928	......	......	......
Anderson, S. E.	Lt Col[2]	O17244	6 Jan 43–18 Apr 43	37	RA	AC	1928	......	......	......
Deputy Chief (Ground)										
Roberts, F. N.[8]	Col	O12734	19 Apr 42–10 Sep 43	45	RA	Inf	1920	1940	......	......
Lincoln, G. A.	Col	O17497	23 Oct 43–29 Nov 44	36	RA	CE	1929	......	......	......
Roberts, T. D.	Col	O15529	30 Nov 44– 2 Sep 45	41	RA	Cav	1924	1940	......	......

(Footnotes at end of table)

DIVISION, GROUP, AND SECTION CHIEFS IN OPD
21 FEBRUARY 1942–2 SEPTEMBER 1945 [1]—Continued

Name	Rank [3]	Serial Number	Period of Assignment	Age [5]	Component	Branch	USMA	C & GS	AWC
Deputy Chief (Air)									
Anderson, S. E.	Lt Col [2]	O17244	19 Apr 43–29 May 43	37	RA	AC	1928		
Todd, W. E.	Col	O17121	1 Jun 43– 5 May 44	36	RA	AC	1928		
Ritchie, W. L.	Col	O16059	5 May 44–29 Nov 44	42	RA	AC	1925	1940	
Cary, J. B. [4]	Col	O19352	30 Nov 44– 2 Sep 45	33	RA	AC	1934		
Executive Officer									
Tasker, H. P.	Col	O15557	1 Feb 43– 2 Sep 45	41	RA	CAC	1924		
Section Chiefs:									
Future Operations									
Hull, J. E. [7]	Col	O7377	21 Feb 42–30 Jun 42	46	RA	Inf		1936	1938
Smith, G. A., Jr.	Lt Col	O16474	1 Jul 42–26 Jul 42	40	RA	Inf	1926		
War Room									
Smith, C. P.	Lt Col	O252843	21 Feb 42–12 May 42	36	Res	FA			
Webb, L. F.	Maj	O336719	8 Jun 42–30 Sep 42	35	NG	Inf			
Parker, B. W.	Capt	O413926	1 Oct 42– 5 Jan 43	23	Res	Cav			
Strategy									
Nevins, A. S.	Col	O7110	21 Feb 42–26 Jul 42	50	RA	Inf		1933	1936
Blizzard, J. C., Jr.	Col	O7581	27 Jul 42–18 Sep 43	47	RA	Inf		1939	
Billo, J. J.	Col	O12721	24 Oct 43–22 Jan 45	44	RA	Inf	1920	1941	
Wood, R. J. [10]	Col	O18064	22 Jan 45–31 Jan 45	39	RA	CAC	1930	1941	
Johnson, M. S.	Col	O16745	1 Feb 45– 2 Sep 45	42	RA	CE	1927	1938	
Army Section (JUSSC-JWPC)									
Maddocks, R. T.	Col	O7291	21 Feb 42–10 May 43	46	RA	Cav	1920	1938	
Bessell, W. W., Jr.	BG	O1261	11 May 43– 2 Sep 45	42	RA	CE	1920	1940	
Combined Subjects									
Kibler, A. F.	Col	O6668	21 Feb 42–20 May 42	50	RA	FA		1935	1938
Rogers, E. J., Jr. [10]	Lt Col [2]	O16622	20 May 42–26 Jul 42	38	RA	AC			
Lindsay, R. C.	Lt Col [2]	O17845	27 Jul 42– 2 Jun 43	36	RA	AC			
Woolnough, J. K.	Lt Col	O18709	3 Jun 43–30 Jun 43	32	RA	Inf	1932		

Position	Rank	Serial No.	From	To	Age	Comp.	Br.			
Policy										
Woolnough, J. K.	Lt Col	O18709	1 Jul 43	10 Jul 44	32	RA	Inf	1932	....	....
Jones, C. L.[10]	Lt Col	O19074	10 Jul 44	31 Jul 44	35	RA	FA	1933	....	....
Zimmerman, D. Z.	Col	O17499	1 Aug 44	11 Jul 45	40	RA	AC	1929	1943	....
Bonesteel, C. H., III	Col	O18655	11 Jul 45	2 Sep 45	35	RA	CE	1931	....	1936
Missions										
Russell, C. A.	Col	O5144	10 Mar 42	1 Apr 42	49	RA	Inf	....	1931	1936
Implementing										
Martell, L. E.	Capt	O1000621	9 May 45	2 Sep 45	31	AUS	AGD	....	....	....
LOGISTICS GROUP										
Chief										
Miller, L. W.	BG	O3773	10 Mar 42	24 Jun 42	50	RA	CE	1915	1932	1940
Davis, T. D.	Col	O8223	25 Jun 42	31 Jul 42[10]	49	RA	Inf	....	1936	1938
			1 Aug 42	4 Dec 42				....	....	....
Tansey, P. H.	BG	O9299	4 Dec 42	17 Jun 45	48	RA	CE	1918	1936	....
Esposito, V. J.	BG	O16053	19 Jun 45	2 Sep 45	45	RA	CE	1925	1939	....
Assistant to Chief										
Haskell, J. H. F.	Col	O222339	14 Dec 42	1 Mar 43	39	NG	Inf	1925	....	....
Deputy Chief										
Daly, J. C.	Col	O4911	2 Mar 45	2 Sep 45	54	RA	Cav	....	1928	1939
Executive Officer										
Fair, F. L.	Lt Col²	O17029	29 Aug 42	29 Jan 43	44	RA	AC	....	1937	....
Gallant, E. B.	Lt Col	O257020	29 Jan 43	10 May 43	36	NG	CAC	....	....	....
Peploe, G. B.	Col	O16246	10 May 43	16 Sep 43	42	RA	Inf	1925	1939	....
Bomar, E. C.	Col	O6733	17 Sep 43	15 Sep 44	47	RA	Ord	....	....	....
Daly, J. C.	Col	O4911	16 Sep 44	1 Mar 45	53	RA	Cav	1928	1928	1939
Section Chiefs:										
Current[11]										
Frederic, R. T.	Lt Col	O17196	9 Mar 42	16 Jun 42	34	RA	CAC	1928	1939	....
North, T.	Col	O11879	16 Jun 42	31 Jan 44	49	RA	FA	....	1935	....
Resources & Requirements[12]										
Townsend, J. R.	Col	O6357	21 Feb 42	15 Apr 42	48	RA	CAC	1939	1939	....
Davis, T. D.	Col	O8223	15 Apr 42	15 Jun 42	49	RA	Inf	1936	1936	1938
Troop										
Davis, T. D.	Col	O8223	15 Jun 42	31 Jul 42	49	RA	Inf	1936	1936	1938
Fair, F. L.	Lt Col²	O17029	31 Jul 42	30 Oct 42	44	RA	AC	....	1937	....
Clark, C. I.	Col	O196442	30 Oct 42	17 Jan 44	49	Res	CAC	1932	1932	....

(Footnotes at end of table)

DIVISION, GROUP, AND SECTION CHIEFS IN OPD
21 FEBRUARY 1942–2 SEPTEMBER 1945 [1]—Continued

Name	Rank [2]	Serial Number	Period of Assignment	Age [3]	Component	Branch	Graduated USMA	Graduated C & GS	Graduated AWC
Materiel									
Tansey, P. H.	Col	O9299	15 Jun 42– 4 Dec 42	48	RA	CE	1918	1936	....
Peploe, G. B.	Col	O16246	4 Dec 42–20 Apr 43	42	RA	Inf	1925	1939	....
Daly, J. C.	Col	O4911	20 Apr 43–17 Jan 44	52	RA	Cav	....	1928	1939
Plans and Assignment									
Esposito, V. J.	Col	O16053	15 Apr 43–17 Jan 44	42	RA	CE	1925	1939	....
Projected Logistics									
Esposito, V. J.	Col	O16053	17 Jan 44–16 Jun 45	43	RA	CE	1925	1939	....
Barney, K. R.	Col	O16377	22 Jun 45– 2 Sep 45	41	RA	CE	1926	1942	....
Operational Logistics									
Daly, J. C.	Col	O4911	17 Jan 44–15 Sep 44	52	RA	Cav	....	1928	1939
Poorman, D. A.	Col	O17631	16 Sep 44– 2 Sep 45	37	RA	Inf	1929	1942	....
CURRENT GROUP [11].									
Chief									
North, T.	BG	O11879	1 Feb 44– 2 Sep 45	50	RA	FA	....	1935	....
Deputy Chief									
Walker, W. A.	Col	O16410	5 Dec 44– 2 Sep 45	43	RA	FA	1926	1941	....
Executive Officer									
Connor, W. M., Jr.	Lt Col	O20137	1 Feb 44–31 Oct 44	31	RA	FA	1936	....	....
Thompson, P. W.	Col	O17506	31 Oct 44– 5 Dec 44	37	RA	CE	1929	....	....
Section Chiefs:									
Combat Analysis									
Walker, W. A.	Col	O16410	1 Feb 44– 5 Dec 44	43	RA	FA	1926	1941	....
Paige, B. L.	Col	O18704	5 Dec 44–20 Jun 45	35	RA	FA	1932	1941	....
Thielen, B.	Col	O18782	21 Jun 45– 2 Sep 45	37	RA	FA	1932	....	....

Coordination & Reports

Leihy, C. W.	Col	O236216	1 Feb 44–14 Sep 44	38	Res	FA	......	......	......
Bishop, G. H., Jr.	Col	O19239	15 Sep 44– 9 Jul 45	35	RA	Inf	......	1933	1941
Heriot, J. J.	Col	O18047	9 Jul 45– 2 Sep 45	38	RA	FA	......	1930	......

Operations Analysis & Projects

Low, R. M.	Lt Col	O902219	30 Jul 45–17 Aug 45	33	AUS	Cav	......	......	......
Barnes, C. DeM	Capt	O1284450	17 Aug 45– 2 Sep 45	33	AUS	Inf	......	......	......

Troop Control (Theater Group) Chief 10 May 1945–28 May 1945 while assigned as Deputy Chief (Air), Theater Group; Brig. Gen. J. E. Hull served as Chief of both European Section (Theater Group) and Future Operations (S&P Group) during the period April 1942–June 1942.

1 The Division was organized tentatively on the OPD pattern as of 21 February 1942, though this organization was not official until 9 March 1942 and the name Operations Division was not used until 23 March 1942.

2 Rank denoted is the highest AUS rank which the officer reached while serving as Chief, based on "date of rank." Notation "2" beside the officer's rank indicates that the officer had received promotion to higher AUS (AC) rank than the AUS rank listed.

3 Age is given as of date officer became Chief.

4 Second tour of duty in WPD/OPD.

5 No formal designation of Deputy Assistant Chief of Staff, OPD, was made under General Handy, but General Hull acted for General Handy when necessary.

6 For Current Section after March 1942, see Logistics Group.

7 Indicates current assignment to more than one position: Maj. Gen. H. A. Craig was appointed Deputy Assistant Chief of Staff, OPD, on 25 November 1944 in addition to his assignment as Theater Group Chief; Brig. Gen. J. Def. Barker served as

8 First tour of duty in WPD/OPD for officers serving more than one tour of duty.

9 American Section (Theater Group) became Pan-American Group on 1 April 1945.

10 Acting Chief.

11 See Executive Group for Current Section before March 1942. Current Section became Current Group on 1 February 1944.

12 Resources & Requirements was initially and briefly carried as an independent group 21 February 1942–9 March 1942. After 9 March 1942 this section was one of the two original sections in Logistics Group, the other being Current Section.

Source: OPD History Unit Study D.

Appendix B

U. S. ARMY COMMANDERS IN MAJOR THEATER COMMANDS, DECEMBER 1941–SEPTEMBER 1945

There is a mass of detailed information concerning major and minor U. S. Army commands set up in World War II, but a simple table of the few highest headquarters and the U. S. Army commanders in them, with dates and explanatory notes, does not exist in Department of the Army files. This appendix presents the names of the superior headquarters in which U. S. Army officers held command positions in every part of the world. For the most part OPD's links with the "overseas theaters" served to establish liaison between the War Department and the Chief of Staff in Washington and these headquarters and these commanders overseas.

Unless otherwise indicated, the "Date Established" signifies the date the official order for the setting up of a particular command was sent out by the War Department, the JCS, or the CCS. These dates, based largely on orders from Washington, do not coincide necessarily with the dates of the arrival of troops, the actual assumption of command by the commanding general, or the beginning of the effective functioning of the command headquarters. Unless otherwise indicated in the accompanying notes, the dates beside the name of the commanding general signify the period of actual assumption and relief from command. The rank of the commanding general listed is the rank he held upon his actual assumption of the command indicated.

The sources of information on which this table and the accompanying notes are based are varied and scattered. They present so many technical problems in citation that documentation has been omitted. Nevertheless, the information given is considered reliable within a small margin of error. For basic information, with an informal system of documentation, see OPD History Unit Study Z.

EUROPEAN THEATER

Name of Command	Date Established	Commanding General
U. S. Army Forces in the British Isles (USAFBI)	8 January 1942	Maj Gen J. E. Chaney [1] (8 Jan–8 Jun 42)
European Theater of Operations, U. S. Army (ETOUSA)[2]	8 June 1942	Maj Gen J. E. Chaney (8–20 Jun 42) Maj Gen D. D. Eisenhower (24 Jun 42–3 Feb 43) Lt Gen F. M. Andrews (4 Feb–3 May 43) Lt Gen J. L. Devers [3] (10 May 43–8 Jan 44) Gen D. D. Eisenhower [4] (15 Jan 44–1 Jul 45)
Supreme Headquarters Allied Expeditionary Force (SHAEF)	15 January 1944	Gen D. D. Eisenhower [5] (15 Jan 44–16 Jul 45)
U. S. Forces European Theater (USFET)[6]	1 July 1945	General of the Army D. D. Eisenhower (1 Jul–11 Nov 45)

[1] General Chaney had been serving as the Special Army Observer in the United Kingdom and head of the American mission called the Special Observer Group (SPOBS) since May 1941. British-American military staffs agreed during their meetings in Washington, January–March 1941 (ABC–1 Conversations), to exchange military missions to facilitate planning for the eventuality of American entry in the war. General Chaney arrived on 18 May 1941, and on the following day Headquarters, SPOBS, was established in London. After the United States entered the war, SPOBS was succeeded by USAFBI, actually SPOBS under a new name. At the time of the ARCADIA Conference, December 1941–January 1942, the decision was made to place the MAGNET force (U. S. Forces for North Ireland) under the command of Maj. Gen. E. L. Daley, and make him in turn responsible to General Chaney, designated as CG, USAFBI.

[2] ETOUSA (successor to USAFBI) was a joint command in which, by agreement of U. S. War and Navy Departments, the Army exercised planning and operational control under the principle of unity of command over all U. S. Navy forces assigned to that theater. Iceland (INDIGO) was included in the ETO in June 1942. General Eisenhower, while he was commanding the invasion of North Africa, remained in command of ETO through a deputy, Maj. Gen. R. P. Hartile, until 3 February 1943.

[3] General Devers assumed command in ETO, after the death of General Andrews on 3 May 1943 in an airplane accident.

[4] TAG issued orders on 31 December 1943 transferring General Eisenhower to duty as CG, ETOUSA, and relieving General Devers from that theater and assigning the latter to command U. S. Forces in NATO. The effective date of the exchange was to be arranged between these officers. General

Devers was relieved of the command on 8 January 1944, but General Eisenhower did not arrive in London until 15 January 1944.

[5] General Eisenhower was notified by the CCS on 10 December 1943 that he had been appointed Supreme Commander, Allied Expeditionary Force (for OVERLORD), a combined command, and that prior to his assuming command early in January he was to return to Washington for conferences with General Marshall and the CCS. Soon after his notification in early December 1943 that he had been appointed supreme commander, General Eisenhower began to lay his plans and arrange for the adjustment of command and staff assignments for his organization for OVERLORD. Following a hurried trip to the United States at the beginning of the new year, he arrived in London on 15 January 1944. His appointment as supreme commander did not become "formally official" until his receipt of a directive from the CCS on 14 February 1944. In the period 15 January–14 February 1944 General Eisenhower conducted planning for OVERLORD with the COSSAC staff, the Allied planning agency, which had come under his control upon his arrival in the United Kingdom and which he proceeded to expand into the headquarters which became known as SHAEF. COSSAC formally changed its name to SHAEF on 15 January 1944. SHAEF was not officially activated, however, until 13 February 1944. SHAEF was inactivated on 16 July 1945.

[6] JCS 1400, approved and dispatched to General Eisenhower on 27 June 1945, provided for the redesignation of ETOUSA as USFET. This message also designated General Eisenhower as Commander in Chief, U. S. Forces of Occupation in Germany. Gen. Mark Clark was designated as Commander in Chief, U. S. Forces of Occupation in Austria. ETOUSA was redesignated USFET effective 1 July 1945.

Africa-Middle East Theater

Name of Command	Date Established	Commanding General
U. S. Army Forces in the Middle East (USAFIME) [1]	16 June 1942	Maj Gen R. L. Maxwell [2] (16 Jun–4 Nov 42) Lt Gen F. M. Andrews (4 Nov 42–31 Jan 43) Maj Gen L. H. Brereton [3] (31 Jan–10 Sep 43) Maj Gen Ralph Royce (10 Sep 43–10 Mar 44) Brig Gen B. L. Giles (10 Mar 44–1 Mar 45)
U. S. Army Forces in Central Africa (USAFICA) [4]	16 June 1942	Brig Gen S. W. Fitzgerald [5] (16 Jun 42–23 Jun 43) Brig Gen E. S. Hoag (6 Jul–4 Sep 43)
Persian Gulf Command (PGC) [6]	10 December 1943	Maj Gen D. H. Connolly (10 Dec 43–24 Dec 44) Brig Gen D. P. Booth (24 Dec 44–15 Aug 45) Col G. A. M. Anderson (15 Aug–1 Oct 45)
U. S. Army Forces Africa-Middle East Theater (USAFAMET) [7]	1 March 1945	Maj Gen B. L. Giles (1 Mar 45–15 Feb 46)

[1] On 16 June 1942 the War Department created within the Africa-Middle East Theater, which had been designated by the CCS as an area of British strategic responsibility, two commands: U. S. Army Forces in the Middle East and U. S. Army Forces in Central Africa. USAFIME was by far the larger and, in terms of proximity to critical military operations, more important command.

[2] General Maxwell had been serving as head of the U. S. Military Mission in Africa, with headquarters at Cairo, Egypt, since the fall of 1941.

[3] Upon the departure of General Andrews for his new assignment in ETO on 31 January 1943, Maj. Gen. L. H. Brereton, in accordance with previous War Department instructions, assumed command as CG, USAFIME. General Brereton had been designated commander of the Middle East Air Force (later 9th Air Force) in June 1942.

[4] USAFICA, established at the same time as USAFIME, was the U. S. Army command assigned responsibility for the area of the trans-African air ferry route.

[5] General Fitzgerald was concurrently Commanding General, African-Middle Eastern Wing, AAF Ferrying Command. In the latter part of June 1942 Brig. Gen. Percy L. Sadler served briefly as CG, USAFICA. On 4 September 1943 the War Department dissolved USAFICA, the defense of the trans-African air ferry route being no longer critical, and placed the area it had covered under USAFIME.

[6] PGC was set up as a separate command directly under the War Department effective 10 December 1943. General Connolly, who had been serving as commander of the Persian Gulf Service Command (PGSC) since 20 October 1942 became CG, PGC. PGSC, a service subcommand in USAFIME, had been set up on 13 August 1942. PGSC was a redesignation of the Iran-Iraq Service Command, activated 24 June 1942, which in turn was a redesignation of the U. S. Military Iranian Mission. The U. S. Army had accepted the responsibility for developing and operating transportation and port facilities in the Persian Corridor to expedite lend-lease to the USSR, as outlined in CCS 109/1, 22 September 1942. Between 24 June 1942 and 10 December 1943 the American organization in the Persian Corridor was within the jurisdiction of USAFIME. PGSC was largely autonomous in fact, although it was not until December 1943 that PGSC, designated as PGC, became an autonomous command in name as well as in fact. PGC ceased to be a separate command on 1 October 1945, when it was again designated PGSC and placed under USAFAMET. Its operations ceased in December 1945.

[7] The War Department redesignated the Middle East theater as the Africa-Middle East theater with new boundaries, effective 1 March 1945. The mission and boundaries of the Africa-Middle East theater were redefined by the War Department 20 November 1945. The War Department issued orders inactivating the Africa-Middle East theater, effective 31 May 1946.

NORTH AFRICAN-MEDITERRANEAN THEATER

Name of Command	Date Established	Commanding General
Allied Force Headquarters, North Africa (AFHQ)	11 August 1942 [1]	Lt Gen D. D. Eisenhower [2]
North African Theater of Operations, U. S. Army (NATOUSA) [3]	4 February 1943	Lt Gen D. D. Eisenhower (4 Feb 43–8 Jan 44) Lt Gen J. L. Devers [4] (8 Jan–22 Oct 44) Lt Gen J. T. McNarney [5] (22 Oct–1 Nov 44)
Mediterranean Theater of Operations (MTO) [Allied]	10 December 1943	*CinC* Gen D. D. Eisenhower [6] (10 Dec 43–8 Jan 44) *Deputy CinC* Lt Gen J. L. Devers [7] (8 Jan–22 Oct 44) Lt Gen J. T. McNarney [8] (22 Oct 44–23 Oct 45)
Mediterranean Theater of Operations, U. S. Army (MTOUSA)	1 November 1944	Lt Gen J. T. McNarney (1 Nov 44–23 Oct 45)

[1] General Eisenhower's combined headquarters for TORCH was formed on 11 August 1942 in London. General Clark's suggestion that the title "Allied Force Headquarters" (AFHQ) be adopted for this headquarters was accepted by the British on 24 August 1942. The word "expeditionary" contained in the directive to the commander in chief for TORCH (General Eisenhower) was omitted for security reasons. The Advance Echelon, AFHQ, arrived in Algiers on 9 November 1942. AFHQ was in ETO until the formal separation of NATO from ETO on 4 February 1943. AFHQ remained a combined administrative headquarters for the Allied commander in the Mediterranean after the establishment of the Mediterranean Theater of Operations (Allied) in December 1943 and after a British officer, initially Gen. Sir H. Maitland Wilson, succeeded General Eisenhower in early 1944 as Commander in Chief, Mediterranean Theater (later designated SACMED).

[2] General Eisenhower was formally designated Commander in Chief, Allied Expeditionary Force (for TORCH) by a CCS directive, CCS 103/1, approved in 36th meeting CCS, 13 August 1942. This directive, which General Eisenhower received from the CCS on 14 August 1942, officially confirmed an assignment upon which in reality he had been engaged since July 1942.

[3] NATOUSA was separated from ETO on 4 February 1943. General Eisenhower (AUS general, 11 February 1943) was designated CG. By agreement between U. S. War and Navy Departments, NATO, like ETO, was a unified American command. In NATO the U. S. Army commander exercised planning and operational control of the U. S. Navy forces, Northwest African waters, under the doctrine of unity of command.

[4] General Devers relinquished command of ETO and assumed command of NATOUSA on 8 January 1944, simultaneously becoming Deputy Allied Commander in Chief, Mediterranean.

[5] General McNarney succeeded General Devers both as Deputy Supreme Allied Commander, Mediterranean, and as Theater Commander, NATOUSA, 22 October 1944. General McNarney served as CG, NATOUSA, until 1 November 1944 when NATOUSA was redesignated Mediterranean Theater of Operations, U. S. Army.

[6] CCS 387/3, 5 December 1943, provided in effect for the combination of the U. S. North African Theater of Operations and the British Middle Eastern theater to form the Mediterranean Theater of Operations. In this directive General Eisenhower as Commander in Chief, Allied Forces, North Africa, was given command of the Mediterranean theater. This directive brought the whole offensive in the Mediterranean under a single command and gave General Eisenhower responsibility for all operations in the Mediterranean other than strategic bombing. He retained command of NATOUSA. Effective 10 December 1943, a unified command was established in the Mediterranean theater under a Commander in Chief, Allied Forces, who was redesignated Allied Commander in Chief, Allied Forces, and still later, 9 March 1944, renamed Supreme Allied Commander, Mediterranean Theater (SACMED). Shortly after General Eisenhower left the theater for a visit to the United States prior to assuming his new post as Supreme Commander, Allied Expeditionary Force (for OVERLORD), General Wilson succeeded him in the supreme command, Mediterranean Theater (8 January 1944).

[7] At the same time that General Wilson succeeded General Eisenhower in command of Allied forces in MTO, 8 January 1944, General Devers began his duties as CG, NATOUSA, and as General Wilson's deputy (Deputy Allied Commander in Chief, Mediterranean). Field Marshal Sir Harold Alexander relieved General Wilson of command of MTO on 12 December 1944, and another British officer, Lt. Gen. W. D. Morgan, was appointed Supreme Allied Commander, Mediterranean Theater, in early October 1945.

[8] General McNarney assumed his duties as Deputy Commander in Chief, Mediterranean, when he relieved General Devers as CG, NATOUSA. When the North African Theater of Operations was redesignated MTOUSA General McNarney automatically became CG, MTOUSA.

Name of Command	Date Established	Commanding General
U. S. Army Forces in the Chinese Theater of Operations, Burma and India	2 February 1942	Lt Gen J. W. Stilwell [1] (also CofS to Generalissimo, Supreme Commander, China Theater) (4 Mar 42–21 Oct 44)
Southeast Asia Command (SEAC) [Allied]	21 August 1943 [2]	*Deputy Supreme Allied Commander* Lt Gen J. W. Stilwell (16 Nov 43–21 Oct 44) Lt Gen R. A. Wheeler [3] (12 Nov 44–4 Oct 45)
U. S. Forces, China Theater (USFCT) [4]	24 October 1944	Maj Gen A. C. Wedemeyer (also CofS to Generalissimo) (31 Oct 44–1 May 46)
U. S. Forces, India-Burma Theater (USFIBT)	24 October 1944	Lt Gen D. I. Sultan (27 Oct 44–22 Jun 45) Lt Gen R. A. Wheeler (23 Jun–28 Sep 45)

[1] At the same time that General Stilwell was appointed U. S. Army Representative in China, the War Department, by directive of the President, appointed him to be chief of staff to the Supreme Commander, China Theater (Generalissimo Chiang Kai-shek). General Stilwell arrived in Chungking, China, to assume his command on 4 March 1942. At the end of June 1942 he designated his American command as USAFCBI. He was notified of his relief from responsibilities in Asia in a message received from General Marshall, 18 October 1944. He left Chungking on 21 October 1944.

[2] At QUADRANT Conference provision was made for setting up SEAC, a combined Allied command, under Admiral Lord Louis Mountbatten as Supreme Allied Commander (SACSEA). General Stilwell, CG, CBI, was to be made his deputy. Operations in the Chinese theater were to continue to be under the Generalissimo with General Stilwell as his chief of staff. Through British Chiefs of Staff the CCS were to exercise general supervision over operations in Southeast Asia by SEAC. CCS 308/3, which provided for setting up a supreme Allied command in Asia, was approved by CCS at their 114th meeting, 21 August 1943. Admiral Mountbatten actually took over the command of SEAC on 16 November 1943. General Stilwell assumed his duties as Deputy Supreme Allied Commander at the same time and continued in this capacity until 21 October 1944.

[3] On 12 November 1944 General Wheeler became Deputy Supreme Allied Commander, SEAC, and on 23 June 1945 was given additional duty as the commander of the India-Burma Theater.

[4] In October 1944 General Stilwell was relieved of his responsibilities in Asia, and the American administrative area CBI was separated into the India-Burma and the China theaters. General Sultan was given command of the India-Burma Theater, and General Wedemeyer (former Army planner in the War Department prior to becoming Deputy Chief of Staff, SEAC, in October 1943) was appointed commander of U. S. Forces in China, and succeeded General Stilwell as the Generalissimo's chief of staff. General Stilwell was brought back to the United States, assigned to the post of CG, AGF, and later returned to the field in command of the Tenth Army upon the death of General Buckner on Okinawa. American forces, under the command of the CG, USFIBT, were, as directed by CCS, to be under the operational control of SACSEA. Certain units in China, such as Navy Group China and the XX Bomber Command, were not to be under the full control of the CG, USFCT, but to continue their status as shown in directive to CG, CBI. Similar exceptions from the full control of the CG, USFIBT, were made. General Wedemeyer arrived in the theater and actually assumed command as CG, USFCT, on 31 October 1944. USFCT was inactivated 1 May 1946 and its duties taken over by U. S. Army Forces China. USFIBT was inactivated on 31 May 1946 with remaining functions taken over by detachment, U. S. Army Forces India.

PACIFIC THEATER

Name of Command	Date Established	Commanding General
U. S. Army Forces in the Far East (USAFFE)	26 July 1941	Lt Gen Douglas MacArthur [1]
ABDA Command (ABDACom) [Allied] [2]	3 January 1942	*Deputy Commander* Lt Gen G. H. Brett [3]
U. S. Army Forces in Australia (USAFIA) [4]	5 January 1942	Maj Gen G. H. Brett (5–12 Jan 42) Maj Gen L. H. Brereton (12–27 Jan 42) Maj Gen J. F. Barnes (27 Jan–25 Feb 42) Lt. Gen G. H. Brett (25 Feb–18 Apr 42) Maj Gen J. F. Barnes (18 Apr–10 Jul 42)
GHQ, Southwest Pacific Area (SWPA) [Allied] [5]	30 March 1942	Gen Douglas MacArthur (CinC SWPA) (18 Apr 42–2 Sep 45)
U. S. Army Forces in South Pacific Area (USAFISPA) [6]	7 July 1942	Maj Gen M. F. Harmon (ComGenSoPac) (26 Jul 42–8 Jul 44)
Hawaiian Department [7]		Lt Gen W. C. Short (8 Feb 41–17 Dec 41) Lt Gen D. C. Emmons (17 Dec 41–1 Jun 43) Lt Gen R. C. Richardson, Jr. [8] (1 Jun 43–17 Mar 46)
U. S. Army Forces in Central Pacific Area (USAFICPA) [9]	14 August 1943	Lt Gen R. C. Richardson, Jr. (ComGenCentPac) (14 Aug 43–1 Aug 44)
U. S. Army Forces, Pacific Ocean Areas (USAFPOA) [10]	1 August 1944	Lt Gen R. C. Richardson, Jr. (ComGenPoa) (1 Aug 44–17 Mar 46)
U. S. Army Forces, Pacific (AFPAC) [11]	3 April 1945	General of the Army Douglas MacArthur (CinC AFPAC) (6 Apr 45–31 Dec 46)

[1] The Philippine Department had been in existence for many years before the outbreak of the war as the outlying U. S. Army command in the Pacific. The Philippine Department, which had been under Maj. Gen. George Grunert May 1940–October 1941, was reduced to the status of a services of supply organization for USAFFE shortly before Pearl Harbor. In January 1942 it was redesignated the Bataan Service Command. On 26 July 1941 General MacArthur, retired, was placed on active duty, appointed lieutenant general (AUS), and designated as CG, USAFFE. The USAFFE command included troops in the Philippine Department and the forces of the Philippine Army as they were inducted into American service. It had the task of organizing the defense of the Philippines. From 18 April 1942 to 26 February 1943 USAFFE, with General MacArthur still in command, was inactive. Effective 26 February 1943 all units of the U. S. Army in the Southwest Pacific areas, and all elements of the Philippine Army called into the service of American forces were assigned to USAFFE which had been constituted by the War Department on 26 July 1941.

²For a short period in 1942, a separate command under General MacArthur existed in the Philippines. Established 21 March 1942, with Lt. Gen. J. M. Wainwright in command, it was called U. S. Forces in the Philippines (USFIP). General Wainwright surrendered 6 May 1942. ABDACom for the Southwest Pacific was set up during the meeting of British-American authorities at the ARCADIA Conference 24 December 1941–14 January 1942 and approved by the Australian, British, Dutch, and American Governments, whose initials formed the name of the command. Designed to stem the tide of Japanese advance, it was composed of American, British, Dutch, and Australian forces, and included all the land and sea areas in the general region Burma-Malaya-Netherlands East Indies and the Philippines. A British officer, Gen. Sir Archibald Wavell, was selected as supreme commander. General Wavell arrived in Batavia on 10 January 1942 and actually assumed command on 15 January 1942. ABDACom was short-lived. After the fall of Singapore, CCS proceeded to dissolve this command. It ceased operations on 25 February 1942.

³ General Brett, the newly appointed commanding general, U. S. troops in Australia, was ordered to report to General Wavell as Deputy Supreme Commander, ABDACom. General Brett was promoted from major general to lieutenant general 7 January 1942, after he was designated Deputy Commander, ABDACom. In mid-January General Wavell, with General Brett as his deputy, took over ABDACom.

⁴ Great confusion surrounded the establishment of the American command in Australia and the designation of a commander. It resulted partly from haste, in both Washington and ABDACom headquarters in the critical early days of the war and from dual responsibilities of American commanders in Australia to ABDACom and to other U. S. Army commands in the Pacific. On 12 December 1941 American troops aboard a convoy originally scheduled for the Philippines were constituted a task force, Task Force South Pacific, and placed under the command of General Barnes, senior officer in the convoy. The convoy was ordered to proceed to Brisbane, Australia, and General Barnes was instructed to assume command of all American troops in Australia and place his forces under CG, USAFFE. He was given the primary objective of aiding in the defense of the Philippines. When the convoy docked at Brisbane, Australia, on 22 December 1941, the Task Force South Pacific became at that point the U. S. Forces in Australia (referred to as USFA or USFIA) with General Barnes in command.

While the convoy was still en route to Brisbane, the War Department was drawing up a plan for using Australia as a supply base for Philippine operations. WPD recommended, 17 December 1941, that General Brett, an Air Corps officer then at a military conference of Allied military leaders in Chungking, assume command of American troops and military facilities in Australia, thus relieving General Barnes who was temporarily in command of the forces headed for Australia. As Commanding General, American Troops in Australia, General Brett was to be under General MacArthur who commanded all U. S. Army forces in the Far East (USAFFE). General Marshall approved this plan for the Australian base, and WPD sent out the messages and directives, 17 December 1941, to put this plan into effect. Pending General Brett's arrival, Brig. Gen. H. B. Claggett, an Air Corps officer on General MacArthur's staff, was to be sent from the Philippines to Australia to take temporary command in Australia. General Claggett arrived in Brisbane by air on 22 December 1941 and took over the command of USFA (USFIA) from General Barnes on 24 December 1941. General Barnes thereupon became General Claggett's chief of staff.

General Brett finally reached Australia 31 December 1941 and on 5 January 1942 assumed command of American troops in Australia as CG, USAFIA. This command was set up under General Brett on the basis of War Department instructions of 17 December 1941 and subsequent modifications and elaborations. The USAFIA command was basically an air services of supply, with a primary mission of logistic support of American air units operating in Northwest Australia and in the Netherlands East Indies. General Barnes, previously General Claggett's chief of staff, became chief of staff to General Brett. General Claggett served briefly as commander of the supply base at Townsville and then returned to the United States.

Confusion in mid-January 1942 increased when General Brett began to function as Deputy Commander in Chief, ABDACom. General Brett reported for duty in Batavia on 12 January and remained General Wavell's deputy until ABDACom headquarters was dissolved (25 February 1942). The War Department, 12 January, without co-ordinating with General Wavell or General Brett, instructed General Brereton, Commanding General, U. S. Far East Air Forces, then operating from the Philippines to Australia and in the Netherlands East Indies (ABDA) area, to assume command of all U. S. Army Forces in Australia. General Brereton actually was CG, USAFIA, 12–27 January 1942. At General Wavell's request, however, General Brereton was designated commander of U. S. Air Forces in the ABDA area. General Barnes succeeded General Brereton as CG, USAFIA, on 27 January 1942. In the last week of February 1942 General Brett, following the collapse of ABDACom, resumed command as CG, USAFIA, with General Barnes as his deputy commander. General Brereton became CG, 10th Air Force in India. Upon General MacArthur's assumption of command as Commander in Chief, Southwest Pacific Area, on 18 April 1942, General Barnes replaced General Brett as CG, USAFIA. General Brett became commander of Allied air forces, SWPA, holding this position until Maj. Gen. G. C. Kenney took over in August 1942. On 10 July 1942 General Barnes was relieved as CG,USAFIA, and USAFIA was redesignated more descriptively the U. S. Army Service of Supply, Southwest Pacific Area (USASOSSWPA). This change became effective 20 July 1942.

⁵ JCS, by directive of 30 March 1942, approved by the President on 31 March 1942, divided the Pacific theater, which had been designated by the CCS in CCS 57/2, 24 March 1942, as an area of American strategic responsibility, into two areas of responsibility: the Southwest Pacific Area (SWPA) and the Pacific Ocean Area (POA). Both the directive for the Southwest Pacific Area and the designation of General MacArthur as supreme commander of the armed forces of the governments whose units were operating in the area, were contained in a War Department message to General MacArthur, 3 April 1942, as amended by a War Department message of 5 April 1942. According to the directive contained in the 3 April message, the CCS would exercise general jurisdiction over grand strategy policy, allocation of forces and war materials, while the U. S. JCS would exercise jurisdiction over all matters of operational strategy. The Chief of Staff, U. S. Army, was to act as the executive agency for the U. S. JCS. Final approval of the SWPA directive by the Australian Government was received in Washington 14 April 1942. General MacArthur assumed command of the Southwest Pacific Area on 18 April 1942.

General MacArthur's combined command in SWPA consisted of Allied ground forces (including Australian and Dutch forces), Allied air forces with General Brett commanding, Allied naval forces, U. S. Forces in the Philippines (USFIP) under General Wainwright, and U. S. Army Forces in Australia (USAFIA), virtually a service command, under General Barnes. Admiral Nimitz was designated Commander in Chief, Pacific Ocean Areas (CinCPoa) on 20 April 1942, effective 8 May 1942. U. S. Army forces in the Pacific Ocean area directly concerned were to comply with directives issued by that commander in chief. General MacArthur was relieved from command of SWPA on 2 September 1945.

⁶ USAFISPA was set up as a separate army command in the South Pacific 7 July 1942, paralleling the naval subcommand in the southern part of Admiral Nimitz' POA command. SOPAC was the short title for the South Pacific Force and Area used by the U. S. Navy. At the time of the establishment of U. S. Army Forces, Pacific Ocean Areas (USAFPOA) on 1 August 1944, Army Air Forces, Pacific Ocean Areas (AAF/POA) was set up with General Harmon (then lieutenant general) as commanding general under CG, USAFPOA. AAF/POA was to consist initially of the U. S. AAF units assigned to the Central Pacific Area and to the South Pacific Area. Under the principles of unified command (JCS 263/2/D) CG, AAF/POA was to be responsible directly to CinCPoa for all matters concerning the preparing of plans, operations, training, and disposition of his forces. In addition General Harmon was designated Deputy Commander, 20th Air Force, on all matters relating to those units of the 20th Air Force based in the Pacific Ocean Areas. In the latter capacity he was to deal directly with CinCPoa in co-ordinating 20th Air Force activities with other activities in his area.

⁷ For many years before World War II the Hawaiian Department controlled all Army activities in the Hawaiian area. Until the creation of USAFISPA, General Emmons as Commanding General, Hawaiian Department, was in effect administrative commander of U. S. Army forces in Admiral Nimitz' POA command, exclusive of the special USAFISPA subarea.

⁸ General Richardson remained in command of the Hawaiian Department along with his successive assignments in command of the U. S. Army Forces in Central Pacific Area, USAFPOA, and U. S. Army Forces, Middle Pacific (AFMidPac).

⁹ General Richardson was formally designated CG, USAFICPA, under Admiral Nimitz, 14 August 1943. The primary mission of this Army command under General Richardson was training.

¹⁰ Effective 1 August 1944 the USAFPOA was established, consolidating and initially consisting of all U. S. Army forces previously assigned to the Central Pacific Area and South Pacific Area. General Richardson as ComGenPoa was to exercise command under CinCPoa under the principle of unity of command (JCS 263/3/D).

¹¹ JCS, 3 April 1945, designated the Supreme Commander, SWPA, as Commander in Chief, U. S. Army Forces, Pacific (CinCAFPac), a post held concurrently with his SWPA command. All U. S. Army resources in the Pacific theater (less the Southeast Pacific Area and resources under the command of the Commanding General, Alaskan Department) were placed under his command. All American naval resources in the Pacific (less Southeast Pacific Area) were placed under the command of CinCPoa. Both General MacArthur and Admiral Nimitz, commander of naval forces in the Pacific, were to prepare for final operations against Japan. AFPAC absorbed the forces assigned to USAFFE and USAFPOA. Headquarters, USAFPOA, was amalgamated on 1 July 1945 with Headquarters, AFMidPac, a command established on the same date under AFPAC. General Richardson was in command of AFMidPac from 1 July 1945–17 March 1946. USAFPOA was not formally dissolved until 1 September 1946, when the functions of the CG, USAFPOA, were simply taken over by the CG, AFMidPac. General MacArthur also created AFWesPac 7 June 1945 to replace USASOSSWPA which had come under General Styer's command on 30 May 1945.

Western Hemisphere

Name of Command	Date Established	Commanding General
U. S. Army Forces, South Atlantic [1]	20 November 1942	Brig Gen R. L. Walsh (20 Nov 42–15 May 44) Maj Gen R. H. Wooten (16 May 44–30 Oct 45)
Caribbean Defense Command (CDC) [2]	10 February 1941	Lt Gen D. Van Voorhis (10 Feb–18 Sep 41) Lt Gen F. M. Andrews (20 Sep 41–9 Nov 42) Lt Gen G. H. Brett (12 Nov 42–15 Oct 45)
Alaska Defense Command (ADC)	4 February 1941 [3]	Brig Gen S. B. Buckner, Jr. (4 Feb 41–31 Oct 43)
Alaskan Department	1 November 1943	Lt Gen S. B. Buckner, Jr. (1 Nov 43–12 Jun 44) Lt Gen D. C. Emmons (21 Jun 44–30 Jun 46)
Continental Defense Commands [4]		

[1] The organization of USAF, South Atlantic, with head-quarters at Recife, Brazil, was established under the command of General Walsh by War Department letter dated 20 November 1942. Headquarters, USAF, South Atlantic, was discontinued 31 October 1945.

[2] In the years before World War II, overseas departments controlled all Army activities in the Panama Canal region and in the Puerto Rican region. Early in 1941 the defenses of the Puerto Rican Department and the Panama Canal Department were inegrated, along with the base commands which had been set up in the American leased bases in British Caribbean territory, under the Caribbean Defense Command. In mid-1941 General Van Voorhis commanded the Panama Canal Department, and Maj. Gen. J. L. Collins commanded the Puerto Rican Department. Prior to Pearl Harbor, however, General Van Voorhis was replaced by General Andrews. Subsequently the Commanding General, Caribbean Defense Command, was concurrently the Commanding General, Panama Canal Department. The Puerto Rican Department became part of the Antilles Department, a subordinate command within the Caribbean Defense Command.

[3] The Alaska Defense Command was designated in February 1941 as part of the War Department move to organize Western Hemisphere defenses on a defense command basis. Before and during the first months of World War II, Alaska was under the 9th Corps Area command, commanded by Lt. Gen. J. L. DeWitt, who also commanded the Fourth Army, stationed on the West Coast. Upon the creation of the Alaska Defense Command, General DeWitt exercised control over Alaska as Commanding General, Fourth Army. After the Western Defense Command (WDC) was constituted 17 March 1941, General DeWitt as commanding general had a planning responsibility for the defense of Alaska, which was still in the 9th Corps Area, as well as WDC. Upon the activation of WDC after Pearl Harbor (11 December 1941) and its designation as a theater of operations, the Alaska Defense Command was placed under its control with General DeWitt still in a superior position of responsibility. General Buckner was ordered to Alaska in the spring of 1940 to assume command of American troops there, and became successively Commanding General, Alaskan Defense Force, Alaska Defense Command and Commanding General, Alaskan Department. The Alaska Defense Command was redesignated effective 1 November 1943 and separated from WDC. Upon the establishment of the Alaskan Department in 1943, the Army activities in Alaska came to be administered separately very much on the same basis as those in Hawaii. General Buckner was relieved from command of the Alaskan Department 12 June 1944, assumed command of the Tenth Army in August 1944, and was killed on Okinawa in June 1945.

[4] WDC headquarters was combined with Fourth Army headquarters with station at San Francisco. Each became a separate headquarters on 12 September 1943. The status of WDC as a theater of operations was authorized by War Department radio to WDC 11 December 1941 and was terminated 27 October 1943. WDC was discontinued 1 March 1946. General DeWitt remained in command of WDC from March 1942 to September 1943. Lt. Gen. D. C. Emmons succeeded him, serving from September 1943 to June 1944. Maj. Gen. R. H. Lewis was in command briefly in June 1944, Maj. Gen. C. H. Bonesteel II was in command from June until November 1944, and Maj. Gen. H. C. Pratt was in command from December 1944 until November 1945, after the close of hostilities. The Eastern Defense Command, originally called Northeast Defense Command, was constituted on 17 March 1941, along with the other continental U. S. defense commands. It was redesignated the Eastern Theater of Operations on 24 December 1941. During all this period Lt. Gen. H. A. Drum was concurrently Commanding General, First Army and Eastern (Northeast) Defense Command (Theater of Operations). The Eastern Theater of Operations was reconstituted the Eastern Defense Command 11 March 1942. General Drum was succeeded in both capacities in 1943 by Lt. Gen. George Grunert, who served as Commanding General, Eastern Defense Command, 8 October 1943–31 July 1945. Brig. Gen. K. P. Lord became Acting Commanding General, Eastern Defense Command, 1 August 1945 and held the post until 15 March 1946, when the command was discontinued. The Central and Southern Defense Commands, the remaining continental U. S. commands, were never theaters of operations.

Bibliographical Note and Guide to Footnotes

This history is based almost entirely on documentary source material. While research ranged into every major category of the official records of the Department of the Army, most of the documents cited in this volume are in the records of the War Plans Division and the Operations Division of the War Department General Staff accumulated between 1921 and 1945. At present these files are in the custody of the Departmental Records Branch, Adjutant General's Office. Permission to consult them must be secured from the G–3 Division, General Staff, U. S. Army (the present successor to OPD). The other main document collections used in writing this history were the files of the offices of the Secretary of War, the Assistant Secretary of War for Air, the Chief of Staff, the G–1, G–3, and G–4 Divisions of the General Staff, the Army Service Forces, the Army Air Forces, and The Adjutant General. All of them are in the custody of the Departmental Records Branch, Adjutant General's Office.

Very few histories or other secondary sources treat in detail any of the topics covered in this study. For this reason no formal bibliography of published materials or secondary sources is presented. Nevertheless, when such sources provide evidence missing in the official files, confirm points of general significance, or present background material of more than casual interest, they are cited in the footnotes. The most notable are three historical memoirs, Dwight D. Eisenhower, *Crusade in Europe* (New York, 1948), Robert E. Sherwood, *Roosevelt and Hopkins* (New York, 1948), and Henry L. Stimson and McGeorge Bundy, *On Active Service in Peace and War* (New York, 1947). Also very useful and frequently cited are four historical studies that present parallel treatments of some of the major developments discussed here: Maj. Gen. Otto L. Nelson, Jr., *National Security and the General Staff* (Washington, D. C., 1946); W. F. Craven and J. L. Cate, *Plans and Early Operations,* Vol. I of THE ARMY AIR FORCES IN WORLD WAR II (Chicago, 1948); and two volumes of the series U. S. ARMY IN WORLD WAR II, K. R. Greenfield, Robert R. Palmer, and Bell I. Wiley, *The Organization of Ground Combat Troops* (Washington, D. C., 1947); and Mark S. Watson, *Chief of Staff: Prewar Plans and Preparations* (Washington, D. C., 1950).

The primary sources for this history, the records of the War Plans Division and the Operations Division, fall into six main categories: (1) the official central correspondence file of the War Plans Division; (2) the official central correspondence file of the Operations Division; (3) the WPD and OPD Message Center file; (4) the plans file of the Strategy & Policy Group of OPD; (5) the informal high-policy file of the Executive Office, OPD; and (6) the periodical reports file of the Current Group, OPD. The following paragraphs describe the nature and arrangement of these files:

(1) The War Plans Division file, containing documents of the 1921–42 period, is identified in footnotes by the symbol "WPD" followed by the numerical designation of the subject file in which a particular paper appears and—if there is one—by the case number indicating the position of the paper within that file. Papers are arranged in the WPD file according to a rather limited group of subject headings and within each subject file are roughly chronological. There is a detailed card index of subjects that can be trusted to provide initial leads and cross references to related files.

(2) The Operations Division file, containing documents of the 1942–45 period, is arranged in three subgroupings according to security classifications. Thus physically there is a Secret file, a Secret Security file, and a Top Secret file, and each must be consulted separately. Each of these OPD files is arranged by subject under the numerical headings of the War Department decimal system. An OPD file is identified by the symbol "OPD" followed first by a decimal number referring to the specific subject file and then by the case number within that file, as OPD 320, 2; OPD 320 Sec, 2; OPD 320 TS, 2 (second case of the Secret 320 file; the Secret Security 320 file; or the Top Secret 320 file, respectively). Each of the OPD decimal (subject) files contains a master list of the papers in it, and there is a separate cross reference file arranged by decimal (subject) designations. In the field of strategy and matters of high policy, the OPD file is the most important single collection of World War II documents in the custody of the Department of the Army.

(3) The WPD-OPD Message Center file begins 7 December 1941 and covers all of the World War II period. The WPD collection (December 1941–March 1942), very informal in organization, runs to about twenty volumes. The OPD message file, beginning in April 1942, is arranged according to the classified message (CM) number and the date, with incoming and outgoing message volumes in two separate files. The comparatively small number of messages that received special handling (Top Secret, Eyes Only, and BIGOT messages) are separated physically from the rest of the classified messages, and are also arranged in incoming and outgoing volumes. This message file is the most comprehensive collection of wartime radio messages outside the permanent file of the Staff Communication Office, Office of the Chief of Staff.

(4) In matters of joint or combined strategic planning and policy, the most important collection of World War II records in Washington (with the possible exception of the JCS records) is the Strategy & Policy Group file. Covering the 1942–46 period, it is identified by the symbol "ABC" (American-British Conversations) and is arranged by the War Department decimal system. This file contains virtually a complete set of the papers issued by or under the authority of the Joint Chiefs of Staff, the Combined Chiefs of Staff, and the State-War-Navy Coordinating Committee. It is especially valuable because OPD drafts, comments, and related papers appear with the JCS, CCS, and SWNCC papers. Associated with the ABC file, though not actually a part of it, is the plans file maintained by the Army member of the Joint Planning Committee of the Joint Board. It is arranged by the serial numbers assigned by the Joint Board, which makes it roughly chronological. The bulk of the papers in it relate to the 1940–41 period, and it leads directly into the ABC file.

(5) The Executive Group file is an informal collection of papers compiled in the Executive office of the Operations Division, primarily for the use of the Assistant Chiefs of Staff (WPD and OPD). Because of the special, closely restricted use for which it was designed, and because many of the papers in it were considered too "hot" to go through the standard filing machinery, this file was neither arranged nor indexed in any systematic way. In order to make use of it and refer to it, the author arbitrarily divided these papers into ten major subject categories and assigned an arbitrary serial number to each item (Book, Folder, Envelope) in each category. Papers in this file are identified by the abbreviation "Exec," which appears in each citation of item number and category number, as Item 4, Exec 1, Book 2, Exec 8, etc.

(6) The Current Group file is a comparatively limited but frequently useful collection of the various periodical reports put out by OPD, including the complete file of the OPD Diary (March 1942 through 1945). It is located physically with the OPD official correspondence file in the Departmental Records Branch, Adjutant General's Office.

All of these file collections are in the physical possession of the Departmental Records Branch, Adjutant General's Office, with the exception of the early planning papers (Joint Planning Committee of Joint Board) and the Executive Group files, which are still in the possession of the G–3 Division, General Staff.

Citations contain references to four other files by designations which might not readily be understood if inquiry were addressed to the Department of the Army. First, formal strategic plans are Registered Documents of the G–3 Division, General Staff, and are identified as "Reg Doc." Such plans are physically in the possession of the G–3 Division unless they are formally declared obsolete, in which case they are physically in a special collection of the Classified Files, Adjutant General's Office. Second, a random collection of administrative notices, rosters, organization charts, and other ephemeral contemporary documents relating to the history of WPD and OPD was compiled by the author for his own use. Since the official files contained surprisingly little of this ephemeral material, this informal file became a useful reference and is cited as OPD History Unit file, with an item number referring to folder or volume, as item 2b, OPD Hist Unit file. Third, a few otherwise unsupported observations are documented in statements made by informed persons—mostly OPD officers—to the author and incorporated in letters or memoranda labelled as OPD History Unit "Interview file" or "Comments file." Fourth, certain topics treated briefly in this volume were based on such extensive research that meticulous documentation became far too lengthy for publication. In these cases, research studies with full documentation were organized into a special file and referred to as if they were primary sources. These research monographs are lettered serially and cited by name and appropriate letter, as OPD Hist Unit Study B. The OPD History Unit files referred to, including contemporary documents, interviews, comments, and research studies, are now in the custody of the Office of the Chief of Military History, Department of the Army, but will be retired eventually to Departmental Records Branch, AGO.

The file reference, the last element of most citations, includes the symbol identifying the file series, the folder (or other individual file) number, and the case number, or other indication of where the particular document may be found. This is not necessarily a number that appears on the document itself, but is a number that appears on the individual file folder of the series in which the document is located. The symbols that appear in the file citations identifying the series by original custodial organization are OCS, OSW, G–1, G–3, G–4, and WPD for the prewar series, and WDCSA, OPD, etc., for the wartime period. Abbreviations used in the footnotes are explained in the glossary at the end of this volume.

The types of documents which appear in all files cited in this history include memoranda, letters, disposition forms, messages, informal notes prepared by staff officers for each other or for their superiors, and many rough drafts which, though not used officially, give a clear indication of staff thinking. There are also minutes of meetings, notes on conferences, and memoranda for record. In the annotation of sources the type of communication is always indicated and four other kinds of descriptive information is presented if available on the particular document cited—the originator, the addressee, the date, and the subject. The file reference normally is the last element in the citation.

A few special kinds of documents are cited by the identification that appears on the document itself and there is no reference to the file collection of any particular organization. AG letters can best be located by the Adjutant General's Office by the numbers on the letter; the classified messages can be located by classified message number and date in any of several file series; the Joint Chiefs of Staff and Combined Chiefs of Staff papers and minutes can be located by the numbers of the papers as assigned by the Joint Chiefs of Staff and the Combined Chiefs of Staff; and the Joint Board papers and minutes can be located by the Joint Board subject number and serial number. While the author almost invariably used the Strategy & Policy Group (OPD) records for these last two categories, they may readily be consulted elsewhere. The official file of the Joint Chiefs of Staff and the Combined Chiefs of Staff is under the control of the Joint Chiefs of Staff, as is the official set of Joint Board papers.

All printed, widely distributed documents, such as Army Regulations, general orders, handbooks, annual reports, hearings, and board reports, are cited as simply as precision permits. They are available in the Army Library or have been preserved in Departmental Records Branch, AGO, as a part of the records of the agencies responsible for their issuance.

Glossary of Abbreviations

AA	Antiaircraft
AAF	Army Air Forces
ABC	American-British Conversations (Jan–Mar 41)
ABDA	Australian-British-Dutch-American
ACAN	Army Command and Administrative Communications Network
Acft	Aircraft
ACofS	Assistant Chief of Staff
ADC	Alaska Defense Command
Adv	Advanced
AEF	American Expeditionary Forces (1917–18)
AF	Air Forces
AFHQ	Allied Force Headquarters
AFPAC	U. S. Army Forces, Pacific
AG	Adjutant General
AGF	Army Ground Forces
AGO	Adjutant General's Office
AGWAR	Adjutant General, War Department
Almt	Allotment
ANPB	Army-Navy Petroleum Board
AR	Army Regulations
AS	Air Staff
ASF	Army Service Forces
Asgd	Assigned
Asgmt	Assignment
ASGS	Assistant Secretary of the General Staff
ASW	Assistant Secretary of War
ASWA	Assistant Secretary of War for Air
Atzd	Authorized
AUS	Army of the United States
Auth	Authority
AWPD	Air War Plans Division
AWS	Air Warning Service
Bd	Board
Bmr	Bomber
Bsc	Basic
CAD	Civil Affairs Division
CBI	China-Burma-India area
CCS	Combined Chiefs of Staff
Cen	Center
CG	Commanding General
CinC	Commander in Chief

CINCAFPAC	Commander in Chief, U. S. Army Forces in the Pacific
CINCPAC	Commander in Chief, U. S. Pacific Fleet
Com	Committee
Cmd	Command
Comdr	Commander
CO	Commanding Officer
CofAC	Chief of Air Corps
CofAS	Chief of Air Staff
CofS	Chief of Staff
COMINCH	Commander in Chief, U. S. Fleet
Contl	Control
Conv	Conversation
COSSAC	Chief of Staff, Supreme Allied Command
CPS	Combined Staff Planners
CsofS	Chiefs of Staff
DCofS	Deputy Chief of Staff
Def	Defense
DEML	Detached Enlisted Men's List
Det	Detachment
D/F	Disposition form
DSM	Distinguished Service Medal
Dtl	Detail
Dy	Duty
EDC	Eastern Defense Command
Enl	Enlisted
EO	Executive Order
Est	Estimate
ETO	European Theater of Operations
Fld	Field
FM	Field Manual
FY	Fiscal Year
G–1	Personnel Section of divisional or higher headquarters
G–2	Military Intelligence Section
G–3	Operations Section
G–4	Supply Section
GHQ	General Headquarters
GO	General Order
Gp	Group
Gr	Grade
Grd	Ground
GS	General Staff
GSUSA	General Staff, U. S. Army
H Com	House Committee
H Res	House Resolution
Hv	Heavy
Info	Information
Instr	Instruction
Int	Intelligence

Intpr	Interpreter
IPCOG	Informal Policy Committee on Germany
JAdC	Joint Administrative Committee
JAG	Judge Advocate General
JB	Joint Board
JCB	Joint Communication Board
JCS	Joint Chiefs of Staff
JLC	Joint Logistics Committee
JLPC	Joint Logistics Plans Committee
JMTC	Joint Military Transportation Committee
JPS	Joint Staff Planners
JPWC	Joint Post-War Committee
JSSC	Joint Strategic Survey Committee
Jt	Joint
JUSSC	Joint U. S. Strategic Committee
JWPC	Joint War Plans Committee
MAB	Munitions Assignments Board
Maj	Major
M Day	Day when general mobilization of forces should begin
Mil	Military
MIS	Military Intelligence Service
Mun	Munitions
Mvmt	Movement
NATO	North African Theater of Operations
Obsn	Observation
Obsr	Observer
OCS	Office of Chief of Staff
Off	Officer
OPD	Operations Division
Opn	Operation
Ord	Ordnance
Orgn	Organization
OSW	Office of the Secretary of War
P&A	Personnel and Administration Division
Pdn	Production
Pers	Personnel, personal
PL	Public Law
P&O	Plans and Operations
POA	Pacific Ocean Areas
POM	Preparation for Overseas Movement
Prov	Provisional
Rcd	Record
Reasgmt	Reassignment
Reorgn	Reorganization
Reqmt	Requirement
Res	Reserve
SANACC	State-Army-Navy-Air Force Coordinating Committee
S Doc	Senate Document

SEAC	Allied Southeast Asia Command
Ser	Serial
Serv	Service
SGS	Secretary of the General Staff
SHAEF	Supreme Headquarters, Allied Expeditionary Force
Sig C	Signal Corps
SN	Secretary of the Navy
SO	Special Order
SOP	Standing Operating Procedure
SOS	Services of Supply
Sp	Special
S&P	Strategy & Policy Group
Specl	Specialist
Stf	Staff
Str	Strength
Surr	Surrender
SW	Secretary of War
SWNCC	State-War-Navy Coordinating Committee
SWPA	Southwest Pacific Area
T	Theater
TAG	The Adjutant General
TIG	The Inspector General
Tng	Training
Tr	Troops
TS	Top Secret
UK	United Kingdom
USA	United States Army
USAFBI	U. S. Army Forces in the British Isles
USAFISPA	U. S. Army Forces in the South Pacific Area
USASTAF	U. S. Army Strategic Air Forces
USMBW	Munitions Assignments Board
USN	United States Navy
USSR	Union of Soviet Socialist Republics
USW	Under Secretary of War
VLR	Very long-range (bomber)
WD	War Department
WDC	Western Defense Command
WDCMC	War Department Classified Message Center
WDCSA	Chief of Staff, U. S. Army
WDGS	War Department General Staff
WDSS	War Department Special Staff
WPD	War Plans Division

Glossary of Code Names

ANFA — Sometimes used by OPD officers as a code name for the Casablanca Conference of January 1943.

ANAKIM — Plans for operations in Burma.

ANVIL — The planned 1944 Allied invasion of southern France in the Toulon-Marseille area.

ARCADIA — U. S.-British staff conference at Washington, December 1941–January 1942.

ARGONAUT — International conference held at Malta and Yalta, 30 January–9 February 1945.

BIGOT — Code for messages dealing with plans for future military operations.

BLACKLIST — General MacArthur's plan for the occupation of Japan.

BLUE — Prewar plan for the defense of the United States, should war occur.

BOBCAT — Force for Bora Bora Island in the South Pacific.

BOLERO — The build-up of troops and supplies in the United Kingdom in preparation for a cross-Channel attack.

BOSCO — Telephone directory of American and British delegations at QUADRANT.

CAMPUS — Admiral Nimitz' plan for the occupation of Japan.

CORONET — Assault planned for 1 December 1945 on Tokyo Plain.

CRICKET — International conference at Malta, 30 January–2 February 1945.

EUREKA — International conference at Tehran, 28–30 November 1943.

HUSKY — Allied invasion of Sicily in July 1943.

MAGNET — 1942 build-up of U. S. forces in Northern Ireland.

MAGNETO — International conference at Yalta, 4–9 February 1945.

MANHATTAN DISTRICT — Atomic bomb project.

MODICUM — Name for group that went to England in April 1942 to present the "Marshall Memorandum" to the British.

NEPTUNE — Actual 1944 operations within OVERLORD. This code name was used for security reasons after September 1943 on all OVERLORD planning papers which referred to the target area and date.

OCTAGON — International conference at Quebec, 12–16 September 1944.

OLYMPIC — Assault planned for 1 March 1946 on Kyushu.

ORANGE — Prewar plan to be used should war with Japan occur.

OVERLORD — Plan for the invasion of northwest Europe in the spring of 1944.

QUADRANT — International conference at Quebec, 14–24 August 1943.

RAINBOW — Name for various prewar plans of military action to meet situations created by Axis aggression.

RANKIN — Plan for an emergency return to the Continent in event of a collapse of German resistance.

RED — Prewar plan to be used should war with the British Empire occur.

ROUNDHAMMER	Code name used at the TRIDENT Conference in May 1943 to designate a modified ROUNDUP invasion.
ROUNDUP	Various 1941–43 plans for a cross-Channel attack in the final phases of the war.
SEXTANT	International conference at Cairo, 22–26 November and 3–7 December 1943.
SLEDGEHAMMER	Plan for a limited-objective attack across the Channel in 1942 designed either to take advantage of a crack in German morale or as a "sacrifice" operation to aid the Russians.
SYMBOL	International conference at Casablanca, 14–23 January 1943.
TERMINAL	International conference near Potsdam, 16–26 July 1945.
TORCH	Allied invasion of North and Northwest Africa, November 1942.
TRIDENT	International conference at Washington, 12–25 May 1943.

UNITED STATES ARMY IN WORLD WAR II

List of Subseries

*Published by the University of Chicago Press.

Index

U.S. GOVERNMENT PRINTING OFFICE : 1961 O—589727